The Marketing Customer Interface 2001–2002

Rosemary Phipps and Craig Simmons

Published on behalf of
The Chartered Institute of Marketing

OXFORD AUCKLAND BOSTON JOHANNESBURG MELBOURNE NEW DELHI

Butterworth-Heinemann
Linacre House, Jordan Hill, Oxford OX2 8DP
225 Wildwood Avenue, Woburn, MA 01801-2041
A division of Reed Educational and Professional Publishing Ltd

℞   A member of the Reed Elsevier plc group

First published 2001

British Library Cataloguing in Publication Data
A catalogue record for this book is available from the British Library

ISBN 0 7506 5307 8

For information on all Butterworth-Heinemann
publications visit our website at www.bh.com

Typeset by P.K.McBride, Southampton
Printed and bound in Italy

Contents

An introduction from the academic development advisor

Over the past few years there have been a series of syllabus changes initiated by the Chartered Institute of Marketing to ensure that their qualifications continue to be relevant and of significant consequence in the world of marketing, both within industry and academia. As a result I and Butterworth Heinemann have rigorously revised and updated the Coursebook series to make sure that every title is the best possible study aid and accurately reflects the latest CIM syllabus.

The revisions to the series this year include both restructuring and the inclusion of many new mini cases and examples. There are a number of new and accomplished authors in the series commissioned both for their CIM course teaching and examining experience, and their wide general knowledge of the latest marketing thinking.

We are certain that you will find the new-look books highly beneficial study toolS as you prepare for the CIM examinations. They will guide you in a structured and logical way through the detail of the syllabus, providing you with the required underpinning knowledge, understanding and application of theory.

The editorial team and authors wish you every success as you embark upon your studies.

Karen Beamish

Academic Development Advisor

How to use these coursebooks

Everyone who has contributed to this series has been careful to structure the books with the exams in mind. Each unit, therefore, covers an essential part of the syllabus. You need to work through the complete coursebook systematically to ensure that you have covered everything you need to know.

This coursebook is divided into units each containing a selection of the following standard elements:

- **Objectives** tell you what part of the syllabus you will be covering and what you will be expected to know, having read the unit.
- **Study guides** tell you how long the unit is and how long its activities take to do.
- **Questions** are designed to give you practice – they will be similar to those you get in the exam.
- **Answers** (at the end of the book) give you a suggest format for answering exam questions. *Remember* there is no such thing as a model answer – you should use these examples only as guidelines.
- **Activities** give you a chance to put what you have learned into practice.
- **Debriefings** (at the end of the book) shed light on the methodologies involved in the activities.
- **Exam hints** are tips from the senior examiner or examiner which are designed to help you avoid common mistakes made by previous candidates.
- **Study tips** give you guidance on improving your knowledge base.
- **Insights** encourage you to contextualize your academic knowledge by reference to real-life experience.
- **Definitions** may be used for words you must know to pass the exam.
- **Summaries** cover what you should have picked up from reading the unit.

While you will find that each section of the syllabus has been covered within this text, you might find that the order of some of the topics has been changed. This is because it sometimes makes more sense to put certain topics together when you are studying, even though they might appear in different sections of the syllabus itself. If you are following the reading and other activities, your coverage of the syllabus will be just fine, but don't forget to follow up with trade press reading!

Objectives

- Be introduced to the wide range of factors that influence customer behaviour.
- Be introduced to some of the macro- and micro-environmental factors that are currently influencing conditions in the market.
- Look at the driving forces behind customer power.
- Understand how organizations can respond to these pressures.
- Look at examples of customer focused marketing in specific economic sectors.
- Rethink the use of the word 'customer'.
- Be introduced to the concept of role and role relationships.

This unit covers the following parts of the Marketing Customer Interface syllabus:

- 2.1.1
- 2.1.2
- 2.1.3

Study guide

Readers are introduced to the wide range of factors that influence customer behaviour. A number of macro- and micro-environmental forces currently impacting on organizations are discussed, forces that are making organizations fundamentally rethink existing ideas about their external adaptation and internal integration.

Specific research done by the Future Foundation has identified a new drive for a caring and liberal form of capitalism. Trust and the goodwill a company generates as a result of its contribution to society have now become the values on which some consumers will make purchases. Within this framework of values, as markets mature and competitive pressures increase, organizations are discovering that customers are expecting more. Research carried out by the Institute of Customer Service outlines changes in customer behaviour, actions companies are taking in response to these changes and what they should do in the future to become more customer-focused.

Examples of customer-focused marketing from different economic sectors are given. Students are advised to research and add to these examples during their course.

Students are then asked to think about the use of the word 'customer' and to extend their ideas to the concept of role relationships.

Organize your study materials from the beginning of your course:

- Use file dividers to keep broad topic areas indexed and relevant materials and articles with the relevant notes.
- Look out for relevant articles and current examples, you will find these useful to illustrate examination answers.

Factors influencing customer behaviour

Managing the marketing customer interface involves understanding people, the way in which they purchase, interrelate and interact with the interface of the organization. Such a focus is necessary because increasing attention to customer service, creativity, innovation and the management of change demands more from marketers than ever before. The understanding marketers need to have of customers and processes within the organization needs to go far beyond the traditional role played by the

1

marketing department. Throughout the module it is stressed that organizations need to adopt this customer-centred focus throughout the firm so that marketing extends beyond the management of the marketing department to managing an organization that has a marketing focus.

The following factors influence customer behaviour.

External factors

Macro-environmental factors

Political influences, legal constraints, economic conditions and changes in the economy, international developments, socio-demographic changes, cultural influences, technological developments and environmental interests (otherwise known as PEST factors).

Micro-environmental factors

1. The type of market and its characteristics, market life cycle, industry structure.
2. The number of competitors, generic positioning, competitive strategy.
3. The suppliers in the supply chain.
4. The method of distribution and the distribution chain.
5. The number of customers, the way in which the market can be segmented, the degree of market segmentation, the adoption and diffusion curve.
6. Individual psychological factors such as motives, perceptions, approach to risk, attitudes, personality, unique ability, knowledge, demographic and situational factors.
7. Social factors such as roles and family influences, opinion leaders, innovators, reference groups, social classes, culture and subculture.
8. The decision-making process (DMP) and the extent of the decision making involved – extended and limited problem solving (EPS and LPS), routine response buying, impulse buying and the degree of involvement in the purchase.
9. The decision-making process within the decision-making unit (DMU).
10. The influence of stakeholders and the impact the organization has on society.
11. The defining and management of relationships.

Internal factors

1. Values and meta values (the values behind the espoused values) embodied in the vision, mission and enacted in the way the organization manages itself.
2. Objectives, strategy and policies.
3. The marketing mix and other situational factors.
4. Leadership, management and human resource management.
5. Production/operational processes.
6. Financial and resource management.
7. Outsourcing and partners.

Many of these points are discussed in this coursebook, others are discussed elsewhere in the syllabus.

The emergence of customer power in the new competitive climate

Driving forces for change and organizational response

Some of the principal challenges that Kashani (1996) identified in an international study of 220 marketing managers were:

- High and rising levels of competition across virtually all markets.
- Far higher levels of price competition.
- An increasing emphasis upon and need for customer service.
- The demand for higher levels of product quality.
- High rates of product innovation.

- The emergence of new market segments.
- The growing power of distribution channels.
- Growing environmental/Green concerns.
- Increases in government obligations.
- European integration.
- Increasing advertising and promotional costs.

The principal implications of these were seen by managers to be the need for constant improvements to product and service quality, development of new products, keeping up with customers and adding to or improving customer service.

Kashani also asked managers about the sort of changes that were most likely to affect their markets in the future. The three most significant of these proved to be:

1. The consolidation of competition as fewer but larger players emerge.
2. Changing customers and their demands.
3. The globalization of markets and competition.

In order to cope with this sort of change, he suggests that marketing needs to respond in several ways:

1. Marketing should take far more direct line responsibility within the organization, with an emphasis upon segment or product management, where the focus is upon customer segments or particular products or technologies. This would have the effect of integrating marketing thinking and action into day-to-day business decisions.
2. Marketing needs to become more strategic and less specialized so that it becomes part of a more integrated process.
3. Marketing or customer orientation needs to become far more widespread so that marketing would no longer be the isolated concern of a few people but of staff throughout the whole business. This would mean that marketers would need to be more skilled in strategic thinking, communication and customer sensitivity.

As marketing is part of an organization which interacts directly and immediately with the environment it is essential that marketing comes to terms with areas of growing importance.

Doyle (1994) identified the major changes that the marketing planner would be faced with as:

- The fashionization of many relatively traditional markets as model changes occur much faster, obsolescence becomes more rapid and markets become more fickle.
- The replacement of mass markets with micro markets.
- Rising expectations across virtually all markets and a reduced tolerance to accept poorer or poor performance.
- The greater pace of technological change.
- High levels of competition.
- The globalization of an even greater number of markets.
- Differentiation on the basis of service and the soft rather than the traditional hard elements of the marketing mix.
- The increased commoditization of many markets.
- Greater government and legislative constraints.

Kotler's (1997) views on the changing emphasis and priorities within marketing are broadly similar, with the greatest emphasis upon:

- Quality, value and customer satisfaction.
- Relationship building and customer retention.
- Managing business processes and integrating business functions.
- Global thinking and market planning.
- Building strategic alliances and networks.
- Direct and on-line marketing.
- Services marketing.
- Ethical marketing behaviour.

As Wilson and Gilligan (1997) write:

- It is apparent there is a need for companies to adapt as the pace of change increases, the speed of anticipation and response will become ever more important and time-based competition more essential.

- As markets fragment, customization will become more necessary.

- With expectations rising, quality will become one of the basic rules of competition (in other words a 'must have') rather than a basis for differentiation.

- Information and greater market knowledge will provide a powerful basis for competitive advantage.

- Sustainable competitive advantage will increasingly be based upon an organization's core competencies, the consequences of the lack of strategic focus becomes more evident and more significant.

- As market boundaries are eroded, the need to think global would become ever more necessary. In this way, the marketing planner will be able to offset temporary or permanent declines in one market against growing opportunities in another. At the same time, of course, they need to recognize that the strategic significance of size and scale is increasing. However, the marketing planner should not lose sight of the need for tailoring products and services to the specific demands of markets by thinking globally but acting locally.

- Differentiation will increasingly be based upon service.

- Partnerships with suppliers and distributors will become far more strategically significant.

- Strategic alliances will become more necessary as a means of entry and operating within markets, partly because they offer the advantage of access to greater or shared knowledge, but also because of the sharing of costs and risks.

- A far greater emphasis upon product/service and process innovation.

- The need to recognize the greater number and complexity of stake-holder expectations.

Doyle identifies the ten most obvious of these changes being the need to:

1. Break hierarchies and reorganize around flatter structures.
2. Organize around small/smaller business units.
3. Develop self-managing teams.
4. Re-engineer.
5. Focus upon developing networks and alliances.
6. Move towards transactional forms of organization.
7. Become a true learning organization.
8. Emphasize account management in order to integrate specialist expertise across the organization for the benefit of the customer.
9. Recognize the importance of expeditionary marketing (instead of focusing upon what Hamel and Prahalad refer to as 'Blockbuster innovation' designed to get it right first time). The organization concentrates upon developing a stream of low-cost, fast-paced innovative products.
10. Rethink the way in which the board of directors operates so that it is focused to a far greater extent upon strategic direction rather than control and day-to-day management.

Activity 1.1

Read through the analysis done on the oil industry by Juliet Walker and then ask yourself the following questions

- What are the driving forces for change in your industry
- How is the organization responding
- How does this affect the way people are organized and managed
- How does this affect manager
- How does this affect employees

As Wolfgang E. Grulke, Chief Executive, FutureWorld writes, the computer and telecommunications revolution has taken the business world by storm, and has been a critical contributor to the forces that are creating a fundamentally new economy on the planet – the service or information economy. For access to articles by Wolfgang Grulke see www.futureworld.co.za.

Over the past decade we have begun to realize that the 'old' industrial economy has entered the end of its life cycle. In the USA less than 30 per cent of employment is now in the traditional industrial businesses. Analysts estimate that more than 90 per cent of the US GDP this year will come from information and service businesses. We see similar shifts worldwide.

Political pressure to remove international trade barriers is creating a global marketplace for goods and services. With the World Trade Organization acting as enforcer, countries are being increasingly bound by legal agreements which aim to ensure a 'level playing field' for trading on the global market. Opponents of economic globalization point to the deleterious effects on local economies, social and environmental conditions that such 'free' trade can have. Instead they argue for more regionally focused trading, producing locally to meet local needs, and the need for any international trade to be based on strict ethical criteria.

While many consumers still appear to be basing their purchasing decisions on price alone, increasing numbers are demanding goods and services which met stricter social and environmental standards thus bucking the trend towards globalization. Take, for example, the rise in farmer's markets. These showcases for local produced foodstuffs are drawing customers away from supermarket chains – stores which have traditionally sourced produce without thought to their country of origin.

Whether for good or bad, few would disagree that globalization has fundamentally changed the marketplace. A product sold in the Europe could easily have been manufactured in Malaysia by a Japanese company financed by a German bank.

A new global infrastructure

The internet currently links millions of people around the globe. Estimating the exact number of people who use the internet is problematic. Based on analysis of numerous studies, Nua Internet Surveys (www.nua.ie/surveys) estimate that worldwide more than 407 million people were on-line at the end of 2000. This is a staggering increase of more than 350 million over the last five years.

Of course, figures vary significantly by Country as the table below illustrates.

Table 1.1 Figures of online users

Source: Nua Internet Surveys

World total	407.1 million
Africa	3.11 million
Asia/Pacific	104.88 million
Europe	113.14 million
Middle East	2.40 million
Canada & USA	167.12 million
Latin America	16.45 million

Internet growth rates show no sign of slowing down. Even in relatively affluent countries, with a good history of technical innovation, such as the UK, there are still significant numbers of customers eager to get on-line.

New trade routes for a new economy

The trade routes for the new information economy are the electronic networks that span the globe – the telephone, television and computer networks that together make up the much-vaunted information highway.

The traditional value chain, the process of how your product or service gets into the hands of the customer, is being devastated by the drivers of the new economy. In the past the complete value chain was directly under your own control, sequential and somewhat constant and predictable. Today the value chain is fragmenting. The pressure to be competitive by global standards is forcing companies to outsource key components of the value chain to best-of-breed suppliers – wherever in the world they are – with information and communication technologies taking time, distance and cost right out of the equation. The traditional predictable *value chain* has become a chaotic instantaneous *value network,* the *marketplace* has transformed into a virtual *marketspace.*

Today small companies can have access to global networks for a few hundred dollars a month – something that would have cost millions of dollars just a few years ago and would have been available only to the largest of businesses. In future 'size' alone will be less and less of a competitive advantage.

As the physical, geographic *marketplace* moves to being a virtual, global and paperless *marketspace,* the nature of competitiveness is changing fundamentally. National boundaries become almost irrelevant – no more than a nuisance. *The primary limits to business performance are those that exist in our minds.*

Changing cultural values

Recent research carried out by the Future Foundation (future@netcomuk.co.uk) says that the impact of globalization on individual economies and working practices has been one of the key influences on the development of a new political economy.

The steady deregulation of world trade is forcing businesses in all sectors to become more competitive in the face of a greater choice of goods and services in previously protected home markets. Thus in most market sectors there is a growing need to sustain and create a competitive advantage through focusing on core competence, building strong and valued brands and keeping costs under control. This is having a major impact on employment and working practices. Downsizing and the restructuring of corporations has resulted in ever more functions being contracted out. Not surprisingly, employees' perceptions of their own job security have plummeted as a result (see Figure 1.1).

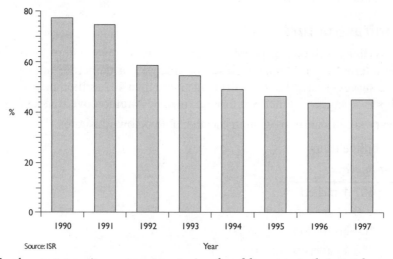

Figure 1.1 Employment security – percentage saying they felt secure in their employment

Globalization has been critical in the development of a new political economy. The reality and seeming inevitability of global competition has forced governments of all political persuasions to adapt their economic and social policies. At the same time, it has increased job insecurity and income polarization and threatened social cohesion and hence has fed the need for a more caring focus.

This reflects the two poles of a new political economy: full hearted acceptance of the global market economy while at the same time searching for mechanisms to protect individual citizens from the ravages of it. This has driven the search for the so-called 'third way' of politics – or social capitalism as the Future Foundation has labelled it. Others have argued for a more radical alternative to globalization – referred to by Colin Hines as 'localization'. More prosaically, Richard Douthwaite has called this approach 'short circuiting' the global economy.

An evolving hierarchy of responsibility

Maslow suggested that as societies develop so people move up a hierarchy from the basic sustenance required just to live in primitive societies through security to socialization, and then through self-esteem to self-actualization. The stage of self-esteem is associated with lifestyles focusing on status driven consumption ('what I have'). Self-actualization is less concerned with appearance and more with personal development and quality of life ('how I am').

The Future Foundation argue that there is a similar process in organizations which matches the needs of individuals in society – after all, organizations are collections of individuals. Thus, in a less developed society, a company's first priority is to provide basic products that people can afford. As society develops, the company takes more notice of its employees, helping to provide security of employment where possible. In UK history, this would be reflected in both the development of labour regulations and paternalistic employers.

As society moves into the socialization phase, companies begin to produce products and brands that express a feeling of being part of society – in effect the mass-market brands of the 1950s and 1960s. The search for status and the development of positional consumption is consistent with the development of designer labels and upmarket brands – arguably, most typified by the UK in the 1980s. The movement to self-actualization – which society is currently engaged in – points to companies, products and brands having a wider perspective, adding to people's personal development and quality of life.

In a sense then we can map the individual's hierarchy of needs with the corporate hierarchy of responsibilities as they have developed in the UK over the last century.

Corporate hierarchy of responsibilities

How does this translate into a company's role? First it re-emphasizes that a company's wider role and responsibilities in society are likely to grow in importance. Second, it suggests a clear hierarchy of responsibilities and tasks a company needs to embrace:

1. Getting the basic offer right in terms of price, quality and service.
2. Getting the right employee focus – an issue that is becoming more important in the less secure job environment, as we discuss below.
3. Getting the right customer focus.
4. Considering and responding to other stakeholders.
5. Assessing responsibilities to the wider society.

Companies need to decide where they are positioned on this hierarchy (Figure 1.2) and where they should be to satisfy their stakeholders and maximize their commercial potential (given that, effectively, the Future Foundation argue that being higher up the hierarchy is likely to be 'good for business'). Those companies wishing to lead the world must aspire to being at the very top of the hierarchy. In this the Future Foundation add that each level is, on the whole, dependent on the level before. You need to get each one right before moving up the scale.

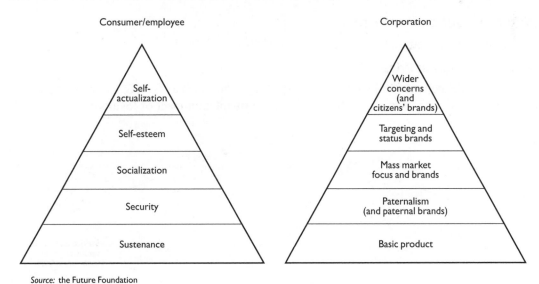

Source: the Future Foundation

Figure 1.2

Customers expect more

Within this changing environmental framework as markets mature and competitive pressures increase, organizations are discovering that customers are expecting more. As competitors catch up with the leaders, customers have a greater range of choices, they react to the homogenization of alternatives by becoming more price sensitive and less loyal.

Customer service demands have increased dramatically over the past five years

Customers have come to expect more and more from the companies selling them products or services. According to a survey carried out for the Institute of Customer Service by Bain and Co., customers now:

- Demand more access time – customers often demand 24-hour service, seven days a week.
- Are less willing to wait – in one organization the average time callers wait on hold before they hang up has fallen in two years from 130 seconds to just 30 seconds.
- Demand faster responses – customers now expect the person who answers the telephone to be able to deal with their request or query, there and then.
- Want more information – they want it delivered directly, and they are less willing to wait to receive something in the post.
- Have less patience with broken service promises – if roadside recovery is promised in 30 minutes, customers ring if the engineer hasn't arrived in 25 minutes. If the water is off for 10 minutes longer than customers were told it would be, customers ring – and water companies only recently told them how long they would have to wait.
- Complain more and more, and are more aggressive in their telephone manner – UK consumers are no longer frightened to complain, and are quicker to demand to speak to the manager, to demand compensation, and to threaten action in the small claims court.

The stereotypical consumer who will wait in silence as they are repeatedly ignored is fast disappearing. And this trend will continue.

Respondents in the survey felt that customer expectations will continue to increase. Some point out that consumers are travelling more and more, and are exposed to the best that the world has to offer. These experiences influence their service expectations from domestic suppliers.

Service advances in one sector now affect other sectors

Service improvements made in one sector influence customer expectations in other sectors. A number of survey respondents point to leading retailers who, by the improvements they have made within their own organizations and industry, have raised expectations in all other sectors.

Retailers entering financial services complain that, although they believe that their service levels are better than those provided by any existing players, they risk upsetting customers if standards don't reach what they expect from their retail brand.

A number of companies are attempting to use service to differentiate themselves from competitors.

Getting the right customer focus

Organizations are responding to these challenges in different ways!

Loyalty enhancing service

Many recent academic texts, and the work of consulting firms such as Bain & Co, have made organizations more aware of the service profit cycle and the financial impact of loyalty-enhancing service (Figure 1.3).

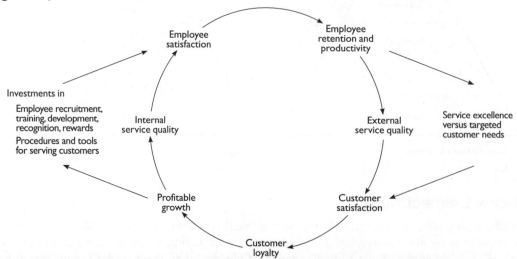

Figure 1.3 *Service profit cycle. Source: The Loyalty Effect,* Harvard Business Review, *Bain & Company*

There is therefore a basis for believing that investments in improved customer service will lead to higher levels of profitability. But given the never-ending supply of investment opportunities to improve service, the challenge for companies will be to identify which will yield the greatest return.

Companies must be able to rate the company's performance against each of these values, and to rate the performance of their competitors and of a variety of leading service firms. What they have yet to do is to relate these 'soft' measures to the 'hard' measure of customer retention.

It is not enough to track customer loyalty. Customer satisfaction measures may not be an accurate indicator of customer behaviour. The real measure of customer value is customer loyalty.

Sophisticated analysis

Better performing companies appear to have more sophisticated customer analysis techniques.

In research carried out for the Institute of Customer Service, those companies that told the Institute that they earn over 15 per cent return on capital (ROC), use annual and lifetime customer profitability calculations, measure customer loyalty and use this information in investment decisions more than other respondents.

Investment in people and technology

If companies are to keep pace with rising customer demands, they need to make significant investments in both people and technology. Before they do this they must understand their customer base:

- Carry out a needs analysis.
- Determine their segment profitability.
- Measure retention.

Technology will be the key to delivering superior service at lower cost. In research done by the Institute of Customer Service, 80 per cent of UK respondents recognize the importance of technology and 72 per cent of respondents felt technology will be vital when it comes to reducing the costs of service. But most organizations surveyed felt they have a problem with the way they use technology. Only 31 per cent of UK respondents consider their use of technology to be good or state of the art in its support of customer service. Systems were described as 'out-of-date', 'completely inadequate', and 'unsatisfactory'. Historic rates of return from IT investments are seen as poor.

The ultimate indictment is the relatively poor rate of return that survey respondents feel they have obtained from IT. Only 23 per cent of UK respondents feel their returns have been good or excellent. It is viewed as an investment black hole. Don't be fooled into thinking that technology alone will solve the people issues.

Despite the far-reaching applications for advanced technology, respondents felt strongly that it will not allow them to use lesser-skilled customer service employees. Companies hope to use technology to simplify processes and practices – 'to put the science on the computer'. This will allow staff to spend more time interacting with customers, particularly on value-added activities. In no way will technology replace the personal touch – which is generally the key differentiator in the consumer experience. The trick is to use technology to create even higher levels of consumer intimacy – via customer prompt screens, for example.

The use of technology is also allowing greater use of multi-skilling. This gives employees more interesting jobs, and means that customers are more likely to be offered solutions with a single call – but it also implies that staff have enough business judgement to take responsibility for a broad range of commercial decisions. The image that technology will completely replace people in the provision of service appears unlikely.

Market segmentation

Understand the profitability of the segments in your customer base. Different types of customers will have different needs, and will be of differential value to an organization. It is therefore very important to understand how much different segments of the customer base contribute towards profitability, to allow prioritization of investment.

Although more than 80 per cent of UK companies surveyed by the Institute of Customer Service segment their customer base, only 40 per cent of them calculate annual profitability by segment, and even fewer – 22 per cent – measure lifetime profitability.

The Institute of Customer Service say that only around 40 per cent of respondents identify customer needs by segment 'to a fair degree/in great detail', and set service standards according to those needs.

Without understanding needs and profitability by segment, it is difficult to prioritize service investments. How do you know whether to invest in next-day delivery or same-day delivery if you don't know if your customers value it and will pay for it. Some respondents use service standard categories such as gold, silver and bronze customers (but often these were fairly crude).

Track customer satisfaction

Customer satisfaction is measured by nearly 90 per cent of UK and US respondents. A variety of means were mentioned:

- Random customer surveys
- Customer focus groups
- Mystery shoppers
- Complaints analysis
- Operational measures such as, on-time delivery
- Abandoned call rates
- Time to turn-round correspondence.

Value analysis

One technology company speaks of the 'value analysis' that they recently embarked upon. They used research to identify customer needs by segment – such as technical advice, speed of response, price and so on – and the relative importance of each need in determining customer value.

Managing people

Respondents see people issues as fundamental to their future success. And it is this area of employee policies that managers are most passionate about. They understand that customer service staff are not just based in the call centre but spread throughout the organization.

Organizations are now recognizing that customer service must be delivered by all staff who have frequent contact with customers, and this requires a significant shift in attitude, culture and approach.

Recruitment

The front-line staff of tomorrow need excellent interpersonal skills, numerical and verbal reasoning, IT competency and general commercial awareness. They must be able to resolve customer problems as they arise – which means they need the self-confidence, latitude and knowledge to do so. This suggests that organizations will have to think very differently about their recruitment and training strategies.

Typical annual staff turnover rates in call centres in the UK are in the region of 30 per cent. But one UK company managed to reduce theirs from 20 per cent to 2 per cent over a two-year period by systematically rethinking the way it ran its centres. They did this by:

- Hiring staff with a different skill and personality set.
- Reducing the management hierarchy and adopting self-managed teams.
- Providing more and different staff training, giving them more responsibility for problem solving.
- Implementing a revised reward structure linked to customer service measures.

Employees found they had more interesting and rewarding jobs with better pay. Employee attrition fell and customer service improved at the same time. The challenge for most organizations will be to replicate this success with their own operation.

Given the demanding specification for tomorrow's front-line staff, the Institute of Customer Service believes there will be a shortage of candidates. This, combining with the high cost of recruiting the wrong people (e.g. cost of training, poor productivity and lost customers) will make it critical that companies adapt their recruiting practices to attract the right sort of people. They will need to investigate new sources for employees (including universities in more technical sectors) and they will need to be sure that their package of job responsibility, training, compensation, and development opportunities will offer potential recruits the most compelling career prospects.

Commercial awareness

'Employees will need a better understanding of business operations, and an appreciation of the financial implications of actions. Staff will need to be empowered to do their job – which means resolving customer issues and making decisions. They'll need training for this.'

'Employees will need to be less functional. They'll need broader product knowledge and more cross-training.'

Team working

'Project management skills are important, to facilitate cross-functional working. They need to know how to run a meeting.'

'We will see more self-managed teams – with each employee having a wider span of control.'

Interpersonal skills

When managers were questioned on the types of skills that were needed they gave these replies:

- Customer care skills – soft skills as well as functional skills.
- How to provide customer advice, and how to communicate.
- Selling skills.
- How to keep customers happy, and increase customer loyalty.
- How to deal with the difficult customer.

Managers are struggling with the rapid development of in-house training programmes to address these varied needs – with existing programmes having focused primarily on functional skills. Enhancing interpersonal skills is particularly difficult, and companies tend to rely on on-the-job coaching and role-playing exercises. It is likely we will see a rise in the provision of third-party training programmes to improve softer skills, and in significant investment in the development of tailored in-house programmes.

Training

There will be a dramatic increase in the training needs of staff if their latent motivation and capabilities are to be unlocked. The status of front-line staff will need to be raised, and measures and incentives will change.

In many organizations the Institute of Customer Services talked to, it appears as if front-line customer service staff are sometimes seen as second-class citizens. Given the increasing importance of service and the need for more highly skilled people in service roles this must change. How? First, through better recognition:

- Immediate recognition by line management is important, as well as by very top management.
- Recognition is critical – through career development and job enrichment opportunities.
- One-off awards can be used to recognize the exceptional achievement. There shouldn't though be specific incentives for customer service itself – that should simply be the 'way things are done around here'.
- The link between variable pay and operating performance and customer satisfaction must be increased.
- Bonuses will be set on service improvement targets.
- Everyone's compensation must be linked to service performance and, in particular, to customer retention.

In one call centre, employees are eligible for a bonus of up to 20 per cent of their total compensation each month. Their performance is measured in terms of:

- Customer satisfaction – every tenth call automatically triggers the mailing of a customer feedback form.
- Abandoned call rate – for the team of which they are a member.
- Amount of time that they are available to speak to customers.

The bonus is big enough to influence employees' behaviour, and the performance dimensions are clearly measurable. The customer services director in the same organization is also eligible for a 20 per cent bonus – dependent upon customer satisfaction, employee satisfaction and profitability.

Companies will be employing new model, high-flier customer service managers

It is not just the front-line staff whose job descriptions are changing. The survey respondents highlight the important and changing role of front-line managers.

- We need 'balanced' managers – result-focused, driven, high-energy commercial champions, yet approachable team workers.

- First-line managers must be able to manage in dynamic environments, and they must be empowered to take responsibility and to make things happen.
- They must be commercially astute, totally customer focused, with excellent management and communication skills.
- They must be able to take a more strategic view – not just deal with irate customers.
- They need to be coaches, team developers and performance monitors – not merely supervisors.

Managers will need to exhibit all the characteristics of good customer service staff, but they will also need a deep understanding of the economies of the business and be able to take balanced decisions rapidly. At the same time, they will need to act as coaches and mentors to ensure high levels of employee satisfaction and retention, particularly while cultural changes in customer service are implemented. Companies will be demanding more and more from these managers – these are tomorrow's high-fliers.

Taking the customer focused approach does not mean just putting a smile on the face of people who are dealing with customers. Yes, it is important for people to be pleasant, and yes, it is important for the environment to be pleasant. However, organizations must put their concentration on the organizational factors necessary that will enable the whole organization to become more responsive.

Examples of customer orientation

National Health Service

Research done by Burns (1992) shows that what bothers patients is not about medical treatment, quality of equipment or general administrative efficiency. What bothers them is that they are kept hanging around and the doctor does not explain what is wrong with them.

This is a classic example of an organization not understanding about customers and their needs.

Local authority

Work by Hall (1992) adapted from Burns (1992) shows that in a comparative study of two borough councils in two affluent middle-class suburbs in the UK (Solihull in the West Midlands and the London Borough of Richmond) customers were more satisfied with Solihull than with Richmond. What emerged was that although Richmond provided more superior services, Solihull treated customers more sensitively.

British Airways

Before British Airways launched its 'Customer First' campaign they carried out a survey whose objectives were to understand how they compared with their major competitors and what factors customers thought were most important when travelling by air. Concern and problem solving, after the above were the top four factors. Customers valued staff being able to break out of routine systems in order to accommodate their individual needs and also to recover after a mistake has been made.

Car industry

Research by Lewis (1994) showed that the fleet owners put a higher value on after-sales service. Ford then put in motion what it called 'Ford business solutions'. This covered a number of separately linked initiatives which were aimed at improving customer service and thereby differentiating it from its competitors. Fleet operators were given one point of contact and not shoved from pillar to post.

> ### Exam hint
> Students should actively seek out examples of customer orientation in profit and not-for-profit organizations.

Service initiatives

Service offerings

- A retailer responds to customer demands by introducing a 'one in front' checkout guarantee, customer service desks, open gates, and a customer call centre.
- An airline offering full-service arrival lounges – including message retrieval, shower facilities,

breakfast – for their business and first-class passengers flying long-haul routes, at no additional cost.

- An internet provider increasing its call centre service hours from six days a week for 12 hours a day to seven days a week for 24 hours a day.
- A retailer setting different service standards at different times of the day, based on customer research that identified the different needs of morning shoppers, lunch-time shoppers and afternoon shoppers.
- A food manufacturer targeting 98.5 per cent service performance, defined as delivery of the right product, in the right amount, at the right time and to the right place – while competitors and retailers tend to use only volume measures, or only record service failures above certain levels.

Employee training and empowerment

- A retailer with more than 10,000 outlets conducting face-to-face training for employees in each and every outlet over a two-year period.
- An insurance company developing in-house a specialized series of training programmes for employees recruited into a new dedicated unit serving all customers won since January 1998.
- A hotel chain authorizing employees to spend up to £1250 to correct a problem affecting customer service.

Feedback

- A telecommunications company conducting over 10,000 interviews a month with customers who have asked for a service or fault repair, made a request or a complaint.
- A building society carrying out regular customer surveys, focus groups, and encouraging complaints as well as compliments. Surveys are simple to understand and kept to one page, and the home telephone number of the CEO is at the bottom of the page. Every customer who completes a survey is telephoned (over 35,000 customers a year), either to thank them or to apologize.
- A life insurance provider using a dedicated team to contact clients when they ask to cash in their policy, laying out alternative options. As a result 55 to 60 per cent of policies stay in force.
- An airline investing in customer relations to increase its approachability, through easy availability of postage-paid comment cards, customer forums, and a programme allowing customer relations staff to fly with customers to experience problems firsthand. Retention rates of customers who complained to customer relations more than doubled, to 80 per cent.

Leadership

- The CEO who is so personally passionately committed to service excellence that he does roadshows, and says 'I'll sack you if you consistently give poor customer service'.
- The CEO who measures his managers in terms of their 'impact on society', namely the extent to which they increase the service performance hurdle rates for others.

(Supplied by the Institute of Customer Service)

Activity 1.2

Now undertake Question 4 from CIM Examination Session June 2000 to be found in the Exam paper appendix.

Discussion on the use of the word 'customer'

Traditionally the word 'customer' was used to define people whom the organization dealt with externally. Today it is used more broadly to include people working within the organization as well.

The Conservatives, when they were last in power, introduced the idea of 'consumers' into schools (John Bazalgette, Grubb Institute). They did this by drawing upon their idea that the 'market' provides the most efficient way of organizing activities of all kinds. Schools were thought of in terms of delivering services to consumers, they were a kind of shop or supermarket. Teachers were traders, parents and employers 'consumers', pupils the product. They used the idea that Marks & Spencer provided – an organizational model of how a nationwide chain should be run.

The Grubb Institute predicted at the time that this idea would be communicated to pupils within the school system where they would learn to be 'consumers' rather than citizens. The Secretary for State for Education at the time (Kenneth Baker) said that was exactly what the government wanted: people who were more like consumers and who knew how to get what they wanted in the marketplace, just as the effective shopper does. As the Grubb Institute said at the time, 'the problem with confusing the two terms is that individual consumers do not take responsibility for the overall quality or type of product; all they need to concern themselves with is their own purchases'. People are social beings, each person participates in society's evolution and is moulded by its features – to function well in a society means a whole hearted involvement in society. If people do not involve themselves in society they will be isolated from society. Society and organizations are there to achieve a purpose and organizations and institutions provide roles in order for this to take place. To be a social being either at work or in society entails one taking on a role and taking on formal and informal responsibilities to other people. The 'customer' role does not allow for this dual responsibility – it is a one-way process.

As predicted by the Grubb Institute the use of the word consumer and customer has entered overall use and is broadly used by society to describe any and every exchange. It has provided a model we use to guide our behaviour irrespective of circumstance. However, if we reintroduce the idea of role and role relationships, in which an exchange is taking place and value is being created we need to think about a number of additional aspects. This is now particularly important as marketing as a discipline has entered the not for profit, government, public and religious institutions and the professional relationships these organizations engage in extend beyond customer and consumer terminology. But before we do this, let us consider the use of the word 'role', and to think about it as the idea one has in one's mind that helps us to manage our behaviour in different circumstances.

Role and role relationships

Role relationships

If one starts to look at customer relationships based on role relationships in which an exchange is taking place and value is being created, we need to think about the following:

1. Role
2. Role relationship
3. Role expectations
4. The creation of value in the exchange
5. The measurement of value
6. The evaluation of value.

We will discuss some of these ideas briefly now, but they will be referred to throughout the book.

Role

Taking a role is about behaving in relation to one's inner understanding of the situation; about monitoring and tuning that behaviour so as to bring about and/or contribute to the aims or purpose of the enterprise from the particular position one is in – as a nurse, doctor, secretary, salesperson, customer care manager.

The role is made up of the components shown in Figure 1.4.

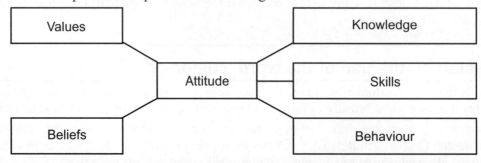

Figure 1.4

Taking on a role does not mean you leave your feelings and values at the door. The role acts as a showcase in which the five components of the individual can be displayed. An understanding of attitudes and attitude change is a key component of the CIM syllabus at all levels – see Unit 4, Modelling customer behaviour, attitudes and dynamics.

Role relationship

As an example of a role relationship, let us take the example of a nurse giving an injection. The ability to perform the nurse role will depend on a number of aspects (see Figure 1.5).

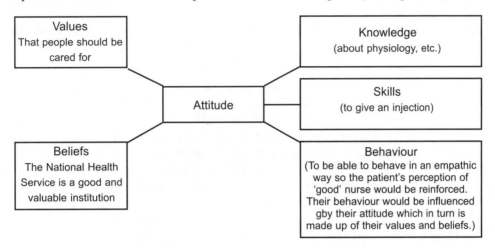

Figure 1.5 *Nurse role*

Similarly, if we look at front-line staff as people who are in contact with customers, we would expect them to have different sets of knowledge and skills and behave in a way in which the customer's idea of a 'good' encounter would be reinforced. Their ability to do this would be determined by their attitudes, which is made up of their values and their beliefs.

This idea of role relationship also brings into consideration the behaviour of the person on whom the service is being carried out. The role relationship is interactive.

The patient should have some idea about how to behave as a patient. Similarly, a customer should have some idea on how to behave as a customer. This is especially important on airlines, trains, and buses, where the passenger role can affect the safety of other people.

The word 'client' is used by accountants, lawyers, psychotherapists and social services. The word 'client' implies a professional role relationship where personal and professional ethics are of prime consideration. Equally, the role responsibilities of both parties need to be considered where disclosure of important facts may be key to ensuring quality and legality.

Role expectations

If one assumes that one is dealing with a 'reasonable' sort of person who understands how to behave, a customer's understanding of the role being performed well, will be determined by their previous experience and any 'ideal idea' they may be carrying in their own mind about what to expect.

When role expectations are not met, or just meet or fall below expectation, there is a gap. When people experience this gap they can feel frustrated, disappointed and angry. Dissonance is created. Part of the success in managing customer relationships is to understand how to manage this gap. It can be done by:

- Understanding what the expectations are in the first place.
- Creating the correct offer and expectation and ensuring they match.
- Being able to manage the disappointment people feel when they go wrong.
- Exceeding the expectation they have and creating excess delight so that dissonance is not experienced.

Ensuring the creation of value in the exchange

The creation of value in the exchange is dealt with in the sections covering quality, management, dealing with organizational barriers and so on.

Measurement of value and evaluation of value

The measurement of value and evaluation of value is dealt with in the section on market research.

The customer is king

Yes, the customer is king/queen if you want to keep their business. And you can take the customer from their throne if you want to and if circumstances allow you to.

Not all customers are kings/queens. Some don't deserve the obsequious behaviour they demand, nor are some of them profitable.

Some customers need to have their role defined. Recent stories about passengers' unruly behaviour on airlines make this imperative.

David Armstrong writes:

> Taking up the pupil role does not mean knowing the ropes, the rules of the system, what behaviour is expected and who is to do what and when. It refers to what happens when one is able to form some idea of the aim and task of the institution, what it stands for, what it seeks to do, to which I can relate my behaviour as a member from my own particular position. A role in this sense is an organizing principle in my mind, which may need continual revision in the light of my experience, through which I can manage my own behaviour to make a contribution to the task of the system of which the role is a part. (*New Directions in Pastoral Care,* Blackwell, 1985)

Enabling this to take place

In order to understand and enable this process to take place we would first have to understand how people conceive their role. Second, we would need to understand the way they relate to the role the institution actually offers. For example, is the role experienced in terms of expectations and the rules of others rather than their own wishes?

The ability to take a role is a two-way process. It is not a one-way process which the word 'customer' implies and it can be belligerent, demanding, self-satisfying and violent. Extending this idea puts a new light on the contribution 'customers' need to make in enabling and contributing to organizational and institutional tasks.

Use of the word 'customer' in the public sector

In relating the word 'customer' to the public sector (government departments and authorities responsible for the administration of local/municipal affairs) the following factors need to be taken into consideration.

The public sector provides a number of services. In some services the word 'customer' is appropriate, for example where there is a choice between using social housing or housing provided or managed by the private sector.

Citizens pay taxes and in some cases are users of the services provided for by the state. They do not have a choice in deciding which services to purchase or not, and they are unable to choose an alternative provider of these services, for example, social benefits. The public sector also markets social causes. For example, stop smoking and birth control. Here they are attempting to make a behavioural change for the overall improvement of society.

In many other aspects the word 'customer' should in fact be replaced by the word 'citizen'. Citizens have a relationship to the overall community. Customers seek to please themselves. The word 'customer' erodes this sense of responsibility and detracts from the role of public service delivery – equity and the cure of social problems. Citizens do however have the opportunity to contribute to the democratic process which decides which political group will manage those services, and although they can vote, they cannot vote with their feet because there is no choice. The adoption of the word 'customer' is an attempt to convince citizens on their primacy. One has to ask the question – are citizens being fooled by this?

The political group in power reflect the culture, values and belief(s) of the society. As such in many cases they are marketing an ideology and taking certain aspects of the marketing mix and marketing terminology in order to carry this out. The developments in certain political campaigns confirm this.

The policy decided on by the political managers of the public sector will determine the need and the level and extent of the services that are provided. Individual citizens are unable to do this. The selection and extent of the overall services provided have in effect to sell themselves otherwise the political group will be removed.

In marketing there is an integrated use of the marketing mix, in politics very often the election promises have little or no bearing on what the citizens receive. Is government, in using the word 'customer', trying to create a form of voter (customer) brand loyalty to the prevailing ideology, consumers of government reform? Or is the government in its drive to privatization, getting control of the public sector by giving itself more choice so that they become the customers, and can choose whom they give the taxpayers' money to?

On a practical and interpersonal level, the way in which the public sector carries out its tasks has to be done in the light of public opinion and the relationships formed in the day-to-day carrying out of these services. The needs of citizens (people) have to be taken into consideration and their right to demand certain standards needs to be encouraged. This puts a pressure on the providers of these services to maintain the level of service citizens have come to expect because of their previous experience of the customer role. This in many cases has led to a situation where citizens behave like the worst type of customer – greedy, belligerent and dependent. Citizens have a responsibility to contribute to society, to look after the resources, not 'consume' them inappropriately. The word 'customer' is inappropriate and can encourage infantile behaviour in certain situations.

Citizens may also have different ideas of the public sector's primary task – the task they must perform in order to continue their existence. For example, the prison service has three tasks:

1. To punish offenders
2. To contain offenders
3. To reform offenders.

The manner in which each of these three tasks are carried out, and the priority given to each of them will determine whether citizens needs are satisfied. It is a political decision as to how the users of the service, the prisoners, should be treated. Very often it does not match what the more punitively minded citizens seek.

Policy making

The policy which guides the public sector is made by political groups whose judgements reflect the values and beliefs of the country. This is done on a macro- and a micro-scale depending on political judgement as to need.

Quantification of those needs must be carried out in order to establish demand and provision, equity and social reform. Market research needs to be carried out in order to assess whether the needs are being met in an adequate way – for example in the provision of public housing, the collection of waste and so on.

Pressure group activity and votes influence political judgement. The various charters help to make citizens aware of the standards they can expect from the providers of these services and their right to be treated as individual people when they use them and in some cases to compensate the users for a fall in standard or provision.

The word 'customer' appears to have been substituted for citizen, and the right people have to be treated politely and with due consideration. The word 'customer' has been used to change the culture of these organizations and has enabled the paternalism of we 'know what is best for you' to be overcome. However, citizens have responsibilities as well and these need to be defined as well.

Use of the word 'customer' in internal organizational role relations

The word 'customer' is also used to denote the role relationships defined by the job description that exist in organizations. A role has specific responsibilities attached to it, the casual use of the word 'customer' detracts from this but on the other hand creates a certain pressure in terms of creating a sense of demand, urgency and standards. As in all role relationships standards are set and role holders need to be made aware of them so that standards can be monitored, evaluated and reviewed. We have role relationships with our colleagues, the term 'customer' does not strictly apply but will be used as a term in this book as it is now used in the literature.

Use of the word 'customer' in charity marketing

The users (recipients of charity) of these services are not customers. They are the recipients of a service which may or may not be asked for.

The donors to these services do so for a number of different reasons. They can be divided into two groups, individual donors and corporate donors. Both of these groups give for their own reasons.

To this extent the range and number of different charities that exist could be looked upon as a cultural reflection of social concern and prevailing values and beliefs. They can be analyzed and segmented using the different systems of segmentation to ensure that the 'psychological needs' of the individual donors and those influencing which charities receive donations are also satisfied.

Some corporate donors may decide to contribute on the basis of recognition of need, or they may wish to tie their donation into a high-profile activity reflecting the organization's social concern and sense of altruism for the recipients of a particular charity. This may be seen as good business practice and form part of their desire to become proactive socially. It may also meet the needs of their employees who wish to work for a socially responsible organization.

The plight of the recipients is used to raise money for charities. In some cases this is possible as the charity is able to use the recipients to promote their own cause. In other cases such as child sexual abuse it is more difficult as it is not possible to use the recipients to promote their own cause and care has to be taken to protect them.

The word 'customer' when applied to the third sector, would apply to the extent that donor and corporate needs are satisfied.

Rethinking the word 'customer'

It is time that marketers began to rethink the word 'customer'. They need to approach it more flexibly and think in terms of roles and role relationships. Some 'customers' in markets need to have their roles defined, for example, passengers, patients, citizens, students and pupils. In many cases they need their roles defined for them so they understand how they can contribute to the institutional and/or organization's task. Colleagues are colleagues – they are not customers, their role is defined by a job description and consists of tasks that contribute to the organizational mission. Role expectations also need to be clarified and opened out for discussion. It is also necessary to understand the Decision Making Unit (DMU) – this is discussed in the following unit.

Question 1.1

You are the marketing officer for either a large hotel or a car dealer. Produce a report for your company's head of marketing in which you explore:

a. the reasons between customer satisfaction and customer delight

b. the reasons why it is so important to create the sensation of delight among your customers

c. the ways in which it could be done.

Illustrate your arguments by examples relevant to your chosen organization, i.e. the hotel or car dealership.

Summary

In this unit we have noted the range of factors influencing customer behaviour and some of the macro- and micro-environmental factors currently influencing organizations. Readers have seen a variety of ideas organizations are developing in order to provide superior customer service. The use of the term 'customer' and the idea of role and role relationships has been introduced.

We will now go on to discuss the classification of goods and services, the decision-making unit, market segmentation, mass customization, one-to-one marketing.

Objectives

- Understand the classification of goods and services. (This links to Marketing Fundamentals and Marketing Operations).

- Examine the use of the term 'decision-making unit' (DMU).

- Examine the process of segmentation in consumer markets and understand the following systems of segmentation: geographic, geodemographics, demographics, behavioural, psychographic, motivation.

- Examine the process of segmentation in industrial and business-to-business markets.

- Consider the uses and tools of segmentation.

- Understand some of the changes that are taking place in market segmentation and product positioning.

- Understand new approaches to classifying customers: mass customization and one-to-one marketing.

This unit covers the following parts of the Marketing Customer Interface syllabus:

- 2.1.1
- 2.3.2

Study guide

This unit introduces readers to the range of variables that effect the buyer decision process and industrial situations. A classification of products and services is then given so that students are able to understand that the type of goods and services that are being supplied will affect the way in which people make their purchasing decision and as a result influence the way in which marketers approach their use of the marketing mix. The concepts of extended problem solving (EPS) and limited problem solving (LPS) are introduced later in the coursebook.

Students are then asked to link their knowledge of the product life cycle, market life cycle and the adoption and diffusion curve to the process of market segmentation.

Traditional methods of market segmentation, target marketing and positioning are then considered for both consumer and industrial/ business-to-business marketing.

Changes currently taking place in market segmentation and product positioning are then discussed and readers are then introduced to the ideas of mass customization and one-to-one marketing.

Product/service classification

To establish marketing strategies for individual products, marketers have developed different classification schemes based on the characteristics of the products.

Purchases are traditionally classified into three groups:

1. *Non-durable goods* – these are tangible and consumed quickly (cold drinks, washing powder, etc.)

2. *Durable goods* – these are tangible and last a long time (washing machines, clothes, etc.)

3. *Services* – these are intangible and can last a long or a short time (accountancy, education, etc.).

A mix of tangibility and services

It is useful to view products and services as a mix of tangibility and intangibility:

- A pure tangible good which has no service attached to it.
- A tangible good with accompanying services to enhance its consumer appeal.
- A service with accompanying goods and services.
- A pure service.

Services are traditionally thought of as being different from products in that they are intangible, heterogeneous, unable to be stored, and simultaneously consumed and produced.

Services

Kotler defines a service as 'any activity of benefit that one party can offer to another that is essentially intangible and does not result in the ownership of anything. Its production may or may not be tied to a physical product'.

A key phrase that encapsulates the essence of a service is that a service does not result in the ownership of *anything*. You will receive a certificate of motor insurance, which is tangible, but you have bought intangible protection. You have been helped to feel really good by the chef but you don't own the ingredients he bought at the same market you visited that morning. The nurse dresses your wound but any ownership of the bandages is only loosely peripheral to the service provided.

Gummesson feels that apart from the simultaneous production and consumption the other three differences do not hold true. Airlines are classified as a service but the aircraft, food and drinks are very tangible. The physical evidence surrounding a service makes it tangible. Services and goods alike can be standardized and produced and still contain customized elements. The pizzeria and the bank offer highly standardized services. However, management consultants, lawyers and architects are highly customized (although they contain standardized modules). Gummesson feels that the claim that services cannot be stored is nonsense. Services are stored in systems, buildings, machines, knowledge and people. The ATM is a store of standardized cash withdrawals. The emergency clinic is a store of skilled people, equipment and procedures. However, he does feel that the simultaneous production and consumption process, the presence of the customer, and the customer's role as co-producer form the distinguishing properties between goods and services. These are also the salient features in total relationship marketing and the new service economy. They require interaction in a customer-provider relationship, sometimes also in a customer-customer relationship. The interaction can be face to face, but it can also take place via IT and other equipment.

Industrial and consumer goods

The classification is further developed by a distinction being made between consumer and industrial goods. Industrial goods are bought by organizations for use in their business or for processing. Consumer goods are bought for people's own use.

It is on this basis that the following classification is made for consumer goods; industrial goods are considered later on.

Consumer goods

Consumer goods can be divided into convenience goods, shopping goods, specialist goods and unsought goods.

> ## Question 2.1
>
> Consumer goods can be divided into convenience goods, shopping goods, speciality goods and unsought goods. How would this distinction help you to decide on the decision-making process and the use of the appropriate marketing mix. Give examples.

Convenience goods

These are items that are purchased regularly with a minimum of comparison and buying effort (matches, bread, soap, etc.). Manufacturers attempt to predetermine the purchasing decisions by promoting them as branded products, so the consumer looks for a certain brand rather than a generic (non-branded) product. Convenience goods are also further classified into staple, impulse and emergency purchases.

- Staple goods are consumed on a regular basis (fruit and vegetables, tomato sauce, baked beans) and product differentiation tends to be minimal.
- Impulse purchases are not pre-planned (magazines and sweets at a supermarket checkout counter).
- Emergency goods are needed at short notice (shovels in a snow storm, umbrellas at an open air concert, etc.).

Shopping goods

These include major durable or semi-durable items which are bought less frequently (hi-fi, clothes, washing machines, etc.). The consumer compares price, quality, style, and suitability. Much pre-planning goes into the purchase. Branding strategies aim to simplify the decision process for consumers. Shopping goods can be further classified as homogenous or heterogeneous.

- Homogeneous goods are broadly similar to each other in technical performance and price, examples are refrigerators and washing machines. Certain brands attempt to differentiate themselves through image or technical or design superiority. Generally price is a major influence on the purchasing decision.
- Heterogeneous goods tend to be non-standard, and price is often of secondary importance. Behavioural factors play an important role in the purchasing decision. A wide range to satisfy individual tastes is important.

Speciality goods

Items which have a unique character (branded clothing, a Porsche). Their purchase is characterized by an extensive search and a reluctance to accept substitutes. Consumers are usually prepared to pay a premium price and it is important to create and preserve the correct image. Customers rarely compare speciality goods.

Unsought goods

Those goods the customer has not considered buying before being made aware of them such as smoke detectors and compact discs, insurance, double glazing. Unsought goods often satisfy a genuine need that the consumer did not recognize existed.

As you have seen, a product's characteristics will have a major effect on the decision-making process and the marketing strategy and techniques used to sell it.

Industrial goods

Industrial goods are divided into capital items, materials and parts and supplies and services.

Capital items

These include installations and accessory equipment.

Installations consist of buildings (factories, offices) and fixed equipment. They are expensive and critical to the long-term success of a company. Purchase is often the result of a very extensive search. Price factors must be viewed as important in such a decision, however it is rarely the single deciding factor. Much emphasis is placed on the quality of sales support and advice, and subsequent technical support and after-sales service. The producers have to be willing to design to specification. They use advertising, but much less so than personal selling. Personal selling is more important than advertising.

Accessories include portable factory equipment (ancillary plant and machinery, office equipment and office furniture) and are usually less expensive than installations. They have a shorter life than installations, but a longer life than operating supplies. Quality, features, price and service determine how suppliers are selected. Middlemen are used as the market tends to be geographically spread. Buyers are numerous and orders are quite small.

Materials and parts

These include raw materials and manufactured materials and parts.

Raw materials (farm products such as wheat, cotton, livestock, etc., and natural products such as fish, lumber, crude petroleum, iron ore, etc.). Farm products are supplied by many different producers to marketing intermediaries who process and sell them. Quality, consistency of supply, service, price and delivery are important. The uniformity of natural materials limits demand creation. They are rarely advertised and promoted. Grower groups promote their own products in campaigns (e.g. potatoes, oranges, milk, eggs). Some brand their goods (e.g. Outspan oranges).

Manufactured materials and parts include component materials (iron, cement, etc.) which are usually processed further, component parts (small motors, adhesives, etc.), and replacement and maintenance items for manufacturing which enter the finished product with no further changes in form. Most manufactured materials and parts are sold directly to the industrial users. Price and service are the major marketing factors and advertising is less important.

Supplies and services

These are industrial goods that do not enter the finished product at all.

Supplies are sometimes called the convenience goods of industrial requirements as they are bought without much effort or comparison, their purchase is routine and undertaken by less senior employees. They include operating supplies (lubricants, stationery, etc.) and maintenance and repair items (paint, nails, brooms, etc.). They have a low unit value, are marketed through resellers and there are a large number of customers who are spread geographically. Price and service are important because of the similarity between suppliers and brand preference is not high.

Business services (also called industrial services) include business advisory services (advertising, legal, professional consulting) and maintenance and repair services (window cleaning, office equipment repair). Generally these services are carried out under contract although some original equipment suppliers include maintenance and repair as an ongoing aspect of their services. Business advisory services are often new-task buying situations.

Business-to-business services can be thought of as tradable services and support services. Figure 2.1 classifies services into a six-cell matrix.

Importance of service

		LOW	HIGH
	Property	*Facility support* Laundry Janitorial Waste disposal	*Equipment* Repairs Maintenance Product testing
Focus of service	People	*Employee support* Food service Plant security Temporary personnel	*Employee development* Training Education Medical care
	Process	*Facilitator* Book keeping Travel agent Packaged software	*Professional* Advertising Public relations Legal

Figure 2.1 *A taxonomy for purchasing business services. Source: Fitzsimmons, Noh and Thies (1998), Purchasing Business Services, Journal of Business and Industrial Marketing, 13*

As the focus moves from property to people to process the following takes place:

- The difficulty of evaluating the service increases
- The seniority of people involved in the decision making increases
- The decision process becomes dominated by surrogate measures like past performance and professional certification
- It becomes more difficult to decide the criteria for purchase in an objective manner
- As the time taken to assess the final outcome of the service increases, the perceived risk and risk handling behaviour increases
- Personal service and sources become more important in deciding purchasing criteria
- As the service becomes more important the need for the supplier to be physically near decreases
- Where importance of service is low, purchasing may be more driven by cost considerations
- The more important the service, the more important non-cost factors such as 24-hour service may be in securing business.

The decision-making unit (DMU)

What is a customer?

Although it is useful to use the word 'customer' as a single unit, it is important from the start to understand that purchases are made both by individuals and groups of people involved in the decision-making process. In the commercial world the term 'customers' is appropriate but marketers need to give consideration to the word 'customer' and how it is now applied in other sectors, sometimes in not a wholly appropriate way.

> ### Definitions
>
> **Customer** refers to the purchaser of a product or service. They may or may not be the consumer. The term 'consumer' refers to the end-user of a product or service.
>
> **DMU** refers to the decision-making unit, that is the group of people who decide whether to buy a product/service.

Internal customers

People working within the same organization are also referred to as customers. This is not strictly correct, internal customers are actually users.

The Decision-Making Unit (DMU)

The DMU ensures that the marketer makes a distinction between the people who are actually buying/paying for the product/service from the people who are using it – the users – and not to confuse the two (although in some cases the user, decider and buyer/payer are the same person).

Autonomous purchase

- Example: individual purchase – face cream
- User: the woman
- Decider: the woman
- Payer/buyer: the woman who pays for it and gets it from the shop
- Influencer: a friend

Family purchase

- Example: a child's purchase – toy
- User: child
- Influencer: child's friends
- Decider: parents
- Payer/buyer: one or both parents who pay for the product and get it from the shop

Organizational purchase

- Example: a photocopier
- Starter/initiator of the buying process: the person who first suggested the idea
- User who is likely to operate the product or service being bought: typist, general office staff, anyone who is the ultimate user
- Advisor: supplies technical and/or professional assistance
- Influencer: anyone who stimulates, informs or persuades at any stage of the buying process
- Decider: purchasing committee or people who actually take the purchase decision
- Buyer/purchaser of the product or service: could be the buying department
- Gatekeeper: receptionist, secretaries who control the flow of information and are between the purchaser and the product/service source
- Financier: supplies the necessary resources, or who reports on their availability and, if necessary, on the mechanisms by which the resources can be acquired.

The concept of 'payer' is explored by Jagdish N. Sheth, Banwari Mittal and Bruce I. Newman (*Customer Behavior: Consumer Behavior and Beyond,* Harcourt Brace 1999). They say that there are three customer roles – user, payer and buyer. The user is the person who consumes or uses the product or receives the benefits of the service. The payer is the person who finances the purchase. The buyer is the person who participates in the procurement of the product from the marketplace. Role specialization occurs when the user lacks expertise, time, buying power or access. It also happens when the product/service is unaffordable and the user then becomes dependent on whatever services are supplied; or it is subsidized and choice is therefore restricted; or where it is free and the user is not the same as the purchaser, for example, library books.

As the examples show a decision-making unit identifies the number of people who are involved in the decision-making process and ascribes a role to them. Each person will have their own concerns, motivations and interests in determining the outcome. These need to be considered when carrying out market segmentation and designing the information carried in promotional material.

Life cycle and the adoption and diffusion curve

The concept of market life cycle, product life cycle and the adoption and diffusion curve are particularly important to marketers. They need to consider these three ideas alongside the concept of market segmentation. As markets and product/services mature new people will be drawn into the market. This means that the needs of the market and the market segmentation will change. Organizations need to be continually updating their offers, and creating new ones so that they are continuously matching the developing needs of their customers and by developing new offers, bringing in new innovators and opinion leaders into the cycle. When markets mature, marketers should look at innovation and improved service, and message modification, not use price in an attempt to retain market share. Otherwise they collectively run the risk of commoditizing the market and ruining profitability.

You will find a number of ways in which market segmentation is defined:

> The process of dividing large heterogeneous markets into smaller, homogeneous subsets of people or businesses with similar needs and/or responsiveness to marketing mix offerings.

Kinnear, Thomas C. and Bernhardt, Kenneth L. (1990) *Principles of Marketing.* 3rd edn, Scott Foresman/Little Brown

> To segment is to divide into parts. In the marketing context these parts may be groups of consumers with like requirements or groups of products/services with like attributes.

Crimp, Margaret (1990) *The Marketing Research Process,* Prentice Hall

Market research

Market research is also covered in the Management Information for Marketing Decisions coursebook.

A market researcher is likely to approach the design of a segmentation study from one or two angles:

1. *Consumer typology* – clustering consumers. Data will be collected and analyzed to sort consumers and group them homogeneously according to geographic, geodemographic, demographic, psychographic and buyer behaviour factors.
2. *Product differentiation* – clustering products. Data relating to the products/services/brands is collected and analyzed with a view to sorting products into groups which in the eyes of the consumer have similar attributes.

> ### Exam hint
>
> The examiners may well use the terms 'target marketing' and 'market segmentation' interchangeably. In this unit we have seen that in fact market segmentation is only one step in the target marketing process. 'Product' or 'market positioning' are also used interchangeably.

Although many marketers can see the rationale of segmentation, many are dissatisfied with it as a concept and often find it difficult to apply to certain markets. It is therefore important to remember that:

- It is a creative tool
- It is different for every situation
- The majority of markets can be segmented in a variety of different ways

- There is no one right way to segment a market
- It is not a one-off exercise and needs constant monitoring to maintain its usefulness.

The marketer has to try different segmentation variables to find the best market view.

Value of segmentation

For the customer

- Provides greater choice of products/services
- Products/services should more closely match the needs of consumers.

For the organization

- Better marketing planning as reactions to marketing activities can be predicted
- It helps organizations to identify prospects who are most likely to buy
- Marketers will get to know their customers better so that they can provide a better service
- Budgets can be more closely allocated on the basis of the investment and return needed from different segments
- Smaller segments may be easier to dominate
- Marketing and sales activity will be closely focused, leading to more sales, lower costs and higher profitability.

There are five major segments variable.

- Geographic
- Geodemographic
- Demographic
- Behaviour in the product field
- Motivation, psychographics and social value groups.

Geographic techniques

Please refer to the Unit 3, The individual, the group and organization as customer for a more comprehensive description of culture. This is the simplest technique and simply involves dividing markets into different geographical units such as nations, states, regions, counties, cities. The marketer then chooses to operate in a few or all of the areas. The marketing mix will change to take into account any regional differences.

Culture

Culture refers to a complex set of values, beliefs and attitudes that help individuals to communicate, interpret and evaluate members of a given society. It has three important features:

1. It includes both abstract (values, beliefs, attitudes, symbols, rituals) and material elements (art, music, literature, buildings).
2. It is socially transmitted and learned.
3. It influences human behaviour.

Since consumption involves behaviour, culture is an important influence. You will need to refer to cultural affinity zones and cultural affinity classes, which are covered later.

Geodemographic techniques

Geodemographics is an extension of geographic techniques in which recognition is given to the fact that, broadly speaking, people with similar economic, social and lifestyle characteristics tend to congregate in particular neighbourhoods and can be considered as micro-cultures.

This technique is useful in identifying new retail sites and the stock they should carry, selecting sales territories, allocating marketing resources, leaflet distribution and direct marketing.

However, in market research, geodemographic systems can only tell the marketer:

- What type of area a brand is doing well or badly in
- Where further research can be carried out once the target has been defined.

Unless the geodemographic technique is linked to attitudinal, behavioural or motivation studies, they do not tell the marketer:

- How to define the target segment in terms of consumer behaviour
- The consumer attitudes which help to explain that behaviour.

Residential neighbourhood classifications

Every one of the postcodes in the country has been analyzed according to the type of housing it represents and classified into a neighbourhood group. Each of these neighbourhood groups now has its own detailed lifestyle profile which lists every type of behaviour from typical marriage and employment patterns, to car ownership and holidays abroad.

Activity 2.1

Go to **www.upmystreet.co.uk.**

One of the best known classifications is ACORN, standing for A Classification of Residential Neighbourhoods (see Table 2.1). This was developed by Richard Weber in 1973, who applied techniques of cluster analysis to 38 separate neighbourhood types, each of which was different in terms of its housing, population and socio-economic characteristics. Kenneth Baker (1982) of the British Market Research Bureau saw how useful it could be and it was used for supervising the field work of the Bureau's Target Group Index. Later Richard Weber joined Consolidated Analysis Centres Inc. (CACI) and developed his ideas.

More sophisticated approaches have been developed including CCNs MOSAIC, CDMSs SUPERPROFILES, Infolink's DEFINE and PINPOINT Analysis's PiN and FiNPiN.

Table 2.1 *ACORN profile of CACI's 2000 population projections for Great Britain*

ACORN Types	% of households	ACORN Groups
ACORN Category A: Thriving		
1.1. Wealthy suburbs, large detached houses	2.6	Wealthy achievers, suburban areas
1.2. Villages with wealthy commuters	3.2	
1.3. Mature affluent home owning areas	2.7	
1.4. Affluent suburbs, older families	3.7	
1.5. Mature, well-off suburbs	3.0	
2.6. Agricultural villages, home based workers	1.6	Affluent greys, rural communities
2.7. Holiday retreats, older people, home based workers	0.7	
3.8. Home owning areas, well-off older residents	1.4	Prosperous pensioners, retirement areas
3.9. Private flats, elderly people	0.9	
ACORN Category B: Expanding		
4.10. Affluent working families with mortgages	2.1	Affluent executives, family areas
4.11. Affluent working couples with mortgages, new homes	1.3	
4.12. Transient workforces, living at place of work	0.3	
5.13. Home owning family areas	2.6	Well-off workers, family areas
5.14. Home owning family areas, older children	3.0	
5.15. Families with mortgages, younger children	2.2	
ACORN Category C: Rising		
6.16. Well-off town and city areas	1.1	Affluent urbanites, town & city areas
6.17. Flats and mortgages, singles, young working couples	0.7	
6.18. Furnished flats and bedsits, younger single people	0.4	
7.19. Apartments, young professional singles and couples	1.2	Prosperous professionals, metropolitan areas
7.20. Gentrified multi-ethnic areas	1.0	
8.21. Prosperous enclaves, highly qualified executives	0.8	Better-off executives, inner city areas
8.22. Academic centres, students and young professionals	0.7	

8.23. Affluent city centre areas, tenements and flats	0.4	
8.24. Partially gentrified multi-ethnic areas	0.7	
8.25. Converted flats and bedsits, single people	0.9	

ACORN Category D: Settling

9.26. Mature established home owning areas	3.3	Comfortable middle agers, mature home owning areas
9.27. Rural areas, mixed occupations	3.5	
9.28. Established home owning areas	4.0	
9.29. Home owning areas, council tenants, retired people	2.7	
10.30. Established home owning areas, skilled workers	4.5	Skilled workers, home owning areas
10.31. Home owners in older properties, younger workers	3.0	
10.32. Home owning areas with skilled workers	3.0	

ACORN Category E: Aspiring

11.33. Council areas, some new home owners	3.8	New home owners, mature communities
11.34. Mature home owning areas, skilled workers	3.1	
11.35. Low rise estates, older workers, new home owners	2.8	
12.36. Home owning multi-ethnic areas, young families	1.1	White collar workers, better-off multi-ethnic areas
12.37. Multi-occupied town centre areas, mixed occupations	1.8	
12.38. Multi-ethnic areas, white collar workers	1.1	

ACORN Category F: Striving

13.39. Home owners, small council flats, single pensioners	1.9	Older people, less prosperous areas
13.40. Council areas, older people, health problems	1.7	
14.41. Better-off council areas, new home owners	2.4	Council estate residents, better-off homes
14.42. Council areas, young families, some new home owners	3.0	
14.43. Council areas, young families, many lone parents	1.6	
14.44. Multi-occupied terraces, multi-ethnic areas	0.8	
14.45. Low rise council housing, less well-off families	1.8	
14.46. Council areas, residents with health problems	1.9	
15.47. Estates with high unemployment	1.1	Council estate residents, high unemployment
15.48. Council flats, elderly people, health problems	0.7	
15.49. Council flats, very high unemployment, singles	0.9	
16.50. Council areas, high unemployment, lone parents	1.8	Council estate residents, greatest hardship
16.51. Council flats, greatest hardship, many lone parents	0.9	
17.52. Multi-ethnic, large families, overcrowding	0.6	People in multi-ethnic, low-income areas
17.53. Multi-ethnic, severe unemployment, lone parents	1.0	
17.54. Multi-ethnic, high unemployment, overcrowding	0.5	

The common element in all geodemographic systems is their use of census enumeration district (ED) data. Other systems are broadly similar although each uses a variety of other variables. MOSAIC for example includes housing data similar to the Acorn system but also includes:

- financial data (county court judgments, finance house/credit card searches)
- socio-economic census data (occupations and car ownership)
- census data (ownership, facilities and size of household, number and ages of residents)
- demographics (people who have moved house)

Activity 2.2
- Go to **www.capscan.com**
- Go to **www.marketinglists.com/eroll.htm**
- Go to **www.anysite.com**
- Go to **www.informationpathwaysinc.com**

Geographic modelling

GMAP University of Leeds

Geographic modelling is different from residential neighbourhood classification systems because it is based on using catchment areas, demographic data within those areas, with information from market research on patterns of behaviour and competitor information. Geographical models then simulate the interaction between supply and demand.

Extending Knowledge

Find out more about GMAP from the University of Leeds. See www.ccg.leeds.ac.uk/linda/geodem/gd_inlvo.html

---

Demographic techniques

Demography studies the measurable aspects of society such as: age, gender, education, occupation, social grade, religion, race, culture, nationality, family size and family life cycle. Most secondary data is expressed in demographic terms and the information helps marketers to:

- Provide an understanding of market structure and potential customer segments
- Identify potential for sales
- Identify trends in population
- Locate a target market.

Data is easy to get hold of, and compared to other segmentation methods it isn't too expensive.

Social class and status

Two of the most commonly used terms in segmentation are class and status.

Social class is the most heavily used segmentation technique used in the UK because it relies on an existing class system and provides an objective measure for classifying people.

Social class gives a hierarchical classification in which each group is stratified into strata or classes (see Table 2.2). The technique relies heavily on a combination of:

- Occupation
- Income
- Educational attainment.

Social grade	Social status	Occupation
A	Upper middle class	Higher managerial, administrative or professional
B	Middle class	Intermediate managerial, administrative or professional
C1	Lower middle class	Supervisory or clerical, and junior managerial, administrative or professional
C2	Skilled working class	Skilled manual workers
D	Working class	Semi and unskilled manual workers
E	Those at lowest level of subsistence	State pensioners or widows (no other earner), casual or lowest-grade workers

Source: Rice, C. (1997) *Understanding Customers,* Butterworth-Heinemann.

Table 2.2 *NRS Social Grade definitions These are the standard social grade classifications using definitions agreed between Research Services Ltd. and NRS. A JICNARS publication Social Grading on the National Readership Survey and National Readership Survey Appendix E describe the definitions and methodology used.* Source: *Rice, C. (1993)* Consumer Behaviour, *Butterworth-Heinnemann.*

The idea of class is complex but some of the key ideas are as follows:

1. The notion of hierarchical distinction which is also expressed in ideas such as social stratification – upper class, middle class, lower class, working class.

2. The use of census data to provide descriptive categories such as those used by the Registrar General in dividing the population of the United Kingdom.

3. The use of occupations to identify socio-economic status groups such as manual and non-manual, or white collar and blue collar.

4. The description of a society in terms of the degree of social mobility. This leads directly to classifications such as open societies (social mobility and movement from one class to another being possible) and closed societies (social class being defined and fixed at (and by) birth as in a caste system).

5. The ideas of Marx which centre on ownership and non-ownership of property and resources and which give rise to the classification of bourgeoisie and proletariat as the dominant classes in capitalistic societies.

6. Weber's use of similar analysis focused on the subdivisions of property, including ideas such as knowledge or education.

Definition

Class is used by the marketer to identify groups of people of similar status to share beliefs, aspirations and values. It is an objective way of classifying people according to such criteria as occupation, education, lifestyle, place of residence and income. It implies an awareness of class consciousness within the group, a degree of uniformity of lifestyle, and social interaction. *Rice, C. (1993) Consumer Behaviour, Butterworth-Heinemann*

Activity 2.3

1. What class are you? On what basis do you make that judgement?
2. Do your colleagues agree with you?
3. What class are the other people living in your neighbourhood?

Allocation to social class categories

Allocating people to a particular category usually involves one of three approaches:

1. The *subjective* approach where participants are asked to decide their own social class.
2. The *reputational* approach where individuals are asked to determine the social class of others in the community.
3. The *objective* approach where non-participants allocate individuals on the basis of pre-determined factors (e.g. occupation, education, income and wealth, lifestyle).

In 1990, the Market Research Society published an up-to-date guide to socio-economic status. The guide defines the pecking order of 1500 jobs and is based not on earnings, but on qualifications and responsibilities.

Activity 2.4

Look at Table 2.3. Do you agree with the classifications?

Status

Status is a subjective phenomenon which is a result of the judgement of the social position the person occupies. Here the distinction from class becomes somewhat blurred as the judgement is usually also based on factors such as power, wealth and occupation.

It is possible to identify three forms of status:

1. *Ascribed status* – this is similar to the ideas of ascribed groups. Individuals have little control over this as it covers the status accorded by society to classifications such as gender (male/female) and race/colour.

2. *Achieved status* – in contrast, is that which has been acquired by individuals through occupation, place of residence and lifestyle.

3. *Desired status* – this is the social status an individual wishes to attain. Here the analogy is with the aspirational group.

Social grade/class

The social grades, class, occupation and percentage of the UK population has already been outlined in Table 2.2.

A: admiral, advocate, air marshal, ambassador, archbishop, attorney, bank manager, bishop, brigadier, chemist shop manager (more than 25 staff); chief constable, chief engineer, chief fire officer, chief rabbi, chiropodist (more than five staff); national orchestra conductor, coroner, university dean, dental surgeon with own practice, chartered estate agent, self-employed farmer (more than 10 staff), financier, general practitioner (own practice/partner), school head-teacher (more than 750 pupils), homoeopath, insurance underwriter, magistrate, hospital matron, judge, MP, professor and town clerk.

B: advertising account director, archdeacon, area sales manager, ballistics expert, qualified brewer, bursar, churchcanon, chef (more than 25 staff), police chief inspector, computer programmer, stock exchange dealer, deputy power station manager, drawing office manager, fund manager, master mariner, orchestra leader, parish priest, parson, prison governor, probation officer, rabbi, senior buyer, senior engineer, qualified social worker, secondary-school teacher, television newscaster, lecturer and nursing sister.

C1: advertising account executive, accounts clerk, announcer (television, radio or station platform), art buyer, articled clerk, athlete, band master, bank cashier, boxer, bus inspector, calligrapher, campanologist, telephone canvasser, cardiographer, cartographer, chef (five to 24 staff), chemist dispenser, chorister, chorus girl, clown, sports coach, coastguard, computer operator, skilled cook, police constable, advertising copywriter, travel courier, curate, cricketer, dancer, dental hygienist, private detective, dietician, driving examiner/instructor, estate agent (not chartered), fashion model, film projectionist, golfer, hospital houseman, book illustrator, disc jockey, juggler, domestic loss adjuster, magician, maitre d'hotel, masseur/masseuse, midwife, monk, nun, staff nurse, non-manual office worker, pawnbroker, plant breeder, RSPCA inspector, receptionist, secretary, telephone operator, sports umpire, youth worker.

C2:AA patrolman, self-employed antique dealer, boat builder, bus driver, shoemaker, bricklayer, carpenter, chimney sweep, bespoke tailoring cutter, deep-sea diver, dog handler, hairdresser, skilled electrician, fireman, thatcher, train driver, Rolls-Royce trained chauffeur, skilled miner.

D: au pair, bingo caller, dustman, bodyguard, bus conductor, chauffeur, croupier, dog breeder, lumberjack, unskilled miner, nursemaid and ratcatcher.

E: anyone brave enough to admit it.

Table 2.3 Some examples from the Market Research Society's occupation groupings. Source: MRS (1990)

Criticisms of social class

The major criticism of class being used is that it is too restrictive and may not reflect the changing nature of UK society. It is also too narrow – six categories cannot possibly provide an accurate reflection of 55 million people. In addition, nearly a third of those earning over £21,000 are C2DE and half those earning £15,000-£21,000 are C2DE. The correlation between social grade and income no longer exists.

People find it difficult to define themselves and most people believe themselves to be a different class. Some people like and cling to the idea of being working class, even though objective data proves this belief to be incorrect.

Head of the household categories don't take into consideration what is happening in society.

Access to education has removed many class barriers.

Although values, attitudes, beliefs and purchasing habits don't change overnight, unemployment has reduced the spending power of many middle class managers. However, class is still reflected in certain types of behaviour, for example eating habits reflect class structure. In a survey of 7000 British households, it was convincingly shown that our eating habits are affected not just by our income, but also by class, gender and age ('social class and change in eating habits', *British Food Journal*, 95(1), 1993).

Example for social class vs eating habits

A recent survey by A. C. Nielsen (www.acnielsen.co.uk), using their Consumer Panel, showed that eating habits differ not only by social class but particularly by lifestage.

Question 2.2

Social class and status

1. What are the differences between social class and status? Of what value are these concepts to the marketer?
2. What criticisms have been made about using social class as a segmentation variable?

Sex

Changes in society brought about by the change in women's role has resulted in a number of marketing campaigns being directed at women (cigarettes, cars, hotels).

Income

Generally income provides a useful guide to the capacity to purchase goods, but other factors such as lifestyle, life cycle, cultural values will determine how it is spent.

Age

Age is a useful discriminator in many consumer markets.

Family life cycle

The idea of family life cycle is that as people progress through their lives their membership of the family and lifestyle will change. These changes will then have an effect on the economic character of the household as well as income and household expenditure. There are various models used (seeFigure 2.2 and Figure 2.3).

Stages in the family life cycle	Buying patterns
1 Bachelor stage: young, single people living at home.	Few financial commitments. Recreation and fashion orientated. Buy: cars, entertainment items, holidays.
2 Newly married couples: young, no children.	Better off financially than they are likely to be in the near future. High purchase rate of consumer desirables. Buy: cars, white goods, furniture.
3 Full nest 1: youngest child under six.	House buying is at a peak Liquid assets are low. Dissatisfied with level of savings and financial position generally. Buy: medicines, toys, baby food, white goods.
4 Full nest 2: youngest child six or over.	Financial position is improving. A higher proportion of wives are working. Buy: wider variety of foods, bicycles, pianos.
5 Full nest 3: older married couples with dependent children.	Financial position is improving yet further. A greater proportion of wives work and some children get jobs. Increasing purchase of desirables. Buy: better furniture, unnecessary appliances and more luxury goods.
6 Empty nest 1: older married couples, no children at home, head of household still in the workforce.	Home ownership is at a peak.The financial situation has improved and savings have increased. Interested in travel, recreation and self-education. Not interested in new products. Buy: holidays, luxuries and home improvements.
7 Empty nest 2: older married, no children living at home, head of household retired.	Substantial reduction in income. Buy: medical products and appliances that aid health, sleep and digestion.
8 Solitary survivor in the workforce.	Income still high but may sell home. Same medical and product needs as group 7.
9 Solitary survivor, retired.	Substantial cut in income. Need for attention and security.

Figure 2.2 The family life cycle and its implications for buying behaviour. *Source: Adapted from Wells and Gubar (1966); Wilson and Gilligan with Pearson (1993), Strategic Marketing Management, Butterworth-Heinemann*

The family life cycle (FLC) has been criticized because the changes taking place in society are not reflected in the basic FLC models. Women's roles have changed, there is also a high divorce rate and a large number of single parent families, many couples are childless and remain so, many marriages take place much later, if at all. The labour market has changed and many families have dual income earners, some are out of work, or retire early.

There is however a distinctive lifetime pattern to saving and spending. When we are in our twenties and thirties – getting married, buying houses, having children – we borrow and spend. When we are old and retired, we 'dissave' and spend. In middle age, therefore, we have to save to repay debts and build up capital for our old age.

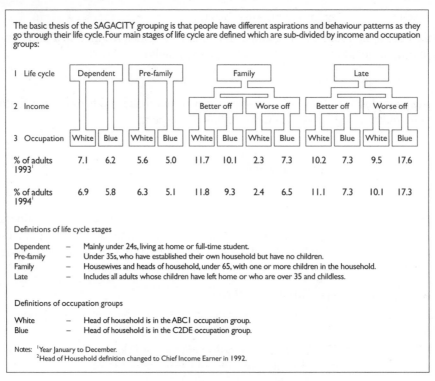

The basic thesis of the SAGACITY grouping is that people have different aspirations and behaviour patterns as they go through their life cycle. Four main stages of life cycle are defined which are sub-divided by income and occupation groups:

1 Life cycle	Dependent		Pre-family		Family				Late			
2 Income					Better off		Worse off		Better off		Worse off	
3 Occupation	White	Blue	White	Blue	White	Blue	White	Blue	White	Blue	White	Blue
% of adults 1993[1]	7.1	6.2	5.6	5.0	11.7	10.1	2.3	7.3	10.2	7.3	9.5	17.6
% of adults 1994[1]	6.9	5.8	6.3	5.1	11.8	9.3	2.4	6.5	11.1	7.3	10.1	17.3

Definitions of life cycle stages

Dependent	–	Mainly under 24s, living at home or full-time student.
Pre-family	–	Under 35s, who have established their own household but have no children.
Family	–	Housewives and heads of household, under 65, with one or more children in the household.
Late	–	Includes all adults whose children have left home or who are over 35 and childless.

Definitions of occupation groups

White	–	Head of household is in the ABC1 occupation group.
Blue	–	Head of household is in the C2DE occupation group.

Notes: [1]Year January to December.
[2]Head of Household definition changed to Chief Income Earner in 1992.

Figure 2.3 The SAGACITY life cycle groupings. Source: RSL (Research Services Ltd) and NRS Ltd

Social and cultural characteristics can make a big difference in the approach to be taken when classifying customers at a transnational or global level. It is important to be aware of varying importance attached to different discriminators in different countries. To get a feel for the sort of demographic dimensions considered important, study recent research in the country under consideration. For example, those interested in the US market could do worse than look at the journal *American Demographics* (available on-line at www.marketingtools.com).

Activity 2.5

Application of life cycle

You have now read through the section on life cycle. Which markets do you think you could usefully apply it to?

Activity 2.6

Cross-national demographics

Pick any two countries. Research how the significance of demographic factors might vary between nations.

Question 2.3

In what way could a portfolio of products for an insurance company be designed for consumers using life cycle segmentation as an approach?

Behaviour in the product field

This method is based on a series of behavioural measures including:

- Attitudes to the product/service – positive, indifferent, negative, etc.
- Knowledge – aware, unaware, interested, intending to buy
- Benefits sought – apply to product/service
- User status – non-user, ex-user, potential user, first time user, regular user
- Usage rate – light, medium, heavy

- Loyalty status – none, medium, strong, absolute
- Purchase occasion – regular, special occasion, critical event
- Adoption process.

A few of these are discussed in more detail, others are fairly self-evident.

Benefit segmentation

Marketers focus on selecting the major benefit on which the unique selling proposition (USP) can be based.

Marketers can however use more than one benefit to position a product/service (see the section on positioning below).

Activity 2.7

How would you segment the soft drinks market? Fill in the space below with some well-known brand names.

	Brand names
Sport drink	
Ice tea	
Nutrition drinks	
Functional drinks	
Fruit juices	

- User status – non-users, ex-users, potential users, first-time users and regular users. First-time users and regular users can also be considered in terms of the rate of usage – heavy, medium, light. This segmentation variable can be used in formulating strategy. For example: a company with a high market share will focus on converting potential users into actual users. A company with a smaller or lower market share will often concentrate on persuading users of competitive brands to switch brands.

- Loyalty status can also be used to segment a market – hard-core loyals, soft-core loyals, shifting loyals and switchers. If consumers are very loyal to a product it is unlikely that they will switch.

- The adoption process could also be used to segment a market – innovators, early adopters, early majority, late majority and laggards.

The US fitness market can be broken into three market segments, covering 50 per cent of families:

Winners who recognize the need to get fit and equate it with their desire to achieve generally;

Dieters who perceive fitness as a way of controlling their weight; and

Self-improvers who perceive fitness as a necessary part of their sense of well-being.

These three segments can be easily targeted by marketers working in health services marketing, such as hospital marketing managers.

Source: 'Benefit segmentation of the fitness market', *Health Marketing Quarterly,* **9**, 1992.

Motivation, psychographics and social value groups

For a detailed description of how motivation theory is applied to marketing see page the section 'Motivation' in *Unit 3, The individual, the group and organization as customer*.

What is psychographics?

The technique of measuring lifestyles is known as psychographics. In the classification shown below the word 'psychographic' has come to cover personality, lifestyle and various other systems of classification.

Psychographics is not the same as demographic analysis as it tends to include qualitative data on motives, attitudes and values.

Although psychographics includes qualitative factors, like motivation, its findings are presented as quantified, statistical data in tabular format. It is different from motivation research as it relies on less intensive techniques like self-administered questionnaires and inventories (ordered listing or catalogue of items that assesses traits, opinions, beliefs, behaviours, etc.).

The term 'psychographic segmentation' is given to the main way in which lifestyle analysis is carried out. It is commonly called AIO analysis and it focuses primarily on developing personality inventories based on attitudes when discussing:

- The relevant activities which are usually observable, measurable and objective and relate to how people spend their time: work, hobbies, social events, shopping habits, sports, entertainment, reading, holidays, club membership.

- Interests which imply all or some of the following: attention, curiosity, motivation, focus, concern, goal-directedness, awareness, worthiness and desire related to – topics, events, subjects, family, home, achievements, food, media, recreation, fashion, community.

- Opinions – where people stand on product related issues. It is a term used to describe something that is intellectually held and based on expectations, evaluations and interpretations about objects, events, people, social issues, or topics such as politics, business, education.

Activities, interests and opinions are different from beliefs where there is an emotional component, and from attitudes which can also be thought of as something internal.

Psychographic segmentation

The number of direct marketing campaigns has increased significantly over the last few years so the need to identify sub-groups of the population has never been more important. By understanding each group's characteristics and motivations the marketing mix can be tailored to meet that its requirements.

Demographics such as Lifestage and Social Class are easy to understand and fairly easy to apply, however these are often insufficiently discriminating for sensitive targeting. Using Psychographics we can move beyond the who, where and what and begin to look at why.

If we use the retail environment as an example, differing attitudes and motivations are essential drivers of behaviour in the arena of pricing and promotional activity. A.C. Nielsen's (www.acnielsen.co.uk) attitudinal segmentation 'Promo*Focus' is a more targeted segmentation which focuses on this particular area of marketing strategy. Seven types of consumer have been identified all with radically different triggers in relation to price/promotion (see Table 2.4).

Table 2.4 Promo*Focus Copyright 2001 A.C. Nielsen

Promo*Focus Type	in GB	Attitudinal description	Characteristics
Branded EDLP Seekers	17.3	"I'm not prepared to compromise even though I'm a bit short, I know what brands I like and I'll search about for them at the lowest price"	Brand loyal Store disloyal Likes shopping
Low Price Fixture Ferrets	13.3	"I know where I'm going to shop and I'll look about for the lowest price when I get there"	Own Label buyers Likes coupons Store loyal
Promotion Junkies	15.6	"I've no need to be thrifty but I love it – I get a buzz out of getting the most groceries for the lowest price. Coupons appeal to me"	Will search for best offers Organized promotions shopper Brand/store disloyal
Stock-Pilers	12.9	"Well it seemed silly not to buy it – it was such a good buy and even though I've got an awful lot of it, well it is our favourite brand"	Price not important Loves multi-buys Brand and store loyal
Budget Bound	12.4	"I hate shopping because I have to be so careful. Money is very tight"	Budget constraints Hates shopping Price driven, no stock-piling
Promotion Opportunists	14.9	"I love promotions and am prepared to buy more to get a bargain. Saving money is key"	Penny watches Shopping not planned Brand disloyal
Promotional Oblivious	13.6	"So what's a promotion then?"	Not interested in offers Traditionalists Store and brand loyal

Understanding these different consumers and their attitudes in relation to a particular brand or shopper franchise will allow manufacturers and retailers to refine and maximize their marketing strategies.

Lifestyle

Lifestyle is the way in which a person tries to achieve their desired self-concept.

The term 'lifestyle' was introduced to marketing in 1963 by William Lazer with the idea that a systematic relationship exists between consumption and lifestyles of a social group. It is important to remember that people in the same demographic group can have very different psychographic profiles.

Max Weber thought of lifestyle as a mark of status which enabled the person to be recognized as belonging to a group and helps them to become socially integrated.

Alfred Adler used the same term but thought of lifestyle as the way in which the individual adapts psychologically to society.

Lifestyle can therefore be looked at in two ways, either as a reflection of personality and motivation (inwardly driven), or a sign of social stereotyping (externally driven).

Lifestyle analysis starts with individual motivation using techniques of group discussion and depth interview, and then links it to groups of people. Once the groups have been defined the marketer is then able to decide on the group and create a stereotype at which the advertising message is to be targeted.

Social value groups

Social value groups are founded on shared values and beliefs but the members of each group also share distinct patterns of behaviour.

Examples of social value groups

The VALS System (SRI International)

This system was developed in the USA by Arnold Mitchell of the Stanford Research Institute.

The VALS framework used the answers of 2713 respondents to 800 questions to classify the American public into nine value lifestyle groups. This framework shows that individuals pass through various stages of development, each of which influences attitudes, behaviour and psychological needs. They move from being driven by needs (survivors and sustainers) to an outwardly directed hierarchy (belongers, emulators and achievers) to an inner directed hierarchy (I-am-me, experientials, societally conscious).

The 9 groups, together with estimates of the percentage of the US population within each group are:

1. Survivors who are generally disadvantaged and who tend to be depressed, withdrawn and despairing (4%).
2. Sustainers who are again disadvantaged but who are fighting hard to escape poverty (7%).
3. Belongers who tend to be conventional, nostalgic, conservative and generally reluctant to experiment with new products or ideas (33%).
4. Emulators who are status conscious, ambitious and upwardly mobile (10%).
5. Achievers who make things happen, and enjoy life (23%).
6. I-am-me who are self-engrossed, respond to whims and generally young (5%).
7. Experientials who want to experience a wide variety of what life can offer (7%).
8. Societally conscious people with a marked sense of social responsibility and who want to improve the condition of society (9%).
9. Integrateds who are psychologically fully mature and who combine the best elements of inner and outer directedness (2%).

Other models have been developed over the years from the insights offered by lifestyle analysis such as Young and Rubicam's 4Cs and Taylor Nelson's Monitor, and Stanford Research Institute's lifeways.

Monitor (Taylor Nelson)

This typology has the following framework and is rather similar to VALS.

1. Sustenance-driven. Motivated by material security, they are sub-divided into:
   a. aimless, who include young unemployed and elderly drifters and comprise 5% of the population;

      b.   survivors, traditionally-minded working class people who comprise 16% of the population;

      c.   belongers, these conservative family-oriented people form 18% of the population, but only half of them are sustenance driven.

2. Outer-directed. Those who are mainly motivated by the desire for status, they are divided into:

      a.   belongers

      b.   conspicuous consumers (19%)

3. Inner-directed. These are subdivided into:

      a.   social resisters who are caring and often doctrinaire (11%)

      b.   experimentalist, who are hedonistic and individualistic (14%)

      c.   self explorers, who are less doctrinaire than social resisters and less materialistic than experimentalist.

Young and Rubicam 4Cs

This is a Cross-Cultural Consumer Characterization based on the following framework:

1. the constrained:

      a.   the resigned poor

      b.   the struggling poor

2. the middle majority:

      a.   mainstreamers

      b.   aspirers

      c.   succeeders

3. the innovators:

      a.   the transitionals

      b.   reformers

The 4Cs define the individual and group motivations and needs. Young and Rubicam have used this to develop marketing and advertising campaigns both domestically and internationally. The British Gas 'Tell Sid' shares campaign and Legal and General's 'Umbrella Campaign' were based on this analysis.

The terms Yuppie (young upwardly mobile professional) and Bumps (borrowed-to-the-hilt, upwardly mobile professional show-off) have been used to illustrate a particular style of life.

The Stanford Research Institute's life ways

This cover the relationship between people and society and suggest that people fall into one of six groups. Kotler (1988) summarized them as follows:

- *Makers* Makers are those who make the system work. They are the leaders and up-and-comers. They are involved in worldly affairs, generally prosperous and ambitious. They are found in the professions and include the managers and proprietors of business.

- *Preservers* Preservers are people who are at ease with the familiar and are proud of tradition.

- *Takers* Takers take what they can from the system. They are attracted to bureaucracies and tenured posts.

- *Changers* Changers tend to be answer-havers; they commonly wish to change things to conform with their views. They are critics, protestors, radicals, advocates and complainers.

- *Seekers* Seekers are the ones who search for a better grasp, a deeper understanding, a richer experience, a universal view. They often originate and promulgate new ideas.

- *Escapers* Escapers have a drive to escape, to get away from it all. Escape takes many forms from dropping out, to addiction, to mental illness, to mysticism.

These life groups differ in many ways and need to be seen as market segments with specific material and symbolic needs.

Practical application of market research

You will remember that the market researcher is likely to approach the design of a segmentation study from one of two angles:

1. Consumer typology – clustering consumers
2. Product differentiation – clustering products.

However, in practice many marketers face a situation where they do not have the information to do this in any depth and a general 'thumb nail' approach is shown to you below under Method 1. The second approach, where the objective is to cluster products, is shown to you under Method two.

Method 1 – a thumbnail sketch clustering consumers

Sometimes students get the target marketing process confused with the marketing mix. So, in order to get these out of the way, first think about the product/service, the place (channels of distribution) and the price. Then think about the target marketing process and follow these steps:

Target marketing process

1. *Market segmentation* Using the segmentation systems explained to you above – geographic, geodemographic, demographic, behavioural and psychographic – think about dividing the market into distinct groups of buyers who might call for separate products or marketing mixes.

   Then see if any natural segments already exist. The most important ones will show you the basic structure of the market.

2. *Market targeting* After the different ways in which a market can be segmented are identified the marketer develops different profiles of the market segments. These are then evaluated and a decision is made on which market segment/s to enter.

3. *Market positioning* The third step is market positioning which involves deciding on the competitive position for the product/service.

4. *Designing the marketing mix* After this has been carried out the marketing mix is designed – product, price, place and promotion.

Example

To help you decide which method to use it is often helpful to lay out the following grid:

Historic site publications

Product features: Photography, illustration, map, postcards, writing style and design, quantity of information, size of publication, language

Price: A range – low, medium and high price

Place of purchase: On-site shop, off-site shops

Target marketing process

1. Market segmentation

   Geographical: UK, Europe, USA, historic site

   Demographic: Family life cycle (child, adult, family), income, language group (home or visitor from abroad), school, class

   Behavioural: Purchase occasion – one-off purchase, could be a collector of a series benefits sought – memento, record of history, entertainment, curriculum related activities

   Psychographic: ? no information available

2. The main segmentation variable here in the UK would be for overseas or home visitor use. Segmentation on home visitor use would be life cycle and schools use. There would therefore be three primary segments – overseas visitors, home visitors and schools.

3. Market target

   These will need to be assessed using the criteria explained to you above in market targeting – how to choose (a) usable market segment/s.

   For example: this information could then be related to other information such as the number of visitors (with or without children), foreign language visitors, schools coming to a site and an estimate of the potential market and market segments made on the basis of an analysis of these figures and the target market/s chosen.

4. Product positioning (this is discussed in more detail below)

    The product would be positioned on:

    o   Price

    o   Quality

    o   Product features.

5. Marketing mix

    Once you have decided on your segments you will need to develop the appropriate marketing mix. You may decide to use:

    o   One marketing mix for the whole market (undifferentiated marketing strategy)

    o   A number of marketing mixes designed to meet the needs of each market segment (differentiated marketing strategy)

    o   Choose a market segment that is your major market segment and allow the mix to filter through to the rest (concentrated marketing strategy).

Home market – family life cycle

	Segment 1	Segment 2	Segment 3
	Child	*Adult*	*Family*
Product	Illustration	Photography	Illustration and photography
Number of pages (roughguide)	Stickers, postcards, poster 12	Map 30/100/200 (3 products)	Map, postcards, poster 30
Price	£1	£3/£10/£20	£2
Promotion Sales promotion, public relations, selling	Possible trade deals sales; press release only; sales visits to outlets		
Place	On-site and immediate surrounds of site		

Schools and foreign language publications developed separately.

Method 2 – product differentiation – clustering products

Here the focus would be on consumer use and perception of types of product or service and, more especially, brands.

In this method the marketer works backwards from the position the product occupies in the marketplace in relation to the competition. They would think about the sequence of variables which consumers may consider when they make a purchase. This information is then related to other geographic, geodemographic, demographic, behavioural and psychographic information.

This could be done by: creating a perceptual map on two (or more) dimensions; or creating a brand map by using attributes.

Creating a perceptual map on two dimensions

The thread that runs through all this is the need for the marketer to understand the structure of the market. This is most commonly done by focusing on three areas:

1. Develop a spatial map of consumers' perceptions of brands within a given market sector.

2. Identify how consumers see existing products/services in relation to this map and put the names of competitors' brands onto this map. You will then be able to use the map either to spot a gap or develop an ideal position for your brand.

3. From this map you will then be able to develop a model which will help you to predict consumer responses to new and modified products/ services.

Example

Here the wine market is positioned on two dimensions – type of drinker, and usage occasion.

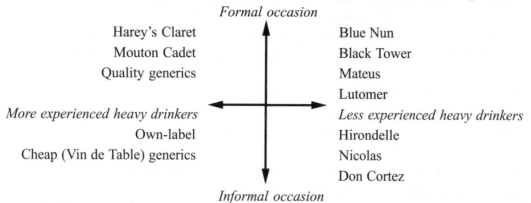

From this map the advertising agency, Abbott Mead Vickers, was able to examine the duplication of brand usage among wine drinkers and establish the degree of overlap between the different brands. By doing this, clusters of brands emerged according to usage and provided the agency strategist with an understanding of the market's structure, the existence of any gaps, the nature and intensity of the competition, and the type of marketing mix needed to establish or support a brand.

This sort of picture of the market can then be taken a step further by superimposing a second map illustrating in greater detail consumer profiles. This might typically include sex (male versus female), age (young/middle-aged, old), income group (high earners versus low earners), and marital status (married versus single).

Source: Wilson and Gilligan with Pearson (1993), *Strategic Marketing Management,* Butterworth-Heinemann

Activity 2.8

Think about the textbooks that you're using on this course and fill in the names of the publisher and titles of the books.

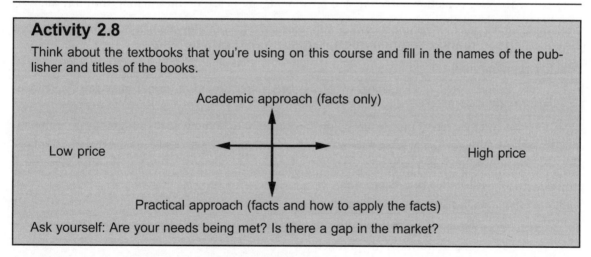

Ask yourself: Are your needs being met? Is there a gap in the market?

Creating a brand map by using attributes

Another way of doing it is to list the attributes and put them into a hierarchy.

Example:

Initial perceptions of instant coffee brands

Expensive			*Cheap*
Gold Blend, Blend 37	Nescafé, Maxwell House	Red Mountain	Own label
The best instants	Popular	Cheaper	Cheap and nasty
Special, expensive, when one has people around, Christmas	Everyday, reliable, the standard, frequent use, old favourites, ordinary	Not as classy, middle of the road, cheap and cheerful	Weak, bitter, lack flavour

Source: Feldwick (1990), p. 210

39

These perceptions led to qualitative research in which the perceptions of Red Mountain elicited the image and personality as being:

Outdoor, rugged, working class, eccentric, ordinary, scruffy, lumber-jack, macho, farmer, normal, dull, boring, rough and ready, strange, untidy, basic.

From these findings the product was repositioned not to compete directly with Gold Blend but at the market occupied by Nescafé and Maxwell House. The brand proposition that was decided on was 'Ground coffee taste without the grind'.

Source: Advertising Works 5, Holt, Rinehart Winston, 1990.

Perceptual maps can be used to:

1. Establish the bases for segmentation.
2. Identify gaps in the market.
3. Identify which brands are perceived to be similar to your own brands.
4. Assess your strengths and weaknesses.
5. Reposition yourself in the marketplace.

Although these methods show the underlying process, the marketer will also have to decide between *a priori* and *post hoc* methods. Both methods have their place.

A priori methods

Segmenting in advance – for example where you know who is purchasing from you, it is then possible to tailor the marketing strategy to the needs and expectations of each group.

The examples of historic site publications, wine and coffee are a priori methods.

Post hoc methods

Segmenting the market on the basis of research findings. Where the market is new, the marketer has no experience of it, or the market is changing or there are no natural segments, a more formal procedure is needed. Segmentation, targeting and positioning are based on information from the analysis (see below for the method).

Seven steps in market segmentation, targeting and positioning

Market segmentation

1. At an individual level, identify what the needs are through informal interviews and focus groups.
2. Based on their needs profile, group the customers into homogeneous subgroups or segments.
3. Based on these findings prepare a formal questionnaire that is administered to a sample of consumers to collect data on:
   o Attributes, and their rating
   o Brand awareness and brand ratings
   o Product usage patterns
   o Attitudes towards the product
   o Demographics, psychographics and mediagraphics.

The needs-based subgroups will then be identified with *other characteristics* that will enable you to reach the segment with your promotional mix.

Market targeting

1. Cluster analysis will then allow you to create a number of different segments (internally homogeneous and externally different). The potential of each segment can be evaluated and the segment selected that will give you the greatest opportunity – this is your target market (see below how to choose a usable market segment).
2. Choose which segment/s you will target.

Market positioning

1. The product/service will then need to be positioned within the selected segment/s.
2. Develop the right marketing mix for each target segment.

Market targeting: how to choose usable market segments

Ideally segmentation bases should allow us to reveal segments that have these characteristics:

- *Measurable* The segments should be measurable. In many markets it can be more difficult to do if there is a lack of specific published data.
- *Accessible* The marketers should be able to reach the segments with promotion.
- *Substantial* The segments revealed should be large enough to serve profitably. This decision is relative because what one organization may consider as being appropriate for them, another may not. Ford may not be interested in custom-built cars whereas a smaller company may be able to target this segment.
- *Stable* Ideally it should be possible to predict how the segment will behave in the future and that it will exist long enough to warrant the time and cost of development.
- *Appropriate* The segment should be chosen so that there is a fit between it and the organization's objectives and resources.
- *Unique* The segment should be distinguishable from other market segments and show clear variations in market behaviour in comparison with other segments.

Activity 2.9

Discuss the factors you think people consider when buying a computer service?

Question 2.5

On what basis would you choose a market segment?

Positioning

- Positioning refers to the way in which a product/service is defined by the consumer in their minds relative to that of the competition.
- Positioning is carried out after market segmentation.
- The message should be distinctive and the customer should understand it as the basis for their buying decisions.
- Positioning should take into account the position of a market leader, follower or challenger – followers should not position themselves too close to or directly against the market leader.

A smaller firm should be able to find its own customers and position in the marketplace.

Positioning strategies can be related to:

- The product attributes
- The benefits they offer
- The price
- The quality
- The application – extending cornflakes from a breakfast cereal to something that can be eaten all day
- The users – extending the eating of cornflakes to adults
- By product class – against another product class (margarine tastes like butter) or with another product class (soap that acts like a moisturizer)
- By competitor – against a competitor (products are compared with a competitor), or away from a competitor (we are not the same we are different).

Very often there is an overlap between the original market segmentation and the positioning, this can cause some confusion as the same ideas are repeated and one gets lost between thinking – is it segmentation I am doing or is it positioning?

Worked examples

Try doing these examples without looking at the answers below. You may or may not agree with the worked examples as they have not been done with any of the added benefits of research. Think about how you would extend or change what has been suggested to you. A question mark has been put in where there is not enough information available.

Remember

It is not always possible to fill all the information into the segmentation systems, either because not enough is known about the market, or the category does not apply.

- Look for natural segments
- Most marketers will segment a market in more than one way and use two or more demographic variables
- Try and think of which method will be most suited to the particular product/service
- Not all the ways in which a market can be segmented are covered in the classifications shown to you above, so use them as a guide
- Segmentation is a creative exercise and must be related to the market with which you are dealing.

1. Clothes washing market
2. Analgesic market
3. Vitamin market
4. Air travel
5. Greeting cards.

First think about the product/service, the place (channels of distribution) and the price in order to get them out of the way so you do not get them confused with market segmentation. They can also be helpful when you consider market positioning and the marketing mix.

Target marketing process

1. *Market segmentation* Using the segmentation systems explained to you above (geographic, geodemographic, demographic, behavioural and psychographic) think about dividing the market into distinct groups of buyers who might call for separate products or marketing mixes.
2. *Market target* These will need to be assessed using the criteria explained to you above in market targeting – how to choose a usable market segment/s.
3. *Market positioning* Now think about the sequence of variables which consumers may consider when they make a purchase, how you think the product would be positioned within that market segment in relation to the competition.
4. *Marketing mix* The marketing mix would be designed on the basis of the above information.

Answers

Clothes washing market

Target marketing process

1. Market segmentation

Geographic:	USA
Demographic:	Age, male, female
Behaviour in the product field:	Benefits and different mixes of benefits – extra action, hot, warm, cold water, enzyme, non-enzyme, concentrated, less suds, fabric softener, mild and gentle, with bleach, with special ingredients (proteins, borax, detergent to get out stains), scented, unscented, extra-scented, liquid/powder, concentrated/ unconcentrated (based on Kotler) – can you think of any more?

Psychographic: ? No information available – would need research

Motivation: Clean clothes, good mothering/fathering

2. The target market would then be chosen.

3. Market positioning

Market positioning would take place on one of these benefits.

Analgesic market

Product ingredients: Aspirin, paracetamol, codeine, etc.

Product features: Size of tablet, shape of tablet, colour of tablet, container size

Place of purchase: Chemist or general distribution

Price: A range

Target marketing process

1. Market segmentation

Geographic: UK

Demographic: Age of user, male, female

Behaviour in the product field:
Purchase occasion: regular, special
Benefits sought: speed of treatment, safety, ease of swallow, frequency of dosage
User status: non-user, ex-user, potential user, first-time user, regular
Loyalty status: none, medium, strong, absolute
The usage: type of ailment (head, period, arthritis, cold, flu, hangover, migraine)
The usage rate: light, medium, heavy usage time: morning, day, evening

Psychographic: ? No information available – would need research

Motivation: Pain relief

2. The main segmentation variables would be the usage (type of ailment), benefits sought. Other demographic information related to this would be age of user and sex. This information should reveal the basic market structure from which the target market would be selected.

3. Market positioning

Market positioning would be done on using a selection/combination of these points:

o Product features

o Product ingredients

o Benefits sought

o Price

o Against a competitor.

Vitamin market

Product ingredients: ?

Place of purchase: Chemist, general distribution

Price: ?

Target marketing process

1. Market segmentation

Geographic: UK

Demographic: Age

Behaviour in the product field: Needs/benefits related to each age group

Psychographic: ? No information available – would need research

Motivation: Health, vitality

2. The main segmentation variables would be the needs/benefits related to each age group from which the target market would be selected.

3. Market positioning

Market positioning would be done on using a selection/combination of these points:
- o Product features
- o Benefits
- o Price
- o Quality.

Air travel – air passenger market

Target marketing process

1. Market segmentation

Geographic:	International
Demographic:	Age, occupation, male, female, cultural differences
Behaviour in the product field:	Purchase occasion – journey purpose: business – corporate, independent, conference and incentive travel Leisure – holiday, visiting friends and relatives Length of journey – long haul, short haul Benefits sought – excess baggage, schedule convenience, in-flight amenities, status recognition, safety, status of airline, type of air craft, punctuality, flexibility Usage rate – light, medium, heavy (frequent flier) Loyalty status – none, medium, strong, absolute (also relate this to country of origin loyalty) Critical event – sudden illness, or emergency back home
Psychographic:	? No information on psychographics
Motivation:	Safety, comfort, reliability

2. The main segmentation variable would be business or leisure. Further development of this would involve looking at all the other variables shown above. This should reveal distinct groups of buyers who might call for separate products or marketing mixes from which the target market would be selected.

3. Market positioning

The product would be positioned within those segments using a combination of these points:
- o Product features
- o Benefits
- o Price
- o Quality
- o Against a competitor (better than)
- o Against a product class (train, road, ship)

Greeting cards

Product features: humour, romantic, cartoon, classic artwork, photography, stickers, badges, electronic music and so on.

Place of purchase: corner shop, greeting shop, garage, giftshop, etc. Price: under £1, over £1, etc.

Target marketing process

1. Market segmentation

Geographic:	UK
Demographic:	Age, class, sex
Behaviour in the product field:	Type of occasion – Christmas, Easter, birth, birthday, Valentine, Mother's Day, bereavement, thank you, just to say hello, remember me, miss you, love you, and so on.
Psychographic:	? No information available – would need research
Motivation:	Just to say hello, remember me, miss you, love you, and so on

2. The major segmentation variables would be on the type of occasion and benefits sought. This would be related to other segmentation variables such as social class, age, sex, race, from which the target market would be selected.

3. Market positioning

   The product would be positioned within those segments using a combination of:
   - Product attributes
   - Price
   - Quality.

Activity 2.10

Now carry out the same exercise on your own organization. Are there any gaps in the information available to you? What can you do to acquire the information that you need?

Exam Hint

1. You must be able to tell the difference between the overall process – target marketing – and the steps involved in carrying this out, which are – market segmentation, market targeting and market positioning.

2. The marketing mix (product, price, promotion, place, and in the case of services, people, process and physical evidence) is designed after this process has been carried out. Not before.

Market segmentation and product positioning have recently undergone several changes:

- Increased emphasis on segmentation criteria that represent softer data such as attitudes and needs.

- Increased awareness that the basis of segmentation depend on its purpose. For example, the same bank customers could be segmented by account ownership profiles, attitudes towards risk taking and socioeconomic variables. Each segmentation could be useful for a different purpose, such as product cross selling, preparation of advertising messages and media selection.

- Greater use of hybrid segmentation methods. For example, a beer producer might first segment consumers according to a favourite brand. Then, within each brand group, consumers could be further segmented according to similarities in attitude towards beer drinking, occasions where beer is consumed and so on.

- Research on dynamic segment models that consider the possibility of competitive retaliation. Such models examine a company's vulnerability to competitive reactions over the short term and choose segment combinations that are most resistant to competitive encroachment.

- A move towards letting the data speak for itself and finding segments through the detection of patterns in survey or in-house data. So called data mining methods have become much more versatile.

Activity 2.11

Go to Market Miner (www.abtech.com). Market Miner helps marketing and sales professionals increase their sales and profitability by 20% to 250% easily and affordably. *Source*: nexis.com.

Insight

Knowing your customers

The more you know about your customers the greater your chances will be to create a product or service that really appeals to them. In fact the web and other technological advances that gather, store and sort data has made it easier and more cost effective than before. For example, Citibank in New York used traditional demographic segmentation, MBNA used affinity segmentation (common interest groups like professional associations and sports teams) and NextCard Inc use self segmentation, allowing customers to configure their own credit card terms. *Source*: nexis.com, sharonfmc@compuserve.com.

Segmenting industrial markets

Much of the work done on consumer market segmentation (see Figure 2.4) can be applied to industrial markets – such as usage rates, benefits sought, geographical location, etc. Other factors which would affect the buying situation would be:

1. Buying situation – new buy, modified rebuy or new task.
2. Type of product and the degree of standardization.
3. Significance of the purchase to the buying organization.
4. Degree of risk and uncertainty involved for the buying organization.
5. Source loyalty.

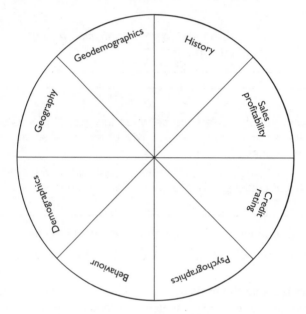

Figure 2.4

Another approach is to look at the major industrial market segmentation variables. A summary of these questions in declining order of importance is shown below.

Demographic

- *Industry* – on which industries that use this product should we concentrate?
- *Company* – on which size of company should we concentrate?
- *Location* – in which geographical areas should we concentrate our efforts?

Operating variables

- *Technology* – which customers' technologies are of greatest interest to us?
- *User status* – on which types of user (heavy, medium, light, non-user) should we concentrate?
- *Customer capabilities* – should we concentrate on customers with a broad or a narrow range of needs?

Purchasing approaches

- *Buying criteria* – should we concentrate on customers seeking quality, service or price?
- *Buying policies* – should we concentrate on companies that prefer leasing systems, systems purchases, or sealed bids?
- *Current relationships* – should we concentrate on existing or new customers?

Situational factors

- *Urgency* – should we concentrate on customers with sudden delivery needs?
- *Size of order* – should we concentrate on large or small orders?
- *Applications* – should we concentrate on general or specific applications of our product?

Personal characteristics

- *Loyalty* – should we concentrate on customers who exhibit high or low levels of loyalty?
- *Attitudes to risk* – should we concentrate on risk taking or risk avoiding customers?

From Bonoma and Shapiro (1983); Wilson and Gilligan with Pearson (1993), *Strategic Marketing Management,* Butterworth-Heinemann.

The decision-making unit is a useful tool for deciding on segmentation variables within the industrial market. People within the unit can be grouped in various ways according to the size of their business and response to variables such as new purchase, attitude to risk, size of order, etc. (See Figure 2.5).

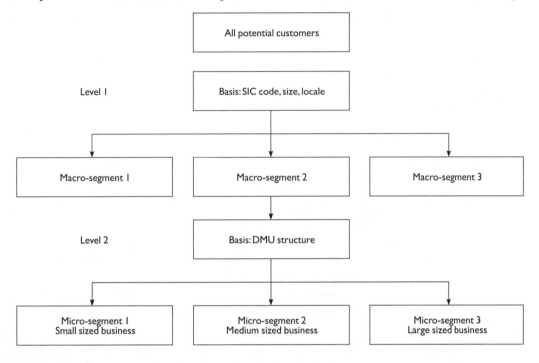

Figure 2.5

One-to-one marketing and mass customization

As markets become increasingly competitive, marketers are turning to methods that will make them increasingly less vulnerable. Companies are focusing on a technique that they hope will satisfy customers so much the price will become irrelevant. The approach is to first differentiate and then focus on target groups of customers with customized products. The next step is to focus on keeping your current customers by providing them with better customer service, better communications and ongoing product differentiation. This technique of one-to-one marketing aims at customizing a product so carefully that it fits the customer perfectly.

Products can be customized in different ways:

1. 'Core' mass customization where products are customized on a mass basis using modular designs and fast, flexible, modular production processes as enabling individual products to be delivered directly to the customer. For example, Motorola has twenty-nine million variations of hand-held pagers. Customization can take place by:
    - o Combinational assembly – customize by assembly
    - o In-house processing – customize by process machining, painting
    - o Information content – customize by onboard software.

2. 'Post-product' customization where standard products are manufactured on a mass basis and customized by having unique services wrapped around the common core, for example, customized software solutions.

3. Mass 'retail' customization where standard products are manufactured on a mass basis and customized at the point of sale or delivery, for example, quick response high street opticians Vision Express where 90 per cent of all glasses are made in house.

4. 'Self' customizing products where the manufacturer, through the use of design and technology capabilities, includes options within the mass-produced product so that the customer may personalize the product at the point of receipt or during the use of the product, for example, personal computers which can be configured to the users choice of screen layout. Vacuum cleaners that can adapt to unique household flooring and carpets.

Why customize? – the drivers

There are various reasons: Panasonic did it because of downward price pressures, inventory obsolescence, increased competition, cheap imports and segmentation complexity; Raleigh did it because of the demand from customers and dealers for specials, which inconvenienced manufacturing whose business processes and IT systems were designed for large batch production.

Imperatives to achieve mass customization are:

- Lean production involving the use of JIT, short set-up times for equipment, minimal work-in-progress inventories.
- Modularity of products and processes
- Successfully integrated IT to cope with the explosion of complexity which mass customization brings
- An intense customer focus
- Supplier partnerships to ensure flexible response to the demands of customization.

One-to-one marketing and mass customization are the extension of traditional target marketing and product differentiation, the only difference is that it tries to fit the customer's needs more perfectly. In order to do business in this way there is a need to change how the business is organized. Information technology is the element which makes this possible and the organization, in order to mass customize, must be able to track large volumes of data.

Levi, Strauss and Co. is making mass customization an instrument of customer satisfaction. They take a woman's measurements, transmit them electronically to the factory and use them to customize a pair of jeans.

One-to-one relationships and mass customization have two different requirements. The first deals with knowing what the customer wants and building a relationship. The second involves providing a mass-customized product and will therefore rely heavily on manufacturing technology.

Marketing one-to-one requires commitment and a culture that is dedicated to treating each customer as the complete focus of the company.

There are four basic steps to go through:

1. Identify customers – identify heavy, medium, light and non-users of your products. It is no use spending money and effort to try and win the wrong customers over.

2. Differentiate each customer – identify what they want and treat them differently.

3. Interact with each customer – every contact that you have with the customer will give the opportunity to learn more about their needs and their potential value to the organization.

4. Customize products/services for each customer – this step is only possible if you have carried out the last three steps and have already identified what the customer wants. It is possible to do this if you integrated the production process with the firm's customer feedback. This will in effect create a barrier of entry as a customer will have to re-invent another relationship with another business in order to get this level of service.

To be able to do this you will need:

- A proper database.
- People working for the organization capable of personal interaction.
- Interactive media.
- Systems that support mass customization.

Individualization doesn't mean adding a layer variety of products which customers can now choose, it is about getting product and services exactly right for those individual customers within the target segment and user group with whom the organization has decided to do business (see Figure 2.6).

M	T	C	I	Unique level 4
M	T	C	Different level 3	
M	T	Similar level 2		
M	Common level 1			

M = Mass, T = Targeted, C = Customized, I = Individualized

Figure 2.6 Reconfiguring the market. *Source: Sanda Vandemerve, John Wiley & Sons, 1996*

Activity 2.12
Have a look at the website **www.1to1.com.**

Question 2.6

Write a memo to the Marketing Director of a major toy manufacturer in which you outline your views on each of the following:

1. The market segmentation system which would be especially relevant for a toy manufacturer (excluding retail).
2. The relevance to your business of the distinction between customers (people who pay for the product) and users (people who use the product but are not the purchasers as such).
3. The importance of understanding the other roles in the decision-making unit, and how your marketing activities might be influenced by them.

Please lay the answer out in a businesslike fashion – the question has three parts and in order to get a decent mark you will need to answer all three.

Market segmentation made easy

	Geographic	Geodemographic	Demographic	Behaviour in the product field	Personal Characteristics
Consumer	Nation State Region Country City	Acorn Mosaic Super Profiles Define Pinpoint	Social class and status Sex Income Age Family Life Cycle	Attitudes Knowledge Benefits sought User status Usage rate Loyalty status Purchase occasion Adoption process	Motivation Personality Psychographics Social value group
	Demographics	Operating Variables	Purchasing Approach	Situational Factors	Personal Characteristics
Industrial	Industry Company size Location	Technology User status Customer capability	Buying criteria Buying policies Current relationships	Urgency Application Size of Order	Motivation Similarity of personalities Similarity of values Perception of risk Loyalty
	General Broad Base				Specific Base Effective

49

Summary

In this unit you have been introduced to the classification of goods and services and will understand how these need to be considered in customer behaviour, market segmentation and the marketing mix.

You have also looked at the decision-making unit and adoption and diffusion curve and been asked to consider them in your market segmentation process.

Traditional methods of market segmentation have been discussed and you have been introduced to the idea of:

- How the whole objective of segmentation is to identify groups of people within the broader market who have needs which are broadly similar to each other and who respond in a similar way to the promotion methods and the rest of the marketing mix.

- How the concept of segmentation is related to consumer and industrial markets and is one of the main cornerstones of marketing.

  1. Segmenting consumer markets
     a. Geographic
     b. Geodemographic
     c. Demographic
     d. Behaviour in the product field
     e. Motivation, psychographics and social value groups.
  2. Segmenting industrial markets
     a. Demographics
     b. Operating variables
     c. Purchasing approaches
     d. Situational factors
     e. Personal characteristics.

- That the market researcher is likely to approach the design of a segmentation study in two ways – by collecting data in order to cluster consumers or by collecting data to cluster products.

- That the process of target marketing calls for four different steps:

  Market segmentation calls for dividing a market into distinct groups of buyers who might call for separate products or marketing mixes.

  Market targeting – the marketer develops different profiles of the market segments. These are then evaluated and a decision is made on which market segment/s to enter.

  Market positioning involves deciding on the competitive position for the product/service.

  Designing the marketing mix.

- You have also considered the limitations of some of the methods that can be used. The importance of mass customization and one-to-one marketing has been shown as being the way forward for certain types of business.

Further study and examination preparation

Now undertake Question 5 from December 2000 to be found in the Exam Paper Appendix.

Question 2.7

As the marketing manager for a soft drinks company, write a report for your Director in which you address the following issue:

a. the factors which your company should take into account when deciding which market segments to address and which ones to leave alone

b. the processes which can lead to the discovery of new and potentially profitable segments

c. the ways in which sales form existing segments may be developed incrementally

Objectives

In this unit you will be:

- Introduced to the concept of culture and explore its constitutional elements.
- Consider the nature of culture – how we acquire it, what membership means, and the cultural consideration required when marketing to different cultures or sub-cultures.
- Consider factors influencing the individual's purchasing behaviour.
- Be introduced to the concept of motivation, self-concept theory, psychoanalytic role theory, trait factor theories and new application to consumer behaviour.
- Look at group influence – how it can occur and its impact on buying behaviour.
- Be introduced to the influence of primary and secondary groups.
- Understand the difference between consumer and industrial buying.

This unit covers the following parts of the Marketing Customer Interface syllabus:

- 2.3.3
- 2.3.4
- 2.3.5

Study guide

In this unit you are introduced to influences on buying behaviour arising from social and cultural aspects of the society. You will explore how it influences and shapes buying behaviour and be able to anticipate problems which can occur when marketing across cultures and sub-cultures. You will also understand the importance of group influence in shaping behaviour and how this influence can be used in marketing.

The motivations that drive customers are also important. To provide what the customer needs requires an understanding of their goals and aspirations. Whereas proven theories of customer motivation are thin on the ground, the general theories of motivation that exist provide useful guidance to marketers. Other theories are touched on.

External factors influencing customer behaviour

These are the social and cultural factors influencing the individual's behaviour as a customer. Sociologists use the term culture to describe the physical and social environment which results in shared attitudes and behaviours, a fact which is of interest to marketers.

Definition

Culture - the values, attitudes, beliefs, ideas, artefacts and other meaningful symbols represented in the pattern of life adopted by people that help them interpret, evaluate and communicate as members of a society.

Culture can be represented graphically as in Figure 3.1)

Influences from institutions and other elements of society (such as education, politics, and the law) combine in complex ways to provide us with culture, customs and rituals which are expressed as attitudes and behaviours.

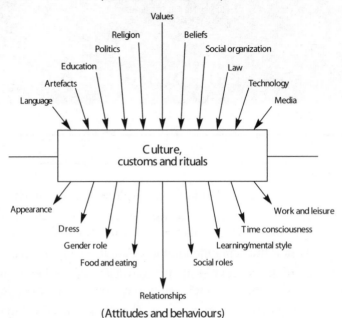

Figure 3.1

(Institutions and elements)

(Attitudes and behaviours)

Keith Williams (1990) *Behavioural Aspects of Marketing* describes five main characteristics of culture:

1. It exists to serve the needs of a society. For example, most cultures have some form of 'wedding' ceremony.

2. It is acquired socially. That is, we are not born with any cultural knowledge but acquire it throughout our lifetime.

3. It is learned by interacting with other members of the culture.

4. It is cumulative. Culture is transferred from generation to generation with new influences constantly being added to the cultural 'soup'.

5. It is adaptive. Culture changes in response to the needs of the society.

Importance of culture in marketing

By understanding the nature of culture, and the cultural differences that exist in the population, the marketer can do much to prevent potential problems arising when marketing to different cultural groups. A thorough understanding of a particular culture can also be used in a positive way to more effectively market within that culture.

Elements of culture

Culture is exhibited by the customs, language, symbols and rituals within a society. These are the observable elements of the culture:

• Customs are the established 'rules' of behaviour within a society. They define what is, and what is not, acceptable.

• Language and symbols are the means by which members of a particular culture communicate with one another. This communication can be verbal (using words) or non-verbal (using images which convey directly, or indirectly, ideas).

• Rituals are patterns of behaviour, often quite complex, which a society shares. Ritual behaviours include religious services, attainment parties (eighteenth birthday, retirement, engagement, etc.) and private routines such as the Saturday morning shopping trip or the Sunday walk in the park.

Customs

Williams (1990) defines four classes of customs:

1. *Folkways* are the everyday customs of the culture. Greetings are one such example.

2. *Conventions* are more formally observed folkways, ones which might start to cause more long-term offence if ignored. For example, the sending of Christmas presents.

3. *Mores* are formally recognized rules of behaviour such as respect for your parents.

4. *Laws* mores which society wishes to control are governed by laws.

Languages and symbols

Marketers involved in multilingual operations must be aware of the implications of selling their products to speakers whose native language is not English. The use of language in advertising copy also requires attention.

Word-plays are very much surface features of a language. It is also common for language, and objects, to have other meanings and associations other than those that might appear in a dictionary. For instance, a crudely drawn heart conveys a meaning of innocent love. The phrase 'he fought like a tiger' only makes sense because of the symbolism we associate with the word 'tiger' (courage, cunning, stealth). Such words and objects are said to be 'symbolic' (see Table 3.1). Symbols add richness to communication within a culture.

Table 3.1 *Some common symbols and their associations in European culture*

Symbol	Associations
Dolphin	Intelligence
Tick	Correctness
Gold	Wealth
Crown	Superiority
Swan	Grace
Owl	Wisdom

Symbols can be simple and blunt or subtle and complex (see Figure 3.2). The richness of symbolic meaning can be used in marketing to associate certain qualities with your product or convey more complex meanings in a shorthand form (which can thus be understood and absorbed more quickly).

Casual *Historic* Boring **Strong**

Figure 3.2 *Even different typefaces can have different symbolic associations*

Rituals

From a marketing perspective, rituals and rites represent a substantial opportunity. In particular, if it is possible to associate an object or other event, known as artefacts, with a ritual then the persistence of the ritual will ensure the continuing use of the artefact (see Table 3.2).

One example is the red and white Santa Claus costume. This has become so closely associated with Christmas that many people believe it to be historic. In fact, the red and white costume was 'invented' by Coca-Cola as a marketing promotion. It has ensured that the combination of red and white (the Coca-Cola colours) has a continuing positive association with fun and jollity.

Table 3.2 *Common UK rituals and typical artefacts*

Rituals	Typical artefacts
25-years' service*	Award ceremony, clock/plaque
Friday night at home	Video, take out meal, beer
Saturday night out	Meal, cinema/theatre/disco/concert
Valentine's day	Red rose, card
21st birthday*	Key, card, presents

* indicate rites of passage

Activity 3.1

If you have ever been abroad, think of the things you found strange about the host country's culture. Try to list five things. Were these customs, language/ symbols or rituals?

Macro- versus micro-culture – the cultural onion

At any one time we are influenced by many different cultures. A person living in England is most probably influenced by 'Western', 'European' and 'English' cultures. The customs and rituals of these cultures are shared with many other people. Such widespread cultures are frequently referred to as macro-cultures. Imagine peeling an onion. The well-defined outer layers are rather like macro-cultures, with one nesting neatly inside anther. However, if we were to peel the onion further we would find that the layers become less distinct. It is rather the same with culture. As we examine smaller and smaller cultural groups the dividing lines become less distinct. A single individual may well be a 'member' of ten or more overlapping sub-cultures, or micro-cultures, as they are known (seeFigure 3.3).

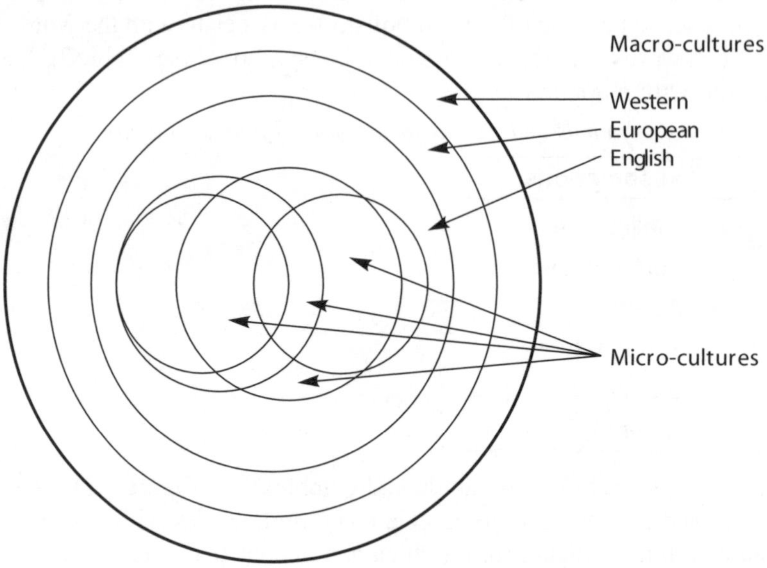

Figure 3.3 *The cultural onion. As the size of cultural groups become smaller and smaller the separation between them becomes less distinct. The position of a hypothetical individual is represented by a black dot*

There are six broad sub-cultures in the UK based on ethnicity, age, geography, religion, gender, occupation and social class:

1. *Ethnicity* – This includes not only indigenous population groups, such as the Welsh and Scots, but also from those groups that have settled in the UK.

2. *Age* – Within society there are certain values and attitudes which are shared by persons of a similar age. For instance, people brought up during the war years shared some very extreme changes in society such as rationing and life-threatening situations which few persons have since experienced.

3. *Geography* – The physical separation of peoples can lead to the development of distinct cultures in different regions.

4. *Religion* – Those whom subscribe to a particular religion are strongly influenced by its customs and practices. Most religions dictate rules which their followers must abide. These often include dietary, social and ethical requirements.

5. *Gender* – Traditionally, in our culture, women have been considered 'home makers' while men have been considered the 'bread winners'. While these descriptions are no longer accurate or relevant, many advertisers perpetuate, or use these stereotypes and other gender differences, to market products.

6. *Occupation and social class* – These characteristics of UK culture are often used interchangeably. Many organizations, such as the Market Research Society, define social class in terms of occupation. Occupation is a product of many things such as the occupation of one's parents, education, intelligence, aptitude and opportunity. People with similar occupations tend to share similar lifestyles and incomes. It is common for insurance companies, for instance, to target specific occupations which have been proven to be of a lower risk. One such occupational group is the police force.

Market segmentation using culture

It is possible to segment a market according to the micro-cultures that exist in the target population.

You might decide to market to women, for instance, to try to increase their consumption of lager. You could get more specific and decide to target businessmen under 35, in the South-East, to increase sales of a new cure for baldness.

Activity 3.2

Think how you might use sub-cultures in the UK to market a new dating service.

Learning culture

As has been stated, all culture is learned. The process of learning one's native culture is termed socialization. The learning of a new culture is called acculturation.

Definition

Socialization is the process by which the culture of a society is transmitted from generation to generation so that each individual not only understands and follows the 'rules' of their culture but is able to pass these on to others.

There are three main mechanisms by which culture is learned:

1. *Social modelling* – Where a culture is learned by copying an existing member of the culture. It may be that this learning is direct (i.e. from a peer or family member) or indirectly from the media (i.e. from television or a magazine). Fashion, for example, is often adopted from the pages of a magazine and rarely from other members of the family.

2. *Role-playing* – A form of social modelling where imitation is allowed to develop further.

3. *Conditioning* – Whereby certain behaviours are rewarded or punished according to their conformance with the rules of the culture. Eating food without cutlery is likely to be admonished by parents.

Social modelling is the mechanism of most use to marketers in gaining acceptance of their product. Showing a prominent member of a culture behaving in a certain manner (for example, Naomi Campbell wearing a new fashion) can increase the acceptability of this behaviour among other members of the culture.

Conditioning can also be used. If purchasers are rewarded for buying a product, through discount vouchers or cashback offers, the purchasing behaviour is more likely to be repeated.

Dynamic nature of culture

Culture is constantly changing but we are so much part of it that the changes often go unnoticed. It is only when we compare our current culture with that of the past that the differences become apparent.

Marketers should be aware of cultural trends so that they do not get 'left behind' or, conversely, do not miss the opportunity to be the first in the field to market a production based on an emerging cultural characteristic. Promotions aimed at young people must be particularly careful in this respect.

Cross-cultural marketing

We have already seen how mistakes can be made, and the benefits to be gained from an understanding of the cultural differences between markets.

There are two strategic approaches to cross-cultural marketing:

1. Global marketing – which uses common cultural characteristics of consumers
2. Local marketing – which makes use of differences in consumers from different cultures.

Local versus global marketing

Figure 3.4 summarizes the sorts of products more suitable for either global or local marketing.

In support of the scheme presented here, some marketers label the products most suitable for global marketing as 'high tech' and 'high touch' (Schiffman and Kanuk 1994). By this they mean that high

Product types more suitable for global marketing
Products aimed at a specific global micro-culture (e.g. the 'jet-set')
Products which are easy to tailor (e.g. foodstuffs)
Products which are novel (e.g. electronics)

Products which are difficult to tailor (e.g. furniture)
Products which appeal to a specific culture only (e.g. greeting cards)
Product types more suitable for local marketing

Figure 3.4 Product types suitable for global or local marketing

technology products (such as computers and cameras) and high touch products (such as perfumes and wrist watches) are more likely to transcend cultural differences and are thus more amenable for global marketing. In contrast, products which are low technology or low touch are more suitable, it is claimed, for a local marketing strategy.

Measurement of culture

The multifaceted nature of culture necessitates that a range of measurement techniques are used:

- *Projective tests* are frequently used to assess motivation and personality.
- *Attitude measurement* is frequently used to determine beliefs and values.
- *Depth interviews and group discussions* are useful to discover emerging cultural characteristics.
- *Observation* can provide valuable insights into the more obscure aspects of culture which may not be amenable to direct questioning. For instance, a consumer may not be aware that certain of their behaviours are ritualized.
- *Content analysis*, as the name implies, uses an analysis of past and present media to identify cultural changes. This can also be undertaken on a cross-cultural basis. Such a survey carried out in the early 1990s found a shift in trends in household furnishings away from greys with primary spot colours towards pastel tones.

The individual as customer

The difference between a brand and a commodity can be summed up in the phrase 'added value'. The added value can be tangible or intangible. In seeking to understand what creates 'added value' marketers need to understand the characteristics of consumers. The understanding of customers and their psychological make-up provides marketers with a richer basis for understanding consumer behaviour than do demographics and other mechanical methods of classification that tell the marketer very little about consumers' actual needs.

It is standard ethnographic practice to assume that all material possessions carry social meaning and a main aspect of cultural analysis would be to concentrate upon their use as communicators. Goods have a double role, they provide subsistence and create lines of social relationships. Goods are the medium that links social relations. As Mary Douglas says (*The World of Goods*, Penguin, 1980):

> Man is a social being, we can never explain demand by only looking at the physical properties of goods. Man needs goods for communicating with others and for making sense of what is going on around him…goods make visible statements about the hierarchy of values to which we choose to subscribe…We need to know how they are used to create an intelligible universe…There is no mention in utility theory about physical enjoyment, spiritual needs or even about envy.

The modern brand secures an emotional involvement rather than only meeting a functional need. The brand links the consumer through the brand to the supplier and its values and to other purchasers as a member of a connected tribe. Brands define who is in the group as much as who is not.

Branding and the post-modern consumer

Gregory Carpenter and Alice Tybout ('Mastering Marketing', *Financial Times*, October 1998), write that we have moved to an era in which brands need to satisfy a greater range of goals than before. They will need to satisfy many goals simultaneously, reconcile conflicting goals or satisfy neglected needs. Many of today's consumers do not see consuming brands as an objective as a previous generation may have done. They see brands as a means to an end.

Classic branded products signalled that one had the money to buy certain goods that were produced to a high standard, that the decision making was simplified and that they formed a common bond within the community. The goods were largely defined by a single goal largely determined by the product function. For example, fast food restaurants satisfied one's hunger with the minimum of fuss.

Contemporary brands then moved to creating a broader benefits base and built the brand around functionality and associated benefits. For example Volvo cars protected self and family.

Post-modern brands enable buyers to attain a much broader range of goals while having less time in which to achieve them. This is largely a reflection of the many roles post-modern buyers play. Working mothers have more active careers, working fathers play a more active role at home. There is less time, more pressure but there is still the expectation of being able to carry out the roles competently.

Some of the goals people are looking for are timeless: membership of a larger community, intellectual stimulation, spirituality, freedom, recognition and responsibility. Others reflect our changing lives, e.g. status, convenience and stress reduction. Post-modern buyers are willing to turn brands into satisfying many of these goals. People therefore try and satisfy more than one goal at the same time.

Multiple goal satisfaction

Products that enable people to satisfy more than one goal at a time are flourishing. Examples are mobile telephones and laptop computers that help people to use downtime and continue doing more than one thing at the same time.

Resolving goal conflict

Brands can be built to help buyers cope with role conflict. Levi jeans for example encouraged companies to implement the concept of 'Casual Friday'. This blurred the difference between business and leisure and enabled workers to integrate these two goals.

Satisfy neglected goals

As a result of the lack of time and the focus on financial security, social responsibility and social acceptance, many people do not have time to develop more internal, self-orientated goals. Brands can be developed that focus on these unsatisfied aspects. For example, Harley-Davidson help people to satisfy the desire for individuality and freedom. Jeep and Land Rover introduce an element of adventure into mundane tasks. Volvo is now changing its advertisement to encompass goals of individuality and self-expression, Volvos still protect but also contribute to psychological well-being by enabling the person to escape to remote and beautiful settings.

People can be said to live in a double environment, the personal inner world of feeling, emotion and thoughts as well as the outer world of people, places and possessions. If customer behaviour is to be understood it is not possible to solely concentrate on the rational, conscious motivations of individuals who react in a calculated way to their environment. It is necessary to also look at their perceptual processes as well, how customers create a mental vision of the brand in their own minds and the feelings that they associate with that image.

To do this one has to be able to look at the mind as being something dynamic. Not something that is static and fixed. The marketer can create a brand and instigate the branding process as an input, but it is the buyer who forms the mental vision of it and what they create (the branding output) may be very different from what the marketer intended. Consumers are certainly not passive!

Internal factors

Most people do not understand either themselves or others very well, our senses are often flawed and limited and our perception is limited. Selection plays an important part in everything we perceive.

The essential problem of enquiring into what may be in other people's minds is captured in this quote:

To try and understand the experience of another it is necessary to dismantle the world as seen from one's place within it, and to re-assemble it as seen from his. For example, to try to understand a given choice another makes, one must face in imagination the lack of choices which may confront or deny him. The well-fed are incapable of understanding the choices of under-fed. The world has to be dismantled and re-assembled in order to be able to grasp, however clumsily, the experience of another. To talk of entering the subjective experience of another is misleading. The subjectivity of another does not simply constitute a different interior attitude to the same exterior facts. The constellation of facts, of which he is the centre, is different.

Source: Berger and Mohr, 1975.

Any enquiry into what is in the minds of others is not only an exploration of what is consciously expressed by people but also about interpreting what is unconsciously believed and felt.

An output process

Successful marketing techniques must be considered in the light of the above. Customers do not receive messages passively. Customers take the messages marketers give them and then actively use them to fit into their own internal world and also to give them clues about the brand's capability. It is what customers do with the marketing mix in their minds that needs to be assessed. The marketer has constantly to say 'What is going on in there?'

The brand becomes the consumers' idea of the product/service, not the marketers. It is what customers perceive, interpret and then believe the values of the brand to be. So much so that the brand then acquires a personality that is so well recognized that even products with very little functional difference are seen as being different.

Attention

The term 'perception' implies the use of direct sensory information but it is not only external stimuli which makes products/services stand out, but our attention is also influenced by our interests, needs, motives and expectations.

The person's interests and motives may lead them to positively select certain information from their environment. The processes involved here are selective attention, selective exposure, selective retention, selective vigilance and perceptual organization.

Expectation

Expectation plays an important part in the selection of what we perceive. It refers to the way people respond in a certain way to a given situation or set of stimuli. This may be the result of either known or unknown past experiences.

People often perceive what they expect to perceive rather than the message they do receive. This concept is particularly important in service marketing where people are involved.

Subliminal perception

This is the expression used to describe something that is below the level of perception. There is a great deal of debate in this area as to whether it works and whether it is legal.

Awareness set

Brand choices do not just depend on brand awareness but also on the consumer's evaluation of the product into distinct groups or sets. Faced with a number of product groups made up of similar brands, consumers will try and simplify their purchase decisions.

Howard and Sheth argue that consumers will select from the brands of which they are aware – the awareness set – a smaller range of brands from which they will make their actual brand choice – the evoked set.

The concept of the evoked set is useful in marketing research as it can help to identify:

- The competitive position of the product
- What the consumer thinks are the competitive products
- Strategies which can be adopted to change the way in which the brand is categorized
- An appropriate marketing mix – such as media advertising, sampling, comparative advertising, redesign of the product – as the marketer will be able to see whether the evoked set or inert set includes their brand or not.

Motivation

Do not buy what you want, but what you need; what you do not need is dear at a farthing.
Marcus Porcius Cato (234-149 BC),*Reliquae*

The study of motivation is concerned with why people choose to behave in a certain way. In particular, it is concerned with:

- The most basic human requirements – referred to as 'needs'
- How these needs translate into behaviours – referred to as 'drives'
- What these behaviours aim to achieve – referred to as 'goals'.

In an organization context, understanding what motivates a work force is of prime importance to ensuring their continued productivity and satisfaction. In a marketing context, understanding what motivates a consumer is equally important. It enables products to be produced which are both desired and satisfying. An understanding of what motivates is also of use in preparing promotions and can be used for market segmentation purposes.

Certainly, this is a broad area of study. The great psychologist George Miller (1957) described the study of motivation as covering all things 'biological, social and psychological that defeat our laziness and move us, either eagerly or reluctantly, to action'.

At a basic level, our body has a need (hunger, for instance) which translates in a drive (in the case of hunger, this is a drive to obtain food). The goal is to satisfy the need (in this example, to feel full). This can be represented diagrammatically as shown in Figure 3.5. Achievement of the goal satisfies the initial needs thus completing the circle. Of course, next time that need surfaces (if the case of hunger, the next meal time) then the whole circular process will start again.

Figure 3.5

Perhaps the most popular theory which links needs and drives with goals is that of Hull. His drive-reduction theory attempts to explain both motivation and learning. He was mostly concerned with the operation of primary needs but the principles he presents are of general interest. Hull's theory is illustrated inFigure 3.6. As we have discussed, a need gives rise to a drive and corresponding behaviour aimed at reducing the drive and thus the need. According to Hull, this act of reducing the drive (drive reduction) reinforces the drive-reducing behaviour thus making the behaviour more likely to occur again in response to reoccurrence of the need.

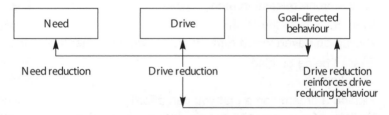

Figure 3.6 *A simplified view of Hull's drive reduction theory*

Suppose we are on a beach and feel thirsty. We will go to find the nearest source of refreshment, a beach bar perhaps. According to Hull's theory we are most likely to drink a product which has satisfied our thirst in the past, Perrier water for instance. If this is not on sale, we may pick something similar, or try something new, and this (if it satisfies us) is then more likely to be selected next time we are thirsty.

As well as positive motivations (in the above example the drink) we can also experience negative motivations or avoidance of certain items or situation. If we are thirsty, for example, we are likely to avoid salty things, which are likely to make us even more thirsty. To give another example, if we are cold we will avoid situations which will make us colder (avoidance of cold) and seek out situations that make us warmer (approach warmth).

On this basis, we can classify objects as either approach objects (contact with these will satisfy our need) and avoidance objects (contact with these will make our need worse). Let us now look in more detail at needs.

Needs

These fall into three broad categories:

1. *Physiological (or primary) needs* – these are the needs that sustain life. They include the need for food, air, sex and self-preservation.

2. *Psychological needs* – these are the needs that relate to our competence to deal effectively with the outside environment, often termed personal competence.

3. *Learned (secondary or cultural) needs* – we have already seen the influence that culture can have on an individual's behaviour. Learned needs are those needs which arise as a result of our socialization. As the name suggests, they are learned and are dependent on the culture we grow up in. Some cultures value power and status, others humility and a structured life. These are all learned needs.

These different categories of needs are related in complex ways. For example, the food a consumer purchases (a primary need) will depend on secondary needs. If you are hungry at breakfast time in the UK, you are most likely to eat cereal and toast. In the USA you may well satisfy your hunger by eating pancakes or even cake – the culturally acceptable breakfast foods in that country. In addition, psychological needs may play a part – does the food look palatable, pleasant and well presented.

The following are examples of how learned and psychological needs interact with primary needs:

- Donating a kidney to save another life.
- Giving up one's life for the greater good (such as with the Japanese kamikaze fighter pilots in the Second World War).

Needs arousal

We are aware of our needs only when they are aroused. They can be aroused by four distinct stimuli; physiological, cognitive, environmental and emotional. Table 3.3 has examples of all four stimulus types.

There at least two prominent theories that address motivation needs which are of use to marketers.

1. Maslow's hierarchy of needs.
2. McClelland's three motivating needs.

Before discussing these we will turn to a description of goals.

Table 3.3 *Types of stimulus and their effects*

Stimulus type	Example of mechanisms	Need aroused
Physiological	Drop in blood sugar levels	Hunger
	Testosterone release in men	Sex
Cognitive	Remembering a loved one	Affection
	Seeing an advert which reminds you to phone a friend	Social
Emotional	Fear of being burgled	Security
	Chaotic life	Stability
Environmental	Finding a dream home that you can afford	Success
	Walking past a shop and seeing clothes you want to buy	Prestige, self-respect

Goals

As already noted, these are the end-points of motivated behaviour. Goals can be generic or specific. If you are thirsty, you may want any liquid or you may want a specific brand of drink (seeFigure 3.7). Some psychologists distinguish between wants and goals, referring to the specific want as the object of desire (the brand of drink in this case) and the goal as the behaviour required to obtain the specific want.

GENERIC   SPECIFIC

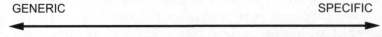

Any drink — Any cold drink — Any carbonated drink — Any carbonated cold drink

Figure 3.7

From the marketer's point of view, we are interested in making goals specific to our products. Different levels of specificity are appropriate to different types of products. For example, many foods are unbranded – potatoes for example. In the case of this food, the Potato Marketing Board presents the purchase of potatoes as a fairly generic goal.

Choice of goal chosen to satisfy a certain need depends on a number of things:

- *Personal experience* If a particular goal has satisfied a need in the past then it is more likely to be selected again. As we have seen with Hull's drive-reduction model, the success of a goal in satisfying a need actually reinforces its use again. For example, if a particular washing powder has been successful in cleaning our clothes we are more likely to buy that same washing powder in the future.

- *Cultural norms and values* We have seen in the previous unit how cultural norms and values affect behaviour. For example, we may shun the purchase of a new washing machine liquid (as opposed to powder) because using such a product is not the 'done thing' in our culture.

- *Personal norms and values* Our personal norms and values, possibly religious or ethical, can also affect the goals we select for the achievement of a particular need. For example, if we are 'green minded' we might choose to select an environmentally-friendly washing powder.

- *Physical and/or intellectual capacity* It might be some goals are unachievable due to our own personal limitations. Suppose we want to own a cat but are allergic to fur. Our need for companionship must find an alternative goal.

- *Accessibility of goal* The goal that we select may be determined on the basis of accessibility. We may wish, for example, to go to a particular play but the distance of the theatre precludes us going.

Maslow's hierarchy of needs

Maslow categorized human needs in five groups which he arranged into a hierarchy of importance (seeFigure 3.8).

Figure 3.8 *Maslow's hierarchy of needs*

These five groups, arranged from lower to higher importance are:

1. *Physiological needs* – such as hunger, thirst, sex and activity.
2. *Safety needs* – freedom from threat, health but also security, order, and stability.
3. *Social, or belonging needs* – relationships, affection, sense of belonging (identification).
4. *Esteem needs* – such as prestige, success and self-respect.
5. *Self-actualization needs* – the fulfillment of personal potential.

He also introduced other categories of 'enabling' needs which provided the channels through which the five categories of needs could be achieved:

- *Freedom of enquiry and expression needs* – for social conditions permitting free speech and encouraging justice, fairness and honesty.

- *Knowledge and understanding needs* – to gain and order knowledge of the environment, to explore, learn, and experiment.

Marketing applications of Maslow

As a theory, Maslow's hierarchy of needs has proved useful in applying a more behaviour-oriented structure to the market. It has found use in market segmentation and brand/product positioning.

Each product/service has a 'natural' needs category which it addresses. Most products only actually address the very basic physiological and safety needs. For example, all the foodstuffs sold only address our physiological need for sustenance. However, it is possible to position products to appeal to just about any needs category which broadens the appeal and can be used to create a brand image.

Table 3.4 provides some examples of positioning by needs category.

As already stated, we can also segment a market using Maslow's needs categories. Table 3.5 gives examples of these.

Needs also translate into benefits which form the basis of benefits segmentation. Furthermore, motivation is also used in psychographic segmentation (see Unit 2, Market segmentation).

Table 3.4 Positioning by needs categories

Need category	Products appealing to this category
Physiological	'Ready Brek' breakfast cereal provides you with a protective 'barrier' against the cold
Safety	AA rescue service stops you being stranded at night in a hostile environment
Social	BT adverts – the telephone keeps you in touch with absent family and friends
Esteem	Rolex watch adverts suggesting that ownership of a Rolex is a sign of success
Self-actualization	Adverts for adult education courses encouraging you to further yourself

Table 3.5 Positioning according to Maslow's needs categories

Needs category	Potential target groups
Physiological	Teenagers eager for sexual experience Old persons worried about health problems
Safety	Wealthy people with valuable possessions to protect Families worried about safety of children
Social	New arrivals in an area looking for social affiliations, clubs, societies, etc. Single parents looking for company
Esteem	Recent high income earners eager for outside signs of prestige High status groups, e.g. company directors
Self-actualization	Those in higher education – likely to be looking for additional education Health conscious teenagers eager to conform to perfect body image

Notwithstanding these problems, Maslow's work has provided a framework which is easy and useful to marketers.

Activity 3.3

In terms of Maslow's categorization of needs (physiological, safety, social, esteem, self-actualization), how would you segment the following products/services:

- Headache tablet
- Household burglar alarm
- Church service
- Typing course
- Cream cake
- Computer
- Wedding ring

For each of the above, think of a way of how you might market position them in at least one other segment. Write this down and explain your decision.

Evaluation of Maslow's hierarchy of needs

Maslow's theory certainly has intuitive appeal. If you are desperate for food you are unlikely to be concerned about social niceties or self-fulfillment. His ideas are also useful in that they consider much of what drives us as individuals. Unfortunately, there are a number of problems with the theory as Rice (1994) explains:

- Lack of empirical evidence to support it. Physiological and safety needs are not always the predominant factor in determining behaviour.
- The absence of money from the list of needs worries some people.
- Self-actualization and esteem needs are likely to be a function of each individual's self-perception.

McClelland's theory of need achievement

Unlike Maslow, some psychologists, such as McClelland and his colleagues, believe in the presence of just three main needs. Whereas these can be subsumed within Maslow's hierarchy, considered as separate entities they are useful for marketers to consider:

- *Affiliation* – this relates to a desire to belong, to be part of a group and to have friends.
- *Power* – this relates to control over both people and other objects in the environment.
- *Achievement* – this relates to the need to achieve.

Activity 3.4

Think of work colleagues, friends and family that you know. How would you classify them in terms of McClelland's three needs theory? Which need motivates them most?

Other theories of motivation

There are two other theories which are occasionally referred to in a marketing context. A brief explanation will suffice for each of these.

Alderfer's ERG hierarchy of needs

This proposes a hierarchy of just three needs – existence, relatedness and growth (hence ERG). While similar in many ways to Maslow, Alderfer introduces the useful notion of frustration. That is, if a need is not satisfied it results in frustration which may result in other behaviours. In a marketing context, we may find consumers dissatisfied with a particular product settling for an alternative or complaining at what they have purchased. It is important to accept that frustration can occur in any buying situation and to plan for it.

Vroom's expectancy theory

This theory is strongly related to the extended Fishbein model of attitudes. Essentially, the strength of an individual's motivation is based on the expectation that a behaviour will lead to a certain outcome and the preference (or valence) for that outcome. For a worked example see Activity 3.5. From a marketing viewpoint, it is clear that to increase the motivation to buy we must increase the perceived value of our products/ service and raise the expectancy of satisfaction that will result from its purchase.

Activity 3.5

In a previous unit we discussed probabilities. Working through an example of the use of Vroom's expectancy theory is a good way of exercising this knowledge.

1. List five outcomes that you might expect from going on holiday to the West Indies. To get you started, outcomes 1 and 2 have already been completed:
   a. Feel relaxed
   b. Get a sun tan
   c.
   d.
   e.
2. Now give each of these outcomes a value. This is known as the valence (*V*). +1 if you like them; 0 if you feel neutral towards them and -1 if you dislike them.
3. Estimate the probability of attaining each outcome. You will remember that a probability of 1 is equal to absolute certainty while 0 is equal to no chance. For example, 0.5 represents a

---

4. Now place your values in the table provided below and calculate $E \times V$, placing this value in the last column. Now add up the values in the $E \times V$ column. The result is called the F score and relates to the motivational value of the holiday.

Outcomes	Expectancy (E)	Valence (V)	E × V
1 Feel relaxed			
2 Get a sun tan			
3			
4			
5			

You might want to experiment with this technique as a way of comparing the F scores from different product brands.

Measuring motivation

The most popular techniques for motivation research are undoubtedly projective techniques such as those discussed in the earlier unit on primary data, such as word association and thematic apperception tests (TAT). However, depth interviews and group discussions are also used. Unlike other uses of these methods, the focus is to uncover why a particular behaviour took place. The group discussion can yield more information than individual in-depth interviews but is not suitable for the discussion of certain topics such as those that might embarrass, are difficult to discuss in company, or require very individual consideration.

Activity 3.6

Try interviewing fellow students about their motivation for undertaking the marketing course. Start by asking the question:

Why did you decide to apply for this particular course at this particular college?

Make notes as they answer. After each answer your aim is to ask another why question about some detail of their previous answer. It is likely that a number of opportunities for further questioning will arise, make sure no opportunity is missed. Note each question, returning to it if necessary. If you have a tape recorder available, you may wish to use this to record the interview to ease later study.

What needs do you identify?

When you try to use ideas from these theories to help you define your customers' needs more accurately, it is important to remember that the concepts you are using come from a therapeutic area where they are used to enable people to make some sense of their lives. These are not theories that are cast in stone but are useful as metaphoric models that help us to capture different aspects of experience. There are many conceptual frameworks that are used to enable people to make sense of their lives, only a few are dealt with in this coursebook and it is also beyond its scope to deal with them in any detail.

Consumer imagery

Self-concept theory

The theory centres around the concept of 'self' which Newcomb (*Social Psychology*, New York, Holt, Reinhart and Winston, 1950) defines as 'the individual as perceived by that individual in a socially determined frame of reference'. This perceived self influences the person's perception of both their environment and their behaviour. The Jungian concept of self is quite different.

Each individual has an idea of themselves as being a particular type of person. Self-concept develops in different ways, from the way we have grown up, from our background and experience. The self-image comes from interactions with other people, starting off from parents and then to other individuals and groups with whom we have contact, including the culture in which we are brought up in – these experiences teach us how to see ourselves. Some people have a high self-image, others have a low one.

One of the most important aspects of self-concept is the individual's level of aspiration, and their own self-perception compared with their perception of others. Once developed, self-concept is reinforced by the process of selective perception, this allows the person to maintain and enhance an internally consistent self-image and the person reacts in a way that is consistent with his or her self-image.

Possessions, brands, people and places have symbolic value for them and are judged on the basis of how they fit with their own personal picture of themselves. There are different types of self-image:

1. *Actual self-image* How consumers see themselves.

2. *Ideal self image* How they would like to see themselves.

3. *Social self-image* How consumers feel others see them.

4. *Ideal self-image* How consumers would like others to see them.

5. *Expected self-image* How consumers expect to see themselves at some specified future time.

Studies show that consumers prefer brands which relate to their self-perception and to their subjective images of brands.

The extended self

Consumer possessions can be seen to confirm or extend the person's self-image. People identify with them by projecting their own meaning and emotion into them, they also identify with them by taking certain aspects of meaning and emotion from them into themselves – they introject them. This can work both positively and negatively.

It has been proposed by Russell W. Belk (1989), 'Possessions and the extended self', *Journal of Consumer Research*, 15 September, that possessions can extend the self in a number of ways:

1. By allowing the person to do things that they would otherwise find difficult or impossible to accomplish (e.g. problem solving using a computer).

2. Symbolically, by making the person feel better or 'bigger' (e.g. receiving an employee award for excellence).

3. By conferring status or rank (e.g. status among collectors of rare works of art because of the ownership of a particular masterpiece).

4. By conferring feelings of immortality, by leaving valued possessions to young family members (this also has the potential of extending the recipient's 'selves').

5. By conferring magical powers (e.g. a ring inherited from one's grandmother might be perceived as a magic amulet bestowing good luck when it is worn).

Altering the self

Self-altering products which help consumers to look better, create a new self or maintain the existing self (e.g. cosmetics). Other self-altering products can make a consumer look like another type of person (e.g. create a yuppie look).

Products, dreams and self-concept

The mind also uses product images in dreams as shown in this example:

The dreamer dreamed about a young woman at work, a single parent, and struggling financially. She wanted to do something for this woman, to show her that there was another side of life and to give her a treat. She decided that she would give her a ride in a Porsche.

One can even go as far as to say that customers are surrounded by a little group of 'friends' and the friends become the medium through which non-verbal communication takes place. They reaffirm the ideas the person has about themselves as they reflect their self-image.

In the same way that products can be owned, services, people (politicians, pop stars and football teams), organizations and places can be owned in the same way – they all become part of the customer's internal world; and in varying degrees this process can be both conscious and unconscious.

Psychoanalytic theory

The structure of psychoanalysis has by far burst the thought boundaries set for it by Freud. He put forward the theory that the human personality system consists of the id, ego and super ego. The id seeks immediate gratification for biological and instinctual need. The super ego representing societal or personal norms that have an ethical constraint on behaviour. The ego mediates between the two.

For example, picture a gorgeous woman next to a car. The car is an extension of male virility and the woman is placed next to the car to emphasize this fact. (The gorgeous woman appeals to the id and the car becomes a phallic extension of the id.)

The sale of insurance on the other hand would appeal to the super ego where it plays to the sense of responsibility. The ego is buffeted between the super ego and id. For example, a family man wants to buy a Ferrari when he turns 40, but super ego realizes that he should put the money in an endowment plan, and the ego makes a compromise between the two. So if the organization selling the endowment policy gave a 'treat' that appealed to the id some compromise could be reached between the two.

Role theory

Historically, individual consumers were thought to have had a single self and to be interested in products and services that satisfied that single self. However, psychoanalytic theory indicates that it is more accurate to think of people in terms of a multiple self and although between the inner and the outer world there is an ego which is a filtering process screening aspects of the outer world, people are likely to behave differently in different situations within the context of their social roles. In fact, acting exactly the same way may not actually be all that healthy.

Role theory is concerned with the roles people act out in their lives. People's behaviour will change depending on different social groupings in which they find themselves.

Role signs

In many situations people are expected to have a specific appearance or uniform – milk and post deliveries, railway guards, and so on. A uniform is an important role sign and various personal possessions (briefcase, organizer) can be used to reinforce a person's perceived role. A product/service image can be enhanced by being associated with particular roles. A marketer needs to know the role signs people want to buy.

> ## Activity 3.7
> How do you use role signs?

Role relationships and models

Role relationships can very often define a relationship quite specifically. For example, a customer will expect sales assistants to behave in a certain manner. Generally people have perceptions of the way in which the role should be carried out, these would be based on the rules of behaviour (norms established by society) associated with that role. Role models who embody the highest expectations of particular roles can be associated with a product.

Products can be used to indicate the nature of the role relationship, intimate and formal.

Role ambiguity and role conflict

When people have multiple roles, problems associated with differing expectations occur. Role conflict occurs when people who have several different roles find that the roles are incompatible. Marketers can provide products that assuage the customer's guilt and sense of inadequacy of not being able to fulfil their different roles. For example, the busy working woman who still wants to cook a proper dinner can use wholesome convenience gourmet foods.

Role conflict can occur between roles, for example having to finish a piece of work and attend a child's birthday party at the same time.

Intra-role conflict arises when there is a conflict arising from different aspects of the same role. For example, a parental role when the parent wants to both love and discipline the child.

Role ambiguity refers to the individual's uncertainty of what is expected in a role, and also to the role sets (the people to whom the role holder is relating to) uncertainty of what is expected in the role.

Brands can be developed to help clarify roles and enable the values associated with the role to be achieved.

Trait factor theory

Trait factor theory puts forward the idea that an individual's personality is comprised of predispositional attributes called traits. These traits are relatively enduring.

Trait theory makes a number of assumptions:

1. Many individuals share the same traits.
2. Traits will vary in intensity between different individuals.
3. Traits are relatively stable in different environments. However, some people believe that personality may be more situational than trait theorists propose.

These assumptions lead then to the belief that traits can be inferred by measuring behaviour.

Trait factor theory is used in marketing personality research to try and find a relationship between purchasing, media choice, risk taking, attitude change, fear and social influence. It is also used in recruitment.

Cattell is perhaps the best known of the supporters of the trait approach to personality. He used the technique of factor analysis to identify what he believed to be the principal factors of personality as set out in Table 3.6.

Table 3.6 *Cattell's 16 principal factors (16PF)*

Cool	A	Warm
Concrete thinking	B	Abstract thinking
Affected by feeling	C	Emotionally stable
Submissive	E	Dominant
Sober	F	Enthusiastic
Expedient	G	Conscientious
Shy	H	Bold
Tough minded	I	Tender minded
Trusting	L	Suspicious
Practical	M	Imaginative
Forthright	N	Shrewd
Self-assured	O	Apprehensive
Conservative	Q1	Experimenting
Group-oriented	Q2	Self-sufficient
Undisciplined self-conflict	Q3	Controlled
Relaxed	Q4	Tense

In addition a number of second order or composite factors are identified which include:

- *Extroversion* The extent to which an individual is socially outgoing.
- *Anxiety* The extent to which an individual is habitually anxious.
- *Tough poise* The extent to which an individual is more influenced by facts than feelings.
- *Independence* The extent to which an individual is aggressive, independent, daring and incisive.
- *Super ego/control* The extent to which an individual tends to conform to the rules and expectations associated with their roles in life.
- *Neuroticism* The extent to which an individual is apprehensive and emotionally reactive.
- *Leadership* The extent to which an individual appears to have the traits that are commonly associated with leadership potential, such as sociable, relaxed, assertive and self-assured.
- *Creativity* The extent to which an individual is imaginative and experimenting.

People are asked to complete extensive questionnaires and the responses are subjected to mathematical analysis. The questions are subjective both in formations and interpretation. There is also a tendency for people to answer questions as they think a normal person would, or how the person wishes themselves to be. However, it seems likely that personality traits should have some effect on purchasing behaviour.

Behaviourist theories

Skinner rejected the idea that each person's behaviour is shaped and determined by internal personality factors. He suggested that each person's behaviour can be explained entirely by reference to the individual's reinforcement history and specific behaviour that has been rewarded or punished.

This concept can be used to explain loyalty marketing. Organizations reward customers for 'good' behaviour, and our ultimate aim is for them to learn brand loyalty.

Primary and secondary groups

People in groups

People are naturally sociable. There is a strong desire amongst most people to form part of a group. This group may be a family, a department at work, or a social club.

Definition

Group – two or more people who interact together and share some common attitudes and/or behaviours.

This definition is by no means comprehensive. It is perhaps easier to define a group in terms of its characteristics. A collection of people which possess most of the characteristics listed are usually deemed to constitute a group:

- More than one person
- Sufficient interaction between members
- Perception of themselves as a group
- A certain set of agreed/accepted values (called norms)
- Allocation of specific roles (different activities) to members
- Social (affective) relations between members
- Shared aims.

Group influence

Most research work by psychologists has shown that groups exert a strong influence on the way we behave.

Undoubtedly, the most quoted experiment performed by Professor Mayo was the drawing office experiment. Chris Rice (1993) explains:

> Here the problem lay in low morale which was blamed on the lighting. Mayo split the department into two – the first group was the experimental group, the second group acted as the control group and their lighting remained unaltered throughout the experiment. When the intensity of the lighting of the experimental group was increased the expected improvement in morale and output occurred. What was unexpected was that the morale and output of the control group rose in exactly the same way. This puzzled Mayo who proceeded to reduce the intensity for the experimental group – output of both groups again rose! His conclusion was that the changed behaviour was nothing to do with the intensity of the lighting, but was a group phenomenon.

Interestingly, culture plays a strong part in the degree of conformance exhibited by an individual. Isolated members of a culture within a group (for example, a white male in a group of black females) are more likely to conform than if they are in a group with members of their own culture. It also seems that certain cultures are more likely to conform than others. Norwegian students have been found to conform more than the French; similarly Russian children were found to conform more than their Israeli counterparts (Gross, *Psychology*, 1989).

Consumer reference groups

From a marketing perspective, reference groups are useful in that they are influential in the formation of consumer behaviour. A teenager may, for instance, decide to dress in a certain way because of the influence of their school mates. In this example the school mates are the reference group.

There are two general types of reference groups:

1. *Normative groups* These are groups which shape the basic attitudes and behaviour of an individual. The most prevalent normative group is the individual's family.

2. *Comparative groups* These are groups which are used to compare and contrast one's existing attitudes and behaviours. In common parlance if you are doing well, in comparative terms, it is often said that you are 'keeping up with the Joneses'. That is, your lifestyle is comparable to others that you perceive to be in the same social class.

Definition

Reference group – a group (or possibly individual) used by a person as a reference point in the formation of their own attitudes and behaviour – subjective norm – see Unit 4, Modelling customer behaviour, attitudes and dynamics.

Reference groups are frequently categorized on the following dimensions:

- *Ascribed versus acquired groups* Ascribed groups are those to which an individual naturally belongs, e.g. gender, family unit. Acquired groups are those to which an individual actively seeks membership, e.g. health club.

- *Formal versus informal groups* A formal group is well defined in terms of its structure and purpose, e.g. parliament. Informal groups are less well structured and exist primarily to fulfil a social function, e.g. a group of drinking 'buddies'.

- *Primary versus secondary groups* Primary groups are usually small and associated with more personal contact, e.g. close friends, colleagues at work. Secondary groups are usually larger with communication which is generally less personal, e.g. colleges, large work groups.

There are two important reference groups to which an individual does not belong:

1. *Aspirational groups* These are groups to which an individual aspires to joining, e.g. rock musicians, artists.

2. *Dissociative groups* These are groups which an individual actively avoids membership of, e.g. for some people the Hell's Angels motorbike club might be such a group, others might actively avoid working in the arms industry.

From a marketer's viewpoint, informal, primary groups are of most interest as they are likely to exert the most influence on an individual's consumer behaviour. In addition, aspirational groups are the most important non-membership groups for the same reason.

Activity 3.8

List five reference groups that you belong to. For each of these decide whether it should be classed as a normative group, a comparative group or whether it fulfils both functions.

The influence of reference groups is summarized in Figure 3.9.

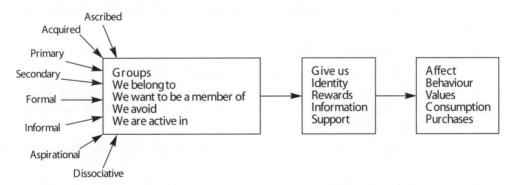

Figure 3.9 *{Reference groups and their influence*

An experiment by Rule et al. (1985) tried to assess the influence that various groups exert. US students were asked to record, both when they felt that someone was trying to influence them and when they were trying to influence someone else. Whereas such experiments are unlikely to be completely accurate (Are students exposed to the same influences as others? Would they recognize all attempts to influence them?), they do provide a useful guide. The results are summarized in Table 3.7. Perhaps not surprisingly, immediate family and close friends were perceived as the groups who made the most attempts to persuade. These groups were also those that the student tried most to persuade.

Table 3.7 *Groups that US students perceived as trying to persuade them and whom they tried to persuade*

	Who tries to persuade you (%)	Whom do you try to persuade (%)
Immediate family	27	35
Extended family	7	5
Close friends	18	24
Occasional friends	7	12
Instructors	13	7
Sales people	11	2
Other professionals	10	3
Trait defined: religious, etc.	5	9
Goal defined: trying to impress them, etc.	2	3

Question 3.1

Categorize the following groups on the dimensions: ascribed/acquired, formal/informal, primary/secondary. Note whether they might also be aspirational or dissociative.

- Dance troupe
- Local branch of political party
- Your college class

Group membership – roles and norms

I would never be a member of any group that would have me as a member.

Paraphrased from Groucho Marx

When you join a group you accept certain norms, which govern the behaviour of the group, and take on a certain role (whether it be active or passive).

Norms may apply to any aspect of the behaviour of the group. If you joined Greenpeace, the environmental action group, you would be expected to agree with their 'direct action' method of campaigning. You might also be expected not to buy environmentally-unfriendly products where alternatives were available, to avoid unnecessary car travel, and to vote for the Green Party. As a member of a local Greenpeace group you might also be given, or take on, a number of roles; as organizer of a door-to-door collection, as press officer and so on.

Norms commonly affect the following aspects of the group culture:

- Physical appearance and dress
- Social and leisure activities (even when these are not the main business of the group)
- Language and gestures used
- General opinions, attitudes and beliefs
- The way in which the group carries out its own business.

Roles within a group are decided, primarily, on how we see ourselves and what others expect of us. If we see ourselves as a leader we are likely to try for this role. Alternatively, if others see us as 'leadership material' we are likely to be offered this role.

Within any groups a number of role types commonly exist. Most roles inevitably fall into the first two categories:

- *Task roles* – a member or members concerned with pursuing the goals of the group (often referred to as the members who 'get things done').
- *Maintenance roles* – a member or members concerned with keeping the group operational and efficient (these may be the group administrators or act as emotional supports for the group).
- *Comedy role* – a member who is a joker or the willing butt of jokes.
- *Observer role* – a passive observer of proceedings.
- *Deviant role* – a member who constantly disagrees and challenges the group norms.

- *Specialist role* – a member who is held as being a specialist in the technical activities of the group.
- *Spokesperson role* – a member who communicates the activities of the group to non-group members.

Communication within groups

The way in which group members communicate with one another is important to marketers. The direction and density of communication affects how quickly decisions are made, the satisfaction of group members and the quality of the decision. Study of communication patterns might also help you to market your products more effectively and efficiently.

The sociometric method is the technique most used to determine communication patterns. Individuals are asked where they obtained advice or information on a certain subject or product and whom they provided with advice or information. Lines are then drawn on a diagram between circles representing the individuals involved to form what is called a sociogram. It might be that you wish to know how knowledge of a particular book spread within a community or how consumers found out about a special offer.

When such studies are undertaken, three common sociogram patterns emerge; circle, wheel (or star) and all-channel. These are illustrated inFigure 3.10 for a five person group. Each line represents a channel of communication, each dot represents an individual.

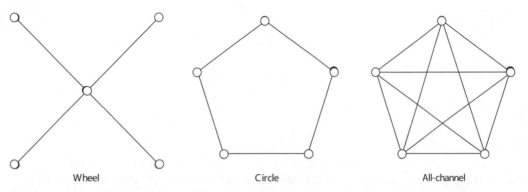

Wheel   Circle   All-channel

Figure 3.10

Consumer-referent groups

Marketers have identified the groups which have the most impact on consumer behaviour:

- *Family* Members in the family take on different roles in the decision making.
- *Peer groups* Through school, our teenage years and on into adulthood we are constantly surrounded by people of our own age and social class. These are usually informal and often social groups of friends. In conjunction with the family, close friends are the biggest influence on our consumer behaviour.
- *Consumer or lobbying groups* In recent years consumers who feel that they are getting a 'bad deal' have formed groups with the specific purpose of bringing pressure to bear on manufacturers and service providers. Such groups may address a single issue or provide a more general service as a 'watchdog'.
- *Work groups* People at work form both formal groups (departments, divisions and so on) as well as more informal groups (company sailing club, after-work drinking 'buddies', office squash league, and so on). The amount of time that people spend at work in the company of their work colleagues provides ample opportunity for influence.

How the mass media uses referent groups

The appeal of certain types of referent groups is used in advertising to influence the consumer (see Table 3.8). Three general approaches are:

1. *Aspirational appeal* – present the product in a situation, or use a celebrity or type of person, to which the consumer aspires. Examples include showing the product in the context of a beautiful house or using an athletic actor.

2. *Peer appeal* – present the product by a person to whom the consumer can relate. For instance, an advert aimed at selling car telephones to working women may show a business women stranded in the middle of nowhere with a broken down car.

3. *Expert appeal* – the product is endorsed by an expert, who may be known or unknown, with the aim of convincing the consumer that the product does the job for which it was designed. The more trustworthy the expert, the more convincing the appeal. Ex-police officers have been used on several occasions for this very reason.

The benefits of using reference groups in the ways described is that they reduce the perceived risk of purchase and increase product awareness. As we have seen in earlier units, these are two of the most important barriers to successful marketing.

Table 3.8 *Some examples of referent group appeal*

Appeal element	Product	Type of appeal
Michael Jackson	Soft drink	Inspirational
Exotic locations	Cars	Inspirational
Ex-police chief Markham	Car tyres	Expert
Ex-police chief Stalker	Alarm systems	Expert
Head of company post room	Courier service	Expert
Scientists	Washing powder	Expert
Driver in broken down car in unsafe area	Car breakdown and recovery service	Peer

Family purchasing

The most comprehensive marketing model on family purchasing and decision making assumes that children are growing up in a two-parent family structure (Sheth 1974, and see Figure 3.11). In reality family structures today include not only married couples with children but also a variety of alternative family structures, including female and male-headed single parent families.

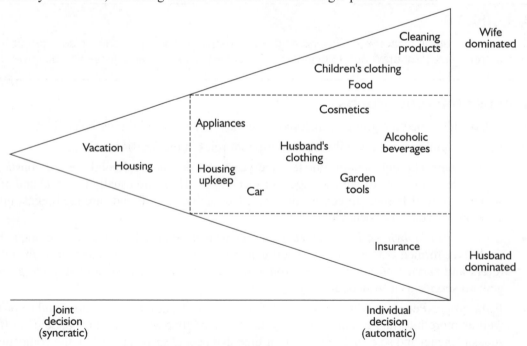

Figure 3.11 Purchasing decisions. *Source: Adcock, Bradfield, Halberg and Ross (1994)*

With family purchasing, decisions can be be made autonomously or jointly: on one's own behalf, on behalf of one or more other family members, or for the family as a unit.

The organization as customer

Differences between consumer and industrial buying

- Many buyers prefer to deal with suppliers who can offer complete systems
- There are fewer customers than the consumer marketer
- The market is clearly segmented – a supplier may know all potential customers and a potential buyer may know all potential suppliers
- Some large organizations have enormous purchasing power
- The practice of reciprocal buying may exist
- The external environment will influence the organization in different ways. For example: the level of primary demand, the cost of money
- Many organizational markets have inelastic demand (see the unit Unit 10, Relationship marketing)
- Decisions are made through a group buying process
- Buying is often carried out by purchasing professionals
- An unsuccessful decision carries much greater risks than the average customer purchase, a bad decision will affect both the individuals, the groups involved in the purchase and the organization itself
- The buying process is more formal – with written reports, detailed product specifications, and purchase orders
- There is an interlinking customer-supplier chain of dependency and counter dependency
- The demand fluctuates quite widely, a small increase in consumer demand will create a large increase in industrial demand
- Much of the purchasing is done on the basis of history and ongoing relationships are of crucial importance. Organizational marketers very often work closely with their customers – they help them to define their needs, customize the offer and deal with the after-sales service
- The organizational culture and structure will influence the buying process and the way decisions are made
- Because organizations consist of many people, individual needs will be more varied and need to be taken into account
- No two organizations are the same. Although the standard promotional material may be the same the people who are in direct contact with the customer need to be aware of the differences
- The buying criteria that will be used to judge 'good value' will be much wider. These criteria could include: price/discounts, technical quality, advantage and advancement, after-sales service, reliability and continuity of supply, back-up advisory service, credit facilities.

The organizational buying process

- The type of buying situation will be different but the categorization in terms of low involvement and high involvement purchases made by individuals is similar:
  1. Routine behaviour or **straight rebuy** where the buyer reorders something without any changes being made. History is a significant factor here and there is an inertia which tends to make it difficult for a new supplier to enter the market – very often price cutting is a way in
  2. Limited problem solving or **modified rebuy** is where the buyer wants to modify the specification, prices, terms or suppliers
  3. Extended problem solving or **new buy** is where the buyer is buying something for the first time; these tend to be lengthy as the buying criteria will have to be established and developed from scratch

See Figure 3.12 and Table 3.9 for some examples of the types and stages of buying situations.

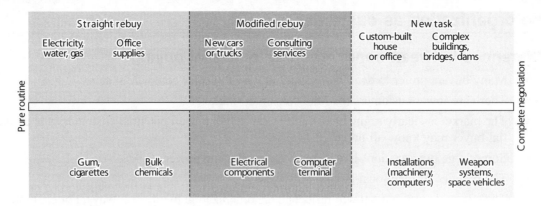

Figure 3.12 Three types of industrial buying situation. *Source: Enis, Ben, M. (1980) Marketing Principles, Copyright 1980, Scott, Foresman and Company. Reprinted by permission*

Question 3.2

In what way does an industrial buying situation differ from the consumer market? Use an example of your choice.

The organizational decision-making unit: internal processes of the DMU

Gatekeepers

Gatekeepers are often able to acquire power that goes well beyond their formal status. For example, many secretaries exert a special influence by controlling what information comes into an organization, or who is allowed into the organization.

The gatekeeper can very often be a specialist who feeds relevant information into the rest of the DMU, so there is an overlap with other roles.

Initiators

The initiator (the person who triggers off an idea or identifies a problem) may have great ideas but may not have the power within the organization to carry out ideas. It is always important to find the decider in the DMU and to involve them as soon as possible.

Table 3.9 *Major stages of the industrial buying process in relation to major buying situations. Source: Kotler (1980),* Principles of Marketing, *Prentice-Hall International, Inc., adapted from Patrick J. Robinson, Charles W. Faris, and Yoram Wind,* Industrial Buying and Creative Marketing *(Boston: Allyn and Bacon, 1967)*

Stages of the buying process	Buying situations		
	New task	Modified rebuy	Straight rebuy
1 Problem recognition	Yes	Maybe	No
2 General need description	Yes	Maybe	No
3 Product specification	Yes	Ye s	Ye s
4 Supplier search	Yes	Maybe	No
5 Proposal solicitation	Yes	Maybe	No
6 Supplier selection	Yes	Maybe	No
7 Order routine specification	Yes	Maybe	No
8 Performance review	Yes	Ye s	Ye s

Influencers

Influencers are people who influence decision making. They perform the role of informing, persuading or stimulating the decision-making process. They can be inside the organization, for example technical people in research and development. They could be outside the organization, for example, stakeholders, pressure groups.

Deciders

Deciders actually make the decision to buy and have the power to decide on what is required and who will provide it.

Buyers

Buyers do not necessarily make the decision to buy, they do, however, make the purchase. They have formal authority from within the organization to select a supplier and negotiate the terms of purchase. In some cases their role is purely administrative.

Users

Users are the people who actually use the product or experience the service. In many cases, they initiate the buying proposal and help define the product specifications and have a high level of technical expertise. They may or may not be the deciders or the buyers.

Financiers

Financiers are the people who determine and control the budget.

Question 3.3

What roles do people take up within the industrial DMU and what part do each play within the DMP? Relate your understanding to an organizational situation you have experience of.

Activity 3.10

Forces influencing organizational behaviour

Choose an organization with which your company has a commercial relationship and see how much of the following information you can find out: (if your work does not provide you with the opportunity to carry out this task, work with another colleague). Remember to look at the whole system, not just one aspect of it.

Past history with your organization

- Records on: sales visits, purchases made, frequency of purchase, time of purchase, credit arrangements, complaints, etc.
- Information on previous relationships they have had with members from your own organization
- Information on the current supplier chain within your own organization – who else in your business has contacts with this customer and are these relationships satisfactory and how has history affected them (misbilling, personal friction, late delivery, etc.)?

Information on the organization

1. Organizational environment
   - How does the macro-environment (PEST) and micro-environment influence their business?
     - i. Economic, commercial and competitive factors such as interest rates, exchange rates, industrial optimism/pessimism
     - ii. Also the political, legal and social environment such as the green movement, equal opportunities policies, ISO9000
     - iii. Technological change
     - iv. Supplier size and flexibility, financial reputation
     - v. Co-operative buying
     - vi. Industry structure – Potter's five forces.

   You will also need to find out about:
   - Their customers – information on their customers and how their needs will have an influence on what your organization produces.
   - Other competitors – information on any other organizations competing for their business.

2. The organization as a whole
   - How does the organization stand commercially?
   - Can you describe the overall size and culture of the organization? (Don't forget different sub-cultures you need to be aware of.) This will effect the structure of the

organization, the reporting relationships, the buying policies, the level of autonomous decision making.

- o What are the needs of their internal value chain?

3. The group DMU

- o What is the type of purchase (straight rebuy, modified rebuy or new buy)?
- o How do they get information?
- o What other sources of information are available to them (any other external influences on their purchasing behaviour like other businesses, journals, cooperative buying, etc.)?
- o How active are they in the search for alternative information?
- o How is the decision-making unit structured and how does it fit into the organizational structure?
    - i. Is the DMU centralized?
    - ii. Is the decision-making process (DMP) formalized to the extent that rules and procedures are stated and adhered to by members of that organization? Are there any meta rules (unseen rules that govern the rules)?
    - iii. Is the DMU specialized to the degree in which different departments take on different aspects of the decision-making process?
    - iv. How does the DMU function?
        - § Initiators
        - § Influencers
        - § Gatekeepers
        - § Users
        - § Deciders
        - § Buyers
        - § Financiers
    - o Is there information on the buying criteria?

Are there any group attitudes to:

- o Time pressure?
- o Price-cost factors?
- o Supply and continuity?
- o Risk and their methods of avoiding risk?
- o Quality?
- o Seeing problems?

What are the relationships between groups?

- o Any record of conflict in the DMU between people or departments?
- o Any record of functional interests in defining the problem?
- o How is conflict resolved (joint problem solving, persuasion, bargaining or politicking)?

4. The individuals

- o The names and roles of the people involved in the decision-making unit
- o How do they see their problems? Different backgrounds and training will influence the way problems are perceived.
- o How satisfied are they with previous purchases and why?
- o The needs of the individuals in the DMU, how they perceive themselves and the quality of relationship they like to have with suppliers. For example:
    1. What is their background (class, age, education and lifestyle)?
    2. How much time do they want spent with them?
    3. How frequently do they want suppliers to contact them?
    4. Do they treat suppliers as peers?
    5. What level of intimacy do they want?

6. Will they want to dominate the relationship?

7. Will they want to become dependent on suppliers?

8. Will they be aggressive?

9. What attitudes do they have towards risk? And how does this show in the way they procrastinate and throw up objections?

10. How will sex, race and other forms of difference influence the relationship?

11. How will they play their professional role and what sort of relationship will their professional role allow the supplier to play

12. How is the supplier expected to behave? Remember you have to create an ongoing relationship with them!

Unforeseen factors

These could relate to the internal and external environment. Is there anything outside the control of the DMU that could affect the decision making (industrial relations problems, cash flow, tax changes, etc.)?

Question 3.4

What role do sales people play in helping customers to make decisions? Use the decision-making process as a structure on which to base your discussion. Consider both a retail situation and an industrial situation.

Summary

In this unit we have considered cultural factors influencing customers' behaviour, theories of motivation, consumer imagery, psychoanalytic theory, role theory, trait factor theory and behavioural theory. We have also looked at the influence of the group on organizational purchasing. There are similarities and differences between buyer behaviour towards consumer and industrial goods and services.

Buyer behaviour is influenced in many different ways – the condition of the economy and other environmental factors, product characteristics, the type of market and its characteristics, the product's stage in the life cycle, the degree of market segmentation, the number of competitors, the number of customers and their geographic spread, the psychological factors operating within individuals such as their motives, approach to risk, attitudes and personality and other personal factors that are unique to a person such as their ability and knowledge, demographic factors and situational factors, social factors influencing the buyer decision process such as roles and family influences, reference groups, social classes and culture and sub-culture. The decision-making process (DMP) and the extent of the decision making involved – extended and limited problem solving, routine response buying, impulse buying and the degree of involvement in the purchase and the decision-making process within the decision-making unit (DMU).

Further study and examination preparation

Now undertake Question 6 from CIM Examination Session June 2000 to be found in the final Exam Paper Appendix.

Unit 4
Modelling customer behaviour,
attitudes and dynamics

Objectives

In this unit you will be introduced to:

- Modelling.
- The concept of attitudes.
- The different models of attitudes and how they can be used to explain behaviour.

This unit covers the following part of the Marketing Customer Interface syllabus:

- 2.3.1

Study guide

The emphasis in this unit is very much on understanding the principles and techniques behind consumer modelling rather than slavishly learning specific models by rote. The only way to gain a thorough understanding of modelling techniques and their application is to try working examples and relate these to your own purchasing experiences.

Any questions on modelling will require students to know why models are used, how they are designed, and what their benefits are. Most of the qualitative data we collect as market researchers relates to the attitudes of current or potential customers to the product or services we offer. To gain acceptance from customers we must present a favourable image and avoid unfavourable associations. How favourable impressions translate into active endorsements of a product or service is a matter of some conjecture. The attitude theories described in this unit all approach this problem in a slightly different manner.

Consumer decision making

We all make decisions every day of our lives: 'What shall I have for breakfast?' 'What sort of career do I want?' 'What brand of potatoes should I buy?' We are so used to making decisions that we rarely think about them. In fact, making decisions has become so automatic that we sometimes have difficulty explaining why we made a particular choice!

The aim of consumer decision-making research is to understand why decisions are made. Not surprisingly, this is not always easy. An understanding of the decision-making process requires a knowledge of consumer behaviour. The contents of this unit tie together many of the basic psychological and social processes that have been described earlier in this coursebook.

Activity 4.1

Ask a friend or colleague (politely!) why they chose the clothes they are wearing. The response may well be 'I just liked them' or something quite specific. List the reasons they give for each item of clothing (underwear excepted!).

This should give an idea of the range of possible reasons for a buying decision being made.

What is a model?

A model is an abstract representation of a process or relationship. A simple example: if we believe that raising the price for crossing a toll bridge will reduce the number of cars using the bridge we have expressed a model which can be represented in one of three ways:

   1. *Verbally*: 'as price increases – cars decrease'

2. *Mathematically*: $C = K1/P$

   where C = number of cars, P = toll price, K = constant

3. *Pictorially*: Price increase Reduction in cars

We all hold numerous models in our heads, most of which we give no thought to, but which allow us to make sense of the world and predict the likely course of events. Consider gravity. We all have a notion about gravity – we know that if we let go of something it will fall to the floor. This allows us to predict what is going to happen when we accidentally knock something over, drop-kick a football, or throw something.

It is possible to have totally different models of the same phenomenon. Keith Williams (1990) gives the example of an atlas where one might find the same country on different pages modelled on its topography, climate, geology, population, and zoology.

Models are of assistance in a number of ways:

1. They assist in the development of theories.

2. They aid the understanding of complex relationships.

3. They provide a framework for discussion and research.

Definition

Model — A physical, visual or mathematical simplified representation of a complex system.
Macmillan Dictionary of Retailing

Consumer decision models

In this unit, we are primarily concerned with the use of models to understand consumer behaviour. In most cases, what is being modelled is the behaviour leading up to a purchasing decision.

We are most interested in understanding how and why certain decisions are made. As such, our models will usually include consideration of many of the topics in this coursebook:

- Attitudes
- Perception
- Learning
- Motivation
- Social and cultural influences.

In most cases, consumer models are expressed pictorially and in this unit, we will discuss the basic principles underlying consumer modelling as well as looking at several specific models.

Classification of models

In 1974, the Market Research Society presented the findings of a study group which had been established to look at modelling. They agreed a classification system for assessing models which identified eleven dimensions:

1. *Micro or macro* In a micro-model each individual or unit in the market or database is represented and processed at the individual level. The output may or may not be a result of the aggregation of individual data. In a macro-model the total market is considered as a whole and the model's output is a global market response.

2. *Data-based or theory-based* Data-based models are the logical outcome of the process of data analysis used. Theory-based models are developed through the application of reason and have their basis in theories adopted from the behavioural sciences.

3. *Low, medium, or high level* This relates to simplicity or lack of it. At the lowest level simple models can be devised that require few variables but they inevitably have certain limitations because of their narrow coverage. They are better regarded as sub-models or component parts of some larger, more comprehensive model. At the other extreme there are 'grand' models that seek to orchestrate all relevant market variables and represent the full range of marketing stimuli. The medium category lies elsewhere between the two.

4. *Descriptive (historical or current), diagnostic or predictive* Here the distinction is made between models that describe market behaviour, those that seek to explain or diagnose why

consumers behave as they do, and those that set out to predict how consumers will behave under specified circumstances.

5. *Behavioural or statistical* In behavioural models, reference is made to underlying assumptions about how the individual behaves. They seek to relate to the total process of consumer responses to a given stimulus. With the statistical model there are no implicit assumptions about how or why consumers behave as they do. The internal parameters are hypothesized as a function of the analytical procedures employed.

6. *Generalized or ad hoc* Here a distinction is made between models that are intended to be, or can be, applied to a wide range of markets and those that are developed in the context of, and for use in, one market only.

7. *Functional or intellectual* The functional model represents the actual function of the object; it is meant to have real world application. The intellectual model need not be rooted in practicability.

8. *Static or dynamic* The static model represents a particular system at a given point in time and cannot take account of time effects. The dynamic model is able to represent systems over time. It can take account of changing values of parameters and even changes in basic relationships between parameters over time.

9. *Qualitative or quantitative* In the case of qualitative models no explicit variables are measured. In the case of quantitative models they are. A quantitative model is therefore more likely to be helpful in predicting behaviour as it should provide an indication of the weighting of importance that should be given to individual variables.

10. *Algebraic, sequential/net, or topological* In algebraic models summation or other manipulation is independent of the order of the variables. With sequential or net models the order of the variables is explicitly taken into account by the model. Topological models are based upon field-theory concepts involving space and geometry, forces and motion. They are gestalt models, that is they are concerned with the total situation.

11. *Successful or unsuccessful* These concepts are indefinable. What constitutes success or lack of it will differ among different people. Nonetheless, it was felt to be a useful criterion.

We would all like a simple model which accurately predicts all consumer behaviour under a variety of circumstances. Unfortunately, the perfect model does not exist and the best we can hope for is to be able to understand the behaviour that most people will conform to under a restricted set of circumstances. Nonetheless, this is better than 'whistling in the wind' and, gaining a better understanding of behaviour, does have other benefits as we have seen in earlier units.

Construction of models

Before looking at models in detail, we must identify the variable types which form the 'building blocks' of these consumer models.

Stimuli   These act as inputs to the consumer's behaviour. Examples include: advertising, environmental factors, reference group influence and physiological factors.

Responses   These are the observable responses of individuals which may be directly due to certain stimuli or arise as a result of internal processes.

Internal   These are variables which arise as a result of either internal physiological or psychological processes. Examples include: attitudes, learning, motivation, hunger and sex.

External   These are variables which arise as a result of external influences. Examples include: economic factors, situational factors and weather.

Endogenous   These are variables which have a clearly defined effect. These are included in the model.

Exogenous   These are variables which have a poorly defined effect. For example, a change in future circumstances, price changes by competitors and so on. These are usually not included in a model.

To these categories we must add intervening variables which act between stimulus and response. They modify the relationship between the stimuli received and the responses made but, by definition, cannot be observed or measured. They are thus exogenous variables which can be both external or internal in origin.

Figure 4.1 illustrates the action of the various variables, the box representing the consumer. In particular, it should be noted how response variables can impact future behaviour and that past and future considerations can be considered as stimuli.

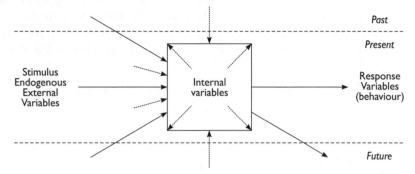

Figure 4.1 *Showing effect on consumer of variable types. Dotted lines represent the possible influence of exogenous variables*

Evaluating models

Before considering specific models in detail, it is worth considering the criteria to be used in their evaluation. The following were proposed by Williams (1990) as being indicative of a 'good' model:

1. *Simplicity* – whether the model is of high or low level, it should seek to break down complex behaviour patterns into simple easily understandable components.
2. *Factual basis* – a model should be consistent with the facts as far as they are known.
3. *Logic* – to be plausible a model must make sense and be internally consistent.
4. *Originality* – if a model is to advance knowledge it should be original, either in its basic construction or in the way in which it links together previously separate areas of knowledge.
5. *Explanatory power* – a model should seek to explain how, and why, specified behaviour takes place.
6. *Prediction* – a model should aid the prediction of a consumer's reaction to a given stimulus.
7. *Heuristic power* – this refers to a model's capacity to suggest new areas of research.
8. *Validity* – if a model is to have validity it must be verifiable. This means that it should be possible, at least in theory, to test the relationships proposed between variables.

It would be unrealistic to expect every model to satisfy all these criteria. However, they do provide a useful framework for assessing the importance and significance to be attached to a particular model. If, for example, a model lacked any factual basis, failed to explain observed behaviour and did little to enlighten our thinking, then we would be justified in dismissing it.

Of course, no set of criteria can be comprehensive or pertain to every situation. As with all such problems, a commonsense assessment, against the background of a general understanding of the components of consumer behaviour, will go a long way.

Simple models

Simple models of consumer behaviour take a 'broad brush' approach to understanding consumers. In contrast with the comprehensive models to be discussed later in this unit, they consider only the main influences on behaviour. Simple models fall into four general categories:

1. *Black box* – this is the generic name for models which do not consider internal processes but rely solely on directly observable stimulus variables and responses.
2. *Decision process* – these types of models enjoy widespread use within marketing. They illustrate the various decision stages a consumer progresses through to arrive at a particular course of action. An example is the AIDA (attention, interest, desire, action) promotional model.
3. *Personal variable* – these, in contrast to black box models, focus on internal variables. They attempt to model particular internal processes. One example is Fishbein's attitude model.
4. *Hybrid decision/personal* – these attempt to combine the features of decision process and personal variable models. In this unit, we will consider Chris Rice's *PV/PPS* model.

Black box models

Perhaps the simplest black box model of behaviour is the stimulus-response (SR) model which is typically illustrated by the experiments of Pavlov. Pavlov found that when a dog was presented with meat it salivated. In this case the stimulus was the meat, the response the salivation. Simple SR relationships also exist in people. For example, a short tap just below the knee (stimulus) will cause the leg to move in a reflex action (response). The basic SR model can be represented as in Figure 4.2.

Figure 4.2 *The simplest black box model*

More complex black box models typically consider more variables and more entities (whether they are single consumers or organizations).

Figure 4.3 is an example of a 'consumer-centric' black box model of a consumer's decision environment. It shows the stimuli which can influence purchasing behaviour. Note that some of the influencing variables can themselves be influenced by the consumer resulting in a two-way interaction.

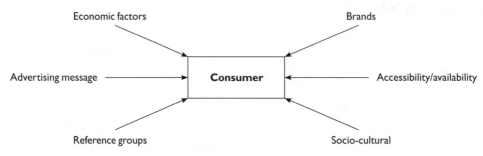

Figure 4.3 *Consumer-centric black box model of consumer decision environment*

Figure 4.4 shows Kotler's model of the buying process showing inputs and outputs. It presents a more considered view of the buying behaviour. It takes into account more influences and details more of the responses.

As black box models concentrate solely on the action of external variables, they are only useful in the investigation of behaviour where internal variables are not deemed significant. When considering black box models researchers are primarily interested in the relative importance of the stimuli involved.

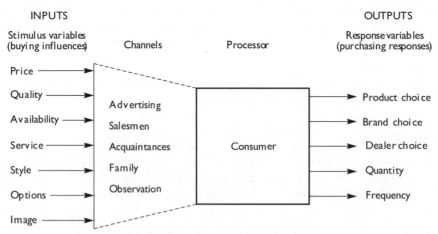

Figure 4.4 *Kotler's Model of the buying process. A complex black box model*

For example, cigarette advertising is banned on British television so, unless a particular consumer is known to be regularly exposed to other sources of advertising (magazines, cinema, etc.), then reference groups, cultural influences and brand experience are more likely to play a part in the brand of cigarettes chosen. Similarly, someone who lives in a big city is less likely to be influenced by accessibility/availability restrictions than a consumer living in a remote village.

Decision process models

Unlike black box models, decision process models represent a process flow. They are derived from the general decision-making/problem solving models of researchers such as Newell and Simon. Figure 4.5 illustrates such a generic model.

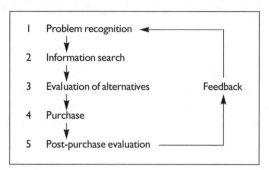

Figure 4.5 *The five-stage model*

This model allows us to consider buying as a process but it makes various assumptions and has therefore been criticized. It assumes:

- That consumers are rational
- That decision processes are simple and sequential
- There are different types of decisions
- It assumes that customers can receive and order information
- Many purchases seem not to be preceded by a decision process.

Decision process models occur in many areas of marketing (both with reference to behaviour and other fields) and form the core of most of the comprehensive models.

Problem recognition

The customer recognizes they would like to change the current situation, they have a need. The stimulus could be internal or external (for example, feels in need of a break and/or sees a holiday brochure).

Search for information

The customer looks for information either from external sources or from memory. The more complex the area the more information will be required. The marketer must be able to get the product/service into the consumer's awareness and choice set (Figure 4.6).

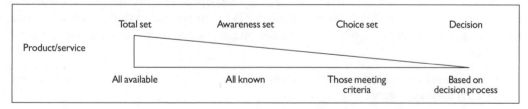

Figure 4.6 *The customer awareness and choice set*

Example

For example, the customer decides they want to go out for a meal. There may be many restaurants within practical reach (the total set) but only a few of which the customer is aware (the awareness set).

Alternative evaluation

The customer looks at alternatives from a need-satisfying perspective – they look for benefits.

Purchase

After evaluation the customer buys the preferred alternative or a substitute. The decision to modify or postpone purchase is influenced by the risk they perceive and any anxiety they feel.

Evaluation

The purchase is then evaluated against the original criteria.

Risk

When consumers make decisions the outcome may be uncertain, purchasing involves risk and anxiety. However, risk is personal and related to the consumer's perception of what they consider to be risky – functional risk (will the product perform?), physical risk (will I be harmed?), financial risk (is it worth the money?), social risk (will the deodorant work?), psychological risk (will it affect my self-image?), time risk (am I wasting my time?).

Managing risk

Consumers may minimize risk by staying with the same brand, buying a well-known brand, purchasing from a reputable dealer, buying a more expensive brand, looking for reassurance (such as money-back guarantees, laboratory test results, prepurchase trial, warranties) and looking for information (such as from family, friends, opinion leaders, consumer reports, testimonials and information found in the media).

Post-purchase dissonance

Often after an important purchase has been made, a phenomenon called 'post-purchase dissonance' is present; this is a feeling of unease that the goods may not represent good value. Consumers frequently rationalize and reinforce their purchase decisions by looking for messages that confirm their past beliefs, or by ignoring the dissonant information by refusing to discuss it or rejecting it. Marketers should therefore reduce post-purchase dissonance by providing reassuring messages, providing after-sales service and general customer care.

Levels of consumer decision making

Extended problem solving and limited problem solving

Not all consumer decision making requires the same degree of information search. The actions at each stage vary and depend on the extent to which customers are engaged in extended problem solving (EPS) or limited problem solving (LPS).

When customers purchase, two factors are particularly useful in explaining how they come to a decision.

1. How involved they are in purchasing the product/service.
2. The difference in their perception between competing brands.

Involvement

The extent to which the customer gets involved in a purchase depends on the individual. Involvement can be transient or enduring especially where the choice is repetitive and past experience produces a brand preference (for example: perfume, cigarettes, magazines and newspapers) (seeFigure 4.7 andFigure 4.8).

For each of the 10 statements, circle the extent to which you agree or disagree.The scale ranges from (1) strongly agree to (6) strongly disagree

1	I would be interested in reading about this product.	1 2 3 4 5 6
2	I would read a *Consumer Reports* article about this product.	1 2 3 4 5 6
3	I have compared product characteristics among brands.	1 2 3 4 5 6
4	I think there are a great deal of differences among brands.	1 2 3 4 5 6
5	I have a most preferred brand of this product.	1 2 3 4 5 6
6	I usually pay attention to ads for this product.	1 2 3 4 5 6
7	I usually talk about this product with other people.	1 2 3 4 5 6
8	I usually seek advice from other people prior to purchasing this product.	1 2 3 4 5 6
9	I usually take many factors into account before purchasing this product.	1 2 3 4 5 6
10	I usually spend a lot of time choosing what kind to buy.	1 2 3 4 5 6

Figure 4.7 *A personal involvement checklist. Source: Engel, Warshaw, Kinnear, Richard D. Irwin, Inc 1994. Adapted from Edward F. McQuarrie and J. Michael Munson, A revised product involvement inventory: improved usability and validity, in* Advances in Consumer Research*, vol. 19, eds John F. Sherry, Jr., and Brian Sternthal (Provo, Utah: Association for Consumer Research, 1992). Used by special permission*

	High-involvement purchase decision	Low-involvement purchase decision
Decision making (information search, consideration of brand alternatives)	Complex decision making (autos, major appliances)	Variety seeking (cereals)
Habit (little or no information search, consideration of only one brand)	Brand loyalty (cigarettes, perfume)	Inertia (canned vegetables, paper towels)

Figure 4.8 *Consumer decision making. Source: Assaell (1987)* Consumer Behaviour and Marketing Action*, Kent Publishing Company*

Extended problem solving (EPS)

When customers are highly involved in the purchase and they can see that the differences between brands are significant. High involvement purchases involve a degree of risk, for example:

- They are highly priced (financial risk), e.g. cars.
- Very complex (psychological risk) the wrong decision will cause stress, e.g. computers.
- They reflect self-image (social risk) and peer group approval is important, e.g. clothing, jewellery.

The stages are as follows:

1. *Problem recognition*
2. *Information search*

   Customers will look for information from a wide variety of media sources and personal selling will influence their choice. The decision making may be carried out over an extended period of time.

3. *Alternative evaluation*

   Multiple criteria will be used to evaluate the brand and each brand will be seen as significantly different from each other.

4. *Purchase*

   Customers will travel and visit a lot of shops. Personal selling will influence their choice.

5. *Post-purchase evaluation*

   Satisfaction will increase their loyalty to the brand.

Limited problem solving (LPS)

Customers are not very involved in the purchase, there are minor perceived differences and the problem that needs to be solved is not large. The stages are as follows:

1. *Problem recognition*
2. *Information search*

   The customer is unlikely to look extensively for information.

3. *Evaluation of alternatives*

   When involvement and interest in a brand is low, brand switching is likely to take place. The brand decision is not considered important enough to warrant pre-planning and will often take place in the shop.

4. *Purchase*

   Customers are likely to try the brand out when they come across a purchase trigger like an in-store display, a coupon, a free trial. Point-of-sale display, price and packaging are important aspects of the marketing mix as buying action is also influenced by brand recognition. Customers may switch brands out of boredom, others may buy the same brand again out of 'inertia' because it is just not important enough to give it any thought.

   It may also be better to position these products functionally (see the section 'Positioning' in Unit 2, Market segmentation).

5. *Post-purchase evaluation*

Beliefs about the brand may be formed by learning passively about it and recalled from memory, or the brand may be evaluated after use and beliefs about it formed by experience.

How much information do customers need?

It is generally believed that customers make decisions to purchase on a small number of selectively chosen pieces of information.

It therefore follows that it is extremely important to understand what information the customer feels will help them to be able to evaluate goods and services. In group decision making it is likely that each member of the group may have different needs for information.

Activity 4.2

This process is now considered in more detail and this activity will enable you to get some hands-on experience of customer decision making. Working with a partner take a recent or planned purchase and work through the five stages answering the following questions.

1. Need recognition

    The customer recognizes they would like to change the current situation.

    o   What is motivating the person? (think about basic psychological needs and benefits, these can be driven internally or externally by the environment).

    o   Are the needs dormant or can the customer express them?

    o   How involved with the product are they? Think about the situation, is it one of extended problem solving or limited problem solving?

2. Search for information

    The customer looks for information either from external sources or from memory to solve the problem. The amount of information that is found will be influenced by a number of factors such as time available, past experience involving ways in which attitudes have been formed and patterns of learned behaviour, and other influences such as social factors which include reference group influence, personal contacts, etc.

    o   Do you understand what information they need to proceed to the next stage of evaluation?

    o   Do you know where information about the product/service comes from?

    o   Do you know what information they have?

    o   Do you know if the customer is motivated enough to look for alternative information?

    o   What criteria (features, benefits) do they use to assess the information?

3. Alternative evaluation – the customer looks at alternatives from the perspective of need-satisfying benefits.

    o   What else is being evaluated at the same time?

    o   What criteria (features, benefits) are the competition using?

    o   Are there existing customer-supplier relationships?

    o   Are the criteria used perceived by the customer as being different or essentially the same?

    o   How important are the differences?

4. Purchase

    After the evaluation has been made the customer then buys the preferred alternative or a substitute.

    o   Do they have the money?

    o   Will the offer have to be adapted in order to clinch the deal?

    o   Will the customer go on looking until they find exactly what they want?

    o   Will they accept a substitute?

    o   Where do they expect to make the purchase?

---

5. Post-purchase evaluation

The purchase is then evaluated against the original criteria. Does it meet the needs and expectations of the customer?

- How satisfied are they and what reasons do they give for their satisfaction/dissatisfaction?
- How does this experience compare with previous experiences with other products/services?
- Have they told anybody else about their satisfaction/dissatisfaction?
- Have they tried to complain? What reaction did they get?
- Will they purchase again or will they use an alternative?

Personal variable models

These focus on modelling specific internal processes such as attitudes, perception and motivation.

The rise in the 1980s of information processing theory has been influential in the development of personal variable models. Information processing theory is mostly concerned with the mind and the way it is organized. It has provided another perspective on the way in which decisions are modelled and in particular in the area of rule development – the rules used in arriving at a decision where alternatives are being considered. There are four basic personal variable models, classified according to the decisions rule types used within the model:

1. *Compensatory, or trade-off, rule* assumes that consumers trade-off products against each other considering all of the features of the products against some hypothetical ideal. The rule implies that sacrifices are made as part of the decision process but that each alternative is considered thoroughly. For example, you may be willing to compromise on the appearance of a new stereo system if the sound quality is good.

2. *Threshold rule* assumes that products can be totally rejected on the basis of just one undesirable characteristic – without further consideration. For example, you may reject the purchase of a new set of kitchen pans out-of-hand if their colour clashes with the rest of your kitchen despite the fact that the other characteristics of the pan may have been ideal.

3. *Disjunctive rule* assumes that a product can be chosen simply because it excels on one characteristic. Returning to the pans example, it may be that a sub-standard set of pans is chosen simply because they are the 'right' colour.

4. *Lexicographical rule* assumes that a product can be selected on the basis of considering just a few characteristics considered in a predetermined order. Taking house buying as an example, you may have a set of criteria such as number of bedrooms, access to shops, garden size and so on, which you have prioritized to determine your choice. If these are satisfactory, then you may not bother considering any further characteristics (for instance you may not mind if it does or does not have a garage, how many bathrooms or if it is a maisonette or house).

Hybrid model – Rice's PV/PPS model

In an attempt to overcome the weaknesses of the personal variable and decision process models, Chris Rice synthesized the two approaches to develop, what he calls, the perceived value/perceived probability of satisfaction (*PV/PPS*) model.

The central notion in this model is that the subjective utility (*SU*) of a particular decision alternative can be calculated from:

1. The value attached to the outcomes (perceived value or *PV*).
2. The perception of the probability of each outcome occurring (perceived probability of satisfaction or *PPS*).

The formula for calculating *SU* is:

$$SU = PV \times PPS$$

The model therefore predicts that the highest utility option will be that where the outcomes are valued highly and are most likely to be satisfied. This can be illustrated graphically as in Figure 4.9, neatly dividing purchases into four categories.

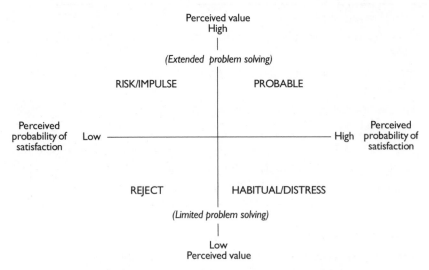

Figure 4.9 *Type of purchase analyzed in terms of the Rice PV/ PPS model*

The following explanation is adapted from Chris Rice (*Consumer Behaviour*):

The lower right-hand quadrant is concerned with purchases which are of low perceived value in themselves, but which have a high probability of satisfaction. Here an example might be the situation of running low on petrol when travelling down a motorway. Government quality standards ensure that there is little to choose between brands so the car is filled with whichever brand is sold in the next service station. Many petrol companies attempt to increase the perceived value of their brand by offering air miles, tokens or similar. This example could be classed as a *distress purchase,* but a similar process would be predicted in *habitual buying* at supermarkets. Low involvement purchases are often made on the basis that there is little, or nothing, to choose between brands.

The top left-hand quadrant is interesting (high value, low probability) as it may go some way towards explaining otherwise apparently irrational behaviour. An example might be gambling on the UK lottery despite the chances of winning a fortune being extremely small. Here the hypothesis would be that, for many people, the very high value of winning a very large sum of money (with its attendant outcomes of travel, giving up work and being able to afford luxuries), more than compensates for the very low probability of that outcome occurring. This can be classed as a *risk* or *impulse purchase.* The top right-hand quadrant is the marketer's dream – high values and high probability of satisfaction – the combination that is most likely to result in *probable purchase.*

Thus, in practical terms this model clearly identifies two key objectives of marketing effort and communication:

1. To raise the perceived value of the outcomes of purchase.
2. To raise the perceived probability of satisfaction following purchase.

An example will illustrate the model. Suppose, we are trying to decide which type of food to purchase on our way home from work. We have two alternatives: either pre-cooked or fresh. However, we are unsure what our partner has planned for this evening. We may be 'watching a video' (in which case we might want something quick and convenient to cook) or we may be having 'a romantic meal' in which case a well cooked, tasty meal is called for. Obviously, a real situation may consider many more characteristics and/or alternatives.

To assess perceived value we could rate the value of each characteristic on a scale of 1 to 10. We might arrive at the results similar to those in Table 4.1. It is important to remember that these are only perceived values and may bear no resemblance to an objective assessment.

Table 4.1 *Rice PV/PPS model – perceived value table*

Food	'Romantic meal at home'	'Watching a video'
Pre-cooked	3	8
Fresh	9	5

We must then assess the probability of each of the conditions occurring. We may perceive that 'watching a video' is more likely and give this a probability of 0.8 (an 80 per cent likelihood of happening). This leaves us with a probability of 0.2 (or 20 per cent) for the 'romantic meal at home' (the complete set of probabilities must add up to 1.0).

To calculate the subjective utility scores (*SU*) we must now multiply each cell in the value table by its perceived probability. Therefore, all the entries in the 'romantic meal' column are multiplied by 0.2; and all the entries in the 'watching a video' column are multiplied by 0.8. Table 4.2 shows the results.

Table 4.2 *Rice PV/PPS model – subjective utility scores*

Food	'Romantic meal at home'	'Watching a video'
Pre-cooked	0.6	6.4
Fresh	1.8	4

According to *PV/PPS* theory we will act on the outcome that will result in the highest *SU* score. In this example, we are certain to buy pre-cooked food.

In this context, the pre-cooked meal is seen as relatively the most probable purchase – it would thus occupy the top right-hand quadrant in Figure 4.9 in that it has both perceived high value and perceived high probability of satisfaction.

Comparison of simple models

	Black box	Decision process	Personal variable	Hybrid decision/ personal
Considers internal variables	No	Yes	Yes	Yes
Considers external variables	Yes	Yes	No	Yes
Good for explanation	No	No	Yes	Yes
Good for prediction	Yes	Possibly	Yes	Yes
Good for structuring marketing strategies	No	Yes	No	No
Simple to understand	Yes	Yes	No	No

Comprehensive, or grand, models of consumer behaviour

There are also, so-called, grand models of consumer behaviour which attempt to comprehensively explain all those aspects of the buying situation which their creators deem to be significant. These are:

- Nicosia model
- Howard-Sheth model
- Engel, Blackwell and Miniard model (which you may see referred to as the Engel, Kollat and Blackwell model – an earlier derivative).

These models are not discussed in this syllabus and are now thought to be rather outdated.

Attitudes and behaviour

Most of the qualitative data we collect as market researchers relates to the attitudes of current or potential consumers to the products or services we offer. To gain acceptance from customers we must present a favourable image and avoid unfavourable associations. How favourable impressions translate into active endorsements of a product or service is a matter of some conjecture. The attitude theories described in this unit all approach this problem in a slightly different manner.

The motivations that drive customers are also important. To provide what the customer needs requires an understanding of their goals and aspirations. Whereas proven theories of customer motivation are thin on the ground, the general theories of motivation that exist provide useful guidance to marketers.

What are attitudes?

> I know what I like and I like what I know
>
> *lyrics from the Genesis album Selling England by the Pound*

Most of us have at some time been asked what we 'think' or 'feel' about a particular object, issue, activity, or person. Our responses to such questions are an expression of our attitudes. That is, whether we generally like or dislike the object, issue, activity or person under discussion.

Formal definitions of attitude try to capture this notion of 'liking and disliking' but, as much of what we say and do can be interpreted as expressing an attitude, such definitions are often broad and/or uninformative. Examples of the more popular definitions are given below.

Definition

Learned orientation – a learned orientation or disposition, toward an object or situation, which provides a tendency to respond favourably or unfavourably to the object or situation (the learning may not be based on personal experience but may be acquired through observational learning and identification) (Rokeach, 1968). Attitudes are likes and dislikes (Bem, 1979). An overall evaluation that allows one to respond in a consistently favourable or unfavourable manner with respect to a given object or alternative (Engel et al., 1990).

Characteristics of attitudes

Attitudes are held by individuals. When similar attitudes are held by many individuals they become embedded in that society's culture. They help us to understand and predict behaviour such as stereotyping, prejudice, behavioural intentions, interpersonal attraction and persuasion.

The following are generally held to be characteristics of attitudes:

- They can be held about any object, person, issue or activity – referred to as the attitude object.

- They may be strongly or weakly held – an attitude is not simply something that is turned on or off, it is an assessment based on a continuous evaluation.

- They are learned – we acquire attitudes in much the same way we acquire culture, through conditioning and social modelling.

- Attitudes change – they are dynamic. We no longer have the same attitudes as we did when we were younger. We are constantly modifying attitudes based on our experiences and acquiring new attitudes as we encounter new attitude objects.

- Some attitudes are more fundamental than others and more resistant to change – certain opinions stay with us throughout our lives, while others change from week to week.

- Attitudes are learned (formed) as a result of information, modelling, classical conditioning and operant conditioning.

Information provides us with the basis for our beliefs on which attitudes rest. For example, if we read in a magazine that a certain red wine is overpriced, then we may well believe that to be true. Several beliefs pertaining to a particular attitude object will go towards forming our overall attitude. The balance of positive and negative information, which in turn leads to a balance of positive and negative beliefs, will determine whether our overall attitude towards red wine is positive or negative.

Modelling is a process that occurs when we emulate the behaviour of other people. If we see people we admire or believe to be similar to ourselves drinking red wine or expressing a positive attitude towards red wine, then we too will be very likely to develop a positive attitude to the drinking of red wine.

Classical conditioning (described below) influences the development of attitudes by associating the attitude object with either a positive or negative stimulus. For example, if we always drink red wine when we are relaxing at the end of the week, we will come to associate the taste and the smell of red wine with feelings of relaxation and pleasure. This will lead to a positive attitude towards red wine.

Operant conditioning (described below) can also influence the development of attitudes. If every time we drink red wine we feel warm and comfortable inside, then the drinking behaviour is being positively reinforced. This process will lead to the development of a positive attitude towards the drinking of red wine.

All four processes may combine to help us form the attitude that we have towards any particular attitude object. There may be conflict to the extent that some factors lead us towards the development of a positive attitude, whereas others lead towards the development of a negative attitude, but the overall balance of positive and negative influences will determine whether our attitude is positive or negative and how strong the attitude is.

Reinforcement

The concept of reinforcement lies at the heart of psychological theories of learning. It was first postulated by Thorndike in 1911 when he stated in *Animal Intelligence*:

of the responses made to a situation, those which satisfy the organism's needs tend to be retained while those which fail to satisfy these needs tend to be eliminated.

In other words, responses which satisfy a need (see motivation) are more likely to be perpetuated. This process is called conditioning. We have already looked at socialization, and the role that conditioning plays in acquiring culture. However, the use of conditioning in other marketing contexts is worth further, brief exploration. There are two prominent conditioning theories:

1. Classical conditioning
2. Operant conditioning.

Classical conditioning

Classical conditioning is said to take place when two stimuli are paired. That is, a stimulus is associated with an event. The work on this form of conditioning arose out of experimentation by Ivan Pavlov with dogs. Naturally, the dogs would salivate on sight of meat. But, by repeatedly preceding the arrival of the meat by a ring of a bell, Pavlov was able to condition the dogs to salivate to the sound of the bell *without the presence of meat.*

Classical conditioning is frequently used in advertising and promotionals. By repeatedly associating a slogan, image, or sound with a particular product it is possible to conjure up the memory of the product by the associated stimulus only. For example, colours have become associated with particular political parties so that the colour alone can evoke thoughts of the party. Similarly, a jingle or other tune associated with a product in an advertisement which goes on to become a 'popular hit' will continue to evoke images of that product (for free!). It is now quite common for music to be scored for commercials with just this goal.

The association between the conditioned stimulus and the original response slowly weakens until it is totally extinguished. This is known as *extinction.* A conditioned response that has been extinguished may, however, *spontaneously recover,* if the original association is again reinforced. In other words, the association will take less time to re-establish than the learning of a new association. It is as if the mind has retained some kind of 'memory' of the association which makes re-establishment easier. For example, offering petrol tokens will reinforce a driver to use that chain of petrol stations although the association will slowly weaken if the promotion is stopped. However, due to the action of spontaneous recovery, a re-introduction of the token scheme will make the original driver more easy to attract back when compared to a driver new to that chain of stations.

Operant conditioning

This is different from classical conditioning in that the learner is instrumental in producing the stimulus (in classical conditioning the stimulus – the bell in the case of Pavlov's dogs – was introduced by the experimenter). Operant conditioning can be explained with the experiments of Skinner on more animals, this time rats, in a cage which became known as the 'Skinner Box'. The box contained a lever which, when depressed, dispensed food pellets. After wandering around the cage for some time the rats eventually pressed the lever, either out of curiosity or by accident, which of course provided them with food (positive reinforcement). As a result, the pressing of the lever became associated with the production of food.

Both positive and negative reinforcement can occur. For example, if the lever delivered an electric shock, the rat would be unlikely to repeat the behaviour.

Sales promotions commonly make use of operant conditioning to reinforce certain behaviours. For example, the 'computers for schools' coupons scheme introduced by Tesco stores reinforces shopping at that store. Operant conditioning is also responsible for much brand loyalty. If a customer is satisfied with a brand or product their purchasing behaviour is reinforced.

Activity 4.3

Go to your local supermarket and try to identify at least three promotions. What type of conditioning is being used in each?

Marketers are most concerned with understanding attitudes (for instance, does a brand have a favourable or unfavourable image), modifying attitudes (to make them more favourable towards certain objects and/or less favourable towards others) and turning positive attitudes towards an object into action, usually involving the purchase of the item in question.

Reinforcement makes a particular behaviour even stronger and may be biological (food, water, sleep), social (attention, approval from others, physical contact or sex), cognitive (stimulation, knowledge, feedback). There are primary reinforcers which are important to us in their own right (food, water, attention) and there are secondary reinforcers such as money, which is useless in its own right and only acts as an exchange. There is also self-reinforcement which comes about through learning about one's own values of good and bad, for example, I did well, I am pleased with myself, with what I have achieved.

Understanding attitudes

An attitude is not a simple entity but is formed from a combination of mental processes and expressed by actions. Most psychologists agree that, at some level, attitudes contain three components:

1. A cognitive component – the knowledge and perceptions about an object. For instance, its shape, colour, price and so on.
2. An affective component – what a person subjectively feels about the attitude object – whether or not they are favourably disposed towards it. For instance, is the colour of the product a 'favoured' colour?
3. A behavioural component – how a person responds to the attitude object (based on 1 and 2).

Suppose we are interested in customers' attitudes to washing powder. The cognitive component to their attitudes may relate to the fact that the powder cleans, that is environmentally friendly and so on. These are what they believe to be the 'truths' about the product. Whether they are favourably disposed to the product overall will depend on how they feel about the cognitive components of the product. If they value both cleaning ability and environmental friendliness highly, then they are likely to feel positive towards the product overall. As a result, of assessing the cognitive and affective components of their attitude they may decide to purchase one brand of powder instead of another (the behavioural component).

Attitudes, beliefs and values

Attitudes are normally thought of as resulting from a combination of beliefs and values.

*   *Beliefs* The body of knowledge we hold about the world (may be incomplete or inaccurate). These underpin the cognitive component within attitudes. Beliefs are often expressed in sentences where the word 'is' appears. For example, the information that 'Guinness is good for you' was presented as a fact in a clever advertising campaign. Undoubtedly, this view now forms part of many people's belief system.
*   *Values* Deeply held views about what is good, desirable, valuable, worthwhile. Unlike beliefs, these are usually ideals to which we aspire and may be expressed in sentences where the words 'should be' appear. For example, 'Health care should be free to all' is an expression of the value of social justice.

The relationship between attitudes and our beliefs and values is a complex one. People typically have thousands of beliefs about the world, hundreds of attitudes although probably fewer than fifty values.

It is interesting to see how advertisers use these values to sell products. Typically, a product is associated with a particular value dimension to give it appeal.

For example, pharmaceutical products are typically sold using the dimension of theoretical (truth). Facts and figures, often in the form of a graph, are shown to demonstrate the effectiveness of the product being sold. It may be that a brand of toothpaste prevents the formation of plaque for six hours or that a shampoo bonds extra proteins to your hair, and so on.

Subjective norm

As we can see people can behave in the way they do for many reasons. These reasons are not just based on attitude, but on something called the subjective norm. This is what other people think we should do (see culture and group influence).

Perceived behavioural control

Another factor influencing behaviour is the control we think we have over our actions. This control may be external to ourselves, or, internal to the extent of believing that one can change things.

Attitude change

Changing attitude needs therefore to take into account:

- The values and beliefs that make up the attitude
- The cognitive and conative behaviour aspects of the attitude itself
- The way in which information, modelling, classical and operant conditions can form and change attitudes
- The influence of groups (subjective norm)
- And the control the person perceives themselves to have over their behaviour

Relationship between attitudes and behaviour

As marketers, we are most interested in being able to predict and alter the behavioural component of attitudes. We want people to like our products but also buy them, remain loyal and recommend the products to others. All these involve action of some sort.

Figure 4.10 represents a simple model of the relationship between attitudes and behaviour. In this simple model, positive cognitive and affective perceptions of an object lead to positive behaviours and vice versa.

Figure 4.10 *A simple model of the relationship between attitudes and behaviour*

Unfortunately, psychological research has found that there is no clear relationship between measured attitudes and behaviour. Perhaps this is not surprising as many of the factors which also influence our behaviour are outside our own control. It might be, for instance, that we would like to take a three-week holiday in Portugal. We are extremely favourably disposed towards the idea but there are a number of reasons why we might not be able to actually book the holiday. Some examples of outside influences, in this instance, might be:

- We have no money.
- We cannot get the time off work.
- The are no more bookings available for Portugal this year.
- Spain has an air-traffic control strike on at the moment which is stopping flights to Portugal.
- A family member is ill and needs our support.

Some of the apparent difference between what we think and what we do may be due to measurement difficulties. We may observe a person buying a product but are they doing so because they are favourably disposed towards that product or because it happens to be the nearest on the supermarket shelf? Interview is the only way of securing attitudes in isolation from behaviour, but such methods also have their problems.

Some elegant experiments have been undertaken by psychologists and sociologists to try and determine the factors affecting the link between attitudes and behaviour. Perhaps most famous of these is the 'Travelling Chinese Experiment'.

In the early 1930s strong feelings existed against the Chinese in the USA. Around this time Richard LaPiere, a sociologist, took a Chinese couple on a tour of America. The trio stopped at 250 hotels and restaurants during their trip. On only one occasion were they refused entry. After returning from his trip, he wrote to each of the establishments he had visited asking them whether they would accept Chinese patrons. Somewhat surprisingly, of the half that responded to his letter, 90 per cent said they would not.

This experiment demonstrates a rather large gap between what the various proprietors said they would do and what they actually did. In other words, their attitudes (as secured by letter) were strikingly different to their behaviour (as demonstrated by LaPiere's visits).

There are a number of methodological problems with LaPiere's informal experiment. For example, had the same person that answered the letter been in a position to refuse service. Nonetheless, the results are strongly suggestive of a real discrepancy between attitudes and behaviour.

Question 4.1

Can you think of any other factors in LaPiere's 'experiment' that may have weakened the link between attitudes and behaviour?

As a result of LaPiere's study and the experiments of others, it is generally agreed that attitudes are only one factor in behaviour. It is said that they are a predisposing factor. In other words, without any other interventions, the attitudes would lead more directly to behaviour. The following intervening factors are said to affect the degree with which attitude leads to behaviour:

- *Unforeseen events* It may be that unforeseen events lead to a change in behaviour. For instance, you may wish to go to a football match but it starts raining so you reluctantly make alternative arrangements.

- *Elapsed time* As attitudes are dynamic, the longer the elapsed time between measurement of the attitude and the behaviour you are trying to predict, the less likely there is to be a link.

- *Situational factors* It may be that the situation you find yourself in precludes action. For example, a consumer may wish to buy a tub of ice cream but the shops have just closed or they may not have enough money to hand.

- *Stability* A particular attitude may be unstable in that you keep changing your mind. For example, one day you may feel like wearing jeans, the next day more formal wear.

- *Conflict of attitudes* It may be that more than one attitude is applicable to a certain situation, the resultant behaviour will inevitably lead to a compromise behaviour. For example, you go into a shop to buy a tub of ice cream. You and your partner both want a different flavour. You equally well want to keep your partner happy and you want your favourite flavour. The behaviour you exhibit will be a compromise between these two contradictory aims (the exact compromise will depend how selfish you are!).

- *Strength* The strength with which an attitude is held can determine behaviour. Also, one attitude can be expressed in many different ways. For example, if you support a particular political party you may or may not become a member depending on the strength of your support.

- *Specificity* The accuracy with which attitudes are measured also affects the degree to which they are able to predict behaviour. This is discussed in more detail below.

We are left with a more complex view of the relationship between attitudes and behaviour than suggested earlier. Figure 4.11 is more representative of the relationship that exists:

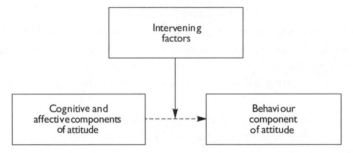

Figure 4.11 *Most likely relationship between attitudes and behaviour*

Specificity of measurement

Fishbein and Ajzen argue that you can predict behaviour from attitudes if the attitudes you are investigating are measured accurately enough. In other words, you need to ensure *specificity* of measurement. This has implications in the design of attitude surveys. Most importantly, questions must ask precisely about the behaviour you are trying to predict. The pill experiment, carried out by Davidson and Jaccard in the late 1970s, on women's attitudes to the contraceptive pill illustrates this point quite well.

A group of women were asked a question about their general attitudes to birth control. There was found to be a very low correlation between positive attitudes towards birth control and their actual use of the pill. When the question was changed to something more specific – it asked about their attitudes to oral contraception – the correlation between attitudes and usage was much higher (0.32). When the question was made more specific again – asking about their use of oral contraceptive over the next two years – an even higher correlation between attitudes and behaviour was found (0.57). When measured attitudes are similar to the observed behaviour, they are said to correspond.

Consistency theories of attitude

There are three prominent attitude theories which address how attitudes change and adapt to changing circumstances:

1. Balance theory (Heider, 1958).
2. Congruity theory (Osgood and Tannenbaum, 1955).
3. Cognitive dissonance theory (Festinger, 1957).

These are all based on the assumption that people seek consistency in their attitudes; i.e. one cannot simultaneously hold two contradictory beliefs. Suppose, a reliable friend recommends a restaurant which you visit and find disappointing. In general terms, consistency theories state that you cannot simultaneously believe that both your friend is reliable yet his recommendation was wrong. You would, according to consistency theorists, be 'forced' to either change your opinion of your friend or make some excuse concerning the performance of the restaurant on the occasion you visited.

Balance theory and congruity theory are described below. For a description of cognitive dissonance theory refer to the unit 'The basic principles of investigative (market) research'.

Balance theory

Balance theory is mainly concerned at the transfer of information between people. This is of use to marketers investigating ways in which recommendations, as well as negative information, are communicated.

Consider a person (A) that receives information from another person (B) concerning an attitude object (O). Depending on whether this information is positive or negative, the four scenarios in Figure 4.12 are possible. The interactions are represented as triangles, the nature of the communications as positive (or favourable) (+) or negative (or unfavourable) (-):

The top triangle (1) is balanced. Persons A and B have a positive attitude, both towards each other, and the object. There is no inconsistency.

Triangle (2) is unbalanced. Persons A and B have a negative attitude towards each other yet they both have a positive attitude to the object. Although their views of the object are consistent (both positive), their views of each other are negative. This is inconsistent.

Triangle (3) is balanced. Persons A and B have a positive attitude towards each other and share the same (negative) attitude towards the object. There is no inconsistency.

Triangle (4) is unbalanced. Persons A and B have a positive attitude towards each other but their attitudes towards the object are different. This is inconsistent.

According to balance theory, where there is inconsistency (situations 2 and 4) this must be resolved either by changing the attitude to a person or the object.

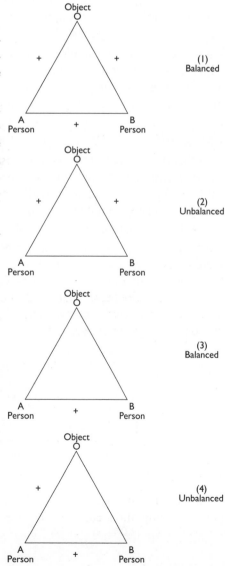

Figure 4.12

95

A selling situation is one context where balance theory can be applied. Suppose a salesman (let us call him David) visits you at work and tries to sell you a new photocopier. He can show you pictures of the copier and talk about its benefits but, ultimately, you are placing your trust in him. After all, the photocopier could turn out to be unreliable, noisy, smelly and expensive to run. How do you decide whether or not to be positive towards the copier? Let us represent this as a balance triangle (Figure 4.13).

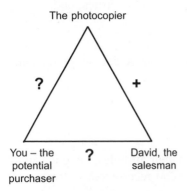
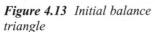

Figure 4.13 Initial balance triangle

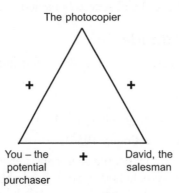

Figure 4.14 Favourable towards David so, to be consistent, we are most likely to feel favourable towards the photocopier

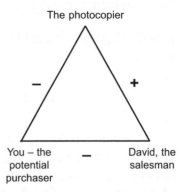

Figure 4.15 Unfavourable towards David so, to be consistent, we are most likely to feel unfavourable towards the photocopier

Initially, only the salesman's view of the photocopier is certain. Over the course of his sales pitch we will undoubtedly make our mind up about David. If we feel favourably towards him then the situation shown inFigure 4.14 is most likely, if we do not feel favourably disposed towards him then the situation shown in Figure 4.15 is more likely.

These scenarios can be applied to any marketing situation where customers do not have direct contact with the product but rely on intermediaries for information. Where a service, rather than a product, is being marketed, the only way in which quality is 'sold' is via the salesperson. There is an old marketing saying which goes 'people buy people first'.

Congruity theory

This theory builds on the notion of positive and negative attitudes and adds the concept of attitude strength. Congruity theory allows us to rate our attitudes towards an object from -3 (highly unfavourable) to +3 (highly favourable) with a middle zero point. To reduce consistency (to obtain congruity), we take into account not only the direction of the attitude (as in balance theory) but also its strength. An example will serve to demonstrate. Let us return to David, our copier salesman.

Suppose we gain the impression from David that the copier is extremely good and meets all our requirements. We might rate it +3 (highly favourable). However, we also take a mild dislike to David, let us say a rating of -1 (slightly unfavourable). To achieve congruity we must adjust both of these ratings. Congruity theory states that the final attitude towards an object is calculated by halving the difference between the ratings. Therefore we would give the copier a rating of +1 (slightly favourable), the mid-point between -1 and +3. This is illustrated in Figure 4.16.

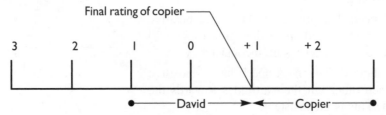

Figure 4.16 Congruity theory

Alternatively, suppose we took a mild liking to David (rating +1). This Would result in a more positive rating of the copier of +2. See Figure 4.17.

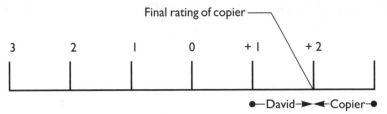

Figure 4.17 Congruity theory

Predicting attitudes

Multi-component models of attitude

These models aim to predict attitudes from any evaluation of their component parts. According to Fishbein, one of the most prominent researchers in this field, an attitude towards an object is a function of:

- Strength of belief that object has certain attributes
- The desirability of these attributes
- And number of attributes.

Attributes are those elements of an object that define it. Some of the attributes of vacuum cleaner might be:

- Has mains cable storage
- Can clean-up liquids
- Colour
- Is floor standing (rather than upright).

Fishbein model

Fishbein's model states that if a consumer believes strongly that an object has many positive, desirable attributes then it will be rated more favourably. This model can be summarized by the formula:

$$\text{Attitude towards an object} = \sum_{i=1}^{n} (b_i e_i)$$

where

b_i = strength of the belief that object contains attribute i

e_i = evaluation of the desirability of attribute i

n = number of attributes.

This can be described as the sum of the multiplication of the belief and evaluations for all attributes.

Usually b is rated on a scale of 1 (strong belief of presence of attribute) to 3 (uncertain of presence) and evaluation of desirability of the attitude on a scale 1 (highly desirable) to 7 (undesirable).

Suppose we are asked to assess attitude towards a particular brand of CD player. These generally have, amongst others, the following attributes:

- Sound quality
- Portability
- Ease of use.

We might then ask a sample of potential purchasers for their opinion on these attributes. If an individual strongly believed that the sound quality was good they might rate it with a 1 (strong belief of presence of attribute). If sound quality was only moderately important to them then they might rate the desirability of it as 4. Continuing in this fashion it is possible to build up data for each attribute.

The following table shows the data from a single individual:

Attribute	Belief (b)	Evaluation (e)	b × e
Sound quality	1	4	4
Portability	3	2	6
Ease of use	3	1	3
		Total = 13	

The attitude score for this particular brand of CD player is thus 13. The higher the figure, the less favourable the attitude towards the object. The maximum (i.e. worst possible) score can be calculated by multiplying the number of attributes by 21. Thus the worse score for a three attribute assessment is $3 \times 21 = 63$.

This method is particularly useful to marketers wishing to do brand comparisons.

Activity 4.5

Find two differently designed telephones – the more different the better. Pick four attributes and assess the phones separately against your chosen attributes. To get you started, one attribute might be 'volume of ringer' another could be 'has dial memories'.

Which phone came out better?

As we have already discussed, attitudes do not necessarily lead to corresponding behaviour. In an attempt to improve the accuracy of Fishbein's original model Williams (1981) modified it so that the ratings referred not to an object but to the behavioural outcomes of taking a particular action. Statistically, the same formula is used but the meaning is very different.

$$\text{Attitude towards an action} = \sum_{i=1}^{n} (b_i e_i)$$

where

b_i = strength of belief that action will lead to particular outcome i

e_i = evaluation/desirability of outcome i

n = number of outcomes.

If a consumer believes that purchasing a product will certainly lead to a large number of desirable outcomes, then they are more likely to purchase it.

For example, you may buy a fast car not because it is fast but because of the outcomes of speed; getting from A to B quicker; to impress friends; to overtake easily on motorways. According to the extended model, we can predict behaviour accurately only if we rate these outcomes rather than any attributes of the car. Based on our earlier concerns about the link between behaviour and attitudes, this model is likely to give more reliable results.

The difference between the standard and extended Fishbein models is best illustrated with an example. Suppose we have been asked to predict voting intentions at the next general election. According to the standard Fishbein model we would find out those attributes of the various political parties that were important to people and then rate the political parties against these attributes. The ratings that the parties received would then be seen as indicative of people's voting intentions, i.e. the party that got the best rating with the majority of those surveyed would win.Figure 4.18 is an example of some of the attributes we might use in our survey.

Attributes	Conservative		Labour		Liberal Democrat		Green	
	b	e	b	e	b	e	b	e
Good leadership								
Honest								
Stable/consistent								
Environmentally aware								
Total sum _b_ _e_ for each party								

Figure 4.18 *Prediction of voting intentions using Fishbein model*

According to the extended model, we would look at the outcomes that are important to people and how likely voting for each of the parties might bring about the desired outcomes. Figure 4.19 is an example of some of the outcomes we might use if we decided to use the extended model.

Attributes	Conservative		Labour		Liberal Democrat		Green	
	b	e	b	e	b	e	b	e
Good leadership								
Honest								
Stable/consistent								
Environmentally aware								
Total sum *b* *e* for each party								

Figure 4.19 Prediction of voting intentions using extended Fishbein model

Activity 4.6

Fill in both of the political rating grids (Figures 4.18 and 4.19) for the Fishbein and extended Fishbein models.

Do the models predict different voting intentions. If so, think why that might be.

Which do you think most accurately predicts your own voting behaviour.

Measuring attitudes

Attitudes can be measured indirectly and directly.

Indirectly:

- Physiological methods
    i. Galvanic skin response
    ii. Pupil dilation
    iii. Heart rate
    iv. Facial electromyograph (EMG).
- Unobtrusive method
    i. Bogus pipe line technique
    ii. Behaviour
    iii. Eye contact.
- Projective tests
    i. Picture completion
    ii. Error test method
    iii. Kelly's Personal Construct Theory (the Reperatory grid was later developed from this).

Directly:

- Thurstone Scale 1929
- Likert 1932
- Guttmen 1944
- Semantic Differential (Osgood, Suci and Tannenbaum, 1957).

The most significant are:

- Likert
- Semantic differential
- Reperatory grid.

(See Unit 6, Quantitative and qualitative methodologies for investigating customer dynamics for further descriptions of these.

Activity 4.7

How would you persuade adult males to switch to a new type of shaving technology? Provide an outline answer.

Summary

In this unit you have learned about:

- Models
- Attitudes – their characteristics and component parts
- The relationship between attitudes and behaviour
- The importance of specificity of attitude measurement.

The motivations that drive customers are also important. To provide what the customer needs requires an understanding of their goals and aspirations.

Unit 5
The basic principles of
investigative (market) research

Objectives

This unit introduces you to the basic principles of market research. You will:

- Learn about the market research process.
- Be introduced to the common experimental design formats.
- Find out about the selection of target populations.
- Consider the wider framework of investigating customer dynamics.
- Appreciate the possible pitfalls with investigative market research.
- Learn about cognitive dissonance.
- Look at the main means of interpreting and presenting results.

By the end of the unit you will be able to:

- Understand the logic of research design and have a basic knowledge of customer dynamics.
- Know how to construct testable hypotheses, select suitable populations and pilot test new research designs.
- Initially interpret results.
- Be aware and take account of the possible problems with investigate research.

This unit covers the following parts of the Marketing Customer Interface syllabus:

- 2.4

Experimental design

Understanding the market research process

The first step in any study is the development of research objectives. These usually arise from the research brief – a description of what information is required – but may be originated by the market researcher. The usual research flow is illustrated in Figure 5.1.

Research briefs often pose questions which are too vague or broad to make good research objectives. For example, 'why are fewer people using high street insurance agents?' It is necessary for the researcher to turn this general question into one or more testable hypotheses (see later in this unit). These may well be initially informed by the intuition, experience or knowledge of the marketer.

Prior experience of a similar problem in another retail sector might lead the researcher to first investigate any changes in local shopping habits – for example, are other high street retailers being affected in the same way? Or, it may be that the researcher focuses on issues of market share – is business being won by the new crop of telephone insurers?

Presumably, though not always, the research brief also wants some answers or pointers as to how to proceed. A good research study will always be proactive in identifying next steps.

The research objectives must be clearly stated. There is rarely enough effort put into the early stages of planning a research study which should clearly define at least the following:

- Type of data required
- What will be done with the data once it is collected
- Who is the audience for the final report
- The target population
- The detailed design of the research process itself.

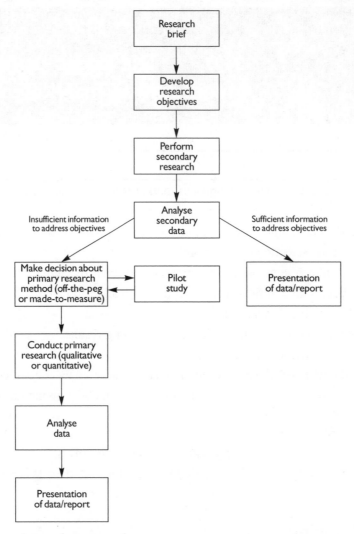

Figure 5.1 *Primary and secondary research process*

Once the research objectives are identified, secondary research is undertaken – that is a review of existing data. If this proves sufficient to address the research objectives then it is possible to move straight to analysis and presentation of a report.

If, on the other hand, existing data is not available to address the research objectives then new, or primary research must be planned and executed to collect more data. This can then be collated, analyzed and reported.

The various types of primary and secondary research are described in the next section.

Pilot testing

Before embarking on primary research or new testing methodology it is important to undergo thorough pre-testing or piloting. This is best achieved by undertaking a peer review followed by limited testing on the intended target population (usually referred to as a pilot test).

A peer review is a review by other market researchers, or colleagues, to ascertain their views on the suitability of the research tools and methods being used. It may be that they are able to identify confusing questions and/or bring to bear their experience from similar research that they have undertaken.

A pilot test on the target population is more costly – in time and resources – but is the best way to identify flaws in procedures and tools. A pilot test can be used to check the following:

- *Data* Is the data you collect of the correct type and format (this avoids later analysis problems)?
- *Analysis* Does your analysis method yield the summary data that you require to address your research objectives?
- *Tools* Is the research tool (i.e. questionnaire) easy to comprehend and use?

- *Resources* Has the research project been allotted sufficient resources (the pilot provides a good indication of the resources that the full project will require)?
- *Time* Has the research project been allotted sufficient time (again, the pilot will give you a feel for how much time the full study will require)?
- *Staffing* Are research staff sufficiently trained and experienced enough to run the full project?

It is important that your pilot gives you the confidence that the full study will yield reliable and sufficient data to address the research objectives. If not, then *run another pilot!*

You may wish to share the results of your pilot with the author of the research brief to check your (and their) understanding of the research objectives.

Basic building blocks

At its most basic level, experimental design focuses on understanding the relationship between two or more factors. Usually one is manipulated while measuring changes in the other(s). For instance, we may pilot test three different promotional pricing structures and measure the effect on sales. In other words, experiments are used to determine if a causal relationship exists (in this case between pricing and sales). Experimental design is a well-established scientific method (see Figure 5.2) with its own established rules and terminology. Many of these are 'borrowed' for use in a variety of market research applications. The main terms used are described below:

- *Hypothesis* This is the 'big question' that your study is aimed at answering. For instance, you might have an intuition that changing the packaging of electric toasters will lead to higher sales? A hypothesis would then be constructed to test this prediction.
- *Variables* These are the factors under investigations. For instance, sales and packaging design.
- *Independent variable* This is the name for the variable(s) we are manipulating. In the toaster example given, this would be the packaging design but we might also change price, colour, product features and measure the effect on sales. These would also be independent variables.
- *Dependent variable* This is the name for the variable(s) we are measuring. In the toaster example given, this would be the sales but we might also want to measure customer feelings towards the new packaging and other aspects of their purchasing behaviour as a result of changing the packaging design. These would also be dependent variables.
- *Intervening (or extraneous) variables* These are those unwanted factors that 'interfere' with your research. For instance, you may be trying to assess people's attitude to changes in product price over a period where there are considerable fluctuations in the national economy. In this example, the economy is an intervening variable. Intervening variables contribute to experimental 'noise', that is, unavoidable variations in the study which affect the accuracy with which the effect of the independent variable can be assessed.
- *Experimenter* This is the term used to distinguish the researcher from those they are studying (i.e. this would probably be you!).
- *Subjects* These are the people being studied (e.g. shoppers, product users and potential purchasers).
- *Control groups* These are groups of subjects which are monitored for the purpose of providing a comparison only. For instance, if we are trying to assess the impact of a new mail order catalogue we might monitor two groups of subjects. One group would be sent the new catalogue while the other group would continue to receive the old catalogue. The group that receives the new catalogue is called the experimental group. The group that continues to receive the old catalogue is called the control group.
- *Field studies* These are studies carried out in the 'real world'. They are the opposite of laboratory studies.
- *Laboratory studies* These are studies carried out under controlled conditions such as in a laboratory or other 'mock-ups'.

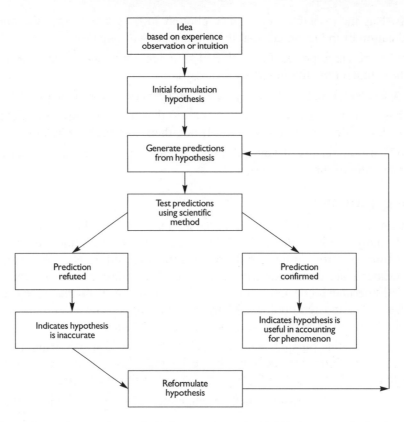

Figure 5.2 *The traditional scientific method. Source: Rice, C. (1993)* Consumer Behaviour, *Butterworth-Heinemann*

Question 5.1

British Telecom ask you to investigate customer satisfaction towards a new 'cheap rate' internet home service which has been given on a trial basis to some of their existing internet customers.

In this example, who, or what, are likely to be the:

- Independent variable
- Dependent variable
- Experimenter
- Control group.

Would the study be classified as a field or laboratory study?

Construction of testable hypotheses

There are three main steps in the design of an experiment:

1. *Decide on your hypothesis*

   This must be expressed in a form which can be tested. For instance, 'some pricing structures are better than others' is *not* a good hypothesis. The use of the terms 'some' and 'better' are vague. An improved version would read something like 'A 10 per cent price discount leads to higher customer satisfaction than a 5 per cent price discount'.

2. *Select your dependent and independent variables*

   The variables must be clearly defined and measurable. The more accurately they can be measured the better. The actual variables used will depend upon the hypothesis. In the pricing example, we would probably choose discount level as our independent variable and customer satisfaction as our dependent variable. However, it is not a sufficient definition of the testing design in itself. The exact pricing structure to be used must be clearly specified as should the method that will be used to measure customer satisfaction.

   Care should be taken that nothing other than the discount level is changed. The service delivered must be identical in all other respects. To introduce any other differences would be to risk introducing intervening variables. For example, if one of the discounts was promoted in a slightly more aggressive manner we would not know whether it was promotional change that had affected customer satisfaction rather than the change in discount.

We may decide to measure customer satisfaction at one particular outlet or across a number of different outlets. We would need to be clear:

- o What was going to be measured. (Whether we are trying to get a more holistic understanding of the effect of pricing structure on customer satisfaction with the service quality or are we just interested in satisfaction with the price. If the former, what aspects of service quality are we interested in?)
- o How this measurement was going to take place (point of purchase, telephone interview, postal survey and so on).
- o The time period over which this measurement was to take place.

3. *Decide on the format that your experiment will take*

There are a number of alternative experimental designs. The design you choose will depend both on your hypothesis and practical constraints (such as time, cost and other resources).

Analytical constraints on hypothesis development

While the traditional experimental method of hypothesis development and testing is ideally suited for the measurement of associations, for example the link between price and packaging design, it is less suited for the exploration of the less tangible and/or open-ended types of investigation.

The difference is essentially that between qualitative and quantitative research as described in the next section.

Common experimental design formats

Five experimental design formats are described by Chris Rice in *Consumer Behaviour*. These cover most of the designs that you are likely to need. In each case the X represents the event – which is usually the purchase decision or other significant interaction with the customer. The T represents the investigation; the point at which the dependent variable is measured.

Case study or survey

An event occurs, such as the purchase of an item, which we later examine by means of a case study or survey. This can be represented diagrammatically as follows (X = the event, T = the study):

$X \rightarrow T$

An example would be the purchase of a mountain bike. This popular style of bicycle became unexpectedly popular in the early 1990s. To try to find out the reason for this we may decide to survey those persons that purchased mountain bikes during this period. It may be that the result of such a survey would help us to develop a new bicycle and/or predict futures sales of existing styles of bicycle.

One group pre-test/post-test design

Sometime referred to as a test-retest design, a group of individuals are surveyed, an event occurs such as a change in our method of service delivery, and then we re-test the same group. This can be represented diagrammatically as follows (X = the event, $T1$ and $T2$ = are tests):

$T1 \rightarrow X \rightarrow T2$

Suppose we wished to determine customer opinions on how well our new telephone support line is performing. It would be sensible to test opinions of our support service both before and after the introduction of the support line so that a comparison could be drawn.

Time series design or survey

In a time series survey, individuals are repeatedly surveyed before and after an event. This can be represented diagrammatically (for 8 surveys) as follows (X = the event, $T1$ to $T8$ = tests):

$T1 \rightarrow T2 \rightarrow T3 \rightarrow T4 \rightarrow X \rightarrow T5 \rightarrow T6 \rightarrow T7 \rightarrow T8$

A common use of time series surveys is in opinion polls. The event may be, for instance, the resignation of an MP due to impropriety or a change of party leader. The aim of a time series survey to understand how responses change over time. The individuals tested may be the same on each occasion, as with consumer panel testing, or different as in the random sampling most commonly used in political polls.

Non-equivalent control group design

This is similar to the one group pre-test/post-test design already described except that two groups are involved. One group, called the experimental group, is exposed to the event, the other group, the control group is not. This can be represented diagrammatically as follows (X = the event, $T1$ and $T2$ = tests):

Experimental group: $T1 \Rightarrow X \Rightarrow T2$
Control group: $T1 \longrightarrow T2$

By using a control group it is possible to eliminate the effect of many intervening variables. Suppose in our telephone support line example we split our regular customers into two groups. Rather than both groups being given access to the support line we would provide this facility to only one group (the experimental group) while the other group (the control group) would continue with the previous support package.

When opinions were re-tested we could therefore be more certain that any difference in opinions was really due to the changes in the support package rather than any other spurious effects such as changes in support needs, differences in the perceptions of the company due to new product developments and so on.

When this control group design is applied to a product, for example a new type of medicine, it is often referred to as a 'blind' or 'double blind' trial. To try and avoid experimental effects (to reduce the number of intervening variables) it is usual to give the experimental group a real medicine and the control group a placebo. Of course the control group believes that they have been administered the real thing – thus they are 'blind' to the reality. If the experimenter and/or evaluators – in this case the persons administering the medicine and assessing their effects – are also unaware of which group has received the real medicine then the experimental design is said to be 'double blind'.

Problems with this method relate to the matching of the groups. We must be sure that the experimental and control groups are similar in all respects otherwise it may be possible to attribute any changes in the dependent variable as an artefact of the group characteristics rather than the manipulation of the independent variable.

Classic experimental design

This design is similar to the non-equivalent control group design but overcomes the problem of matching groups by randomly assigning subjects to the experimental and control groups at the outset. The experimental format is identical in all other respects to the non-equivalent design.

Experimental group (random): $T1 \Rightarrow X \Rightarrow T2$
Control group (random): $T1 \longrightarrow T2$

To comply with this design, the respondents in the telephone support line example would have to have been randomly assigned to the experimental and control groups.

Question 5.2

You have been asked to test the effectiveness of a regional TV advertising campaign for private healthcare insurers who have experienced a drop-off in customers. What experimental design(s) could you use. Who would constitute the experimental and control groups?

Question 5.3

You have been asked to make a prediction as to whether New Labour will win the next general election. What experimental design(s) could you use?

Selecting your target population

Determining your sample

In determining your sample you need to decide whom you will survey and how many people you will survey. Researchers often call this group the target population. In some case, when doing an employee attitude survey for instance, the population is obvious. In other cases, such as when prospective customers are involved, determining the target group is more difficult. Correctly determining the target population is critical. A poorly defined target population will result in unrepresentative results.

Suppose we are commissioned to find out opinions of the recent architectural changes to the entrance of the Ashmolean Museum in Oxford. How would we go about determining our target population? If we were looking for a relative appraisal of the changes then we would need to find people who had seen the Museum entrance before and after the changes. If we were only asked to find out visitors general opinions of the new entrance then it would not matter whether, or not, they had seen the original architecture. Clearly, in this example, our survey goal determines the target population.

To decide how many persons need surveying is both a statistical and commercial decision. Surveying more people costs more money but does increase the accuracy, or precision, of the results (up to a point). To increase a sample from 250 to 1000 requires four times as many people, but it only doubles the precision. The statistic issues are dealt with in detail in the unit *Quantitative and qualitative methodologies for investigating customer dynamics*.

Sampling methods

There are two basic types of sampling:

1. Probability (or random) samples – where individuals are drawn in some random fashion from among the population.
2. Non-probability (or non-random) samples – where individuals are selected on the basis of one or more criteria determined by the researcher.

Probability samples

Within this category there are four sampling methods which are commonly employed in market research:

1. *Simple random sampling* – individuals are randomly drawn from the population at large (for example, by selecting from the electoral register).
2. *Systematic sampling* – individuals (or households) are sampled at intervals based on a random start point. For instance, it might be decided to visit every tenth person on the electoral register starting at number 4. In this case the sampling interval is 10. The individuals that would be sampled are thus numbers 4, 14, 24 and so on.
3. *Stratified random sampling* – the population is first divided into groups based on one or more criteria (e.g. age, gender, or other affiliation) and, from within these groups, individuals are randomly selected. For this method to be possible, the data available on each individual must contain information about the criteria being used to stratify the groups. This is not always the case.
4. *Multistage sampling* – the population is first divided into quite large groups, usually based on geography. A random selection of these large groups is then selected and subdivided again. A random selection of groups is again made from the resulting subdivisions and the process repeated as many times as required depending on the survey requirements. Eventually, individuals are randomly sampled from the small groups arising as a result of the final subdivision.

To select individuals on a random basis it is necessary to construct a sampling frame. This is a list of all the known individuals within the population from which the selection is to take place. Each individual is assigned a unique number then, using random number tables or the computer equivalent, individuals are selected on the basis of the random numbers produced.

Obviously, to list all the individuals within the UK would take forever. Luckily, the electoral roll (or register) comes fairly close to doing that. Its primary purpose is to record those persons eligible to vote. Unfortunately, the electoral register has several drawbacks:

- Those under 18 years of age are only listed if they are approaching their 18th birthday when they will be eligible to vote.

- Many persons choose not to register to vote and are thus not listed.

- Mobile individuals – such as students – are frequently not registered where they live.

- Newlyweds are not listed correctly – a women's maiden name may appear and, if the couple have recently started living together, only one name may appear on the register.

- The register may be up to a year out-of-date.

In an attempt to overcome some of these problems, the postal address file (or PAF) is often used. This is the most comprehensive list of addresses in the UK. Addresses are then randomly selected from the list and the interviewer tries to interview one person from each household. Recently, more and more people are failing to register to vote which has led to increased use of the PAF. Unfortunately, the PAF too has several problems:

- There is no way of knowing who lives at the address.

- There is no way of knowing how many people live at the address.

It is thus left to the interviewer to select a person to interview based on an extensive set of rules provided by the research organization. This can result in error.

Non-probability samples

When a sampling frame cannot be established, or would prove too expensive or time-consuming, one of the following non-random methods are usually used (see also Table 5.1).

1. *Judgement sampling* The researcher uses their judgement to select persons that they feel are representative of the population or have a particular expertise or knowledge which makes them suitable. For example, business leaders, top scientists and so on. This method is commonly used with small sample sizes.

2. *Convenience sampling* The most convenient population is chosen which may be the researcher's friends, work colleagues or students from a nearby college. This method is often used to save time and resources.

3. *Cluster sampling* The population is repeatedly divided into groups rather like the process for multistage sampling. However, cluster sampling is different in that all individuals from the remaining small groups are interviewed rather than just a random sample of those remaining.

4. *Quota sampling* The researcher selects a predetermined number of individuals from different groups (i.e. based on age, gender and so on). This is perhaps the most popular non-probability sampling method used.

Setting quotas

Rather than randomly selecting individuals, you may wish to enforce balance in your population by setting quotas for certain sub-groups. For instance, if you are surveying for a product that you know will be mostly used by under-thirty-fives you can set a quota for this age group in your survey sample. You may decide as a result that 90 per cent of your sample should be in this age group.

Table 5.1 Comparison of different sampling methods

Type	Sampling frame required	Cost	Representative?	Likelihood of bias
Simple random	Yes	High	May not be	Low
Systematic random	Yes	Moderate	May not be	Low
Stratified	Yes	Moderate	Yes	Low
Multistage	Yes	Moderate	May not be	Low
Convenience	No	Low	May not be	High
Judgement	No	Low	May not be	High
Cluster	No	Moderate	May not be	Moderate
Quota	No	Moderate	Yes	Moderate

To give another example, if you are interviewing users about a particular product brand, you may wish (depending on your project goals) to select your sample based on their current brand preferences. Alternatively, you may decide to interview only those individuals that currently use a competitive brand or those that use no brand at all.

Quotas are usually specified to a research organization in the form of a grid. For example, if we have a requirement to interview 50 shoppers we might specify that:

- 25 of them under 45 years of age.
- 25 aged 45 or older.
- 15 in the AB social classes.
- 35 in the CDE social classes.

Alternatively, we might specify how many of a particular age should come from each social class grouping:

	AB	CDE
Under 45	13	12
45 or over	2	23

The structure of the sample is therefore fixed by the researcher.

Deciding the sample size for your survey

There are many factors which affect the size of a sample apart from the statistical considerations:

- *The survey method used.* Large sample sizes are easier to achieve with some methods (i.e. postal surveys and telephone surveys) than with others (i.e. face-to-face interviews and observation).
- *Time and resources may be limited.* This will involve a trade-off between sample size and the amount and accuracy of the information to be collected.
- *Precision required.* There is no point using large sample sizes when only a rough estimate of a population mean is required. Decide on the precision you require and use the formula provided for determining the sample size required.
- *Number of groups sampled.* If you plan to sample a number of groups you may be able to merge the group data to provide a better overall estimate of the population mean.

Investigating customer dynamics

A broader experimental framework

It is important to know not only how to construct an experiment but what to measure and where (and when) comparisons should be made. This section sets experimental design in the broader framework of the investigation of customer dynamics. But first, a brief explanation of why such explorations are important.

In a survey of the UK's 100 leading businesses the most important indicators of future success were reported as 'building long-term relationships with key customers' and 'creating a more customer-centred culture'. Over 90 per cent of respondees reported quality and customer satisfaction to be 'very important' yet these two key aspects of service and product perception are often poorly understood.

The main role of investigative market research into customer dynamics is to understand customer needs so that a product or service can be developed to satisfy these needs and understanding customers' perceptions of the product or service once delivered as part of a quality management process. The basic cycle of needs analysis and improvement is shown in Figure 5.3.

> **Definition**
>
> **Quality** is concerned with supplying superior benefits in the opinion of the customer. Thus, the pursuit of quality is the pursuit of greater customer benefit (Hooley, 1993).

The principles are the same whether the organization involved is a producer of televisions, a supplier of financial services or a healthcare provider. The key to success is understanding the complex dynamics between customer and organization, the interactions that inform or reinforce customer perceptions.

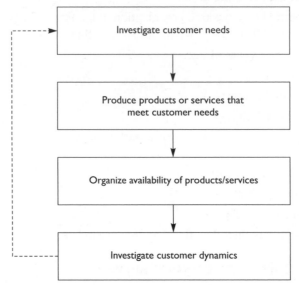

Figure 5.3 *The basic quality improvement cycle*

Such an approach is variously defined as being customer-focused, market-led or a part of a total quality management process. A useful distinction can be drawn between market-driven and market-led research. The former responds to current customer demand, the latter is led by customer needs. The differences in definitions are subtle but have huge implications for the philosophy of organizations and hence the data they seek to gather and their methods of investigation.

Another significant shift is that towards the measurement of service quality. This has come about partly as a result of the change in philosophy highlighted above and partly because of the increasing significance of the service sector to global and domestic economies. We are moving rapidly towards an economy where service providers predominate with the consequence that the measurement and management of service quality becomes more pressing. For example, service industries now account for more than two-thirds of gross national product in the USA. Service sector jobs account for three-quarters of total employment.

> **Definition**
>
> **Service quality** can be defined as 'the ability of the organization to meet or exceed customer expectations' (Christopher, Payne and Ballantyne 1991)

Many of the techniques formerly used to assess product performance and perceptions are simply not up to the job of exploring the less tangible dimensions of service quality. For the purposes of investigating customer dynamics, services are different from products in a number of important ways:

1. Production and consumption takes place simultaneously – the service is delivered at the point of use. A healthcare service, for example, is largely delivered by a direct contact between medical staff and customer.

2. Services are largely intangible – they cannot be tasted, touched, seen or heard. Perceptions of an insurance or banking service are based largely on intangible qualities – feelings of security, reliability, confidence and so on.

3. A service is highly dependent on the person (usually) that delivers it. Unlike a product, consistency and uniformity cannot be centrally controlled or guaranteed. For example, a car hire company will have less control over the quality of their customer service than their rental vehicles!

Although service quality is in many ways more difficult to measure than product quality, the tools and techniques suitable for such investigative research are well developed from their application to the field of social science. Both the modern marketer and scientist want to understand and explore the ways in which perception works at an individual and group level.

Ways in which perception works

According to Parasuraman, there are five dimensions.

- Reliability
- Responsiveness
- Assurance
- Empathy
- Tangibles

These five dimensions have been derived from extensive market research and are in fact produced from 10 service elements as shown below:

- Reliability involves consistency of performance dependability. It means that the firm performs the service right the first time. It also means that the firm honours its promises. Specifically it involves:
  - i. accuracy in billing
  - ii. keeping records correctly
  - iii. performing the service at the designated time.

- Responsiveness concerns the willingness or readiness of employees to provide service. It involves timeliness of service:
  - i. mailing a transaction slip immediately
  - ii. calling the customer back quickly
  - iii. giving prompt service (e.g. setting up appointments quickly).

- Competence means possession of the required skills and knowledge to perform the service. It involves:
  - i. knowledge and skill of the contact personnel
  - ii. knowledge and skill of operational support personnel
  - iii. research capability of the organization, e.g. securities brokerage firm.

- Access involves approachability and ease of contact. It means:
  - i. the service is easily accessible by telephone (lines are not busy and they don't put you on 'hold')
  - ii. waiting time to receive service (e.g. at a bank) is not extensive
  - iii. convenient hours of operation
  - iv. convenient location of service facility.

- Courtesy involves politeness, respect, consideration and friendliness of contact personnel (including receptionists, telephone operators, etc.). It includes:
  - i. consideration for the consumer's property (e.g. no muddy shoes on the carpet)
  - ii. clean and neat appearance of public contact personnel.

- Communication means keeping customers informed in language they can understand and listening to them. It may mean that the company has to adjust its language for different consumers – increasing the level of sophistication with a well-educated customer and speaking simply and plainly with a novice. It involves:
  - i. explaining the service itself
  - ii. explaining how much the service will cost
  - iii. explaining the trade-offs between service and cost
  - iv. assuring the consumer that a problem will be handled.

- Credibility involves trustworthiness, believability, honesty. It involves having the customer's best interests at heart. Contributing to credibility are:
  - i. company name
  - ii. company reputation
  - iii. personal characteristics of the contact personnel
  - iv. the degree of hard sell involved in interactions with the customer.

- Security is the freedom from danger, risk, or doubt. It involves:
  - i. physical safety (Will I get mugged at the automatic teller machine?)
  - ii. financial security (Does the company know where my stock certificate is?)
  - iii. confidentiality (Are my dealings with the company private?).

- Understanding/knowing the customer involves making the effort to understand the customer's needs. It involves:
  - i. learning the customer's specific requirements

ii. providing the individualized attention

iii. recognizing the regular customer.

- Tangibles include the physical evidence of the service:
  i. physical facilities
  ii. appearance of personnel
  iii. tools or equipment used to provide the service
  iv. physical representations of the service such as a credit card or a bank statement
  v. other customers in the service facility.

Assessing internal customer needs

Departmental Process Analysis (DPA) This process tries to find answers to the following questions:

- What purpose do we serve?
- Has our purpose changed?
- How do our internal customers want things done?
- Is there a better way to do this?
- Does our work satisfy any external customers' needs?
- Do our suppliers understand our needs, time and resource constraints?

Principles of service quality measurement – gap analysis

Conceptual model

As we have learned, providing a quality product or service is all about meeting or exceeding customer expectations. Where expectations are met then the customer is satisfied. If expectations are not met then the customer experiences dissatisfaction.

Consider a small, high specification, portable television and a budget wide-screen model. Other things being equal, which is most likely to satisfy a customer? The marketing answer is either one of them depending on the initial customer expectations. If the requirements were for an easily moved unit which could fit in a guest room then the portable TV would probably best meet expectations. If, on the other hand, the need were for family viewing the wide-screen design would probably be perceived as the best choice.

This logic is even more applicable to service provision where there are fewer tangibles. Take, for example, the experience of flying first class. The customer has certain expectations of the level of service that they will receive based, perhaps, on advertising, past experiences or hearsay. Perhaps they expect a separate check-in, a comfortable waiting lounge, personal luggage-handling facilities and so on. When they actually fly they will, consciously or unconsciously, evaluate the performance of the airline company against their expectations. If their expectations and evaluations do not match then there will be a 'gap' leading to satisfaction or dissatisfaction depending on the direction and extent of the gap. Dissatisfaction, so the theory goes, will lead to a perception of poor quality and vice versa. This potential difference between expectations and evaluations is what gap analysis seeks to measure. A basic model of the customer satisfaction gap is shown in Figure 5.4 (Hooley, 1993).

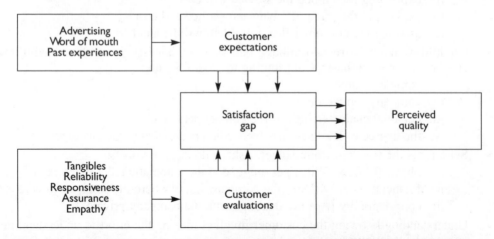

Figure 5.4 *From Hooley, G. (1993)* Market-led Quality Management (*Journal of Marketing Management, 9, 3, July, pp. 315-35*)

The customer satisfaction gap is not the only service quality gap that is said to exist (although it is the key gap directly relevant to consumers). Parasuraman, Zeithaml and Berry (1985) identified five potential gaps in their conceptual model of service quality and more recently Hooley (1993) has suggested that possibly six more could exist. The conceptual model of Parasuraman is presented in Figure 5.5. Gap 5 is the previously mentioned customer satisfaction gap. The other gaps relate more to the work of the organization and marketer.

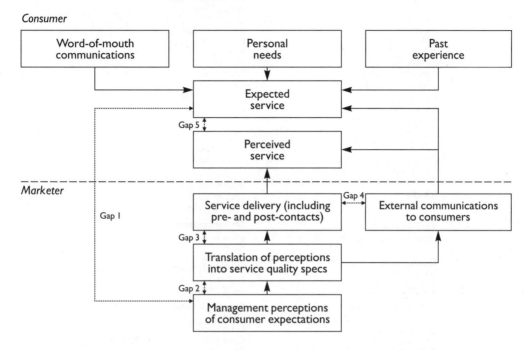

Figure 5.5 *Conceptual model of service quality. Source: Parasuraman, A., Zeithaml, V.A. and Berry, L.L. (1985). A conceptual model of service quality and its implications for future research.* Journal of Marketing, *49, Fall.*

Parasuraman (1998) suggests that the customer satisfaction gap, Gap 5 or the service quality deficiency perceived by the consumer, may be a function of the four key internal (i.e. organizational) shortfalls. The four gaps on the seller's side can be defined as follows:

- Gap 1 Market information gap: due to incomplete or inaccurate knowledge of customers' service expectations.

- Gap 2 Service standards gap: arising from failure to translate accurately customers' service expectations into specifications or guidelines for company personnel.

- Gap 3 Service performance gap: occurs when there is a lack of appropriate internal support systems (e.g. recruitment, training, technology, compensation) that enable company personnel to deliver to service standards.

- Gap 4 Internal communication gap: inconsistencies between what customers are told the service will be like and the actual service performance (e.g. due to lack of internal communication between the service 'promisers' (such as salespeople) and service providers (such as after-sales service representatives).

Methods for the measurement of quality service, discussed in the next section, will focus on Gap 5. However, Gap 5 inFigure 5.4 is influenced by the four preceding gaps.

Service quality benchmarking

As well as identifying service quality gaps within your own organization and customer interactions, it is important to understand how you compete with others. You need to know whether, or not, your performance is better or worse than that of your main competitors (see the checklist in Figure 5.6).

Called service quality benchmarking, performance measurement can be undertaken using a number of methods. Christopher, Payne and Ballantyne favour a five-stage approach whereby the competitive arena is first defined and then the key determinants of customer service identified. Next it is recommended to establish relative weightings for these service elements before actually measuring organizational performance and that of your competitors.

Benchmarks can be created for practically any part of your operation. For example, this list of potential benchmarking categories can help measure your operations against your competitor's.

Advertising
Expenditure
Themes

Sales
Terms
Sales force
  size
  structure
  training/experience
  compensation
  number of calls
  turnover rates
Sales literature
Proposals
  style
  structure
  pricing
Accountability
Cross selling

R&D
Patents
Staff
R&D $/sales
Government contracts

Customers/products
Sales/customer
Breadth of product line
Product quality
Average customer size

Distribution
Channels used
Middlemen

Marketing
Product/brand strategy
Market share
Pricing

Financials/costs
Profitability
Overhead
Return on assets
Return on equity
Net worth
Margins
Cash flow
Debt
Borrowing capacity

Plant/facility
  size
  capacity
  utilization
  equipment costs
Capital investments
Integration level
Quality control
Fixed and variable costs

Organization
Structure
Values
General goals
Expected growth
Decision-making level
Controls

Strategic plans
Short term
Long term
Core business/expansion or stability
Acquisitions

Figure 5.6 *Competitive benchmarking checklist. Source:* Strategic Intelligence Checklist. *Cambridge, MA: Fuld & Co. Inc.*

Finally, the benchmarking results can be mapped in a number of ways to identify relative performance, compared with the competition, as well as performance on those aspects of service quality which are perceived as important by the customer.Figure 5.7 shows a profile mapping for a typical set of customer expectations, shown in the central column. The line on the left shows the relative importance of these elements; the lines on the right show the performance by the organization and a selected competitor.

Weaknesses can be clearly identified as those where importance to the customer is high and organizational performance is low. In this example, 'order cycle time', 'delivery reliability' and 'frequency of delivery' would seem to need attention. The method can also be used to expose areas where unnecessary effort is being expended where the element is of low importance to customers.

For a detailed description of service quality benchmarking the reader is referred to *Relationship Marketing,* Christopher, Payne and Ballantyne (1991), Butterworth-Heinemann.

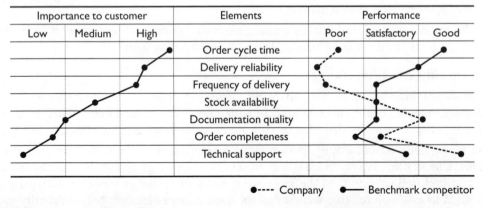

Figure 5.7 *Customer service profile*

Possible pitfalls with investigative market research

Bias in your target populations

If you select a sample population which is not representative then your results may be biased. That is, they will not represent responses in the wider population. For example, if you asked Ford employees whether they preferred Ford cars you would probably get biased results. Totally excluding all bias is extremely difficult but should be the goal in any survey. However, just being aware of bias will allow you to avoid the more obvious sources and interpret certain results more cautiously. There are three main sources of bias:

1. Incomplete coverage – there may be a number of reasons for this:
    1. Sampling frame is incomplete;
    2. Certain outlying areas are excluded (it is common in UK surveys to exclude counties north of the Caledonian canal in Scotland);
    3. The survey method used may place constraints on those that can be sampled, i.e. a telephone survey requires ownership of a telephone!
2. Non-response – low response rates are a problem in any survey. Whether it is a street, telephone or postal survey a significant proportion of those approached will refuse to answer questions.
3. Over-representation – some sampling methods deliberately over-represent certain groups (the non-probability sampling techniques already mentioned). Although this allows detailed examination of a certain sub-group of the population, there is no way of knowing how else the group characteristics might affect the survey responses.

Table 5.2 below shows the ways in which over-representation can introduce bias.

Table 5.2

Sample	Possible source of bias
Existing customers	Customer loyalty may mean that more favourable responses are given
Ex-customers	Possibly no longer customer because of dislike of product/service – may give less favourable results
People in city centre shopping street	Depending on shopping area, may only capture data from certain social classes. May be that only certain members of the family shop
People in out-of-town shopping centre	Unlikely to be used by those without a car or those that have good local shops

Question 5.4

You are asked to gather opinions on a new design of carry-cot for babies. What problems might you experience using your classmates as a convenience sample.

The reliability and validity of customer responses

Questionnaire design

The primary data collection tool is the questionnaire. Whether you are conducting an interview by post, telephone, face-to-face, or even via computer, you will be need to design a questionnaire.

There are two important concepts in the design of measurement methods – reliability and validity.

Validity

If a data measurement tool actually measures what it purports to, then it is said to be valid. For example, time over a 100 metre sprint is not likely to be a valid measure of intelligence. On the other hand, a well-designed intelligence quotient (IQ) test is likely to accurately measure intelligence. The IQ test is therefore said to be a valid measure of intelligence.

Poorly designed questionnaires are often not valid measures – they purport to measure things that they do not. For example, the question, how many times a week do you watch television may seem – on the face of it – a valid way of measuring television viewing time. This is not the case. All the question actually does is measure the *number of times* the television is viewed and not the *length of time* it is viewed for. This question would therefore not be a valid measure of television viewing time. Similarly, surveys on sample populations are said to be invalid if their findings cannot be generalized to the whole population.

Reliability

If a measurement tool consistently measures the same thing then it is said to be reliable. For example, the IQ of a person changes only slowly. Therefore, if we measured it two weeks in a row we would expect it to be approximately the same. A good IQ test would indeed give a similar score week after week. Such a test is said to be reliable. A poorly designed IQ test might give widely differing scores each time it was administered. Such a test is termed unreliable, as it cannot be relied upon to give an accurate answer.

Good questionnaires are both reliable and valid; they measure what they purport to and they do so reliably. Repeat testing of questionnaires, and comparison with other data sources, are methods used to check both validity and reliability.

Cognitive dissonance in the acceptability of research findings

'Cognitive dissonance is a motivating state of affairs. Just as hunger impels us to eat, so does dissonance impel a person to change his opinions or his behaviour. . .' (Festinger, 1962)

According to Festinger, any two pieces of information (say A and B) contained in a person's mind can be related in one of three ways:

1. They can be consonant, or consistent. In this case A implies B.
2. They can be dissonant, or inconsistent. In this case A implies the opposite of B.
3. They can be unrelated or irrelevant to each other. A not related to B.

For example, the two pieces of information 'I like cream cakes' and 'cream cakes make me spotty' are dissonant. Presumably, one does not want to have spots yet one wants to eat cream cakes. On the other hand, 'I like Guinness' and 'Guinness is good for you' are consonant pieces of information.

Cognitive dissonance theory states that people seek to reduce the amount of dissonance they experience, which can be considered as a sort of 'mental discomfort'.

The emphasis in marketing is on post-purchase dissonance, i.e. when information about an accepted or rejected item is received following a purchasing decision. At this point, positive information about the rejected item will generate dissonance, as will negative information about the accepted item.

Suppose, you have to choose between two alternative summer holiday destinations, the South of France or Portugal. After a lot of thumbing through holiday brochures, you finally settle on the South of France. Just after booking the vacation you meet someone who has just returned from the South of France. A negative report from them is likely to generate dissonance as will a positive report from recent visitors to Portugal.

The magnitude of this dissonance will be proportional to:

- The significance of the decision – if you had spent a lot of money on the holiday or perhaps if it was your only holiday for a number of years, the dissonance would undoubtedly be greater.
- The attractiveness of the rejected alternative – if your decision had been a narrow one then positive information from one of the rejected options is likely to create greater dissonance.
- The number of negative characters of the choice made – if the selected destination was seen to have several things 'going for it' then a disappointing report about the weather, for instance, is less likely to create dissonance.
- The number of options considered – the more rejected choices the greater the dissonance. Trying to choose a holiday destination from ten alternatives makes it more likely that one of the rejected options would have turned out better.
- Commitment to decision – if the decision can easily be reversed and/or no public expression of the decision has been made then less dissonance is likely to result.
- Volition or choice – if the choice is 'forced' rather than voluntary then dissonance is minimized.

As with the other consistency theories considered, a person experiencing dissonance will act to reduce the discomfort. There are a number of ways this can be done. They can:

- Change their decision – this may not always be possible or practical.
- Actively seek positive information about the chosen alternative. This is called selective exposure.
- Concentrate on information presenting the positive features of the chosen alternative and ignore information presenting negative features. This is called selective attention.
- Change their attitudes.
- Actively avoid exposure to information that is likely to cause dissonance. This is called selective avoidance.
- Dismiss or devalue ambiguous information about the chosen option. This is called selective interpretation.

For example, the dissonance resulting from the information that 'I like cream cakes' and 'cream cakes make me spotty' can be reduced by one or more of the following. We might:

- Stop eating cakes (change decision).
- Decide that cake eating does not cause spots (change attitudes).
- Convince ourselves that enjoying a cream cake is worth the risk of a few spots (selective attention).
- Question the link between cake eating and getting spots (selective interpretation).
- Eat a cake but then avoid information in magazines and papers which suggests cakes are bad (selective avoidance).
- Eat a cake but then seek information in magazines and papers which suggests cakes are good (selective exposure).

Marketers can use dissonance theory in several ways:

- Post-purchase reinforcement – continue to supply the purchaser with positive information about the product even after purchase thus reducing post-purchase dissonance. This will retain brand and corporate loyalty. This is common among car manufacturers who continue to send owners glossy brochures and owner newsletters after the purchase is made. BMW are known to place car adverts aimed solely at existing owners of their cars.
- Try and buy schemes – offering limited trials, reinforced by coupons and gifts will create a commitment and positive attitude towards the product which is then more likely to be purchased (to avoid dissonance when the product is returned). Book clubs are one example of sales organizations that operate in this way.
- Anticipating and addressing dissonance in the adverting message and product branding – a recent advert for cream cakes actually emphasized that they were a treat which, perhaps, wasn't the healthiest. The message given was 'Go on – you are worth it'. In the area of product branding, one cigarette manufacturer is actually trying to give a similar message with 'Death' cigarettes. This approach acknowledges the health problems with smoking but promotes a devil-may-care image.

However, dissonance also poses problems for those trying to assess customer satisfaction post-purchase – as occurs during the measurement of service quality. Dissonance theory would suggest that post-purchase dissonance might affect the size of the customer satisfaction gap because of the positive attitude which arises from the desire to reduce dissonance.

Take, for example, a person considering a change in their bank deposit account who might rank their identified needs as the following:

1. Polite counter service.
2. Convenient location of bank.
3. High interest rate.

However, having made the decision to shift bank accounts they may find that their expectations were not met in the case of their highest ranked need – for politeness. However, they may find that they have more money than they bargained for due to a higher-than-expected interest rate (their lowest ranked need). Having gone through the effort of changing accounts they might seek to reduce the dissonance associated with the poor performance on 'politeness'.

As with the cream cakes, their later evaluations could be affected in a number of ways. They might:

- Change their attitudes – decide that polite service is not as important as previously thought.
- Selective attention – convince themselves that the service is polite by attending only to examples of good service.
- Selective interpretation – question the link between good service and high quality banking (this notion might be reinforced by the high interest rates).
- Selective avoidance – avoid using the bank's counter service so that possible negative examples of the counter service are not experienced.
- Selective exposure – go only to those branches of the bank known to be the most polite.

Results of post-purchase customer satisfaction surveys must therefore be interpreted with caution. The use of a control group in this instance would be highly beneficial in distinguishing between 'real' and 'dissonance-induced' changes in evaluations.

Question 5.5

How would you construct an experiment, using a control group, to ensure that any bias in findings due to dissonance were clearly identifiable.

Evidence for dissonance theory

Post-purchase dissonance has been demonstrated in a study by Brehm (1956) in which potential customers rated the desirability of several household appliances on an eight-point scale. As a reward for participating in the experiment, the subjects were then asked to choose between one of two items to take home.

When customers were asked to re-evaluate the items after their decision, they rated the chosen items more highly than they had previously, and the rejected items less highly. This is consistent with dissonance theory which predicates that post-decision dissonance will act to reinforce the purchase decision.

A review of literature in this area by Fiske and Taylor (1984) found that people do appear to selectively attend to positive information on their selected alternative (selective attention) and positively interpret ambiguous information (selective interpretation) but little evidence was found to suggest that people go out of their way to find positive information (selective exposure).

Activity 5.1

Have you ever been aware of post-purchase dissonance? How have you coped?

Try to think of three examples.

Activity 5.2

Find one or more people who are intending to buy a lottery ticket. Ask them to rate their chances of winning on a scale of 1 to 10 where 10 is high, 1 is low.

After they have bought the ticket – get them to rate their chances again. Has their rating changed? If so, how can this be explained by dissonance theory.

Ratings should be higher after the ticket is purchased. Research suggests that the act of committing oneself to a bet creates dissonance and leads to a dissonance-reducing boost in confidence in one's choice.

Interpretation of results

Characteristics of data

Each piece of data you collect, whether it is the response to a question on a questionnaire or the weight of produce purchased by a shopper, is called an 'observation'. Each of these observations has a 'value' associated with it. This may be numerical or non-numerical; 'Yes', 'no', 207, 11 kg, 110 mm and 493 widgets, are all valid values. Sometimes non-numerical responses are converted (or coded) into numbers to make them easier to handle and store. For instance, a response of 'yes' may be converted to the number 1; 'no' may be converted to the number 0.

The observations you collect in the course of a particular study, are called a data set. You may collect one, or more, data sets from a series of studies and compare them for changes in attitudes, buying behaviour and identify trends.

Data which has not been altered in any way (that is, it remains unchanged from when it was collected) is called raw data. In most cases, the raw data you collect will simply be pages of numbers or questionnaire responses. This, in itself, is fairly meaningless. Before raw data can be interpreted it must first be summarized. Three main methods are used to describe and present summarized data:

1. Tables
2. Graphics
3. Statistics.

As an example, let us imagine that you have conducted a small survey of ten marketing students to find out how many of the recommended textbooks they have actually read. You find that one student admits to having read only one book, two students admit to having read two of the recommended books, four students say they have read three books, two students say they have read four books and one diligent student claims to have read five books.

Using tables

We could represent the data from the textbook example in tabular form (Table 5.3).

Table 5.3 *Number of recommended textbooks read by marketing students*

Number of books read	Number of students
1	1
2	2
3	4
4	2
5	1

This sort of table is called a frequency table because it records the frequency with which particular values occur.

Using graphics

We also represent the same books data graphically (Figure 5.8).

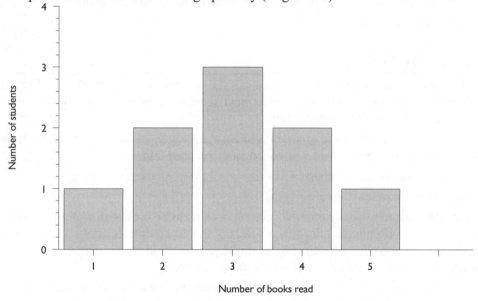

Figure 5.8 *Numbers of recommended textbooks read by marketing students*

This representation of data is called a frequency distribution. Like the tabular equivalent it represents the frequency of unique values found in the data. You will also notice that this particular distribution is symmetrical around the mid-point. That is, the left- and right-hand sides or the distribution are mirror images of each other. This situation is quite rare in market research but important nonetheless as symmetrical distributions (also called normal distributions) have certain special properties.

Using statistics

Complex data is usually interpreted using statistical methods. These range from simple techniques such as calculating the mean result to sophisticated factor analysis techniques.

It is important to have a basic understanding of the correct use of basic summary statistics although it is outside the scope of this coursebook to go into detailed descriptions and present the methods of calculation.

Measures of location

The commonest method of summarizing raw data is to calculate the 'average' response. There are three 'averaging' statistics. These are called the arithmetic mean, mode and median. Collectively, these statistics are known as measures of location. You may well come across these statistics while reading market research studies or literature, however, it is not necessary to know how to calculate them for this unit of the course.

Measures of dispersion

In addition to knowing about the 'average' of a distribution it is also useful to know about the 'spread' of values in the distribution. There are three statistics which are commonly used to describe 'spread'. These are called the range, interquartile range and quartile deviation. Collectively, these statistics are known as measures of dispersion.

As with measures of location, you may well come across these statistics but you do not need to know how to calculate them for this unit of the course.

Proportions, fractions and percentages

Often it is useful to represent values, not in terms of their absolute numerical 'worth', but in terms of their relative value in comparison with other observations. For example, it is all very well knowing that your product sold 250,000 units this month, but of more interest is how it performed in comparison to the competition. For instance, what market share do you have?

There are three ways of representing such information:

1. As a percentage – for example sales are up 10 per cent.
2. As a fraction – one half (½) of our customers are satisfied with our service.
3. As a proportion – 0.25 of our product retail price goes on the packaging.

All of these are in common usage.

Presentation of findings

Invariably, the presentation of research data requires the writing of a report. This will include the graphical presentation of data as described in the next section along with a description of your research and recommendations for further action.

A report is usually the only full record of your research; the purpose of the work, the sample used, all the results, the method of analysis used, the conclusions reached and so on.

Characteristics of a good research report:

1. Objectives of the research are well defined.
2. It is structured and logically ordered. The report should be broken down into sections, each with their own informative title. These sections should be ordered in such a way as to lead the reader through the research. For example, data should be presented and the analysis method described before any conclusions are presented.
3. It is comprehensive (it covers all aspects of the research) but concise (should not be unnecessarily wordy or cover irrelevant areas). A summary or abstract should be provided which summarizes the important findings for casual readers.
4. Accurate, clear and precise language is used throughout (terminology should be appropriate for the intended audience).

These four characteristics can be remembered from the acronym: OSCA (objectives, structure, comprehensiveness, accuracy).

Structure of a research report

In the scientific community, a 'standard' report structure has evolved. While this is not suitable for all purposes, it provides a useful guide under most circumstances.

1. *Title page(s)* This should include the following:
    o   Title of the report
    o   Name of sponsor and/or customer for the report
    o   Title of researcher and organization
    o   Date of publication.

2. *Table of contents* This should include page references for each heading contained within the report.

3. *Executive summary or abstract* This is intended for casual readers who may not have the time or inclination to read the whole report. This often includes the person that makes the decisions!

4. It should summarize the whole of the report, including the findings and recommendations. As a rough guide, this should not exceed one-eighth page for each five pages of report. For example, the summary for a 40-page report should be less than a page long. If your paper is added to an electronic database often the only text available to the reader is the abstract. Some systems limit the 'on-line' abstract to 250 words.

5. *Introduction or background* This should include the following:
    o   Purpose of research (often this is referred to as the 'brief')
    o   Supporting history and background information (i.e. other relevant studies)
    o   Any assumptions made
    o   Specific aims of research.

6. *Methodology* Should include the following:
    o   Details of any material used (questionnaires, interview forms, special equipment)
    o   Sample population (numbers and profile)
    o   Design of study
    o   Procedure used (the sequence in which the study was conducted).

7. *Results and analysis* Should include the following:
    o   Details of analysis method(s) used
    o   Descriptive statistics for raw data
    o   Any advanced statistics
    o   Tabular and/or graphical presentation of data.

8. *Discussion and conclusions* Should include the following:
    o   Discussion of research findings
    o   Conclusions to be drawn from findings
    o   Self-critique of study (e.g. unexpected problems that arose, why not enough people could be surveyed, flaws discovered in a questionnaire)
    o   Additional graphical presentation of summarized or combined data to support discussion or conclusions.

9. *Recommendations* Should include the following:
    o   Actions to take as a result of research
    o   Recommendations for future research.

10. *Acknowledgements* Should include the following:
    o   Thanks to organizations that have funded/supported research
    o   Thanks to individuals that have helped in the preparation of the report (i.e. they may have given useful advice or provided administrative support).

11. *References* Should include full references for all materials and other research studies referred to.

12. *Appendices* Should include all information, such as the full questionnaire text, which, if included in the main body of the text, would have interrupted the flow of the report.

Activity 5.3

Find a copy of the *Journal of the Market Research Society,* or one of the many other journals in this field, and examine the structure of three papers. How do these compare with each other and with the 'ideal' structure outlined in this unit.

Report writing tips

The following tips are presented to assist in the writing of a good report and help assess the reports of others.

- Does the report contain enough information to allow another researcher to replicate the work? If not, then the report should contain more detail. This is, of course, unless the writer wishes for certain aspects of their research method to remain secret.

- The introductory sections to a report, should address at least the following questions:
  - o Why is this report being written?
  - o What does it hope to achieve?
  - o Who is this report aimed at?

- The results and analysis sections of a report should not contain any discussion or conclusions, only an impartial description of the data.

- Conclusions should be based solely on the data reported combined with the findings from other, fully referenced, studies. A clear distinction should be made between the results themselves, the interpretation of the results (which may be contested), and the recommendations being made.

- Recommendations should be concrete and specific, not 'woolly'.

- Are all the graphs and tables properly titled, clearly presented and referenced in the body of the text?

- Does the summary include all the important information from the report?

Summary

In this unit you have learned about:
- The market research process – including hypothesis construction and pilot testing
- Common experimental design formats
- The selection of target populations
- The principles of investigating customer dynamics
- Possible pitfalls with investigative market research
- The main means of interpreting and presenting research findings.

Further study and examination preparation

Now undertake Question 5 from CIM Examination Session June 2000 to be found in the Exam paper Appendix.

Unit 6
Quantitative and qualitative methodologies
for investigating customer dynamics

Objectives

This unit introduces a variety of different primary and secondary research methodologies. You will:

- Learn about the different types of research.
- Explore a wide variety of qualitative and quantitative primary research techniques.
- Be presented with an overview of sources of secondary data.
- Be introduced to the ethical and legal issues surrounding the collection and use of data.

By the end of the unit you will be able to:

- Understand the different types of research.
- Know how to go about conducting secondary research.
- Choose the primary research technique most suited to your research goals.
- Be aware and take account of the possible ethical and legal problems associated with investigative research.

This unit covers the following parts of the Marketing Customer Interface syllabus:

- 2.4.2
- 2.4.3
- 2.4.4

Different types of research

Primary versus secondary

Primary data is information collected for a specific purpose. The process of collection is called primary research. A number of methods of primary research are discussed later in this section.

An example of primary data collection is the research required to identify the market for an innovative new product. It is unlikely that such research has previously been undertaken. Therefore the research is likely to be specially commissioned.

Secondary data is data originally collected for a more general purpose usually by a third party. The process of collection is usually termed secondary research or desk research.

An example is the use of the electoral roll for the purpose of ascertaining, for example, the number of 18-year-olds in a city (people turning 18 in a certain year are marked on the register along with the date of their birthday). This data was obviously collected for the purpose of identifying those eligible to vote but might be of use to a marketer looking at, for example, the best place to site a nightclub aimed at younger people.

Activity 6.1

What primary and secondary research does your organization do?

Internal versus external

The information available within an organization is termed internal data. Internal research is therefore relatively rapid and requires minimal resources. Example of internal data could include:

- Sales, production and distribution records.
- Customer database.
- Historical research reports.

External data is data collected by outside bodies. These might be commercial market research organizations or official bodies such as the Office of National Statistics (ONS).

Examples of external data include:

- Official census data
- Newspaper polls or internet surveys
- Academic research papers.

External data is usually, but not always, secondary data. For example, you may wish to commission a third party to research your corporate image. Similarly, internal data is not always primary data. It may, for example, have been originally collected for a different purpose.

Qualitative versus quantitative

Research is either quantitative (it deals mostly with numerical information) or qualitative (dealing with less tangible data such as interview responses, individual opinions and the outcome of group discussions). Of course, rarely is a particular piece of research either entirely qualitative or quantitative. It may be, for instance, that you conclude a quantitative questionnaire with an open-ended question seeking further comment. The responses to this would be qualitative in nature.

Also, it is possible to 'code' qualitative responses to make them appear quantitative. For example, if you were interviewing a person about a product and, in the course of the interview, they said that they very much liked the packaging you might later rate their opinion by giving it a coding of '3'. If other persons were interviewed who said that they disliked the packaging you might give them a coding of '1'. People who were undecided about the packaging might receive a coding of '2'. Thus, a crude quantitative scale can be built up from qualitative data.

Qualitative methodologies

There are three basic ways of collecting primary data in qualitative research:

1. Depth interviews
2. Focus/discussion groups
3. Projective techniques.

Depth interviews

A depth interview is an unstructured discussion between interviewer and respondent. They are generally lengthy (anything up to one hour) and are best carried out by trained, experienced interviewers.

The interviewing style can vary enormously but the aim is to secure the maximum amount of useful information from the respondent on a particular topic with minimum intervention from the interviewer. The role of the interviewer is therefore to:

- Obtain detailed information on the topic(s) needed within the time available.
- Balance the need for open-ended discussion with the need to address certain topics.
- Avoid biasing the respondent by appearing to favour certain responses or asking leading questions.

The interview is best recorded on audiotape. Recorders which are voice activated are best as they save time when analyzing the tape and, of course, save tape. Transcripts are prepared from the tape, suitably annotated to indicate the emotional content of the voice as required, and studied for ideas, useful comments and subjective opinions on the topic under investigation.

The respondents need to be chosen with care. Some people are not as good at expressing themselves verbally as others. It may be that respondents are chosen from those taking part in a larger study as a result of their 'extreme' opinions, particular knowledge or responsibilities within an organization.

Depth interviews are particularly useful during the early stages of a product/brand development when little has been decided and/or new ideas are required.

Focus groups

Focus groups are similar to depth interviews in many ways. The main difference being that the discussion is not one-on-one but involves a group of seven to ten respondents. The main effect of this is that the group forms its own identity, much of the discussion is among its members. Under these circumstances the researcher facilitates the working of the group rather than actually interviewing its individual members. These groups are sometimes called discussion groups and the researcher leading the group, the facilitator or moderator.

As with depth interviews, the role of the facilitator is to focus discussion on the research topic, directing the group where required but limiting their involvement as much as possible. Certain management of the group is also required:

- The discussion needs to be set in motion.
- Track must be kept of the progress of the discussion (time-keeping, etc.).
- The involvement of all members must be ensured (some people are shy in groups, yet their knowledge or opinions may be just as valuable).
- The discussion needs to be brought to a close in a tidy manner.
- Names and other details of the group members need to be gathered (this may be achieved with a small questionnaire which, of course, must be designed and produced).
- Arrangements for follow-up discussion may also need to be arranged and communicated.
- The practicalities of recording the discussion must be handled (this may involve the use of a flip-chart, tape recorder or videotape).

Focus group members are often chosen to reflect a cross-section of the intended target customers for the product/brand under discussion. In this way, more debate is assured.

The processes that take place in groups, their formation, maintenance, decision making and performance, are called group dynamics. A large number of psychological studies have looked at group dynamics including the roles people play, how groups solve problems and reach decisions, how individual members are affected by their membership of the group and so on. Focus groups are popular amongst marketers because:

- They allow qualitative information from many individuals to be collected in a short period of time.
- They provide a good forum for 'testing the water' with new products/brands.
- The group setting is 'emotionally-charged' in a way that a one-to-one interview can never be.
- They are useful for generating new ideas and, under certain circumstances, problem-solving (suitable techniques are 'brainstorming' and 'synectics').

An advertising executive named Alex Osborn (Osborn, A. F. (1957), *Applied Imagination*, New York, Scribner) was the first to advocate brainstorming as a technique to devise new or creative solutions to difficult problems. His rules for brainstorming are reproduced below:

1. Given a problem to solve, all group members are encouraged to express whatever solutions and ideas come to mind, regardless of how preposterous or impractical they may seem.
2. All reactions are recorded.
3. No suggestion or solution can be evaluated until all ideas have been expressed. Ideally participants should be led to believe that no suggestions will be evaluated at the brainstorming sessions.
4. The elaboration of one person's ideas by another is encouraged.

When brainstorming, it is important that the facilitator write down all suggestions where they can be viewed by all group members. A use for brainstorming might be to devise a new advertising slogan, product name or even a new product. With synectics the aim is to focus on producing creative solutions and to enhance the creative potential of the group, members are usually pre-selected on the basis of their creative abilities and may be recruited from a wide range of disciplines unrelated to the topic under discussion. The problems set before synectics groups are usually of a more complex or technical nature.

Projective techniques

These set of techniques are based on those used by clinical psychologists to understand a person's 'hidden' attitudes, motivations and feelings. In a marketing context, these techniques are used to illicit associations with a particular product or brand. Many psychological techniques have been successfully used for this purpose.

Activity 6.2

You are tasked with finding a new name for a special brew of beer. The beer is to be produced in limited edition to celebrate the eighty-fifth birthday of the brewery owner, a retired man fondly referred to as 'The colonel'. The following information is available about him:

- He is well-known and respected in the brewing industry.
- He has a 'handle-bar' moustache.
- He likes horses (his hobby).
- He was a military man and served in a mounted division.

The following is known about the brewery:

- The popular brews it produces are named with an 'academic' theme.
- The company is well-known nationally but with a strong local image.

Working in a group, set aside 15 to 20 minutes to try and brainstorm a name for the limited edition brew. Appoint a facilitator who writes down suggestions on a blackboard or flip chart. At the end of the allotted time, take your best three suggestions then, as a group, spend five to ten minutes deciding on your preferred, final, name. For each of the three alternatives, give their advantages and disadvantages.

Word association

Respondents are presented with a series of words or phrases and asked to say the first word that comes into their head. This is often used to check whether proposed product names have undesirable associations, particularly in different cultures and languages. You might not wish, for instance, to call a new life insurance policy 'Wish' if it turned out to be associated in many people's minds with 'death' (death-wish) although you might if it brought to mind a 'wishing well'.

Activity 6.3

What is the first word or phrase you associate with each of the following:

- Insurance
- Ice cream
- Computer
- Mineral water
- Psychology

Compare your responses with those of your classmates. Are any of your responses the same? Why do you think that is?

Sentence completion

The beginning of a sentence is read out and the respondent is asked to complete it with the first words that come to mind. To probe the ideas which are important to people in selecting an insurance policy you might provide the sentence: 'The kind of people that do without holiday insurance are. . .'

Activity 6.4

Working on your own, complete the following sentences:

- People who don't own cars are...
- Women who dye their hair are...
- A couple who go on holiday to Spain are...

Now compare your answers with those of your classmates. Are your answers similar or different? What information does this technique provide?

Third-person technique

Respondents are asked to describe a third person about whom they have little information. This technique was used by Mason Haire when instant coffee was first introduced in 1950. Two groups of housewives were given a shopping list to examine. The list given to each group was identical except that one contained instant coffee, the other ground coffee. The housewives perceived the writer of the list that contained instant coffee as 'lazy' and 'poor' whereas they perceived the writer of the list that contained ground coffee as being 'thrifty' and generally a 'good' homemaker. This research demonstrated the negative attitudes associated with convenience foods in the 1950s. A later replication of this study in 1970, when instant coffee was more widely accepted, no longer found these negative associations.

Activity 6.5

The picture is of a man called Dave Rodwell. He is a lecturer at the Oxford College of Marketing. He teaches 'consumer behaviour' on the CIM Marketing courses run at the college.

Without discussing your thoughts, or your answers, with your classmates please answer the following questions. Do not worry if you feel you cannot answer all the questions.

1. What sort of car do you think he drives?
2. What political party do you think he supports?
3. How old do you think he is?
4. What do you think is his favourite sport?
5. Which country do you think he was born in?
6. What do you think his father's job was/is?
7. What do you think is his favourite colour?
8. What sort of place do you think he lives in?
9. What pets do you think he has?
10. What newspaper do you think he regularly reads?

Once you have answered as many questions as you can, compare your responses with those of your classmates. Are there any similarities? Why do you think that is?

Thematic apperception test (TAT)

Respondents are asked to interpret an ambiguous picture or drawing or fill in a blank 'speech bubble' associated with a particular character in an ambiguous situation. A television recruitment advertisement for the UK police force showed a black man in casual clothes running followed by a white policeman running. The footage was presented in an ambiguous way (was the policeman chasing the man? or were they both chasing a third party?) to highlight the problem of racial stereotyping and the need for a multiracial police force. The advert was part of a campaign to increase the number of non-white police.

Activity 6.6

In not less than fifty words, describe this picture. Also, what might the woman be saying?

Now list the 'themes' in your response (what is happening, who is speaking, what they are saying, etc.).

Compare your themes with those of your classmates. What information could this technique provide?

Reperatory grid (rep grid)

A modification of the method first developed by Kelly in 1955 to support his theory of personality, the rep grid is useful as a projective technique in many marketing situations. Respondents are presented with a grid and asked to title the columns with brand names or types of a particular product (e.g. flavours of ice cream, types of car). They are then asked to take three of these products and think of a phrase which describes the way in which any two are different from the third. For instance, a Porsche and a Jaguar might be described as 'speed machines' when compared to a Volvo. This description is then used as a row title and each of the other products/ brands rated accordingly. By repeatedly selecting and describing three items, the way in which an individual perceives the market is found. It might be that an individual perceives the car market as consisting of 'speed machines', 'safe but boring', and 'comfortable' cars. This information can be used in a number of ways for planning a promotion, identifying the attitudes associated with established products and identifying where gaps in the market exist.

Suppose we have been asked to investigate the various ice cream flavours in the market place and determine what characteristics any new flavour should have to be successful. We know the sales figures for the various flavours but we do not know what it is about the ice cream flavours that people like. This is where the rep grid technique can help.

A rep grid is a table with the columns as elements and the rows as constructs. If we were investigating different ice cream flavours, the flavours themselves would be the elements. In this example we will limit ourselves to four flavours although, of course, a real study would take into account all the flavours on the market. To start with, our rep grid would look something like Figure 6.1.

Figure 6.1 Rep grid for ice cream example

Constructs	Elements			
	Nuts and cookies	Strawberry	Roast peanut	French chocolate

To generate the constructs we take any three flavours (elements) and find a way in which any two are different from the third. If we took Strawberry, French Chocolate and Roast Peanut we may decide that the Strawberry is different from the others in that it is 'fruity'. We would therefore write in 'fruity' as a construct and place a tick against 'Strawberry' and any other of the elements which we consider to share the 'fruity' construct. In this example, none of the others would probably be considered 'fruity'. By taking another three elements and comparing them we might come up with the following additional constructs: 'has bits in', 'doughy', 'chocolate-taste' and so on. It must be emphasized that constructs are a very personal thing. No two persons' will look the same. After three constructs are generated, the grid may end up looking something like Figure 10.2.

Figure 6.2 Rep grid for ice cream example with three constructs added

Constructs	Elements			
	Nuts and cookies	Strawberry	Roast peanut	French chocolate
Fruity		yes		
Has bits in	yes		yes	yes
Doughy	yes			

By comparing the high-selling flavours with others we can determine what constructs are the most popular and use this information to determine what constructs any new flavour should match. For instance, we might decide that it should be 'doughy' and 'have bits in'. From this information we might decide to test cookies and chocolate as a combination.

Role-playing

Respondents are asked to imagine that they are an object (e.g. a fridge or car) or a different person (e.g. a bank manager or supplier) and asked to describe their feelings, thoughts and actions. A variation on this technique is the 'friendly Martian' role play where respondents are asked to imagine that they are a Martian and describe what they would do under certain circumstances. For example, the following question could be asked to secure information about the appeal of different supermarkets:

'Imagine you are a Martian who has just landed in a shopping centre close to Sainsbury's, Tesco, Asda and Budgen supermarkets. You need food. How would you decide which supermarket to visit?'

Comparison of different qualitative research methods

Depth interviews	Focus/discussion groups	Projective techniques
Very time-consuming to administer	Moderately time-consuming to administer	Relatively quick to administer (depending on technique)
Can only administer one person at a time	Can administer up to ten people at a time	Can administer many people at a time (depending on technique)
Needs trained interviewers to administer	Needs trained facilitators to administer	Needs few trained staff to administer (depending on technique)
Danger of interviewer bias	Group may be biased towards opinions of stronger members	Low likelihood of bias
Time-consuming to analyse	Time-consuming to analyse	Relatively quick to analyse
Possible to obtain very detailed information	Possible to obtain very detailed information	Information limited by technique used
Indirectly useful for generating new ideas	Can be used for brainstorming new ideas directly	Indirectly useful for generating new ideas

Quantitative methodologies

There are two basic ways of collecting primary data in qualitative research:

1. Observation
2. Surveys and questionnaires (including interviews, telephone, diary and postal surveys).

Observation

We all learn by observing the things that happen around us. Observation, as a market research method, is the formalization and refinement of this process.

We can clearly observe the behaviour of individuals but what observation cannot tell us is what people are thinking or feeling. For instance, we can observe which shoppers buy lottery tickets but we can't distinguish between shoppers who may be thinking, 'If I don't win this week I'll stop' from those who are thinking, 'I'm going to keep buying tickets until I win'. These alternatives are obviously of interest because they will affect future behaviour, but observational techniques are not able to distinguish these two groups of shoppers. Observation is therefore quite limited as a technique but, nonetheless, can be useful under those circumstance where we are more interested in behaviour than in any mental processes.

There are three basic types of observation:

1. *Secretive* – where the subjects of the study are unaware that they are being observed. For instance, the behaviour of shoppers is observed via a hidden camera or by an experimenter pretending to be another shopper. This may pose ethical problems.

2. *Non-participatory* – where the subjects of the study are aware that they are being observed but the experimenter takes no part in the behaviour being observed. For instance, shoppers are observed by an experimenter with a clipboard sited prominently, perhaps near the checkouts. It is possible that the presence of the experimenters may affect the behaviour of the subject.

3. *Participatory* – where the subject and experimenter interact. A shopper might be approached by an experimenter and asked what they are buying and why. This can provide useful additional information but the behaviour of the experimenter may actually change the behaviour of the subject they are trying to observe.

Observations can be carried out in the field or in the laboratory. The latter overcomes many of the ethical problems associated with such studies but risks interfering with naturally occurring behaviours and can appear contrived. It may be, for instance, that meeting friends has an influence on supermarket buying behaviour. This aspect of shopping would be difficult to re-create in a laboratory.

One successful example of the use of observational research was that done by the Postal Service in the USA. They found that most people were on first-name terms with their postmen and women. This led to a successful promotional campaign which prominently featured post deliverers.

Observational data is usually collected using recording sheets. A predetermined set of behaviours are identified and printed on these sheets. The experimenter is then able to mark down quickly the behaviours as they occur.

Suppose we were trying to determine the order in which shoppers visit the various areas within a supermarket as part of a study to reorganize shelving (wet fish, deli counter, fruit and vegetables, tinned food, etc.). In this instance we would be wise to prepare our recording sheet with a list of the various areas in which we are interested. It is then easy to indicate, with a number, the order in which they were visited. It is also good practice to prepare for the unexpected by adding space on the recording sheet for behaviours which were not anticipated. For instance, it might be that a shopper visits an area more than once. You may wish to record which area they re-visited as well as the reason why.

Observations that are difficult to record in 'real time' because they happen too fast or are obscured can be recorded on video for later analysis.

Mystery shopping

One special kind of secretive observation is termed 'mystery shopping'. It is, in fact, one of the least mysterious research methods. Researchers simply pose as customers and report on the nature and quality of the service they receive.

They are normally briefed on the various points that it is important to observe. Examples include:

- The appearance of the store and staff
- Employee product knowledge
- Speed of service
- Whether correct sales procedure is followed.

Mystery shopping provides a welcome opportunity for a business to see itself through a customer's eyes.

The technique is not restricted to personal shopping, it can just as easily be used to assess responses to telephone enquiries, service call-outs, order lines and so on.

One well-known company, Abbey National, uses mystery shopping extensively. Each of its branches is 'inspected' twice a year as part of a broader customer satisfaction programme.

Activity 6.8

Observe students in your college canteen. In what order do they make decisions about what to eat and drink. Are these decisions influenced by the people accompanying them?

When and where do they pick up their cutlery, condiments? Where and how do they pay?

On the basis of the answers to these questions, how might the canteen improve its image and the degree to which it meets the needs of its customers?

Survey methods

A survey is the most commonly used method of gathering quantitative data. It is essential to approach the design and administration of surveys in a structured way to avoid errors, wasted time and poor quality responses. The process of undertaking a survey project is similar in many ways to that for an experiment.

Steps in a survey project:

1. Decide on your survey goals – what you want to learn.
2. Determine your sample – who you will ask.
3. Select interviewing methodology – how you will ask.
4. Design your questionnaire – what you will ask.
5. Pre-test the questionnaire, if at all practical (known as piloting).
6. Administer interviews – ask the questions.
7. Enter the data.
8. Analyze the data.
9. Present the data.

Deciding on your survey goals

The first step in any survey is deciding what you want to know. This will determine whom you will survey and what you will ask them. If you are unclear about what you want then your results will be unclear. Researchers rarely take the time necessary at this stage of the project to consider their survey goals properly. Some general goals could include finding out more about:

- Consumer ratings of current products or services
- A company's corporate image
- Customer satisfaction levels
- Television viewer opinions
- Employee attitudes
- Opinions about political issues
- The potential market for a new product or service.

These sample goals represent general areas of investigation only. The more specific you can make your goals, the easier it will be to get usable answers. Specific goals are usually phrased as questions:

- What do the supporters of the different political parties feel about the level of defence spending?
- What do the employees of UserData Limited feel about the new salary scales?
- Do consumers prefer the services offered by Orange or BT Cellnet?
- Which washing powder do customers think washes their clothing best – Persil or Ecover?

Even at this stage, it may be necessary to get clarification on certain concepts. For instance, in the last question, what is meant by 'washes their clothing best'? The person commissioning the research should be consulted on such questions of interpretation. The 'best' in this context may mean 'cleanest' or 'whitest' or may be to do with how the powder handles sensitive or coloured fabrics.

SERVQUAL – measuring service quality

One example of a survey tool widely used to measure service quality is SERVQUAL, developed by Parasuraman et al. (1988). This is made up of a series of questions; 22 on expectations and 22 on performance.

Each set of 22 questions contains items on five basic dimensions:

1. Reliability
2. Responsiveness
3. Empathy
4. Assurance
5. Tangibles.

These are phrased as statements to which responses are given using a seven-point Likert-type scale. For example, the pair of questions measuring reliability for a bank could be something like Figure 6.3.

Figure 6.3

Question pair	Strongly agree						Strongly disagree
Expectation: Banks should be dependable							
Performance: Anytown Bank is dependable							

There is much debate over the reliability and validity of the SERVQUAL instrument but it remains a popular tool for exploring and measuring service quality and identifying gaps.

For a critique of SERVQUAL read Asubonteng et al. (1996) 'SERVQUAL revisited: a critical review of service quality', *The Journal of Services Marketing*.

Interviewing methods

Once you have decided on your sample you must decide on the method of data collection. The main methods are:

- Personal interview
- Telephone surveys including computer assisted telephone interviewing (CATI)
- Computer assisted interviewing (CAI)
- Postal surveys
- Internet surveys.

(See Table 6.1)

Personal interviews

What distinguishes this type of survey is that the questionnaire is administered 'face-to-face' with the interviewee. Such interviews are often categorized according to where they take place. The following examples are given:

- *Household survey* – The surveyor goes door-to-door, either randomly, or according to some pre-arranged sampling method, and interviews people on the doorstep.
- *Home survey* – Takes place in the interviewee's home. They are normally arranged in advance. This is obviously time-consuming but guarantees a response. Advantages are that, in the comfort of their own home, conversation is likely to be freer and the interviewee will be more tolerant of a longer interview.
- *Hall survey* – As its name suggests, these take place in a hall or hired room. Individuals are invited to attend or called in off the street to take part.
- *Shop surveys* – these take place in shopping centres, inside a particular shop or at the entrance to a particular shop. In many cases a 'stall' is set up for this purpose and/or individuals are approached and asked to participate.
- *On-street surveys* – Otherwise known as 'clipboard' surveys, individuals are approached in the street. In busy, hectic streets this can be problematic. Surveying at busy times, such as lunchtime, is difficult as many people would rather have something to eat! On-street surveys need to be particularly short and to the point.

The use of a prompt card is common in personal interviewing. These are usually a verbal or pictorial representation of the response choices. For example, an interviewee might be asked for which political party they intend to vote. In this case, the response card would contain a list of political parties. The advantage of the prompt card is that it reduces the bias that can be introduced as a result of the changing voice intonation of the interviewer and, by having a number of different cards with different arrangements of responses, the effect of response ordering can be reduced. A further benefit is that 'wayward' responses are avoided. For example, a response to an unguided voting question might be 'Tony's Party'. The interviewee is probably referring to the Labour Party – a prompt card would help to clarify this without a possible biasing intervention from the interviewer.

Telephone (including CATI)

Telephone surveys are probably the most popular interviewing method. The majority of homes and businesses have a telephone which makes coverage almost complete (although about 10 per cent of people are not on the phone – most notably students and old persons but also those who are ex-directory).

Sampling is easy using a telephone directory. Most libraries carry a full set of telephone directories for the whole of the UK. The telephone also makes the sampling of international interviewees easy.

Increasingly popular is computer assisted telephone interviewing (CATI) where the interviewer reads questions from a computer screen and enters the responses directly in the computer. In this way, results can be analyzed rapidly. CATI can also assist the interviewer in structuring their interview by only displaying those questions which are relevant based on earlier responses. Unfortunately, the growth of 'junk' telephone calls is increasing refusal rates amongst potential interviewees.

Computer assisted interviews (CAI)

These are interviews in which the interviewees enter their own answers directly into a computer. They are popular at exhibitions and in large organizations where 'electronic mail' is used to send out the questionnaire. This method is convenient and, as with CATI, no post-survey data entry is required allowing for a rapid analysis. Obviously, CAI is limited by the availability of a suitable computer. The novelty and convenience of CAI leads to moderately high response rates.

Postal surveys

These surveys are generally inexpensive. Postal surveys are seen as less intrusive than personal interviews and telephone surveys but response rates are generally low. More often than not, response rates are less than 10 per cent which provides an opportunity for considerable bias. In an attempt to boost return rates, all manner of offers and incentives are used. One American researcher found that enclosing a one dollar bill massively increased response rates (and no doubt also the cost!).

Low levels of literacy are no doubt one reason why responses are reduced – a good reason to keep questions simple. English is not everyone's first language and, in areas where problems with language are envisaged, it may be worth producing multi-lingual questionnaire variants.

However, much of the low response rate is simply due to the high volumes of 'junk' mail people receive. Try to make your survey look as little like junk mail as possible. Better still, and wherever possible, save some trees and use the telephone!

> ### Question 6.2
> What are the advantages of postal surveys compared with telephone surveys?
> What are the advantages of CAI compared with personal interviews?

Internet surveys

Similar in some respects to postal surveys, obtaining information over the internet (either by e-mail or via online questioning) is inexpensive although response rates can be low.

Unsolicited 'junk' e-mails are rarely responded to and, therefore, the best way to secure a response is to link completion of a questionnaire into some sort of registration or subscription process. This approach, while potentially increasing response rates does result in a slower response time. Internet usage is increasing all the time but ownership of a suitable computer is still relatively low when compared, for example, with the telephone.

Ownership varies by region and is typically lower in poorer households.

Table 6.1 *Comparison of different interview methods*

Internet surveys	Postal survey	Telephone (including CATI)	Computer assisted interviewing (CAI)	Personal interviews
Respondees can see and hear (with a suitable computer)	Respondees can see, feel and/or taste	Respondees can hear	Respondees can see and hear	Respondees can see, feel, hear, and/or taste
Moderately long interviews tolerated	Moderately long interviews tolerated	Moderately long interviews tolerated	Moderately long interviews tolerated while still novel	Longer interviews tolerated in comfortable surroundings (i.e. own home) otherwise only short interviews tolerated (on-street).
Quick to receive responses	Long time to receive responses	Quick to receive responses	Quick to receive responses	Quick to receive responses
Fast analysis	Analysis moderately fast if survey is electronically readable, else slow	Fast analysis (CATI)/Slow analysis (non-CATI)	Fast analysis	Slow analysis
Easy to survey random sample	Easy to survey random sample	Easy to survey random sample	More difficult to survey random sample	More difficult to survey random sample
Poor, but increasing coverage (including international)	Full coverage (including international)	Good coverage (including international)	Poor coverage (have to go out and find individuals)	Poor coverage (have to go out and find individuals)
Requires certain level of literacy	Requires certain level of literacy	Requires comprehension of spoken language (usually English)	Requires certain level of literacy	Requires comprehension of spoken language (usually English)
Allow respondees to answer at their leisure	Allow respondees to answer at their leisure	Forces respondees to answer at time of call	Forces respondees to answer at time of interview	Forces respondees to answer at time of interview
Low response rate unless tied in to some process	Low response rate	Medium response rate	Medium response rate	Medium response rate
Virtual elimination of interviewer bias	Virtual elimination of interviewer bias	Possibility of interviewer bias	Virtual elimination of interviewer bias	Possibility of interviewer bias
Low cost	Low cost	Medium cost	Medium cost	High cost
No special interviewer training required	No special interviewer training required	Special interviewer training required	No special interviewer training required	Special interviewer training required
People more likely to answer sensitive questions (but more difficult to guarantee anonymity)	People more likely to answer sensitive questions	People less likely to answer sensitive questions	People more likely to answer sensitive questions	People less likely to answer sensitive questions

General comparison of different quantitative research methods

Observation	Surveys
Time-consuming to undertake	Relatively quick to undertake (depending on technique)
Restricted in the number of people by the circumstances of the observation	Can administer many people at a time (depending on technique)
Requires trained observers to collect data	Requires no specially trained staff to collect data (depending on technique)
Danger of responses being biased by presence of observer	Generally, low likelihood of bias (depending on technique)
Time-consuming to analyse	Relatively quick to analyse (depending on technique)

Questionnaire design

The following 'fifteen golden rules' are provided as a general guide to the design of questionnaires:

1. Keep the survey short – long surveys are often indicative of poorly defined survey goals. As a rule of thumb, keep the number of questions below forty. Go through each question. If you do not know, or care, what you will do with the result then leave the question out.

2. Design the questionnaire to match the survey method being used – for example, CATI and CAI are able to 'branch' to different questions depending on the responses given to earlier questions which can increase the amount of data collected with the same number of questions and make errors less likely.

3. Keep the questionnaire simple – do not mix topics – for example, combining a survey on smoking with one on political issues simply serves to confuse the interviewee.

4. Do not combine two questions in one – for example, 'How do you feel about the Prime Minister and the Government?' should be asked as two questions (a) How do you feel about the Prime Minister (b) How do you feel about the Government?'

5. Avoid unnecessary terminology, abbreviations, technical words and jargon – these should only be used where questions are intended for specialist groups that would be expected to understand. For example, 'Have you ever owned a PC 486DX 66 computer?' is probably an acceptable question for a computer buff but not a member of the general public.

6. Do not present biased questions – For example, 'How satisfied are you with your new, super fast, hi-tech Swan toaster?' assumes that people already have a positive perception of the toaster and thus is likely to bias their response. A more correct way of phrasing this question would be to ask 'How satisfied or dissatisfied are you with the Swan toaster?' – a suitable response scale would then be provided.

7. Make sure your questions are grammatically correct – poor grammar can lead to confusion, annoys certain people, and creates a poor impression.

8. Each question should have a 'Don't know or 'Not applicable' response unless you are absolutely certain that you have covered all possibilities. For example, in response to the question 'What make of car do you own?' 'Don't know' and 'Not applicable' response categories should be provided. Some people may not actually know, or care, about the make of their car. Similarly, some people do not own a car. You would rarely want to include 'Don't know' or 'Not applicable' in a list of choices being read over the telephone or in person, but should usually accept them when given by respondents.

9. Provide example questions at the beginning of the questionnaire to demonstrate the method of completion. If a number of different question formats are used, provide examples of each and instructions for completion within the body of the questionnaire to avoid confusion.

10. Be specific in your questioning – 'woolly' questions lead to 'woolly' results. For example, 'Have you recently bought a can of cat food' might be better re-phrased 'Have you bought a can of Possum cat food in the last two weeks?'

11. Always allow for the interviewee to make their own comments at the end of the questionnaire – this will often provide useful leads for follow-up studies or allow you to more accurately interpret the data you collect.

12. Take care when laying out your questionnaire – a neat and tidy layout creates a good impression and reduces error.

13. Take care with the ordering of your questions – make sure that the response on a question is not affected by a previous answer or pre-empts a response to a later question. For example, a question which mentions blue packaging should not be succeeded by a question which asks for preferences on packaging colour.

14. Always start your questionnaire by explaining who you are and what you intend to do with the data you collect. This is polite as well as being ethically correct.

15. Always include a question asking whether the interviewee would mind being contacted further – you never know when a quick follow-up study may be required.

Question 6.3

You are stopped in the street by an interviewer. The first thing they say is 'Good afternoon Sir (or Madam), Where have you come from?' What is wrong with this?

Question types

Researchers use three basic types of questions:

1. Multiple choice – where the interviewee has to select from a set of responses (also called closed questions).
2. Open-ended – where the interviewee is allowed to enter anything.
3. Hybrid – a combination of the above two.

Multiple choice

Which destination would you choose for your ideal holiday? (please tick one response only)

- London ☐
- Paris ☐
- Caribbean ☐
- None of the above ☐
- Don't know ☐

Sometimes more than one response is required. This needs to be made abundantly clear to the respondee as in the following question example:

Which of the following qualifications do you possess? (please tick all the responses that apply)

- CSE ☐
- GCSE/O-level ☐
- A-level ☐
- Diploma ☐
- Degree or equivalent ☐

Open-ended

What destination would you choose for your ideal holiday? (please write response below)

Again, it might be that more than one response is required, as in the following example:

Please list the three things you like best about your new toaster:

1. ....
2. ....
3.   ....

Hybrid

Which destination would you choose for your ideal holiday? (please tick or write one response only)

- London ☐
- Paris ☐
- Caribbean ☐
- Other (please specify) ....
- Don't know ☐

Comparison of question types

Multiple choice	Open-ended	Hybrid
Easy to analyze	Difficult to analyze	If choices well researched then moderately easy to analyze
Likelihood of bias	Low likelihood of bias	Likelihood of bias
Difficult to design	Easy to design	Difficult to design
Suitable for quantitative data collection	Suitable for qualitative data collection	Suitable for quantitative data collection

Response scales

Depending on the sort of data you are collecting, you may need to use one of following types of response scales:

- *Likert scale* – developed in 1932 this scale is perhaps the most commonly used attitude response scale. A series of statements are rated in the following five-point scale: *strongly agree, agree, undecided, disagree, strongly disagree.*
- *Semantic differential* – developed by Osgood, Tannenbaum and Succi in 1957 this scale is commonly used where an attitude object rather than a statement is being rated. The semantic differential consists of nine pairs of bipolar adjectives or opposites. Each is given a seven-point scale. The adjectives used vary but typically consist of pairs such as good/bad, active/passive, strong/weak and so on.
- *Rank order scales* – here the interviewee is asked to rank items in terms of some specific property or attribute. Rank ordering can provide useful competitive information and is therefore useful in product positioning.

Likert scale

A number of different formats are favoured for Likert scales. Two examples are given below:

1. Using the scale given indicate how strongly you agree or disagree with the following statement (please circle your preferred response):

I enjoy studying marketing

Strongly agree   (Agree)   Neither agree nor disagree   Disagree   Strongly disagree

2. Place a cross in the box which best indicates how strongly you agree or disagree with each of the statements given:

	Strongly agree	Agree	Neither agree nor disagree	Disagree	Strongly disagree
I enjoy studying marketing	X				
I enjoy attending college			X		
I think the canteen food is over-priced				X	

Semantic differential

As noted, various adjective pairs are used as rating scales. Research has found that the scales used fall into one of three categories:

1. Evaluation – examples are good/bad, clean/dirty.
2. Potency – examples are weak/strong, large/small.
3. Activity – examples are active/passive, fast/slow.

Sometimes the scales seem rather unusual when applied to certain objects or ideas but, being able to apply similar adjectives across a range of items is one of the strengths of the technique. One example question is given below. Here attitudes to nuclear weapons are being measured.

Place a cross on one of the seven scale points for each of the adjective pairs given:

Nuclear weapons

Bad							Good
Fair							Unfair
Clean							Dirty
Worthless							Valuable
Active							Passive
Cold							Hot
Fast							Slow
Large							Small
Weak							Strong

You may wish to fill this in yourself.

One of the attractions of the semantic differential is that the results can be graphically represented by joining up the crosses on the scale points. This is called a profile. Figure 6.4 is an example of how this is done.

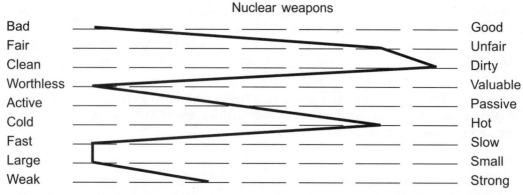

Figure 6.4 *A sample profile derived from a semantic differential scale – attitudes to nuclear weapons*

Using this profiling method it is easy to compare two 'objects' that have been rated on the same scales. This is particularly useful for brand comparisons. Figure 6.5 shows a profile comparing nuclear weapons with conventional weapons. With more than one line, a key is required.

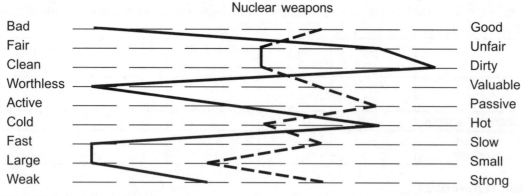

Figure 6.5 *Profiles derived from a semantic differential scale: Attitudes to nuclear and conventional weapons*

Rank order scale

Rank order scales can be used for rating anything from political parties to chocolate bars. Any number of items can be ranked but it is usual to keep the number below ten, and ideally below seven, to reduce the effort required to answer the question. Figures 6.6 and 6.7 are two examples of rank order questions.

Rank the following political parties in terms of their honesty. Place a 1 alongside the party you believe to be the most honest, a 2 alongside the party you believe to be the next honest, and so on until all the parties have been ranked.

Liberal Democrat	3
Conservatives	5
Labour	4
Green	2
Plaid Cymru	1

Figure 6.6 *Rank ordering political parties by honesty*

Rank the following washing powders according to their ability to keep white cottons clean. Place a 1 alongside the powder you believe to be the most effective, a 2 alongside the powder you believe to be the next most effective, and so on until all the powders have been ranked.

Persil	_____
Ecover	_____
Tide	_____
Ariel	_____

Figure 6.7 *Rank ordering washing powders by their ability to clean white cotton clothing*

No	Question	Answer	Code	Skip to
36	SHOW CARD 5 Can you tell me, very roughly, how much money you have saved or invested altogether in these forms of saving?	£50 or less £51–£200 £201–£500 £501–£1000 £1001–£3000 More Don't know	(69) 1 2 3 4 5 6 7	37
37	In which form of saving do you have *most money*	Only one form held Premium Bonds National savings Certificates Building Society P.O.S.B. Ordinary Account P.O.S.B. Investment Account Bank Deposit Account National Development Bonds Defence Bonds Unit Trusts Stocks and Shares Trustees S.B. Ordinary Account Trustee S.B. Special Investment A/c Local Authorities Other	(70) 1 2 3 4 5 6 7 8 9 0 X V (71) 1 2 3	38
38	SHOW CARD 6 What is this saving for? For any of these purposes (CARD) or for other purposes?	For emergencies For meeting large household bills For holidays, Christmas, etc. For security in later life To provide an income Other	(72) 1 2 3 4 5 6	39
39	Why did you choose that particular form of saving? PROBE!		(73) (74)	40
	IF ONLY ONE FORM OF SAVING, GO TO 41. IF MORE THAN ONE, ASK FOR EACH REMAINING IN ORDER OF SIZE. ASK SEPARATELY FOR ALL OTHER TYPES OF SAVING HELD	(WRITE IN TYPE) Type of saving	(10)	
40a	SHOW CARD 6 what are savings in .... for?	For emergencies For meeting large household bills For holidays, Christmas, etc. For security in later life To provide an income Others	(11) 1 2 3 4 5 6	

Figure 6.8 *National Savings Survey (excerpt)*

Real questionnaires

To conclude the discussion on questionnaires, it is only right to include one or two examples of questionnaire that are in use. Figure 6.8 is an excerpt from the National Savings Survey which appears in the third edition of the *Consumer Market Research Handbook* edited by Worcester and Downham. This is part of the interviewer's sheet. Figure 6.9 is a recruitment advert for a US *Family Circle* consumer panel which appears in *Consumer Behavior* by Schiffman and Kanuk.

Figure 6.9 A recruitment advert for a US Family Circle consumer panel

Join Our Consumer Panel!

Dear Reader:

We are about to form the 1994 FAMILY CIRCLE Consumer Panel. The 1993 panelists answered two very lengthy questionnaires over the year and received samples of our advertisers' products to evaluate. The 1994 panelists will be asked to do the same - to tell us about y ourself, your home, family, work, likes and dislikes.

Please take a few minutes from your busy schedule to answer all the questions below. Although we cannot select everyone who responds, I can assure you that those readers who are scientifically selected will have an interesting and rewarding year. When you've answered all the questions, mail the completed questionnaire by March 1, 1994, to:

FAMILY CIRCLE
6400 Jericho Turnpike
Synosset, New York 11791

Thank you and I hope to hear from all of you!

Jackie Leo, Editor

1. Which of the following do you regularly buy? (Please "X" all that apply.)

Cold/flu/cough remedies	(06) 1	Cigarettes (07)	1
Hand/body lotion	2	Feminine hygiene products	2
Home permanents	3	Children's food products	3
Low-calorie products	4	Children's clothing	4
Haircolouring products	5	Home fix-it materials	5
Low-fat products	6	Jeans	6
Athletic shoes	7		

2. Where do you ususlly buy cosmetics and fragrances?

	Cosmetics	Fragrances
Drug store	(08) 1	(09) 1
Department store	2	2
Discount department store	3	3
Supermarket	4	4

3. Please indicate below which activities you regularly do.

Bake from scratch	(10) 1	Cook using convenience foods	5
Cook from scratch	2	Read romance novels	6
Watch pre-recorded videos	3	Exercise at home	7
Exercise at club/spa	4	Buy collectibles	8

4. When will your household most likely purchase/lease your next vehicle?

0-3 months	(11) 1	1- 2 years	4
4-6 months	2	No definite plans	5
7-12 months	3		

5. What will your next vehicle most likely be?

Full size (12) 1	Midsize 2	Minivan 3

6. Do you own a Dog (13) 1 Cat 2

7. Do you have children?

Under 6 years (14) 1	No children under 18	3
6 years or older 2		

8. Are you: Female (15) 1 Male 2

9. Please "X" gr oup that best describes your age.

18 to 24	(16) 1	40 to 44	5	55 to 59	8
25 to 29	2	45 to 49	6	60 to 64	9
30 to 34	3	50 to 54	7	65 or older	0
35 to 39	4				

10. What is your current marital status?

Married	(17) 1	Widowed	3
Single (never married)	2	Divorced/Separated	4

11. What is the highest level of education you have completed?

Some high school or less	(18)	1
Graduated high school		2
Some college		3
Graduated college		4
Post-graduate study or more		5

12. Are you employed either full-time or part-time outside your home for a wage?

Employed full-time (30 hours or more per week)	(19)	1
Part-time (less than 30 hours per week)		2
Not employed/Retired		3

13. Please "X" the bo x below that best describes your total estimated household income before taxes in 1994 for ALL family members. (Please include your own income as well as that of all other household members. Income from all sources such as wages, bonuses, profits, dividends, rentals, interest, etc., should be included.)

Less than $20,000	(20) 1	$40,000 to $45,999	6
$20,000 to $24,999	2	$46,000 to $49,999	7
$25,000 to $29,999	3	$50,000 to $74,999	8
$30,000 to $34,999	4	$75,000 to $99,999	9
$35,000 to $39,999	5	$100,000 or more	0

14. Have you participated in a consumer *panel* or *council* in the past 12 months?

Yes (21) 1 No 2

15. Do you currently subscribe to FAMILY CIRCLE?

Yes (22) 1 No 2

Name _____

Address _____

_____

Phone # (_____) _____

Activity 6.9

Keep any questionnaires you find in magazines, newspapers or on the internet. Act as 'devil's advocate' and list the flaws in each. Decide how these flaws might have affected the accuracy of the data collected.

Secondary information sources

Sources of secondary data can be placed into one of six categories:

1. Government statistics
2. Popular media
3. Technical or specialist publications
4. On-line and electronic databases
5. Third party data
6. Casual research.

Government statistics

In the UK most official statistics are provided by the Government Statistical Service (GSS). The two main organizations within the GSS, the Central Statistical Office (CSO) and the Office of Population Censuses and Surveys (OPCS), merged in 1996 to form the Office of National Statistics (ONS).

Although the GSS existed originally to serve the needs of Government, it makes much of the data it collects widely available to businesses and the general public through the ONS. This data, and the analyses provided, are extremely useful sources for marketers.

The GSS publishes the *Guide to Official Statistics* listing all government sources of statistics. It is more than 500 pages long! The main publications are listed in the pamphlets *A Brief Guide to Sources* and the *ONS Publications Catalogue*.

Those interested in statistics for Northern Ireland should go to the Northern Ireland Statistics and Research Agency (NISRA) rather than the GSS.

Government statistical publications can be broadly divided into nine categories:

1. *Digests* – that is collections of UK and regional statistics.
2. *The economy* – statistics relating to the general economic indicators, financial and companies data, public sector, production industries, housing, construction and property industries and agriculture and fisheries.
3. *Defence* – statistics covering forces personnel and defence expenditure.
4. *External trade* – statistics covering overseas trade both within and outside Europe.
5. *Transport* – statistics covering transport trends, road expenditure, road traffic figures, accidents and casualties, shipping passenger and freight information, and details of air traffic.
6. *Society* – a large category covering the labour market, earnings, retail prices, taxation, standard of living, population and household statistics, family spending, education, home affairs, justice and law, health and safety and social security.
7. *Environment* – statistics covering countryside, land use and planning decisions.
8. *Distribution and other services* – statistics covering retailing, wholesaling, motor trade, catering and allied, and service trades.
9. *Overseas* – statistics covering overseas aid and comparisons of European regions.

Altogether, the government regularly publishes over 400 statistical sources in these areas. Included amongst these sources are many regular surveys. Those of particular interest to marketers include:

- *Social Trends* – brings together key social and demographic series.
- *Business Monitors* – summary statistics covering a number of business sectors.
- *New Earnings Survey* – earnings of employees by industry, occupation, region etc.
- *Retail Prices Index* – measures the average change from month to month in the prices of goods and services bought by consumers.
- *National Food Survey* – food consumption and expenditure.
- *Population Trends* – includes a broad range of family statistics (births, marriage, divorce), mortality and morbidity (deaths from various illnesses), electoral statistics and other population data.
- *Family Expenditure Survey* – income and expenditure by type of household.
- *General Household Survey* – continuous sample survey of households relating to a wide range of social and socio-economic issues.

Using government statistics

The chief advantage of government statistics is that they cover the complete United Kingdom. The disadvantage is that they cannot give tailor-made answers to a specific problem. The following list indicates some example marketing uses for these statistics:

- Using the *Business Monitors* you can compare your own performance against general sales trends.
- Those involved in consumer products can gain valuable information on trends and expenditure from the *National Food Survey* and *Family Expenditure Survey.*
- For test marketing, information from the *Population Trends* and *General Household Survey* can provide regional data on consumers.
- General trends in retail prices can be obtained from monitoring the *Retail Prices Index.*

It would take a book a least the size of this to explain all of the published government statistics and their uses. Some useful further Web sites are contained at the end of this unit.

Popular media

Much information can be gained from keeping an eye on the popular media. Much of this information is not going to be numerical, but may provide leads to previously undiscovered sources of data. The main sources are:

- *Newspapers* – The broadsheet newspapers can provide much useful information. Occasionally, these papers contain regional or national supplements which are especially useful for marketers operating in these specific areas. For financial and business information, try the *Financial Times* or *Wall Street Journal.* For social information, try the *Guardian.* For information on Europe, try *The European.* Local papers can also be a good source of regional business information.
- *Magazines* – There are popular magazines on subjects covering most business and leisure interests. If you are interested in learning about developments in yachting, for instance, you have a choice in the UK of *Practical Boat Owner, Yachting Monthly* and *Yachting World* plus several others. Business interests are perhaps most comprehensively covered by *The Economist,* and US titles such as *Business Week, Forbes* and *Fortune.*
- *Radio and television* – Current affairs, consumer programmes and news broadcasts are all potentially good sources of information.
- *Internet* – Many publications are now available, in some form or another, on the internet. Often the information exceeds that of the hardcopy version. For example, the *Guardian* web site (www.guardianunlimited.co.uk) often has special reports and links to further information not contained within the daily printed version.

Figure 6.10 shows some information gleaned from the *Financial Times* concerning regional house prices. This information might be extremely useful for anyone involved in the construction or allied trades and is of general use to marketers as an economic indicator. Note that the source is shown as the Halifax Building Society. It might be possible to get further information by contacting them.

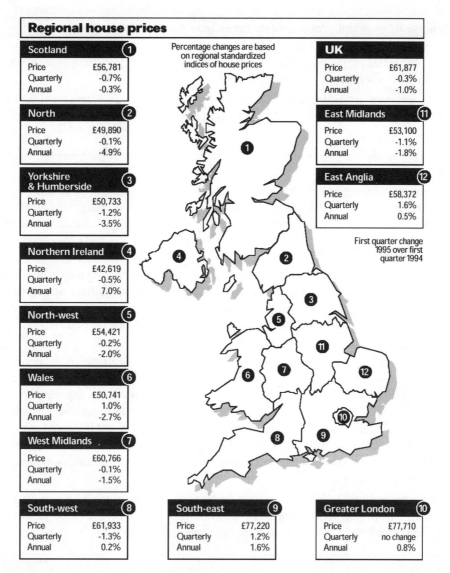

Figure 6.10 *Regional House Prices: Secondary data from the Financial Times*

Technical or specialist publications

For in-depth information about a particular field, a visit to a library, bookshop or internet search can provide technical and specialist data. The main sources are:

- *Market research and academic periodicals* – such as the *Harvard Business Review, Journal of the Market Research Society, Journal of Marketing* and *Journal of Consumer Research.*

- *Trade journals* – such as *Campaign, Computer Weekly, The Grocer* and so on.

- *Specialist books* – these can often provide summarized data along with an opinion on marketing opportunities and operations. Marketing books on Europe are particularly popular at this time.

- *Internet* – many societies, trade associations and private companies have web sites which contain archive copies of hardcopy journals and periodicals, electronic copies of published articles or specialist online publications (for example, see the Organic Trade Association: www.ota.com). One needs to be aware of the date of these online references – just because they are available in such an immediate format it does not mean that they are any more up-to-date than their printed counterparts!

The disadvantage of such publications is that they may be out of date by the time they are printed. However, they can provide useful information on subjects where change is slow. The Market Research Society, for instance, produce a series of Country Notes with general information, and the data sources available, on specific regions of the world.

Internet search engines are fast becoming the best place to start data research. Most useful data services are subscription only, so as with other data providers, do not expect to get quality data for nothing.

Activity 6.12

Read one of the research journals mentioned above. What useful information does it contain? How might this information be used by marketers in certain market sectors?

Third-party data services

Many market research companies sell data as a major part of the services they offer. Typically, such data comes from consumer panels. Panels exist which monitor a wide variety of purchases, opinions, and activities by gathering data from a group of representative consumers. Such data is collected either continuously or at fixed, regular intervals so that trends can be determined and/or special analyses performed at the request of the data purchaser.

Data is collected either by personal visit, postal questionnaire, telephone or, increasingly, by electronic means. One example of a particularly hi-tech consumer panel is *Superpanel* run by Taylor Nelson AGB, the largest UK consumer panel. Superpanel monitors consumer purchases in 8500 homes. Each house is equipped with a hand-held bar code reader which provides full details of items purchased and brought into the home. Details of the items purchased are retrieved over the telephone system each night making the information available to the data purchaser the next day. This rapid turn-around of data is essential for those monitoring the effects of special offers, targeted advertising, and general economic factors.

A competitor to Superpanel is *Homescan,* run by Nielsen which works in a similar fashion. Figure 6.11 is an excerpt from a typical Homescan analysis that might be provided to a data purchaser interested in the performance of their brand (in this case Brand B).

Activity 6.13

Does your organization use any third-party data? If so, what is it used for?

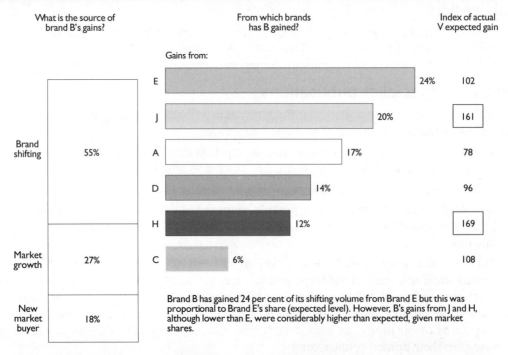

Figure 6.11 A page from an example Nielsen Homescan analysis

Casual research

Much information can be gained by casual research. As its name suggests, this is not formal research nor strictly primary data collection, but occurs 'naturally' in the course of carrying out one's work as a marketer. There are numerous sources of information available to the 'casual researcher' and some of these are listed below:

- *Conferences and fairs* These will often highlight previously unknown sources of data and may provide valuable information on competitive products and services via literature or direct contact.

- *Contacts* Friends and associates in the marketing business and other business sectors of interest can provide valuable information. For instance, a solicitor friend may be able to tell you the journal that most solicitors read or a friend in the CIM may be able to tell you where to go for a particular type of data if they have done similar research.

- *Special interest groups* Most societies and associations, such as the Market Research Society, have special interest groups (or SIGs) which can provide a valuable source of information. The MRS has twelve SIGs including postal research, census, international and financial. This category includes persons that subscribe to electronic mail 'news groups' (such as those on the internet) where information is frequently exchanged among forum members.

Activity 6.14

How did you first find out about the marketing course you are now enlisted on? What research did you carry out and how would you classify it?

On-line and electronic databases

In recent years, more and more data has become available via computer. A collection of such data is called a database. It is said to be an electronic database if it is available on disk or CD-ROM. It is called an on-line database if it is available 'live', usually via a modem and through the internet.

The ONS, for instance, now provide Databank – a service selling data in an electronic format. This allows you to get the most up-to-date data available and, because this system is so flexible, the ONS are able to offer a broader range of data than is possible in print. Another such service is StatBase®. Most of the surveys previously mentioned are also available in a complete or summary form on the internet. See the ONS web site for more details (www.ons.gov.uk).

Third-party suppliers are also offering data in an electronic form. For example, Dun & Bradstreet International offer a European Marketing Database with information on over three million businesses in 17 countries.

Most of the publications that are printed are now also available on-line; newspapers, journals, magazines and so on. In this form, information about specific topics can easily be found by searching for 'keywords'. For instance, fairly sophisticated news clipping services are now available whereby you choose the topics you want to read about and an electronic 'newspaper' is automatically assembled for you containing information from around the world according to your chosen 'keywords'. Such a service is the CompuServe 'Executive News Service'.

For those with access to a suitable computer, the advantages of on-line and electronic data outweigh all other secondary sources:

- On-line data is immediate and therefore up-to-date – financial prices, for instance, are often transmitted instantaneously.

- Information is global – data is available from much of the world in many languages.

- Open all hours – on-line services never close at night or for lunch.

- Data can be used directly – many statistical and spreadsheet computer packages are capable of loading on-line and electronic data for further analysis or presentation.

- Searching on-line and electronic data is quick and easy – within a matter of seconds it is possible to search the equivalent of more than 1000 conventional publications. This is sometimes cited as a disadvantage. A search on an ambiguous keyword, 'culture' for instance, may return articles covering everything from 'bacterial culture' to the 1980s pop group 'Culture Club'.

- Convenience – most places of work now have a computer capable of reading electronic data or obtaining data on-line. With such a facility, trips to the library and other data suppliers are greatly reduced saving time and resources.

National and international data

Many of the following notes about government data sources are specific to the UK. Supranational organizations are good sources for cross-national data; the UN and its daughter organizations, particularly UNESCO and the ILO (International Labour Organization), produce many tables of statistics, and the EU is becoming increasingly important as a source of European data. The ESRC Data Archive gives access to data from many North American studies as well as research done in the UK. The data sources listed here do not, in general, give you access to raw data that you can analyze for yourself, though in some cases you may be able to specify what kind of analysis you would like.

- The CIA World Fact Book is a well-known web resource, which gives basic data about almost every country in the world. Its web address is **www.odci.gov/cia/publications/ factbook/index.html**

- European Union information can be found at the Europa site; the English language version is at http://europa.eu.int/index-en.thm. Directorate-General X of the European Commission carries out a number of regular surveys: for information about these try **europa.eu.int/en/comm/ dg10/infcom/epo/org.html**. A well-known one is the Eurobarometer; there is an index to recent reports on the web at **europa.eu.int/en/comm/dg10/infcom/epo/eb.html**. The EU's comparative statistics on the labour market in Europe are also useful.

- A simple summary of facts and figures about the UK can be located at the UK in figures web page, whose address is **www.statistics.gov.uk/stats/ukinfigs/ukinfig.htm**. More detailed information comes from the Office of National Statistics' Statbase service at **www.statistics.gov.uk/statbase/mainmenu.asp**

- Most local councils in the UK have web pages that will include some statistics about their areas. Tagish Ltd have collected a list of local government web pages at **www.tagish.co.uk/ tagish/links/localgov.htm**.

Surveys with some access to underlying data

UK government statistics are collected by the Office of National Statistics. There is a comprehensive web site describing its activities at **www.ons.gov.uk**, and a catalogue of the statistics it makes available at **www.ons.gov.uk/data.htm**. For most of the following surveys, results are published in book form, and these regular publications can be found in most university libraries. However, accessing the data over the web can be much more convenient.

- UNESCO provides a variety of database services; there is an introduction to them at **www.unesco.org/general/eng/infoserv/db/index.html**

- Information about the International Labor Organization's database services is at **www.ilo.org/ public/english/190bibl/index.htm**

- The World Bank produces the World Tables of socio-economic data; for information see **www.ciesin.org/IC/wbank/wtables.html**

- The European Union's Europa website gives access to a number of databases of European statistics; for a list see **europa.eu.int/geninfo/search/databases_en.htm**

- The most important data source any national government provides is the Census. In the UK, researchers can access summary tables over the web, and also get access to the detailed data. Access for academic purposes is generally free at time of use; commercial users have to negotiate paid access. Academic users go through the Midas gateway at the university of Manchester (**www.midas.ac.uk**), and need to register as users of Midas first. In the UK as in many other countries, the main census takes place every ten years (2001 is a census year), but a percentage sample (still very large by academic standards) is taken in mid-cycle. Further details of census data availability are at **www.midas.ac.uk/census/census.html**

- The ONS makes regular economic data available in electronic format – but this is a subscription service: for information see **www.ons.gov.uk/databank.htm**

- The UK General Household Survey, which has been undertaken annually since 1971, covers health, housing, education, employment, and many other matters in detail than the Census.

Data from 1977 is available online through Midas; for information see **www.midas.ac.uk/surveys/ghs**

- The UK Family Expenditure Survey, undertaken annually since 1957, has its primary focus on the income and expenditure of households. Data is collected partly by interview and partly by diaries. The data is very detailed, including for example information about children's pocket money, gifts, books, etc. Raw data is available through Midas; for information see **www.midas.ac.uk/surveys/lfs**

- The UK National Child Development Study, also available through Midas; for information see **www.midas.ac.uk/surveys/ncds.**

- British Social Attitudes (an annual survey), whose results are held in the ESRC Data Archive

- Social Trends: An annual book publication summarising a variety of UK statistics. Underlying data is available to subscribers, see **www.ons.gov.uk/subdata/strends/index.htm**

- The Longitudinal Study, conducted by ONS, has its own website at **www.cls.ioe.ac.uk/Ls/lshomepage.html**

- The VSB panel study, being carried out in the Netherlands, focuses on economic behaviour and is of particular interest to economic psychologists. It is organized by CentER at the Katholieke Universiteit Brabant (Tilburg University), and it is possible for researchers to go and work at Tilburg for short periods to make use of the data. It is also possible to access the data over the Internet, though you have to register as a user.

Activity 6.15

Log on to the internet and access a search engine by typing the web address into your browser. Try using the Google search engine (type in www.google.com) if you are unfamiliar with any others. In the search box type in the words 'free market research data'. Does this return anything useful?

Competitive market intelligence

This is the general name given to data collected about your competitors. The information can be obtained in any one of the ways described above. Additional sources can include:

- *Competitive benchmarking* – where your product or service is compared with that of your competitors.

- *Company accounts* – these are lodged annually at Companies House and application to their Cardiff office can provide information on the financial performance of your rivals.

- *Patent applications* – these can provide a useful source of information about corporate technology developments.

- *Job advertisements* – these can provide useful information on the skills required by a competitor organization and their growth rate. However, it is not unknown for fake ads to be placed to allay fears about a struggling company!

It is most important to keep a 'watching brief' on the activities of your competitors so that you can spot opportunities, learn from their mistakes and not get caught out by new developments in the marketplace.

Activity 6.16

What market intelligence does your company have about its competitors? Do you think it has enough information? How might you find out more?

Limitations of secondary data

There are a number of general points to be aware of when using secondary data:

- *Age of the data* – some secondary data is offered for general sale only when it is of no more use to the leaders in the field. Historical data can be of use but only for certain types of research.

- *Survey method used* – not all surveys are well designed or administered. You should be aware of the survey details (for instance, number of respondees, geographical sampling, etc.) so that you can be confident that the data is reliable and representative for your purposes.

- *Original purpose of data* – the data may well have been collected by an organization with a particular viewpoint which may have led to bias in the collection method used. For example, surveys by the pro-smoking lobby always seem to find no link between smoking and disease!

Despite these limitations, secondary research is still a vital and valuable first step in any research activity. In many cases, it may be all the research that is needed.

Activity 6.17

Cut out and keep any graphs or data tables you find in magazines or newspapers or the internet. Look at the 'source' quoted for the data. Make a note of the type of data (social, financial, political and so on) and relate this to the source. Is the source private or government? Does the source specialize in this sort of data gathering, or not? If you wanted to find out details about the data not contained in the article, how would you contact the source?

Ethical and other issues concerned with the acquisition, manipulation, interpretation and application of customer-dynamic evidence

Ethical responsibilities of interviewers

The Market Research Society publishes a code of conduct which specifically addresses the responsibilities of those carrying out interviews. In summary interviewers shall:

- Be honest and not mislead the interviewee in order to procure information.

- Not use the information collected for any other purpose without the consent of the interviewee.

- Take steps to ensure that interviewees are not embarrassed or adversely affected as a direct result of an interview.

- Carry an identity card or badge including a photograph, name and organization.

- Send a leaflet, card or letter to the interviewee thanking them for taking part in the interview.

- In the case of telephone surveys, at the end of the interview, the name of the survey organization, a name and contact number should be given.

- Provide a means by which the interviewee may verify that the survey is genuine without incurring any cost.

- Allow an interviewee to withdraw from a survey. Where appropriate, the research organization shall confirm that their data has been destroyed.

- Make no calls in person or by telephone before 9am weekdays, 10am Sundays, or after 9pm on any other day unless an appointment has been made. Those carrying out research overseas should respect the equivalent customs of the host country.

- Only interview children under the age of 14 with the permission of their parents, guardian, or other person responsible for them (i.e. teacher). The responsible person shall be informed of the general content of the interview before the interview itself takes place.

The various types of research, such as mystery shopping, raise their own ethical issues. It is advised by the MRS, for example, that employees should be notified in advance that their employer intends to undertake mystery shopping. Guidelines also state that the results of mystery shopping research cannot be used for disciplinary purposes.

Data protection and confidentiality – legal issues

Principles of data confidentiality and protection are embodied in a new Act of particular relevance to market researchers – the *Data Protection Act 1998*. The following details are extracted from a factsheet which has been prepared by BSI/DISC in conjunction with the Office of the Data Protection Registrar (ODPR).

The new Act will implement the EU Data Protection Directive, which has been in effect in the UK from 24 October 1998, and will lay down detailed conditions for the processing of personal data and sensitive personal data, strengthen the rights of the individual, extend data protection to certain manual records and set new rules for the transfer of data outside the EU.

The new Act applies to anyone holding data about living individuals on computer or on some manual records. Those holding such personal data (i.e. data controllers) must comply with the eight data protection principles, and, with some exceptions, register with the Data Protection Commissioner (formerly the Registrar).

The new Act contains eight enforceable data protection principles. As previously, personal data must be processed fairly and lawfully. There are important new conditions that must be satisfied for the processing of personal data. Data can only be processed for example with consent or where it is necessary in certain specified circumstances.

- There are stricter conditions for the processing of sensitive data.
- As previously, data must be relevant, adequate and not excessive, accurate and up to date and kept for no longer than is necessary. These principles will, however, also apply to manual records.
- The security principle is strengthened with a specific requirement that data controllers have a formal contract with third-party processors.
- Exports of data are only permitted if an adequate level of protection can be guaranteed.
- The right of subject access to your own personal data has been retained and expanded.
- Explicit rights to object to processing, for example, for the purpose of direct marketing.
- The right not to be subject to purely automated decisions.
- Increased rights to seek compensation for breaches of the Act.

Further information on the Data Protection Act 1998 can be found on the web site http://www.open.gov.uk/dpr/dprhome.htm

Principles of data presentation – the use and abuse of statistics

Bias in the presentation of data

Data which is presented in a misleading fashion is said to be biased. Bias can be introduced unintentionally or, in certain cases, on purpose.

The Market Research Society's Code of Conduct states that:

A member shall not knowingly communicate conclusions from a given research project or service that are inconsistent with, or not warranted by, the data (paragraph B.3).

There are four main ways in which bias can occur:

1. Omission of information
2. Manipulation of graph axes
3. Failure to present comparative data
4. Using an inappropriate presentation method.

Omission of information

Omitting certain important information from a graph is not only bad practice but can mislead your audience. Three examples are given below:

- *Number of respondees* – Your audience should be told both the number of respondees to a survey and the proportion of those questioned whom responded. Different importance would be attached to a survey where only 20 people where questioned, and one where 2000 people were surveyed. Similarly, if a postal survey of 2000 attracted only 20 replies, we might suspect that the responses represented the opinions of some special interest group only.
- *Who the respondees are* – Whether your respondees are potential buyers of your product, potential users, randomly selected members of the public, or some other sub-set of the population, may change the interpretation of the results. For instance, comments on price are more relevant if they originate from potential buyers. Other respondees may have no idea of the market value of a particular product.

- *Scale units* – Your audience can be misled by the omission, or incomplete labelling of, the units used in your graph. For example the vertical axis on a sales graph should be clearly labelled with the units used. It may be that this axis represents some monetary value or unit sales. If monetary, it should be clear whether the figures given represent turnover, profit, or some other financial indicator.

Manipulating graph axes

Sometimes called 'stretching the truth', expanding or contracting the scales on chart axes can make small changes in values seem larger, or smaller, respectively. For example, the three sales graphs in Figure 6.12 all show the same data, the sales of 'Possum' cat food during the four quarters of 1994. Which do you think looks most impressive?

All the graphs are technically correct but give very different impressions of 'Possum' sales. To avoid misleading your audience, always present your data in a consistent fashion. For example, in the above example, a scale should be used which allows the data from a number of years to be plotted on the same chart. Thus, one could not be accused of exaggerating this year's sales. Also the zero point on the vertical (Y) scale should be labelled even if part of the vertical scale is then omitted, as long as this is clearly shown. In such an example, it may be more appropriate not to show absolute sales figures but give an indication of the percentage increase in sales during 1994 or moving averages.

Figure 6.12 *Three line graphs, showing sales of 'Possum' cat food, which demonstrate how expanding or contracting scales can mislead*

Failure to provide comparative data

Often data can only be accurately presented when a comparison is made with some 'base line' or other comparative data. This may require one, or more, sets of data to be displayed on the chart or the inclusion of a caption.

Suppose we wish to represent the number of shoppers using the 'Shop-Til-You-Drop' (STUD) chain of supermarkets. We would probably use a line graph as shown in Figure 6.13

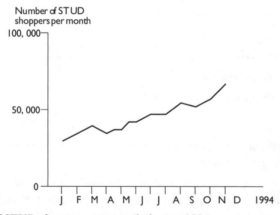

Figure 6.13 *Number of STUD shoppers per month during 1994*

On the face of it, this increase looks promising. However if, over the same period, the number of shoppers using supermarkets had risen greatly, the increase shown on the graph might actually represent a decrease in market share. Of course, the reverse is also possible. If there had been a general decline in the number of shoppers using supermarkets, the figures shown would indicate that STUD was doing very well indeed, 'bucking the trend'. To assist in the interpretation of this data, and to avoid being misled, it is therefore best to provide some comparative data, perhaps the performance of the competition or an indication of the general market trend.

Using an inappropriate presentation method

Using an inappropriate method of presentation can, under certain circumstances, mislead your audience. Suppose a survey is conducted to find out the most acceptable cost for annual tickets to a new leisure centre. Responses fall into a number of categories, the results could be shown with either a pie chart or bar chart, as shown in Figure 6.14.

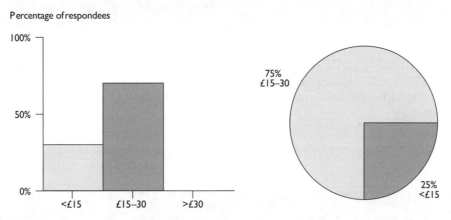

Figure 6.14 *Bar chart and pie chart showing responses to survey on leisure ticket cost*

The pie chart is, in a sense, misleading because it does not show the response categories where no one responded (in this case none of the respondees thought that more than £30 was an acceptable price). This information is lost in the pie chart presentation but appears, or should do, in a bar chart.

Summary

In this unit you have learned:

- About the different types of research
- How to go about conducting secondary research
- How to choose the primary research technique most suited to your research goals
- The best way to construct a survey tool
- To be aware and take account of the possible ethical and legal problems associated with investigative research.

Further study and examination preparation

Now undertake Question 7 from CIM Examination Session December 2000 to be found in the Exam paper Appendix.

Unit 7
Strategy and methods to produce customer focused behaviour

Objectives

- To understand the need for marketing strategy to be aligned with human resource management strategy.
- To understand the range of options that enable organizations to become customer focused.

This unit covers the following part of the Marketing Customer Interface syllabus:

- 2.2.1

Study guide

The unit introduces students to the link that needs to be made between marketing strategy and human resource management strategy in order to meet customer needs. The framework of thinking has been extended from the traditional marketing audit to the use of the 7S McKinsey framework and extended to the customer care audit. The customer care audit and the EFQM excellence model take into consideration aspects of the external and internal environment that need to be considered in order for a diagnosis to be made. This allows the organization to decide what it needs to do in order to improve. Following the diagnosis, a range or menu of different ideas are presented on the methods that organizations have used to encourage quality, and customer focused behaviour.

The unit is structured so that readers can see the following linkages between analysis, identification of core competencies, business philosophy, structure, technique and integration.

1. Analysis – marketing audit, 7S McKinsey framework, customer care audit, EFQM excellence model, success models, balanced scorecard.
2. Identification of core competencies, recruitment, performance management, training and development, rewards and recognition (see Unit 8, Additional techniques for mobilizing performance).
3. Philosophy – vision and leadership, culture, marketing, Kaizen, total quality management (TQM), relationship marketing (RM) (see Unit 10, Relationship marketing).
4. Structure – business process reengineering, value chain analysis, customer activity cycle (CAC).
5. Techniques – benchmark, ISO9000, just-in-time (JIT), IIP, MBO, empowerment, learning, 360° feedback, self-directed teams, Ishikowa.

Strategy

All organizations are in an interdependent relationship with their environments, and it is through the strategic planning process that an organization comes to understand what adaptations it should make in order to stay in business. Organizations need to consider the realities of both the external environment and the internal organizational environment and the way they interrelate (see Figure 7.1).

The development of services, technology, globalization, homogenization of markets, increased competition, mass customization and one-to-one marketing, and the advent of the more demanding customer, have meant that the discipline of marketing now needs to understand and develop new skills to enable the organization to manage the interface between itself and the external environment.

Creating strategy traditionally consists first of auditing the macro-environment, the micro-environment and the internal environment of the organization's marketing department.

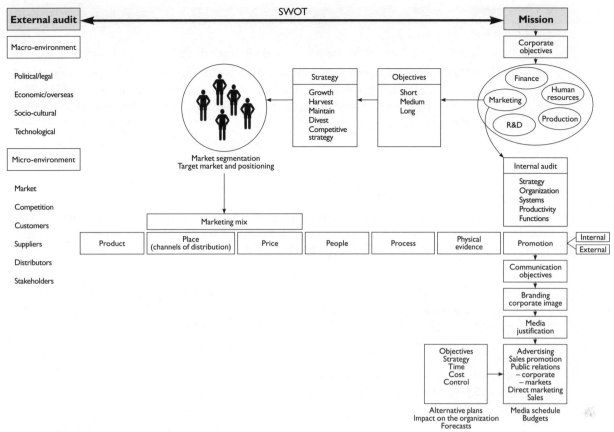

Figure 7.1 *Strategic and tactical framework illustrating the aspects considered in marketing planning.*
Oxford College of Marketing

Components of the audit

Within the general framework of the external and internal audits, Kotler et al. (1989) suggest there are six specific dimensions that are of direct interest to the auditor. These are:

1. The marketing environment audit, which involves an analysis of the major macro- and micro-economic forces and trends within the organization's task environment. This includes PEST factors and markets, customers, competitors, distributors, dealers, and suppliers.

2. The marketing strategy audit, which focuses upon a review of the organization's marketing objectives and strategy, with a view to determining how well suited they are to the current and forecasted market environment.

3. The marketing organization audit, which follows on from the previous point, and is concerned specifically with an evaluation of the structural capability of the organization and its suitability for implementing the strategy needed for the developing environment.

4. The marketing systems audit, which covers the quality of the organization's systems for analysis, planning and control.

5. The marketing productivity audit, which examines the profitability of different aspects of the marketing programme and the cost-effectiveness of various levels of marketing expenditure.

6. The marketing functions audit, involving a detailed evaluation of each of the elements of the marketing mix – the 7Ps outlined below.

Information from the audit is then analysed into the SWOT framework. From this analysis the process of matching organizational strengths to the market place and overcoming weaknesses takes place. The objectives are then set, strategies decided and the relevant marketing mix consisting of the 7Ps is put into place:

- Product/service
- Price
- Place (distribution channel)
- Promotion
- People

- Process
- Physical evidence

This analytical framework is covered in the *Marketing Operations 1990-2000* coursebook.

The traditional marketing audit touches only a limited number of organizational aspects mostly related to the marketing department. However, we now need to extend our thinking outside the marketing department into the whole organization and into the relationships surrounding it so that we create not only a market-focused marketing department, but also a market-focused organization.

Marketing needs to take a broader view and, as suggested by Christopher, Payne and Ballantyne, the 7S McKinsey framework can provide a model on which this view could be based.

The 7S McKinsey framework

Drawing on their work at McKinsey & Co., Waterman, Peters and Phillips (1981) argue that effective organizational change depends on the effective assignment of seven variables that have come to be known as the 7Ss, or 7S McKinsey framework. These are:

- Structure
- Strategy
- Systems (and procedures)
- Style (management style)
- Staff (people)
- Skills (corporate strengths and skills)
- Shared values/superordinate goals.

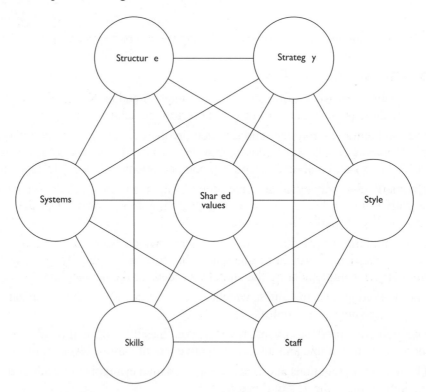

Figure 7.2 *7S McKinsey framework*

The strategic and tactical dimension of market planning can be covered in the traditional framework illustrated in Figure 7.2. However, the 7S framework can be adapted to take into account the variables that need to be aligned to create a model that extends beyond the management of marketing to managing an organization that has a marketing focus.

Customer care audit (OxfordCollegeofMarketing.ac.uk)

It is suggested that the specific elements outlined in the McKinsey framework cover shared values, structure, style, staff, skills training and systems that could be used as the basic structure for conducting a customer care audit.

This audit needs to take place within the context of the external environment – macro- and micro-, so that an understanding of how environmental pressures and various relationships can affect the feelings, behaviour and the effectiveness of the people working within the organization.

The difference between this audit and the traditional marketing audit is that it focuses mainly on the factors that can effect processes and positive feelings within the organization that may ultimately impact on customers and operational effectiveness. It takes marketing out of the box of the 7Ps and puts it firmly into the centre of the organizational strategy.

The presenting problem – customer complaints

When an organization has a problem with customer care it needs to look at the whole organization. It is no use at all to go in for a mere facelift or trying to put a smile on Tutankhamun by redoing the corporate image! Loss of customers and customer complaints must be treated as the presenting symptoms, and in order to carry out a proper diagnosis a proper audit needs to be done.

From the text below it can be seen it is necessary to approach the organization in a number of ways.

External environmental factors affecting the organization

Macro-environment

Political

Political groups reflect the values and beliefs of the people they represent. What is happening politically that will affect the way in which people expect to be treated in their role as customers, citizens, passengers, patients, employees and so on? How do these dominant values and beliefs influence the way in which the organization conducts itself in the wider environment? For example, what do people feel that government should be doing more of? Does your organization need to think in terms of helping to create local job schemes, supporting charity, supporting housing, a disabled scheme, etc?

Legal

What laws are being enacted that will affect people's legal rights as customers and as employees? For example, what is happening with pollution control, equal opportunity, disability and anything else related to the way in which the organization conducts itself internally that will influence the way it is perceived in the wider environment and affect the way employees feel about their own organizational practices?

Economic

What effect is the economy having on customers in terms of their mood and a propensity to spend? How does the mood of the country affect the way in which they treat front-line staff? What effect is high/low unemployment having on employees' morale?

Overseas

What effect is global competition having on the organization and how are employees reacting to an increasingly competitive environment? Is the organization thinking globally? Is management creating some understanding in the workplace about the external environment and the need to adapt and integrate their work practices in a different way? How will the process of change affect people?

Socio demographic/cultural

What effect is a multicultural company having on different national groups and the way in which they are managed? How is cultural difference dealt with in the organization? Does the organizational culture override the national culture?

How does culture affect frontline staff? Are frontline staff aware of how to behave in different circumstances? Are frontline staff aware of how their own projections and tendency to stereotype can interfere in a genuine role relationship? Is the organization training staff to reflect and understand their own reactions to customer behaviour? Is the organization adapting its HR policies to match the needs, values and lifestyle of younger employees?

Technology

What changes are there in technology? How is the company approaching the use of technology? How will technology affect the working of groups? What effect is this having on staff and are there any behavioural changes that they need to adopt while dealing with customers? What new skills need to be learned? What action is the organization taking to create this understanding?

Environmental concerns

What concerns are there about the environment? What effect are environmental practices within the organization having on staff? How is the company responding to this, and to the wider environmental concerns of staff? What action is the organization taking to improve its own work practices? Do their employees feel proud of what they are doing? What action is the organization taking to ensure this?

Micro-environment

Market

- What effect are conditions in the market having on employees?
- How do employees handle themselves in a new market as opposed to a mature market? If the market is depressed what effect is this having on employees and does this mood communicate itself to customers and affect their buying?
- Are employees aware of the position their organization holds in the market and what they need to do to increase income and reduce costs? How does this understanding affect them?
- What action is being taken by the organization to bring some understanding of the marketplace to employees?

Competition

- Does the organization know what the competition is doing? What is it doing to bring this knowledge to its employees, so that they can discuss what they need to do in order to become more competitive, especially in relation to customer retention? Can competition be defined globally?
- What effect are the organization's own competitive strategies and tactics having on its employees? How do they feel about the way in which their organization behaves?

Customers

- Does the organization understand the needs and wants of its target market?

  Ask customers If you are starting from scratch, carry out some market research:

  1. Old customers – those who have left
  2. Existing customers
  3. Potential new customers
  4. Competitors' customers.

  If you are dealing with an organization you will need to ask people in the decision-making unit or take another slice of the organization consisting of people who are using the service or interact with it in some way.

  If potential new customers are dealing with the competition find out from them what they get and what they like and dislike. Find out from old customers why they have left. Market research is discussed in detail in other units. Use your research to find new ways of segmenting your market.

- Does the organization create its products and services from the customer's point of view?
- Does the organization develop customer relationships and retain the loyalty of existing customers?
- Is market research related to customer care ongoing – customer care questionnaires, monitoring of complaints, focus groups, random customer surveys, mystery shopper, complaint analysis, operational measures such as time deliveries, abandoned callouts, time to turn round correspondence, etc. Is this information fed back into the organization to the people who look after customers, and acted upon?
- Are standards specified to customers so they know what to expect?
- How do front-line staff respond to customers' needs and buying processes?
- Are there any particular behavioural skills that staff need to know about in order to cope competently with their customer group? What training is the organization giving staff to help them do this?

- What ongoing support does management give staff who have to deal with difficult or unpleasant situations?
- Do you understand the value of customers and their profitability?

Suppliers

- How do suppliers behave towards the organization?
- What sort of relationship does the organization seek to have with its suppliers and vice versa?
- Are they treated as adversaries or are they seen as part of the whole quality system?
- Are relationships long term?
- How committed are suppliers to the organization?
- What actions has the organization taken to establish long-term relationships with its suppliers?

Distributors

- How do distributors behave towards the organization and vice versa?
- Is there any inter-group conflict within the distribution channel?
- How is conflict managed and resolved?
- Are customer needs being met within the distribution chain?
- What action has the organization taken to establish long-term relationships with its distributors?

Stakeholders

- Which stakeholders present particular opportunities or problems for the organization?
- What steps has the organization taken to satisfy their concerns?
- What effect is the behaviour of stakeholders having on employees?

Internal analysis of the organization

The approach to internal factors is based on the use of the 7S McKinsey framework as an analytical model and adapted by Rosemary Phipps, www.OxfordCollegeofMarketing.ac.uk.

Strategy

- Objectives – is there agreement on reaching them?
- Portfolio planning – is there agreement on the following – growth, harvest, maintain, divest, new product development, partnering?
- Resources – is there agreement on money, people, machines? Are there any? Is there enough?
- Market segmentation – is there agreement on which segments are developed, and by whom?
- Value chain – is there agreement on where value is being created in the organization?
- Generic strategy – is there agreement on whether the organization is a cost, a differentiator, or a focus cost, or focus differentiator?
- Competitive position – is there agreement on whether the organization is a leader, challenger, follower or niche player?
- Market planning – is there agreement about the methods and frequency this is carried out?

Shared values

Mission statement

- Does the mission statement have values and behaviour written into it that relate to customer care? Is marketing and the principle of meeting customer's needs accepted as a business philosophy?
- Is the mission statement something that employees can visualize, articulate and internalize so that it gives them a sense of purpose and an expectation of success?
- Does each job description carry the mission statement with its customer care objectives outlined in such a way that employees are able to translate it into clear actions? Can the success of these actions be quantified and be of use in the appraisal process.

Culture

- Is there a philosophy within the organization of putting customer needs first?
- Is there a culture of innovation and learning?
- Is this culture embodied in policy, routines and rituals?
- What sorts of stories circulate around the organization about its treatment of customers – are they positive or negative?

Corporate image

- Is there any conflict between the image the organization presents and the way employees perceive it to be? How does this dissonance affect them?
- How are other symbols used to link a customer-focused culture with customer perception and employees' perception?

Structure

Organizational structure

- Does the organization have an agile, simple structure that will help it to follow up opportunities?
- Are the marketing positions market segment or key account manager?
- Is the structure able to give fast support to customers?
- Does the work process (value chain) support the needs of the customers' value chain?
- Are roles within the organization interlinked to facilitate a customer-centred focus?
- Does the structure make it easy to get in touch with decision makers?

Style

Leadership

- Does the CEO spend time with customers?
- Does the CEO champion customer care?
- Does the CEO (and management) create a climate of high morale?
- Is customer service represented at top management level?
- Does the CEO view products as part of an integrated product and service offering?
- Does the CEO ensure that non-marketing staff are rotated through the organization to customer contact points?

Management

- Does management make any provision to help employees discuss and come to terms with any stress and anxiety that can arise from customer contact? Are employees encouraged to admit to such stress?
- Does attending to customers' needs and employees' well-being take priority in the internal running of the organization?
- Do managers have the skills to manage people (motivation, empowerment, discipline, coaching, facilitating, counselling, etc.)?

Systems

Recruitment and induction

- Are recruitment practices geared towards acquiring people who understand about marketing and customer care?
- When people join the company does the induction process reinforce the climate and culture the organization wishes to perpetuate?

Appraisal and reward

- Is the appraisal process linked to key performance indicators and other customer care issues?
- Is the reward system linked to customer retention, customer care and other key performance indicators?

Information, communication, decision making and financial

- Are systems for information, communication and decision making focused to enable the meeting of customers' needs?
- Are these systems used to formulate marketing strategy?

Skills

- Has the organization identified its core competencies?
- Is training in place that enables employees to perform well in a customer-focused way?
- Is marketing and customer care (assertiveness, conflict management, negotiation, etc.) training given?
- Are staff trained to expand their role and empower themselves in a manner in line with the organizational objectives?
- Are managers trained to delegate and empower front-line staff? Are they doing it, not just talking about it?

Staff

Interfunctional relationships – inter group

- Is there harmony between groups?
- Are there any interfunctional conflicts that are affecting customer care?
- Are groups given the opportunity to mix and meet professionally and socially?
- Do cross-functional groups work well together?

Group – intra group

- Is there a good atmosphere in front-line teams?
- Do they understand how to work in a team?
- Do they all share the same understanding of what it means to be successful as an individual and as a team member?
- Are people told how they are doing so they can know what they are achieving?
- Are customer complaints fed back to the team so they can learn from experience?
- Is any role conflict within the team discussed so that jobs are not left undone?

Individual employees

- Do employees working directly with customers enjoy their work?
- Are employees empowered and trained to be able to deal with customers flexibly?
- Does the job description carry specific and measurable customer care objectives?
- Is the mission statement translated into actionable tasks?
- Do employees understand what they need to do in order to be successful within the organization and with customers?
- Are employees encouraged to think about their customer care relationships in order to improve their ability to relate to customers?
- Do all employees understand that customer care is the responsibility of the whole organization?
- Do employees understand that customer care takes precedence over the internal needs of the business?
- Do people agree on what they must do in order to keep customers satisfied?
- Is there any intra-role conflict (for example, employees being asked to carry out policies with which they disagree)?
- Are individuals empowered to expand their role?
- Are employees motivated and skilled so that they continually improve their processes, quality and response times?

Once the audit is carried out the marketer will become aware of the organizational fit, and the internal linkages that enable an organization to become more effective to meet the needs of the customers.

The organization will then be able to view its products and services not only in terms of the behavioural aspects discussed in the customer care audit and look after its intangible assets, but also in terms of understanding the new capabilities it needs to develop in order to be successful. From this analysis you will be able to decide on the relevant philosophy structure, technique, managerial process, market research, customer relationship programme, internal marketing programme, customer care programme, marketing mix and other aspects to achieve customer focus.

The EFQM excellence model (previously EFQM business excellence model)

A core approach to analysing organizational performance is the model designed by the European Foundation for Quality Management. The EFQM excellence model (see Figure 7.3) has become best practice in leading organizations and helps you to understand the cause of change and effect within the business and that matters if you are the managing director or a newly appointed sales assistant.

This model provides a framework for assessment and continuous improvement for all organizations, whatever their size or type, and whether they are in the public, private or voluntary sectors. It focuses on a number of performance measures which range from financial and operational areas to the following commonly accepted factors of measuring business excellence. These are leadership, people management, policy and strategy, partnerships and resources, business processes, customer satisfaction, people satisfaction, impact on society, and key performance business results. The data collected involves both qualitative and quantitative measures of performance, giving a comprehensive initial analysis of an organization's situation. Information about the model can be obtained directly from http://efqm.org and your local Business Link.

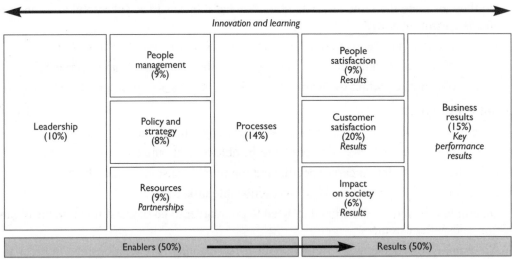

Figure 7.3 *EFQM excellence model.* For further information: http://efqm.org

Self assessment can be taken by a whole organization, or by a department or division or operational unit. It allows an organization to identify both its strengths and those areas in which improvement can be made. It provides an effective means of coordinating and integrating an organization's quality initiatives.

The benefits of self-assessment against the excellence model can include:

- More focused leadership
- Development of concise action plans
- Greater motivation of people
- Identification of process improvement opportunities
- Direct input to the business planning process

- More integrated policy and strategy development
- Quantification of the impact of improved customer satisfaction on organizational performance.

There are various ways to undertake self-assessment and the method you adopt will depend on the culture and objectives of your organization. There is a range of software and paper-based products. The foundation runs workshops, conferences and seminars to help choose the best way for each organization to take.

There is a questionnaire (available from EFQM consultants) and the data from it allows you to come up with an analysis of the organization. This will enable you to pinpoint areas that need to be improved. The relevant techniques can then be used in order to improve performance.

The EFQM excellence model and the balance scorecard (see Figure 7.4) will, in the future, be joined together to form a new business model.

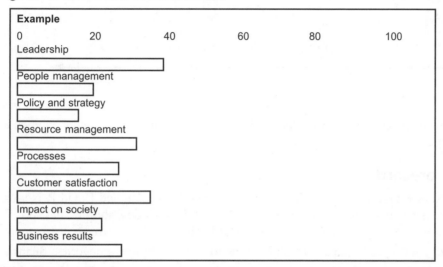

Figure 7.4

Success models – improving the quality and performance of businesses

Background

The term 'success model' comes from the RSA inquiry report, *Tomorrow's Company* and is central to their definition of 'inclusivity' – their vision for how organizations will sustain competitive success in the future. Tomorrow's company 'uses its stated purpose and values, and the understanding of the importance of each [Stakeholder] relationship to develop its own Success Model from which it can generate a meaningful framework for performance management'.

What is the success model approach?

Essentially the success model approach (see Figure 7.5) is a diagnostic which attempts to help managers to understand an organization or a team more deeply so as to plan *effective* change. In particular to identify:

- The business agenda – what matters and why?
- The people agenda – what value is added and by whom (internal and external)?
- The culture – how does the organization make decisions, learn and change?

The outputs from the diagnostic are:

- A diagrammatic framework showing all the relationships, interdependent activities and how these link to the desired outcome (vision/mission?).
- A scorecard which captures the key measurements necessary to plot that the right value is being added in every part – in order to aid learning.

The success model approach helps clients to focus on and identify more definite and measured change and improvement in:

- Commercial performance (sales and productivity)
- Internal/external customer ratings (and loyalty)
- People commitment and capability.

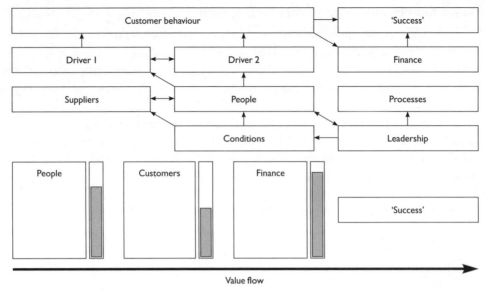

Figure 7.5 *The Oxford Group's Success Model*

In particular the use of the success model has helped to identify and accelerate the implementation of real learning and change.

The balanced scorecard

The balanced scorecard (see Figure 7.6) was developed by Robert S. Kaplan and David P. Norton. The balanced scorecard is a management system that can channel the energies, abilities and specific knowledge held by people throughout the organization toward achieving long-term strategic goals.

The balanced scorecard guides performance and shows how to measure in four categories: financial performance, customer knowledge, internal business processes, and learning and growth – to align individual, organizational, and cross-departmental initiatives and to identify new processes for meeting customer and shareholder objectives.

The balance scorecard emphasizes that financial and non-financial measures must be part of the information system for employees at all levels of the organization. Front-line employees must understand the financial consequences of their decisions and actions; senior executives must understand the drivers of long-term financial success.

The objectives and measures for the balanced scorecard are derived from the top-down process driven by the mission and strategy of the business unit and it translates mission and strategy into tangible objectives and measures.

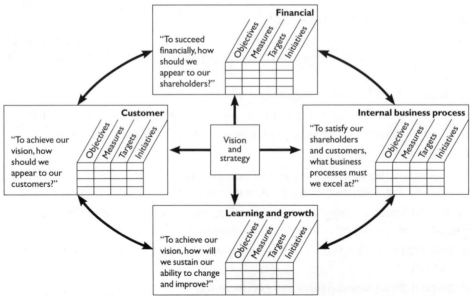

Figure 7.6 *Source: Robert S. Kaplan and David P. Norton, 'Using the Balanced Scorecard as a Strategic Management System', Harvard Business Review (January- February 1996): 76. Reprinted with permission*

As you can see from Figure 7.6 the balanced scorecard provides a framework to translate a strategy into operational terms. It can then be used to:

- Clarify strategy
- Gain consensus
- Communicate strategy to the organization
- Align departmental and personal goals to the strategy
- Link strategic objectives to long-term targets and annual budgets
- Identify and align strategic initiatives
- Perform periodic and systematic strategic reviews
- Obtain feedback to learn about and improve strategy.

Cause and effect relationships

The balanced scorecard enables an organization to see causal relationships. Figure 7.7 illusrates this perspective. Customer measures are shown in Figure 7.8.

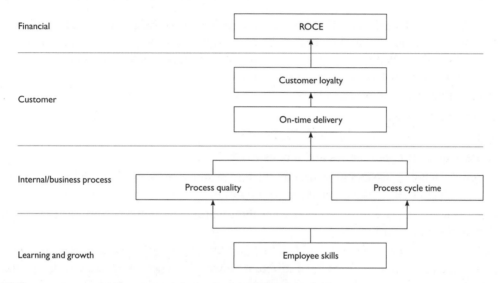

Figure 7.7

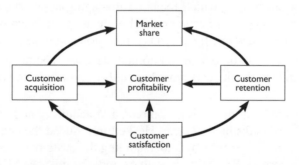

Market share	Reflects the proportion of business in a given market (in terms of number of customers, dollars spent, or unit volume sold) that a business unit sells.
Customer acquisition	Measures, in absolute or relative terms, the rate at which a business unit attracts or wins new customers or business.
Customer retention	Tracks, in absolute or relative terms, the rate at which a business unit retains or maintains ongoing relationships with its customers.
Customer satisfaction	Assesses the satisfaction level of customers along specific performance criteria within the value proposition.
Customer profitability	Measures the net profit of a customer, or a segment, after allowing for the unique expenses required to support that customer.

Figure 7.8 *The customer perspective – core measures. Source: The Balanced Scorecard, Kaplan and Norton, Harvard Business School Press, 1996*

The need for a performance management system in the public sector

Best value has placed authorities in the position of having to implement some form of performance management system. Legislation is to be introduced which will require authorities to adopt a performance measurement framework which will necessitate a continuing need to undertake fundamental performance reviews (FPRs) for all services (see Figure 7.9).

For further information see **www.barony.co.uk** or e-mail barry.hill @barony.co.uk

Financial perspective How should we appear to those who fund the services?		Customer perspective How should we appear to our stakeholders who receive the service?	
Actions	Performance measures	Actions	Performance measures
Continuous improvement perspective How can we sustain our ability to grow and improve?		Internal business perspective What service delivery processes must we excel at?	
Actions	Performance measures	Actions	Performance measures

Figure 7.9

Review

Marketing audits, SWOT analysis, EFQM, success models and the balanced scorecard allow us to take a systematic, critically unbiased review of the basic objectives and policies of the company, the marketing function, the organization, the finance methods, procedures and personnel employed to implement those policies and to achieve those objectives.

The objectives of the analysis are as follows:

1. Know where we are now

2. Understand our own strengths and weaknesses

3. Appreciate what opportunities and threats exist

4. Determine whether we can improve our existing business by rectifying weaknesses and capitalizing on strengths, taking advantage of opportunities and preparing for threats.

The remedies that are taken will depend on what the organization believes and understands to be effective for its particular business.

In their book, McKinsey consultants John Hagel III and Marc Singer (*Net Worth,* Harvard Business Press, 1999) argue that different firms have different economic logic. There are customer relationship businesses, which focus on building and maintaining relationships with customers. There are infrastructure management businesses, which focus on managing assets such as factories to minimize costs and maximize revenues where economies of scale are vital. There are product innovation and commercialization businesses, where the focus is innovation and where being first is the essence.

Transaction marketing with its short time focus on immediate sales is being questioned as companies are now beginning to understand that it costs more to acquire a new customer than it does to keep an old one.

Activity-based costing, in which all the activities directed at acquiring and maintaining a customer are separately costed, makes this distinction clear. Heskett introduced the concept of market economies, by which he means achieving results by understanding the customers instead of by concentrating on developing scale economies. Reichald gives an example of this: 'At MBNA (in the credit card business in the USA), a 5 per cent increase in retention grows the company's profit by 60 per cent by the fifth year' (Christian Gronroos, MCB University Press, *From Marketing to Relationship Marketing – towards a paradigm shift in marketing*). The questions that businesses must now ask are:

1. Which customers do I want to do business with?

2. With which ones can I make a profit?

3. How do I protect my profit?

4. Which tasks am I going to carry out myself and which ones will I outsource or work with a business partner?

The marketing mix is recognized as having limitations especially in service sectors where work systems have to be more directly responsive to customers, and non-routine decision making has to be given to front-line staff in order to maintain flexibility.

Service, quality and the management of costs are key strategic issues on which to establish competitiveness and maintain differentiation in the market place.

Matching business strategies, employee role behaviour and HRM policies

Human resource strategy involves deciding on the way in which the people in the organization are managed. These ideas are then translated into policies and procedures that are integrated with the business strategy (see Table 7.1). Porter (1974) defines three generic business strategies – and each generic strategy implies different skills and requirements for success. These would translate into different organizational structures and cultures. Schuler and Jackson (1987) summarize these approaches.

Environment

Human resource strategy also needs to be placed within the context of the external environment, and display an understanding of what is happening within the macro- and micro-environments. It also needs to be considered in relation to situational factors within the organization. Figure 7.10 illustrates this process.

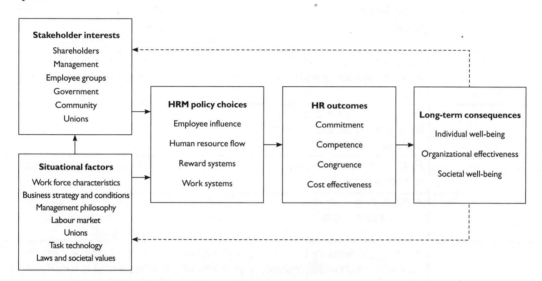

Figure 7.10 The Harvard Framework for human resource management. *Managing Human Assets by Michael Beer, Bert Spector, Paul R. Lawrence, D. Quinn Mills, Richard E. Walton. The Free Press, 1984*

Methods to stimulate customer-focused behaviour

Following on from the analysis of the organization's strengths and weaknesses using a combination of the marketing audit, customer care audit and EFQM excellence model, the organization would think about its human resource policies in relation to its competitive positioning and its core competencies (core competencies are covered in the unit 'Additional techniques for mobilizing performance').

The organization would then consider its guiding philosophy and structure and then decide on the relevant techniques to stimulate customer-focused behaviour.

Before discussing these philosophies and techniques we will first need to place the development of management ideas into an historical context.

Historical development of ideas – the search for quality

Since the early days of industrialization and mass production there has been a struggle between making the most of mechanized production and technology and creating jobs which enrich human experience.

Economic pressure and the culture in which we live have allowed technology and machines to dominate at work, so that very many workers have no opportunity to use all their abilities and gain very little satisfaction from their work. However, the growth of service industries is forcing businesses to look at the way in which they have been influenced by the ideas of organizing labour in mechanized production, and to rethink and create new ways of dealing with people at work and of improving quality.

Table 7.1 Business strategies, and associated employee role behaviour and HRM policies

Strategy	Employee role behaviour	HRM policies
1 Innovation	A high degree of creative behaviour	Jobs that require close interaction and coordination among groups of individuals
	Long-term focus	Performance appraisals that are more likely to reflect longer-term and group-based achievements
	A relatively high level of cooperative, interdependent behaviour	Jobs that allow employees to develop skills that can be used in other positions in the firm
		Compensation systems that emphasize internal equity rather than external or market-based equity
	A moderate concern for quality	Pay rates tend to be low, but allow employees to be stockholders and have more freedom to choose the mix of components that make up their pay package
	A moderate concern for quantity and for processes and results	Broad career paths to reinforce the development of a broad range of skills
	A greater degree of risk-taking; a higher tolerance of ambiguity and unpredictability	
2 Quality enhancement	Relatively repetitive and predictable behaviours	Relatively fixed and explicit job descriptions
	A more long-term or intermediate focus	High levels of employee participation in decisions relevant to immediate work conditions and the job itself
	A moderate amount of cooperative, interdependent behaviour	A mix of individual and group criteria for performance appraizal that is mostly short term and result oriented
	A high concern for quality	A relatively egalitarian treatment of employees and some guarantees of employment security
	A modest concern for quantity of output	Extensive and continuous training and development of employees
	High concern for process; low risk-taking activity; commitment to the goals of the organization	
3 Cost reduction	Relatively repetitive and predictable behaviour	Relatively fixed and explicit job descriptions that allow little room for ambiguity
	A rather short-term focus	Narrowly designed jobs and narrowly defined career paths that encourage specialization, expertise and efficiency
	Primarily autonomous or individual activity	Short-term results-oriented performance appraisals
	Modest concern for quality	Close monitoring of market pay levels for use in making compensation decisions
	High concern for quantity of output	Minimal levels of employee training and development
	Primary concern for results; low risk-taking activity; relatively high degree of comfort with stability	

Customer satisfaction

The determining of strategy, especially a competitive one, requires an understanding of what customers value, or might value, and at what price. Costs, quality and price are inextricably linked. Quality is the means by which a firm sustains its position among competing offers over time and it is quality that gains uniqueness and value in the eyes of the customer.

In an increasingly competitive world, the distinguishing factor between organizations is often the service they provide for their customers or clients. This not only affects retail and sales outlets, but every aspect of industry and institutional life. All members of an organization, not only staff in direct contact with customers, have a part to play in improving standards of quality.

Organizational efficiency

The question of creating organizational efficiency can be considered in different ways as this brief history shows.

We often talk about organizations as if they were machines – efficient, reliable and predictable. But they are not, and with the development on the emphasis of service and relationships within the area of business, it would be foolish to think they are.

Until the nineteenth century craftspeople understood and carried out their tasks in different environments, but with the Industrial Revolution there was an increasing trend towards bureaucratization and routinization of life generally. The diversity, complexity and size of operations meant that tasks were splintered and knowledge was channelled into specific tasks – to match the efficiency of machines and maximize profits. Changes were made to the design and control of work so that people no longer organized their own work, and the discretion of the workers was reduced in favour of control by their machines and supervisors. The whole shift was to take responsibility for the organization of work, from the worker, to the managers, who would do all the thinking and then train the worker to do it effectively; workers would then be monitored.

The most famous of these management gurus was Taylor (1856-1917) and he was fond of telling his workers: 'You are not supposed to think – there are other people paid for thinking around here'. This method of working splits the worker and separates the hand from the brain. What was lost was the idea that people have a natural ability to work and manage their own resources, that hand and brain are able to work together and should be encouraged to do so. The whole thrust of many of the management theories of the time was that organizations can and should be rational, efficient systems – little attention was given to the human aspects.

Organizations where people are treated as machines have the following limitations (Gareth Morgan, *Images of Organizations,* Sage):

- They have difficulty adapting
- Workers are forced into mindless unquestioning attitudes
- Personal interests take precedence over organizational goals
- They can have a detrimental effect on the workforce, especially those in the lower levels of the hierarchy.

However, if the work environment is stable, the task simple and repetitive precision is required, a mechanistic approach can work efficiently – provided that the human machine parts are willing to do as they are told. Management must also live with the consequences. There are some organizations where knowledge and process skill is protected and delivered successfully as these examples show but in different ways!

Asda

Archie Norman, chairman of Asda, believes that good relations with customers depend on good relations with employees. In his business he says 'it means bringing back those old craft skills to which we can all relate and which are fulfilling and are challenging. Being a master baker is a really difficult thing – colleagues are entitled to enrich themselves in their work and to make it more interesting and varied' (Annual Convention 1998).

McDonald's – developing and transferring best practices

Source: Jonathan D. Day and James C. Wendler (1998) 'Best practice and beyond: knowledge strategies', *McKinsey Quarterly*, 1, 19-25, **http://www.mckinseyquarterly.com**

In many service industries, the ability to identify best practices and spread them across a dispersed network of locations is a key driver of value. Such a strategy can create powerful brands that are continually refreshed as knowledge about how to serve customers better travels across the network. In these circumstances, it may be all but impossible to tell whether value has been created by the brand or by knowledge. The two are inseparable. How much does McDonald's brand depend on, say, network-wide knowledge of how best to cook French fries?

The thoroughness of McDonald's best practice approach is legendary. By the time restaurant managers attend Hamburger University in Illinois, they will have received between 1500 and 3000 hours of regional training.

The company also gets comparable outlets to work together to benchmark performance, set aspirations, and make product mix and service decisions. These peer groups are supported by a real-time information system that transmits sales to headquarters hourly. Thanks to this system, the location of group members is immaterial; one group could include branches in Warsaw and Rio de Janeiro. At the same time, the system enables corporate headquarters to keep a tight grip on the valuable knowledge that links its outlets.

However, McDonald's is pursuing an essentially centralist model in which the corporation defines rigid standards not only for its products but for the processes that deliver them. The company's squabbles with franchisees over the introduction of the Arch Deluxe product and the 55 cent sandwich promotion illustrates the degree to which this formula can conflict with entrepreneurialism.

Traditional wisdom maintained that knowledge is held implicitly in the management role and tasks such as analyzing, planning and organizing, controlling output and measuring effectiveness can only be done by managers. Current thinking, with its emphasis on relationship management and empowerment places many of these tasks at the front line. Isabel Menzies Lythe says 'rather like a football team – the manager is not on the field passing the ball, the captain and the team are. However, time framework is an important decider. Traditional management relates to a different time framework. The football team has to do it now'.

Many franchising systems have used the Tayloristic approach, and scientific methods to determine how work should be performed with manuals that set standards providing a recipe for success, provided the service or product can be controlled in this way. Surgical wards, courier firms, organizations in which precision, safety and clear accountability are at a premium, are often able to implement mechanistic approaches successfully, at least in certain aspects of their operations (Gareth Morgan).

However, when circumstances keep changing and flexibility and creativity are valued, a different type of response will be needed. Standardized procedures and bureaucratic hierarchies are not the best way to deal with an environment that is constantly changing and where responsiveness is valued.

Taylor's scientific management came under criticism and the Human Relations School suggested that workers should be involved in decision making and could carry out work without close supervision because they could become self-motivated.

The 1960s brought job enrichment, the 1970s an interest in industrial democracy and legislative backing (though not in the UK) and the 1980s emphasized quality circles, team briefing and profit sharing. The 1980s also heralded the dawn of the enterprise culture and theorists such as Peters encouraged businesses to involve everyone in everything and to lead by empowering people. *In Search of Excellence* (Peters and Waterman, 1982) emphasized autonomy and entrepreneurship and managers were told to trust and involve employees. The end of hierarchy was heralded; delayering and decentralization became the thing to do. In the meantime an interest in the Japanese Kaizen, and total quality management approach introduced ideas of bottom-up identification of problems and TQM began to empower by delegating aspects of the managerial role to employees and giving them responsibility for quality control. Managers became facilitators, team work and participation were encouraged. Responsibility and accountability were delegated and pride, job satisfaction and quality were said to improve.

Human resource management now has a range of options that have been developed over the years. Continuous relationship marketing (where applicable) seeks to embed these relationships so they are ongoing.

The challenge to increase productivity, lower costs and improve quality within a global framework of increased competition needs a workforce who can enable an organization to differentiate on quality and add value by providing superior service. Organizations if they choose to go along this route will need to build cultures that are flexible, built on trust, cooperation and a commitment to organizational goals. Organizations that follow another model can choose to minimize costs by exploiting insecurity over employment so that the balance of power lies within the hands of the managers and changes to working practices can be more easily implemented. Other approaches could include:

- Lowering wages in order to become more competitive.
- Laying staff off.
- Speeding up work processes.
- Investing in technology so as to increase output and reduce labour costs.
- Relocating plant to a country where wages are low, labour unorganized and passive and workplace standards low (and leave the government and local community in the home country to pick up the pieces).
- Rewarding employees so what they earn is related to output (piecework, speeding up the assembly line, profit share or share ownership).
- Introducing a market model into the workplace so people in the same organization are pitted against each other.

Atkinson's flexible firm model provides a dual labour market approach with the distinction between 'core' (primary) and 'peripheral' (secondary) groups of workers. These ideas have been challenged on ideological and empirical grounds (Williams, 1993). But the fact remains – if you are a core worker with the relevant skills and knowledge and are in high demand, life may be good. Peripheral workers will face a life that is less secure.

There are a number of strategic themes that run through the various approaches used by organizations to create customer-focused behaviour. Many are interlinked and organizations will choose and use what they need in order to fulfil their objectives.

They include:

- Philosophies:
  - Vision and leadership
  - Culture
  - Kaizen
  - Total quality management (TQM)
  - The marketing philosophy that puts customer needs at the heart of the business is not discussed here
  - The learning organization
  - Relationship marketing (see Unit 10, Relationship marketing).
- Structure:
  - Business process re-engineering (BPR)
  - Value chain
  - Customer activity cycle.
- Techniques:
  - Benchmarking
  - ISO 9000
  - Just-in-time production and distribution systems
  - Investors in People (IIP)
  - Flexibility
  - 360° feedback systems
  - Self-directed teams
  - MBO
  - Employee empowerment
  - Time-based competition, lean production/lean enterprise, and activity-based cost management.

Most of these ideas are discussed in the remainder of this unit, but it is important to understand that although some are applicable to all organizations, others may not be. Many organizations have more than one initiative running at a time. The organization decides on its core competencies, its philosophy and then uses the most suitable measurements and technique to ensure that it is achieving relevant results. Organizational structure, the role of the manager and many other aspects of organizational life are contextual. Do not be lulled into uncritically accepting what you read.

Philosophy

Vision and leadership

As you can see from Figure 7.22 at the end of the unit the role of the leader is key to creating any organization. The leader chooses markets, decides on roles (which are then structured), decides on the systems throughout the organization and recruits people. This then begins to create the culture. The vision the leader has of the organization, and which stakeholders then carry in their minds, will provide a guiding sense of the organizational purpose. We only need to think of the Body Shop and Virgin, for example, to understand how such vision has entered our culture and can embody certain values both in society and in the people who work for these organizations.

Culture

Organizational culture can be broadly thought of as the way in which people working within an organization learn to cope with adapting to their environment. This includes the problems that arise from the external environment and also the way in which the organization integrates its activities internally. New members of the organization are taught that the way in which the organization operates is correct. In a customer-focused organization people come to believe that meeting customer needs is essential. Culture is a learned product of group experience and is discovered, invented and developed by members of the organization as it develops over time. One of the tasks of leadership is to create and also manage culture. Any change in culture needs to be led by management. The recruitment, induction, appraisal and reward systems support it.

Culture is therefore a product of:

- The context – macro- (PEST factors) and micro- (markets, competitors, customers, suppliers, distributors, stakeholders) environments.
- The structures and functions found within an organization – for example, a centralized organization will have a different culture from a decentralized one, marketing has a different culture from sales, finance and production and so on.
- People's attitudes to their work and the individual and occupational role defences developed by them to protect them from undue stress.
- The individual's psychological contract with the organization – people are attracted to jobs which fit their personalities, in which they can implement their self-concepts and from which they can obtain the outcomes they desire, both conscious and unconscious. Individuals are in a process of self-selection when they choose an organization and organizations tend to choose people who mirror their own self-concepts.
- Leadership – leaders choose markets, they structure organizations, recruit staff and act as behavioural models for employees to follow. They organize the adaptation to the external environment and internal integration.

Marketing creates some of the symbols of culture:

- Corporate image
- Promotional material and branding
- Customer philosophy, market orientation, strategic thinking, marketing research belief in planning and evaluation
- An understanding that marketing activities need to be carried out within the context of the wider social/cultural environment and as such reflect its concerns.

Marketing also guides the organization on its external adaptation – its strategy and marketing mix; and internal integration – structure, systems and design of the value chain necessary to meet customer needs, and create a competitive advantage.

Culture is an important ingredient in the service delivery process. It is 'the way we do things around here'. The following points outline what customers expect from a service-oriented culture:

- No buck passing, people are responsible and flexible
- It is an open, non-defensive culture in which people can admit mistakes
- You can expect the same level of service from everyone in the organization; employees know what standards they are working to
- Common values and beliefs underline the attitudes of employees
- Customers are asked how they feel and their feelings are acted upon
- Managers are exhibiting the behaviour they wish others to follow
- Employees are friendly to the customers and make them feel welcome.

Kaizen

Kaizen is a system of business thinking and behaviour developed by the Japanese and is based on ten principles (Patricia Wellington, 1996, *Kaizen Strategies for Customer Care*, Pitman Publishing):

1. *Focus on customers* It is everyone's responsibility in the company to meet customer needs.
2. *Make improvement continuously* A Kaizen company always looks for improvements. Once found they are built into the formal performance standards immediately.
3. *Acknowledge problems openly* Problems can only be dealt with in the open if the organization fosters a supportive, constructive, non-confrontational and non-recriminatory culture.
4. *Promote openness* As Patricia Wellington says, there tends to be less functional compartmentalization or ringfencing in a Kaizen company than in a Western counterpart. Similarly working areas are more open plan in Japan (only the most senior executives will have individual offices), the usual symbols of rank or status are rarely seen and communality is favoured – all of which reinforce leadership visibility and communication.
5. *Create work teams* All employees belong to a work team and are managed by a team leader. They also belong to a year group (people who joined at the same time), a quality circle and cross-functional teams. This draws people into the life of the organization.
6. *Manage projects through cross functional teams*
7. *Nurture the right relationship process* They look for harmony.
8. *Expect employees to develop self-discipline*
9. *Inform every employee about what is going on* This covers mission, culture, values, plans and practices. Employees are then given the skills and the opportunity to apply the information they have been given.
10. *Enable every employee* Kaizen employees are empowered to influence materially their own and their organization's affairs. Employees are encouraged to multi-skill, given access to data and budgets, and encouraged in decision making.

The difference between a Kaizen, a total quality management and an ordinary organization

The change from a conventional Western organizational model to a Kaizen one can be significant, as Table 7.2 shows. This model throws up a number of differences, how would you feel about them? And what sort of problems do you anticipate having at work in order to change the way in which the organization manages itself?

Many of the new Western practices such as total quality management are based on Kaizen – other TQM programmes are called, as Patricia Wellington says, by many names:

- Continuous improvement
- Working together
- Our contribution counts
- Total involvement
- Focus on quality
- Focus on customers
- Putting customers first

- 560 brands are better than one
- Customer first
- We all make the difference.

Table 7.2 Comparing Western culture and management to Kaizen. Source: Patricia Wellington (1996) Kaizen Strategies for Customer Care, Pitman Publishing.

Western culture	Kaizen culture
Self	Team
Own department	Company
Immediate profit	Long-term gains
Short-term RoI	Market share
Stasis	Change
Making do	Continual improvement
Results	Process
Introspection	Customer satisfaction
Imposed discipline	Self-regulation
Annual appraisal	Continuous performance management
Proprietorial information	Information sharing
Them and us	Harmony
Rigidity	Flexibility

Western management	Kaizen management
Unitary leadership	Delegation, participation, consensus
Authoritarian decision making	Democratic decision approving
Support for and promotion of individual high fliers	Support for and promotion of teams
One-way communication	Two-way communication
Focus on implementation and outcomes	Focus on planning, preparation and process
Individual and territorial specialism	Cross-functional collaboration
Acceptance of certain margin of error and subsequent corrective action as the norm	Striving for continuous improvement to produce error-free outputs; doing things right first time

Total quality management

The best-known quality management philosophy is total quality management (TQM) because it is concerned with all work processes and the way they can be improved to meet customers' needs more effectively.

The TQM approach involves the following:

1. Understanding what customers want
2. Having detailed specification of what customers want and being able to deliver it to them
3. Understanding and managing the processes of manufacture/service delivery so variation can be traced
4. Keeping records so that it is possible to rectify the variables.

It is important to remember that when people want changes any quality system that only conforms to expectations could soon run out of steam. An organization can only maintain its differentiation if it constantly seeks to add value to what the customer says is important. The question is how to create a quality system that has the flexibility to constantly exceed expectations. However, Deming (one of the original quality gurus) said that formal performance measurement could actually produce bad quality because people who feel they are judged by others may not give of their best. He adds that measurement systems sometimes measure the wrong things.

The importance of quality has been reflected in the growth of TQM and the ability to think about organizations and their internal and external relationships as one system.

The core of TQM is the customer-supplier relationship, where the process must be managed. The 'soft' outcomes of TQM – culture, communications and commitment – provide the foundations of the TQM model. The process core must be surrounded by the 'hard' management necessities of systems, tools and teams.

In order to achieve this, attitudes to work and skills have to be changed so that the culture of the organization becomes one of preventing failure – doing the right things, first time, every time.

TQM means achieving total quality through management's ability in gaining everyone's commitment and involvement and ensuring that a continual effort is made towards improvement. This will result in a reduction of total costs as waste is avoided by eliminating errors, and value is added to what is being produced because actions are carried out which add value to the production process.

TQM involves training people to understand customer-supplier relationships (the role relationships), not buying on price alone, managing systems improvement, modern supervision and training, managing processes through teamwork and improved communication, elimination of barriers and fear, constant education and expert development, and a systematic approach to TQM implementation.

The role of marketing

The TQM process starts with marketing and forms part of the foundation framework. Marketing must take the lead in establishing the true requirements of a product or service. This must be communicated properly throughout the organization in the form of a specification. It also calls for market research and the ongoing assessment of customer satisfaction.

The main pillars of TQM are:

1. The foundation framework:
    *   A customer focus
    *   Quality chains
    *   Quality design and conformance to design
    *   Process understanding
    *   Working together with suppliers and customers
    *   Leadership and commitment to TQM
    *   Empowerment.
2. A quality system
3. The tools and the improvement cycle
4. Organization and team work
5. Implementation.

The learning organization

The creation of the learning organization is another philosophy enabling customer-focused behaviour and continuous improvement to take place. There are many different approaches to describing the characteristics of a learning organization. Pedlar, Burgoyne and Boydell (1991) identified eleven characteristics:

1. The formulation of strategy, implementation, evaluation and improvement are structured as in learning experiences. Feedback loops enable the organization to see how they can improve.
2. Participative policy making – everyone is involved in creating policy, differences are aired and the participation process opens things out so that customers and supplies save involvement.
3. Informing technology is used to empower and inform employees.
4. Formative accounting and control – accounting, budgeting and reporting systems are designed to assist learning.
5. Internal exchange – all internal units see themselves as customers and suppliers of each other.
6. The rewarding of flexibility.
7. Enabling structures – roles need to be structured in relation to the needs of internal customers and suppliers so that personal growth and experimentation are encouraged.
8. Boundary workers as environmental scanners – employees in contact with suppliers, customers and neighbours of the organization need to collect data and feed it back.

9. Inter-company learning – employees join with customers and suppliers for training, job exchanges, research and development. Benchmarking is also used.

10. Learning climate – new ideas are tried out, everything is questioned, mistakes are allowed and the importance of continuous improvement is emphasized. Feedback is requested and acted upon.

11. Self development opportunities for all – individual learning is encouraged at all levels – coaching, mentoring, counselling, peer support and feedback all support this.

Further reading: Argyris (1992), *On Organizational Learning,* Blackwell Publishers.

Difficulties of implementation

People may need to be helped in dealing with the implementation of TQM and relationship marketing. The expansion of role and responsibility and the increased expectation that colleagues may have regarding their role as 'customers', may create additional stress within the organization. Increased contact with external customers may also create anxiety. 'Industrial intimacy' is not everyone's cup of tea.

Role development leads to a situation where people can be empowered to take authority for themselves. The concept of empowerment is fundamental to the development of TQM and relationship marketing and the ethos of the customer-centred organization. Good management should help and not hinder this process and managers may need to learn new skills as facilitators to enable people to take more responsibility for themselves.

Activity 7.2

1. Identify your internal customer-supplier chain so that you can look at your role and role relationships.

2. Write down the tasks you are expected to carry out. Think about the expectations other people have about the way you behave and carry out your work.

3. Now think about your own ideas about your own role. You may want to use your job description as a starting point.

4. When you have done this, concentrate on:
   o What helps you to perform your role;
   o What stops you from carrying out, or expanding your role.

5. Are these constraints external, or do they merely exist in your own mind? Have you developed any ways of protecting yourself from the anxiety or stress that comes from carrying out your role? Is the way you have protected yourself (by creating a role defence) stopping you from carrying out your work more effectively? Are the defences you are using the same as those used by everyone in the organization? What constraints are coming from the organization and the external environment.

6. Once you have carried out this exercise, think about how it made you feel. Did you feel comfortable or uncomfortable? How do you think your colleagues would feel if they carried out a similar exercise?

7. What effect is the way you perform your role having on the customer supply chain?

Management of sub-cultures and sentient systems

Many different cultures often coexist in an organization. Some examples of subcultures include:

- Managerial cultures
- Occupationally-based cultures
- Group cultures based on geographical proximity
- Worker cultures based on shared hierarchical experiences
- Unions.

These subgroups very often have different objectives, different concepts about time, different ideas about what is important to them, different values, attitudes and beliefs about themselves, they often share secrets, and share cared-for rooms and possessions. They are groups of people to which an individual feels they belong, to which loyalty is shown and in which they feel to some degree at home. These subcultures are also called sentient systems – groups that people invest feeling or sentiment in.

Leadership or management of any organization entails identifying its constituent task and sentient systems and understanding the relations between them. When a sentient system is threatened by change, its defences will increase. Sometimes there is a conflict between a subculture and the objectives of the organization, e.g. loyalty to a union can often outweigh loyalty to the organization itself.

These sentient groups exist within the organization and also extend outside it. For example, an organization may find an unexpected resistance to change coming from other stakeholders. Management has to manage the individual sentient groups, as well as the relationships between them, the overall organization and the outside groups that feel they have a relationship with the activities of the organization itself. Public relations and other methods of communication play a part in this by recognizing the interests of consumer and pressure groups and other 'relationships'. Other barriers to role change and organizational change are discussed throughout the book.

Intergroup behaviour

Groups feel and believe that they have a relationship with each other. Individuals tend to idealize the groups that are important to them. Very often this means suppressing less satisfactory aspects. Some groups may be treated with suspicion, others are treated neutrally. Individuals in the group build up pictures of other groups from hearsay, guesswork and projected aspects of their own minds. When the task systems of different groups have different priorities, groups may find that they are at odds with each other (see Table 7.3).

Table 7.3 *Interdepartmental conflicts. Adapted from Kotler (1980),* Principles of Marketing, *Prentice Hall International Inc.*

Research and development wants	*Marketing wants*
Product quality	Customer perceptions to lead the definition of quality
Research for its own sake	Ideas that can be applied
Plenty of time in which to develop their ideas	Products that have features that add value to them and differentiate them from their competitors
Manufacturing wants	*Marketing wants*
Plenty of time	Short lead times
Long runs	Short runs
Only a few models	A variety of models
Orders that are standard	Custom made orders
Average quality control	Tight quality control
Few changes	Changes made when they need them
Finance, accounting and credit wants	*Marketing wants*
Standard transactions	Special terms and discounts to suit different customers' needs
Few standard reports	Many reports tailored for specific information needs
Fixed budgets	Flexible budgets so plans can be changed to suit developments in the market place
Pricing to cover costs	Prices that will help them to develop the market
Low credit risks	Easy terms of credit
Controlled and tough credit terms	Methods of examining credit that will not upset customers
Strict procedure for collecting money	Procedures for collecting money that will not upset customers
Strict reasons for spending	
Full financial disclosure by customers	
Purchasing and inventory wants	*Marketing wants*
Narrow product lines	Broad product lines so that customers can have variety and products can be delivered that will suit each customer's needs
Standard parts	Non-standard parts
Material that is bought on price, not necessarily quality	Material that will meet customers' perceptions of quality and add value to the product
Lot sizes that are economical	Large lot sizes and a high level of stock so that nothing runs out
Purchasing at infrequent intervals	Purchasing that can be carried out relative to customers' needs

Envy

The success of one department may not always be encouraged or supported by another that is less successful. This envy operates like a hidden spanner in the works. It can manifest itself by active sabotage or by actively (or unconsciously) withholding necessary cooperation.

The effective group is one that is in contact with reality and knows the boundary between what is inside the group and what is outside it. Individuals also need to know the boundaries between themselves and the outside world. In the same way that individuals use projection as a defence against anxiety, so do groups.

Application

The marketing concept tries to blend everything in the organization towards meeting customers' needs. However, other departments can sometimes put more importance on their own tasks. An understanding of their priorities will help marketing go some way to understanding their internal customers a little more.

Activity 7.3

1. What interdepartmental barriers or conflicts exist in your own organization?
2. Which of these impact specifically on the marketing department?
3. How do they affect your ability to satisfy your external customers' needs?
4. What do you do to help other departments understand customers' needs in order to help things go more smoothly?

John Macdonald ('TQM, does it always work? Some reasons for disappointment', *Managing Service Quality,* 6(5), **www.emerald-library.com**) says that many companies have been disappointed with the results of their drive for quality improvement. The principal reasons for disappointment are:

1. Lack of management commitment, all talk and no action.
2. Lack of vision and planning-people apparently become 'born again' quality managers and this clouds their vision.
3. Satisfaction with the quick fix – the quick fix mentality dashes off and puts in quality circles, customer care programmes and empowers the people. As John Macdonald says, 'each of these approaches is valid and can be powerful contributors to an overall process, but only if the operating environment is conductive to their success'.
4. The process becomes tool bound – people become so involved in collecting statistics they have no time to do the real work.
5. Quality is too constraining – TQM addresses the whole organization and the way in which it is organized. Managers do not see it as a strategic imperative but delegate it to a department.
6. Complacency with customer satisfaction – Macdonald gives the example of IBM who was so concerned about customer surveys on product and service quality and satisfaction they missed out that customers wanted something else – small computers.
7. Culture change versus project approach – Macdonald points out that it is important to take a whole view approach.
8. Quality management institutionalized – people who initiate TQM as a process to achieve continuous improvement should not remain responsible for it. It should subsequently be absorbed by the whole organization.
9. People do not really get involved.
10. Lack of real business manageables – aspects of the TQM process not being measured in a meaningful way.

Structure

From an everyday point of view the way in which an organization develops is mainly determined by the product it produces and the technology it uses. But from a psychological point of view the culture, the structure and the way in which it functions are determined by the psychological needs of the management and staff.

In a customer-centred organization the way in which the organization structures itself should be determined by the needs of customers and the market in which it operates. Creating this balance between two needs – those of customers and those of employees – is the challenge organizations now face.

There is no one way to structure an organization but structure and strategy influences the way in which people work and also the way in which they are managed. Human beings are the product of social structures but they may also form them. Flatter structures have advantages as decisions are taken more quickly and performance can be more related to rewards. Organizations that are very large tend to behave more slowly and can demotivate people who are in contact with customers and so work within a different time framework of flexibility and quick decision making. It is not that certain types of structures are wrong; it is the way people behave in them.

Structure and hierarchy

(Adapted from E. Jacques, *In Praise of Hierarchy*)

It is important to remember that hierarchies exist internally to:

- Separate out jobs that have different complexity.
- Separate out jobs that have different types of mental activity.
- Ensure that people are accountable for what they do.
- Add real value to work as it moves through the organization through the various layers.
- Provide a structure in which evaluation and coaching are done by people who are genuinely perceived as being above those they evaluate and coach.

Without these factors in mind overlayering can create difficulties like too much passing of problems up and down, bypassing, poor task setting, frustrated subordinates, anxious managers, inadequate performance appraisals and personality problems.

In trying to create flatter structures and give employees that face the customer more responsibility managers need to understand that people will have to be able to do the following:

- Carry out more complex jobs and use different types of mental activity.
- Become more personally responsible and accountable and manage themselves.
- Create real value to their jobs rather than passing it up the hierarchy.
- Work in different frameworks of time (see Figure 7.11).

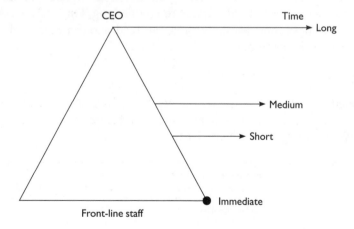

Figure 7.11

In a flatter structure senior managers will be responsible for coaching, training and evaluation. There will be less promotion, giving employees a sense of not knowing where their career will lead to next, and senior managers will become much closer to the customer.

This means that organizations adopting flatter structures will have to think about the following:

- Creating a learning organization that grows and empowers its own staff and develops and multi-skills people to take on a variety of roles.
- Ensuring that people take professional exams, go on secondments and carry out on-the-job training.

- Encouraging people to manage their own career portfolios, to develop wider portfolios and also to get experience in outside roles, for example with charities, when the organization itself is not in a position to help the person get that experience (people need more than one group, one 'organizational basket', so to speak, to identify with – obviously there needs to be a balance in terms of prioritizing individual needs and organizational need).
- Making sure that its bonus structures are geared to multi-skilling and not managerial grades and that the acquisition of new skills is rewarded.

Structure is the extension of culture. It is merely a working relationship that has arisen out of the idea of how an organization should be organized in the process of adaptation to the external environment and internal integration. It is as much a construction as it is a symbolic form. Take, for example, a management organization where the belief is that the managers are the sole depositaries of decision making. The form arises from the ideas leaders have about themselves and about other people. It is important that the culture and the structure that it produces can respond to the needs of the customers and the market, and at the same time take into account the hierarchical systems within the organization that allow it to function effectively within different frameworks of time and complexity.

Organizations can be structured by function, product, territory or market sector and customer segment. There is no one best method. Formal structures are also influenced by the:

- Size of the business
- Location of the business
- Type of staff, abilities and skills
- Age of the organization
- Type of technology
- Type of market – stable or unstable
- Current fashion in managerial thinking – downsizing, flatter structures, matrix organization etc.
- Leader and managerial cultures – see Charles Handy, *Gods of Management* – Apollo, Zeus, Dionysus and Athena.

Business process re-engineering (BPR)

BPR is a method that strips away the hierarchical structure of a company and looks at the way in which processes flow. The company then allows the new processes to define how it should be structured. Michael Hammer, co-author of *Re-engineering the Corporation* and and *Beyond Re-engineering* is among the acknowledged experts of process re-engineering. On the Booz Allen & Hamilton website (www.strategy-business.com/casestudy) you can read about a case study that Dr Hammer carried out at GTE Telephone Operations.

Value chain

Porter (1985) introduced the value chain as a way of breaking down strategically relevant activities in order to understand the behaviour of costs and the sources of differentiation as alternative approaches to securing competitive advantage (see Figure 7.12).

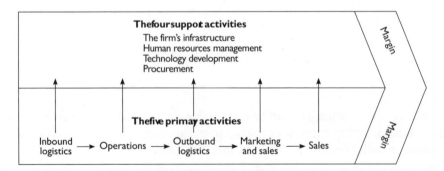

Figure 7.12

The traditional value chain (Figure 7.13) starts with the company and moves to the customers. The customer-centred value chain (Figure 7.14) begins with the customer so that customer priorities drive the business.

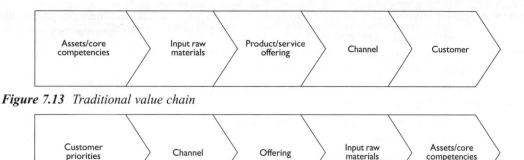

Figure 7.13 *Traditional value chain*

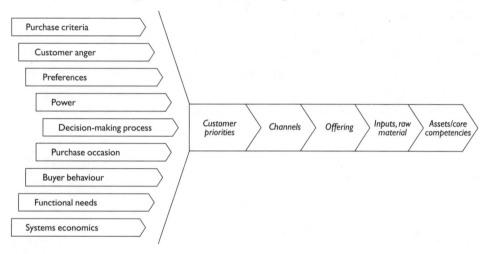

Figure 7.14 *The customer-centred value chain*

This can be extended further to look like Figure 7.15.

The value chain of the organization should be designed to meet the customer's value-chain.

Figure 7.15 *The modern value chain. Source: Slywotzky and Morrison,* The Profit Zone, *Times Books*

Cross-functional work flows

If you were working on your own there would be no need for any structure or functional differentiation within your organization because the whole organization would be integrated into your head. However, once an organization grows, controls come in and work then has to be integrated between people and across departments. When one person's activities are not matched with another person's needs there is a quality gap. These gaps can occur between departments and within departments and contributes to increasing costs, delays, and quality failures along the firm's value chain.

If tasks are put on a flow chart, these links or gaps can be studied and can give organizations a real opportunity to improve their quality. By carefully defining the way in which customers use what the organization is offering, modifications can be made within the firm in terms of designing jobs, working environments, and training, to name a few areas.

The customer activity cycle (CAC)

In her book, *The Eleventh Commandment* (John Wiley and Sons, 1996), Sandra Vandermerwe says that the transformation to 'owning customers' (customer loyalty) is more important than restructuring of the organization into new neat categories. She feels that no amount of traditional restructuring will lead to the fundamental deep changes in mindset that will lead to the notion of 'owning customers'. This involves boundarylessness and an active sharing of ideas.

This statement of hers is quite true. However, rather like the difficulties encountered in TQM, readers are pointed to acquiring a real understanding of role, role defences and institutionalized organizational defences.

She mentions Paul Allaire, CEO of Rank Xerox as saying, 'there is a formal structure and then there's the way the company really works. You have to change the way it really works'. Vandermerwe warns against restructuring at the start of a customer transformation process as it takes energy and resources at a crucial time.

Building new processes involves:

- Identifying what you do now and how you can do it better by understanding what your customer wants – start from the customer activity cycle (see Figure 7.16) and work backwards. Imagine you are starting from scratch, and don't graft improvements onto existing processes.

- Learning how to improve on an ongoing basis and build in new processes all the time.

- Involving people who are in contact with customers as early as possible and letting them tell you how to do it differently.

- Looking at key request areas and ensuring that people are really doing what they were employed to do in the first place.

- Helping people identify what they need to do differently on an ongoing basis.

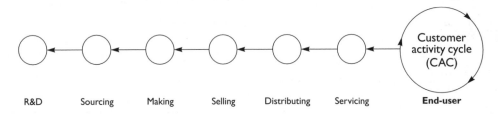

Figure 7.16 The customer activity cycle (CAC) tool

Figure 7.17 and 7.18 illustrate two starting points.

Sandra Vandermerwe's methodology provides a general framework which begins with end-users. The CAC methodology serves different purposes:

1. People see the difference between what they have been doing and what is now needed.

2. As an educational tool, it forces people into the customer's space and provides a common view and tool to see what customer value really means and what it would take to add to this.

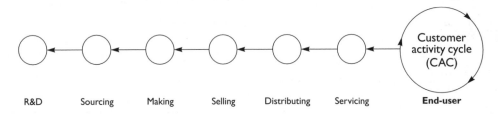

R&D   Sourcing   Making   Selling   Distributing   Servicing   **End-user**

Figure 7.17 The CAC as the starting point for creating value internally

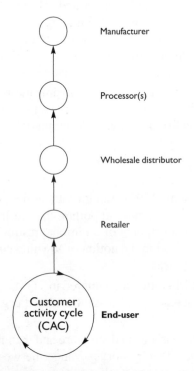

The Customer Activity Cycle (CAC) Tool

Manufacturer

Processor(s)

Wholesale distributor

Retailer

Customer activity cycle (CAC)   **End-user**

Figure 7.18 The CAC as the starting point for creating value externally

Figure 7.19 illustrates the basic model used to analyze the CAC cycle for Citibank.

Figure 7.19 *Customer activity cycle: Citibank global customer (simplified)*

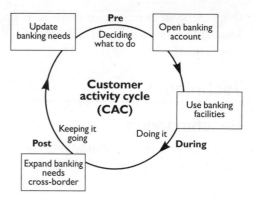

Figure 7.20 shows some of the value add-ons Citibank has developed at each of these critical points.

Figure 7.20 *Value add-ons, customer activity cycle: Citibank (simplified)*

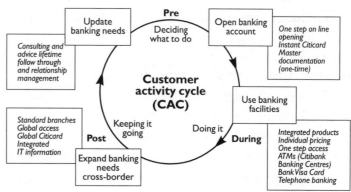

The Fishbone or Ishikowa diagram

The fishbone structures work processes by mapping all the problem cause and effect relationships into a simple diagram. It can be used for analyzing problems and for finding solutions (see the example in Figure 7.21).

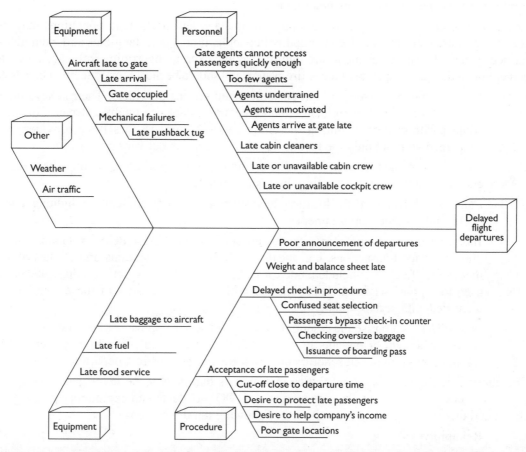

Figure 7.21 *Causes of flight departure delays. Source: Wyckhoff, D. (1984)* New tools for achieving service quality

Once the system of service delivery is understood standards can be set and the service monitored. Standards need to be looked at in terms of the pre-transaction, the transaction and the post-transaction demand.

Techniques

Benchmarking

Benchmarking is an analytical process organizations use in order to compare their performance with that of their competitors. It is used to:

- Identify key performance measures for each business function.
- Measure the organizational performance as well as that of competitors.
- Identify areas of competitive advantage/disadvantage by comparing respective performance levels.
- Improve key issues.

Benchmarking can be divided into five stages:

1. Determining what to benchmark.
2. Forming a benchmarking team.
3. Identifying benchmarking partners.
4. Collecting and analyzing benchmarking information.
5. Taking action.

The features of service include intangibles and people-oriented factors which make quality improvement more elusive and difficult to achieve.

Services need to be analyzed and benchmarked in the following ways.

Front-stage and back-stage operations: the back stage refers to the system which supports front-stage operations, including systems of decision support, physical support, and management support. The front stage is characterized by customer contacts.

Key elements of service operations: although front-stage and back-stage operations may differ in content, they are both intimately concerned with people, time, place, tangibles and intangibles in the service system. These five elements are interrelated and exert an overriding influence on customers' perception of the service quality of the entire system and should be the major concern of benchmarking.

1. *People* – 'people' refers to both customers and service providers. Their behaviour, appearance and attitude often influence the perception of service quality. Because of their close contact with customers during the entire servicing process, a service provider should be concerned with not only the results but also the service delivery process.

2. *Time* – this element concerns whether the time of service offering is convenient for customers; and whether a given waiting time is acceptable.

3. *Place* – such factors as the location, environment, d´ecor, temperature, lighting, and atmosphere of the service environment.

4. *Tangibles (physical evidence)* – goods provided in the service delivery. Goods are received during service transactions, e.g. meals in McDonald's restaurants and clothes in a department store. Tangibles include name cards, business brochures, server's dress and certificates used to support service transactions. As with place, the quality of these tangibles may be identified with service quality.

5. *Intangibles* – comprise the essential functions of service processes, for example, the diagnosis and treatment of patients in a hospital, the legal consultation in a lawyer's office, the teaching programmes in school, and purchase transactions in a department store.

The above five elements highlight the crucial matters that need to be investigated for quality improvement in service systems. Parasuraman et al. (1985) conducted an exploratory investigation and concluded that service quality comprised the following ten dimensions:

1. Reliability
2. Responsiveness
3. Competency

4. Access
5. Courtesy
6. Communication
7. Credibility
8. Security
9. Understanding
10. Tangibles.

The quality level of a service is a function of the gap between a customer's expectations and the perceived service. Parasuraman et al. (1988) subsequently developed a quality measuring instrument SERVQUAL and reduced the ten dimensions into five factors: tangibles, reliability, responsiveness, assurance, and empathy.

Marketing quality assurance (MQA)

MQA is a third-party organization specializing in:

- Providing assessment services to organizations wishing to develop quality systems for their marketing, sales and customer service activities.

- Assessing companies in the service sector to the ISO9000 series of quality systems standards. Developing third-party certification guidelines for specific areas, such as public relations (see Figure 7.22).

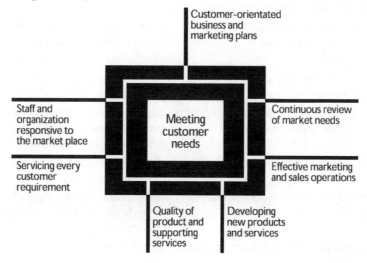

Figure 7.22

ISO9000 series

The market need for accredited quality programmes increases. As Japanese manufacturing rose, many Western companies became interested in quality management, and total quality management (TQM) as a philosophy for continually improving quality and getting the commitment of employees began to grab people's attention. As the interest in TQM grew the International Organization for Standardization (ISO) developed an internationally recognized standard of quality management ISO9000 (originally based on the British System BS 45750).

ISO9000 is based on the idea of quality by inspection. It controls people's performance by controlling their activity. ISO starts with a view of the organization compared to a set of requirements and then decides that if the requirements are met they will have a beneficial impact on performance. Documentation of activities then becomes the method of monitoring performance. It is a method of control which ensures consistency of output. Critics of ISO9000 say that because it starts from an attitude of control it demotivates, introduces bureaucratization and sub-optimization of standards – people do what counts towards ISO not what doesn't. Critics believe that ISO9000 reinforces the idea that work is divided into management and worker roles and that control is now maintained by adherence to procedures, budgets, targets and standards.

Evidence suggests that it adds to costs, makes customers unhappy and demoralizes staff, but most of all it prevents organizations taking opportunities to improve performance which they might otherwise have seen, 'blinding' them to the means for improvement.

QS-9000

QS-9000 is the common supplier quality standard for Chrysler Corporation, Ford Motor company, and General Motors Corporation. QS-9000 is based on the 1994 edition of ISO 9001, but it contains additional requirements that are particular to the automotive industry.

Key players in the development of QS-9000 include:

- Supplier quality requirements task force
- International automotive sector group (IASG)
- Automotive industry action group (AIAG)
- ASQ automotive division.

Just-in-time production and distribution systems (JIT)

The ability to deliver defect-free components exactly when they are required provides the edge needed in this new competitive environment. For any supplier who can become an effective supplier to a JIT customer, the impact is significant – a possible single-source position in a long-term relationship in which the supplier is viewed as an extension of the customer's company. (Table 7.4 compares JIT with traditional operations.)

Table 7.4 *Comparison of traditional manufacturing operations to JIT systems*

Elements	How the elements are viewed in:	
	A traditional manufacturing system	*A JIT manufacturing system*
Inventory	Seen as an asset; insures against errors, late delivery	Seen as liability and indicates operational problems; seen as unnecessary
Production steps	Set-up time is long and value is placed on maximum output	A critical goal is to reduce setup time to the absolute minimum
Suppliers	Multiple sources of supply for 'protection' of relationships often adverserial	Suppliers are partners and one or only a very few are used and are incorporated into the quality standards
Quality	Toleration of small percentage of rejects and scrap	Quality expected to be 100 per cent
Equipment	Maintenance reactive; inventory kept and breakdowns occur	Maintenance proactive; strict maintenance schedules are followed and breakdowns are tolerated
Lead times	Long lead times built in to compensate for problems	Short lead times
Workers	Managers control	Emphasis on management by consensus; workers have a say and a proprietary interest in the firm's operation

Investors in People

According to Investors in People UK (the organization responsible for the administration of IIP) the standard:

> provides a framework for improving business performance and competitiveness, through a planned approach to setting and communicating business objectives and developing people to meet these objectives... [It] draws on the experience of some of the UK's most successful organizations both large and small [and] therefore provides a comprehensive benchmark of best practice against which an organization can audit its policies and practice in the development of people. (Investors in People UK, 1994)

Organizations achieve recognition through a process similar to that of BS EN ISO 9000, involving documentary and auditing assessment, in this case by their local Training Enterprise Council (TEC). The standard is based on the four key principles that an investor in people should:

1. Make a public commitment from the top to develop all employees to achieve its business objectives.
2. Review training and development needs of all employees.

184

3. Take action to train and develop individuals on recruitment and throughout their employment.

4. Evaluate investment in training and development to assess achievement and improve future effectiveness.

In order to carry this out they will need a business and training plan. For further reading see Simon Down and David Smith (1998), 'It pays to be nice to people. Investors in People: the search for measurable benefits', *Personnel Review,* **27**(2), **www.emerald-library.com**

Employee empowerment

In the rapidly changing business world the process of defining strategies for the development of the workforce is becoming ever more important. One such strategy which is being used is the move from control to empowerment and learning.

Empowerment cannot be looked at on its own but needs to be seen as a way of introducing a new type of contract into the organization. Charles Handy talks about the psychological contract that individuals make when they join an organization. 'Empowerment' is the cornerstone for motivating people to take a new approach to their work so that the competitiveness of their organization can be maintained. Empowerment can be seen within the context of society and developing political and cultural values, and also within the context of what has been happening in businesses where a focus on cost-cutting and efficiency has resulted in downsizing and restructuring, and where the employment contract changed from loyalty and long service to an emphasis on knowledge and skills – multi-skilling. This has resulted in a greater choice and freedom for some employees in the marketplace but it has also created an atmosphere of job insecurity and lack of trust.

Conger and Kanungo define empowerment as 'a process of enhancing feelings of self-efficacy among organizational members through the identification of conditions that foster powerlessness and through their removal by both formal organizational practices and informal techniques of providing efficacy information'.

Wellins proposes that an organization empowers people when it enables employees to take on more responsibility and to make use of what they know and can learn.

Randolph defines it as 'recognizing and releasing into the organization the power that people already have in their wealth of useful knowledge and internal motivation'.

Burke states 'to empower implies the granting of power – delegation of authority'.

Geroy, Wright and Anderson define empowerment as 'the process of providing employees with the necessary guidance and skills, to enable autonomous decision making (including accountability and the responsibility) for making these decisions within acceptable parameters, that are part of an organizational structure'.

Vogt defined empowerment as the act of giving people the opportunity to make workplace decisions by expanding their autonomy in decision making.

Empowerment can therefore be seen as a two-way process – as both coming from the organization and also enabling employees to make use of the power they already possess. It is also influenced by employees' perception as to whether they indeed feel empowered to take actions that they have defined and recognized as empowering, and which are also recognized externally by the organization and peer group.

Empowerment will therefore be situational and defined by the organization and the contextual environment. It will also be relative to what employees already have experience of and their ability to reach beyond self-limiting attitudes – which some of them may not want to.

The extent to which empowerment takes place within an organization will also relate to the overall structure of the organization and the way in which power is perceived and has been historically distributed.

Empowerment in a customer service environment

Cook and Macaulay (1997), 'Empowered customer service', *Empowerment in Organizations,* 5(1), found at www.emerald-library.com gives the following example of empowerment.

A customer went into a food store to buy some ingredients for a special meal she was preparing that evening. On returning home from the store she discovered that the cream which she had just purchased was sour, although the sell-buy date on the packaging indicated it should still be fresh.

The customer telephoned the store and explained her predicament. She was too late to go back and still prepare the meal she had intended as the cream was a vital ingredient. The customer complained that the store should ensure in future that the cream was fresh.

Imagine the customer's surprise when, twenty minutes after telephoning, she opened the door to the member of staff who had answered her call. He had decided to make an apology in person on behalf of the store and also to bring the customer two replacement cartons of fresh cream so her dinner party could go ahead.

This is a true story and one which epitomizes empowered behaviour: an employee has the authority and takes the responsibility to do what is necessary to satisfy the customer.

Empowerment is a change-management tool which helps organizations create an environment where every individual can use their abilities and energies to satisfy the customer. It is a method of developing an environment where customers' needs and concerns are addressed and satisfied as quickly as possible at the point of customer contact. Staff are free to take opportunities to exceed customer expectations without referring upwards or fearing repercussions from their manager.

In an empowered company people share responsibility for problems and are proactive in their response to the customer. The customer recognizes empowerment through the way they are treated in the course of doing business with the organization and experiences its positive, proactive, innovative attitude through:

- The ability of employees to provide information and make decisions
- The speed of problem resolution
- An increase in creative new ideas and improvements
- Standards being set and maintained by self-discipline, not centralized enforcement
- Being dealt with by staff who listen actively and show willingness to understand the customer's point of view
- Being greeted with enthusiasm and a positive attitude by members of staff
- Seeing evidence of teamwork and the willingness of staff members to support each other to service the customer.

Empowerment, therefore, will be visible to the customers through employee behaviour, their attitudes and the values which underlie them. Examples of empowerment can be found across a wide range of organizations. At the AA, for example, customer interfacing staff are empowered to deal with members' complaints and difficulties in the best way they see fit. If, for example, a customer experiences a delay in the arrival of a patrol and the customer is a woman on her own, the call operator may suggest that she goes into the nearest café or restaurant and buys a meal at the AA's expense while waiting.

Characteristics of an empowered organization are:

- Shared vision and values
- Customer-focused strategy
- Leadership – where everyone has a chance to be leader in their areas of responsibility
- Structure – where there are as few as possible layers between the organization and the customer, processes are simple and customer-focused and information is readily accessible
- Teamwork
- Learning – where opportunities are given to grow, mistakes can be acknowledged and managers do not pretend they know everything.

Mohammed Rafiq and Pervaiz K. Ahmed (1998), 'A customer-oriented framework for empowering service employees', *The Journal of Services Marketing,* 12(5) say that the special nature of services, and in particular the simultaneity of production and consumption, is one of the major reasons that many services marketers argue that contact employees should be allowed a degree of discretion when dealing with customers. For instance, Grönroos (1990) argues that the interactive nature of services provides empowered employees with an opportunity to rectify mistakes and increase sales.

Ideally, the front-line employee should have the authority to make prompt decisions. Otherwise, sales opportunities and opportunities to correct quality mistakes and avoid quality problems in these moments of truth are not used intelligently, and become truly wasted moments of opportunity to correct mistakes, recover critical situations and achieve re-sales and cross-sales. (Grönroos, 1990).

However, other authors argue that service employees should have little or no discretion. For instance, Smith and Houston (1983) propose a 'script based' approach to managing customer and employee behaviour, to control behaviour and process compliance. That is, they envisage little or no room for participation by employees. Levitt (1972, 1976) forcefully argues for a 'production line' approach and the 'industrialization' of services if their productivity is to be improved. One of the key elements in this approach to services is that it leaves little room for discretion for service employees.

Mills (1995) argues that the degree of management control over service employees (or conversely the degree of employee empowerment) should depend on the structure of the service system. For low-contact, standardized services, behaviour can be controlled by mechanistic means such as rules and regulations. For high-contact, highly divergent services (that is those requiring a high degree of customization) Mills (1985) suggests that employee self-management and peer-reference techniques are more successful. Even Grönroos (1990) recognizes that not all decision making can or should be decentralized as 'chaos may follow in an organization if strategic decisions, for example, concerning overall strategies, business missions and service concepts, are not made centrally' (Grönroos, 1990).

The above suggests that the approach to participation is a contingent one.

Interestingly, the move towards empowerment is reflected in the increasing way that the government, with its use of focus groups, has become not so much a leader as a follower of group opinion. Similarly, the same process is reflected in organizations where empowerment and 360° appraisal now give those lower down the hierarchy some measure of control. The managing of change in political power in an organization needs to be thought through, otherwise lip service may be paid to new words that ultimately in practice have no meaning at all.

Flexibility

Many organizations are trying to build flexibility into their organizations. Flexibility can be looked at in a number of ways. Blyton and Morris (1992) concentrate on four key types of flexibility.

1. *Task or functional flexibility* – Where employees may be multi-skilled and involved in a wide range of tasks, with fewer boundaries between jobs. This type encourages team working practice, and in its ultimate form removes the distinction between cost and operator jobs and tasks.

2. *Numerical flexibility* – Where the labour supply is made flexible by the use of different types of employment contracts and subcontracting.

3. *Temporal flexibility* – Where the number and timing of hours worked can be varied to meet organizational needs.

4. *Wage flexibility* – Where wages offered are individualized rather than standardized.

360° feedback systems

Simon Hurley (1998), 'Application of team-based 360° feedback systems', *Team Performance Management,* 4(5) www.emerald-library.com, explains that the term '360° feedback' is a registered trademark of TEAMS, Inc, a company that did some pioneering work on the theory and its application (Edwards and Ewen, 1996). The term '360° appraisal' can also be applied to a similar process; however, 360° feedback implies that not only is assessment performed, but the results are shared with the individual being assessed/rated (the ratee). Multi-rater assessments are used and information on an individual and their performance is gathered from more than one source or person. The individuals who perform the rating have some degree of familiarity with the person being rated – they know the ratee, interact with them frequently and are qualified to assess their performance. In most cases the ratings are multi-directional – they can come from the ratee's supervisors and co-workers (peer assessment), internal and external customers (customer assessment), and/or sub-ordinates (upward assessment). When used effectively, 360° feedback can improve leadership and management abilities, increase communication and learning and assist employee and organizational development, productivity and efficiency (Edwards and Ewen, 1996; Yukl and Lepsinger, 1995). When performed correctly, it is also efficient (about 15 minutes per survey to complete), equitable, balanced, and participative (Edwards and Ewen, 1996).

Self-directed teams

Downsizing has stripped middle layers from business organizations. These positions, created as co-ordinating and integrating roles, have been lost where middle managers became defenders of functional perspectives and criteria. Now the operating core in many organizations is expected to produce with less supervisory coordination. Executives hope self-regulating teams are a solution to overheads and a mechanism to push accountability down, to focus decision making at the grass roots of the organization.

A self-directed work team is a structure in which members regulate their work around a relatively whole task. The team design is around a whole task of interdependent activities rather than individual jobs. Another characteristic is that the control of the task is located within the work group rather than externally to it. This allows the overall task integration and permits quick responses and flexibility to achieve goals.

What is known about self-directed work teams is an outgrowth of two basic premises about work. The first premise is that work groups accomplish tasks through a joint operating system, called a socio-technical system. Work performance requires both a technology made up of tools, techniques and methods, and a social structure which relates people to both technology and each other. The second premise is that effective groups must be open to influence from the environment and must maintain an environmental relationship to work so that they can improve. This requires learning the system properties needed to relate to an environment.

The following principles should be observed:

- *Responsibility* – If you want a system where the people assume responsibility, then people have to be involved responsibly in creating the work system.

- *Delegation* – Decisions must be made by the people involved. They decide the vision and management fixes as little as possible.

- *Solving problems* – Effective teams need to find out where things go wrong and to deal with problems themselves, not export them.

- *Clear goals and flexible strategies* – Employees need to know where they are going and be able to adapt.

- *Boundary location and control* – The consistent, social-technical message is that if there are supervisors, they manage the boundaries as a group resource, ensuring the group has adequate resources, coordinating activities with other groups and foreseeing coming changes. These resource positions are disappearing as groups become more self-regulating.

- *Information flow* – Teams need information for self-direction.

- *Goals, reward and support systems* – These need to be aligned and consistent.

- *Values, both design and human* – Design must address variation and meaning in work – continuous learning, involvement in decision making, help and support between colleagues, meaningful relationships between work and outside society and a desirable future in the organization.

- *Review* – Ongoing review and learning are necessary prerequisites to managing change.

How to understand the diagram in Figure 7.23

If you were the leader you would:

1. Assess the macro and micro environment

2. Decide on the strategy and work processes you needed …

3. and the roles to carry out your plans

4. You would then design a structure that would be customer-facing

5. The systems they need – such as information, communication, financial and those covering HR, IT, etc. would then be designed

6. You would then recruit staff

7. When they were in place you would manager them – managerial process

8. However, once all this is in place – the culture would emerge

9. If things were not working well, you would need to do an analysis

10. Perhaps you needed to understand more about the structure and change it

11. Once the analysis was done, in order to have customer-focused culture you would need to have a philosophy…

12. and use various techniques to keep this in place.

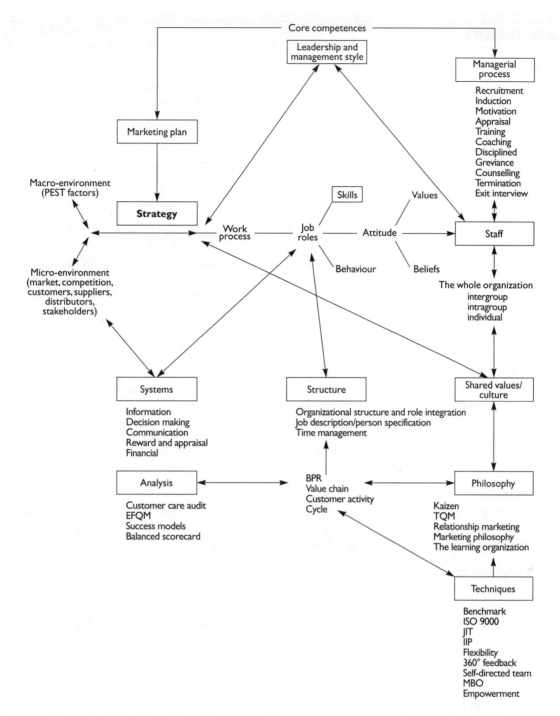

Figure 7.23 *Strategic model integrating marketing and human resource management* Source: Rosemary
Phipps www.OxfordCollegeofMarketing.ac.uk

An understanding of role, role defences, institutionalized organizational defences and other unconscious processes enable us to understand what is going on. It takes skilled management and special
skills to be able to work with them and create a new organizational reality.

Figure 7.23 illustrate the organization's relationship to the environment, not in terms of a marketing
plan but in terms of how it organizes itself in relation to the marketplace in order to create a customer
focus and illustrates how the philosophy, structure and techniques we have been discussing link into
an overall framework.

As Charles Handy says leaders decide on markets, create roles, system, structure and recruit people.
Once the people are in place culture is created. Culture is then both a product of the social and
technical environment as it is of the organization, which in its process of adaptation, chooses to
integrate its activities in a specific way.

In the following unit we will consider additional managerial techniques to mobilize performance.

Case history

Lay-By Chef

Please read the following case study, and using the 7s Customer Care Model as a structure, suggest what you would do to improve things. You may need to remember and apply material that you learned in the Marketing Operations syllabus as well.

Current mission

To refresh and revitalize the motoring family and the business traveller.

Background

The Lay-By Chef group operates a nationwide chain of restaurants. They are located along-side main roads at busy intersections (but not as yet on motorways); there are 250 Lay-By Chef units and the figure is expected to reach 300 within a further five years.

Each restaurant is built to a common standard and is intended to provide identical meals and service. Head Office supplies detailed instructions about every aspect of the Lay-By Chef operation, including safety in the children's play area, cleanliness and inspection of toilets, the amount of make-up the (female) staff can wear, portion control, and so forth.

The group is a well-managed and successful company in a very competitive business, and is in good shape financially. Success has not made the Board complacent and the need to develop and expand is being actively investigated. There is one major weakness in the organization, namely, the level of staff turnover, currently in excess of 30% per annum: this is helping to push the company into a downward performance spiral (the opposite of a circle of virtue) which could ultimately threaten its profitability.

Customer segments

As the Lay-By Chef mission statement suggests, the company has hitherto targeted its product/service principally towards families and business travellers.

Competition

Lay-By Chef shares its marketplace with one dominant competitor, the Granada group (branded as Little Chef), which has around 50% of the total market. Lay-By Chef has 30%, and the remainder is divided among a host of small, localized players.

The current situation

You are a project team leader charged by the Lay-By Chef directors with the task of producing some strategic breakthrough proposals for the company which will ensure that its current market strengths are not jeopardized and that it can, as it were, leapfrog over Granada.

Memo

TO: Lay-By Chef Directors
FROM:
DATE: 13th March 2000
RE: Breakthrough proposals for Lay-By Chef

Before I move forward to breakthrough proposals, I feel it is vital to take stock of the current situation. I have therefore analyzed the company using the McKinsey 7S model as my base and I have also undertaken a SWOT analysis of Lay-By Chef (LBC). This audit and evaluation can be used as the basis for further discussion.

1. Analysis – company audit based on the Mckinsey 7S Model

The key factors on which the McKinsey 7S model focuses are **Shared Values, Structure, Style, Systems, Skills, Staff** and **Strategy**. I will look at each theme in turn in relation to Lay-By Chef.

1.1. Shared Values

The mission statement of Lay-By Chef "To refresh and revitalize the motoring family and business traveller" is focused on two specific market segments and pays no reference to the many other current users of Lay-By Chef, nor to any other potential market segments. Thus the mission statement limits the target market from the outset.

The mission statement contains no reference to customer satisfaction, levels of service provided nor the quality of the product. While it does aim to meet customers' needs for rest and food/drink, it does not provide any quality or satisfaction goals. However, it is important to add that the strict emphasis on adhering to the daily running instructions means that customers who expect a certain Lay-By Chef standard will not be disappointed.

The current mission statement is easy to quantify and so from that point of view gives employees a purpose which is both measurable and attainable. However, it only encourages employees to focus on the customers' physical needs and there is no inspiration for quality customer care. The mission statement does little to encourage staff to develop customer loyalty to Lay-By Chef, nor to satisfy customers who do not fall into the family or business categories.

The homogeneity of the product in all the 250 restaurants (identical meals, floor lay-out, play area) imposes a degree of rigidity which is at odds in many ways with a culture of putting customers first. A degree of flexibility must be allowed if staff are to meet the different needs of different customers to the best of their ability.

1.2. Structure

The brief provided gives little information about the structure of Lay-By Chef and its effects on customer service. Therefore further research would have to be undertaken to gain a better understanding of this aspect of the company. However, it is clear that Lay-By Chef is run out of head office and that all significant decisions are made centrally. The information is then communicated by head office to the network of 250 restaurants. Thus decision making is very centralized and this will affect the ability of individual restaurants to adapt to local and individual customer needs and also the speed at which they can react.

1.3. Style

As all decision making takes place at head office, it would seem that there is a great distance between the CEO and the customers. The head office personnel do not appear to have close links with the customers and this gives the impression that decisions are made "out of context" i.e. without focusing on the customer in the restaurant. Standardization and strict control by head office of all aspects of the individual Lay-By Chef restaurants have been championed to the detriment of customer care.

The very high staff turnover is an indication that staff morale is low and that employees are dissatisfied and/or do not feel valued. This may be a result of the employment policy or may be a symptom of a deeper problem within the company.

We have little information on the interaction between the restaurant managers and the individual staff members. This is an aspect which requires further investigation.

1.4. Systems

Again, little information is provided in the brief on this aspect of the company so I would need to look into this theme further.

1.5. Skills

Significant training must be provided due to the stringent standards set by head office for all aspects of Lay-By Chef activities. Staff must be instructed on how to perform their tasks so that they meet head office's rigid requirements.

On the other hand, there is no indication that employees are trained to focus on customers and on meeting their needs, nor to deal with the wide variety of situations which can arise when in contact with customers. Due to the very precise standards and requirements imposed by head office, there seem to be few opportunities for staff empowerment as their roles seem very fixed. There is very little local autonomy.

However, I would need to gather further details before evaluating this area fully.

1.6. Staff: GROUP AND INTERGROUP

We do not have any indication as to the levels and success of interaction between staff members nor to their functions as either individuals or team members. However, we do know that the most glaring problem facing Lay-By Chef is the high staff turnover. This would indicate that they are not happy with their jobs.

The individual restaurants work very much in isolation from each other. Each restaurant receives information/instructions from head office but there seems to be very little interaction between the 250 restaurants in the group. In this way, the individual restaurants will not see themselves as key points in an active and dynamic network but instead will perceive themselves to be isolated at the beck and call of head office. The lack of links between the different restaurants means that it is difficult to move between different restaurants or to be promoted across the chain.

1.7. Strategy

Lay-By Chef's strategy seems focused on providing a very regulated product so that customers always know what to expect (and they will not be disappointed) and also expansion of the chain. There is no mention of innovation, where value is created in the value chain. The company is well-grounded financially but has very little focus on customer care and exceeding customer expectations. The target markets are defined but we are unclear as to the positioning.

We have no information about their human resource strategy.

Following my brief 7S study based on the brief provided, I have now done a SWOT analysis on Lay-by Chef:

STRENGTHS

- Company has a strong structure and is in good financial strength
- Company is in a position to expand the number of outlets by 20% over the next five years – very positive growth
- People can be assured of certain standards in LBC
- Company is not stagnant nor complacent
- National coverage of restaurants.

WEAKNESSES

- Very high staff turnover – particularly significant as people are the key to an organization
- Very focused on families and business travellers and not taking advantage of opportunities with other market segments
- No indication given on product/service innovation, value chain, relationship marketing or positioning.

OPPORTUNITIES

- Road travel is increasing (convenience, more cars, dissatisfaction with public transport, reduced public transport facilities) so we can capitalize on the increased number of potential consumers.
- People more selective about the food and service they receive in restaurants and are more willing to go out of their way for a more desirable restaurant.
- Greater tendency to eat out rather than cook at home or prepare picnics – greater potential market.

THREATS

- We are the no. 2 player in the market. Little Chef has a greater market share and we can't assume they will be resting on their laurels.
- High staff turnover may damage our reputation.
- Motorway travel on the increase as people try to avoid A and B roads – LBC not located on motorways.
- British people more discerning about their food and are demanding better quality and variety – LBC is very standardized.
- General move to make a journey a more pleasant experience by combining it with a nice meal etc.
- People are looking for some originality, something different – LBC is very standardized.

2. Strategic solutions

2.1 Staff

The company must first try to understand why staff are leaving. The problem is not so much one of recruitment but of retention.

- Why are employees not happy in their work?
- Are Lay-By Chef recruiting the wrong type of people?

Staff should be recognized as offering considerable competitive advantage. There are two approaches to gaining employee commitment.

2.1.1. Production line approach

A good example of this is McDonald's where workers are taught how to greet customers and how to take their order. Staff learn set procedures which they must follow, such as assembling cold drinks first then hot ones. Also there is a script for saying thank you and asking the customer to come again. This approach is argued by many to make customer service interactions uniform and to give the organization control over them. It is also easily learned so workers can be quickly put to work.

2.1.2. Empowerment approach

This involves turning the frontline loose by encouraging frontline service staff to exercise initiative and imagination and rewarding them for it. Tom Peters stated that it is impossible to get people's best efforts such as involvement and caring concern (important to your restaurant customers) if you write policies and procedures that treat your staff like thieves and bandits. The empowerment approach looks to frontline staff to suggest new services and products to solve problems.

2.1.3. What is right for Lay-By Chef?

I believe that Lay-By Chef differs from McDonald's, Lay-By Chef caters for families and businessmen who have chosen not to go to McDonald's, they are therefore looking for a more personal and friendly service. I would therefore suggest the empowerment approach. However it may not be possible to use this approach because for empowerment to work it must have the full support of senior management. Also important, the organization must be able to recruit the right people to whom empowerment and customer service are important. These criteria must go together. If staff are unable to work under their own initiative their performance will be low and they will suffer stress and leave, as will customers. In addition, if empowered staff join a company where management tries to enforce strict rules then they will leave too, with the customer also not being satisfied. To get the right staff requires careful recruitment by using psychological tests and having a recruiter who can spot customer focused people. Also they will need to be trained so that expectations are met and they are not simply left to get on with it. For empowerment to work Lay-By Chef must therefore recruit the right people but it must also create team work and motivate the teams by switching individual members' roles so that they do not get bored with the same task. It will also be a good idea to get individual Lay-By Chefs to compete with each other either on a regional or national basis. Care must also be taken to make sure that service level are kept high and that empowerment does not lead to big differences in service between restaurants. This will be the job of restaurant managers who will report to senior management.

2.1.4 Review and assessment of empowerment

Management needs to survey staff regularly to assess the success of an empowerment approach. It will also need to give staff the opportunity to voice their opinions/concern on a one to one basis with supervisors.

People are the key to a successful business – they personify the company and effect the objectives and strategy of the company on a day-to-day basis. The high staff turnover is the most glaring problem facing LBC. High staff turnover is a major issue as:

- The time, effort and money invested in training people is lost
- Skills that have been developed and perfected at LBC are no longer available
- Continually recruiting people is very expensive
- Lack of continuity and development of skill base – ideas and knowledge cannot be shared
- Demoralizing for other employees – leaving becomes 'catching'.

Before we look at the individual case of LBC in greater depth, I would suggest that there are three general factors which are leading to this high level of staff turnover:

a. The wrong people are recruited for LBC – they don't share the corporate culture

b. There is a mismatch of skills and jobs – people are put in the wrong position for their skills and abilities which leads to dissatisfaction and frustration

c. Employment practices and day-to-day working ethic cause people to leave.

Before jumping to conclusions as to the particular cause of the problem at LBC, I feel that it is very important to undertake surveys to discover what is at the root of the issue. Once this is known, strategy can be developed to overcome it. Approaches I suggest are:

a. Survey employees anonymously at all levels regarding their perceptions of their jobs, satisfaction levels, practices they have issue with and elements of their employment which they would like developed further.

b. Survey ex-employees as to why they left (again anonymously to ensure the most truthful response).

Send senior managers to work 'hands on' in an LBC restaurant so that they fully comprehend the daily reality of working in LBC and ensure that all employment strategy and practices are based on this daily reality.

3. Mission

A customer-focused culture can only be achieved if the CEO is committed to spreading a positive message. He will need to champion the new training programmes and communicate the benefits to the whole company. The mission needs to state clearly what these are and be incorporated into the job descriptions in obtainable and measurable objectives that can be used in the appraisal process.

4. Audit

Skills and core competency gaps need to be identified and then training arranged accordingly. This needs to be marketed internally.

5. Training

5.1 Senior management and directors

Once the training gap has been measured, directors must be sent on training sessions accordingly. Priority will be given to Change Management training, as this will be pivotal to ensuring a smooth implementation of the training programmes and culture shifts.

5.2 Middle management and supervisors

Priority should be given to Customer service training, as this will be pivotal to the whole process of introducing the new changes in culture.

- Customer service
- Teambuilding
- Internal secondments – job swapping
- Stress management/conflict
- Role play
- Appraisal.

5.3 Frontline staff

- Induction
- Teambuilding
- Customer service
- Stress management and complaints handling.

6. Reward and recognition

It will be vitally important to find out how successful the training programmes have been and how they have matched up to the original objectives. These need to be linked into the appraisal and reward system.

Recruitment procedures and training must be linked in with staff reward systems and incentives to encourage loyalty and offer recognition to those whom retain high standards of customer service.

There are a number of reward systems that can be offered:

- Pay increases/extra holiday entitlement
- Prizes awarded for improvement ideas
- Social evenings – funded by Lay-By-Chef, which will also encourage social interaction between staff members
- Distance learning courses – in other areas of interest, e.g. language skills or pottery lessons.

Rewards and recognition may be enough to encourage staff to be more customer-focused in the short term but opportunities for career advancement and promotion may provide the ultimate incentive for staff motivation.

Failure to offer ongoing support and recognition will result in de-motivated staff, which will ultimately impact on the customer. Today's customer is extremely demanding; they are far less likely to 'tolerate' low standards such as sloppy service, poor quality food and dirty surroundings.

Directors must be encouraged to make site visits so that they are not so removed from the frontline staff and the customers.

7. The current market segmentation

This needs to be addressed because there are sectors of the market which are not being served. LBC's mission is aimed at the motoring family and business traveller. However, this leads to two main questions:

a. Are these the most profitable sectors (and if not, who is)?

b. Are our main customers from our target market (and if not, which market sector are they)?

In order to answer these questions, it is necessary to undertake some market research into profitability of different travelling sectors and also into our customer base. The latter is easier, and cheaper, as it involves surveying actual customers whereas the former involves wider market research.

Once it has been discovered who the most profitable sectors are, I feel it is important to target them, if they are not already the main customer base.

However, we also need to look at expanding this customer base to target additional travellers who would complement our current target market. Suggestions include:

- *Group visitors e.g. from coach tours, school trips, etc.* – these could be targeted by directing promotional material, money-off vouchers to the coach companies (which include details of all LBC locations) and special group meal deals, e.g. offer a free tea, coffee or soft drink to all coach party members having a full meal/ spending over £10 per head (this would, of course, have to be costed in first).

- *Haulage companies, especially small, light freight* – we could target this group by sending promotional material to the freight forwarding companies with frequent visitor schemes for the drivers such as half-price meal with five meal receipts. Free newspapers provided as lorry drivers frequently travel alone so won't have anyone to talk with while having their meal.

- *Non-travelling restaurant customers* – we could try and attract local residents to dine at LBC when they would like a good meal out at reasonable prices. This could be done by sending flyers to local areas (undertake studies to identify the most viable areas) with special introductory offers.

Introducing frequent visitor incentives could further encourage businessmen. An example might be a club card which gives them points each time they eat at Lay-By Chef which they can use for air miles or clothes vouchers etc…

All these options would have to be investigated thoroughly to ensure that they would be cost-effective and viable before proceeding to implement the plan.

8. Market research and an understanding of the value chain and customer activity cycle

We also need to find out why people visit LBC so that we can build on these attractions and emphasize others which may not be so obvious. In addition, we need to survey our competitors (especially Little Chef) to find out what they offer which LBC is lacking. This information can be found through customer surveys, random public surveys, surveys of target market group (e.g. business travellers) and mystery visitors to get a fresh, unbiased impression of LBC and our competitors.

Once people have visited LBC we need to ensure that they return. There are many ways that this can be done but three I would suggest are:

- Developing a customer database and sending updated material regularly with vouchers for our target markets, e.g. buy one coffee, get one free for business/group travellers, kid's meal half price with an adult meal for family visitors.

- Present all customers with a leaflet outlining the location of all LBC restaurants when paying the bill – perhaps put receipt inside the leaflet to encourage retention/consideration.
- Provide a stamp for each transaction over a certain level and 5 stamps (for example) lead to a discount or free product (aimed at target market).

9. Build on our nationwide cover and localize

A particular strength of LBC is its nationwide cover. Nationwide cover means that we are able to target our market across the country and customers are able to find LBCs throughout the British Isles. However, this national spread needs to be played upon to develop customer loyalty and to encourage repeat visitors.

LBC currently produces a very homogenized product throughout the country. LBC customers can expect certain standards and they won't be disappointed but, as things stand, they will not experience any pleasant surprises or local variations. Our customers are guaranteed that when they visit LBC their expectations for product and service will be met. However, we need to surpass these expectations by adding extra value to the visit.

LBC's customers, are by the nature of the business, travellers moving around from one area to the next. We can build on local traditions and specialities to personalize a visit to each LBC restaurant. This may be in the form of a 'local special' on the menu, local flowers for decoration or information on local places of interest.

Moving forward in this way will also help involve employees more in the running of each individual restaurant and enable them to feel that they are really inputting into the organization through their ideas for local features.

We can develop this scheme to encourage people to use LBC when they visit new areas as they will be able to enjoy a personalized visit for each place but with guarantees of quality and service.

Conclusion

Many of Lay-By Chef's difficulties lie in its culture of production line approach to customer service. Staff are not happy and they are leaving. This will effect the profitability of the business. By carefully introducing the empowerment approach to its frontline staff and motivating them I believe that this problem can be solved. However it must receive the full support of top level management. Other strategic issues need to be addressed as well, namely market segmentation, relationship building, and value chain analysis and an understanding of the customer activity cycle.

However, one point which I would like to leave you to think about is that common standards of excellence does not mean total homogeneity across the chain and no room for individual expression and local adaptation. Standards are good but people must have the freedom to surpass these standards if truly excellent service is to be provided.

LBC needs to develop happy, satisfied and empowered staff who are fully committed to the company and are focused on providing excellent customer service. The aim is that people should go out of their way to visit LBC because they know they will enjoy great service from committed, fulfilled employees, rather than just happening on LBC as it is conveniently on route.

This must be our goal.

Summary

This unit has covered an extensive range of issues which need to be considered in the context of developing a true customer orientation. There are downsides and upsides to all these methods and the balance and interest conflict between capital and labour, and the observation of it in organizational life, need to be considered. Conflict resulting in lack of competitiveness, low performance, low quality, and lack of motivation, loyalty and commitment is a problem with which most organizations are beset.

Further study and examination preparation

Now undertake Question 3 from CIM Examination Session December 2000 to be found in the Exam paper Appendix.

Unit 8
Additional techniques
for mobilizing performance

Objectives

- To understand core competencies and relate them to culture, recruitment, training and development, appraisal, reward and recognition.
- Think about motivation, empowerment and the setting of objectives.
- To be able to reflect on job design for frontline customers and reflect on the balance between decision autonomy versus standardization of response.
- Understand and criticize the use of internal service level agreements.

This unit covers the following part of the Marketing Customer Interface syllabus:

- 2.2.1
- 2.2.2

Study guide

A customer-centric organization aligns all aspects of the organization with the customer's needs and expectations. Business success is customer satisfaction and customer referrals. In order to maximize the corporate benefits from the organization/customer interface information competence must be identified. Recruitment, performance management, training and development, and rewards and recognition are the four pillars of human resource strategy. You will also learn about motivation and accountability and internal service level agreement. The recruitment process is covered in the Effective Management for Marketing module.

Marketing working with HR

David Ulrich, the world's foremost thinker on people management, uses concepts from marketing to draw a more direct link between the competitiveness of companies and their HR policies.

The objective of any business is to build a brand that customers are loyal to – because they think of you as delivering high quality, keen prices, good design or whatever. But increasingly, he says, brands are becoming focused not on individual products or services (which change so fast), but on firms themselves. At this level, a brand is the identity that a company projects.

It follows that organizational culture is crucial to this type of brand. The attitudes and behaviour of managers when they make key decisions, and of employees in their everyday dealings with customers, could do a lot either to strengthen or weaken the brand. A vital role for HR is to ensure that they strengthen it.

'Marketing people may build the organization's brand identity, but translating that into company behaviours and employee practices needs HR people', Ulrich told *People Management*. It is up to personnel professionals to work out what that identity means in terms of recruitment, pay, training and so on.

Sooner or later, traditional forms of competitiveness – cost, technology, distribution, manufacturing and product features – can be copied. They have become table stakes. You must have them to be a player, but they do not guarantee you will be a winner.

'Winning will spring from organizational capabilities such as speed, responsiveness, agility, learning capacity and employee competence. Successful organizations will be those that are able to quickly turn strategy into action; to manage processes intelligently and efficiently; to maximize employee contribution and commitment; and to create the conditions for seamless change.' *David Ulrich*

Maximizing corporate benefits

Key factors in maximizing the corporate benefits from the organization/customer interface are information technology, people management, value chain efficiencies and sustained leadership.

Once the business has been understood in terms of the linkages that exist between enablers, processes and results, as outlined for example in the EFQM model, they can reach an understanding of where they are now. This needs to be put in the context of their capability, environment and culture. Everyone is different. The organization can then decide where it wants to be.

Nigel Purse (The Oxford Training Group) says that the senior team must have a clear vision, mission and values that can be expressed in a competency model (or framework) that provides a language for describing people's behaviour and their characteristics. Once this has been done the key pillars of human resource strategy can be constructed. These are:

1. Recruitment (internal and external)
2. Performance management
3. Training and development
4. Rewards and recognition.

The competency framework will then be designed and managers trained to bring them to life.

Recruitment

Behavioural interviewing

The best predictor is behaviour as behaviour tends not to change over time. If an organization has a language to describe behaviour they can use the selection process to acquire information to gain evidence of the behaviour in a job. For example, the ability to listen, innovate and measure outcomes.

It may be necessary for interviewing skills to be changed from hypothetical questions of 'What would you do if ...', to 'Tell me about your most recent experience of ...', 'What did you do?' Behavioural interviewing, gathering evidence of how they have dealt with is an important skill to learn.

Use of simulation

Behavioural interviewing followed by a simulation exercise of what it would be like is the second most important aspect. For example, if a person is being interviewed for a call centre they should be asked to make an outbound call, take an inbound call, and a team exercise should be simulated so that the person can be observed working in a team. These sort of exercise need to be custom designed. Assessors would be line managers in the business who are trained to observe, record and classify the behaviour the person is demonstrating against competences defined for that role.

Use of tests

Test are used after behavioural interviewing and simulation. They can be used to assess personality, skills and aptitude. Tests complement the process, they should not be used on their own.

Performance management

This term appears to mean different things to different people. On one side there is the performance-related pay philosophy where everything is just fine if we give big bonuses for high performance. The other side is about coaching and setting people up for success. The elements that need to be considered here are as follows:

Objectives and clarity

People need to have a clarity about what is expected from them, they should have objectives (management by objectives). Managers use coaching to help staff understand what is expected from them. It is the process of coaching that provides this clarity.

How to do it

Objectives need to be SMART and objectives need to be linked to the business success model. Staff need to understand the drivers of customer behaviour and what they can do to cause customers to deepen their relationship with the business. They also need to know how to behave.

Measures of performance

Measures of performance are there to help people learn. The measures are self-measurement and self-monitoring – not measures that punish people. Feedback, both qualitative and quantitative is used for learning.

Reviewing performance

Performance is reviewed so that staff understand how to learn and how to improve. Managers use a coaching style to help people to understand what is successful and why things went well or badly. This process can be supported by paperwork in the appraisal and performance review records.

Training and development

Many organizations have resources for training such as libraries, open learning and their own programme of courses. What they generally don't have is a gateway that enables people in the organization to access resources and make the most of them. A learning philosophy is about raising self-awareness so people know what they want in the way of knowledge, skills and behavioural training.

Self-awareness-raising such as 360° assessment can be used, but also psychometric tests and development training and simulations. For example, to change sales behaviour and enable sales people to move to a more consultative style, an event could be run simulating how customers in the future would prefer to be treated, and what it would be like for them to behave differently. They can then be given feedback so they can see what they need to do and why it mattered.

Principles of effective training

1. Most effective training experiences come from doing rather than being lectured at. It is participative and practical.
2. Training needs to be designed around three components – knowledge, behaviour and skills.
3. People need to be able to prepare to learn. They need the opportunity before an event to think about why they are coming to a course.
4. Training needs to be reinforced and followed up afterwards by a telephone call, focus group, self-help group or involvement with a line manager.

Developing a corporate learning strategy

Colin Coulson-Thomas, a professor at Luton Business School, says corporate learning is at a crossroads. Existing courses and facilities are nearing the end of their useful lives, and there are new learning approaches and technologies to consider. A survey of the corporate learning plans and priorities of 69 organizations suggests there is widespread confusion and a lack of direction. Many courses are excessively general and fail to address particular requirements. The focus is overwhelmingly internal and on organizational needs. Individual aspirations and the requirements of customers and business partners are being overlooked. Existing information and knowledge are being shared, but training and development activities are contributing little to the creation and exploitation of new knowledge and intellectual capital. Opportunities for collaboration are being missed. In many companies training and development remain a cost although they could provide the basis for generating new income streams and become a significant business in their own right. (Source: *Industrial and Commercial Training*, vol 32, no 3, 2000, pp. 84-88.)

Rewards and recognition

Money is not a motivator but lack of fairness in reward and recognition can be a demotivator. Reward systems must be seen to be fair. Pay should reflect the contribution people make to a business. Line managers should be asked to make judgements about peoples' pay. They need to look at the relative position of the employee within the salary band and relate what they have achieved back to the performance management system.

Core competences

The definition of core competence and core values

In their article, 'Is your core competence a mirage?' Kevin P. Coyne, Stephen J. D. Hall and Patricia Gorman Clifford, *McKinsey Quarterly*, 1997, 1, pp. 40-54 say:

'A core competence is a combination of complementary skills and knowledge bases embedded in a group or team that results in the ability to execute one or more critical processes to a world-class standard.'

Such a definition excludes many skills or properties often cited by organizations as core competencies. Patents, brands, products and technologies do not qualify; neither do broad management capabilities such as strategic planning, flexibility and teamwork; nor do high-level corporate themes like quality, productivity and customer satisfaction.

They say that core competences so defined can be grouped into two categories.

Insight/foresight competences

These enable a company to discover or learn facts or patterns that create first-mover advantages. Such insights might derive from:

- Technical or scientific knowledge that produces a string of inventions
- Proprietary data
- Information derived from having the largest share
- Pure creative flair in inventing successful products
- Superior analysis and influence.

What distinguishes this kind of competence is that value ultimately derives from the insight itself. A company may have to go to great lengths to exploit it, but others could do so just as effectively if they had access to it.

Frontline execution competences

These arise in cases where the quality of an end product or service can vary appreciably according to the activities of frontline personnel. Insight/foresight and frontline execution competences can coexist in the same company, but each will require its own managerial focus. McDonald's, for instance, uses its frontline execution competence to engineer the food delivery system at individual restaurants and its insight/foresight to identify winning sites for outlets.

How to evaluate core competences with frontline execution:

1. Establish what your competency is. You can do this through market research and benchmarking. Find out what you are valued for and if it matches your customers' value chain and where you stand in relation to your competitors.

2. Establish how easily you could be imitated by the competition. Remember, to change cultural value, train personnel, change policies and create the type of frontline environment in which customer care is the core value can take a long time.

3. analyze the economic value of frontline competence (output).

4. Find out if the competence matches your existing position differentiation in the marketplace and ascertain the gap.

How to create core competences

Coyne, Hall, Gorman Clifford say that:

1. A world-class competence must steer the power structure in a company. The keeper of the skill drives all the company's major decisions, even in unrelated functions. At Procter & Gamble, for instance, the core consumer marketing skill resides in the advertising department (their name for brand management). Brand managers exert a dominant influence on all decisions throughout the company. And at Wachovia Bank, even relatively new credit officers routinely block loans proposed by experienced senior line officers.

2. A core competence strategy must be chosen by the CEO, not by department heads acting independently.

There are three distinct routes to developing a core competence.

1. *Evolution*, where a company attempts to build skill at the same time as the individuals involved perform their tasks.

2. *Incubation*, where a separate group is formed to focus exclusively on the chosen competence.

3. *Acquisition*, where one company purchases another to obtain the skills it needs.

Recruiting the right person

If one thinks about customer service as being the ability to 'satisfy customer needs (real and perceived) in a dependable manner', an ideal front-line person would have the following profile (Martin, W. and Fritz, E. (1989), *Managing Quality Customer Service*, Crisp):

- A genuine liking for people
- An enjoyment of working for and servicing others
- A sharing social need
- An ability to feel comfortable among strangers
- A sense of belonging to a group or place
- An ability to control feelings
- A sensitivity towards people and ability to show compassion and empathy
- A general sense of trusting others
- A high record of competence.

Choosing a test

There are many tests and in most selection processes systematic selection is essential to reduce numbers to a manageable level. Most selection is about elimination, not by choice.

Some tests are more reliable than others and it is a good idea to contact a reputable company and to take their guidance on the most appropriate methods. However before a test can be chosen you will need to have a clear idea of the range of qualities of characteristics required for the job to be performed well. Details of the work to be done are put together in a job description, while the qualities and characteristics required to perform the job form part of a person's specification. We will not deal with the tests in detail, but give a general description of the main types.

Psychological tests

Psychological tests fall into two different categories (*Source: Psychological Testing*, Institute of Personnel Management):

1. *Psychometric tests.* These determine performance such as tests of general intelligence and special aptitude or, ability, verbal, spatial, diagnostic, mechanical, manual dexterity, clerical speed and accuracy, word processor aptitude, computer aptitude, language aptitude
2. *Personality assessment and psychometric questionnaires.* Personality is defined here as the way in which an individual's behaviour is organized and coordinated when they react with the environment – characteristics which are assessed would include emotional adjustment, motivation, social relations, interests, values and attitudes. These factors are relevant to occupational assessment. Some cognitive (intelligent) scales are included in some questionnaires as some psychologists believe these need to be taken into account.

Personality profiling can help organizations understand and manage their staff. Use the web to find out more:

- managementtech.com/personalysis.html (services)
- http://www.opusmarketing.com/24reasns.htm (general)
- http://www.massprofiles.com/page2.html (general)
- email: *info@thomas.co.uk* and ask for the free personal profile analysis, Martin Reed the MD has made this special offer to CIM students.

Customer care training programme management

Training can be structured in the following ways:

1. It can grouped by hierarchy.
2. It can be grouped by customer supply chain.
3. A vertical slice can be taken of the hierarchy or the customer supply chain.
4. Or a combination of the above may be used.

Training group size

Organizations tend to arrange for large groups (80-150) to be at each session so that employees can see themselves within the context of the whole organization and also to understand how their own actions impact on other people. Smaller groups are used after this for training in particular skills. Group dynamic change in different group sizes, generally described as small (10-12), medium (18-25), and larger groups. The size of the group should be suited to the training event.

Planning

Customer care training should be planned so that it is ongoing, and retraining arranged well into the future. Internal marketing should be used to keep interest in customer care alive, with up-to-date research provided on customer feedback, ongoing developments on innovations and improvements generally. Various techniques could be used as new initiatives to keep the idea of customer service alive (see Unit 7) Benchmarking could also be used.

Organization

Analysis

From the analysis it will be clear where some of the weaknesses within the organization lie. Attitude surveys held with customers and with employees will enable the organization to pinpoint where they need to improve. An understanding of the core competences will clarify this further.

The setting of objectives

The setting of training objectives will then enable the organization to decide what they need to achieve. What they need to do in practice may well fit into the philosophy, structure, and techniques they have decided to use.

Discussion groups

Discussions will then need to take place at a senior level on how the achievement of these objectives then fit into the job descriptions, recruitment, induction, reward, appraisal and promotion procedures; as well as the specific training programmes.

Middle management will also need to be involved and the results from the analysis and attitude surveys relayed. Barriers to change will have to be overcome and managers may have to be trained in many of the techniques of leadership, team building, delegation and empowerment and the encouragement of innovation.

Implementation

Action plans for change will need to be drawn up and the outcome of these decisions will have to be marketed internally so that the rest of the staff are prepared for change. Ideas on how to become involved need to be promoted so that they are able to integrate the ideas, identify with them and ultimately own them.

Internal marketing

Internal marketing could also include promotional material such as newsletters outlining the benefits, badges (the programme could be branded), posters and so on. Workshops could be held to enable employees in direct contact with customers to understand why this training programme is being undertaken. Results from the analysis and attitude surveys can be relayed back, core competences explained, performance standards clarified, the linkages into the recruitment, appraisal, reward and promotion systems explained. The training programmes could then be outlined, for example, verbal and non-verbal skills training, complaint handling, etc.Personal action plans could also be used.

See Unit 7, *Strategy and methods to produce customer focused behaviour*.

What can go wrong?

Introducing new ideas into organizations is not easy. As Ted Johns, the Senior Examiner says in his book *Perfect Customer Care* (Arrow books) problems include:

1. Complacency and arrogance about studying the competition and understanding the need for strategy and training.

2. Conservatism and the lack of receptiveness to new ideas.

3. Production orientation and suspicions about marketing.

4. Interdepartmental rivalries and tight boundaries.

5. Status and seniority of high-ranking employees held in awe, and company cars thought to be more important.

6. Secretive closed attitudes to information and excessive confidentiality.

7. Tolerance of inadequate achievement.

8. Scepticism about people as managers think that organizational effectiveness has nothing to do with staff, their commitment, or their involvement.

9. Rules and procedures treated as ends in themselves with strict job descriptions.

10. Lip service paid to equal opportunity.

11. Customers seen as the enemy and the organization exists for the benefit of its members.

12. Lack of support from senior management and managers too involved in the day-to-day work of the organization.

13. Staff cynical.

14. Results take time.

15. Training seen as a once-off exercise.

16. Attention put on external customers but internal relationships remain the same.

17. Quality improvement teams bogged down in detail.

18. Absence of performance feedback.

Ted Johns feels that the CEO must provide a role model, be personally visible and convey the message in company newsletters, posters, manuals and so on. The CEO should personally look for customer feedback and be involved in the recruitment, promotion and training policies. The role should be used for showmanship and symbolism

Training and coaching

Training covers activities such as:

- Courses, workshops, seminars
- Planned personal development
- Management development
- Team building
- On-job instruction
- Induction.

On- or off-the-job training

The decision to have on-the-job or off-the-job training will need to be taken – it does not necessarily mean an either/or situation.

There are advantages and disadvantages to both. On-the-job training has the advantages of:

- It is totally related to the workplace and therefore real – costs can be measured.
- It would be supervised.

Off-the-job training has the advantages of:

- As it is reviewed people may feel more protected and able to experiment.
- Trainers may be more able to instruct.
- Other people may be there who share the same problems.

Coaching skills

There are three principal reasons for coaching:

1. Correction of weakness
2. Short-term development
3. Long-term development.

The benefits of coaching to team members are numerous:

- They know where they stand
- They know what is expected
- They know they are valued
- They are challenged
- They are supported
- They know where they are going
- They are given feedback on progress.

Coaching can be used to help team members:

- Perform a new task
- Improve performance
- Develop a skill
- Solve a problem
- Build confidence.

In order for coaching to be effective it must take place in an atmosphere of mutual trust and support. This atmosphere must be created so that to seek help is not viewed as being weak or wrong.

The process must be learner-centred. The sessions are designed to meet the needs of the learner, and this must be kept in mind. The benefits of the coaching may be useful to the coach but the process should be conducted in order to develop the learner.

Abilities, experience, goals and values, energy and rewards all affect an individual's behaviour. Abilities and experience indicate how the person is likely to perform. Goals and values will channel the person's behaviour in particular ways.

Table 8.1 *Training or coaching?*

	Training	Coaching
Focus of learning	Task	The results of the job
Timeframe	1-5 days	A month to a year
Approach to activity	'Show and tell', supervised experience	Explore problems together and set up opportunities to try out new skills
Associated tasks	Analyzing task, clear instruction, supervise practice and give feedback immediately	Jointly identify the problem; create and develop opportunities and review
Ownership	Instructor	Shared
Benefits to company	Standard, accurate, performance continuous development and creative	Goal-directed performance, a process of the problem solving

Front-line staff interact with customers and their ability to interact will be determined by their abilities, experience, goals and values.

Customer care is a byproduct of internal relationships and culture. Training should therefore start at the top and courses designed for the outcome that is required at each level.

Training from the top down requires that the organization understands its core competences and has some strategic vision of the marketplace, its customers and its positioning.

In order to implement a customer-focused training programme the following steps need to be taken:

1. Strategic vision and definition of core competences and core value and where they relate in the customers' value chain and the organization's value chain.

2. Understand the operational and managerial behavioural requirements needed to support the core competences and core values.

3. Implementing relevant managerial training such as coaching, facilitating, consulting, changes in managerial style, empowering, delegation, etc.

4. analyze the gap between what the organization wants in the way of the customer-focused behaviour and what it is getting.

5. Deciding on standards and training.

6. Motivating staff to take part.
7. Internal marketing to ensure continuous communication takes place.
8. Identifying how success will be measured.

Staff training is as much about attitudes as it is about skills and leadership and management need to be able to show their commitment so that the relevant modelling of behaviour can take place.

In the same way as recruitment is tailored to the needs of the market in order to ensure core competences and values are maintained, the type of training needs to be specific to the market and to the organization so that core competences and values are protected. Market research can then be carried out in relation to these skills and appropriate training given if standards are seen to fall. The example below from Yellow Pages illustrates the process.

Roles outside the organization

Smaller, leaner organizations with flatter structures may mean that employees are unable to use all their skills at work, or indeed be given the opportunity to develop new ones.

It is also a good idea for employees to be encouraged to use roles in organizations in the voluntary sector to gain experience or develop new skills.

This will need balancing, as the interests of the voluntary sector role may take more energy from the employee than good sense should allow. Psychologically it is healthier emotionally for individuals not to put all their eggs/ambitions into one 'organizational egg basket'.

Counselling – when training is not the solution

Counselling is a useful skill and can be learned but how can counselling help at work? People face problems such as the following at work:

- *Poor job fit.* A poor promotion, secondment or placement decision can lead to a person being placed in a job to which their skills, abilities or motivation are not well suited. The symptoms may be poor performance but the cause may be that the person is being asked to perform in areas where they lack competence or interest.

- *Role defences.* Very often these may interfere with the behavioural requirements of the role and counselling may enable the person to reflect on these aspects.

- *Poor job design.* A poorly designed job can ask the person to meet inconsistent or conflicting demands. Counselling – an external person may bring these problems to light.

- *Relationships.* Relationship problems with the boss may be centred on the boss's inadequacy or incompetence. Maladaptive behaviour in the client may be a coping response, i.e. breaking rules seeking to disprove the boss's viewpoint.

- *Insufficient training.* Again the symptoms are likely to be poor performance but the lack of the necessary education or training could be the cause. In this case it is important to establish that potential exists before reaching a judgement that training is the solution.

- *Adaptation.* To new work methods, people, systems, type of work.

- *Job stress.* The pressures in the job may be too great for one person to sustain. Poor relationships (through irritability) or poor work performance may be symptoms.

- *Personal life stress.* Problems at home, for example marital or financial, can have a very direct effect on performance and relationships at work. A change in performance for no apparent reason is usually a good indicator.

The role of counselling

Although the real root of the problem may lie outside the employee's control, i.e. job design, the employee nevertheless has to live with the consequences. Counselling is therefore concerned with developing ways of helping them to cope with the situation and to find means of changing the circumstances if possible. The focus should be particularly strong on organizational contacts and resources that can be exploited.

Background

The Point of Sale Satisfaction Monitor has been set up to provide an ongoing measure of customer satisfaction with the behaviour and effectiveness of Yellow Pages salespeople. The research is conducted through an independent Market Research Agency. Over a six-month period sufficient interviews are carried out to provide each salesperson with an individual customer satisfaction rating. The sample for each salesperson is carefully monitored to ensure the balance of advertiser types within each score is equal. These ratings are sequentially combined to provide measures for sales teams, sales areas, sales regions and finally, national figures.

Attributes that are used in the Monitor have been identified through qualitative research amongst Yellow Pages' customers to determine specifically what it is they want, in terms of service, from Yellow Pages' salespeople. A total of fourteen attributes are included in the survey, ranging from 'is courteous in their dealings with you' through to 'is knowledgeable about your business and industry' and, of course, 'effectiveness in writing/designing your advertisement'.

Feedback to salespeople is conducted regularly through regionally based news-sheets containing positive comments that have been made about individual (named) salespeople. A national newsletter is planned that will provide more detail on the progress of the research and how it is contributing to the overall improvement in customer service. This newsletter will also include a 'bouquets' section to recognize those salespeople who understand the importance of their work and the benefits of providing good customer service.

Finally: on a regular basis there are what we call 'hot e-mails' where a customer may have a particular concern that requires immediate contact from Yellow Pages. With the customer's permission their name and phone number, along with the details of their concern, are transmitted back to the relevant sales manager and, if necessary, another Yellow Pages department, for action. This action takes place within 48 hours of the date of the interview.

Feedback on the actual ratings achieved by salespeople is provided on a six monthly basis through the Regional and Area managers' regular meetings. Managers will then take their teams' ratings and discuss these with their individual salespeople. The figures will track performance over time as each new period is completed, generating performance over league tables for each of the seven sales channels within each of the regions. Awards will be given both to those achieving the highest results and those who realize the greatest improvement in results over time. Those who do not improve will have the opportunity to identify training and development needs to help them improve in the future. Throughout the introduction and launch of the Monitor it has been stressed that its overall purpose is to help the Company improve customer satisfaction.

Yellow Pages – Point of Sales Satisfaction Monitor 98/99, ©Anne Wolfe, Yellow Pages. March 1999.

Questionnaire summary

Overall

1. In general terms how would you rate the quality of service you received overall from them (the salesperson you had dealings with)?

   o **Attributes**

   How would you rate the salesperson for:

   a. listening to and understanding your needs and concerns

   b. being prepared to work hard to try and help your business succeed

   c. giving you enough time to make your own decisions

   d. giving their time to you, but understanding your time is valuable

   e. communicating well with other support staff to deliver what they promised

   f. having good creative ability to help design and write your advertisement

   g. being courteous in all their dealing with you

   h. inspiring confidence that they are experienced and know what they are doing

   i. knowing your previous history with YP – your pattern of advertising or problems you may have had

Types of training

Empowerment training

Empowerment from a service perspective, gives employees the authority to make decisions regarding customer service. True empowerment means that the employees can bend and break rules to do whatever is necessary (within reason) to take care of the customer. There are three variables that need to be considered:

1. Coaching and mentioning

2. Peer and supervisor modelling

3. Career path development and strategies must be present to provide employees with the guidance and skill necessary to become empowered employees.

The main skills that customer service personnel need are understanding role behaviour, telephone skills, telemarketing, the use of technology, customer service and customer retention, problem solving and maintaining customer satisfaction.

Anne J. Broderick (1998), 'Role theory, role management and service performance', *Journal of Sales Marketing*, 12(5) www.emerald-library.com

Role training

Role theory draws on a behavioural perspective by focusing on explanations of social interaction as behaviours associated with specific social positions (Biddle, 1979). Role theory would argue that the social interaction which occurs between two people in an exchange is principally determined by the roles which each adopts (Goffman 1959; 1967), thus leading to a role script within the encounter. By identifying the dramaturgical aspects within social encounters, it offers an opportunity to examine how role behaviours and choices within the role script can encourage positive service encounter experiences.

Role analysis and planning

Within the internal service process, the efficiency of internal role sets can be identified through an analysis of a role commitment within service teams, the identification of role discrepancies between service providers doing the same job and a comparison of how service providers evaluate their own role performance.

A useful application of role analysis is evident in the training approach at Imperial Hotel Tokyo. Part of the service role training at this hotel focuses on the etiquette and psychology of guest contact, where role playing is used as a preparation tool. Guest psychology such as guests anticipating a level of prestige, feeling possessive about the hotel's facilities and requiring warmth in interactions are considered carefully. Demonstrations of appropriate non-verbal communication and body language are a standard part of the service role preparation. What the management engage in is a meticulous analysis, planning and preparation for desired behavioural outcomes in service roles. The training specified the improved interaction with customers which was sought, identified some verbal and non-verbal role interactions designed to achieve this and addressed these in both the internal service process and at the client interface. In addition, they had a clear idea of the role outcomes to be achieved by employees and how to monitor them.

A practical mechanism for this is through self-assessment and group role analysis (similar in format to quality circles). Similarly, role analysis within the service encounter is useful for specification of role learning needs on the part of client and service provider. Adaptation of the role script can lead to improved customer retention.

Role management during the service life cycle and issues of role identity, appropriate role development and role preparation are important considerations in the management of service life cycles.

Role consistency and service performance

The personal approach of service providers needs coordination, demanding role consistency throughout the service delivery cycle to underline good successive service experiences.

Role outcome measures

These three areas of role management: role analysis and planning, adaptation of role script and role management/role consistency in service performance (during the service life cycle) require some clear measurement criteria, both qualitatively and quantitatively determined.

Telephone skills

Most contact with customers takes place over the telephone. Operators must be able to greet, listen effectively, ask questions, address people, manage objectives, negotiate, manage different types of behaviour and end the conversation.

Telemarketing

Very often contact with a customer offers the opportunity to sell other products. Staff must be able to use these opportunities proactively.

Customer service and customer retention and problem solving

Customer service is not about complaint handling, it is about proactively engaging with customers. For example, finding out if they are happy with a service, ensuring that they know if anything goes wrong they are able to bring back goods for replacement. Problem solving and being able to answer questions, alternatively knowing who to involve so the problem can be solved and ensuring it has been attended to is an important aspect of proactively relating to customers.

Other types of training for frontline staff could include assertiveness training, handling aggression and conflict management, counselling skills, negotiation and sales skills, stress management and personal organization.

This is especially important for new technology which requires constant learning on the job as workers need to keep up with specific skills, but also have a need for general education.

Motivational issues and job design for frontline staff

The ongoing debate about work very much depends on the assumptions people make about the nature of man. Two views that have helped to support the idea that organizations should be made for people and not the other way around have been those of Maslow and Herzberg.

The ideas of Maslow and Herzberg are represented in Figure 8.1. Maslow suggested that various needs need to be satisfied in order to move on to the satisfaction of higher needs. Herzberg developed Maslow's ideas into what he called the motivation-hygiene theory. Here he said that men have two sets of needs which they continually try to satisfy. The need to avoid pain and discomfort and the need to grow and develop psychologically. The need to avoid pain and discomfort is satisfied by organizational factors such as policy, supervision, salary, inter-personal relations and working conditions – these are called hygiene factors and must be avoided if they are to give any long-term feelings of satisfaction. But they do not motivate people to work well. In order to do this people need to grow and develop psychologically. These needs are met by factors such as achievement, recognition, responsibility, advancement and the work itself. It is these motivators that result in positive long-term feelings of satisfaction. Leadership and empowerment are key skills in enabling this process to take place.

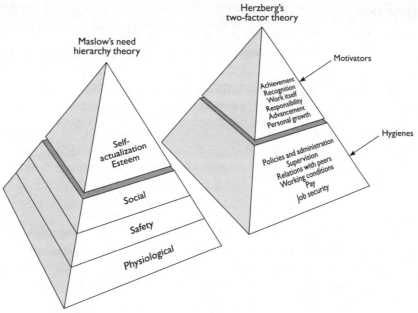

Maslow's need hierarchy theory

Self-actualization
Esteem

Social

Safety

Physiological

Herzberg's two-factor theory

Motivators

Achievement
Recognition
Work itself
Responsibility
Advancement
Personal growth

Hygienes

Policies and administration
Supervision
Relations with peers
Working conditions
Pay
Job security

Figure 8.1

Herzberg has listed job disassatisfiers, also known as maintenance factors. These include physical conditions such as not enough to do, shift systems, hours of work, rota duties, overtime, holidays, heating, lighting, ventilation, arrangement of plant and office layout, car parks and protective clothing. There are ones that affect security such as inadequate technical supervision, unfair supervisors, unfair promotion policies, unhappy working groups, unhappy relationships with supervisor, the conditions of employment, the length of notice, redundancy policies, sick pay, pension scheme, profits sharing and social opportunities. There are economic factors like pay rises, bonuses, piece work, the use of flat rates, increments, fringe benefits, lunches, housing and cars. There may be other factors such as the duplication of effort, struggles for power, waste and inefficiency, company policy and administration. There are also job satisfiers. These might include ones that give a sense of achievement, perhaps by encouraging workers to feel a sense of pride in their work, or allowing all to get on with the job they have been allotted, giving freedom to plan work as they think best, setting achievable goals in consultation with those who have to perform them, creating positive projects which are examined and, where necessary, implemented, delegating responsibility and rewarding enterprise, giving encouragement where assignments are difficult and praise when successful, showing understanding and assisting projects to success, while making each subordinate feel that their contribution has been largely instrumental in reaching a goal. Recognition is another satisfier. This involves giving each employee self-respect, confidence in themselves and their role in the company and making all tasks, including mundane operations, truly important in the eyes of all members of your organization and saying so in public. It also includes granting status to all those deserving it (clothing, tools, sick pay, pensions, merit pay) and showing appreciation for loyalty and long service and difficult tasks accomplished by public acclaim. Participation is another satisfier. This means you recognize that all members of your staff are an essential part of the team with a distinctive role to play, keeping a flow of information up/down, consulting wherever possible, explaining tasks to be tackled, giving real roles to all, which seem to be fair and being available when needed and when help is required. The last satisfier is growth. This might mean providing opportunities for individual initiative, giving opportunity for self-development within the present job, planning personnel development and providing opportunities for promotion and making this known to all members of the group, developing and showing interest in each member of your staff according to their capabilities and appraising performance and setting new goals.

Management can satisfy the needs in Maslow's hierarchy. Self-fulfillment can be encouraged by providing growth, career opportunities, training and development and encouraging creativity and empowerment. Self-esteem can be helped by managers praising high performance, publicizing individual achievement, giving feedback, providing appraisal and giving greater responsibility. Social recognition can come through a manager who provides for working in groups, where there is interaction at different levels or the chance for social/social events, or where a manager encourages participation in informal structures. Safety is enhanced by the provision of safe working conditions, job security and a manager who treats employees equally and fairly. On the physiological front a manager needs to pay fair wages, provide reasonable working conditions and provide rest breaks.

Other theories

There are many other theories about motivation, for example:

- Roethlisberger and Dickson add on the need for justice, fair treatment and dependence-independence
- McClelland emphasizes power affiliation and achievement
- Ardery draws attention to identify, security and stimulation.

You could well add to these lists. The most important point to remember is that each person has their own list and these may differ widely and change as their life develops. Their needs are also influenced by their background, early environment, education, the person's self-concept and experience. Motivation of a person needs to be put into the context of the organization and environment they are working in. Also, the role the person has defined for them by the organization and the 'role idea' carried in their minds will determine how they carry out their work. If you want to find out about people you must talk to them to find out how they feel about themselves and their work.

Maslow's theory is said to not apply outside Western, industrialized economies and cultures and the hierarchy has been criticized. Herzberg (1987) argues his theory holds up in diverse cultures and that there are some common characteristics among workers throughout the world.

Role analysis

Before looking at how to motivate a person one needs to understand the concept of 'role'. The role being the way in which people organize their behaviour in relation to a specific situation. This definition makes the taking up of a role into something that is internally determined – the role is in the mind.

The subjective aspects of the role rely on:

1. The person's ability to understand what the job is in terms of the work to be done.
2. The person's understanding of where they are within a given organizational system – the role relationships.
3. Their realization of how people expect them to behave.
4. The understanding of the environmental considerations that impact on an organization externally.
5. The reality of the pressures that impact on them from within the organization itself.
6. An understanding of any intra-role conflict.
7. An understanding of inter-role conflict.

The role idea which individuals carry in their mind and which motivates them, and relates them to some inner meaning which helps them to manage their behaviour, is affected by:

- The individual's own view of their relationship with other people (e.g. if a person feels threatened they will define their role more tightly and vice versa).
- The individual's own assessment of their performance – if they think they are doing well they will expand their role.
- A change in working environment or a new colleague could be threatening and cause them to redefine the role.
- A change in the macro-environment, micro-environment, mission or primary task may frighten the individual and inhibit them from performing the role.

It is therefore important to always speak to the person to find out about how they view themselves in their role. Some people feel in order to carry the role they need to leave their feelings and personality at the door of the office. This is not the case and if it is the *role idea* that people are using to guide their behaviour, their ideas of how to behave will need to be reassessed. Taking on a role does not mean people have to become stereotypical imitations.

Motivating individuals

Four suggestions to motivate your staff are:

1. Get to know them
2. Help them to achieve success
3. Give them a feeling of control over their work
4. Build their self-esteem.

As a manager one of your first tasks should be to get to know the individual members of your team. Make the effort to find out. Ask the right questions. How do they see their jobs? Where are they in their lives? What aspirations do they have? What do they expect of you? What problems do they have at work? Don't sit in your office, pondering on the answers to these questions. Observe your staff; talk to them; listen to what they have to say.

Vroom's expectancy theory

Motives = Behaviour = Goals

Vroom's theory is also concerned with the complex process of behaviour.

Whether a person will be motivated to achieve a goal is dependent on their *expectations* of the effect their *effort* will have on their *performance* and of the *reward* to be obtained.

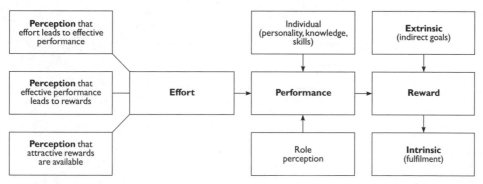

Figure 8.2

Rewards can be:

- *Extrinsic* – can be short term or fail to live up to expectations, e.g. pay rise.
- *Intrinsic* – are more fulfilling, e.g. responsibility, challenge, feedback, autonomy, variety and interaction (Torrington, 1987, p. 358).

An individual's perception of the process will depend on what their 'unsatisfied needs' are. Does the reward satisfy the need?

Summary

1. Vroom takes a wide view of the motivational process.
2. Individuals are motivated when they perceive their behaviour will lead to the desired outcomes.
3. The individual's perception of reality is crucial.
4. Good performance = job satisfaction (not the other way round).
5. Concentration on intrinsic rewards is needed because extrinsic rewards are short lived (Cole 1990).

As you can see from Vroom's expectancy theory shown in Figure 8.2 individuals are motivated when they perceive their behaviour will lead to what they want. Therefore, the individual's perception of reality, what they want, is absolutely crucial. If a person performs well they will be satisfied. Therefore, the more enabled a person is to be able to do a better job, the more satisfied they will become with their own achievements. The more positive feedback they get the more satisfied they will be. Part of this is empowering people, giving them challenges and so on. But one of the most important things is for them to know what they are trying to achieve. This goes back to proper objectives so that the person understands what they are there to do.

If people understand what they are there to do the inability to carry out the task then needs to be thought about in different ways. If they can't do the job, you need to sort out if it is due to ability or motivation…

Is the lack of ability due to:

- Lack of resources?
- Lack of training?
- Inadequate aptitude?

Is the lack of motivation due to:

- Poorly understood or unrealistic expectations?
- Rewards not being linked to the job or unfairly distributed?
- Rewards not salient to this person?
- Role defences?

Enhancing performance

It is important to remember that when you consider role performance that it is part of a 'role three-some' – knowledge, skills and behaviour (Figure 8.3).

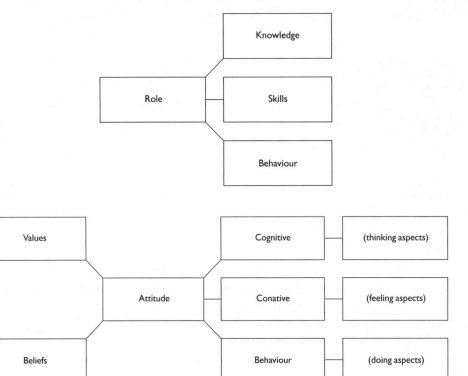

Figure 8.3

Figure 8.4

Behaviour is based on attitudes which in themselves consist of different components (Figure 8.4).

This model allows us to look at enhancing role performance in a number of different ways. It also enables market research around role performance to be linked in specific ways:

1. Values
2. Beliefs
3. Attitude
4. Behaviour:
   - o knowledge (cognitive)
   - o feeling (conative)
   - o behaviour (doing).

The recruitment process can also be built around this process as values, beliefs and attitudes leading to the behavioural side are powerful determinants of organizational culture.

How to enhance role performance

Key guidelines for enhancing role performance and creating a motivating work environment are:

1. Clearly defined acceptable performance of behavioural objectives must be decided by the person (management by objectives). Everyone must know where they are going so that *success* is clearly defined – without understanding what constitutes success you will have an unhappy person. The actions that people take in order to carry out a task must link into the overall mission.

2. The person must be able to internalize these objectives (key result areas) and will have to work on their own self-improvement in order to get better – perceived behavioural control .

3. The organization must remove barriers in the organization that will prevent the person doing their job and make sure that the person has resources and support from their colleagues in order to do their job properly. Unless frustration is removed the person will find it difficult to do their job – perceived behavioural control.

4. If people lack the knowledge, skills and can't behave in the required way, they must be given education, training, mentoring and coaching, to be able to acquire them.

5. They must be given direct feedback from customer research so that they can personally become involved with what customers say and how they are feeling.

6. For example, in teaching the results of student feedback are given to the teacher so that they can personally take on board what they need to do in order to improve. In most cases they do this themselves and read what is said – feedback is immediate and reflection immediate.

7. This is a sensitive process and the person will need to understand how their own defences will come up in order to protect themselves from the emotional pain of criticism. If this process is not understood and talked about openly there is the likelihood of a 'name and blame', 'them and us' culture growing. This type of climate is not conducive to positive customer relations.

8. Rewards must be linked to achieving objectives. People are in fact being 'conditioned' to behave in a certain way.

9. Appraisal and ongoing reflection are used as a learning method to encourage self-discipline. By helping people to identify problems themselves and getting them to explain how they should improve their own selves they will be able to internalize what is needed to make things better. This is in line with the principle of self-actualization outlined by Maslow.

10. Rewards must again be linked to each level of improvement – these do not have to be monetary.

Self-actualization and empowerment

The whole idea of self-actualization and empowerment is based on the individual doing it themselves – systems are then structured into the organization to facilitate this enabling progress to take place.

Design of jobs

Job design for customer-facing roles can be thought about in two different ways.

Fragmentation

Taylor's ideas (he was called the 'Enemy of the American Working Man') would be to fragment a job into different tasks and employees would be trained to carry out the fragmented task in precisely the manner determined best. This method achieves control, a one-task job can be proficiently done, very little skill is needed, the worker remains unskilled so low pay can be given. However, for the worker it is repetitive, boring, the individual's part in the organization is almost meaningless, people get dissatisfied and careless and the person remains undeveloped and unable to progress.

Whole tasks

Whole tasks, on the other hand, allow the person to conceive the job and experience the outcome of their actions. This means that:

- Individuals can be given autonomy in their work instead of allocating aspects of it to supervisors.

- Contact with customers and feedback from customer questionnaires can be given to them so they know how well they are doing and can provide a basis for improvement.

- Meaningful sequences of work will increase the significance of the job and create more job satisfaction.

Managing by objectives

Setting objectives

It is obvious that everybody at work should know what objectives they are working towards and have some measure of knowing how successful they are. It is quite simple – if you do not know what you are supposed to be achieving how will you ever get a feeling of satisfaction about doing a good job? How will you ever be happy with yourself? How will other people know how good you are at your job? How can they praise and reward you.

Objectives are in the main defined by the employee, and not imposed from above, so that there is an implicit democratic and participative element. Thus, hopefully, the employee's wishes in the development of their own future and realization of personal aims are integrated with the organization's need to clarify and achieve its goals of profitability or social unity in relationship with their customers.

By setting objectives that are jointly determined you will be setting a scene in which individuals will be able to motivate themselves because they have been given responsibility and the opportunity to develop themselves. Control is therefore given to the individual over themselves and is not imposed on them from the outside. The person is in fact treated as a grown-up and is doing something because they want to do it, not because someone has told them how to do it.

Five dimensions of empowerment

1. *Self-efficacy.* A feeling that you possess the capability and competence to perform a task successfully.
2. *Self determination.* A feeling of choice, you have the ability to initiate your own actions and processes.
3. *Personal control.* A belief in your ability to effect change.
4. *Meaning.* A belief in the value of the goals which you are pursuing.
5. *Trust.* A belief that you will be treated fairly and equitably.

This approach treats human beings as human beings, not as mechanistic robots.

How to do it

The first step of the organization is to understand where it is going. This may be specific or be expressed as a general aim. Within this organizational plan, each function/department will construct their own plan.

Key results/areas need to be identified which will reflect the success of the department. In order to do this, go back and look at job descriptions. The job description should list five to six key areas which will define what the person is there to do. These need to be checked and updated. They can also be linked to time management so people understand what they should be spending their time on.

Each team member can then work out a job improvement plan. This will consist of:

- Objectives they have for the period under review (normally one year)
- Improvements they can make
- Actions they need to take to achieve them
- Constraints under which they have to work.

This is all taken to the manager, discussed and agreed. It is important that the manager does not interfere in establishing performance levels if they think they are too low. The essence of MBO is that the person has set their own objectives. The manager, sometimes with a consultant, may help to clarify the person's thinking, and can fairly insist they keep within the overall aims of the organization but must as a general principle give way in cases of disagreement. If the manager is right it will become apparent later.

At the end of the period under question to be determined, the person meets their manager and together they look at the performance of the department, the extent to which the targets were achieved, reasons why some were not, ways in which this can be rectified, and on the basis of all this, the person (not the manager) rewrites his job improvement plan for the next twelve months.

However at any time in the twelve months person and manager can meet to amend the plan if it is proving inappropriate to the situation. So the stages can be represented as shown inFigure 8.5.

To see how this works out in practice we might take a few short examples as shown inFigure 8.6.

There are numerous problems if MBO is applied incorrectly but if it is instituted correctly then the main problem is that it takes up a lot of time, particularly in the collaborative process of working out each individual's management plan, but the results will speak for themselves.

Reflection and review

Reflection and review are critical aspects of following the path towards empowering staff – being able to give and take constructive feedback is a necessary part of this process.

Constructive feedback

Feedback is a way of learning more about ourselves and the effect of our behaviour on others. Constructive feedback increases our self-awareness, offers options and encourages development; it is important to learn to give and receive it. Constructive feedback does not mean only positive feedback. Negative feedback, given skilfully, can be very important and useful.

Destructive feedback means that which is given in an unskilled way and leaves the recipient feeling bad with nothing on which to build options for using the learning.

Giving skilled feedback

1. Start with the positive. Most people need encouragement; to be told when they are doing something well. When offering feedback it can help the receiver to hear first what you like about them and what they have done well, e.g. 'I really like how well you listen to Jim; however, on that occasion I did feel that you made an assumption about him without checking it out.'

    Our culture tends to emphasize the negative. The focus is likely to be on mistakes more often than strengths. In a rush to criticize we may overlook the things we liked. If the positive is registered first, any negative is more likely to be listened to and acted upon.

2. The specific. Avoid general comments which are not useful when it comes to developing skills. Statements such as 'You were brilliant' or 'It was awful', may be pleasant or dreadful to hear, but they do not give enough detail to be useful sources of learning. Pinpoint what the person did which led you to use the label 'brilliant' or 'awful', e.g. 'The way you asked that question at that moment was really helpful' or 'At that moment you seemed to be imposing your values on the other person.' Specific feedback gives more opportunity for learning.

3. Refer to behaviour which can be changed. It is not likely to be helpful to give a person feedback about something over which they have no choice, e.g. 'I really don't like your face – height – the fact that you are bald' etc. This is not offering information about which a person can do very much. On the other hand to be told that 'It would help me if you smiled more or looked at me when you speak' can give the person something on which to work.

4. Offer alternatives. If you do offer negative feedback then do not simply criticize, but suggest what the person could have done differently. Turn the negative into a positive suggestion, e.g. 'The fact that you remained seated when Ann came in seemed unwelcoming. I think that if you had walked over and greeted her it would have helped to put her at ease.'

5. Be descriptive rather than evaluative. Tell the person what you saw or heard and the effect it had on you rather than something was 'good, bad, etc.' For example, 'Your tone of voice as you said that really made me feel that you were concerned' is likely to be more useful than 'That was good.'

6. Own the feedback. It can be easy to say to the other person 'You are . . .' suggesting that you are offering a universally agreed opinion about that person. In fact you're entitled to give your own experience of that person at a particular time. It is important that you take responsibility for the feedback you offer. Begin the feedback with 'I' or 'In my opinion' thus avoiding the impression of being the giver of universal judgement about the other person.

7. Leave the recipient with a choice. Feedback which demands change or is imposed heavily on the other person may invite resistance. It is not consistent with a belief in each of us being

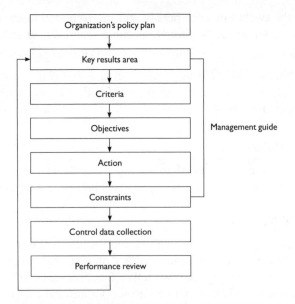

Figure 8.5

Position	Front-line staff in a retail outlet
Key area	To achieve sales by delivering a high level customer service
Criteria	Sales from area Returns Customer opinion Shrinkage
Objectives	a) £x January–June per month b) £x July–October per month c) £x November–December per month d) Zero customer complaints e) Shrinkage reduced by _____ f) Returns reduced by _____
Action	a) Analyse sales per category b) Analyse returns per category c) Analyse shrinkage per category
Control data	Quantitative a) Sales by day, week, month, period b) Shrinkage c) Returns Qualitative a) Customer complaints b) Customer satisfaction c) Customer retention

Position	Regional Sales Manager
Key area	To achieve gross profit and sales volume targets in the region
Criteria	Gross profit as against sales value per customer Regional selling expenses Volume of regional sales Ratio of order to quotation Customer satisfaction/retention
Objectives	a) £x January–June per month b) £x July–October per month c) £x November–December per month d) Zero customer complaints
Action	a) Analyse costs, compare with other regions and make recommendations by January b) Institute new customer campaign aiming at 25 new customers per sales territory by August – ongoing c) Carry out customer satisfaction survey by June
Control data	Quantitative a) Monthly regional accounts b) Daily invoiced sales returns c) Statistical analysis monthly sales by salesman/by customer d) Cost of gaining new customers e) Cost of retention f) Number of referrals Qualitative a) Customer complaints b) Customer satisfaction c) Customer retention

Figure 8.6

216

personally autonomous. It does not involve telling somebody how they must be to suit us. Skilled feedback offers people information about themselves in a way which leaves them with a choice about whether to act on it or not. It can help to examine the consequences of any decision to change or not to change, but does not involve prescribing change.

8. Think what it says about you. Feedback is likely to say as much about the giver as the receiver. It will say a good deal about your values and what you focus on in others. Therefore you can learn about yourself if you listen to the feedback you offer others.

Appraisal

Organizations are increasingly setting staff performance standards based on customer care indicators and appraising staff against these.

The balance between looking at performance as an outcome of work systems and an outcome of team performance rather than the difference in performance between different staff needs to be argued. For example, how does teamwork balance the personalization the 'empowered' worker is expected to give customers?

Data used for appraising employees is gathered in a number of ways:

- Customer survey such as customer focus group, telephone surveys, postal surveys and complaints.
- Electronic surveillance such as taping telephone conversations.
- Direct encounter with a mystery shopper.

Some organizations are also using internal service level agreements. See the Effective Management syllabus.

Service level agreements

Service level agreements are used by organizations internally and externally. Many of the characteristics, benefits and dangers of external service level agreements can be applied to those used externally. Visit Naomi Karten's site (www.nkarten.com) to find out about external service level agreement.

Internal service level agreements

A service level agreement helps to identify responsibilities between a service provider and its customers. It is an agreement between departments that is aimed at:

1. Giving both sides the opportunity to identify their needs and priorities and expectations.
2. By creating an understanding that is shared by both sides it hopes to reduce conflict.
3. As it is a written document it gives people the opportunity to communicate its content to other people.
4. It provides an objective way to monitor and review progress.

It should not be used as a way to stifle progress, procrastinate about updating and changing, get what you want by improving standards or service deliverers. It will take time to develop as both parties need to get together in order to formulate it. Used flexibly, such agreements can increase understanding, used inflexibly they build delay into the system.

Transfer pricing

The concept of transfer pricing is that, within an organization one department is transferring its output to another. This should be regarded as a sale and there should be a definite policy on setting the selling price. The most usual methods of transfer pricing – cost, cost plus, market price and dual pricing need to be evaluated.

The human resource model

Gijis Houtzagers ((1999), 'Business models for the human resource management discipline, a key instrument for selection, implementation and optimizing your HRM system', *Empowerment in Organizations*, 6(7)) has designed a model to capture the processes of the organization that administers and manages the HR components of the workforce. The model is referred to as the 'Employee and Organization Management Model'. This human resource management information system (HRMIS) defines eight components:

1. Organization – its staffing, position related responsibilities, compensation and benefits linked to positions, performance appraisal structure and the company policies.

2. Human resource logistics – budget authorization, establishing position recruitment and selection methods, maintaining applicant data, facilitating the necessary interview scheduling and documentation processes and negotiating the process.

3. Compensation and benefits.

4. Employability – this supports the ongoing development of the active workforce.

5. Relations – this covers internal and external relations such as communication, collective bargaining, procedural justice communication structure, subjects, definition of internal target groups, communications with external agents and relations between defined organizational entities.

6. Health, safety and environment.

7. Information strategies.

8. Employee administration.

The model outlined in this paper provides the following benefits:

1. It provides a tool for bridging the gap between IT and HR.

2. Reduces consultancy support as the model offers a picture of what customers want to implement and guidelines for how data is administered.

3. Training can be tracked more easily and related to all kinds of legislative and tax rulings.

4. It can provide a best practice guide for the selection process.

5. The centralization enables self service and less data maintenance.

Managing across borders

Most, if not all of best management practice can provide useful frameworks for managing across borders. The key success factor is to use these tools and techniques of management in the international context. As marketing responds to the need of external customers and stakeholders, management must respond to the needs of internal employees and external stakeholders.

1. *Planning for differences.* When moving across national boundaries, managers will be expected to manage people from different cultures.

2. *Customer service is significantly influenced by culture.* For example, self-service has become part of Western life. In other parts of the world, customers do not expect to serve themselves. National culture can influence many aspects of organizational life:
   o   negotiation
   o   time management
   o   job titles
   o   job description
   o   job status
   o   hierarchy
   o   structure
   to name but a few.

3. Even the subject of motivation will change. While Maslow's hierarchy of needs is still valid, the order of the needs changes depending on the culture. Hertzberg's theories also change. While security in a Western culture may be a hygiene factor, in other cultures it is a motivator.

4. How far an organization can override a national culture with its own culture is an interesting question.

5. There are two main critical success factors in managing across borders:

- o **The role of training programmes**

    Factors to consider will be:

    a. learning styles and expectations

    b. training methods available

    c. training skills available

    d. attitudes to training.

- o **The role of communication programmes**

    Factors to consider will be:

    a. language and interpretation

    b. style and tone

    c. expected forms of communications

    d. technology availability

    e. symbolism and cultural influences e.g. meaning of colour, use of humour.

6. Although there is talk about global convergence, the work done by Gerte Hofstede in the 1980s is worth considering.

7. Hofstede's research focused on some 40 IBM companies around the world and in it he tried to identify the influence of national culture on organization culture and managing people. He identified four dimensions of national culture:

   - o Individualism dimension

     High Individualism – emphasis on being a good leader, on personal initiative and achievement. Everyone has the right to a private life and their own opinions. The emphasis is on recognition and achievement. Employees are motivated by personal recognition, promotion and through rewards for being successful. Italy, Ireland, Netherlands.

     Low Individualism (collectivist) – emphasis is on belonging and the aim is to be a good group member. Tight social frameworks and people are members of extended families/clans with protection given in exchange for loyalty. There is an emphasis on team work and team building. The social structure is reflected in the job description – work routines are important. Pakistan, Taiwan, Peru.

   - o Power distance dimension

     High power distance – employees tend to be afraid to express disagreement and prefer managers who take the decisions and tell them what to do. If outcomes are successful the boss takes the credit, if not he takes the blame. India, Mexico, Philippines.

     Low power distance – inequality should be minimized and those in power are expected to try to look less powerful. Employees are not afraid to express their opinions and expect to be consulted. Denmark, Canada, New Zealand.

   - o Uncertainty avoidance dimension

     High uncertainty avoidance – people need clarity and order and feel threatened by uncertain situations. They combat uncertainty by hard work, career stability and are intolerant of deviancy. Management aims to maintain the status quo. Procedures, rules, regulations and systems are designed to avoid risk and minimize change. Portugal, Greece, Japan.

     Low uncertainty avoidance – uncertainty is inherent in life. There is a pragmatic view about keeping or changing rules, employees expect shorter working periods with companies. There is an expectation that management will encourage continuous improvement and innovation by fostering greater freedom to experiment. Employees are more likely to embrace change. Singapore, Australia, S. Africa.

   - o Masculinity dimension

     Masculine cultures – sex roles are clearly differentiated, women caring nurturing and men assertive and dominating. Performance is what counts and money and material standards are important. Ambition is a driving force. Women are not expected to play the same roles as men, career progression is not possible as are other activities such as negotiating contracts, making decisions or take customer interface roles. Status symbols are important. Germany, Japan, Venezuela.

Feminine cultures – sex roles more flexible and there is a belief in equality of the sexes. Quality of life is what matters. Service provides motivation. Small is beautiful and unisex attractive. Women can progress and expect to have the same rewards as men. Sweden, Norway, Finland.

8. High context and low context

    Cultures are also described in terms of high context or low context.

    High context – patterns of behaviour reflect cultural norms and expectations in a more explicit non-verbal way. Small rituals in every day life convey more than the spoken word. For example:

    v. who can speak first at a meeting

    a. the exchange of business cards

    to name but two

What is going on in the background can be more important and convey more than the spoken word.

Examples of high context cultures include Japan and Arabian countries.

Low context – words are used much more to convey messages and meaning. Verbal messages are much more explicit and there is little reliance on what goes on in the background. Examples of low context cultures include Germany, USA and UK.

Few countries are entirely one thing or another in terms of culture and even within some countries there will be cultural variances that reflect a number of these dimensions.

However the frameworks described will give the manager some insights on problems and how people might be managed given their different attitudes and expectations.

Developing the management leadership team in a multinational enterprise

John R. Darling is President and Professor of Management and Arthur K. Fischer is Associate Professor of Management, both at Pittsburgh State University, USA. They write that management team-building within a multinational enterprise is greatly enhanced if the interactive style reflected by each person is considered. The blend of behavioural styles can affect the collective achievements of the entire management team, as well as the accomplishments of each member of the team. In this context, behavioural style is a pervasive and enduring set of inter-personal characteristics focusing on how one acts – on what one says and does. There are four behavioural styles – Relater, Analyzer, Director, Socializer – no one of which is necessarily better or worse than any other. Effective management leadership teams are made up of and value individuals who reflect each of the four styles. *Source*: *European Business Review*, vol. 98, no 2, 1988, pp. 100-108.

Activity 8.1

Discuss what the advantages and disadvantages are in cultures where management are expected to take responsibility.

Discuss what the advantages and disadvantages are in cultures where management are expected to involve subordinates.

Case study: Image Makers

Image Makers is an American owned, full-service international communications consultancy, providing everything from research to the implementation of campaigns for clients based in over forty countries worldwide. Billings annually from the European Division, with headquarters in Paris, have reflected the hard times faced by the industry generally. These figures have been corrected for inflation and are quoted in millions of dollars.

Sales in $ million from European Division

1989	1990	1991	1992	1993	1994	1995	1996
89 95	103	103	99	89	91	91	

The agency's salesforce in Europe consists of 30 Key Account Managers who are responsible for building and retaining existing business and 15 New Business Development Executives who operate across Europe from three offices in Paris, London and Rome.

An analysis of Image Makers carried out in May 1996 uncovered weaknesses in the organization of its European sales activity. The following findings emerged from this analysis:

- There was no clear 'leader' of the sales activity and no identifiable strategy for this function.

- Although the agency uses English as a common language, the 45 individuals who make up the operational sales team had little else in common. There were problems with communication between individuals, no evidence of team spirit and very little exchange of information. This situation was worse because the group came from eight different national cultures and opportunities for integration of activities were not being taken.

- Resentment between the Key Account Managers and New Business Development Executives was clearly identified. It was found that both groups thought the other had the easier job and the fact that a sales bonus system was only available to the New Business Development Executives fuelled the resentment further.

- Within the groups there was also tension related to perceptions over 'best' accounts and easier geographic regions.

A customer care survey, carried out by external consultants in the same month showed the company was perceived by clients to be:

- Arrogant in its dealings with clients

- Unable to communicate internally

- Uncaring about its public image

- Falling below competitors on most of the aspects of customer care surveyed.

The survey concluded that Image Makers had only survived because of its recognized reputation for technical excellence.

Brief

You have been appointed as Manager of Client Relations, with responsibility for the Key Account Managers (KAM) and New Business Development Executives (NBDE) as the first step to putting these weaknesses right.

The management team in the USA have asked you to present a report covering the following points:

1. Your proposals for building the Key Account Managers and New Business Development Executives into an effective working team. The management team have indicated that you are free to propose changes which cut across the current organization and remuneration structures. You should include recommendations for improving motivation and team spirit. (25 marks)

2. The actions you recommend to improve customer care for clients of Image Makers and a timetable for their implementation. (15 marks)

Summary

This unit has discussed some of the managerial implications of adopting a customer orientation. It is essential that all staff are consulted and customer focused if such strategies are to succeed. This will require managers to be active to ensure staff are motivated to perform at the best level of their ability. However the organization cannot stand still as the best applications of a customer focus will become eroded over time. Some insight has also been given into the differences between managing in different countries and the critical role training will play if organizational culture is to override national culture. Unit 9 looks at the issues of innovation and the need for continual improvement, if competitive advantage is to be sustainable.

Further study and examination preparation

Now undertake Question 4 from CIM Examination Session December 2000 to be found in the Exam paper Appendix.

Unit 9
Innovation and the culture
of continuous improvement

Objectives

- To understand the concept of innovation
- To understand some of the barriers to creating an innovative and continuously improving culture.

This unit covers the following parts of the Marketing Customer Interface syllabus:

- 2.3.1
- 2.4

Study guide

Innovation is a process whereby new ideas are developed and applied. Innovative products, processes and services are spreading rapidly across the globe and in order to remain competitive organizations need to understand and consider themselves within the context of the external and internal environment. Management research suggests that innovative firms – those which are able to use innovation to differentiate their products – are on average twice as profitable as other firms. However, the management of innovation is inherently difficult and risky: the majority of new technology fails to be translated into new products and services, and most new products and services are not commercial successes. In short, innovation can enhance competitiveness, but it requires different sets of management knowledge and skills from those of everyday business administration. Innovations need to be introduced into the marketplace in a manner that reduces customer barriers and they also need to ensure that strategy, leadership, rewards and mission, recognition, soft organizational feeling issues, structure, culture, role and organizational barriers are addressed.

Innovation and conservatism in customer behaviour

Definition

Innovation is any new idea, product, or service which is perceived, by the receiver of communication concerning its existence, to be new.

The definition of *innovation* has several important implications:

1. An innovation can be anything – from a novel type of paper clip to a new postal delivery service to a truly genuine response to a customer's need.
2. The innovation is in the eye of the receiver:
   - The 'innovation' does not have to be novel to the receiver of the communication
   - The 'innovation' does not have to be new, it may have existed for some time before the receiver became aware of its existence.

While new products are seen as the cutting edge of innovation in the marketplace, process innovation plays just as important strategic role.

In customer-focused organizations, innovation can take place within the continuous interactions between frontline staff and their customers. Creativity and flexibility need to be built into the very fingertips of the organizational culture.

Being able to offer better service, faster, cheaper, high quality has long been seen as a source of competitive advantage. Innovation means that change takes place in two forms:

- Change in the products and services that an organization offers
- Change in the ways they are created and delivered.

There are then two key questions in innovation management:

1. How does an organization structure its innovation process. This covers:
   - Scanning and searching externally and internally for opportunities
   - The strategic selection
   - Resourcing it
   - Developing and launching
   - Learning from experience.
2. How does an organization develop routine patterns of behaviour that will ensure it can operate in an innovational way on a day-to-day basis.

Diffusion of innovations

The process of diffusion is concerned with how innovations spread within a market. There are four main parts to the diffusion process:

1. The innovation
2. The time taken for the innovation to be adopted
3. The channels of communication through which information about the innovation spreads
4. The social systems involved.

Most writers refer to the receiver of the innovation as the 'adopter'. A simple 'one-step' communication is illustrated in Figure 9.1.

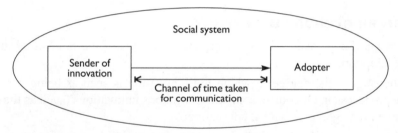

Figure 9.1 *An illustration of a simple diffusion process*

Adoption stages

The consumer does not adopt an innovation immediately. They may, indeed, not adopt the innovation at all. Rogers, in his book *Diffusion of Innovations,* identified the following stages in the adoption process:

- *Awareness* – the consumer is aware of the innovation but little is known about it.
- *Interest* – the consumer becomes aware that the innovation may satisfy a need.
- *Evaluation* – the consumer forms an attitude about the innovation which may be positive or negative. On the basis of this, they decide whether they are going to try it or reject it.
- *Trial* – if a trial is possible, and wanted, then the product is tried by the consumer.
- *Adoption* – the innovation is accepted or rejected. If accepted, the consumer becomes committed to the innovation (if it is a product – then this usually means purchase).

Product life cycle

The product life cycle concept implies different emphasis on innovation.

- *Early stage* – characterized by rapid and frequent product innovation with a proliferation of variety
- *Later stage* – characterized by a relatively stable concept with only incremental change and more of an emphasis on process innovation and cost reduction.

Types of innovation

There are generally acknowledged to be three types of product innovation:

1. *Continuous* – the product is being continuously upgraded in small increments. 'New' products in this case are actually only slight modification on existing products. The use of the product changes little, the consumer does not have to adapt, or modify in any substantial way, their use of the product. Examples include 'new improved' washing powders, new versions of established software.

2. *Dynamically continuous* – the product innovation is more disruptive on consumer usage patterns but does still not substantially alter them. Examples include disposable nappies, cordless telephones.

3. *Discontinuous* – the product requires the consumer to adopt new behaviour patterns entirely. Examples include the introduction of video recorders and computers.

Activity 9.1

How would you classify each of the following innovations – continuous, dynamically continuous or discontinuous?

1. Petrol car → electric car
2. Toothbrush → electric toothbrush
3. Telephone → mobile telephone
4. Matches → pocket lighter
5. Video player → video camera
6. Television → remote control television

What makes an innovation successful?

According to Rogers and Shoemaker, the following characteristics of the innovation influence the speed and extent of adoption:

- *Relative advantage* – the degree to which the innovation is seen as being superior to any comparable predecessor. Of course, some discontinuous innovations (such as the video camera) may have no single, or obvious, comparator.

- *Compatibility* – the degree to which the innovation is compatible with existing culture. Products which are not compatible with existing practices (the use of chopsticks in the UK for example) are likely to take longer.

- *Complexity* – the more complex the innovation, the longer it will take to adopt. A simple-to-understand innovation (such as the pump-action toothpaste tube) will be more rapidly adopted.

- *Trialability* – if it is possible to sample an innovation it is more likely to be adopted rapidly. Free samples of a whole range of products and services are provided on this basis.

- *Observability* – products which are highly visible in the society in which the diffusion is taking place will be adopted more rapidly.

Thus, a continuous innovation, which is compatible with the culture, can be trialled, yet is simple and observable, is most likely to get broadly adopted most rapidly. Table 9.1 rates several innovations on these criteria. It is important to realize that these are perceived values. One person might, for example find the complexity of a particular pocket calculator 'high' while another might find it 'low'.

Multiplicative innovation adoption (MIA) model

The authors propose the theoretical model of innovation adoption in Table 9.1, which is based on the Roger and Shoemaker criteria. It assumes that each of the criterion makes an equal contribution to the success, or otherwise, of the innovation. It also assumes that they combine in such a way that the presence of positive ratings on more than one criterion has a multiplicative effect on success.

Table 9.1 *Rating of innovations based on Rogers and Shoemaker criteria*

Innovation	Relative advantage	Compatibility	Complexity	Trialability	Observability
Compact disks	High	Low	Low	High	Medium
Sinclair C5	Low	Low	High	Low	High
Pocket calculator	High	High	Medium	High	Medium
Post-it notes	High	High	Low	High	Medium
Ford Sierra	Low	High	Medium	Medium	High

To assess an innovation using the Simmons and Phipps MIA model it is first necessary to rate the innovation on the Rogers and Shoemaker criteria using the following scheme:

- *Relative advantage* – rate the innovation with a 3 if the relative advantage is high, 2 if it is judged to be medium and 1 if it is low. This rating is referred to as RA.

- *Compatibility* – rate the innovation with a 3 if the compatibility is high, 2 if it is judged to be medium and 1 if it is low. This rating is referred to as CT.

- *Complexity* – rate the innovation with a 3 if it is simple, 2 if it is judged to be of medium complexity and 1 if it is judged to be highly complex. This rating is referred to as CL.

- *Trialability* – rate the innovation with a 3 if the opportunity to trial is high, 2 if it is judged to be medium and 1 if it is low. This rating is referred to as TR.

- *Observability* – rate the innovation with a 3 if the observability is high, 2 if it is judged to be medium and 1 if it is low. This rating is referred to as OB.

The ratings for each innovation are then multiplied together to obtain an overall prediction of the speed and extent (SE) to which the innovation will be adopted:

Speed and extent (SE) rating = RA × CT × CL × TR × OB

Referring back to Table 9.1 and using the MIA rating scheme, we obtain the SE ratings seen in Table 9.2. The higher the SE rating, the higher the predicted success of the innovation.

Table 9.2 *Speed and extent (SE) ratings using the Simmons and Phipps MIA model,* Oxford College of Marketing

Innovation	Speed and extent (SE) rating
Compact discs	3 × 1 × 3 × 3 × 2 = 54
Sinclair C5	1 × 1 × 1 × 1 × 3 = 3
Pocket calculator	3 × 3 × 2 × 3 × 2 = 108
Post-it notes	3 × 3 × 3 × 3 × 2 = 162
Ford Sierra	1 × 3 × 2 × 2 × 3 = 36

Based on the example ratings provided, it is predicted that the most successful innovation would be Post-it notes and the least the Sinclair C5.

Assessment of success criteria and MIA model

Success is a difficult concept to define and thus any criteria or model are open to criticism on the basis that what they attempt to describe is itself vague. To one person it might be high sales figures, to another high profit margins, high public profile or something else. For example, one-off designer label clothes may not sell in high volumes but may be valuable in that they build up the reputation of the designer. In a sense, they are therefore a success. We could redefine success as meeting the aims that the originator of the innovation themselves set. However, this risks diluting the concept and it is probably best to accept a general definition based on cultural expectations.

The MIA model presented is theoretical and requires validation. Tools do not yet exist to measure the five criteria but could no doubt be simply constructed.

The model and criteria are powerful in that they are based on perceived characteristics. Thus, different individuals could rate the same innovation in a variety of ways. This would make the application of the technique particularly suitable for target marketing.

Categories of adopters

Research on the diffusion process (by Rogers) has found that adoption follows a bell-shaped curve of normal distribution among adopters. This is illustrated in Figure 9.2. Initially, only a very few people adopt an innovation but the numbers steadily, then dramatically increase until they reach a peak. The number of people adopting over time then declines. This normal distribution has been approximately divided into five categories (see Table 9.3).

This information can be most useful in targeting new product campaigns. It also forms a critical basis for understanding the product life cycle and market segmentation.

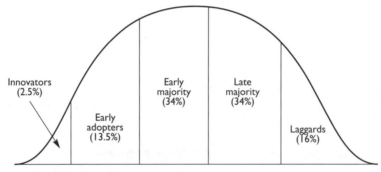

Figure 9.2 *Adoption curve*

Table 9.3 *Categories of adopters*

	Population (%)	Characteristics of group
Innovators	2.5	Risk-takers, more adventurous, more spending power, take most publications
Early adopters	13.5	Highest proportion of opinion leaders, above average education, tend to be younger than later adopters, well-respected, greatest contact with sales staff
Early majority	34	Slightly above average age, education, social status, and income. Rely on informal sources of information
Late majority	34	Above average age but below average education, social status and income. Rely on informal sources of information
Laggards	16	Lowest group with respect to education, income, and social status. Are the oldest group

226

Opinion leaders

As we can see from the characteristics of the adopter groups, opinion leaders are crucial in the diffusion of innovations.

Opinion leaders are those individuals who are instrumental in changing the consumer behaviour of others. If there were no opinion leaders then behaviour would stagnate with no new fashions, ideas or attitudes emerging. Marketers are interested in targeting opinion leaders as, once these are convinced of the benefits of a new product or service, the rest of the adopters will then follow.

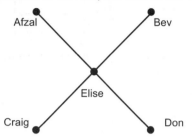

Figure 9.3 Sociogram of flow of information concerning recommendation of book

In the example shown in Figure 9.3, Elise was the opinion leader. Her knowledge of the book led to the purchase of four further copies. Obviously, you do not always buy everything that is recommended to you, the source of the recommendation must possess other qualities. Research has shown that opinion leaders generally possess certain similar characteristics:

- *Personality traits* – Opinion leaders tend to be self-confident individuals. They are confident about their own decisions and opinions and are thus more able to convince others. Leaders are also sociable, indeed they must be to enable the network of acquaintances required for communication.

- *Demographic characteristics* – Not surprisingly, people tend to seek information from those whom they perceive to be most knowledgeable in a particular subject matter and who have similar demographic characteristics. Thus, if you were buying a computer you might seek the advice of a computer-literate friend.

- *Social class* – Most commonly the opinion leader is of the same social class as the people they are influencing. This may be because advice from those of a similar status is more valued or simply that we more regularly communicate with persons in our class.

Activity 9.4

What demographic characteristics would you imagine an opinion leader in the following purchasing decisions might possess?

1. Who would you consult about purchasing Top 10 chart music?
2. Who would you consult about purchasing a violin?
3. Who would you consult about purchasing a sewing machine?

Shiffman and Kanuk (1994) present a multi-step model of how an opinion leader receives and disseminates information (Figure 9.4). Most importantly it shows that some consumers receive information directly from mass media rather than 'consulting' an opinion leader. Note also that the communication between opinion leader and consumer is two way, accurately demonstrating that opinion leaders are themselves open to influence from other sources.

Persuasive communication

We have seen in this unit, and earlier, how communication occurs between members in a group. We will now consider what affects the persuasiveness of that communication. For instance, if a lecturer told you to keep quiet in class you (probably) would. However, if a classmate told you – would you be as likely to obey?

If a persuasive message is successful it leads to an attitude change. For attitude change to occur, a persuasive message on its own is not enough. During the early 1950s the social psychologist Carl Hovland undertook a large volume of research in this area. With colleagues he devised the process model shown in Figure 9.5 which shows the stages required for a message to lead to attitude change.

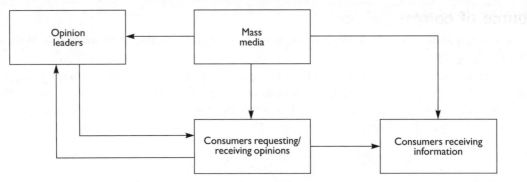

Figure 9.4 *Communication path from the mass media to different consumer groups via opinion leaders. Adapted from Shiffman and Kanuk (1994) Consumer Behaviour*

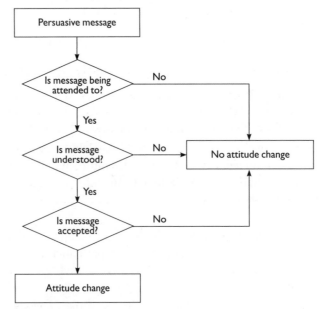

Figure 9.5 *Hovland model of attitude change. Adapted from Deaux, Dane and Wrightsman (1993),* Social Psychology in the 90s, *Brooks/Cole*

Persuasive message

Figure 9.6 shows a communication model where a referent, one or more members from a reference group (possibly an opinion leader), is trying to influence a consumer. The content of the communication is the message with the whole discourse taking place within a particular context. You will notice the similarity with the earlier model of diffusion (Figure 9.1) which is, essentially, the same communication process.

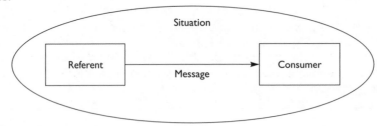

Figure 9.6 *Communication model*

The persuasiveness of the communication can be affected by the characteristics of all those elements shown in Figure 9.6:

- *Referent* – known as the source of the communication, the person trying to persuade.
- *Message* – the content of the communication.
- *Consumer* – known as the recipient of the communication, the person who is being persuaded.
- *Situation* – the immediate context within which the communication is taking place.

Source of communication

The following characteristics of the source affect its persuasiveness:

- *Status and credibility* – if the source is perceived as an expert then they are more persuasive. Thus stories in 'reputable' newspapers are more likely to be believed, as are endorsements from professionals in the topic being communicated. Experiments have shown a 'sleeper effect'. The difference between high and low credibility sources is forgotten over time. However, when the recipient is reminded of the source, the original status effect returns.

- *Attractiveness* – the more attractive, charming, humorous the source the more persuasive (generally) they are likely to be. Of course, these characteristics are as perceived by the recipient.

- *Trustworthiness* – the more trustworthy the source is perceived to be the more persuasive they are. The trustworthiness is assessed on the basis of the perceived intentions and motives of the source.

- *Non-verbal behaviour* – non-verbal behaviour relates to trust. A 'shifty' disposition, for instance, does not instill trust.

- *Similarity with recipient* – if the source is perceived as being of a similar culture and social status as the recipient, then this can increase the persuasive power of the message.

Advertisers make use of all of these beneficial characteristics when formulating their advertisements. As we have already seen, certain individuals are used as experts or aspirational figures to gain appeal, as are people from the same ethnic or social grouping as those in the target audience.

Content of communication (the message)

The following characteristics of the message affect its persuasiveness:

- *Non-verbal aspects* – Face to face communication is more effective than mass media. In this situation the source can react to the recipient (via eye contact, body posture, etc.) and is thus able to anticipate and modify their message accordingly.

- *Implicit or explicit* – This is concerned with whether the recipient is left to draw their own conclusion from the information provided (implicit) or presented with a conclusion by the source (explicit). Thus, advertising aimed at people of high intelligence should not dictate choice but provide information for the recipient to make their own mind up.

- *Emotional appeal* – Emotions, such as fear, humour, sympathy and, of course, sex can be used to increase the persuasiveness of a communication. Experiments with smokers, concerning the danger of cancer, has shown that, somewhat surprisingly, 'high fear' messages are not the most effective way of persuasion. Scaring a smoker into thinking they are 'going to die' (high fear) is less likely to persuade them to stop smoking than a message with a lower fear content (such as 'smoking puts you at a high risk of cancer'). It appears that recipients 'switch off' when presented with high fear messages but are more receptive to messages where the fear content is more regulated.

- *One-sided versus two-sided arguments* – Whether a communication should make any reference to the competition (two-sided communication) seems to depend on the recipient.

- *Primacy-recency* – The order in which information is presented can affect its persuasiveness. The first and last slots in an advert break are the most sought after as research has shown that they are more likely to be remembered.

Recipient

The following characteristics of recipients effect the persuasiveness of the communication:

- *Level of education* – The more educated respond better to more complex arguments.

- *Resistance to persuasion* – Resistance to persuasion is strongest when counter-arguments are available and weakest when they are not.

- *Latitude of acceptance and rejection* – It is easier to persuade people where large shifts in their existing attitudes are not required.

- *Compatibility with self-concept* – Related to the above, if we have a certain self-concept (that is we believe we possess certain attributes or characteristics) then messages which support our self-concept are more likely to be accepted.

- *Individual differences* – Opinions differ, but some psychologists believe that there is a personality factor which equates to 'persuadability' thus some people are, inherently, more difficult to persuade than others.

Situations

The following aspects of the situation affect the effectiveness of the persuasive communication:

- *Informal situations* – These are generally more effective than formal ones for persuasion. The example of 'Tupperware parties' and other home shopping is one common way in which communication is made less formal and thus more persuasive.
- *Role-playing* – Trying to put the recipient in the shoes of the source can increase persuasion.
- *Small groups* – As we have seen people are more likely to be persuaded if they are part of a small group that already shares these norms and values.
- *Public commitment* – Making a public commitment is more likely to lead to attitude change. Political parties make good use of this at election time.

Activity 9.5

Think of a recent purchase you have made. What influencing factors can you identify from among those listed? Were there other influencing factors as well? List them.

Similarly, can you remember any occasion when you resisted persuasion? What went wrong in the persuasive process? List the factors involved.

Customer barriers to innovation

Customers do not necessarily resist a particular innovation because they dislike it, but rather because they do not like change and disruption. It is therefore important to understand what disruptions are caused so that the innovation or change can be directed with minimal interruption to existing practices and values. Sheth and Ram identify five areas of customer concern; they can be grouped into two categories – functional (usage pattern, economic value and risks), and psychological (cultural tradition and image).

Functional barriers

Usage barrier

It takes time for innovations to be accepted by customers as they need to absorb them into their daily lives. The service sector also faces usage barriers and Sheth and Ram cite video teleconferencing and car pooling as examples which disrupt our workflow. They say that these barriers can be overcome by thinking about the following:

- *The whole system* – The whole system needs to be considered so that the new offering fits into and interacts with what is already there (e.g. dishwashers into kitchens).
- *Integration* – Rather than sell to an end user a solution would be to integrate the innovation into the preceding activity or product (e.g. car telephones to car makers).
- *Force* – Make usage mandatory through government legislation (e.g. seat belts, lead-free petrol, smoke detectors).

The value barrier

Sheth and Ram say innovation, must offer greater value in that products or services must have better performance; a better price, or be positioned against a different competition.

The risk barrier

Purchasing a product or service always entails a degree of risk – there is economic risk, physical risk, performance risk and psychological risk. Marketers, in order to overcome these risks, can offer free trials, present testimonials, or introduce the offer as a component in a system so that the end user does not, or cannot, evaluate it. Examples include selling independent services under a well-known brand name, or introducing medical supplies into a hospital where people have no opportunity to choose treatments.

Psychological barriers

The tradition barrier

Sheth and Ram say that an innovation is resisted when it requires making changes in the traditions established by the corporate or societal culture. They say 'as the US economy becomes more and more service-oriented, we see more evidence of customers erecting cultural or tradition-based barriers to the increasing number of innovative services'.

They give as examples advertising for a spouse, singles bars, eating alone, co-ed health spas, the use of surrogate mothers, adoption of interracial children, organ transplants and other socially integrative medical practices.

Time erodes traditional barriers but changes to traditions must be approached with the right attitude. Understanding and respect, education and the use of change agents are required.

The image barrier

Image barriers may be associated with the origins of a product or service – product class, industry and country can create unfavourable stereotypes. Ways around this are to make fun of the image, create a unique image, or to associate the product/service with something or someone who has a positive image.

Innovation and the culture of continuous improvement

Innovation is a process whereby new ideas are developed and applied. An innovating organization must be able to:

1. Reflect on what it is doing and seek feedback
2. Acquire new ideas
3. Be open to change
4. Implement new ideas.

Avenues to customer-focused innovations

Innovation might not involve entering new markets and it is about more than product development. It can come from a number of avenues and the marketer needs to be constantly looking for:

- New forms of segmentation, reaching the target market and positioning
- New types of product or service linked to providing solutions to customers' problems
- New mechanisms for product or service delivery
- New techniques for creating supplier to customer continuity
- New ways of increasing the perceived value
- New ways of ensuring operational excellence
- New ways of motivating frontline staff.

An innovating organization needs to take the whole system into account. It needs to consider what it is doing within the context of the external and the internal environments of the organization and how the component parts work together and influence each other. Everything is interdependent and, as Gummesson says, an organization needs to think of itself as both interacting with the environment and being integrated with it.

External environment

Understanding the market

Innovation is systemic and linked with the macro-environment (PEST factors). It is also linked to an understanding of the micro-environment (markets, competition, suppliers, distributors, customers, stakeholders).

When an organization is open to influence from the environment and staff are seen as integrated into it there will be positive relationships with suppliers, buyers, customers – even competitors – and there will be a two-way flow of ideas and feelings between these different networks of people. This openness stops an organization becoming stale and enables it to remain boundaryless. Exchanges can be facilitated in different ways: focus groups, customer feedback forms, joint meetings with professional associations and other specialists in the field, benchmarking, think tanks, brainstorming and so on. An integrated communication plan that regards communication as a two-way process is fundamental to establishing this type of feedback.

Internal environment

There is no one way of creating an innovating customer-focused organization, but there are some aspects that can be broadly identified as contributing to the process. These include the following.

Framework of thinking

The framework of thinking with which a marketer approaches this task will depend on there being a conceptual understanding of the marketers' role. This is changing from marketing management to the management of an organization with a marketing focus. This extension of thinking means that marketers need to think of the organization as a whole, not just what the marketing department is doing. When the whole organization is thinking marketing, innovation and improvement are likely to follow.

Vision and mission

A different vision now drives a customer-centric organization. This focus requires a new integrity, it has a greater urgency and is related to providing real service and value that customers and employees can relate to.

In much the same way as customers carry a product/service idea in their minds, within an organization individuals carry both a 'role idea' and an 'organization idea'. The vision which individuals carry in their minds of the organization helps them to manage their behaviour. The organization in the mind is not a replication of the hierarchical structures we are familiar with. However, it is as much of a reality as any organizational chart and may well create a different sense of organizational purpose for each and every member belonging to it. Internal realities, because they exist in people's minds, are difficult to change.

It is largely because organizations develop to satisfy the needs of the people working within them that very often it is difficult to change the people within an organization without first structurally changing the organization itself or indeed finding new members.

Leadership vision, commitment and internal marketing are essential to creating a focus on which this 'idea in the mind' can be developed into a mental picture that inspires and guides customer-focused behaviours.

The gap between strategic intent and reality

Many marketing activities fail to get off the ground because the organization suffers from inertia and has no energy; there is no time to do anything, and the strategy is not aligned around a central guiding idea.

The central guiding idea that helps to define what the organization does and how it goes about its business is a mission statement. The mission statement and an understanding of core competences creates a mindset that links the interests of customers, shareholders, and staff together into a network of relationships.

In an innovating organization that seeks constant improvement, these values, like those that guide the core competences, need to be articulated and marketed internally.

The mission statement needs to be translated into actionable points in each person's job description so that they know what they need to do in order to contribute to the organization's objectives. Similarly, if the philosophy is that of a learning organization ongoing learning objectives must be treated in the same way. Other relevant policies and procedures will then support these values.

Leaders

Gummeson (*Total Relationship Marketing*, p. 128) says that consumers and companies need a basic level of security. Security is associated with words such as:

- Promises
- Honesty
- Trust

- Reliability
- Predictability
- Stability
- Fear of being swindled or let down
- Reduction of uncertainty or risk.

Leaders need to embody the values of a customer-centric organization. They must be able to model the right behaviour so that their colleagues understand in their bones the key values of customer-focused behaviour. Leaders also need to support and be supported by shareholders in changing the focus of the organization. Their support is pivotal to creating this vision and, as far as innovation is concerned, creating these cultural values so that employees feel secure being innovative. Leaders should establish a dedicated innovation manager/director. Responsibilities should include:

- Building innovative teams
- New ideas, processes
- Pulling departments together.

Rewards and the mission

The mission determines what values are to drive the imagination and behaviour of employees. It lies behind the objectives, the strategy, the tactics and the job descriptions of the organization. If the mission is to be thin and lean, one would imagine that the organization would be concerned with costs. If the mission is to be customer driven, statements on customer care and fulfilling customer needs should be the driving idea behind the jobs that people carry out. Similarly, if the organization values innovation this should be reflected. Rewards need to be linked to what people achieve on behalf of the organization and hence to what the organization values.

Organizations place a value on different aspects of their activities:

- Market share
- Profit
- Sales turnover
- Cost reduction
- Training
- Customer satisfaction
- Customer loyalty
- Initiative
- Entrepreneurial spirit
- Team working.

People join organizations because they encompass values that match their aims (the Body Shop) or in other cases give them the opportunity to carry out a professional task. When the mission and values of an organization change this can create resistance or stress. For example, when the National Health Service changed to a market model, people whose values centred around patient care had to absorb the idea of a 'financial transaction' into their understanding of their role – this transition has created a lot of stress.

Recognition and happiness

When rewards are linked to the organizational purpose, recognition can be given. When people are recognized for their contribution they will feel successful – this in turn will breed further success.

Soft issues

The customer-care audit focuses on the soft organizational issues – feelings of trust, commitment, support, concern, envy, anger and resentment. These are all relationship issues that must be addressed alongside the harder issues of IT, profitability, market segmentation, branding, etc.

Structure, training and skilling

Structures may need to be developed that respond to change and structural issues addressed so that people in the frontline are able to be innovative and imaginative in satisfying customer needs (not only the needs of the managerial hierarchy). Before organizations restructure they need to think about factors such as:

- Empowering frontline staff
- Multi-skilling and training
- Ensuring rewards are related to the right values and tasks
- Being able to manage the change in balance of power from middle management to front-line staff.

Developing new ideas

If an organization wants to develop new ideas it may be helpful for subsystems, differentiated from routine work, to come together to focus on new ideas. These could include project teams and network structures; which may need to be developed in order to get the mix of specialists necessary to develop new ideas.

Every part of the organization has an effect on every other part. It is no good just looking at the departments who are in touch with customers directly or in charge of innovation strategy. The beliefs and values of every department in the organization will either support or hinder the process of customer focus and innovation. Innovation and customer focus affect all the interests that various stakeholders may have in an organization. These interests need to be thought about and taken into account. People may need training to be able to negotiate, become more creative, and handle conflict and differences of opinion, so people are able to participate in the process and not just cut themselves off because it feels too dangerous to step outside what everybody else is doing.

Organizational culture

Organizational culture can be broadly thought of as the way in which the people working within an organization learn to cope with adapting to their environment. This includes the problems that arise from the external environment as well as the way in which the organization integrates its activities internally. New members of the organization are taught that the way in which the organization operates is correct. Culture is therefore a learned product of group experience and is discovered, invented or developed by members of an organization as the organization develops over time. One of the tasks of leadership is to create and also manage this culture. Any change in culture needs to be implemented by management – this is why management must lead any change and training process. The recruitment, induction process, reward systems and appraisal process support this.

The culture in these new customer-focused organizations is different from a bureaucratic hiearchy. The rules for getting along have changed. People may have to learn them if they are not naturally born team players.

Organizational culture as a defence against anxiety

The term organizational defence is used to describe the way in which the members of an organization protect themselves from anxiety. They are built up from the individual role defences.

Once organizational culture and working methods are in place it is very difficult to get the members of an organization to adapt to changes brought about by the macro- and micro-environments. Very often working methods are created to protect people carrying out the work from the anxiety and stress that is inherent in the work itself. Resistance to change does not only happen with individuals and departments, it can also affect the whole organization. It can also create a 'them and us' situation when dealing with customers.

As Isabel Menzies Lyth, Tavistock Institute (www.tavinstitute.org) says:

> The members of an organization use culture, structure and operating methods to create working methods that help them to deal with any struggles they have in coping with the stresses that can arise from carrying out the job itself; and changes in, and threats from, the environment. New members to the organization will either quickly fit into the existing work practices or find themselves out on a limb. Some may even leave. (Menzies Lyth, I. (1988). *Containing Anxiety in Organizations,* Free Association Books)

Creating a customer-focused innovational culture in which there is an attitude towards continuous improvement will involve looking at the way in which the organization protects itself from stress and anxiety. Innovation is not linear, it muddles through, people have to struggle with themselves to

234

adapt to change and half-baked ideas as people struggle to formulate them. If the organizational culture and management style does not allow for this, people will feel unsafe. Managers have to be able to facilitate creative problem solving. They need to be able to use coaching skills. If this is contrary to the way in which they normally behave (directive and controlling) they may need training.

Sheth and Ram (*Bringing Innovation to Market,* John Wiley & Sons) identify five major barriers to innovation that are inherent in the structure of many organizations. The specialization trap tends to lead to rigidity because it reinforces the expertise barrier and the operations barrier. Barriers associated with the environment are identified as the resource barrier, the regulation barrier and the market access barrier. Before choosing the organization will need to consider the advantages and disadvantages of the different methods:

1. *The expertise barrier* People with a highly vested interest in a highly specialized technology tend to be unable or unwilling to disrupt established procedures radically enough to produce truly market-driven innovations. Peters and Waterman suggest they should be put into an autonomous task force called 'Skunk Works' where they can be free to experiment outside established corporate behaviour. It is also common to form strategic research alliances. Acquisitions and mergers are another way forward but it is important that they do not provide new barriers to implementing change.

2. *The operations barrier* Operational barriers will also prevent change. For example, resistance to changing work processes such as marketing products that are operationally continuous rather than market driven and customer focused. Ways of overcoming these barriers could include starting afresh with a new and separate facility, modifying procedures as the industry updates itself with the use of new technology. Selective modification is another alternative.

3. *The resource barrier* If acquiring funds could be a problem there are other ways to break through this barrier including:
   o License agreements and franchising
   o Consortiums
   o Venture capital.

4. *The regulation barrier* Regulations – both industry self-regulation relating to codes of business practice, and also government regulations – control various aspects of a business. Regulations can sometimes be changed by effective lobbying. Alternatively, organizations can avoid legislation by marketing in another area, or by reorganizing the holding company so it is free to offer product or service innovations not allowed in the regulated entity.

5. *Market-access barrier* This type of barrier includes factors as various as access to shelf space and difficulties for customers switching to new products because technology is embedded in their existing products. Porter discusses all sorts of barriers that organizations use to prevent new market centres. International trade barriers also keep competition out. Sheth and Ram suggest the following solutions:
   o Forming alliances with the dominant vendor
   o Developing an in-house distribution system
   o Jumping the barrier by marketing directly to the customers.

Role

Innovation requires an expansion of role. People in the organization must be able to take personal responsibility for organizational problems. This is the organizational equivalent of good citizenship – people take responsibility for themselves and society. This means they must be able to expand the role idea that helps them to manage their behaviour. For this to occur they will need to feel safe so they do not spend time defending themselves and protecting their backs. They may also need training on how to help them think about what prevents them from expanding their role. There could be personal, organizational and environmental factors – the three are interrelated.

Mixed role teams

Create teams with mixed roles and you avoid the trap of recruiting people who all think the same way. This approach to recruitment encourages diversity in which difference is accepted. Belbin identified nine team roles – people are naturally stronger in some roles than others. Using this approach to selecting team players, people are enabled to identify their strengths and weaknesses, and these can be taken into account, dismissed and 'difference' allowed for and managed.

Belbin's roles:

1. *The shaper* This individual plays the role of a task-oriented leader, concerned to influence or shape the cause of events through getting their own way – often seen as autocratic in style.

2. *The coordinator* Also a leader but one who succeeds by drawing out the ideas of others, rather than imposing their own views.

3. *The plant* is the individual who has plenty of ideas and enables the team to become more imaginative.

4. *The resource investor* Also gets ideas but from outside the team, the resource investigator is not a technical type but a creative, social type – a Mr or Mrs Fixit.

5. *The team worker* This individual keeps the team in harmony.

6. *The implementor* The individual who carries things through.

7. *The monitor and evaluator* This individual is good at helping the team evaluate less suitable ideas that emerge within the group from shapers and plants.

8. *The completer finisher* This very necessary individual enables teams to carry through on implementation and detail.

9. *The specialist* Whose presence in the team is confined to the supply of technical/professional guidance.

Activity 9.6

Carry out an innovation audit on your own organization and write a report.

Summary

This unit has examined the critical role played by innovation and continuous improvement in maintaining a customer focus over time. It has addressed the barriers to innovation that may occur in organizations and suggested ways in which such barriers can be overcome. We will now introduce modelling, the concept of attitudes and how attitude modelling can be used to explain behaviour.

Unit 10
Relationship marketing

Objectives

To understand:

- How to communicate with customers
- Customer/supplier partnerships and agreements.

This unit covers the following parts of the Marketing Customer Interface syllabus:

- 2.2.1
- 2.3.3

Study guide

This unit introduces the concept of relationship marketing, where the priority has shifted away from transaction marketing to creating ongoing relationships with customers to create lifetime values. Relationship marketing is considered in both consumer and industrial markets. Situations are analyzed in terms of their suitability or unsuitability to relationship marketing. The benefits are considered and difficulties of relationship marketing are considered.

Creating positive relationships with customers

The rules for business success are changing fundamentally. Forces such as globalization, technological change and the rising power of the customer are stimulating marketers to find new ways to retain, satisfy and work with customers so that their needs can be anticipated and products and services customized more accurately. One of the most reliable indicators of the success of a company is whether it retains its customers. It is estimated that it costs between five to fifteen times as much to acquire a new customer as it does to keep a current one.

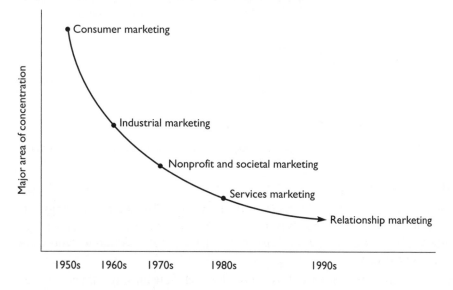

Figure 10.1 *Historical applications in marketing*

The result of this concern is relationship marketing (see Figure 10.1). Priority is shifting from products to people and processes aimed at creating delighted customers. Companies are now realizing that like every other organism they exist in a feedback loop with their environment. This is the underlying theory of using a systems approach towards organizational behaviour, in recognition that every aspect of the system will have an effect on another.

Marketing is moving from transaction marketing to relationship marketing. Each of these approaches has its own characteristics.

Transaction marketing:

- Focus on single sale
- Orientation on product features
- Short time scale
- Little emphasis on customer service
- Limited customer commitment
- Moderate customer contact
- Quality is primarily a concern of production.

Relationship marketing:

- Focus on customer retention
- Orientation on product benefits
- Long time scale
- High customer service emphasis
- High customer commitment
- High customer contact
- Quality is the concern of all.

Relationship marketing is the process of building and managing collaborative customer and other value chain relationships to increase customer value, retention and profit. The relationship process moves customers up a ladder of loyalty, as shown in Figure 10.2.

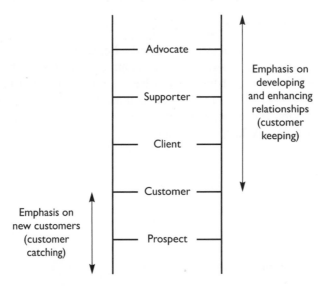

Figure 10.2 The relationship ladder. Christopher, Payne and Ballantyne, Relationship Marketing

Collaborating internally

Companies, instead of just being led by their production capability, their technology, or their financial departments, are looking at the needs of their customers and are breaking down walls internally to develop value chains based on relationships. As we have learned communication, empowerment and teamwork are key issues.

These customer-focused companies are thriving on their relationships, or rather the strength of their relationships both internally and externally so that there is a good match between the external and internal environment. Relationship marketing involves taking a broader view of this match.

The key to successfully implementing a relationship marketing strategy is to organize and motivate your workforce so they are interested in and understand the concept then:

1. Carry out an industry analysis.
2. Carry out an audit of relationship markets (see Gummesson).

3. Analyze internally.
4. Collect information on your customers.
5. Identify customers for RM strategy.
6. Understand individual customer profitability.
7. Market internally and externally.
8. Measure and evaluate the results.

Relationship marketing in consumer markets

Up until recently the idea of relationship marketing was mainly applied to industrial and services marketing, but it may also have some relevance for consumer marketing. This will depend on the characteristics of a market segment and the product field in question. It is important to understand and distinguish between actions that would aim to develop marketing relationships and actions that are interpreted and evaluated as sales promotion and merely create sales in the short term.

Marketing relationships are often initiated by the supplier, but sometimes consumers make the first move and take responsibility for maintaining and developing a relationship. This is termed reverse marketing, good examples are the relationship between a private consumer and a local builder, or the relationship patients may build up with a dentist as they seek further treatment over a lifetime.

It is this trust and confidence that relationship marketing seeks to build with larger groups of customers. Although this one-to-one, individualized marketing communication is more expensive per person to undertake, in the long term it may be less of an expense, if analyzed in terms of lifetime value.

The use of technology

Falling IT costs now make it possible to offer customers the recognition that was formerly only possible in businesses where the customer base was relatively small. Organizations are now using refined information about current and potential customers to anticipate and respond to their needs. Continuous relationship marketing now gives marketers a range of information about their customers. It is then possible to rearrange the information in many different ways.

The elements of a marketing relationship – when is it possible?

1. *Time frame* In considering whether a relationship marketing approach is possible one needs to consider the opportunity for a long-term relationship with the customer.
2. *Differentiation* The product or service must be able to be differentiated from the competition in some way.

Recognizing a natural RM possibility

It should be clear that some products and services naturally offer the opportunity for a relationship to form, and suppliers in the marketplace who are unable to satisfy and manage these relationships in a competent way will suffer in a competitive marketplace.

High involvement products/services

Some products and services offer the opportunity for a personal relationship to develop. For example, a musician may go to a music shop for advice about instruments. The help and care that the assistant can give is a natural opportunity to create a long-term relationship with that particular customer.

Risk

Purchasing must be considered in terms of generating anxiety and putting the consumer at risk. There are different types of risk: social, psychological, financial, and product failure. It is obvious therefore that customers may prefer to have previous experience of an organization before committing themselves to purchasing. In terms of ongoing purchasing they may be reluctant to change.

The desire to pay for more than just the core product

The essence of marketing is to turn a commodity into a brand. It is in the branding process that the product/service is augmented in such a way that customers are prepared to pay a premium price.

Customization

Some products/services need to be customized. With the growing understanding that customers wish to be treated as individuals, organizations should look at how they can tailor what they give to meet individual needs.

Training

When customers purchase products that are complicated, they may perceive a need for training. This need offers an opportunity for relationship marketing.

Psychological need

A relationship may be sought out by customers for very many reasons. For some it may be loneliness: with the breakdown of family, and the development of home working, some people may not have a large network of people in their personal lives to relate to. Others may wish to attach themselves to various organizations for reasons as varied as status, a better deal, or even the reluctance to look elsewhere. The research done by the Future Foundation indicates that we now live in a wider environment and that many of the values we once treasured in personal relationships we now look for in society and the relationship business creates with its social environment. The language used: 'industrial intimacy', 'making corporate love', is suggestive of this.

Regular maintenance and repair – ongoing services

Hairdressing, dressmaking, accountancy, law, fitness training, massage – there are any number of services where there is an ongoing interaction – a product requiring maintenance or repair throughout its life, or whose ongoing nature engages customers in a relationship with the providers.

Frequency of purchase

The higher the frequency of purchase the higher the opportunities will be to create a relationship.

Differentiation

The more a product or service is adapted to the particular tastes of a customer the greater will be the opportunity to create a relationship. Hairdressing, interior decoration and architecture are good examples.

Inconvenience

The more a supplier knows about a customer and their particular tastes the greater the opportunity for forming a relationship. For example, lawyers hold detailed client histories and clients may be reluctant, or too busy, to have to go through telling another lawyer about their life; the same holds true for accountants.

High switching costs

There may be costs involved in changing a supplier. For example, the new supplier may need to go through some sort of learning curve where mistakes will have to be made. There may be equipment costs where the old supplier has provided the customer with equipment free of charge.

Extended problem solving

Suppliers can add value to products/services in which the customer is deeply involved in an extended period of decision making, where there is a high degree of risk (social, psychological, financial and product failure) and where expertise is valued as a supplier.

Extended problem solving and a high level of involvement in product/services occurs where there is a perception of high risk and customers have a need to have things explained to them. Suppliers can add to the relationship by showing a real interest in the product area perhaps by visiting a customer, ensuring that the product is being used in the right way and sending invitations to further demonstrations, updates on product information and even a Christmas card.

Even where the level of involvement may not be high, for example in buying a tube of wallpaper paste, the customer may value advice. This in itself gives the retailer the opportunity to build a relationship on an ongoing basis, and then focus on linking these intangible benefits with a tangible benefit as a reward to purchase loyalty.

Role relationships

At all times the provider of the service must be aware that the relationship is based on the financial transaction, and the boundaries that delineate that relationship from one based on personal preference must be considered. The role relationship, and the behavioural expectations arising from a performer of the role, must be analyzed in detail. For example, a nurse or a teacher is expected to behave in a particular way. The possibility of relationship marketing must be viewed from both the customer's side and that of the market/product/service field and what is deemed suitable. Further consideration to some of the difficulties involved in relationship marketing, and how to manage them will be given in 'Relationship marketing in organizational markets'.

Customer and product influences on relationship potential

In approaching consumer markets, the traditional categorizations of products and services can be viewed in terms of their 'relationship possibilities'. These relationship possibilities may well be tangible or intangible.

There are thus two different types of incentives:

1. Incentives that offer tangible benefits.
2. Incentives that offer intangible benefits.

Tangible benefits

Tangible benefits attempt to encourage customers to enter into a relationship or to remain in one for a longer period of time. They can include:

*   *Money or near-money benefits* Examples include the British Telecom 'Family and Friends' scheme, the Air Miles benefits that participants can collect, and product discount-based schemes such as that run by Homebase. All these types of scheme give extra supplies at a better price or other products at a preferential price.

*   *Access to extra features* Examples include the British Airways Executive club member scheme which gives access to a special lounge, or the special shopping evenings which some shops have from time to time.

*   *Access to customized products or services*.

*   *Access to special customer service arrangements* For example, ordering by telephone, chauffeur-driven car to the airport, late check-in facilities.

*   *Extra information* Companies can send existing customers information on special deals or new product information, or produce a leisure magazine containing such information.

*   *User groups* Common interests create common bonds, the creation of user groups is another way of giving people the opportunity to relate to each other.

Intangible benefits

Intangible benefits could centre round self-esteem, using the relationship to reflect or imply quality, reducing risk such as social, psychological, economic and quality.

Social status, self-esteem and social concerns

Charities and fundraising offer opportunities to fund-givers to improve their social status. Royalty is associated with the voluntary sector and becoming involved may provide the chance to meet the rich and the famous in a well-known place not normally accessible. Charities following this path of fundraising need to look at sponsorship, or holding events such as operas and recitals where the great and the good are able to display themselves. At the other end of the scale it may mean joining in local activities and finding a sense of community. They also need to send ongoing information in order to keep donors involved and identified with the project.

Raising money for charity or doing something for a particular cause may well give a person a greater sense of self-esteem as well as the opportunity to show to the world that they are doing something. At a more symbolic level it may give the donor the opportunity to work out deep-felt social concerns, and sometimes concerns that they have experienced personally in the course of their lives.

Relationship marketing in organizational markets

Industry and relationship analysis

An industry and relationship analysis, including an examination of competitors, is an essential step prior to making a decision about your own strategy. In undertaking an analysis of any industry, its characteristics and long-term prospects can be analyzed in terms of five dimensions:

1. The nature and degree of competition.
2. The barriers to entry to that business.
3. The competitive power of substitute products.
4. The degree of buyer power.
5. The degree of supplier power.

Through analysis of these five dimensions insights can be gained into relationship with a number of key market areas, in terms of both opportunities and threats, as well as the specific key factors for success in the industry under consideration.

The five forces which contribute to industry profitability are summarized by Christopher, Payne and Ballantyne:

1. *Potential entrants* Two factors determine how strong this force will be – the existing barriers to entry and the likelihood of a strong competitive reaction from established competitors. The threat of entry tends to be low if barriers to entry are high and/or aspiring new entrants can expect extremely hostile retaliation from the established firms within the industry. If the threat of entry is low, profitability of the industry tends to be high.

2. *Buyers* The bargaining power of customers (buyers) is high when a number of critical factors are present. These include: the products that a company purchases forming a large proportion, in terms of cost, of its own product; the buyer group is operating in an industry of low profitability; the products supplied are undifferentiated, making it easy for the buyer to switch between suppliers at little cost; the products being purchased in large volumes; and the buyers having the potential to integrate backwards. Such conditions of high buyer power will result in lower industry profitability.

3. *Suppliers* Similarly, the bargaining power of suppliers can be high if there are relatively few suppliers; if the industry is dominated by only a few suppliers; if the industry is not an important customer of the supplier group; if the supplier has the potential to integrate forward into the customer's business; if there are few or no direct substitutes for the product, or if the supplier group's products are sufficiently differentiated that the firm being supplied the goods cannot easily switch to another supplier. Conditions of high supplier power lead to reduced industry profitability.

4. *Substitute products* In many markets it is possible to identify products which can serve as substitutes. In industries ranging from telecommunications to car making, the threat of substitution is present. The higher the threat of substitution, the lower the profitability is likely to be within the industry. This is because threat of substitution generally sets a limit on the prices that can be charged. The factors which influence the threat of substitution include the substitute product price-performance trade-off, and the extent of switching costs associated with changing from one supplier to the supplier of the substitute. If the threat of substitution is low, industry profitability will tend to be high.

5. *Industry competition* The degree of industry competition is characterized by the amount of rivalry between existing firms. This can vary considerably and is not related necessarily to whether or not the industry is highly profitable. Intense rivalry can exist if there is slow growth within the industry; if competitors are evenly balanced in size and capability; where switching costs are low; where there is a high fixed-cost structure and companies need to keep volumes high; where exit barriers are high such that unprofitable companies may still remain within the industry; and where competitors have different strategies – the result of which is that some firms may be willing to pursue a strategy that results in considerable conflict within the industry with price wars being a common outcome. A high degree of rivalry depresses industry profitability.

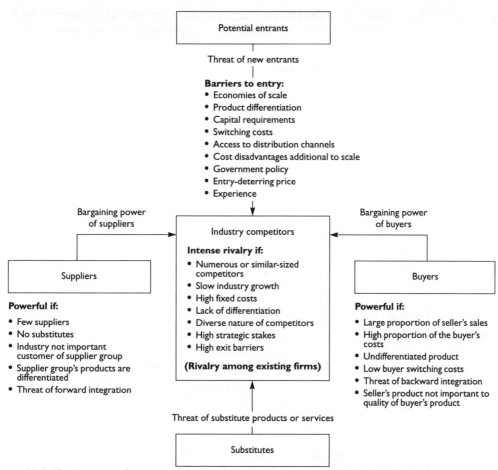

Figure 10.3 *The Porter industry analysis model. Based on Porter, M. E. (1980),* Techniques for Analyzing Industries and Competitors, Competitive Strategy. *New York: Free Press*

Porter argues that the goal of the corporate strategist is to find a position in the industry where their company can best defend itself against these five forces, or alternatively influence them in its favour.

A complete and balanced analysis of the competitive environment in which a firm is operating would include an examination of barriers to entry, the relative power of buyers and suppliers, the power of substitutes, and the degree of rivalry within the industry (see Figure 10.3). This understanding needs also to extend to the relationships that exist between all these players so that the marketer understands that they are not entering an empty playing field. This would lead to a good understanding of the key factors for success, and give managers a sense of the strengths and weaknesses, opportunities and threats within the industry. The power structure in an industry may result in conflicts being structuralized or institutionalized. This may, or may not, be insurmountable and affect the shape relationship marketing is able to take. In some industries it may even affect the relationships the distribution channels have with their customers.

It is also of importance to consider relationships with competitors. The type of relationship with competitors, is often the result of the degree of rivalry and the competitive structure of the industry. Rivalry is usually strong where there are numerous or equally balanced competitors but may also be intense under other conditions. Poor relationships can manifest in deep-seated antagonism between firms in the way they use their resources to attack one another, to their mutual detriment.

Better relationships between two seemingly implacable rivals in a given market sector may restore industry profitability. Porter points to the need to adopt strategies relating to competitors that could be called 'cooperative', and that make the industry as a whole better off. Kevin P. Coyne and Somu Subramaniam, 'Bringing discipline to strategy', *McKinsey Quarterly,* (www.mckinseyquarterly.com) point out that the traditional Porter model needs to be reassessed.

Evert Gummesson (Stockholm University, School of Business) says, 'although the frameworks presented in marketing books claimed to be universally valid, they dealt with consumer goods marketing: cola drinks, pain killers, cookies and cars. Contrary to common belief, consumer marketing is the smallest part of all marketing; services marketing and business marketing account for the major share...' Relationship marketing is becoming a general marketing approach and customers need to be seen as living within a network of relationships where people enter into active contact with each other. Figure 10.4 illustrates the complexity of relationships and shows how they exist as intertwining networks.

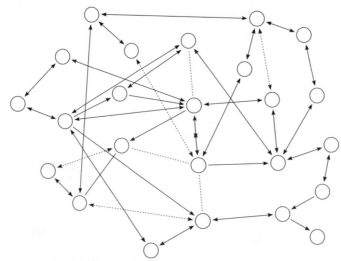

Figure 10.4 *Source: Gummesson, E. (1999),* Total Relationship Marketing, *Butterworth-Heinemann*

Table 10.1 *TRM as a paradigm shift in marketing. Source: Gummesson, E. (1999)*

Definition	RM is marketing seen as relationships, networks and interaction.
Characteristics	Value for the parties involved – of which the customer is one – created through interaction between suppliers, customers, competitors and others; parties in a network of relationships are co-producers, creating value for each other.
Making RM tangible	Specification of 30 relationships, the 30Rs, both operational market relationships, and mega and nano non-market relationships.
Relationship portfolio	As part of the marketing planning process, a selection of focal relationships is made for the planning period in the marketing plan.
Values	Collaboration in focus; more win-win and less win-lose; more equal parties; all parties carry a responsibility to be active in the relationship; long-term relationships; each customer is an individual or a member of a community of like-minded people.
Theoretical and practical foundation	Built on a synthesis between traditional marketing management, marketing mix (the 4Ps) and sales management; services marketing (3Ps); the network approach to industrial marketing; quality management; imaginary organizations; new accounting principles; and the experiences of reflective practitioners.
Links to management	RM is more than marketing management, it is rather marketing-oriented management – an aspect of the total management of the firm – and not limited to marketing or sales departments; the marketing plan becomes part of the business plan.
Links to accounting	The balanced scorecard and intellectual capital provide tools for measuring return on relationships.
Links to organization structure	RM is the marketing manifestation of the imaginary organization and vice versa.
Advantages to a firm	Increased customer retention and duration; increased marketing productivity and thus increased profitability; increased stability and security.
Advantages to the market economy	RM adds collaboration to competition and regulations/institutions; the symbiosis between these three contributes to a dynamic marketing equilibrium.
Advantages to society, citizens and customers	RM is the marketing of the value society and the postmodern society; increased focus on customized production and one-to-one marketing, diminished focus on standardized mass manufacturing and anonymous mass marketing
Validity	By focusing on relationships, networks and interaction, RM offers a more realistic approach to marketing than currently prevails in marketing education. In practice, business is largely conducted through networks of relationships.
Generalizability	RM can be applied to all kinds of organizations and offerings, but the relationship portfolio and the application is always specific to a given situation.

Gummesson suggests that the traditional audit needs to carry additional questions. His definition of relationship marketing is as follows: 'Relationship marketing is marketing seen as relationships, networks and inter-action' (Gummesson, E. (1999) *Total Relationship Marketing,* Butterworth-Heinemann).

In his book he outlines 30 types of relationship, and suggests that marketers should look at them and their constituent parts and answer the following questions:

1. Is the composition of our relationship portfolio satisfactory?
2. How well are we handling specific relationships and their parts?
3. Are specific relationships or parts of them crucial for success?
4. Could specific relationships add to our performance if we improve them?
5. Should certain relationships be terminated?
6. Do we measure return on relationship (ROR) in the best possible way?

His framework of thinking adds an additional understanding to the audit and also takes marketing into a wider framework. Gummesson has extended the term relationship marketing to total relationship marketing (TRM) and he says that it represents a paradigm shift in marketing as illustrated in Table 10.1 .

Another consideration in relationship marketing is to understand when it is appropriate, and indeed how much of the relationship the customer actually wants. Within the context of business-to-business marketing it is important to understand that:

1. Activities that would create commitment take time and therefore money.
2. Organizations interact with more than one department in the course of doing business. It may be difficult to ensure in a relationship marketing programme that the whole organization is singing from the same song sheet.

In setting up a relationship marketing programme within a business it is important to communicate that the time, effort and cost of carrying it out is probably less than would be spent looking for new business and carrying out discrete transactions.

For relationship marketing in business-to-business marketing, the same question applies as in consumer marketing – does the customer actually want a relationship? Because if the customer does not want one, or is not getting the one they would like, an organization may well waste a lot of money supplying the wrong thing.

Communication

Gummesson in his book *Total Relationship Marketing,* Butterworth-Heinemann (p. 236) says that the 30R approach (see Table 10.2) allows marketers to go beyond suppliers and customers and see marketing relationships as embedded in a network of multiple relationships:

- Classic market relationships (R1-R3) are the supplier-customer dyad, the triad of supplier-customer-competitor, and the physical distribution network, which are treated extensively in general marketing theory.

- Special market relationships (R4-R17) represent certain aspects of classic relationships, such as the interaction in the service encounter or the customer as a member of a loyalty programme.

Table 10.2 The 30 relationships of TRM – the 30Rs

Classic market relationships
R1 The classic dyad – the relationship between the supplier and the customer. This is the parent relationship of marketing, the ultimate exchange of value which constitutes the basis of business.
R2 The classic triad – the drama of the customer-supplier-competitor triangle. Competition is a central ingredient of the market economy. In competition there are relationships between three parties: between the customer and the current supplier, between the customer and the supplier's competitors, and between competitors.
R3 The classic network – distribution channels. The traditional physical distribution and modern channel management including goods, services, people and information, consists of a network of relationships.

R4   Relationships via full-time marketers (FTMs) and part-time marketers (PTMs). Those who work in marketing and sales departments – the FTMs – are professional relationship makers. All others, who perform other main functions but yet influence customer relationships directly or indirectly, are PTMs. There are also contributing FTMs and PTMs outside the organization.

R5   The service encounter – interaction between customer and the service provider. Production and delivery of services involve the customer in an interactive relationship with the service provider, often referred to as the moment of truth.

R6   The many-headed customer and the many-headed supplier. Marketing to other organizations – industrial marketing or business marketing – often means contacts between many individuals from the supplier's and the customer's organization.

R7   The relationship to the customer's customer. A condition for success is often the understanding of the customer's customer, and what suppliers can do to help their customers become successful.

R8   The close versus the distant relationship. In mass marketing, the closeness to the customer is lost and the relationship becomes distant, based on surveys, statistics and written reports.

R9   The relationship to the dissatisfied customer. The dissatisfied customer perceives a special type of relationship, more intense than the normal situation, and often badly managed by the provider. The way of handling a complaint – the recovery – can determine the quality of the future relationship.

R10   The monopoly relationship: the customer or supplier as prisoners. When competition is inhibited, the customer may be at the mercy of the supplier – or the other way around. One of them becomes a prisoner.

R11   The customer as 'member'. In order to create a long-term sustaining relationship, it has become increasingly common to enlist customers as members of various loyalty programmes.

R12   The electronic relationship. Information technology – telecoms, computers, TV – are elements of all types of marketing today and they form new types of relationships.

R13   Parasocial relationships – relationships to symbols and objects. Relationships exist not only with people and physical phenomena, but also with mental images and symbols such as brand names and corporate identities.

R14   The non-commercial relationship. This is a relationship between the public sector and citizens/customers, but it also includes voluntary organizations and other activities outside of the profit-based and monetarized economy, such as those performed in families.

R15   The green relationship. Environmental and health issues have slowly but gradually increased in importance and are creating a new type of customer relationship through legislation, the voice of opinion-leading consumers, changing behaviour of consumers and an extension of the customer-supplier relationship to encompass a recycling process.

R16   The law-based relationship. A relationship to a customer is sometimes founded primarily on legal contracts and the threat of litigation.

R17   The criminal network. Organized crime is built on tight and often impermeable networks guided by an illegal business mission. They exist around the world and are apparently growing but are not observed in marketing theory. These networks can disturb the functioning of a whole market or industry.

Mega relationships

R18   Personal and social networks. Personal and social networks often determine business networks. In some cultures, business is solely conducted between friends and friends of friends.

R19   Mega marketing – the real 'customer' is not always found in the marketplace. In certain instances, relationships must be sought with governments, legislators, influential individuals, and others, in order to make marketing feasible on an operational level.

R20   Alliances change the market mechanisms. Alliances mean closer relationships and collaboration between companies. Thus, competition is partly curbed, but collaboration is necessary to make the market economy work.

R21 The knowledge relationship. Knowledge can be the most strategic and critical resource and 'knowledge acquisition' is often the rationale for alliances.

R22 Mega alliances change the basic conditions for marketing. The EU (European Union) and NAFTA (North American Free Trade Agreement) are examples of alliances above the single company or industry. They exist on government and supranational levels.

R23 The mass media relationship. The media can be supportive or damaging to marketing and they are particularly influential in forming public opinion. The relationship to media is crucial for the way media will handle an issue.

Nano relationships

R24 Market mechanisms are brought inside the company. By introducing profit centres in an organization, a market inside the company is created and internal as well as external relationships of a new kind emerge.

R25 Internal customer relationship. The dependency between the different tiers and departments in a company is seen as a process consisting of relationships between internal customers and internal suppliers.

R26 Quality providing a relationship between operations management and marketing. The modern quality concept has built a bridge between design, manufacturing and other technology-based activities and marketing. It considers the company's internal relationships as well as its relationship to the customers.

R27 Internal marketing: relationships with the 'employee market'. Internal marketing can be seen as part of TRM as it gives indirect and necessary support to the relationships with external customers.

R28 The two-dimensional matrix relationship. Organizational matrices are frequent in large corporations, and above all they are found in the relationships between product management and sales.

R29 The relationship to external providers of marketing services. External providers reinforce the marketing function by supplying a series of services, such as those offered by advertising agencies and market research institutes, but also in the area of sales and distribution.

R30 The owner and financier relationship. Owners and other financiers partly determine the conditions under which a marketing function can operate. The relationship to them influences the marketing strategy.

The next two types are non-market relationships which indirectly influence the efficiency of market relationships:

- Mega relationships (R18-R23) exist above the market relationships. They provide a platform for market relationships and concern the economy and society in general. Among these are mega marketing (lobbying, public opinion and political power), mega alliances (such as the NAFTA, setting a stage for marketing in North America), and social relationships (such as friendship and ethnic bonds).

- Nano relationships (R24-R30) are found below the market relationships, that is relationships inside an organization (intra-organizational relationships). All internal activities influence the externally bound relationships. Examples of nano relationships are the relationships between internal customers, and between internal markets that arise as a consequence of increasing use of independent profit centres, divisions and business areas inside organizations. The boundary is sometimes fuzzy; it is a matter of emphasis. For example, the physical distribution network (R3) is part of a logistics flow, concerning internal as well as external customers.

Gummesson has a unique way of looking at relationships. He uses the metaphor of the Russian doll and says that Vandermerve, in her book *From Tin Soldiers to Russian Dolls* (Butterworth-Heinemann, 1993), uses the metaphor of tin soldiers and wooden dolls to describe the management of an emerging service society. The metaphor points to connections and dependencies that must be considered when a company organizes its marketing. The doll becomes a symbol of the imaginary organization where the borderline between organization, market and society is not as clear as in traditional organization theory and economics.

Recognizing a natural relationship marketing possibility

There are a number of factors within organizational markets that may lead to the opportunity for a relationship marketing approach:

1. *Uncertainty* When an organization feels that the product supplied is not homogenous there will be a certain amount of uncertainty. The uncertainty, or rather the management of risk and spreading of the risk within the organization, will determine the complexity of decision making and the need for relationship marketing.

2. *Unequal power* In some business relationships one organization may have more power than the other; the weaker organization may then need to appoint people within its own ranks who have influence in the stronger organization.

3. *Environmental uncertainty* Raw materials may vary in terms of price. A relationship could be developed as a way of handling this so that variability is absorbed.

4. *Legitimacy* Creating a relationship with a powerful organization and being able to publicize this fact will give an organization legitimacy as far as quality, financial standing, or reliability is concerned to such an extent that other customers may feel they no longer need to check their credentials.

5. *Inconvenience* A relationship may develop between two organizations because they are tied into each other by the way of shared equipment, shared knowledge or a shared expertise.

Risks involved in relationship marketing

There is a danger of only thinking about marketing in terms of relationship marking. The objective of relationship marketing is to turn new customers into advocates for a company on a long-term basis. Hopefully, this will ensure that they stay with the company and refer other people. Relationship marketing therefore adds an additional concept to customer service and quality to the traditional marketing mix.

Some aspects of role relationships are dealt with in the section 'Role and relationships' in the unit 'Macro and micro-environmental forces driving change'. Other aspects that need to be considered are as follows.

Personal and professional dimensions of role relationships

It is obviously easier for relationships to form if the people concerned get on well together – it is another matter when they do not, or even when they start off getting on well, and for their relationship to deteriorate as a result of some personal or professional disagreement.

The question is: how does the organization put in systems to deal with this (like taking a temperature reading) before the situation becomes confrontational? The relationship itself will need to be maintained, and feedback on the functional, professional and the feeling side, to do with the personal relationship that is forming or has formed, needs to be considered.

Creating an atmosphere in which these discussions can take place can only be done in a 'no blame' environment. Human beings are not like machines. Very often things go wrong that, with an opportunity for reflection, we can learn to manage.

Within this context of understanding organizations need to meet on a regular basis to look at:

1. The task elements – is the job going well, are contractual and legal obligations being met?

2. The feeling elements – how are people feeling? Are the behavioural criteria being met? If they are not it may be time to move key individuals out of the relationship. In a no-blame culture where people are open to discussing the vagaries of human nature it should be possible to do this less painfully than in a blame culture where scapegoating is the norm.

Relationships and innovation in role

Relating in any personal relationship requires people to adapt and be innovative within the relationship. It is truly interactive, the success of the relationship is two way as two people are involved. Relationship marketing involves a fundamental change in the philosophy guiding the organization's behaviour. When there is a change in values and beliefs in an organization a certain amount of discomfort will be created. An understanding of stress and anxiety, role and role relationship will enable this process to be understood.

Changes in role

Relationship marketing and empowerment involve a devolution of power to the front line. However, when an organization changes its philosophy and structure so that more power, authority and autonomy reside with the staff in contact with customers, middle managers may feel threatened. Managers need to understand that changes like these will release them from day-to-day tactical responsibilities so they have more time for strategic planning and playing a facilitative role. Conversely, employees who are given more responsibility may feel overwhelmed and will need to be given training in order to enable them to expand their roles.

Membership of a primary group

Sociologists have long said that membership of stable primary groups is essential to the well-being of every society. It is through membership of groups that basic needs for affiliation, security and recognition are satisfied. If we accept this, we can look at organizations as groups of people who come together to satisfy their own psychological needs.

It is these psychological needs that prevent change from taking place within the organization. A customer-centred organization seeks to satisfy the needs of its customers and its employees and tries to create a balance between the two. Nonetheless, there may be some difficulty in adjusting because change affects people in different ways and many employees may feel stressed and anxious.

The outcome of any change process will be determined by the way in which an organization manages these feelings.

Stress and anxiety

The stress that people feel at work is an area that is receiving a considerable amount of attention. Stress on the personal level causes real pain and suffering. On an organizational level it causes disruption and loss of production.

Anxiety arising from stress is a response to perceived danger – the physical symptoms are a pounding heart, sweating palms, rapid breathing, and all the other bodily dysfunctions anxiety can produce. Externally, anxiety manifests itself in low productivity, lateness, absenteeism, illness, depression, etc.

External danger will automatically result in a person feeling anxiety; however from within the person, unconscious feelings and memories can also cause intense feelings of anxiety.

For example, you may be asked to carry out a new task at work which, by overcoming your anxiety, you are able to complete. However, a different person in the same situation may experience such intense anxiety that they are unable to complete the task.

The new service culture puts many people in touch with customers and expects them to behave in an unfamiliar way, we are being asked to be friendly to strangers. This increased contact, for people who have not been specially recruited with such skills in mind, and who do not like or find it difficult to engage with their feelings with strangers in this way, may lead them to feel under increased pressure when they are asked to expand their roles.

Defences

When people are anxious and stressed they will understandably try to protect themselves from anything that may result in emotional pain.

When individuals suffer from anxiety they externalize their feelings and attribute them to an external cause. Other people or social groups become repositories for these projections.

The conceptual framework that underlies this approach to organizations is based on Melanie Klein (1959) who explained that people divide feelings into differentiated elements. She called this 'splitting'. By splitting emotions people can gain relief from internal conflicts. Projection often accompanies splitting, and involves locating feelings in others rather than oneself.

Projection blurs the boundaries between people because it distorts reality and makes what is inside people appear to be outside them. Their actions are therefore based on an assessment of a situation that is unreal.

These processes can make it difficult for people to open up and create an innovative organization involved in a process of continuous change. This type of reaction creates a blame culture. Organizations can change this by making it acceptable to talk openly about feelings, and by giving people proper real information about the external environment (macro, micro and internal organizational factors) so they can adapt accordingly.

Taking up a role

(Adapted from work done at the Grubb Institute by Reed and Palmer)

The idea of role can be looked at as an idea held in the mind of individuals through which they are able to bring together their skills, knowledge and resources (such as people, machinery and money) in order to deal with an external task. Role training is covered in the unit 'Additional techniques for mobilizing performance'.

The key to the way in which people perform their tasks at work lies in their ability, or inability, to take up and perform their roles.

The subjective psychological aspect of a role relies on:

- The person's ability to understand what the job is in terms of the work that must be done.
- The person's understanding of where they are within a given organizational system (the role relationships).
- The person's realization of how others expect them to behave (the role set's expectations).
- The person's understanding of the environmental considerations that impact upon an organization externally.
- The reality of the pressures that impact on them from within the organization itself.
- The ability to reflect on their self-management within their role.
- An understanding of any intra-role conflict (conflicting demands of the different requirements of the same role – for example, a manager may feel that drinking with the boys will inhibit him from managing).
- An understanding of inter-role conflict (for example a salesperson who is required to travel a great deal might find their work role conflicts with their role of parent, which requires them to be at home)
- An understanding of intra-role conflict when the ethics of an organization conflict with personal values and beliefs.

In order to manage themselves 'in role' people need to understand the feelings they have about their roles, and the reactions they have to the way in which others behave towards them because of their role.

For example, it can come as a total surprise to experience how people change their behaviour towards others when they become part of 'management', or when they have to deal directly with customers.

People will need training to look at their roles, learning to manage behavioural aspects of a role and understanding how people will expect them to behave so they do not upset others and are able to handle any conflicts inherent in the role itself.

Similarly, the increase in tasks and responsibilities that people are asked to take on may make them very anxious and therefore unable to take on their roles.

When people are unable to make the most of their roles either because of fear, reprobation or risk there will be stagnation on a personal level and on an organizational level.

The understanding of role and the expectations of customers will enable organizations to ensure that customers only meet with people who know how to behave in role. Similarly, the person in role will understand what these expectations are and be prepared for them – for example, customers who feel that the role holder should be prepared for aggressive, demanding and infantile behaviour (for example, drunkenness in a pub).

Role management

The role idea is the idea which individuals carry in their minds and which motivates them, and relates them to some inner meaning which helps them to manage their behaviour. The way in which a person manages their role will be influenced by:

- Their own view of their relationships with other people. If a person feels threatened by others the role will be defined more tightly – if the person feels encouraged they may well expand their role.

- Their own assessment of their performance. If a person thinks they are doing well they are likely to expand that role.
- A change in the working environment, or a new colleague either of which can threaten people and thus lead to a redefinition of roles.
- Similarly a change in culture may inhibit people or help them to look at the roles in a new way.
- A change in the micro-environment (this includes changes to the primary task or mission of the organization) or macro-environment may frighten people individually and inhibit them from performing their roles.

Role defence – the avoidance of pain

Role may appear to others as an objective reality, but people experience roles as a subjective reality; we do not see roles, we see people doing things. Role involves both a task and a behavioural requirement in the way the task is performed. It also has an imaginative element which depends on the way in which the individual sees, creates and performs their role.

The term 'role defence' is used to describe the way in which the members of an organization protect themselves from anxiety. When individuals face situations that are too difficult, too threatening or too painful to acknowledge, they defend themselves against them. Central among these defences is denial, which involves pushing certain thoughts and feelings and experiences out of conscious awareness because they have become too anxiety-provoking. When attention is brought to them, there is an emotionally charged refusal to accept them – this is called resistance.

Managing and monitoring one's own behaviour and taking feedback is an essential skill for frontline staff. People may well need help in order to be able to do this.

Role relationships

It may be helpful for people to think about their roles as being able to provide them with some protection. For example if we rely on our personal relationships to get things done and then people fall out with each other, work will suffer. However, if people look at each role and the specific tasks that need to be carried out by the holder of that role it is then possible to move into a role relationship and not have only a person-to-person relationship on which to rely on (see Figure 10.5). Although the two can be managed together it of course helps if the people get on as people

Old – Relying on making personal relationships to get things done. If people fall out with each other the work suffers.

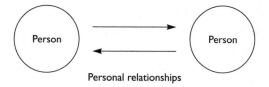

New direction – Using role relations to achieve the task of organization.

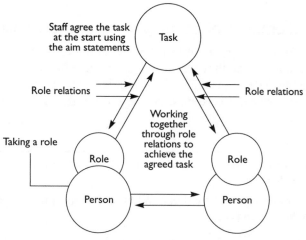

Role relations enable people to be frank,
truthful and tough with one another,
without damaging personal relationships.

Figure 10.5 Source: Grubb Institute

251

Role conflict

Role conflict occurs when two sets of pressures occur simultaneously making one aspect of the role more difficult. There may be a great relationship but the service manager may also have to say things that may cause a negative reaction.

Role definition

Role definition covers the degree to which roles are interrelated and the way in which people relate through their roles. The relationship roles need to be defined – in terms of the contractual elements related to the task and also in terms of contact. (See Patching and Chatham (1998) 'Getting a life at work: developing people beyond role boundaries' *Journal of Management Development,* 17(5), www.emeraldlibrary.com).

Role interdependence

Role interdependence is a measure of the information one person must receive from another so that they can both perform their roles.

Role ambiguity

This arises when there is a discrepancy between the information available to the person and that which is required to perform the role adequately. It is particularly prevalent in situations where disclosure is necessary to the professional performance of the role.

Role suction

Very often when an organization places people on customers' premises or they get involved with the relationship aspects of managing a customer, supplier, distributor or any other stakeholder, they may be sucked out of their role of representing the interests of the organization who is paying their salary and feel they belong more to the organization they are serving. Obviously, this balance must be carefully considered and employees given the opportunity to discuss what is happening.

Parallel process

Picking up on how the organization feels about issues – if the people working within an organization feel badly about it, customers will tend to feel the same way. If customers feel badly about an organization, the employees will feel the same way as well.

Picking up how customers feel about themselves – people working for an organization tend to pick up the same feelings and dilemmas as their customers. For example, a management school very often practises the worst kind of management. Organizations need to be able to talk about the effect their client group is having on people. If the client group is particularly demanding, for example, in an unemployment office or a customer complaints department, the organization must provide for space and time for these issues to be addressed and allow people to talk about their feelings.

Understanding the dilemmas of other people and organizations

Close business relationships provide opportunities for a greater understanding about how other people feel about the organization for which they are working. It is clear that while remaining empathetic a relationship marketer must be able to manage the boundaries between their own organization and that of the customer/supplier/distributor/stakeholder's organizations.

References

'Relationship marketing in consumer markets', R. Christy, G. Oliver and J. Penn, *Journal of Marketing Management* 1996, 12, 175-187.

'Relationship marketing in organizational markets: When is it appropriate?', K. Bliss, *Journal of Marketing Management 1996,* 12, 161-173.

Case History: The Platinum Print Company

Read the following case study brief and answer the questions beneath.

Background

Platinum Print is a privately-owned company, with the majority of the shares held by John Rush; the other shareholder is his brother, but he plays no active role in the business. The Board consists of John Rush (as Managing Director) plus three Executive Directors responsible for Operations, Marketing/Sales, and Finance. Established in 1970, the company now has around 80 employees; it has grown very slowly but now stands poised, potentially, for more spectacular expansion, because it has acquired a bankrupt competitor.

The equipment used by Platinum Print enables it to print in a maximum of two colours (plus black); its machines are fairly old and the company's profit margins have not been sufficient to justify their replacement. Platinum's field of expertise is concentrated in such products as 'café pads' (the notepads used by waiters and waitresses in restaurants for taking customer orders), invoice books, envelopes, and standard or customized office stationery.

Customer segments

Four-fifths of Platinum Print's sales are conducted through stationery supply companies, both wholesale and retail; the remaining 20 per cent is fragmented among a number of direct clients, such as owner-operated restaurants, small fast food chains, and family businesses of various kinds (e.g. in retailing, distribution, and the building trades). The vast majority of the firm's customers are located within 50 miles (80 kilometres).

Competition

Printing is highly competitive. Overall, the market is static or in decline, as organizations become capable of in-house document production through desktop publishing equipment, and as companies communicate increasingly through electronic media rather than by conventional correspondence. Many of the items in Platinum's 'catalogue' are distress purchases (i.e. clients order them as a matter of necessity rather than because they want to). Winning orders, in what is virtually a commodity market place, is widely seen as being dependent on price. No single competitor has more than a very small share of the total sales in printing.

The current situation

You have been engaged by John Rush to re-energize the Platinum Print business and capitalize on the opportunities generated through the acquisition of its bankrupt former competitor.

Produce a report for the Managing Director of Platinum Print, John Rush, in which you supply responses to the following four issues which he has put in front of you.

a. At present the company has no systematic mechanisms for obtaining, analyzing and acting on customer feedback. Outline the methodological options available and indicate (with reasons) the approach you would recommend to Platinum Print, given its customer profile.

b. John Rush has heard of relationship marketing and thinks that it may offer some opportunities for his company. Briefly summarize the generic rationale for relationship marketing and assess its potential for Platinum Print.

c. Platinum's employees are immersed in the crafts of printing, typesetting, typographical design and the other technical skills associated with the company's operation. In the view of John Rush they display insufficient concern for customers. What can be done to encourage them to be much more customer focused, so far as the company's external clients are concerned?

d. At present, Platinum Print has no particular competitive advantage which differentiates it from other printing companies. How could it create one?

It is permissible to make assumptions by adding to the details given above, provided that the essence of the case study is neither changed nor undermined in any way by what is added.

Summary

This unit has introduced the concept of relationship marketing and its increasing importance in the context of developing sustainable competitive advantage. We have considered where it can be applied in consumer and industrial markets, and discussed some of the difficulties that can be encountered.

Objectives

To enable students to understand the benefits of building a customer focus.

- To understand the operational aspects of achieving a customer focus.
- To explore aspects of outsourcing and partnering.

This unit covers the following parts of the Marketing Customer Interface syllabus:

- 2.2.1
- 2.2.2
- 2.2.3

Study guide

The benefits of achieving a customer focus are made clear and the operational organizational aspects of achieving a customer focus are considered. First of all, organizations must find out if, and where, they have a problem. They need then to understand the value of customers and their profitability. Once this has been established, organizations need to lock their customers into the business. Once existing customers are locked in, the organization can develop ideas about increasing income by increasing sales and improving profit. The use of technology, customization and one-to-one marketing, outsourcing and customer/supplier partnership agreements are explored as a method of decreasing costs and improving customer service.

Key ingredients to achieving a customer focus

The benefits to building a customer focus are clear:

1. *Customer loyalty and retention* enables the customer and the organization to get to know each other better. This means that the organization is able to match its offer more closely to customer needs and customers are likely to feel greater satisfaction.

2. *Customer satisfaction* in turn makes people working in the organization feel as if they are doing a great job and this in turn makes them more motivated to provide better service.

3. *Customer service* is improved because work becomes a good place to be. Employee stress decreases, absenteeism drops, productivity increases, profits go up, shareholders are happy and don't withdraw their money, the organization pays more tax and the economy benefits.

4. *Stability* The organization is therefore in a more stable position. We all benefit: society, the economy and you.

The outcome will be:

- Existing customers:
  1. Increased loyalty
  2. Increased retention
  3. Lower rates of loss
  4. And, in some cases, higher share of customer spend
  5. Lower levels of complaints
  6. Greater satisfaction in the way complaints are handled
  7. More spontaneous referrals from people who have heard about you
  8. More referrals from customers who when asked, are willing to refer the organization to other people they know.

- New customers:
    1. Improved rate of conversion.
- Old/lapsed customers:
    1. The improvement in reputation and the return of customers who have drifted away.

The functional/organizational aspects of customer focus

In order to harness the idea of customer focus, organizations need to consider the 'how' of getting it done. The following steps need to be considered (adapted from Charles Wilson, *Profitable Customers,* Institute of Directors):

1. Find out if and where you have a problem.
2. Deal with customer complaints.
3. Make sure you understand the value of customers and their profitability.
4. Communicate with customers, create relationships where possible and understand their objectives.
5. Ensure first class service is provided, look at your value chain and match it with the customer activity cycle..
6. Look at increasing income.
7. Improve profits.
8. Re-evaluate your distribution channels.
9. Help your customers to save money.
10. Investigate the use of technology.
11. Ascertain if customization and one-to-one marketing are for you.
12. Investigate outsourcing and customer/supplier partnering agreements.
13. Ongoing: look at the macro and micro environment and make sure you understand the context in which your customers are operating.

Find out if and where you have a problem

See Unit 7, Strategy and methods to produce customer focused behaviour for external and internal analysis (customer care audit). From this analysis you will be able to decide on the relevant philosophy, structure, technique, managerial process, market research, customer relationship programme, internal marketing programme, marketing mix and other aspects covered in this unit.

Dealing with customer complaints

1. *Spot problems before they happen* Ensuring that you get customer feedback is one thing, but you also need to ensure that sales and profit are constantly tracked as well. This means that you need a financial system that gives this information. Once you know there is a problem it will be possible to find out whether any decrease in business is due to an internal problem and is controllable or an external problem and therefore uncontrollable. For example, a customer of a customer going out of business.

2. *Make it easy to complain* Most customers hate complaining, they just move their business. If there is a complaint make sure you move quickly. The complaints process needs to be fast, friendly and work with a minimum of administration. Staff should be encouraged to be supportive and to act in a responsive way. Immediate compensation is effective.

Encourage your customers to help you provide a better service

Ted Johns, *Perfect Customer Care* (Arrow Business Books, 1995) provides the following advice:

1. Make it easy to complain: use complaint forms and 0800 (free) telephone numbers. Try video talk back and suggestion schemes.
2. Ask for complaints: seek out customers at random and ask them for their views.
3. Pretend to be a customer.
4. Listen to the complaints without becoming defensive: ask questions, ask for suggestions (what can we do to put it right?), ask what you should have done, ask what the customer expected in the light of the behaviour of other organizations.

5. Act quickly and with goodwill to solve the problem.

6. Replace defective products immediately or repeat the service.

7. Take positive steps to prevent a recurrence – don't assume that the first complaint is a one-off.

8. Use some imagination in finding ways to secure feedback. If you're in the personnel function you could ring people who come for interview (and who have been rejected) to ask them how they were treated and if they have any suggestions about how their processing could have been improved.

9. Award positive recognition for customer feedback: small prizes for completed questionnaires drawn out of a hat.

You may need to check:

1. Product service failure or performance

2. Method and efficiency of delivery

3. Delivery time and frequency

4. Intensity and effectiveness of promotion

5. Quality of the sales force and their methods of selling

6. The after-sales service

7. The skills and experience of the staff employed

8. The technology employed

9. Procedures governing the action of staff

10. Speed and value of order processing

11. Mechanisms for dealing with complaints

12. Employee satisfaction.

Business to business marketing

If you are part of a supply chain, look for weaknesses in the linkages and think about how you can overcome them. Move from being an available supplier to becoming an approved supplier, to a preferred supplier, to a partner agreement. Think about IT links, or look at strengthening the relationship in other ways (see 'Investigate outsourcing and customer/supplier partnership agreements').

Think about the future

Close contact with your customers will enable you to understand their vision. This information will then make it possible for you to match your supplies with their needs. If a new product is being developed try and work alongside your customers. Get your R&D people involved with customers – get them close to them so they can listen to real problems experienced by real people.

Look at www.crm-forum.com and www.ecademy.tv.

How do you understand your customers better and deliver what they want, when they want it, and how they want it – visit www.Delanotech.com to hear how Delano and third party experts use CRM to maximize customer value.

Make sure you understand the value of customers and their profitability

It is a fundamental rule that if you do not know how much your customers are worth to you, you will not be able to understand how to serve them.

Some organizations take a short-term view of a customer's value, per transaction, others take a longer view. If an activity costing is carried out it will be clear that although customers appear to make a profit in the short term they may not once all the costs are allocated directly to them.

There are four ways to approach calculating the value of a customer:

1. *Acquisition cost* This is the amount that needs to be spent to acquire the customer in the first place. It would include all promotion and sales costs.

2. *Revenue stream* This is the amount of money the customer pays you for the goods/service that have been purchased.

3. *Cost stream* These would include all the costs incurred to provide the goods and services to the customer.

4. *Time* Time is the length of the relationship between a customer and the organization.

Customer value can then be calculated once an estimate of the revenue and cost stream have been calculated. The estimate can then be used to discount back to the present to get a net present value (NPV) estimate of expected profit during the time the customer is with the organization – this is called lifetime customer value.

In order to calculate lifetime value you will need to think about the following:

1. Decide who your customers are.
2. Estimate how you expect them to purchase (frequency, volume spend) over the period of time.
3. Estimate how much your costs will be to retain them.

From this analysis you will be able to work out a marketing strategy that will enable you to target your most profitable customers. This method allows you to create a value based segmentation system. The right level of customer service can then be given to customers who represent a higher lifetime value.

Note: Net present value calculations are covered in the module *Management Information for Marketing Decisions*.

Table 11.1

Calculation per customer /trade channel	Comment
Annual sales	Sales for the last financial year (including after sales income)
Gross income	(Net sales after discounts – cost of product + overheads but excluding costs to interface)
-	
Costs to interface	Marketing, selling, distribution, service, administration, stockholding, customization, promotions etc. (allocated by customer)
=	
Net customer profitability (NCP)	Gross income – costs to interface
×	
Expected length of relationship	How long will the customer remain loyal?
=	
Discounted customer profitability (DCP)	£NCP × expected length of relationship (adjusted for internal cost of capital)

Source: Charles Wilson (1996), *Calculating Discounted Customer Profitability,* Institute of Directors/Kogan

Alan Mitchell points out, (*Marketing Business,* May 1999), that like most great ideas, implementing lifetime customer value is turning out to be more difficult than enthusiasts first predicted. Many companies still can't identify individual customers let alone individual revenue streams. Loyalty schemes have proved invaluable, but they only scratch the surface. Projecting how current revenues will pan out over a 'lifetime' involves a lot of guesswork, albeit data-driven, educated guesswork.

Key account management portfolio analysis

Portfolio analysis is simply a means of assessing a number of different key accounts, first according to the potential of each in terms of achieving the organization's objectives and, second, according to the organization's capability for taking advantage of the opportunities identified.

Key account attractiveness is a measure of the potential of the key account for yielding growth in sales and profits.

Business strength/position is a measure of an organization's actual strengths in each key account, that is to say the degree to which it can take advantage of a key account opportunity. Thus, it is an objective assessment of an organization's ability to satisfy key account needs relative to competitors.

Ten steps to producing the key account management portfolio:

Step 1   Define the key accounts which are to be used during the analysis.

Step 2   Define the criteria for key account attractiveness and the weight for each.

Step 3   Score the relevant key accounts out of ten on the attractiveness factors.

Step 4   Define the critical success factors (from the customer's point of view) for each key account and the weight for each.

Step 5   Score your organization's performance out of ten on each critical success factor relatively to competitors.

Step 6   Produce the position of key accounts in the portfolio.

Step 7   Position the key accounts on the box assuming no change to current policies. That is to say the forecast should be made of the current position of the key accounts (this step is optional).

Step 8   Should redraw the portfolio to position the key accounts where the organization wants them to be in, say, three years' time. That is to say the objectives they wish to achieve for each key account.

Step 9   Set out the strategies to be implemented to achieve the objective.

Step 10 Check the financial outcomes resulting from the strategies.

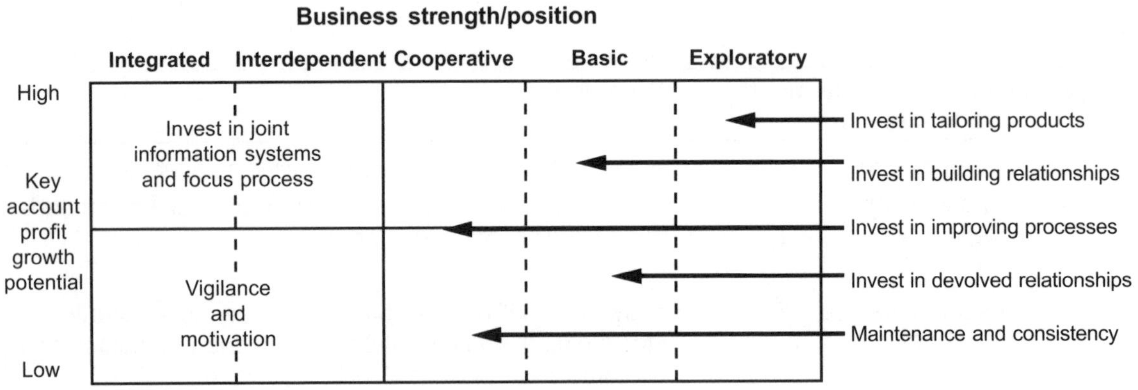

Figure 11.1 *Produce the position of key accounts in the matrix*

Communicate with customers and create relationships where possible

Planning

Before embarking on creating your communication plan you will need to do the following.

Define your relationship target/network

In business to business marketing, protect your business with multiple contacts. Develop relationships with your customers by ensuring there are multiple personal links. Look at the interface between the two organizations as a network of exchanges so that personal contacts run between the organizations at many different levels. Think of it as networking into a spider's web. This will make it more difficult for frontline staff to take a customer with them if they leave the organization.

Multiple linkages make relationships more difficult to manage as all the communication linkages will have to be monitored This needs to be thought through on an organizational level to ensure your communications are integrated and ensure that these linkages are maintained and the messages are consistent.

analyze and define your relationships and networks so that you know who they are and the type of relationship you have with them. Refer to Gummesson's work *Total Relationship Marketing* to help you match them with the context in which the organization is working. A summary of the different types of relationships is shown in the unit 'Relationship marketing'.

Create a database

It is much easier if all marketing information is on one database. Examples are:

- Trends, opportunities, strategic decisions such as calculating the value of customers, developing profiles and programmes for customer segments and analysing purchasing patterns can all be done more easily.

- Date triggered mailings can be made, responses to various promotions can be coded and respondents identified. Customer awareness can be increased by advising customers of special events or offers, keeping people up to date, rewarding customer loyalty and increasing customer loyalty.

- Customers can be monitored and followed up on an ongoing basis. Special customers can be highlighted in terms of their annual spend and special deals could be offered to them on the basis of their sales history by being able to match your offer with their needs more closely, encourage cross-selling.

- Reports can be tailored and analyzed on hard facts: such as number of responses, profit, key ratios, customer retention and so on.

Data can be obtained from internal sources:

- Contact name and address and postcode.
- Frequency – how often do they buy from you?
- Recency – when did they last buy from you?
- Amount – how much did they buy from you?
- Category – what type of product or service did they buy?
- Promotion history – when did you promote to that customer?
- Response history – what was the response?

This information is needed to calculate the value of the various customer segments. Once these are classified they can be ranked and contact strategies devised. Tactical activities such as upgrading customers and cross-selling can also be looked at. The customer database is a vital strategic tool which enables organizations to generate high levels of customer retention by using an individually tailored approach.

The organization could also try and increase its database by organizing events in which potential customers provide their names and addresses.

Set objectives

Set your objectives. These will be quantitative and qualitative. Quantitative related to specific measures like the marketing objectives and communication objectives and relationship objectives, and qualitative related to how you want people to think, feel, experience and do with your offer. Objectives will change depending on various factors. For example, customers could be segmented in different ways and objectives will need to be related to market segments.

- Whether they are past, new, existing, potential
- Where they are in the purchasing cycle before, during, after
- Where they are on the loyalty ladder
- Their purchasing history
- Their total sales, profitability
- Their geodemographics, demographics, motivational and psychographic profile.

Information and response

You will need to think through the type of information you want back from them. They may need certain inducements to reply. Confidentiality and security will need to be thought about. Response handling will affect the whole organization.

Method

The suitability of method will depend on the relationship/network targets, the objective and the scale of the response required.

Time

Target market, objectives, information and response, and method will need to be thought through in the context of time – short, medium and long term.

Organizational aspects

The communication will need to be placed within the context of the organization as the response aspect will have an impact on the processes, systems and procedures.

Building relationships with technology

David Miller of Miller, Bainbridge and Partners Ltd, says that in what might otherwise be considered a delightful coincidence, the growth of the customer who demands to be listened to has gone hand in hand with the growth in technology, which allows brands to listen, understand and respond to customers.

In fact, the move from mass marketing to mass customization is nowhere more evident nowadays than in the new communication channels which technology is opening. Integrating database, call centre and, increasingly, web-site technology means that as marketers, we are able to treat our customers as individuals – albeit, on a mass scale. In the past, we used technology just to talk at people en masse – television being the prime medium. Now we can use technology to listen to our customers – understand what they are saying – and respond accordingly.

So suddenly, brands that had only a mouth, and therefore could only talk, have now been given a set of ears, so now they can listen. We now have the ability to move from talking at customers, to talking with customers.

If brands at their best are commercial friends, then they now can begin properly to behave as friends. They can now listen, understand, as well as talk.

Brands can now begin to come to life in a real way, which the customer can experience – not just as a thirty-second commercial on TV. Impersonal selling is being replaced by personal relationship marketing.

Richness and reach – no longer a constraining factor?

Philip Evans and Thomas S. Wurster think that the internet can blow away practically any business, and in Blown to Bits, they examine how e-commerce can 'deconstruct' industries such as newspapers, auto retailing, and banking while creating new business opportunities. They write that the 'glue that holds today's value chains and supply chains together' is melting, and that even 'the most stable of industries, the most focused of business models and the strongest of brands can be blown to bits by new information technology.'

Their reasoning is based on the idea that the internet provides the potential for reaching a much wider set of potential customers without sacrificing 'richness' – the depth of information and service provided to each. Traditionally, these goals are traded-off when determining a business strategy.

Evans and Wurster go as far as saying that success in e-commerce will be determined by just three factors: reach, richness and affiliation.

Evidence that richness and reach can now go hand-in-hand is found in the many on-line newspapers which are appearing. These provide both the general news 'review' services found in a printed newspaper but also the ability to tailor content to suit individual interests. This potential is fully realized in on-line news clipping services which allow for your own personal 'newspaper' to be constructed from selected keywords. Thus if you are only interested in financial news from the Far East the stories meeting these criteria can be automatically presented from among a larger library of content (see www.customscoop.com).

Sales promotion

Some promotions, such as price reductions, do not reinforce the belief that the brand is worth paying for and draw particular attention to price as a choice determinant.

Continuous, indiscriminate and badly-executed price cutting is clearly dangerous. However, to ignore the role of normal price and short-term price reduction as a key weapon in the marketer's armoury is equally dangerous at a time when more and more purchasing decisions are being made at the point of sale.

1. With some brands price reductions can *devalue* the brand so as to cheapen its character.
2. A difference must be made between strategic long-term decisions to cut the price in order to undercut the competition (for example, if one wanted to establish a reputation for low prices, or promoting the fact that your store offered the best price in town), and short-term tactical pricing to encourage new buyers or persuade lapsed buyers to return to you.

The role of promotion is to encourage purchase by temporarily improving the value of the brand. Added-value promotions can enhance people's perceptions of the brand, whereas price reductions may reduce it.

Loyalty programmes

Many organizations have developed loyalty programmes. Some of these like the loyalty cards supermarkets use have been said to erode margins and are the equivalent of the old green shield stamps. Other loyalty programmes have a high perceived value but a low actual cost.

When a loyalty programme is chosen make sure it has the following features:

- It bears some relationship to the product/service and customers find it relevant.
- That customers get some choice.
- That the customer finds it easy to use.
- That customers are told what to expect and the results are monitored and the cost and profitability are measured.
- That you choose one that competitors will find hard to copy.

Corporate image

A corporate image doesn't simply refer to the design of a company's letterhead. In reality a corporate image goes much deeper and covers the way a business relates to its whole internal and external social and cultural context. You may need to revise your corporate image so that it reflects your new values.

A corporate image adds value. It is not only brands that customers create a relationship with, but the organization itself. As much as brands become 'in the mind' so do organizations – both for the people working within them and their customers.

Public relations

Good business is based on achieving good relationships within the environment it operates. Good relationships alter the perceived values. Public relations is a marketing technique which is used to add value not only to a brand but also to the organization. Public relations influences opinion in such a way that people who have a stake in the business are happy to support it – the relationship portfolio (see Gummesson).

Ongoing customer mailings

These could cover the following:

- Customer service updates and factsheets
- Newsletters
- Christmas, birthday cards and so on.

Customer service manual

This document and manual outlines the customer service goals. It also goes through the business procedures so that each party knows what they are getting. Documents and facts that could be included are:

- Service objectives
- Lead times
- Delivery notes
- Invoices
- The names and telephone numbers of key people
- Hot line services
- Order status enquiry systems.

Workshops and focus groups

Problem-solving workshops can be held on a regular basis to iron out any problems and improve the quality of the services being provided. Role swapping can also be used as a learning exercise.

User groups

User groups or customer groups are groups of people who come together to help each other resolve problems. They communicate via the internet and meet at conferences. They also provide information for new product development and product modifications. They have mostly been used in business-to-business selling, for example in the computer industry but the idea is moving into consumer markets where a club feel can be created. For example, the General Motor launch of Saturn cars, owners were encouraged to come along to barbecues and sports events. The Harley Davidson club is another example.

Football cards and stickers are an old fashioned application of the same principle, children who collected them would join together to swap them.

Other methods of achieving feedback are covered in the section on market research.

Ensure first class service is provided (process and people)

Look at your value chain and make sure it matches the needs of the customer activity cycle (see Unit 7). Customer service is a serious business. Earlier units have given you an idea of the complexity of creating an organization that is focused on customer service. Remember that you will need to keep it going by retraining, giving constant customer feedback, constantly improving procedures, policies and systems, maintaining contact with outside bodies so that you can see what is going on, inviting professional bodies in, benchmarking and keeping the internal marketing going. Recognize your frontline staff as professionals in their own right. They are the ambassadors, the public face of their organization. More often it is the attitude, approach and determination of frontline staff that determines whether an organization will succeed or fail. Encourage them to work towards an Institute of Customer Service award. They do not have an easy job – provide them with training, support and above all, respect. Read the Senior Examiner's book – Ted Johns, *Perfect Customer Care,* Arrow Books.

Look at increasing income

Market penetration

Sell more to existing customers

If it is possible you will need to find out how much business they do with other suppliers. Once you have done this you will need to find out what is standing in the way of your acquiring it.

Find more customers in the same market segment

Once you know who your customers are likely to be, you will be able to put together a communication plan that enables you to attract more of the same type of person.

Get customers from the competition

If you know what your competitors are providing then you will be able to create an offer that meets the customer needs of the market segment more closely. Suitable tactical competitive measures will then need to be taken.

Market development

New market segments

Marketers should be constantly looking out for new ways to segment the market. This requires a constant updating and understanding of new needs so new people can be brought in. The concept of the product life cycle and the adoption and diffusion curve should give you some perspective on this. New people are constantly being brought into the market – they may have different needs from the customers who first brought from you. You need to keep your market segmentation up to date.

New geographic areas

Think about marketing your product or service in a new geographical area in the same market or overseas.

New distribution channels

The internet offers one new way for organizations to extend.

New product/service modifications for existing customers

Even if you do have a sound relationship with your existing customers you should constantly be monitoring any shifts in their value chain which would entail realigning yours. Looking for improved ways to deliver your offer, perhaps redeveloping it or modifying it in some way is an ongoing process. New product development offers the opportunity to work in tandem with your customers.

Diversification

Diversification can be looked at in three ways – horizontal, backward and forward integration. Joint venture, merger, acquisition and franchising fall into this section.

Improve profits

Income can also be increased by restructuring pricing and terms, by reducing costs and by improving negotiations. Pricing and negotiation are covered in other parts of the Advanced Certificate. A brief summary on pricing is given here.

Pricing

Price is the chief source of revenue for the organization. However, apart from being a simple component of the marketing mix and source of profit, price is a communications channel to the customer in its own right. Correct use of price communicates value derived, and product quality to the customer. It needs to be supported by other elements of the marketing mix.

The future of pricing in the customer relationship

As the development of marketing channels shapes the transaction options of the future, many pricing options will be removed. Catalogue selling over the internet will enable pricing structures to be reviewed and novel pricing methods to cope with this transparency will be developed. Tradable services (those that do not need to be delivered in the customer's premises) and international pricing may lead to some form of bartering or counter-trade system of pricing (see for example, Tofler). Customizing requirements to segments of one, or tailoring products and services for individual customers throughout a customer relationship, will offer different challenges to the price setting structures. What will remain however, is the basic premise that price is a reflection of the value of continually satisfying customers needs and not a function of the delivery cost set in absence of market expectations. (Contributed by Graham Cooper, FCIM, marketing consultant and lecturer at Oxford College of Marketing.)

The Ansoff growth matrix in Figure 11.2 is a useful model to use for clarifying ideas.

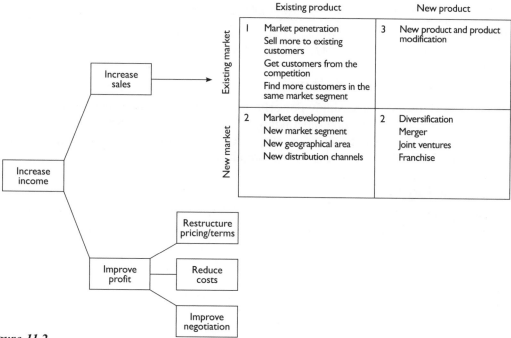

Figure 11.2

Re-evaluate your distribution channels (place)

Re-evaluate your distribution channels to ensure your customers are receiving superior service.

1. Reassess your customers' requirements along your distribution chain.
2. Rethink which type of intermediaries are possible, including direct sale. For example, have you investigated e-commerce?
3. analyze your costs and establish the following:
   a. Is it possible to satisfy all your customers' requirements?
   b. What type of supplier support will be required to do this?
   c. What will the costs be for supporting each alternative channel system?

4. Specify your constraints and outline your objectives and look at your channel system with these in mind. Ensure you think long term.

5. Compare your ideal system, the one operated by your customers, to the feasible one specified by your constraints and objectives.

6. Evaluate the gaps between the existing and feasible systems and consider the impact on your customers and the business.

7. Review all your assumptions and talk to other experts.

Help your customers to save money

Helping your customers to save money does not mean you must cut your price but you can look at ways in which the customer could cut the cost of acquiring a product, possessing and/or using a product/service. Table 11.2 illustrates the routes to reduce total costs for customers.

Table 11.2 Routes to reduce total costs for customer

Customer cost area	Cost/risk	Opportunity for a supplier to help the customer make savings
Acquisition	Cost of goods	Reduce customer wastage/increase product longevity
	Buying cost	Minimize paperwork/buying administration costs
Possession	Storage/obsolescence	Cut customer inventory
	Interest	Offer favourable interest charges
	Handling	Easy to store and handle
Usage	Direct	Simplest, quickest, cheapest to use
	Indirect production costs	Minimal training, back up, administration, etc.
Total		Lowest total cost for customer

Source: Wilson, C. (1996) *Profitable Customers,* Institute of Directors (based on a framework developed by Frank Cespedes in *Concurrent Marketing,* 1995)

Investigate the use of technology

Recent advances in IT include increasingly powerful microcomputers, sophisticated software packages based on Windows, the information superhighway on the internet, powerful organizational tools (databases/fax/mobile telephones), newly IT educated 'knowledge workers' and new organizational concepts (the remote office and voice responsive computers).

Internet technology

Where should you invest?

Figure 11.3 illustrates the dilemma facing decision makers looking at internet technology for the first time.

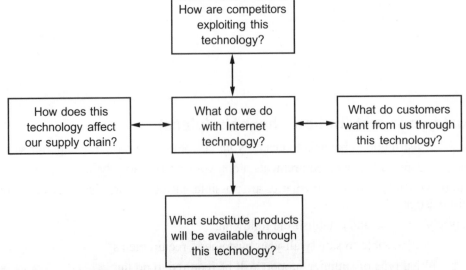

Figure 11.3 What decisions does your organization face? Source: Bickerton, P., Bickerton, M. Simpson-Holley, K. (1998) Cyberstrategy, Butterworth Heinemann.

It is crucial to know what your competitors are already doing, how you can match and better them and provide something of value to your clients. Of course this must relate to and support the long-term aims of your business. The Cyberstrategy Model is a tool developed directly as a result of working closely with a wide range of innovative companies.

Supportive case studies are available at www.marketingnet.com/cyberstrategy to show how various companies have exploited different areas of Internet technology to develop their business aims and achieve not only long-term solutions but real, quantifiable benefits including profit generation and rationalization of internal structures and procedures. Downloadable worksheets are also available.

By developing a model like the one in Table 11.3 for your organization, you will have a clear understanding of where the best return on investment is likely to come.

Table 11.3 *An overview of the business benefits of the varying applications and stages of development of networked or internet technology. Source: Bickerton, P., Bickerton, M. Simpson-Holley, K. (1998) Cyberstrategy, Butterworth Heinemann.*

Use Stages	Internet	Extranet	Intranet
Presentation	International presentation and positioning; name and image, products and services	Cost-effective fast publication of material to a specific target audience	Consistent corporate communication managed centrally
Interaction	Two-way communication with the visitor	Channel which elicits feedback and communication with specific target audience	Open communication channel across the organization
Representation	Cost-effective sales and order processing	Cost-effective targeted selling; replacement to a core business activity	The benefits of remote working

1 Develop an extranet

Table 11.4 *Specific examples and benefits of extranet developments for customers. Source: Bickerton, P., Bickerton, M. Simpson-Holley, K. (1998) Cyberstrategy, Butterworth Heinemann.*

Stage 1 Presentation		
What questions are you answering?	*Examples*	*Benefits*
Would you like to see behind the front door? Why should you stay loyal to our organization?	Company policy Business plan News, Awards Annual report and accounts Demonstration of expertise	Strong corporate image Credibility building Persuasion
What products and services do we sell and are looking to sell?	Catalogue Special offers Product development plan	Fast and cost-effective customer update and communication
Why come back and visit us again?	What's new? Briefings/newsletters New product updates Special offers	Fast and cost-effective customer update and communication
Stage 2 Interaction		
What questions are you answering?	*Examples*	*Benefits*
Talk to us about our service	Complaint handling Market research/opinion	High quality feedback Cost-effective complaint handling
What can we do for you?	Decision tree taking customer to the most appropriate product/service	Feedback on the client's specific needs
How can you solve some of my specific needs	Newsgroups/conferences Automatic responders E-mail subscriptions	Cost-effective information provision Consistent and easy communication

Stage 3 Representation		
What questions are you answering?	*Examples*	*Benefits*
How can I conduct business with your organization?	Direct links into back office systems Integrated funnel into existing sales system Online ordering or quotation system	90-100 per cent of traditional business communications is conducted online

Table 11.5 *Specific examples and benefits of extranet developments for suppliers. Source: Bickerton, P., Bickerton, M. Simpson-Holley, K. (1998)* Cyberstrategy, *Butterworth Heinemann.*

Stage 1 Presentation		
What questions are you answering?	*Examples*	*Benefits*
Would you like to see behind the front door? Why should you stay loyal to our organization?	Company policy Contractual process Our supplier policy Awards Annual report and accounts	Credibility building Persuasion Corporate communication
How can you become more involved with us?	Supplier needs Product development plan	Ease of communicating needs from suppliers
Why come back and visit us again?	What's new? Briefings/newsletters New product updates Special offers	Fast and cost-effective supplier update and communication
Stage 2 Interaction		
What questions are you answering?	*Examples*	*Benefits*
Feedback what you can do for us Changes in your prices	Remote update to supplier records	High quality supplier data because it is maintained by the supplier
Apply for on-line tenders Feedback what you think about us	On-line tenders Market research/opinion Voting mechanisms	Fast response to tender in electronic format Feedback Cost-effective supplier complaint handling
Talk to us Let us help you	Newsgroups/conferences Online supplier support	You obtain feedback as to what specific needs the supplier has Cost-effective centralized communication Quality supplier support
Stage 3 Representation		
What questions are you answering?	*Examples*	*Benefits*
How can ordering products and services from you be made electronically and automatically?	Direct links into back office systems for EDI Potential connection of customer direct to supplier Automatic purchasing	90-100 per cent of traditional business communications is conducted online

2 Develop an intranet

Stage 1 – Intranet presentation

- Disseminate a consistent message more effectively then ever before
- Centralize all corporate communication in one arena
- Make a stronger impact with animation, video, audio and use of graphics, communication

Stage 2 – Intranet interaction

- Change the culture of the organization by diagnosing employee attitude, providing reaction and implementing culture change.
- Help internal marketing of people and projects
- Everyone is 'singing from the same hymn sheet'

Stage 3 – Intranet representation

- Reduction in sales costs through remote working
- Create a virtual organization with no centralized office expenses and conduct all administration and queries remotely, even within the client's premises
- Rationalization and cleaning up of internal processes and procedures

Table 11.6 *Specific examples and benefits of intranet developments. S1ource: Bickerton, P., Bickerton, M. Simpson-Holley, K. (1998)* Cyberstrategy, *Butterworth Heinemann.*

What questions are you answering?	Examples	Benefits
Stage 1 Presentation		
Who are we?	Company history	Reinforce the corporate image, message and mission
How are we doing?	Annual report and accounts Sales results	Employee understanding and education
What products and services to we sell?	Catalogue Features and benefits	Induction training Remote access to product information for sales people Pricing updates are instant
What makes us unique?	Reviews Press articles Product features and benefits compared to industry Consolidated market research information	Communicate market positioning
What competitors do we have?	Marketing information system Competitor information	Market awareness throughout organization
What's going on?	What's new? Briefings/newsletters New product updates Special offers/promotions Fun section	Instant and consistent communication across the company
What systems and procedures do we use here?	ISO9000/BS5750/IIP manuals Forms to print off and fill in Changes in procedures	Cost-effective centralized procedure management
Who is using what in the organization?	Meeting room availability Car pool availability Resource allocation	Fast and easy management of scarce resources Instant and consistent communication across the company
Who's who in the company? What jobs are available?	Telephone/e-mail directory CV and skills database database with easy update for person outlined Outline job application for internal vacancies	Ease of information access Ease of induction training
Who are our customers?	Sales and marketing database read only Overview of sales by industry, sales by company size, etc.	Instant and consistent communication across the company about client details

What questions are you answering?	Examples	Benefits
Stage 2 Interaction		
What do people think about the company	Employee satisfaction questionnaires Quality improvement suggestions	Anonymous collection of employee attitudinal data and suggestions
How are we doing?	Sales results with comments from sales people Projected figures	Direct news from the frontline
What products and services could we sell? How could we improve our business?	Product development suggestions	Ideas from employees Quality improvement suggestions
What are competitors doing?	Business lost to competitors Activity by competitors Pricing updates	Employees motivated to discover about the competition for themselves
What's going on?	What's new from you? Social events arranged Fun section – gossip and things to buy and sell	News desk which people can contribute to means a high usage rate
What can we do better?	Suggestions for ISO9000/BS5750/IIP manuals Online forms Changes in procedures	Quality systems implemented online throughout organization with instant publication
Where is everyone in the company?	Networked diaries	Improved communication Improved customer service
What is happening with out customers?	Sales and marketing database with controlled update facility	Instant and consistent communication across the company about client activity
Stage 3 Representation		
How can I work remotely?	All software accessible from one centralized area with remote access Video/audio presentations of company and products Integrated funnel into existing sales system Online ordering or quotation system/hybrid CD applications	People can perform all major elements of their jobs remotely. Offices used for face-to-face communications only

Example

If airports are to compete in today's commercial environment, one of the key elements is information and communications technology (ICT). It is the information networks that provide the means to enhance revenue, reduce costs and improve safety. And there is plenty of new ICT technology that can help the airport become more profitable.

High-speed networks are necessary to copy with the capacity demanded by a typical airport. Hong Kong Chek Lap Kok Airport installed a very high speed asynchronous transfer mode (ATM) network in order to support the range of services available at the new facility. The most successful networks are all-embracing rather than islands of automation. Single central databases on single airport networks offer the best opportunities to maximize services.

Applications are growing. The internet is becoming a more important part of airport services. Wireless networks are extending the reach of the hard-wired network, with the new wireless LAN, Bluetooth, offering a common standard worldwide. Vienna International uses a wireless network that covers almost the whole airport to manage its ground support equipment activities.

Airport revenue is derived from a range of services. These include shared systems (such as common use terminals), baggage track and trace, radio frequency identification, security monitoring, retail sales and so on. The process of news gathering, authentication and transaction services two purposes.

It can be used to generate revenue, for example through targeted advertising and better understanding of passenger flow, but it can also help to identify and resolve congestion points and delays. At Boston Logan International, commercial vehicles are radio tagged and charged according to the time spent on the airport.

Other examples include advertisements, interposed with flight information data, and smart cards used by frequent flyers to bypass the busy check-in terminals. While many systems are still in trial stages, new revenue opportunities are already apparent. Sophisticated information technology, such as WAP-enabled telephones is behind many of these opportunities and heralds a new generation of technology.

'*Profitable New Airport Technology*' is published by Footnote Analysis: www.footnoteanalysis.com.

Source: www.nexis.com

Ascertain if customization and one-to-one marketing are for you

To answer the question of whether to customize or not to customize the Foundation for Manufacturing and Industry, Department of Trade and Industry, IBM Consulting Group 1997 asked organizations to consider their business from two points of view – production and the customer.

Is your production:

- Increasing in range?
- Experiencing both core and cosmetic changes?
- Reducing customer order sizes?
- More specials than standard?
- Shortening life cycle for new varieties?
- Prone to technical and/or fashion obsolescence?

Is your customer:

- Knowledgeable about the capabilities and products and processes?
- Concerned about the latest features and who can provide it?
- Loyal as long as you provide exactly what they want?
- Reluctant to want to pay a hefty price premium for their exact needs to be met?

If the answers are yes – then mass customize.

The study also draws attention to the following issues.

Important issues for businesses supplying consumers

- Innovate in support
- Customize services
- Achieve a shorter time to market
- Provide a higher product choice.

Important issues for companies supplying other businesses

- Innovate in service
- Customize service
- Innovate in manufacturing and engineering
- Customize products.

The organizations in the survey who have customized experienced the following:

- Increase in profitability – 14 per cent
- Reduction in manufacturing costs – 5.5 per cent
- Market share increase – 21 per cent
- Decrease in response time to customer order – 24 per cent.

When not to do it

The study points to three reasons not to do it:

1. Companies in a stable market providing commodity products where individuality is neither needed or valued by the customer

2. Companies which are not lean manufacturers
3. Companies unable to contemplate the change required.

Internal organizational barriers to mass customization

1. Factories not flexible enough
2. Product too expensive
3. Information systems incapable of supporting customization
4. Incapable of managing the change required
5. Insufficient management skills and attention
6. Problems with understanding what the customer really wants
7. Suppliers unable to meet the challenge.

It is clear that in order to meet market needs and remain competitive, companies need to customize wherever applicable and possible.

Investigate outsourcing and customer/supplier partnership agreements

Managing Service Quality, 8(1) (1998)

Strategic assessment of outsourcing and downsizing in the service market

Donald F. Blumberg says that before taking the decision to outsource organizations need to think about:

- The importance of service to the organization's customers and users
- The market or community's observed perception of the vendor's service quality and responsiveness
- The current levels of service efficiency and productivity compared to other equivalent service organizations in the market.

Outsourcing has a number of real and perceived benefits, as well as disadvantages.

Outsourcing benefits and disadvantages

Outsourcing can create a number of economic advantages: eliminating investments of fixed infrastructure; allowing for greater quality and efficiency of services; and more significantly, cost savings. However, the concept of outsourcing is not for everyone. There are a number of risks in outsourcing which may create perceived disadvantages. However these disadvantages are mostly of a psychological nature and if managed effectively, do not lead to financial losses. Partnering with a third-party introduces a host of new outlooks, personalities, and demands that can produce new problems. These challenges include a more complicated level of communication, insecurity in the workforce, and the risk of alienating customers. Therefore, systems must be put in place to monitor and evaluate the performance of vendors.

There are a total of eight major classifications of service providers to the general outsourcing market:

1. Computer systems providers including VARs, TPMs and integrators
2. Office automation manufacturers
3. Telecommunications providers
4. Specialist management consultants
5. Functional support vendors
6. Facilities management firms
7. Systems software vendors
8. Systems consulting firms.

Factors that need to be considered when selecting a partner:

- Breadth and depth of experience
- Financial solvency
- Commitment to quality improvement and customer satisfaction
- Unique service capabilities

- Understands customer's business and market
- Commitment to technological innovation
- Willingness to offer performance guarantees
- Long-term service commitment
- Availability of customer references
- Reputation
- Skill and experience of service personnel
- Full range of service portfolio.

Creating a partnership with the supplier could involve a fundamental change in attitude for both parties. The whole idea of having common objectives and sharing some of the risks in order to participate in the rewards may be a little strange for managers too used to working with suppliers on an adverserial basis. This is a critical area for relationship marketing especially when organizations are locked into each other and have to manage irregularities in the market.

As Dull, Mohn and Noren (1995, *McKinsey Quarterly*) state, teaming up with suppliers was a first step, marketing's eighth P (partners) is a direct link to strategy. Customers and channels can be partners too, even competitors. They define partnering to be 'when two or more parties agree to change how they do business, integrate and jointly control some part of their mutual business systems and share mutually in the benefit'.

Partnering originated in customer-supplier relationships but many companies have now moved beyond this to intermediaries and/or channels, peer companies and/or allies and also directly with suppliers.

International markets

Overseas markets may need a different approach.

'China – Seven Keys to the Middle Kingdom' (Patrick Medley, Lim Teck Ch'ang, *Business Times*, Singapore, 31 January 2001, www.nexis.com)

1. *Cultivate guanxi at all levels* central government, local government, local partners and key customers.
2. *Segment the market* China is not one market, its many markets reflect its many geographical differences and the rural-urban income gap.
3. *Localize the marketing mix* for example 30% of the shampoo business done by MNCs is in single-serve shampoo sachets. Unlike bottles, these are affordable and allow customers to experiment with new products.
4. *Manage local partners* local partners can break or make a business. They need to be managed.
5. *Invest in sales and distribution* China's multi-level distribution system and under-developed supply chain infrastructure are major challenges in getting products to market. Investment will need to be made to build a sales presence.
6. *Invest in people* training, a transparent career development process, attractive pay and promotion.
7. *Strategies for growth* to protect against cheap, 'copy-cat goods' MNCs need to innovate products, processes and services.

Ongoing

Look at the macro and micro environment and make sure you understand the context in which your customers are operating. Refer back to forces influencing behaviour in the unit 'Strategy and methods to produce customer focused behaviour'.

Activity 11.1

Here is an example of analysis, recommendation and evaluation carried out on an organization using the Customer Care Audit. Carry out your own analysis on your own organization.

Sample analysis

Report

To: Rosie Phipps

From: Linda Cordeaux

Date: 13 February 2001

Re: Customer Care Audit – XYZ Instruments and suggestions for achieving a customer focused organization

Background

XYZ Instruments is a manufacturer of industrial measurement equipment and medical monitoring devices based in Japan. They have subsidiaries for the distribution of their products worldwide including offices in England, America and Australia.

Although XYZ Instruments have had massive success in the industrial measurement market in Japan and the medical monitoring marketing in America, the UK subsidiary has not managed to build the same market share or corporate image that the other divisions of the company have achieved.

The UK subsidiary had seen growth in market share in the industrial measurement market up until 1998 when there was a change in management and positioning strategy. Since this time, market share and turnover has dropped. This is coupled with a general depression in the industrial measurement market.

The medical monitoring market is growing and offers a real opportunity for XYZ Instruments, but a lack of strategic direction and customer focus could prevent them from taking advantage of these market conditions.

The employees at XYZ Instruments are demoralized and this shows in their attitude towards their customers. Decision-making processes are slow and this effects the speed of service offered to customers. There is a lack of co-operation between individuals and departments in the organization.

Summary

This report examines the UK division of XYZ Instruments. The report starts with an analysis of XYZ Instruments' current situation, encompassing both an analysis of the external environment and an internal audit using the McKinsey 7S structure. I then go on to make recommendations for XYZ Instruments to achieve a customer focus.

1 External analysis

1.1 Macro environment

1.1.1 Political

The restructuring of the NHS into Primary Care Groups has lead to new opportunities for XYZ Instruments to target the professional market. The announcement of the government's spending of £20 million on the refit of cardiology departments and equipment for heart monitoring within PCGs will create additional market potential for XYZ Instruments.

More government support for training schemes both for youth and long-term unemployed could benefit XYZ Instruments as they could take on more trainees for their training intensive roles within the technical service department.

The recent publicity of health issues and awareness campaigns regarding heart disease could give rise to an opportunity for enhancing XYZ Instruments' company image by supporting relevant charities such as the British Heart Foundation and the British Hypertension Society.

1.1.2 Legal

XYZ Instruments have recently been granted permission to verify their own balances, which will save both time and money.

The clinical validation of medical monitoring equipment is very important, with most doctors only using and recommending clinically validated monitors. There are stringent requirements to be met before making claims as to clinical validation; this could create advantage for XYZ Instruments, as they are careful about making these claims unlike their major competitor.

All products have to be checked and verified due to the importance of their accuracy of measurement, this is time-consuming but must be upheld to ensure meeting legal requirements.

1.1.3 Economic

There is a general downturn in the profitability of the industrial measurement market as a whole. Spending on medical monitoring products, both professional and consumer is increasing.

The recession in Japan is hitting the company hard. Banks are not granting any loans for investment in new projects and withdrawing credit where they can. This means that the money available to XYZ Instruments' subsidiaries is limited and this, coupled with a decrease in industrial instrument sales, is creating a sense of unrest within the company.

1.1.4 Overseas

Although XYZ Instruments is a global organization, each subsidiary is managed as if it were a separate company. The organization is starting to realize that they need to work as a team as customers that operate on a global scale are now noticing differences between their operations.

XYZ Instruments can also achieve economies of scale by operating as an integrated group.

There are problems caused by distributors with a global network sourcing from cheaper suppliers worldwide.

XYZ Instruments could learn more from their parent company who have achieved great success in their home market where they are market leader in the industrial measurement industry. They could also learn from the American subsidiary, as they are market leader in the home healthcare market.

1.1.5 Social/demographic

There are many cultural differences and different ways of doing things across the global organization, this needs to be addressed and there is a need to have a greater understanding of each other.

The ageing population in the UK creates a great opportunity for XYZ Instruments with their home health monitoring equipment. This is coupled with a general increase in health awareness and preventative medicine.

The growing skills shortage is a concern for XYZ Instruments due to the technical knowledge needed for a number of service jobs and also for management positions. This is accentuated by the company's very high rate of staff turnover.

1.1.6 Technological

XYZ Instruments are operating in a highly competitive technical environment. Technical innovation is strong at XYZ Instruments in Japan.

XYZ Instruments are currently investing in a new ERP system but this is only for managing information on physical resources, they also need to develop systems for customer data management and marketing information as they are lacking in this area.

1.1.7 Environmental concerns

Given the current environmental concerns, XYZ Instruments must ensure that all its manufacturing processes and packaging are environmentally sound and they should publicize this fact.

Internal employee concerns about the environment also need to be considered. This could be addressed by introducing the recycling of waste paper, not using plastic cups for water and coffee machines, encouraging employees to switch off lights and equipment when they are not using an area (such as toilets and meeting rooms).

1.2 Micro environment

1.2.1 Market

The market for industrial measurement equipment is depressed and XYZ Instruments' market share has decreased over the last two years. XYZ Instruments' image in the market is poor and this is reflected in their employee's negative attitudes, which in turn increases the poor company image in the market.

The market for medical products is growing but employees are not confident that we can use this to our advantage due to the generally poor company performance.

Employees are confused about the company's position in the market due to changeable positioning strategies and the lack of communication to employees regarding the marketplace.

1.2.2 Competitors

XYZ Instruments' competitors are well defined but not enough information is collected about them.

The threat of new entrants to the marketplace is low due to the high investment in technology and technological expertise needed.

The company's competitive strategies (e.g. positioning) are vague and changeable.

There is almost a situation of employees being embarrassed in the face of such strong competitors who are perceived as having better service, salesforce and corporate image than XYZ Instruments. Many employees leave XYZ Instruments to work for one of their major competitors.

1.2.3 Customers

XYZ Instruments are not in touch with the end-users of their products as they only deal through distributors. This is short-sighted, as they need to be aware of and cater for the needs of the end-user even though they do not have direct contact with them.

No customer research is undertaken either with end-users or distributors (any research used is that undertaken by Japan or America).

There is very limited input from subsidiaries regarding customer needs when developing new products. The customers' point of view is therefore one taken from the Japanese market and does not consider global customers. This leads to products being produced that will not sell in international markets, often the feedback from distributors indicates that very minor modifications would have made the product 'sellable'.

Standards are not currently set so that customers know what to expect. The only indication of quality standards is conformance to ISO9000, which can in itself be a limitation to developing new innovative processes.

Distributors need to be in contact with frontline staff who have technical knowledge and knowledge of the particular market segment they are serving. This is rarely the case and staff need technical, product and market training to fulfil this need.

XYZ Instruments' customers are often disgruntled due to poor delivery and service times and staff are not offered any support from management for the stress of dealing with these customers, this leads to absenteeism and demotivation.

There is no communication across the company on who key customers are.

1.2.4 Suppliers

Suppliers tend to be loyal as XYZ Instruments try to pick smaller suppliers with whom they are a larger account. Relationships with suppliers tend to be long term. Obviously XYZ Instruments' main supplier is their parent company and this means they are guaranteed the best possible prices when buying in products.

1.2.5 Distributors

XYZ Instruments' distributors are their main customers. The distributors are therefore very powerful as they can decide which brand of product they stock, this power is increased in XYZ Instruments' case as they do not sell directly to the end-user, unlike their competitors, so have no other channel to reach the end-user.

There is often much conflict over prices (especially now distributors can source products globally) and lack of support.

XYZ Instruments could actually turn their lack of direct sales into an advantage when dealing with distributors. They could develop strong marketing partnerships with their distributors sharing systems and resources to reach niche segments. The dealers would allow XYZ Instruments more access to their customer base due to the fact that they would not have the risk of XYZ Instruments selling to their customers directly. Dealers would also be less likely to switch to another supplier if they were working in partnership with XYZ Instruments.

1.2.6 Stakeholders

XYZ Instruments need to build a more positive image with all of their stakeholders.

They need to communicate and work with associated organizations and charities such as the British Weighing Federation, British Hypertension Society and British Heart Foundation.

XYZ Instruments need the hospitals and practices within the NHS to see them as a credible supplier, a hard task to achieve without a direct sales force.

They need to make sure that their reputation with Trading Standards in kept intact to ensure that they can continue to self-verify their equipment.

It is important that XYZ Instruments' image with both the parent company and other subsidiaries is improved.

Employees' attitudes to the company are very poor; this is an issue that needs to be addressed before any external improvement to company image can be achieved.

Media relations need to be improved. Relationships are built up with key publications but then damaged by booking and then cancelling advertising space. This is caused both by lack of strategy and instantaneous changes to strategies that do exist, meaning that existing plans are scrapped and changed on a regular basis.

2 Internal analysis

2.1 Shared values

2.1.1 Mission statement

XYZ Instruments' mission statement is:

XYZ Instruments is a technology driven, market oriented, manufacturer of measurement equipment, catering to multi-national needs, providing better value to those it serves.

There is no mention of customer care or values and behaviour within the mission statement. Although the company may be 'market oriented' in Japan it certainly is not in the UK where it is sales oriented.

Marketing and customer needs are accepted as business philosophy on paper only, the MD understands these concepts and writes about them in his annual appraisal letter to all employees but this philosophy is not applied to the organization or communicated to employees.

Employees' job descriptions do not contain reference to the company mission statement nor do they have customer care objectives outlined.

During the annual appraisal process the MD asks that employees relate how they have contributed to company objectives and show how they reflect the 'customer service concept' in their daily work. This has been included over the past two years, although most employees are not even aware of the company's objectives and certainly do not understand the customer service concept. Employees have to take advice from their managers on how to fill in this section. This is also fairly unhelpful, as most of the management team do not understand the philosophy of marketing and customer focus or how to apply this to the organization.

2.1.2 Culture

The philosophy of putting customer needs first is certainly not evident at XYZ Instruments. Employees are concerned with getting their tasks done, increasing sales, using resources as sparingly as possible and leaving on time at the end of the day.

There is a culture of innovation in Japan but not in the UK. The MD can be quite verbose in his rejections of employee's ideas, which does not encourage a culture of continuous innovation. Employees are not encouraged to embark upon personal development and have to push to be put on any form of training course.

Most employees have a negative perception of the company and the way it treats its customers.

2.1.3 Corporate image

There is conflict between the way the organization presents itself and the way employees perceive the organization. This causes staff to be embarrassed and demoralized.

There is also a lack of continuity in the company's positioning in the marketplace also causing confusion among staff.

The company is trying to position itself against the market leaders, who offer higher quality products and have a large amount of resources at their disposal. It started to build an image of being of a much higher quality than its competitor at the lower end of the market but offering similar prices, which seemed to be successful and market share was growing substantially.

Due to a change in leadership about two years ago this strategy was changed and without cause employees were told the company was positioning itself against the two market leaders who operate at the high quality, higher priced end of the market.

Had the strategy of filling a gap in the market with a high quality low priced product been followed the company may have gained the highest market share in the UK.

It would seem tempting to re-position the company again and use the competitive strategy that it used two years ago, however this would probably lower customer's perceptions of the company as they keep changing their strategy.

There may have been some confusion when changing this positioning strategy between gaining market share by filling a gap in the market and competing in the overcrowded premium end of the market. This could have been due the new management's hedonistic pursuit of being perceived as having the highest quality products in the market.

2.2 Structure

There is a high ratio of managers to frontline staff. There should be a flatter structure within XYZ Instruments as it is a small company. The MD likes to be involved with every decision and can 'make a fuss' when decisions are made without his authority even if the consequences of the decision were not detrimental to the company or the customer, or indeed may have increased customer satisfaction.

Sales positions are based on geographical area, not market segment. This means that account managers do not have specialist market knowledge and conflicts can develop over customers that operate in more than one geographical area.

Due to the size of the organization you would think that XYZ Instruments would be able to give fast support to its customers, this is not the case due to their approvals process.

There is no match between work processes (company value chain) and the customers' value chain as there is no understanding of the latter due to a lack of customer research.

There is poor communication between departments and roles are not interlinked to facilitate customer service. There is an attitude of 'it's not my job' meaning that tasks can be left undone leading to customer complaints and dissatisfaction.

The size of the company means that managers are accessible but they are often wary of making decisions due to the MD changing strategic direction and even forgetting what he has agreed to, this leads to conflict and time-consuming approvals processes.

2.3 Strategy

Objectives are formulated and stated in the business plan, however these are only communicated once a year during the appraisal process. Employees are unclear on the company's direction as strategies have been changed many times, causing unrest among the workforce and a lack of continuity in trying to achieve objectives. There also seems to be some confusion in the business plan between objectives and strategies.

XYZ Instruments' positioning strategy is not strong, as mentioned above. The company does not seem to focus on its core competencies but tries to compete with the premium end of the market to which it is unsuited.

2.4 Style of leadership

The MD rarely spends time with distributors; when he does salesmen often complain about his methods of communication and tendency to want to have 'power' over the situation.

The MD talks of the customer care and marketing philosophy and seems to understand these concepts but does not know how to communicate them to the organization or create a customer-focused organization.

The MD creates low morale, he shouts at employees (including managers while in front of their subordinates), changes his mind over decisions and has little respect from employees.

The MD does not consider the service side of the business enough. He views products separately from service (i.e. he does not view them as a combined offering). This leads to 'pushing' products to customers regardless of their needs (which is typical of a sales orientation) and a lack of investment in the human or 'soft' elements of the marketing mix.

Managers do not encourage employees to admit problems in carrying out their roles or with stress and personal problems.

Customer needs and employees' well-being is not a priority in the internal running of the organization, there is more concern with profit and resource management. Managers are more concerned with physical resources and problem solving than with people management.

2.5 Systems

2.5.1 Recruitment and induction

Recruitment processes are geared towards finding people with the right technical and administration skills or a good sales record rather than those with an understanding of the marketing and customer care concept (even for sales and marketing positions).

The induction process is more about introducing processes and products rather than any sense of company culture and values.

XYZ Instruments do not have a human resources department.

2.5.2 Appraisal and reward

During appraisal, employees are asked to relate their performance to how they have contributed to the 'customer service concept' this is a daunting task, as most employees do not understand what this is.

appraisal is not a continuous process; it is a process that is performed once a year. This does not lead to continuous improvement or training to improve performance. Employees are not regularly given feedback on their performance so do not know if they are achieving an acceptable standard.

The reward system is based on sales and use of resources, not on customer care or retention. There are very few intrinsic rewards offered and employees are becoming very demotivated due to this lack of personal development and attainment.

2.5.3 Information systems, communication and decision making

XYZ Instruments do not have an official management information system. They are introducing a new database system to manage resources and orders but there is very limited market, customer or competitor information.

XYZ Instruments do not undertake any marketing research and there is no clear marketing strategy. Internal communications are poor, with many staff not even being aware of new products that are about to be launched.

When staff do not have adequate information on which to base decisions, deal with customer enquiries or to appear competent they are told, 'Don't use the excuse "nobody told me".' This is also stated in the MD's annual appraisal instruction letter. Employees are expected to seek information even though there is not an information system for them to refer to.

2.6 Skills

XYZ Instruments do not offer customer service training to enable employees to act in a customer-focused way (skills such as assertiveness, conflict management and negotiation are needed).

It is stated (once again in the annual appraisal instruction letter) that employees should expand their role, but they are not given any encouragement or training to increase empowerment.

Managers tend to retain many tasks rather than pass them to frontline staff as the MD does not tolerate mistakes and they would rather take responsibility and ensure things are done right first time. This does not lead to an atmosphere where people are not afraid to take on new tasks, expand their roles, make decisions and feel they can learn from their mistakes.

2.7 Staff

2.7.1 Inter-functional relationships

There is a certain lack of harmony between groups. Groups tend to be critical of each other and will only undertake tasks that are in their job description, this means that tasks that overlap between functions are often not done or are delayed by the time it takes to communicate it to a member of another group.

Groups do mix socially, mainly at social events when a member of staff is leaving or at Christmas but there is much 'sniping' and 'back-biting' during day-to-day office life.

2.7.2 Intra-group relationships

Again there is an attitude of 'it's not my job' even within departments. There is some evidence of teamwork but self-advancement or an attitude of being 'above' certain tasks is prevalent.

Managers do not regularly communicate with their team about performance except during their annual review. Customer complaints are taken and dealt with by the appropriate person, but are not often communicated back to the team that caused the problem so that they understand what went wrong.

Certain tasks that are seen as menial can be left to one side as no one wants to do them; these tasks can seem unimportant but may make a big difference to a customer.

2.7.3 Individual employees

Most employees are demoralized and only remain employed by XYZ Instruments for security and fear of the unknown.

Employees are not trained to deal with the customer flexibly and do not have customer care objectives stated in their job descriptions. There are no performance measures in place so employees do not know what level of attainment should make them feel successful.

Employees do not have an understanding that customer care is the responsibility of the whole organization; although this is stated in the appraisal letter the concept is not clearly communicated to staff and they do not fully understand it.

Employees are more concerned with achieving day-to-day tasks and using minimum resources than with customer care, as their job descriptions focus on these areas.

There is a lack of motivation throughout the workforce.

3 SWOT analysis

3.1 Strengths

- Technological advances and innovation (such as the new sensor industrial measurement equipment that reduces the cost of manufacture and maintenance)

- Success of parent company in their home market for industrial measurement products
- Success of American subsidiary in the medical market
- Growth in medical business
- Staff with good technical or administration skill base
- Good distributor base

3.2 Weaknesses

- Lack of strategic direction
- Lack of skills in customer service
- Leadership
- Structure
- Lack of human resources department
- Cash flow

3.3 Opportunities

- Expanding healthcare market
- Office move to large premises, meaning that there will be larger stock holding facilities allowing quicker deliveries to customers
- New resource management system under development. Customer contact management and marketing information system could be developed alongside this system to provide a full management information system
- Opportunity to build an empowered, motivated and customer-focused workforce from a base of multi-skilled employees
- Developing strong partnerships with key dealers.

3.4 Threats

- Japanese recession and lack of funds
- Decline in weighing business
- Employee demoralization and high staff turnover
- Skills shortage emerging in workforce.

4 Suggestions for transforming XYZ Instruments into a customer-focused organization

4.1 Culture

XYZ Instruments need to try to develop a culture similar to that of their Japanese parent company, which seems to be based around the principals of Kaizen, which are:

- A focus on customers
- Making improvements continuously
- Acknowledging problems openly
- Promoting openness
- Creating work teams
- Managing projects through cross-functional teams
- Nurturing right relationship process
- Expecting employees to develop self-discipline
- Informing every employee about what is going on
- Enabling and empowering every employee.

This is obviously going to be a huge task and will require work in all areas of the organization.

4.2 Vision and leadership

The company's vision needs to be communicated to all employees and needs to be championed by a strong leader.

Respect for the current leader may have dwindled too much for this to be possible and a new visionary leader may be needed to lead the organization through the period of change.

A mission statement should be developed that relates to customer care and the customer focus/marketing philosophy.

Core competencies should be identified and developed and communicated, these could be:

- Technical innovation
- Low cost of manufacture and maintenance
- The opportunity to work in partnership with dealers as there are no direct sales

The management team needs to be the first to take on board the customer focus concept and should be trained in people management skills such as motivating employees, discipline, coaching, facilitating and counselling so they have the skills necessary to develop their staff into a motivated, empowered, customer-focused workforce.

4.3 Information

A management information system needs to be developed, information on customers, competitors, market conditions and other environmental factors needs to be collected continuously and quality information needs to be available to management and all employees. This should be developed alongside the resource management and customer contact systems.

4.4 Strategy

Clear objectives and strategies need to be developed and communicated to all employees. Strategies need to take into account environmental issues and internal capabilities.

Once strategies have been formulated each employee's job description needs to have specific and measurable customer care objectives, with tasks translated into how they are contributing to achieving the company's mission. Staff should be encouraged to look for improvements they can make and have their objectives translated into an action plan that helps them to achieve the objectives. They also need to be made aware of the constraints and resources available to undertake these tasks.

4.5 Structure

A human resources department should be established this could just involve the recruitment of a qualified human resources professional.

The marketing philosophy needs to be put at the centre of the organization, every employee has to have marketing skills and the marketing function should not just be seen as sales support, rather sales should be a functional department of marketing. To ease the transaction period the current sales manager could be named sales and marketing manager, with the marketing executive having more input into the department's decisions. This will help to ease any hostility from the sales team to this change.

The marketing department needs to work in conjunction with HR to ensure that the HR policies being developed match with the corporate and marketing strategies.

Once clear strategies and policies have been developed, put in writing and communicated, managers should be able to take ultimate responsibility for departmental decisions making it easier for frontline staff to get immediate decisions and to ease the process of managers empowering their team to make their own decisions.

HR needs to recruit people who understand the customer focus/marketing concept or who have the potential and 'people' skills necessary to be trained.

Account management should be allocated by market segment rather than geographical area, allowing for specialist knowledge of both customers and markets to be developed. This means that account managers will be able to understand their customers' needs and market developments and act as a credible partner for dealers operating in specific and niche markets. This will allow stronger relationships to be developed with key dealers, working in partnership to penetrate and develop markets.

Cross-functional teams should be developed to work on projects. It is particularly important to have expertise from each department to allow teams to utilize each skill/knowledge base to come up with the best customer-focused solutions. A mix of technical, financial, resource management and marketing skills within project teams will create a good balance. This will lead to the organization working as a whole to achieve customer satisfaction rather than seeing themselves as independent departments working for individual goals. It should also help to eradicate inter-group envy, with attitudes such as that 'marketing have the fun jobs'.

4.6 Service standards

XYZ Instruments could set both external and internal service level agreements.

Competitor analysis can be undertaken in order to benchmark XYZ Instruments' service standards against those of their competitors, standards could be those such as:

- People
- Time
- Place
- Tangibles
- Intangibles.

Customer research needs to be conducted to establish how customers feel about existing service levels and the importance they place on the different elements of service.

Once this analysis has been completed, service levels can be set, ensuring that they *at least* measure up to competitors' standards and customer expectations and that the elements that are most important to customers are given the highest priority.

A service level agreement can be drawn up between XYZ Instruments and its distributors helping to inspire confidence in XYZ Instruments' new initiatives and publicizing their new commitment to customer service.

Internal service level agreements should be drawn up. These should be flexible and should only indicate the *minimum* levels of service each department can expect from the other and enable measurement of internal service standards.

4.7 Training

An internal marketing programme needs to be developed to communicate the customer focus concept and objectives to all employees. This process needs to be continuous and integrated into every process, training session, and internal communication to ensure it becomes part of the company culture. This also needs to be incorporated into the induction process so that new employees have an understanding of the company vision and culture.

Employees should be given both on and off the job training. On the job training should encompass empowerment and role training. Off the job training could include professional certification, language skills and any other personal development that will motivate and fulfil employees.

Counselling should be used and staff should feel able to discuss their problems and work stresses.

4.8 appraisal and rewards

Line managers should appraise employees on a regular basis in addition to the official yearly appraisal. Employees need constant feedback on their performance and training to address any performance gaps.

Feedback can be given from other employees regarding achievement of or surpassing internal service level agreements. Feedback can be obtained from customer surveys, customer complaints, mystery shopping or recording telephone conversations (although the later could increase hostility towards management by them being perceived as having a 'big brother' mentality).

The yearly appraisal should be based on a 360° feedback system whereby employees are assessed by team members, customers, suppliers, subordinates and supervisors to ensure a balanced perspective of an individual's performance.

Rewards to employees should be balanced. Monetary rewards should relate to the individual's contribution to company objectives, profits and customer satisfaction and retention. Other rewards given should be responsibility, challenge, autonomy, variety, interaction and self-development.

XYZ Instruments could also consider introducing a 'service star' award for those consistently exceeding both internal and external service level agreements.

4.9 Evaluation of results

Evaluation of results will be similar for the organization as a whole. Measurement will be needed to ascertain whether corporate objectives have been achieved. This can be done by analysing financial performance ratios both for XYZ Instruments and in comparison to their competitors, benchmarking against competitor customer service levels, customer acquisition and retention levels, customer surveys, number of customer complaints and attainment of and exceeding customer service level agreements.

XYZ Instruments could also look at their market share and whether this has increased or decreased.

'Soft' measures such as working atmosphere, employee motivation, innovation and levels of understanding of the customer service concept among employees could also be used.

Summary

This unit has focused upon the operational/functional aspects of building a true customer orientation. It illustrates it as a proactive process providing opportunities for profit and savings in cost. The following unit will explore future patterns for segmentation arising from changing demographic and social trends, and e-commerce.

Objectives

- To understand how changes in social and demographic behaviour affect patterns of consumption and market segmentation
- To understand the value and relevance of trade cycles
- To understand how technology can influence a business
- To be introduced to e-commerce and global marketing
- To understand that the delivery of outstanding customer service will form a critical part of tomorrow's business strategy.

This unit covers the following parts of the Marketing Customer Interface syllabus:

- 2.5
- 2.5.1
- 2.5.2
- 2.5.3

Study guide

This unit introduces you to the socio-cultural factors that influence structures of the market and customer demand. It attempts to give you an idea of the types of market opportunities that can arise from changes in the environment. Customer concerns about ecological, environmental and ethical issues are covered. We also look at the idea of globalization and the growth of e-commerce and examine how the internet can enable exporting.

Introduction

The future pattern for market segmentation depends on changes reflected in society and their needs. Change will affect society's expectations and open up different markets.

We are already experiencing customers whose expectations are putting continual pressure on organizations to increase their quality, service standards, response times, restitution processes and so forth. Some customers are very demanding and understandingly totally intolerant of broken promises and delays. Standards set in one market sector are transferred into another market sector so that all round there has been a greater sense of urgency as customer service becomes more innovative and more flexible.

Bill Gates, in *Business at the Speed of Thought,* creates a sense about the expected velocity of change. Customers are also more willing to complain. Legal enhancements to consumer power and the availability of media outlets make complaining much easier to do. Customers are more concerned about ethical issues, about employment conditions and ingredients in food. However, their ideas are not always reflected in their purchasing behaviour (see 'Attitudes and behaviour' in Unit 4). Sometimes attitude and behaviour do match and when they do customers will stop purchasing, as recently witnessed with Nike, genetically modified foods and the BSE crisis.

Access to the internet allows customers to call up a vast array of services. Many of the new competitors are coming from outside traditional competitors and are setting new standards of service, quality and speed (for example, CD-Now and Amazon.com). Others are redesigning their market interfaces, cutting costs and doing business based on new infrastructures, such as Federal Express. Value chains are moving to value networks so that many processes happen simultaneously so that customer service has improved. It is important that marketers keep an eye on the environment.

Market life cycle, product/service life cycles, the process of innovation and diffusion need to be thought about together so that organizations are defining new market segments as an ongoing process. Lazy thinking leads to organizations finding themselves in a mature market selling to laggards where differentiation on price is the sole criteria for purchasing.

Changing customer needs

Changes in the marketing mix

Changes in lifestyle and demographics will create changes in the marketing mix. If this is so, then as culture and values change and people look more to understand themselves, the brands created today already contain the seeds for their own destruction.

Culture is dynamic, it changes and marketers must be aware of changes in society. If and when people change their ideas of who they are, the social and political culture will change as well and there will be a demand for different goods/services and the marketing techniques across a whole range of dimensions will need to change as well.

Socio-cultural factors

The demographic environment

Demography studies populations in terms of age structure, geographic distribution, balance between males and females, future size and characteristics. Marketers need to know this for the following reasons.

1. *The demand side* The size, structure and trends of the population exert an influence on demand and the size of market segment. There is a strong relationship between population growth and economic growth, and the absolute size of the population determines potential or primary demand.

2. *The supply side* Labour is an essential resource. For example, in retailing the decrease in young low-paid staff has already led to the employment of older people.

Changes in population growth are caused by:

- Changes in birth rate and/or fertility rate
- Changes in death rate
- Emigration and/or immigration.

Growing populations often require fast economic growth in order to maintain living standards, they need more resources for capital investment, they stimulate investment as the market size increases, they can also lead to greater labour mobility and overcrowding on land and in cities.

Falling populations need to be more productive, they put a greater burden on young people to support an older population; they show changes in patterns of consumption and make some scale economies difficult to achieve.

Important trends to appreciate include changes in:

- The growth of world population
- Developed as against less-developed country growth rates
- The future size of a population
- The age and gender structure of a population
- Its distribution by region and locality
- Migration within and between national borders.

Size of population

The population of the United Kingdom has increased since 1991 with the biggest increases being observed in the very elderly age group of 85 and over, in the working population of age 30 and over and in children aged 5-15. The increases of ages 30-64/59 can be traced back to the high birth rates during the 60s and as a result of the post-Second World War baby boom. Despite the overall increase in the population some age groups have decreased since 1991. These are the 0-4, 16-29 and 65/60-74 age groups. The 16-29 age group has declined as a result of low fertility rates during the 70s. The 65/60-74 age group has declined as a result of low birth rates during the 30s.

Geographical shifts in population

In Britain there is a north/south divide which is characterized by different levels of economic activity and employment.

There has been an increase of 10 per cent in the number of people living in Cambridgeshire, Buckinghamshire, Dorset and Cornwall in England and Co. Down in Northern Ireland.

Find out if your market is likely to be affected by geographical shifts in population?

A country may also suffer from overpopulation in some areas and underpopulation in others. In the UK city centres are facing a fall in population. Other areas, such as the ex-mining towns, are becoming depopulated.

The key marketing factor to emerge from this is the swing from teenagers and young adults to middle-aged marrieds. The increased life expectancy has increased the demand for products and services catering for the elderly, such as entertainment, health products and holidays.

The household as a unit of consumption

Marketers focus attention on the household as a unit of consumption. In household structure several changes have occurred:

- Growth in the number of one-person households – one-person households include single, separated, widowed and divorced. This section has grown over the last few years partly as more people are getting divorced and partly because more young adults leave home early. At the same time the number of pensioner one-person households is expected to have increased from 2.9 million in 1979 to almost 4 million by the mid-1990s.

- There has already been a demand for more starter homes, smaller appliances, food that can be purchased in smaller quantities and a greater emphasis on convenience products. Other needs for this sector include single bars, physical fitness centres, holiday clubs, radio talk shows, drugs, meditation, adult-oriented television programmes, redesigning of products and services for one person, lifestyle magazines rather than family magazines.

- Rise in the number of two-person cohabitant households – several sociologists propose that cohabitation is the first stage of marriage. At the same time there is an increase in the number of households with two or more people of the same sex sharing. Married couples with one or two dependent children comprised 30 per cent of households in 1961 compared with 20 per cent in 1991.

- Rise in the number of group households with members of the same sex sharing expenses and living together, particularly in larger cities.

- Dual-income families – time is now spent working or preparing for work instead of home making and shopping. Purchasing and consumption take place in the evening and at weekends. This effects opening hours, home visits to service people, childcare, cooking, cleaning, eating out, frozen dinners. Time matters more and people quickly become impatient and find waiting intolerable. This means that organizations that take time processing will be open to competition by those who solve these problems. Sheth and Ram in their book, *Bringing Innovation to Market,* point out that there is a redistribution of wealth in the community, the middle class is on the decline and is supplemented by a larger affluent class and a larger low-income class. They say the bulge in the middle of the income distribution is being pushed to two ends. As a result there are three distinct market segments: premium (affluent), best value (middle class), and affordable (new poor) products and services in virtually every sector of the economy.

Family structure changes have come about through:
- Later marriages
- Fewer children
- Increased divorce rates
- More working wives
- Careers for women.

Changing role of women

The role of women in the UK has changed with many women working or pursuing further education either on a full- or part-time basis. Women now have more money but less time. The following is a list of trends together with the associated impact on a large retailer's marketing operations:

1. Women becoming better educated and pursuing careers
   o Greater recruitment of professional women into the marketing department to fill emerging skill gaps and take advantage of their comparative skills in interpersonal relationships
   o Demand for a greater geographical variety and quality of product range due to greater travel overseas
   o More environmentally aware consumers impact on green policies, e.g. biodegradable packaging, dolphin-friendly tuna
   o Health and fitness consciousness impacts on fat-free products
   o Increased home computer ownership supporting development of home shopping – building on principle of mail-order catalogues
   o Retail marketers may consider home delivery
   o Purchasing products that were within the traditional male domain such as cars.

2. More women working pre/post childbearing and later marriage
   o Impacts on demands for convenience foods/in-store preparation
   o Impacts on late/weekend/Sunday opening times/faster checkouts
   o Impacts on car park security/creche/mother and baby provision
   o Impacts on spending power due to second incomes – demand quality
   o Impacts on attraction to one-stop shopping/financial services
   o Impacts on the identity of the decision-maker, choice and the focus for promotional activity.

3. Women require increasing flexibility
   o Impacts on employment conditions for women
   o Impacts on recruitment and retention policies – how the store's image is marketed
   o Flexitime, flexiyears and career breaks may be the required marketing response.

4. More single parents
   o The rise in divorce and single parenting produces a very different segment
   o Low disposable income suggests value for money ranges
   o Impacts on store location given more frequent visits
   o May impact on the provision of smaller 'metro' type stores.

An ageing population

In 1961, 12 per cent of the population were 65 or over. This will rise to 24 per cent before 2021. Table 12.1 illustrates trends for the age structure of the UK.

Table 12.1 UK population age structure

	Under 16 %	16–24 %	25–34 %	35–44 %	45–54 %	55–64 %	65–74 %	75+ %	Total (millions)
1961	25	12	13	14	14	12	8	4	52.8
1996	21	11	16	14	13	10	9	7	58.8
2011*	18	12	12	14	15	12	9	8	60.9
2021*	18	11	13	12	13	14	11	9	62.2

*Projected

Ageing of the population means that the average age is increasing. Japan, Europe and, to a lesser extent, the USA are facing a sharp increase in the proportion of pensioners. The main causes include falling birth rates but a greater life span. By 2050 there will be some 70 million West Europeans aged

65+, representing over 20 per cent of the population. In Britain there are forecast to be more over-65s than under-16s by the year 2016. This will affect marketing operations in a number of ways:

- The age profile of the shopper and the target population changes. The key resource of shelf space must be redeployed to reflect this changing balance.

- Older customers tend to be more experienced and discerning in their buying habits. They focus on value for money and quality. This needs to be reflected in the marketing mix. Relationship marketing to retain such customers is an obvious strategy. The spread of store and loyalty cards reflects this attention.

- Retailers have tended to rely on younger people for recruitment. The marketing function must turn their attention to the use of 'older' employees to match the customer profile, e.g. B&Q.

- A sports and leisure retailer would have to consider repositioning its product range. Athletic sports such as squash and football would tend to grow slowly compared to fitness and 'social' sports. Tastes would become more conservative but with a preference for quality and durability. Older consumers may tend to be laggards and resist unreasonable change suggesting fewer layout changes or innovatory new products.

- Ageing brings larger numbers into the 'empty nest' category and significantly higher disposable incomes. Retailers such as Marks & Spencer have already moved to exploit financial services.

- Ageing will impact on the style and facilities of the retailer. Those retiring early will shop during the day and expect restaurant facilities and, in many cases, individual assistance.

- The ageing population will be diverse and segmentable. Retailers must invest in information systems to help identify their changing needs and assist in focusing promotional activity.

The grey market has considerable financial power but this marketplace is not homogenous and there are large variations within it. It is important to remember that ageing is a process that occurs over a period of time on many levels – biological, social and psychological. According to the Henley Centre, estimates suggest that the over-45s have nearly 80 per cent of all financial wealth, and are responsible for about 30 per cent of consumer spending. Much of this is concentrated in the 55-64 age group. They have higher levels of home ownership and possession of private or occupational pensions.

The future of ageing

- Improvements in healthcare could help to prolong life expectancy even further. Cosmetic surgery and hormone replacement therapy (HRT) will minimize ageing and reduce aesthetic distancing between the generations.

- According to www.nexis.com (PR Newswire, 29 January 2001) more consumers now surf the internet to look for health information than sports scores, stock quotes or online shopping. Healthy Newsletters Direct based in Evanston, Illinois, has developed the first direct marketing e-mail letter that targets key segments of the health care consumer market (www.hndweb.com).

- Cruise and alternative holidays may increase rather than beach holidays.

- We now live in a more liberal society which allows adults to enjoy being young. The older generation will have more in common with their children than their parents.

- Durability may replace fashion as a key attribute.

- Improvements in technology and the growing movement of the workforce away from the traditional workplace into the home will change work patterns. It will also mean that it is not just the old who stay at home all day.

- If people are unwilling or unable to drive, home delivery may intervene.

- Alternative media networks such as the internet, and cable may lead to more dedicated programming for the older consumer by the older consumer.

- A new form of spirituality may emerge to accompany the ageing population. Possibly the development of a post-modern, post-materialist culture will evolve as the older generation seeks to influence society to satisfy this need.

- Social and political groups may emerge to protect the interests of the elderly – organizations that have real political clout.

An increase in health care reflected in services and extending outside this to food, drink, clothing, personal care, appliances, cars, home, creation and leisure. Older people eat less meat so there could be demand for more vegetarian foods. They also drink less caffeine which would lead to tea and coffee substitutes or caffeine-free drinks. They have more capital and are therefore able to start a business and invest on the stock exchange. They are more concerned about safety, security of themselves and their property.

The conventional segmentation that has evolved has been of three groups, with some rough age brands, namely:

- The 'young old' (55-64)
- The 'mature old' (65-74)
- The 'old old' (75+).

While the total population of England and Wales has been projected to increase by 8 per cent between 1991 and 2001, the population aged 75-84 is projected to rise by 48 per cent and that aged 85 by over 138 per cent.

Increased middle class

Higher levels of education have created more people who are middle class, this is linked to the slow down of birth in developed nations. Family size is decreasing as many families are only having one child.

Influence of children in family purchasing

Taking children with you to the supermarket can affect what you buy, recent research has shown. Fathers spend on average 13 per cent more when shopping by themselves with their children. Mothers spend less.

Since the number of under-15s is estimated to grow by 10 per cent in the 19902 in the UK, with an estimated disposable income of £9 billion by 1998, this is a crucial influence on buying behaviour.

Generation X

American teenagers, a group sometimes called Generation X, have economic clout – with an estimated $115 billion to spend this year. Not surprisingly teen magazines are now filled with ads from national credit card companies, offering credit cards and prepaid debit cards, which require parental consent. (Source: www.nexis.com).

Education and achievement

It is likely that more and more people will become qualified. In 1977 to 1978, 33 per cent of school leavers left school without any GCE/SCE or CSE qualifications. By 1991 to 1992 this had changed to 12.5 per cent. Fewer girls leave school without qualifications than boys.

There will be a rise in the demand for 'knowledge' workers, which has led to the government expanding vocational and higher education in an effort to avert critical shortages in skills. The trend in university education is that there are more women, more mature students, more from non-conventional backgrounds (for example, there are increasing numbers of unemployed doing Open University degrees).

Ethnicity

Aspects of an ethno-marketing environment that could be used to formulate a market segmentation strategy would include demographics, lifestyle, culture, education and employment.

- *Demographics* 21 per cent of the white population are 60 years and over; the figure for ethnic groups is less than 6 per cent, although this would vary as the ethnic minority population has a younger age structure than the white population. It is being suggested that the minority/majority divide may disappear in many of our cities in the future. For example, ethnic minorities may well make up the majority in half of London boroughs.

- *Lifestyle* Many ethnic minority groups have a larger average household size with more dependent children than the white population. Although the figure will vary between different ethnic groups, the common feature among them is the importance they place on the extended family. The ethnic population is steadily moving up within the British socio-economic hierarchy. Asians, particularly the Indian community, have overtaken whites as the people most likely to have their own businesses and professional qualifications. Their culture, which embraces and reinforces the extended family system, helps them to get ahead in business. An understanding of the DMP, the DMU and whether it is hard to initiate, influence and to carry out marketing exchanges will be needed by businesses seeking to engage in ethnic marketing.

- *Education/and employment* The government's labour force survey shows that higher proportions of the young people from India, black and Asian Africa and Chinese origin stay in full-time education after 16 than their white counterparts. This is now reflected in such professional areas as accountancy, medicine, legal services and computer consultancy.

This means that marketers must question some stereotypes and outdated assumptions.

Healthy living

There is an increased concern for healthy living which has led to a demand for sporting facilities, low-fat products and natural foods.

There has been an increase in vegetarianism, 'green consumerism' and a concern with organic food.

The increasing interest in health has stimulated the market for sports-related goods. Sporting shoes have become fashion accessories. Some employees are providing gyms and offering help to employees who abuse alcohol.

Employment trends

- Increased numbers of part-time employees.
- More people choosing to work from home as telecommunications improve.
- Flexible working hours – this flexibility is in both employee and business interests. It is underpinning much less standardized lifestyles and demanding a marketing response to cater for three-day weekends, all-night and even all-day entertainment as well as the late-night banking and retailing we increasingly take for granted.
- An increase in the numbers of self-employed people. Ethnic minorities from Asia have higher than average rates of self-employment.
- Jobs are no longer 'jobs for life' – increasing numbers of people are employed on short-term contracts which are often renewed at the end of the term.
- The emergence of flexible organizations.
- The rise of the knowledge worker – since most jobs in future will require brains rather than brawn in the next century, the government is belatedly expanding vocational and higher education in an effort to avert critical skill shortages from inhibiting high-technology growth opportunities.
- The self-service economy – non-standard work patterns imply non-standard leisure patterns and more of this leisure time is being absorbed doing tasks which were previously undertaken by business. Interactive computer systems linked to databases offer dramatic potential to transform the way in which many services are currently marketed, sold and performed. Home banking, direct insurance and distance learning are just a sample of leading-edge applications.
- Short-term contracts will need to be reflected by the creation of managers who take into account the needs of a variable work pattern.
- Computers that are aimed at the business/leisure use.
- Financial services for the self-employed.

Changes in lifestyle

Albrecht (1979) has distinguished five major lifestyle changes taking place which have increased the level of stress. These are:

1. From rural to urban living
2. From stationary to mobile
3. From self-sufficient to interconnected
4. From isolated to interconnected
5. From physically active to sedentary.

Quality of life

There are changes in lifestyle such as, for example, a demand for recycled products, gourmet foods, an increased demand for classical music.

Convenience and self-service

There is an increased demand for convenience such as more ready-to-use products, more convenient sizes and easier methods of payment.

Informality

There is a greater style of informality which has resulted in a demand for more casual clothing, less formal restaurants and less formal furnishings.

Local government

Services which have been traditionally provided by local government employees are having to go out for commercial tender. This has opened up a number of opportunities for the UK private sector.

Pensions

The government is trying to get citizens to take responsibility for providing for their own pensions. This is essential because of the growing number of elderly people.

Private medicine

This area is still covered by the NHS although private medicine has increased. It is unlikely that the majority of people, while they are still being taxed for medical services, will want to pay for them twice.

Environmental priorities

As Mary Douglas says (*World of Goods*):

> Consumption has to be recognized as an integral part of the same social system that accounts for the drive to work, itself part of the social need to relate to other people, and to have mediating materials for relating to them. Mediating materials are food, drink and hospitality of home to offer, flowers and clothes to signal shared rejoicing, or mourning dress to share sorrow.

We live in a world of goods, but people are becoming more and more concerned about our physical environment. In the 1960s Rachel Carson's book *Silent Spring* (1963) drew attention to the possible irrevocable damage being done to the planet and the possibility that we would exhaust the world's resources. The concern was echoed in the coining of the term 'eco-catastrophe'. Subsequently pressure groups formed, such as the Friends of the Earth, who have had a major impact on business practices. The four major areas of concern are:

- An increasing shortage of raw materials
- Increasing costs of energy
- Increasing levels and consequences of pollution
- An increasing need for government to become involved in the management of resources.

The question facing us is how our need for goods balances with our need to protect our environment, and how this need will be taken up by the rest of the developing world?

Behavioural aspects

Most opinion surveys show a clear growth of environmental consciousness among the public. In the UK, this has been substantiated by research carried out by Market and Opinion Research International (MORI).

Environmental consciousness is an element of the individual's belief system and is part of the social consciousness which is in itself a complex system of values and attitudes. Environmental consciousness would therefore have cognitive, affective and conative components.

The results of surveys only show a change of values on a global level, these are not always reflected in the consumer purchase behaviour. New judgements, for example, about environmental compatibility, occur only after the consumer has developed an awareness of the inconsistency between values and product choice criteria.

Private and social cost

The costs of production do not solely include rent, rates, labour, material and transport costs – these are relatively simple and easy to calculate. The true costs are not borne by industry, the true costs are the social costs of production.

The costs that businesses impose upon society have included damage to the environment: Global warming, acid rain, depletion of the ozone layer, waste, the catastrophes of oil spillages, nuclear incidents (e.g. Chernobyl), noise, congestion, air and water pollution, industrial pollution, to name but a few. Businesses therefore need to become increasingly involved in developing solutions for the resource and energy problems facing the nation and indeed the world.

Industrial activity will almost always damage the natural environment. The public's great concern for a non-polluted environment, apart from being absolutely necessary from an environmental point of view, will also create marketing opportunities for companies. New markets can be developed and companies should ensure that customers, employees, other stakeholders and the public are informed about their compliance with environmental standards.

One example would be the growth in renewable energy business, energy conservation and labour-intensive repair industries.

A corporate response

Change should not only be driven by law-makers, by environmental standards, by pressure groups and consumer demand. Businesses should become proactive and make care for the environment part of their core beliefs and values and these should form part of the mission statement. Protection of the environment requires a corporate response that will affect all areas of a firm's activities.

Environmentalism must be seen as being distinct from a 'fad'. It will not disappear overnight and if it is not to become a corporate burden it must be addressed head on.

Marketing expresses the company's character, environmentalism is now an integral part of the corporate image. Businesses which fail to respond to these changes will be at a significant competitive disadvantage and run the risk of being commercial dinosaurs. People are realizing that pollution is not only a question of 'not in my back yard' but that it is a matter of global concern. Agreements are being reached on this.

New markets

Green marketing is seen by some as a transparent marketing activity. To many consumers and business people it is not, it is marketing listening to and responding to customers' needs. People buy goods for material welfare, physical welfare and display. We all need recreation and work, to be fed, clothed, sheltered, but we also need peace of mind. Green marketing, taken seriously and with honest intent, is part of this process.

A potential market exists for pollution control systems and recycling systems. Also new ways need to be developed for packaged goods. Demand from consumers is also creating a market for greener products and consumers say they want environmentally-friendly goods and the government is increasingly demanding them.

Activity 12.1

Carry out this activity within your own organization and find answers to the following questions:

1. How has the environmental movement affected the business?
2. What has it meant to your organization to have to become environmentally friendly?
3. If changes have been made were they brought about by a change in core belief and values, consumer demand or legislation?
4. Were there any costs involved in making the changes, or indeed any savings?
5. Have the changes been communicated internally and externally?
6. Does your organization only do business with environmentally friendly suppliers?
7. Are any more changes anticipated?

If it is at all possible try and present and discuss your findings in class. It is extremely interesting being able to get some feedback on what other organizations are doing.

In order to carry these programmes, out businesses will obviously reduce some costs, but will need in some cases to increase prices as plant is changed and products redesigned to create less damage on the environment. Prices will have to be borne by the consumer. All this will involve a cost, marketers need to find out what their competitors are doing and also to establish what consumers will pay for.

Training

Employees working for organizations will also have to change, for example, work practices. In some cases new technology and processes will result in redundancies and jobs becoming obsolete. This should open up areas for retraining. A major area of training is environmental management.

Sustainable development

This term refers to the interface between the natural and the economic environment. For development to be sustainable it suggests that any growth or improvement in the standard of living of current generations must not be achieved at the expense of reduced welfare for future generations.

Development which proceeds without regard to the depletion of non-renewable resources or the generation of wastes beyond natural absorptive capacities cannot be sustained and current generations are, in effect, stealing from the future.

High profile examples of non-sustainable development include the depletion of rain forests, fish stocks and nuclear wastes.

Commentary on significance to the marketer:

- Marketers should be aware of rising environmental concerns.
- Consumers increasingly recognize unsustainable behaviour.
- Marketers, such as those at the Body Shop can achieve an edge by promoting an ethical image and taking their social responsibilities seriously.
- Product development should consider designing sustainability into products – consider life-time impacts.
- Efforts to re-use and recycle materials form part of sustainability. Legislation will eventually enforce compliance.

There is a saying in the Green movement that 'if we are going to have any future then it has to be Green'. What is meant by this is that the goal of Green policies is to provide a future which is sustainable in environmental, social and economic terms. Therefore, almost by definition, if we are to have any future then it must be Green!

This fundamental idea has widespread implications for consumer lifestyles, commercial activity and our values systems in general. Marketing too must 'go Green' if it is to meet future challenges.

Green Marketing, as this new approach to marketing has been termed, has evolved in the last ten years, or so, to try and address issues relating to sustainability.

What is sustainability?

Chambers, Simmons and Wackernagel in their book '*Sharing Nature's Interest*' (see www.ecologicalfootprint.com) describe how sustainable development is about ensuring 'quality of life for all within the means of nature'. That is, the aim of economic progress should be to ensure that all of the global population are able to live satisfying lives but that this must be achieved within the constraints of the natural world. This definition clearly prioritizes the social and environmental dimensions of sustainability. The third, economic dimension should, it is argued, be focused on furthering the other two aims rather than being an end in itself (as is so often the case now).

It is generally recognized (for example, visit the Worldwatch Institute web site www.worldwatch.org) that society is currently unsustainable in that our natural resources are being destroyed at a faster rate than they can regenerate. Examples of this include:

- Climate change
- Soil erosion
- Water scarcity and contamination
- Falling fish stocks
- Deforestation
- Loss of biodiversity (animal and plant species).

Most environmental scientists agree that society must reduce its consumption of energy and materials and share the available resources more equitably. Currently more than 80% of the available resources are consumed by less than 20% of the population.

What is Green marketing?

Green marketing means many things to many people. There are, however, two distinct views. On the one hand Green marketing is seen somewhat narrowly as the promotion or advertising of products with environmental characteristics. A product might, for instance, be labelled as 'environmentally-friendly', 'recycled' or 'ozone free' and so on. This can be considered as 'light' Green marketing. A broader view of Green marketing is that it applies to the whole supply chain for both goods and services. Micahel Polonsky (1994b. '*A stakeholder theory approach to designing environmental marketing strategy*', unpublished working paper, available from www.marketingcustomerinterface.com) defines Green marketing as consisting of 'all activities designed to generate and facilitate any exchanges intended to satisfy human needs or wants, such that the satisfaction of these needs and wants occurs, with minimal detrimental impact on the natural environment'. This latter view can be termed 'dark' Green marketing in that it takes in account more completely, the range of environmental impacts associated with delivering a product or service.

The term Green marketing is increasingly being used to refer to both environmental and social dimensions of products and services. However, some people do make the distinction between these aspects of sustainability and refer to social dimensions of marketing using the term ethical marketing.

Ethical marketing

This covers a range of social aspects of marketing as they relate to individuals and communities. Ethical marketing aims to safeguard human rights and promote equity. Therefore it can refer to everything from data protection and the right to privacy to poverty alleviation. Much ethical marketing is therefore focused on improving the lots of those in poorer countries but it can equally well refer to, for example, the ethics involved in marketing products to children in the richer parts of the world.

One prominent example of ethical marketing is Oxfam's Fair Trade brand. According to Oxfam (www.oxfam.org.uk):

> Fair Trade is Trade which promotes sustainable development by improving market access for disadvantaged producers. It seeks to overcome poverty and provide decent livelihoods for producers through a partnership between all those involved in the trading process: producers/workers, traders and consumers.

> The aim of Oxfam is to build 'awareness among consumers of the inequalities of trade and the implications of their buying decisions, Fair Trade empowers people to challenge the ways trade works and choose to make socially responsible choices'.

For the sake of clarity, when talking about Green marketing we will define the term in the broadest sense – though the reader must realize that finer distinctions are made in some other literature.

Green marketing standards

What can, and cannot, be called 'Green', is largely unregulated and there are understandably many people calling for more clarity on the use of terms such as 'environmentally-friendly' to avoid loss of consumer confidence and create consistency in the marketplace. As a result various labelling schemes, standards and regulatory frameworks have been implemented although there is, as yet, no consistent approach across sectors or countries.

A UK government-commissioned study published in 2000 divided the available consumer information in to three broad categories:

i. **Self-declared claims** made by individual businesses about the environmental or social performance of their product. These account for most of the 'product sustainability' information currently in the market. They vary in quality from the clear and informative to the vague, unhelpful and misleading.

ii. **Standardized labelling schemes:**

   o **Pass/fail ecolabelling schemes** – awarded for products reaching a specified level of performance. They fall into two broad categories:

a. **Single-issue labels,** such as the Forest Stewardship Council (FSC) label on timber products, the 'Freedom Foods' label of the RSPCA, or the German 'Blue Angel' scheme.

b. **Multiple-issue labels,** such as the EU ecolabel, which look at the overall impacts of a product across its life cycle.

o **Eco-rating schemes**, under which products are awarded a rating, on say a scale of 'A' to 'G', based on their environmental performance. Most are single issue (e.g., the EU energy label).

o **Eco-profiling schemes,** which provide factual information in a standardized format (e.g. the current voluntary car label in the UK, which shows fuel efficiency and emissions).

o **Social or ethical rating schemes**, in which a number of social or ethical standards are met in order to satisfy an external assessment (e.g. 'fair trade' labels).

iii. **high-level award schemes,** at the very top of the market, which are designed to reward just a few outstanding performers (e.g. the UK's Queen's Award for Sustainable Development).

Some systems such as the Canadian 'Terra Choice' scheme combine some aspects of all three approaches providing pass/fail, eco-profiling and eco-rating information to cater for a range of consumer sophistication.

What follows are examples of some consumer information schemes.

Organic

Organic standards are designed primarily to encourage the spread of organic agriculture and do not enforce any particular social forms of production. However, most organic standards now include social guidelines, which recommend that workers should have decent minimum conditions of employment, consistent with international conventions. Such issues are not monitored as rigorously as the organic standards. Organic labelling does not exclude large, well-organized producers and is not limited to 'Third World' products. www.soilassocation.org

Wood

Standards to encourage the sustainable management of forests have been developed by the Forest Stewardship Council – which operates internationally. The standard has been perhaps one of the biggest successes in that it is both international (although regional variations are permitted) and deals with both environmental and many social aspects of forest management. For example, the FSC standard requires that the right of indigenous peoples are respected, cultural features of any forest are protected, that the long-term viability of wood harvesting is considered. It also states that waste and pollution is minimized. The standards also talk about the need to take into account local economic factors. See the FSC UK web site for more information (www.fsc-uk.demon.co.uk)

FairTrade

FairTrade standards have a social goal: they are primarily designed to ensure that disadvantaged producers – small farmers or plantation workers – in the Third World can gain more control over their lives. The standards therefore cover issues such as working conditions, fair prices and conditions that allow producers to participate in decisions that affect them. Many producers seek to use organic practices, but FairTrade does not require them to do so. www.fairtrade.org

EU energy label

EU energy labels give consumers clear and easily recognizable information about the energy consumption and performance of appliances and light bulbs. The most important part of the label is the energy efficiency rating scale, which shows a simple index of efficiency from 'A' (most efficient) to 'G' (least efficient). By law the label must be displayed on all new domestic refrigerators, freezers and fridge-freezer combinations, lightbulbs, washing machines, electric tumbledryers, combined washer dryers, and dishwashers. In the UK, the introduction of energy labels has been found to have a measurable effect on consumer choice.

Environmental managements and reporting

As well as product information, many consumers are also seeking information about the manufacturer or supplier companies. International standards are being developed in the area of environmental management which meet these needs.

ISO14000 are a series of environmental management standards that consist of voluntary standards and guideline reference documents addressing environmental management systems, environmental audits, eco-labelling, environmental performance evaluations, life cycle assessment and environmental standards for products.

The ISO standards have become an affirmative marketing benchmark for suppliers and manufacturers; eventually the ISO14000 environmental standards may become an absolute condition precedent to participation in the global market.

Alongside the development of environmental management standards, companies are also coming under increasing pressure from customers and stakeholders to report their environmental and social performance. Standards for reporting of sustainability are under development as part of the Global Reporting Initiative (www.globalreporting.org).

Activity 12.2

Get hold of several equivalent packs or jars of coffee which claim to have some environmental or social credentials. Are these claims credible and widespread, and why?

Activity 12.3

Obtain copies of several company environmental reports. Evaluate them and determine which is the most helpful in evaluating all three dimensions of sustainability (environmental, social and economic).

Successful Green marketing

Jacquelyn Ottman (www.greenmarketing.com) defines 7 principles for successful Green marketing:

1. Do your homework – understand the full range of environmental, economic, political and social issues that affect your consumer and your products and services now and over the long term.

2. Create new products and services that balance consumers' desires for high quality, convenience and affordable pricing with minimal environmental impact over the entire life of the product.

3. Empower consumers with solutions – help them understand the issues that affect your business as well as the benefits of your environmentally preferable technology, materials and designs.

4. Establish credibility for your marketing efforts.

5. Build coalitions with corporate environmental stakeholders.

6. Communicate your corporate commitment and project your values.

7. Don't quit – continuously strive for 'zero' environmental impact of your products and processes; learn from your mistakes.

Activity 12.4

How would the application of Ottman's 7 principles transform the following common product types?

1. A portable radio
2. A system for heating domestic hot water
3. A car.

Examples of successful Green marketing given by Ottman in her book *Green Marketing:Opportunities for Innovation*, include the outdoor clothing supplier Patagonia. Patagonia has it headquarters in Ventura, California. The company has a reputation for innovative social and environmental action and is both successful and enjoys a high level of customer loyalty.

The company makes a point of scrutinizing all aspects of its business. Its retail stores, for example, are carefully designed to maximize material re-use and minimize waste. It has an extensive recycling programme, uses natural or energy efficient lighting and even has low flush toilets.

Patagonia also works closely with suppliers to make sure that its products also cause minimum environment impact. They have a range of clothing made out of recycled plastic bottles, for example, and use only organically grown cotton.

Customer education forms part of Patagonia's marketing activities. Each store stocks not just clothing but informative environmental and social literature, books and displays.

Most radically of all, Patagonia has capped its own growth – mimicking a primary natural principle. In founder Yvon Chouinard's own words, this decision stems from the desire 'to avoid cluttering the world with a lot of things people can't use'. High quality, durable products don't have to be replaced often and when outgrown can be passed along for further use.

Patagonia reinforces its strong ties to consumers by supporting the 'good causes' they care most about. Patagonia does not shy away from supporting controversial issues, such as population growth or direct action, relying on the respect and mutual support of its customers.

The company publishes an annual 'Green Report' detailing progress against all key environmental-related goals.

Patagonia is both successful in financial terms and acclaimed for its pioneering approach.

Activity 12.5

Research details of another company that makes Green claims from the products or services that it delivers. How does it compare with Patagonia?

Pressure groups

There have been sharp increases in membership of consumer pressure groups. Consumers are better educated and have learnt to demand their rights. Retailers have become larger and more remote from the individual, encouraging membership of formal and informal pressure groups. Membership of the Consumers Association is a sectional interest group since the member is seeking economic advantage/better value for money. Membership of cause groups is more transitory. Examples include:

- Local people resisting the building of an edge-of-town store
- Environmental groups concerned over issues such as animal testing for cosmetics/packaging and recycling/animal friendly foods/ozone free, etc., sustainable products
- Health and safety causes, e.g. E. coli and BSE
- Genetically modified foods.

Consumer pressure groups will tend to apply primary pressure on legislators and planners as key decision makers. These may have an effect on marketing operations as follows:

- Customer orientation means that customer needs must be taken seriously
- Image and behaviour is important in reassuring customers
- Codes of conduct might be considered, e.g. Sainsbury's regarding environmental policies
- Positive steps should be promoted and efforts made to work with serious groups to achieve balanced progress for all stakeholders
- Pressure to be proactive in terms of recycling and re-use and seek a competitive edge through good practice and clear ethical values
- Failure to respond to pressures may lead to lost customers and a tarnished image.

The next revolution in the marketing customer interface

Reconciling the discipline of marketing with the need to consume less and share more is undoubtedly difficult. It requires nothing less than an overhaul of the entire customer marketing interface. Yet the push from legislation, pull from customer demand, and the realities of the finite nature of our planet, strongly indicate that change is inevitable if not yet widespread.

Hawken, Lovins and Lovins, in their book *Natural Capitalism*, set out four principles which they argue companies must adopt if they are to survive and prosper in a world of limited natural resources and which respects social values.

1. *Radical resource productivity* Business must learn to do more with less. This has three main benefits; resource depletion is slowed, pollution is reduced and employment opportunities

increased. For example, in Denmark most glass bottles are re-used rather than thrown away. This uses less resources, less waste is produced through disposal and jobs are created in the bottle-cleaning and distribution industries.

2. *Biomimicry* Waste must be reduced and eventually eliminated. Biological systems provide the model for the ideal industrial/commercial process. All materials are re-used in 'closed loops'. For example, some public buses in France are run on bio-diesel, a form of diesel made from plants. The gas produced when the fuel is burned does not add to atmospheric pollution as the plants are part of a natural cycle.

3. *Investing in natural capital* The existing damage to the environment must be repaired and, where possible, stocks of natural resources expanded.

4. *Service and flow economy* A fundamental change must take place between supplier and consumer. This transaction, currently based primarily on the purchase of goods, must change to one based on the principles of 'service' and 'flow'.

Although all four principles are interrelated and interdependent the latter is of most relevant to Green marketing and will therefore be explored further.

Moving from products to services

Hawken, Lovins and Lovins envisage a more eco-efficient and socially-responsible economy where the consumers no longer buy goods but secure services by renting or leasing. This profound change in the relationship between manufacturers, suppliers and consumers is best illustrated with some real-life examples.

- Xerox lease many of their copiers to their customers charging a fixed or per copy rate. The copier remains the property of Xerox and they handle the servicing and maintenance.

- Interface Carpets have started to lease recyclable carpet tiles to companies. Their charge includes the cleaning and maintenance of the floor covering. When tiles get worn they re-place them and recycle the carpet and backing into making new tiles.

- Communications company NTL now lease high-speed computer connections to domestic users. The service they are providing is fast access to the internet. The fee structure includes the rental of the necessary modem (there is also the option to buy it for a one-off charge). This remains the property of NTL and is replaced by them in the event of failure.

- The three examples given show how the concept of a service and flow is already manifesting itself in some sectors of the economy. Of course, merely delivering something as a service does not in itself guarantee a greener economy – the other principles of natural capitalism must also minimally be applied.

As Hawkin, Lovins and Lovins write:

> In a service economy the product is a means, not an end. The manufacturer's leasing and ultimate recovery of the product means that the product remains an asset. The minimization of material use, the maximization of product durability, and enhanced ease of maintenance not only improve the customer's experience and value but also protect the manufacturer's investment and hence its bottom line. Both producer and customer have an incentive for continuously improving resource productivity, which in turn further protects ecosystems. Under this shared incentive. Both parties form a relationship that continuously anticipates and meets the customer's evolving value needs – and meanwhile rewards both parties for reducing the burden in the planet.

Natural Capitalism, Hawken, P., Lovins, A.B., Lovins, L.H., Earthscan, 2000

Let us take as an example one purchase which does not follow the principles of service and flow and consider how it might change: the buying and selling of a home computer. Computer technology is moving so fast that models quickly go out of date. Old computers are dumped, generating a huge and mounting waste problem to the extent that new EU legislation is being drafted to deal with the problem. The average working life of a computer is now between two and four years. In 1998, 6 million tonnes of waste electrical and electronic equipment were generated (4% of the municipal waste stream). The growth in electronic waste is about three times higher than that of average municipal waste. How could the principles of service and flow be applied? Here are some suggestions:

- The computer could be engineered to make the components easier to re-use
- Construction could be modular to facilitate easier upgrades

- Customers could be leased the service of 'computing power' rather than sold a particular model
- This 'computer power' lease could include maintenance and upgrade options
- Fixed price internet access could also be included in the lease.

Activity 12.6

Think of some other supplier-customer relationships which already apply some principles of 'service and flow'. How could they be further improved?

Activity 12.7

How would you apply the principles of 'service and flow' to the following existing products and services:

- Household natural gas supply
- A private car
- Disposable baby nappies (diapers).

Protection of consumer interests

'Consumerism' is the term used by the consumer movement to describe what they do and is concerned with the protection of consumers' interests. These range from:

- Ensuring the availability of product and price information
- Ensuring the labelling is correct
- Ensuring that advertising does not misinform
- Ensuring that products are safe
- Ensuring that businesses do not indulge in sharp practices
- Ensuring that businesses abide by the law
- Encouraging government to intervene on consumers' behalf.

The ethical consumer

Go to www.wdm.org.uk and you can find out about the World Development Movement. Some of the issues they have achieved success in are:

- Convinced Del Monte to allow unions on its banana plantations in Costa Rica.
- Led the fight against the new MAI treaty which would have guaranteed multinationals more power
- Helped Indian campaigners block P&O's megaport that would have destroyed the local economy
- Secured a High Court victory to stop the squandering of aid on Malaysia's Pergau Dam.

Issues they are currently campaigning for:

- Persuading big business to put people before profits: such as voicing the concerns of Third World farmers whose lives could be devastated by genetic modification of their staple crops.
- Fighting for government policies that support the poor: such as a fifteen-year battle for an end to the injustice of Third World debt.
- Justice in the twenty-first century: giving voice to brave and principled campaigners in their struggle against exploitation.

The emergence of the ethical consumer can be traced back to the 1980s when official reports, such as that by the Brundtland Commission (*Our Common Future,* 1987, (World Commission on Environment and Development, chaired by the Norwegian Prime Minister Gro Harlem Brundtland), New York, Oxford University Press), started to highlight issues of sustainability. For perhaps the first time this report officially linked social, economic and ecological concerns. For example, depletion of natural resources was associated with poverty and trade with employment conditions in the developing world. This had the effect of boosting the credibility of the established environmental and development-oriented non-governmental organizations (such as Oxfam and Friends of the Earth) and made it more politically acceptable for them to operate on a broader campaign base.

Ethical purchasing campaigns were one beneficiary of these changing circumstances, leading to the publication of numerous guides for concerned consumers. Examples include the popular *Green Pages* (Button, J., 1988, Optima) an ethical equivalent of the *Yellow Pages*, and the *Green Car Guide* (Nieuwenhuis, Cope and Armstrong, 1992, Greenprint).

Ethical consumers can generally be considered to be those who make purchasing decisions based on a broader set of criteria than just price. Value to them goes beyond the intrinsic qualities of any purchase (quality, packaging and so on) to the extrinsic taking into account the environmental and social 'life cycle' of the product or service. Thus, they may be willing to buy fairly traded, organic coffee at a premium price, even though the taste might not be totally to their liking, because they perceive that wider benefits will accrue. In this case coffee workers will have an improved quality of life, better working conditions, and fewer harmful chemicals will be used during production.

Ethical consumers are sometimes categorized into 'light' and 'dark' Greens depending on the depth and breadth of their beliefs. The latter often eschew consumer culture in favour of a more do-it-yourself, minimalist approach to living. In the United States it has been reported that anything up to 10 per cent of the population have adopted this lifestyle – often termed 'voluntary simplicity'. In the UK and Europe the numbers are likely to be similar, as suggested by the growing number of 'sustainable communities' projects, although little official data exists. One telling trend is the very high membership of social and environmental pressure groups within the UK. Approximately one in nine of the population (11 per cent) is a member of one or more groups which ranges from the Royal Society for the Protection of Birds (RSPB) to Greenpeace.

The ethical consumer is likely to have many of the following ten key values acting on them to varying degrees. (Adapted from several sources including the book *Seeing Green* (Porritt, J., 1984, Blackwell) and the key values of the Green Committees of Correspondence and International Green Parties. A selection of definitions of key values can be found on the web site www.greens.org.)

1. *Social justice* The realization that there is a need to redistribute wealth and provide access to the benefits of society to all the peoples of the world. Thus, it is recognized that, rather than reinforcing existing developed-world supply and demand structures, purchasing decisions should aim to encourage and support self-reliance amongst the less fortunate. Thus, companies such as The Body Shop aim to deal direct with local cooperatives in developing countries and link with other initiatives aimed at providing, for example, clean water and education.

2. *Community-based economics* The belief that, in economic terms, 'small is beautiful'. A recognition that buying locally adds financial value to the community and has social and environmental benefits. Examples are the growing number of vegetable 'box schemes' and community farms where residents and local food growers enter into a supply agreement often including doorstep delivery and sometimes in exchange for occasional farm-hand work.

3. *Non-violence* The commitment to resolve disputes at a local, national or global level without resorting to violence. An example is of consumer demand for ethical investment funds which do not invest in companies which manufacture weapons.

4. *Decentralization* The belief that the balance of power should be shifted in favour of local communities rather than being centralized to a national or global level. One example of this is the concerted internet campaign credited with forcing the multilateral agreement on investment (or MAI) out of the European Parliament. The MAI aimed to give more power to multinational corporations to the detriment of national and local governments potentially denying the rights of local authorities to 'buy local'.

5. *Future focus/sustainability* Thinking in terms of the future. Recognizing the rights of future generations to live comfortably on the planet. This usually manifests itself in a product or service guarantee which claims to offset pollution and replace or recycle the natural resources being consumed. Examples include the many products which use all, or a percentage of recycled materials such as newspapers, plastic carrier and bin bags, and even clothing. Another interesting example is the 1997 concert tour of musician Neneh Cherry where a number of trees were planted to offset the carbon dioxide pollution emitted from the electricity consumed during the tour.

6. *Post-patriarchal values* Replacing the traditional ethics of dominance and control with those of cooperation and spirituality. This key value gets to the heart of ethical consumerism. It recognizes that the consumer is not all-powerful and has no more rights than any other person in the supply chain. Thus the emphasis is shifted to take account of the needs of those working to grow, manufacturer and distribute products or deliver services. An example is the recent concern over Sunday working which was not just religious but also recognized the need for shop staff to have time off to relax and spend time with their families.

7. *Personal and global responsibility* Taking personal responsibility for the effects of our actions on the whole of society. Again, this key value gets to the heart of ethical consumerism – the belief that individuals should be selfless and consider the impacts of their decisions on other people and the environment. An example of how this has been used is in the selling of paper products where the promise is often made to plant more trees to replace those logged to manufacture the product. This recognizes that consumers perceive the link between purchase and the impact on the natural environment.

8. *Respect for diversity* Honouring cultural, ethnic, racial, sexual, religious, spiritual and biological diversity. Covers a broad spectrum of concerns from the banning of one of Salman Rushdie's books in some countries, on the basis that it was offensive to certain religious groups, to the issue of racial and gender equality and the conservation of endangered animal species. One example is the Worldwide Fund for Nature's link with a range of product manufacturers to ensure a donation to conservation efforts.

9. *Grassroots democracy* A belief that individuals must have the ability to control the decisions that affect their lives. Pertains to consumer issues such as employment rights, human rights and political conditions in country of manufacture. An example of consumer action was the boycott of South African products while the country was under minority white rule.

10. *Ecological wisdom* Living within the ecological and resource limits of the planet. Pertains to issues such as energy-efficiency, organic agriculture and waste minimization. An example of consumer action is the pressure for eco-labelling of products and low energy appliances.

The ethical consumer exerts power not only directly – in their choice of products or service – but also indirectly through the political and legislative process.

A related type of consumer is the healthy consumer. There is a strong overlap between what is considered healthy for an individual to consume and what is healthy for the environment. Thus the enormous public outcry over the introduction of genetically-modified foods brought together those concerned with both the possible effects on the health of those eating GM foods and those concerned at the effect of releasing GM materials into the wider environment. The latter were more concerned with effects such as the development of pesticide-resistant weeds and the impact on wildlife.

In most cases the concern of the healthy consumer revolves around their personal consumption of food. There may be ethical reasons for not wishing to eat certain foodstuffs, for example vegetarianism and/or a desire to eat locally-grown produce, but the healthy consumer is equally as interested in diet. They may seek to avoid certain ingredients, artificial sweeteners, mono-sodium glutamate (MSG), excessive salt, saturated fats, or actively consume others such as vitamins, wholefoods, mineral water and so on.

The healthy consumer may also be seeking to control their weight through their levels of consumption.

The FairTrade mark – A new dimension to shopping

The FairTrade symbol is an independently-assessed mark awarded only to those products that meet a strict set of criteria including:

- Decent wages
- Minimum health and safety standards
- A fair price
- A long-term trading commitment
- Good environmental standards.

The FairTrade mark arose as a result of pressure from ethical consumers to assist them in making socially and environmentally-sensitive purchasing decisions. Products with FairTrade marks include coffee, tea, chocolate and cocoa.

The FairTrade Foundation – 020-7405 5942.

World population

Global population has grown exponentially over the last two or three centuries. As industrial economies matured, however, they enjoyed a demographic transition whereby customarily high birth rates fell to levels closer to already-reduced death rates. This process has yet to be completed in many less-developed countries, especially in Africa, meaning that world population will continue to rise, although at a reducing rate, for a good number of years. Less-developed countries account for a steadily increasing proportion of total population. There is an annual and exponential growth rate of 1.8 per cent. The world population grew from 4.4 billion in 1980 to 6.2 billion in 2000. The share of the industrialized countries of this overall total will shrink from 25 per cent to 17 per cent by 2005.

Technology

Marketing research is made easier through the use of analysis packages such as SPSS. The changing technology also affects marketing operations, for example:

- Supply side:
    o Supply chain management
    o Electronic data interchange (EDI) links suppliers and retailers – enables JIT
    o EPOS/barcode systems allow automatic reordering
    o EFTPOS systems to improve cash flow and customer convenience via cash back
    o Computer-linked intelligent trolleys and self check-out.
- Personnel side:
    o Marketing staff have more processing power
    o Direct marketing is facilitated via loyalty databases
    o Productivity increases in all areas.
- Demand side:
    o Opens up the potential of home shopping
    o Product range fine-tuned
    o Automated telephone ordering systems
    o In-store secure automated banking services
    o Sales opportunities.

As Bill Gates says in his book, *Business at the Speed of Thought*,:

If the 1980s were about quality and the 1990s were about re-engineering, then the 2000s will be about velocity. About how quickly the nature of business will change. About how information access will alter the lifestyle of consumers and their expectations of business. Quality improvements and business process improvements will occur far faster. When the increase in velocity of business is great enough, the very nature of business changes. A manufacturer or retailer that responds to changes in sales in hours instead of weeks is no longer at heart a product company, but a service company that has a product offering. These changes will occur because of a disarmingly simple idea: the flow of digital information.

For the technically minded, see www.speed-of-thought.com

Changes in technology have an impact on:

- The environment
- The types of products that are marketed
- Methods of production

- The type of work that is done
- The way in which the work is carried out
- The way in which human resources are deployed
- Techniques used for marketing
- Consumers and society in general.

Economic environment

The economic environment can affect consumer spending and purchasing power. Total spending power includes:

- Current income
- Savings
- Credit
- Prices.

A major determinant of demand income is widely used as a measure of potential demand.

- Net disposable income is all earnings (earned from salaries) and unearned (from investments) health and welfare benefits and so on, less tax.
- Discretionary income is the amount available after all 'essential' (mortgage, rent, food, basic clothing, etc.) expenditure has been met.

Consumer behaviour and marketing strategy will influence whether a product/service falls in the discretionary or non-discretionary sector.

Marketers should be aware of:

1. Patterns of real income distribution
2. Inflationary and deflationary pressure
3. Changing consumer expenditure patterns
4. Changes in the saving/debt ratio
5. Concern over Third World debt
6. Different consumer expenditure patterns.

These changes must not be looked at in isolation but be viewed against a background of change in the political/economic balances of power worldwide and major changes in the physical environment.

Economic factors

You should be able to understand how consumer behaviour is affected by economic factors both domestically and abroad. It is important to understand that it is not the objective nature of the economic context but rather the way in which that context is perceived and interpreted by consumers.

Economic forecasting involves looking at the impact and relationship of the following:

- The industrial structure
- The income distribution
- GNP per capita
- Rate of growth of GNP
- Ratio of investment to GNP
- Business cycles
- Money supply
- Inflation rates
- Unemployment
- Energy costs
- Patterns of ownership
- Exchange rates
- Taxation
- Currency stability
- Export and so on.

Make sure that you read the quality press and trade and business magazines on a regular basis to keep track of what is happening in your market. Collect articles and put them into your folder. You will be expected to include up-to-date examples in the exam.

The business cycle

This refers to the periodic fluctuations in economic activity that occur in industrialized countries. At times we have economic growth and at other times we have high unemployment and falling production. The word cycle implies that there is something regular about it.

Many different cycles have been identified by various economists, for example Kuznets highlighted a 15-25 year cycle, while Kondratieff identified a 50-60 year cycle. For much of the post-war period most advanced economies have suffered fluctuations of economic activity that last about 4-5 years, these are called business cycles (see Figure 12.1).

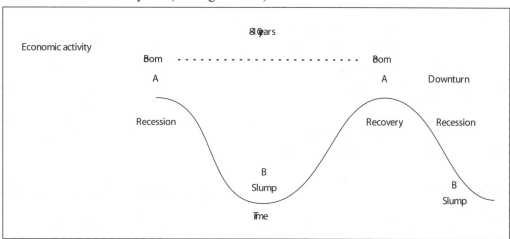

Figure 12.1 *Phases of the business cycle*

The marketer must be able to try to anticipate fluctuations, especially the stages at which the economy is moving into or out of recessions and booms.

The stage of the cycle will determine the policies you should be pursuing:

- *Downturn* Control stock in line with order slowdown, analyze weak products and channel outlets (Pareto analysis), stop recruitment and further long-term commitments.
- *Recession* Retain skilled core staff and upgrade their skills, order capital equipment for future installation.
- *Recovery* Orders start coming in, start building stock and encourage distributors to do likewise, start hiring and prepare new products for launch.

Exam Hint

Certain businesses do not follow the pattern of a normal trade cycle and run counter to it. These include debt collection, receivership, discount stores. Some are very cyclical, e.g. construction, others are less so, e.g. food.

The business cycle represents the average of many individual industry cycles. It is important to remember that any one cycle may be in advance of or lag behind the main cycle.

Forecasting the cycle

Unfortunately no way has been found to do this accurately. However, the marketer can take a careful note of present trends of the following:

- GDP
- volume of retail sales
- level of unemployment
- changes in stocks, and so on.

Surveys of business opinion such as the CBI survey can help. The marketer may also be able to predict trends from changes in statistics. There are a number of statistical trends that are thought to be significant in measuring business cycles – these are called economic indicators. Some react ahead of the trend and are known as leading indicators (housing starts), others lag behind the business cycle (investment and unemployment).

In the UK a range of indicators are published quarterly by the Central Statistics Office in the journal *Economic Trends*.

Globalization

The term 'globalization of markets' (Levitt, 1983) refers to:

1. Tastes, preferences and price-mindedness becomes increasingly universal
2. Products and services becoming more standardized and competition within industries reaches a worldwide scale
3. The way in which organizations try and design their marketing policies and control systems for global products, consumers and competition on a global scale.

Jean-Claude Usunier writes in *International Marketing,* Prentice Hall (1993):

Globalization means homogenizing on a world scale. The implicit assumption behind the globalization process is that all elements will globalize simultaneously. A central assumption of globalization is that the mostly artificial trade barriers (non-tariff, regulation, industrial standards, etc.) have kept many markets at the multidomestic stage. If these barriers are removed, which is the aim of 1992, 'insiders' who hold a large market share just in their home market may only be protected from new entrants by natural culture-related entry barriers.

Electronic commerce and its impact on the organizational customer interface

Martin Butler and Thomas Power have very kindly supplied much of this information from their book The *E-Business Advantage* (Martin Butler – www.butlergroup.com and Thomas Power – www.TheEcademy.com).

Martin Butler and Thomas Power are IT and e-business analysts who work closely with Europe's leading companies. They can see clearly that the internet has truly created a new, completely electronic economy. It has unique financial models, strategies, structures, politics, cultures, combatants, regulations, successes, failures, opportunities and problems.

They define e-commerce as the buying or selling of products, goods, information and services over the internet and e-business as the transformation of an organization's internal processes through the application of web technologies.

- E-commerce:
  - Home page
  - Catalogue
  - Order taking
  - Secure transactions.
- E-business:
  - Intranet and extranet
  - Electronic procurement
  - Customer acquisition
  - Catalogue management
  - Merchandise planning and analysis
  - Order entry – confirmation and fulfilment
  - Returns
  - Shipping and freight
  - Warehousing and inventory management
  - Pricing – promotions, taxes, duties, freight
  - Payments – credit cards, digital cash, bank transfers

- o Financial accounting
- o Reporting
- o Customer profiling and customer relationship
- o Customer service.

The internet

The internet is transforming the way we do business across all sectors. Unfortunately, many businesses still see the internet as *just* another channel of communication with their customers. In fact, it has the potential to be much more than that and needs to be recognized as such.

Trading over the internet fundamentally affects the relationship between business and consumer – the customer relationship.

Doing business over the internet is referred to as e-Commerce. Putting an 'e' (which originally stood for 'electronic') in front of just about any term is fast becoming a common means of indicating that we are talking about the involvement of the internet. For example, you may see references to e-business, e-marketing, e-customers, the e-world and even the e-tailing!

As well as creating new ways of working, e-Commerce is arguably the main driver behind a paradigm shift in the way we do business.

Table 12.2 shows the sorts of transitions that are occurring as we move towards a wired up world.

Table 12.2 *Adapted from Christine Willard, 'Strategic Management', Computerworld, 12 July 1999.*

Issue	Old business way of working	E-business way of working
Basis of competition	Driven by the 'bigger is better' philosophy	Driven by innovation
Barriers to entry	Typically need to invest in substantial capital infrastructure Physical location largely dictates type of business	Very few funds actually needed to set up an e-business Constraints are more intellectual than physical
Control	More producer-control	More customer-control
Marketing, sales and service	Mass marketing	Mass personalization
Time to market	Dependent on chain of raw materials supply, tooling up, production and distribution	Time to market more dependent on people-resources
Product/service/pricing	Based on costs of raw materials, labour, and distribution	Based on development costs. Transaction costs approaching zero
Operations	Based around the actual process of creating the product	Based around 'knowledge engineering'
Organization	Hierarchical departments	Multifunctional teams connected by the web

The fundamental difference is the ease with which one is able to create an e-business. This has, of course, led to a proliferation of new online businesses. The key question is no longer whether one can afford to start a new business but whether it is worth doing it. Finding and keeping customers is now more important than ever. As Chris Fox (www.chrisfoxinc.com) has argued that, we are moving from an industrial age, where success is dictated by the ownership and availability of natural resources, to the information age where success is measured by the number of customers. Whereas value was once vested in physical assets it is now to be found in relationships (business to customer, customer to customer or business to business) and intellectual capital (knowledge, ideas and skills).

Advantages of doing business electronically

From both the business and customer's perspectives, using the internet to trade has many inherent advantages:

- *Convenience* – almost anyone armed with a credit card and internet connection can sit in front of their computer any time of the day or night and surf the web. For example, the emergence of electronic banking allows you to check your account balance, transfer money, and even arrange a loan outside bank opening hours. Examples include Barclays Bank

Insight: The e-consumer rules OK

Extracted from The Guardian web site (published 29 September 2000)

The internet challenges the fundamental premises of marketing, and marketers will have to do more than just set up a website to keep their consumers interested, writes **Lindsey Roberts**, (founding partner of the FRESH ideas consultancy lindsey.roberts@letstalkfresh.com).

How are businesses gearing up for a new kind of consumer power that is emerging from the electronic revolution?

I undertook research on behalf of Marketing Forum 2000 to answer that question and found real dilemmas for marketing and businesses in their quest to come to terms with the growth in consumer power heralded by changes in electronic media. The research, which was conducted among both marketers and consumers, found that the rules of marketing haven't fundamentally changed but many of the processes marketers use are now too bureaucratic and ponderous.

Some companies are simply hiving off the electronic division to keep the 'e-types' from being too disruptive a force in the existing corporate culture. This is, in effect, a kind of corporate denial. A better solution is to embrace the need for change and become quicker and less bureaucratic. Size is important in the e-world but speed and agility are vital too. The winners will be those companies that succeed in combining both. There are implications for ways of working too. In the words of one senior marketer: 'This is the death of precedent.' Everyone in marketing will have to find quicker, more original ways of working with more emphasis on creativity.

… As far as consumers are concerned, few companies are getting their electronic offering right. There is too much emphasis on design and too little on functionality in websites. One of the consumer respondents summed it up: 'Your website is your shop – whether or not you are planning to sell from it. Most people who visit are looking for information and help and they need to be given it. Then they may stay to browse and even buy. If they don't like the feel of your place, they have the biggest shopping mall in the world on their desktop.'

However, this pales into insignificance against the biggest single conclusion from this research. We are witnessing the start of a seismic shift in the balance of power in marketing. We are only feeling the first distant rumbles, but as more people become e-enabled the closer we will get to the epicentre of a major earthquake that has the potential to shake the very foundations on which marketing has been built.

The marketing industry may soon look back with nostalgia at the good 'old' world ruled by brands and built on inspiring confidence and reflecting consumer aspirations. Since the arrival of the e-world there has been much talk of building deeper relationships based on the previously undreamed of quality and quantity of data, providing a new depth of knowledge and the ability to anticipate consumer needs.

Attractive as this model may seem to today's marketers, based on the consumer research, I believe it is unlikely that this will be the future of marketing. While it is no news that the new, emergent e-consumer is becoming empowered, marketing has not yet fully understood the implications of meeting the needs of consumers who feel omnipotent rather than in awe.

(www.barclays.co.uk), and exclusively online banks such as Egg (egg.co.uk) which claims to be the UK's largest with 1.33m customers (Guardian 14 December 2000).

- *Improved access to information* – every computer connected to the internet is theoretically in contact with every other either directly, via e-mail, or indirectly via third-party content posted on web sites. Whether you are trying to find the lowest price for a CD, or looking for a difficult-to-find antique, the internet gives you access to massive amount of information. There are more than 1.3 billion web pages that can be searched. The converse of this is that a web page displayed by a giant corporation such as Microsoft (www.microsoft.com) is just as accessible as one posted by a radical anti-advertising group such as Subvertise which sets out to parody big business (for example, see www.subvertise.org/technology/stec0004m.htm).

- *Interactivity* – the internet has the potential to be more interactive than other written or visual forms of media. Web sites can now combine sound, animation, and even 'remember' earlier sessions with repeat users. A good source of information about web interactivity (and web site design issues in general) is that of Jakob Nielsen (www.useit.com). And try www.webpagesthatsuck.com.

- *Low startup and transaction costs* – you can, at least in theory, set up an online business in an evening with nothing more than a £1000 ($1500), That will buy you a computer, internet connection and some modestly priced software. Whether or not you will attract any customers is another matter! Once established, transaction costs are generally much lower than with traditional business models. Estimates vary, but typically taking and processing an order online is said to be about a third of the cost of traditional methods.

Disadvantages of doing business electronically

People are often so overwhelmed by new technology that they can overlook the downsides.

Intangibility – although the internet is a more powerful medium than, say, a direct mail flyer, it cannot match the richness of communication that results from face-to-face communication. It would be very difficult, for example, to sell a new brand of perfume over the internet. The intangibility of online buying puts off those customers who like to get more physically involved in the process.

Expertise – as with any other 'new' area of knowledge, there can be difficulty recruiting web designers and strategic thinkers (whether marketers, project managers or others) with sufficient expertise to successfully implement an e-commerce solution.

Security – the main concern of customers purchasing goods online is security. Many customers fear that their personal credit card or account details might become publicly available or their financial transactions intercepted or even 'lost'. Customers' concerns are occasionally stoked by the reporting of a security breach such as that experienced by the on-line bank Egg in 1999.

Legal issues – legal issues still can act as a barrier to successful e-commerce. Some of the issues are strictly internet-related, such as that battles over domain name ownership and the use of trademarks, and the legalities of the inter-linking of site. Others are traditional issues applied to the internet, such as copyright, consumer rights, licensing, privacy, taxation, regulation and jurisdiction. For more information on this see www.cybercrime.gov/ecommerce.html)

Product/service delivery – the ease with which purchases can be made on-line is often offset by the difficulties experienced when trying to deliver to the customer. This problems can be overcome by regionalizing distribution (as with www.dominos.co.uk) but at some cost to the supplier.

Customer exclusion – some people are simply unwilling or unable to shop online. Some people are merely slow to embrace new technologies, others have a fundamental dislike of this use of technology, others still may simply lack access to a suitable computer through choice or circumstances.

E-commerce models

What is an e-commerce model?

An e-commerce model is a framework for doing business on the internet. This framework is usually taken to include an organization's goals and strategies as well as its products, services, processes, technologies and structure.

Thus when doing business on the web it is important to make sure that the implications on the company as a whole are taken into account.

Type of models

Many different e-commerce models exist and new one are emerging all the time. No agreed classification system exists but there is considerable agreement on the general features which distinguish the different ways of working on the web.

Table 12.3 categorizes models according to the way in which revenue is raised by the web site owner. Columns in the table describe the model, give outline details of the value perceived by the purchaser or viewer, and provide examples.

Of course, it is possible to combine different types of e-commerce models. This can both add to the value experienced by the user and increase the potential for revenue generation. For example, Yahoo! (www.yahoo.com) provides an auction facility, sells advertising space, and offers direct sales.

Activity 12.8

Think about a hobby that you have. How might you turn it into a revenue-generating web site? What e-commerce model would you select?

Table 12.3

Model	Description	Value to purchaser/viewer	Examples
Direct Sales	'Shopping cart' style web sites which sell products via a 'virtual storefront'	Buyers feel they are getting a good price, inherent value in the product or service. Value is often added by providing background information on items, reviews and ratings, and customized interfaces which 'remember' a customer's preferences and may suggest new or alternative purchases	www.Amazon.com – books, CDs www.domino.co.uk – pizza delivery
Brokerage or Auction sites	The brokerage (or auction) model works by bringing together potential buyers and sellers Revenue is usually raised by advertising on the site or the broker charging the seller a fee	The value to the web site user is that they can easily reach lots of potential buyers or sellers Value is often added by permitting traders to see images of the items and previous or current sale prices	www.ebay.com – auction site www.mondus.com – business to business exchange
Advertising	The development and maintenance of content is funded from advertising, in the form of links to sponsors, on-screen banner adverts or intrusive pop-up windows	The value is inherent in the content, for example, news information, which is, first and foremost, what brings people to the site	www.guardianunlimited.co.uk – online version of the Guardian newspaper www.sheknows.com- a site for women
Subscription	A fee is paid to permit access a restricted site, which will provide access to information, products or services	Again, the value is inherent in the content which is often of a technical or specialist nature	www.nexus.com – an online library www.consumerreports.org – ratings and recommendations of products and services
Company	Revenue is primarily raised indirectly through the business generated for the company This might be in the form of 'offline' product sales, consultancy services or even securing membership of an organization	Users find the site useful in obtaining organizational information, job vacancies, investor information, event details, market intelligence or maybe even 'free offers' Often the 'links' maintained by an organization can be the most useful resource	www.shell.com – the Royal Dutch/Shell Group www.peevish.co.uk – a web design company
Informational (or Vanity)	No revenue is raised and there is no expectation of revenue – usually campaigning sites or personal homepages promoted through informal networks such as families, friends or campaigning groups.	The value is inherent in the content which is often of a campaigning, entertaining or personal nature	www.subvertise.org – anti-advertisement site Use a search engine to search for a common name, e,g, 'John Smith' and you will find lots of personal and family homepages
Infomediary	Revenue is raised by selling information about, or access to, an individual and/or their online behaviour	Users are usually attracted to the site by a 'free' service – such as free internet access or a search facility. Such services provide the opportunity to collect more information about a user than a content-only site	www.netzero.com – free email www.google.com – their adwords programme provides for targeted adverts
Affiliate	Revenue is generated by directing potential customers from your site to another site – usually a direct sales site Payment is usually a percentage of any purchases made	Customers are usually first attracted to the affiliate site for a number of reasons, e.g. the author of a book may set up a web site to promote the book and then affiliate themselves to an online book seller to provide a 'click to buy' facility	www.ecologicalfootprint.com – affiliated to Amazon www.magicbutton.net – a site for affiliates

Insight: Public sector applications of the internet

There is much talk at a local and national government level, in the public health sector and government agencies about the electronic delivery of services and information to the public. Referred to as e-Government, the public sector is particularly interested in the efficiency saving that can result from web delivery. In the UK, all branches of the government have been told to move services on to the internet by 2005.

For more information, go to the website: **www.centre-for-egovernment.com**

To see some examples of online public sector service delivery go to:

www.nhsdirect.nhs.uk – online delivery of health information

www.oxon-tss.org.uk – Oxfordshire's award winning trading standards site

www.ennis.ie – the web site for Ennis – an 'information age town' in Ireland where there has been massive investment in information technology.

New ways of marketing

There are many ways in which the web can be used to market a product or service. Such channels of communication are an integral part of the business models described earlier.

E-mail marketing

Marketing using e-mail is, or should be, a two way process.

The key to dealing with inbound email is to respond to it – the quicker the better. Even a holding response (or a mere thank you) is better than no response and gives the sender an impression of quality and efficiency.

Ideally, your web site should provide different e-mail addresses to assist in directing enquirers to the correct person. Sales enquiries should NOT end up in the inbox of support staff!

Make sure you glean whatever information is possible from all those people who send you e-mails. Many e-mails are 'signed' with company details, job titles, web sites and so on which might prove useful. Try to categorize contacts to assist in future marketing efforts.

Online businesses should be actively encouraging people to contact them. The usual method is by putting a 'click to e-mail' button or link on your web site and widely distributing your e-mail and/or web address as part of your promotional work. Ideas for generating/finding email contacts include:

- Place an e-mail address under your phone book entry
- Put an e-mail address on your business cards and brochures
- Start up an e-mail discussion group or join an existing group
- Search the web for the e-mail addresses of target customers
- Provide a 'free' gift to those people who provide their contact details
- Make access to an interesting part of your web site conditional on contact details being provided
- Set up a business card box at a trade show or fair.

Be creative in your efforts to gather addresses. Why not, for example, create several company e-mail addresses to help you track where leads are going from.

Building up such a list of contacts is a vital part of e-mail marketing. Good e-mail software will allow you to create selective groups of contacts to make email targeting easier. For example, say you would like to promote your services in North America. You should be able to search on addresses and extract all contacts that are in this region and create a custom e-mail list.

You can, of course, buy e-mail lists but these are rarely as good as a list you build from scratch.

Remember that you must provide details of your Privacy Policy wherever e-mail addresses are collected online. Under the European Data Protection Act this must state what you intend to do with the data (including whether you intend to sell or rent it). Legally you cannot process or use personal data without the provider's explicit permission.

The content of any e-mails you send out should be carefully thought through. The last thing you want to do is annoy a potential customer or have your e-mail placed straight in the electronic waste basket!

Consider including the following in your email:

- Useful events listings
- Promotions or deals
- Notice of new services or products
- Helpful information of a more general kind
- Above all, keep outgoing e-mails brief. If necessary provide links to further information. Be sure that the format of your email is compatible with the email software of the recipient. If you are in doubt then use a simple text-based approach.

Here is an example of a simple, professional, concise e-mail promoting the sale of music CDs:

===========The Best Jazz Music of 2000 from CDBUYER =============

Year 2000 was a good year for Jazz and Jazz Rock music

In association with Jazz Player Monthly, CDBUYER is selling the year's bestselling Top 10 masterpieces, for a limited period only, at 20% off list price.

Find out more about the artists, the music and the specially selected Top 10 by clicking on the link below:

Take me to the year 2000 Top 10

Other special offers

From Friday, September 5, 2001 through Monday, September 8, 2001, save 10% on ALL U.S. releases by these past and present legends of rock and jazz; Duke Ellington, Pat Metheny, Charlie Parker, Louis Armstrong, Lyle Mays. Click on the link below to find out more:

 CDBUYER Special Offers

Guide to Upcoming Jazz Concerts and Festivals

Consult CDBUYER's free listings to when and where the best jazz is to be found. In many cases CDBUYER has been able to negotiate discount ticket prices. Click the link below for more details.

CDBUYER Jazz Listings

Thank you

Dave Duke
Chief Executive, CDBUYER (www.cdbuyer.co.uk)

The prices of the items featured in this e-mail were accurate at the time the e-mail was sent, but may be subject to change.

You received this e-mail because you are an account holder at CDBUYER. If you'd prefer not to receive this weekly Special Offers message in the future, click here.

Or, if you'd like to receive different information from us, you can always update your music preferences by simply going to the CDBUYER website

For questions regarding your account, order status or to contact our Customer Service department, please visit our Help Desk.

It is particularly important to supply a succinct, friendly and appropriate e-mail subject line (the first thing a reader will see) which will increase the chances of your e-mail being read. The more subtle 'Top Jazz Hits at Cool Prices' is probably better than 'Cheap CDs For Sale'.

Remember that all e-mails, by law, should include an explanation of how to avoid getting further unsolicited e-mails.

Finally, remember that every business is different. Experiment by trying out different styles and approaches to writing and distributing e-mails.

Link building and affiliate schemes

What is affiliate marketing?

Put simply, a supplier signs up a number of affiliates to act as a virtual salesforce. Each affiliate displays a link to the merchant site and, every time a customer clicks through and makes a purchase from the merchant, the affiliate earns a commission.

The basic e-commerce model, described from the point of view of the affiliate, has already been outlined. As a merchant, you may wish to consider entering into affiliate partnership to increase the number of visitors to your web site. An affiliate partnership is a win-win arrangement:

- The merchant increases audience and sales
- The affiliate earns commission (typically 5 to 10% on sales)
- The customer is provided with easier access to product and service information

Companies such as MagicButton.net (www.magicbutton.net) use their expertise to broker deals between merchants and affiliates.

Most merchants provide their affiliates with a full set of monitoring and reporting tools. Amazon, for example, the king of affiliate marketing, has a special area of their web site for affiliates which provides all the tools necessary to setup affiliate links and report on the web site traffic.

Insight: UK Watch News

Adapted from www.affiliatemarketing.co.uk/news.htm (accessed February 2001)

BT to launch first-ever B-to-B affiliate marketing solution in the UK

MagicButton.Net to aid British Telecom in selling its StoreCentre and TrustWise services through the UK with an innovative affiliate marketing program.

British Telecommunications has signed an agreement with MagicButton.Net, Europe's leading affiliate network, to create a merchant branded affiliate program. Through these affiliations, BT.com will sell the telecommunications company's eBusiness services. The agreement marks the first-ever, business-to-business affiliate marketing solution in the UK, and the first affiliate marketing solution launched by a telecommunications company.

MagicButton.Net will recruit a network of web sites to BT as potential affiliates to sell its online services, and has already had interest from a number of leading partners. By creating an online affiliate program, BT will cost-effectively drive traffic to BT's product offerings, increase sales and brand awareness through partnerships, and acquire new customers.

'We decided upon an affiliate network approach, as it gives us the flexibility to partner with a wide variety of on-line vendors, retailers or service providers in line with our rapidly expanding portfolio of Internet and eBusiness services,' states Alison Cleland, strategic marketing manager at British Telecommunications.

Sponsorships, partnerships and alliances

There are other kinds of relationships that can be effective in marketing your e-business. Typically these involve some sort of reciprocal arrangement. Often these are informal 'deals' whereby web site links are exchanged.

It is well worth spending the time building up such links. Many of these sites can be encouraged to link to yours for free. Some are hobby sites, others are directories of shops maintained by other companies such as the Guardian's shopping site at www.shoppingunlimited.co.uk

Link building requires nothing more than finding and politely e-mailing sites who you feel may be interested in telling their visitors about your site. Some may agree, some may refuse, some may suggest you pay to advertise with them (see below) and others may ask if you have an affiliate scheme (see above).

Most search engines allow you to find out who has linked to your site.

Search engine submission

If you are a retailer of sports shoes in Canada it would be good if your business came top of the list when web users typed the words "sport shoes Canada" into a popular search engine.

If you are in a competitive business then ensuring a top listing will be difficult, if not impossible. However you can do many things to increase you chances of being noticed.

Meta tags, the keywords used by search engines, should be chosen carefully.

Submit your page directly to the popular search engines. This can be done manually (one at a time) or automatically. Neither guarantees success but the former is the more reliable method. Start with the following search engines; www.google.com, www.yahoo.com, www.altavista.com. Look for an 'add URL' or 'add site' button and follow the instructions.

Don't expect an instant, or even a noticeable, response. Changes to ranking can take several weeks.

Activity 12.10

Pick a company with a web site. Using its main products or services as keywords, run a search at a search engines such as www.google.com. Does the company's site appear in the results, and if so, where in the rankings? Go to the site and see if you can find out what meta tags are used on its home page (most web browser provide you with a 'view source' option which will display the tags). Can these meta tags be improved?

Banner advertising

At the top of many web pages you will find 'banners' tempting you to take a holiday, switch your bank or buy books. These banner adverts remain the most used form of promotion. Some web sites have valuable 'real estate'. To get your banner advert on to the Wall Street Journal home page can cost thousands of pounds. Targeting and placement issues are much the same as they are in any other media. The difference is that customers can simply and easily click through to your web site.

Response rates to banners are, however, very low. Fewer than 1% of users will click on a banner advert.

The design of banners has become quite an art form with colourful, animated banners now the norm. The following will increase the chance of a hit on your banner:

- Change your banner regularly
- Try out different designs and monitor success
- Include an eye-catching message or promotion
- Clearly indicate that the banner can be clicked
- Make your banners interactive.

Banners are slowly being replaced by affiliate schemes as the main form of advertising revenue.

Measuring success

As with any other type of marketing it is important to asses the effectiveness of your approach. There are many free tools on the internet that will help you do this. For example try www.thecounter.com. This company provides free counters that can be placed anywhere on a web site. The counter logs 'hits' on the web page and produces regular reports.

You will probably need to involve your web designer in setting up a web site counter but, once incorporated, reports can be automatically e-mailed to you.

Web counters are not able to record much detail about a particular site visitor but can, for example, tell you their last visited site. This helps you track down the source of the hits.

The success of banner ads can similarly be monitored. The most common measure here is the 'click through rate' (ctr). This is the percentage of people seeing a banner who click on it.

Making e-commerce happen in your company

E-commerce requires a well-developed strategy:

1. *High level support* Companies recognize the need for high level support at board level and a budget. This will need senior management vision and understanding.

2. *Need for an enterprise-wide approach* The organization may have to be redesigned to provide an appropriate customer interface and order fulfilment. Responsibility for e-commerce must be allocated to individuals with cross-business unit responsibilities who report to the board. However, in French companies, for example, e-commerce was more likely to be led by the marketing department and to be a joint venture between departments than in companies from other countries.

3. *Organization* E-commerce is not just about internet-based transactions. It is the creation of a whole way of thinking. A programme needs to be set up that outlines how the whole organization will evolve within the networked economy, embracing the issues of marketing, technology, training and resources.

4. *Integration* The point of customer contact – the web front end – needs to fully integrate with existing systems, sales order processing, purchase ledgers and so on.

5. *Technology* E-commerce demands additional security levels. Authentication and non-repudiation are also areas that need to be thought about.

6. *Payment systems* Ensure that the payment system you adopt is flexible.

7. *Use of designated resource* Even when companies identified that electronic commerce is an enterprise-wide undertaking, they still designated a resource to implement it. The largest companies (in terms of employees) were more likely to rely on the IT department for electronic support.

Useful world wide web links

Hear are some web sites that will hopefully provide you with further information, ideas for business opportunities or ideas for web page design:

- www.baynetworks.com/Solutions/
- www.bt.com/business/
- www.eca.org.uk – Electronic Commerce Association
- www.ibm.com/e-business/what/how/ns.html
- www.isi.gov.uk – Information Society Initiative for Business
- www.itforall.gov.uk – IT for all Programme
- www.interforum.org
- lucent.com/enterprise/
- www.opentext.com
- marketplace.unisys.com/coolice/index.html
- www.microsoft.com/siteserver/commerce/default.asp
- www.springboard/solutions
- www.sun.com/e-commerce/solutions
- www.unisys.com/execmag

Examples of electronic business:

- www.buckinghamgate.com – shopping
- www.eaglestardirect.co.uk – insurance
- www.ecn.dk – publishing
- www.fs-on-line.com – travel
- www.ideal.co.uk – distribution
- www.nationwide.co.uk – banking
- www.sparbanken.se – banking
- www.waterstone.co.uk – booksellers
- www.blackwell.co.uk – booksellers

Shift in customer behaviour

The internet is forcing both traditional and new players to get away from the narrow, technology-driven approach of telecommunications to the far broader marketing-oriented view of electronic trading and information highways. The internet has seen a phenomenal increase in the number of users. This is changing all the time and students should be reading the press in order to keep up to date.

Worries

However despite some success, a significant number of people have doubts about shopping over the internet. These doubts include:

- Worry about iffy retailers
- Hassle of returning
- Worry about credit cards
- Worry about junk mail
- Want to see and touch what they will buy.

In order to get shoppers to come back for more there needs to be strong brand awareness, brand association and brand interaction. Brand interaction has several components:

- Don't keep your shoppers waiting
- Don't hide the goods
- Build trust
- Don't hide the prices
- Make human contact.

There is a matching of objectives with online strategy and tactics:

- Brand awareness and traffic generation
- On- and offline campaign integration
- Product promotion and customer acquisition
- Build brand in editorial environment
- Promote product through event sponsorship
- Promote product trial and add value via interactivity
- Build qualified prospect database
- Distribute product and services
- Expand into international markets.

Many of the dot.com failures can be attributed to a lack of flexibility within the organization. Blinded by available new technology and the ease with which businesses can be set up, dot.com entrepreneurs often forget some of the marketing basics listed by Ted Johns in his book Perfect Customer Care (Arrow Books).

According to ZDNET (www.zdnet.co.uk) dot.coms around the US and Europe are closing at the rate of one each day. According to analysts Webmergers, the failed companies have lacked consumer focus: 'Most of the companies are not being snapped up by better-established or more traditional competitors because they simply have no assets – such as an audience base, a brand or proprietary technology – worth buying'. In-depth coverage of specific technology company failures and mergers is available from Webmergers (www.webmergers .com) and the less serious, but still informative, www.dotcomfailures.com.

Market segmentation

In assimilating internet survey data, PSI Global determined six core consumer segments and their characteristics. These categories and their breakdown of the total surveyed are:

- *Power users* (13 per cent) spend the most time online; have high trust in technology and the safety of online transacting; use the internet for financial transactions, information and entertainment; and are early adopters.
- *Proficient transactors* (20 per cent) have less experience with PCs and online services; are slightly less affluent than proficient transactors; are interested in or use online banking, bill payment and investing; and have less interest in online shopping than the previous category.
- *Online novices* (10 per cent) are the most marginal online group; have low use or interest in online banking, bill payments, shopping and investing; consist of a mix of professionals and blue-collar workers with moderate-income levels; do not have a lot of experience with PCs or online services; and are not very trusting of technology or online security.

- The *disintereseds* (15 per cent) are similar to the previous category but are much more likely to be professionals; have a higher income and are more experienced with PCs than online novices; have higher interest in online investing than online novices; are concerned about fraud and do not trust current security measures; and have a low use of banking technology such as automated teller machine and debit cards.

- *Entertainment seekers* (25 per cent) use the internet as an entertainment outlet, with low interest in transacting; have an income lower than the US household average; consist of a high number of retired persons, students and blue-collar workers; have a high online time at home but little at work; and have low use and interest in online shopping, banking, bill payments and investing.

Summary

Competing in the information age

As you can see we are in the midst of a revolutionary transformation. The combination of globalization, deregulated markets, markets wired together by a converging information highway is being dominated by new and transformed organizations. Customers expect more and are becoming more demanding. This has increased competitiveness based on innovative customer service, and flexibility providing better quality, cheaper products and quicker services tailored exactly to customer needs.

During the industrial age, from 1858 to about 1975, companies succeeded by how well they could capture the benefits from economies of scale and scope. Technology mattered but it was used in a different way – companies would use technology to offer efficient mass-produced standardized goods. Over the last couple of decades market power moved to channels and now market power has moved to the consumer.

Global information and communication resources are becoming available to everyone at extremely low cost. As big business shrinks, small- and medium-sized businesses grow. A new management challenge requires competency to manage alliances with multiple business partners and tie them together into a business network. Companies can use opportunities created by trade deregulation and the internet to make their companies global operations. Organizations can team up with designers in one country, cheap labour in another and take advantage of low tax duties in different countries.

New capabilities

Organizations need new capabilities to be successful. For example they may include:

- New market segments need to be identified and served effectively and efficiently.

- Products and services must be designed to meet the specific needs of targeted customer segments and designed and customized at low cost with short lead times.

- Organizations need to try integrating production and delivery processes so that operations are triggered by customer orders, and not by production plans that push products and services throughout the value chain.

- Some companies may need to compete globally against the best companies in the world – the competition needs to be redefined.

- As product life cycles shrink, companies who compete in industries with a rapid technological innovation need to be able to anticipate future customer needs and be able to innovate product and service offerings very quickly.

- Information technology and databases and systems must be used as the driving force that links many of these ideas together.

- Organizations need to be looked at as whole systems in an open relationship with the environment.

Gummesson says that in the future, less than 10 per cent of the working population of a mature industrialized nation will work on the shop floor. In order to meet customer needs, the total offer of goods and services must be made. Services are now key aspects of differentiation and have a strategic marketing role. Internally within organizations, services have been broken up so that very often each section works as a profit centre, with many services being contracted out.

The network approach sees industrial marketing, in a network of relationships between people in the network, accentuate:

- The longevity and stability of relationships
- The importance of collaboration as a means to an effective market economy
- The importance of transaction and switching costs
- The active participation of the parties in the relationship
- The importance of power and knowledge and how it is managed
- The importance of technology, procurement and logistics
- The management of trust, risk and uncertainty.

Currently 80 per cent of business on the internet is business to business, it is expected to extend to consumer markets. Marketing needs to extend itself out of the marketing department to managing an organization that has a marketing focus, where people are seen as an asset, and the key ingredient to success is providing superior service.

Further study and examination preparation

Undertake Question 1 from CIM Examination Session December 2000 to be found in the Exam paper appendix.

Undertake Question 3 from CIM Examination Session June 2000 to be found in the Exam paper appendix.

Appendix 1
Curriculum information

Syllabus

Aims and Objectives

- To address the marketing opportunities presented through effective interaction between the organisation and its customers

- To equip students with a conceptual framework which enables them adequately to distinguish between different stakeholder groups across a variety of marketing environments.

- To develop a sophisticated understanding of customer dynamics, in which customer behaviour is viewed as an interactive process influencing product/service innovation.

- To acquaint students with the range of methodologies through which customer dynamics may be investigated, measured, analysed and interpreted.

- To examine the strategic, managerial and operational implications of customer-focused marketing.

- To explore trends in customer behaviour over the foreseeable future, both incremental and transformational.

Learning Outcomes

Students will be able to:

- Describe and interpret the significance of the differences between 'customers', 'users', 'consumers' and 'payers'.

- Critically appraise the relationship between customer dynamics and marketing.

- Evaluate the effectiveness of the marketing/customer interface within specific product sectors, and propose cost-effective performance improvements where appropriate.

- Understand the (psychological, social, cultural and economic) factors influencing customer dynamics in particular marketing scenarios and the impact upon product/service improvement or innovation.

- Analyse key issues in customer dynamics including segmentation, relationship marketing, and the behavioural patterns found within the Decision Making Unit.

- Design and carry out operational investigations into customer dynamics, customer perceptions of product/service performance, and customer satisfaction/delight.

- Develop visionary yet practical strategies for mobilising customer-focused marketing programmes within defined organisational settings.

- Maximise returns from investments in IT and people within the arena of customer-focused marketing and customer service.

- Comprehend the directions for customer dynamics in the foreseeable future and identify related marketing opportunities.

Indicative Content and Weighting

2.1 Overview, concepts and background (10%)

2.1.1 Terminology and Definitions:

- Identifying 'customer', 'user', 'consumer' and 'payer': Interpretations of customer focus in organisations.

- Assumptions, stereotypes and myths about the marketing/customer interface and customer dynamics.

315

2.1.2 The Emergence of Customer Power in the New Competitive Climate:
- Driving forces and organisational responses
- Significance for the marketing/customer interface

2.1.3 Customer-focused marketing in specific economic sectors:
- Customer orientation within major profit-seeking and competitive arenas and within not-for-profit organisations

2.2 Managing the marketing/customer interface (30%)

2.2.1 The Strategic Dimension: Vision and Leadership
- Corporate strategy, culture and structure; the role of top-down leadership, vision, empowerment and related processes.
- Systems for stimulating customer-focused behaviour within and across organisations.
- Customer focus, customer relationships, retention, and customer service as key ingredients in the drive for sustainable competitive advantage.
- The functional/organisational aspects of customer focus: accountability in the fields of customer focus and customer service.
- The strategic rationale for outsourcing: benefits, risks, applications, goal-setting and monitoring.
- Customer-related measures as part of the corporate scorecard

2.2.2 The Managerial Dimension: Mobilising Performances:
- Key factors in maximising the corporate benefits from the organisation/customer interface. Information Technology and people management.
- Motivational issues and job design for front-line customer- facing roles.
- The impact and implications of electronic commerce in the field of customer relationships – the richness/reach dilemma.

2.2.3 Creating Positive Relationships with Customers:
- The features, benefits and costs of relationship marketing.
- Methods of communicating with customers.
- Customer/supplier partnerships and agreements.

2.2.4 Innovation and the Culture of Continuous Improvement:
- Sources of customer-focused innovation; barriers to implementation and how to overcome them.
- The role of information-gathering and analysis in generating customer-focused product/service innovation.

2.3 Customer Dynamics (25%)

2.3.1 The Holistic Perspective of Customer Behaviour:
- Modelling customer dynamics: rationale, objectives, applications, limitations.
- Individuals, groups, and organisations as customers.
- Innovation and conservatism in customer behaviour: why new products/services succeed or fail.
- Customer expectations and perceptions: dissatisfaction, satisfaction and delight.

2.3.2 Classifying Customers for Competitive Advantage
- Customer segmentation: rationale, objectives; features of effective customer segments.
- Segmentation systems for individual consumers, customer groups and organisations.
- New approaches to classifying customers.

.3.3 The Individual as Customer:
- Attitudes and behaviour: relevance to the marketing/ customer interface.
- Factors influencing the individual's behaviour as a customer.
- Personality profiling for individual customers.

2.3.4 The Group as Customer:

- Power, influence and authority within the primary group: targeting the decision-making unit (DMU).
- Secondary groups: their significance for customer behaviour and implications for national, international and global marketing.

2.3.5 The Organisation as Customer:

- Special features of business-to-business transactions and related customer dynamics.
- The organisational DMU: characteristics, roles, decision processes and marketing implications.

2.4 Investigating Customer Dynamics (20%)

2.4.1 Basic Principles

- Systematic techniques for investigating customer dynamics.
- The creation of meaningful populations (based on market segments).

2.4.2 Quantitative Methodologies for Investigating Customer Dynamics:

- Questionnaires, surveys, interviews and other primary methods of data/information collection.

2.4.3 Qualitative Methodologies for Investigating Customer Dynamics:

- Projective techniques: features, benefits, risks and applications.
- Focus groups: features, benefits, risks and applications.

2.4.4 Secondary Information Sources

- Sources of secondary data: government statistics, market research agencies, the media, etc.

2.5 Customer Dynamics and the Future (15%)

2.5.1 Trends in Customer Behaviour and Expectations:

- Enhancement of customer expectations and organisational service standards and performance delivery.
- Increasing opportunities for customer complaints and legal enhancements to consumer power.
- Customer concerns about ecological, environmental and ethical issues.
- Emergent customer attitudes and their impact on (re)purchasing behaviour.
- Future patterns for segmentation: customised products and services, demographic and social trends, etc.

2.5.2 Market Trends with Customer-facing Implications:

- The global marketplace and global products and services
- Customer service as a sustainable competitive advantage
- The decline of manufacturing and the emergence of new service-sector industries.
- The decline of manufacturing and the emergence of new service-sector industries.

2.5.3 The Marketing Implications of E-Commerce:

- Emergent business models in the age of e-commerce
- Trends in e-commerce with special reference to business to consumer, business to business, utilities and public sector applications.
- Strategic, organisational and managerial issues associated with the achievement of competitive advantage in an e-commerce market place.
- Internet marketing and the significance of e-commerce for supplier/customer relationships.

Reading list

- J Frazer-Robinson, *It's all about Customers (Paperback version of J Frazer Robinson Customer Driven Marketing)*, Kogan Page, 1999, essential reading
- A Payne, M Christopher, M Clark, H Peck, *Relationship Marketing for Competitive Advantage*, Butterworth-Heinemann, 1998, essential reading
- E Gummesson, *Total Relationship Marketing*, CIM/Butterworth-Heinemann, 1999, essential reading
- R Phipps, C Simmons, *The Marketing Customer Interface*, CIM/Butterworth-Heinemann, 2001, coursebook
- *The Marketing Customer Interface*, BPP, 2000, Study Text
- JN Sheth, B Mittal, BI Newman, *Customer Behaviour: A Managerial Perspective*, Harcourt Brace, 1998, additional reading/resources
- C Daffy, *Once a customer always a customer*, Oak Tree Press, 1999, additional reading/resources
- C Wilson, *Profitable Customers (2nd Edition)*, Kogan Page, 1998, additional reading/resources
- T Johns, *Perfect Customer*, Random House, 1999, additional reading/resources
- P Weinzimer, *Getting it right – Creating Customer Value for Market Leadership*, Wiley, 1998, additional reading/resources
- D Peppers, M Rogers, *The One to One Manager*, Capstone, 2000, additional reading/resources
- P Gamble, M Stone, N Woodcock, *Up Close and Personal?*, Kogan Page, 1999, additional reading/resources
- S Godin, *Permission Marketing*, Simon & Schuster, 1999, additional reading/resources
- M McDonald, B Rogers, D Woodburn, *Key Customers*, CIM/Butterworth-Heinemann, 2000, additional reading/resources
- M Stone, N Woodcock, L Machtynger, *Customer Relationship Marketing*, Kogan Page, 2000, additional reading/resources
- *The Marketing Customer Interface Practice & Revision Kits*, BPP, 2000,
- *Learning Cassettes*, BPP, 2000, additional reading/resources

Preparing for your examination

You are now nearing the final phase of your studies and it is time to start the hard work of exam preparation.

During your period of study you have been used to absorbing massive loads of information, trying to understand and apply aspects of knowledge that are very new to you, while information provided may be more familiar. You may even have undertaken many of the activities that are positioned frequently throughout your text, which have enabled you to apply your learning in practical situations. Whatever the position is of your knowledge and understanding and level of knowledge application, do not allow yourself to fall into the trap of thinking you know enough, you understand enough or even worse, thinking you can wing in on the day.

Never underestimate the pressure of the CIM examination, getting into the examination hall, and wishing it had all been different, that indeed you had revised and prepared for this big moment, where all of a sudden the Senior Examiner becomes an unrelenting question master!

The whole point of preparing this unit for you is to ensure that you never take the examination for granted, and that you do not go into the exam completely unprepared for what you find what might come your way for three hours at a time.

One thing for sure, is that there is no quick fix, no easy route, no waving a magic wand and finding you know it all.

Whether you have studied alone, in a CIM study centre, or through distance learning, you now need to ensure that this final phase of your learning process is tightly managed, highly structured and objective.

As a candidate in the examination, your role will be to convince the Senior Examiner for this subject that you have credibility. You need to demonstrate to the examiner that you can be trusted to undertake a range of challenges in the context of marketing, that you are able to capitalize on opportunities and manage your way through threats.

You should prove to the Senior Examiner, that you able to apply knowledge, make decisions, respond to situations and solve problems. The list of solutions you will need to provide to prove your credibility could be endless.

Very shortly we are going to look at a range of particular revision and exam preparation techniques, methods, time management issues and encourage you towards developing and implementing your own revision plan, but before that, lets look a little bit a the role of the Senior Examiner.

A bit about the Senior Examiners!

You might be quite shocked to read this, or even find it hard to understand, but while it might appear that the examiners are 'relentless question masters', but they actually you to be able to answer the questions and pass the exams. In fact they would derive no satisfaction or benefits from failing candidates, quite the contrary, they develop the syllabus and exam papers in order that you can learn and utilize that learning effectively in order to pass your examinations. Many of the examiners have said in the past that it is indeed psychologically more difficult to fail students than pass them.

Many of the hints and tips you find within this unit have been suggested by the Senior Examiners and authors of the coursebook series, therefore you should consider them carefully and resolve to undertake as many of the elements suggested where possible.

The Chartered Institute of Marketing has a range of processes and systems in place within the Examinations Division to help to ensure that fairness and consistency prevail across the team of examiners, and to ensure that the academic and vocational standards that are set and defined are indeed maintained. In doing this, CIM ensures that those who gain the CIM Certificate, Advanced Certificate and Postgraduate Diploma, are worthy of the qualification and perceived as such in the view of employers, actual and potential.

Part of what you will need to do within the examination is be 'examiner friendly' and you will need to ensure that they get what they ask for, doing this will make life easier for you and for them.

Hints and tips for 'examiner friendly' actions are as follows:

- Show them that you understand the basis of the question, by answering precisely the question asked, and not including just about everything you can remember about the subject area.
- Read their needs – how many points is the question asking you to address?
- Is the question asking you to take on a role? If so, take on the role and answer the question in respect of the role. If you are asked to be a Marketing Manager, then respond in that way. For example, you could be positioned as follows:

  'You are working as a Marketing Assistant at Nike UK' or 'You are a Marketing Manager for an Engineering Company' or 'As Marketing Manager write a report to the Managing Partner'.

  These are actually taken from questions in past papers, so ensure you take on board role-play requirements.

- Deliver the answer in the format requested. If the examiner asks for a memo, then provide a memo, likewise if the examiner asks for a report, then provide a report. If you do not do this, in some instances you will fail to gain the necessary marks required to pass.
- Take a business-like approach to your answers. This enhances your credibility. Badly-ordered work, untidy work, lack of structure, headings and subheadings can be offputting. This would be unacceptable in work, likewise it would be unacceptable in the eyes of the Senior Examiners and their marking teams.
- Ensure the examiner has something to mark, give them substance, relevance, definitions, illustration and demonstration of your knowledge and understanding of the subject area.
- See the examiner as your potential employer, or ultimate consumer/customer. The whole purpose and culture of marketing is about meeting customers' needs. Try doing this, it works wonders.
- Provide a strong sense of enthusiasm and professionalism in your answers, support them with relevant up-to-date examples and apply them where appropriate.
- Try to differentiate your exam paper, make it stand out in the crowd.

All of these points might seem quite logical to you, but often in the panic of the examination they 'go out of the window', indeed out of our minds, therefore it is beneficial to remind ourselves of the importance of the examiner. They are the 'ultimate customer' – and we all know customers hate to be disappointed.

As we move on some of these points will be revisited, and developed further.

About the examination

In all examinations, with the exception of Marketing in Practice at Certificate Level and Analysis and Decision at Diploma level, the paper is divided into two parts.

- Part A – the mini-case study = 40% of the marks
- Part B – Option choice questions – choice of three questions from seven = 60% of the marks.

Let's look at the basis of each element.

The mini-case study

This is based on a mini-case or scenario with one question possibly subdivided into between two and four points, but totalling 40 per cent overall.

In essence, you, the candidate, are placed in a problem-solving role through the medium of a short scenario. On occasions, the scenario may consist of an article from a journal in relation to a well-known organization, for example in the past, Interflora, EasyJet, Philips, among others, have been used as the basis of the mini-case. Alternatively they will be based upon a fictional company, which the examiner has prepared in order that the right balance of knowledge; understanding, applications and skills are used.

Look at the examination papers at the end of this book and see the mini-case.

Approaches to the mini-case study

When undertaking the mini-case study there are a number of key areas you should consider.

Structure/content

The mini-case that you will be presented with will vary slightly from paper to paper and of course from one examination to the next. Normally the scenario presented will be between 400-500 words long and sometimes will centre on a particular organization and its problems or may even specifically relate to a particular industry.

The length of the mini-case study means that usually only a brief outline is provided of the situation and the organization and its marketing problems, and you must therefore learn to cope with analysis information and preparing your answer on the basis of very limited amounts of information.

Time management

Your paper is designed in order that you are assessed over a three-hour period. With 40 per cent of the marks being allocated to the mini-case, it means that you should dedicate somewhere around 70-75 minutes of your time to write up the answer, on this mini-case, plus allowing yourself approximately 20 minutes reading and analysis time. This takes you to around 95 minutes, which is almost half of your time in the exam room.

Do not forget that while there is only one question within the mini-case it can have a number of components. You must answer all the components in that question, which is where the balance of times comes in to play.

Knowledge/skills tested

Throughout all the CIM papers, your knowledge, skills and ability to apply those skills will be tested. However, the mini-cases are used particularly to test application, i.e. your ability to take you knowledge and apply it in a structured way to a given scenario. The examiners will be looking at your decision-making ability, your analytical and communication skills and depending on the level, your ability as a manager to solve particular marketing problems.

When the examiner is marking your paper, he/she will be looking to see how you really differentiate yourself, looking at your own individual 'unique selling points' and to see if you can personally apply the knowledge or whether you are only able to repeat the textbook materials.

Format of answers

On many occasions, and within all examinations, you will most likely be given a particular communication method to use. If this is the case please ensure that you adhere to the requirements of the examiner. This is all part of meeting customer needs.

The likely communication tools you will be expected to use are as follows:

- A memorandum
- A memorandum/report
- A report
- Briefing notes
- Presentation
- Press release
- Advertisement
- Plan

Make sure that you familiarize yourself with these particular communication tools and practise using them to ensure that on the day you will be able to respond confidently to the communication requests of the examiner. You may look back at the Customer Communications Text at Certificate level to familiarize yourself with the potential requirements of these methods.

By the same token, while communication methods are important, so is the meeting the specific requirements of the question. **Note the following carefully.**

- **Identify** – select key issues, point out key learning points, establish clearly what the examiner expects you to identify

- **Illustrate** – this means the examiner expects you to provide examples, scenarios, and key concepts that illustrate your learning.

- **Compare and contrast** – look at the range of similarities between the two situations, contexts or organizations. Then compare them, i.e. ascertain and list how activities, features, etc. agree or disagree. Contrasting means highlighting the differences between the two.

- **Discuss** – questions that have 'discuss' in them offer a tremendous opportunity for you to debate, argue, justify your approach or understanding of the subject area- *caution* it is not an opportunity to waffle.

- **Briefly explain** – This means being succinct, structured and concise in your explanation, within the answer. Make your points clear and transparent and relevant.

- **State** – present in a clear, brief format

- **Interpret** – expound the meaning of, make clear and explicit what it is you see and understand within the data provided

- **Outline** – provide the examiner with the main concepts and features being asked for and avoid minor technical details. A structure will be critical here; or else you could find it difficult to contain your answer.

- **Relate** – show how different aspects of the syllabus connect together.

- **Evaluate** – This means review and reflect upon an area of the syllabus, a particular practice, an article, etc, and consider its overall worth in respect of its use as a tool or a model and its overall effectiveness in the role it plays.

Your approach to mini-cases

There is no one right way to approach and tackle a mini-case study, indeed it will be down to each individual to use their own creative minds and approaches to the tasks which are presented. What you will have to do is use your initiative and discretion about how to best approach the mini-case. However having said this, there are some basic steps you can take.

- Ensure that you read through the case study at least twice before making any judgements, starting to analyse the information provided, or indeed writing the answers.

- On the third occasion read through the mini-case and, using a highlighter, start marking the essential and relevant information critical to the content and context. Then turn your attention to the question again, this time reading slowly and to carefully assess what it is you are expected to do. Note any instructions that the examiner gives you, and then start to plan how you might answer the question. Whatever the question ensure there is a structure: a beginning, structured central part of the answer and finally, always closing with a conclusion.

- Always keep in mind the specifics of the case and the role which you might be performing, and keep these contexts continually in mind.

- Because there is limited materials available, you will sometimes need to make assumptions. Don't be afraid to do this, it will show initiative on your part. Assumptions are an important part of dealing with case studies and it can help you to be quite creative with your answer. However, if you do use assumptions, please explain the basis of them within your answer so that the examiner understands the nature of them, and why you have arrived at your particular outcome. **Always ensure that those assumptions are realistic.**

- Now you are approaching the stage where it is time to answer the question, tackling the problems, making decisions and recommendations on the case scenario set before you. As mentioned previously, these will often be best set out in a report or memo type format, particular if the examiner does not specify a communication method.

- Ensure that your writing is succinct, avoids waffle and responds directly to the questions asked.

Part B

Again, with the exception of the Analysis and Decision case study, each Part B is comprised of six or seven, more traditional questions, each worth 20 per cent. You will be expected to choose three of those questions, to make up the remainder of the 100 per cent of available marks.

Realistically, the same principles apply for these questions, as in the case study. Communication formats, reading through the questions, structure, role-play, context, etc. everything is the same.

Part B will cover a number of broader issues from within the syllabus and will be taken from any element of it, the examiner makes the choice, and no prior direction is given to students or tutors on what that might be.

As regards time management in this area, you should have approximately one and a half hours left, i.e. 90 minutes. If you do have, this means you should give yourself seven minutes to read the question and plan out your answers, with 22 minutes to write and review what you have put within your answer.

Keep practising – use a cooker timer, alarm clock or mobile phone alarm as your timer and work hard at answering questions within the timeframe given.

Specimen examination papers and answers

To help you prepare and understand the nature of the paper, you will find that the last two CIM examination papers and specimen answers are included at the end of this unit. During your study, the author of your book may have on occasions asked you to refer to these papers and answer the questions, providing you with a specimen answer for guidance. Please utilize every opportunity to undertake and meet their requirements.

These are vital tools to your learning. The specimen answers are not always perfect, as they are answers written by students and annotated by the Senior Examiners, but they will give you a good indication of the approaches you could take, and the examiners provide annotation to suggest how these answers might be improved in the future. Please use them. You can also access this type of information through the Virtual Institute on the CIM web site using your student registration number as an access code.

Other sources of information to support your learning through the Virtual Institute are 'Hot Topics'. These give you scope to undertake a range of associated activities related to the syllabus, and study areas, but will also be very useful to you when you are revising.

Key elements of learning

According to one Senior Examiner, there are three elements involve in preparing for your examination.

- Learning
- Memory
- Revision

We are going to look at what the Senior Examiner suggests, by examining each point in turn.

Learning

Quite often, as students, we can find it difficult to learn. We passively read books, look at some of the materials, perhaps revise a little and regurgitate it in the examination. In the main this is rather an unsatisfactory method of learning. It is meaningless, useless and ultimately leaves us mindless of all that we could have learned had we applied ourselves in our studies.

For learning to be truly effective it must be active and applied. You must involve yourself in the learning process by thinking about what you have read, testing it against your experience by reflecting on how you use particular aspects of marketing, and how you could perhaps improve your own performance by implementing particular aspects of your learning into your everyday life. The old adage goes something like 'learning by doing'. If you do this, you will find that passive learning does not have a place in your study life.

Below are some suggestions that have been prepared to assist you with the learning pathway throughout your revision.

- Always make your own notes, in words you understand and ensure that you combine all the sources of information and activities within them.
- Always try to relate your learning back to your own organization
- Make sure you define key terms concisely, wherever possible

- Do not try to memorize your ideas, but work on the basis of understanding and most important, applying them.
- Think about the relevant and topical questions that might be set – use the questions and answers at the back of each of your coursebooks to identify typical questions that might be asked in the future.
- Attempt all of the questions within each of your coursebooks since these are vital tests of your active learning and understanding.

Memory

If you are prepared to undertake an active learning programme then your knowledge will very probably be considerably enhanced, as understanding and application of knowledge does tend to stay in your 'long-term' memory. It is likely that passive learning will only stay in your 'short-term' memory.

Do not try to memorize parrot fashion, it is not helpful and even more important, examiners are experienced in identifying various memorizing techniques and therefore, will identify them as such.

Having said this, it is quite useful to memorize various acronyms such as SWOT, PEST, PESTLE, STEEPLE, or indeed various models such as Ansoff, GE Matrix, Shell Directional, etc., as in some of the questions you may be required to use illustrations of these to assist your answer.

Revision

The third and final stage to consider is 'revision', which is what we are now going to concentrate on.

Revision should be an ongoing process rather than a panic measure that you decide to undertake just before the examination. You should be preparing notes throughout your course, with the view to using them as part of your revision process. Therefore ensure that your notes are sufficiently comprehensive that you can reuse them successfully.

For each concept you learn about, you should identify, through your reading and your own personal experience at least two or three examples that you could use; this then gives you some scope to broaden your perspective during the examination. It will of course, help gain you some brownie points with the examiners.

Knowledge is not something you will gain overnight, as we saw earlier, it is not a quick fix; it involves a process of learning that enables you to lay solid foundations upon which to build your long-term understanding and application. This will benefit you significantly in the future, not just in the examination.

You should ensure that you do the following prior to the real intensive revision process commencing.

- Ensure that you keep your study file well organized, updated and full of newspaper and journal cuttings that may assist you formulate examples in your mind for use during the examination.
- Practise defining key terms and acronyms from memory
- Prepare topic outlines and essay answer plans
- Read your concentrated notes the night before the examination.

Revision planning

You are now on a critical path, hopefully not too critical at this time, with somewhere in the region of between four and six weeks to go to the examination. Hopefully the following hints and tips will help you plan out your studies.

- You will, as already explained, need to ensure that you are very organized and therefore before doing anything else, put your files, examples, reading material in good order, so that you are able to work with them in the future and of course, make sense of them.
- Ensure that you have a quiet area within which to work. It is very easy to get distracted when preparing for the examination.
- Give up your social life for a short period of time, as the saying goes 'no pain – no gain'.
- Take out your file along with your syllabus and make a list of key topic areas that you have studied and which you now need to revise. You could use the basis of this book to do that, by taking each unit a step at a time.

- Plan your time carefully. Ideally you should start you revision at least six weeks prior to the exam, so therefore work out how many spare hours you could give to the revision process and then start to allocate time in your diary, and do not double-book with anything else.

- Looking at each of the subject areas in turn, identify which are your strengths and which are your weaknesses. Which areas have you really grasped and understood, and what are the areas that you have really struggled with. Split you page in two and make a list on each side of the page. For example:

Planning and control

Strengths	Weaknesses
Audit – PEST, SWOT, Models	Ratio analysis
Portfolio analysis	Market sensing
	Productivity analysis
	Trend extrapolation
	Forecasting

- However many weeks you have left, break down your list again and divide the points of weaknesses, giving priority in the first instance to your weakest areas and even prioritizing them by giving them a number. This will enable you to master the more difficult areas. Up to 60 per cent of your revision time should be given over to that, as you may find you have to undertake a range of additional reading and also potentially gaining tutor support, if you are studying at a CIM Accredited Study Centre.

- The remaining time should be spent reinforcing your knowledge and understanding of the stronger areas, spending time testing yourself on how much you really know.

- Should you be taking two examinations or more at any one time, then the breakdown of your time and managing of your time will be critical.

- Taking a subject at a time, work through your notes and starts breaking them down in to subsections of learning, and ultimately down into key learning points, items that you can refer to time and time again, that are meaningful and that your mind will absorb. You yourself will know how you best remember key points. Some people try to develop acronyms, or flowcharts or matrices, mind maps, fishbone diagrams, etc. or various connection diagrams that help them recall certain aspects of models. You could also develop processes with that enable you remember approaches to various options.

   (But remember what we said earlier about regurgitating stuff, parrot fashion.)

You could use the type of bomb-burst in Figure A2.1 as a way of remembering how the key components of STEEPLE break down in your learning process.

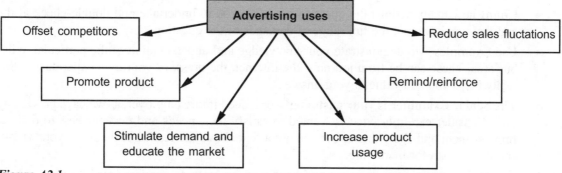

Figure A2.1

Figure A2.1 is just a brief example of how you could use a flow chart diagram which, in this case, highlights the uses of advertising. It could be a very helpful approach to memorizing key elements of learning.

- Eventually you should reduce your key learning to bullet points, from which you can revise. For example: imagine you were looking at the key concepts of Time Management – you could eventually break them down into a bullet list which contains the following key points in relation to 'Effective Prioritization:'

   1. Organize
   2. Take time

3. Delegate
4. Review

Each of these headings would then remind you that you need to discuss elements associated with the subject area.

- You should avoid getting involved in reading too many textbooks at this stage, as you may start to find that you are getting a little confused overall.

- Now refer to the end of this book and look at some of the exam questions listed, and start to observe closely the various roles and tasks they expect you to undertake, but more importantly the context in which they are set.

- Without exception, find an associated examination question for the areas that you have studied and revised, and undertake it, more than once if necessary.

- Without referring to notes or books, see if you can draft a answer plan with the key concepts, knowledge, models, information, that are needed for you to successfully complete this answer and list them. Then refer to the specimen answer to see how close you are to the actual outline presented. Planning your answer, and ensuring that key components are included, and that the question has a meaningful structure is one of the most beneficial activities that you can undertake.

- Having done this, now write the answer out in full, time constrained and in hand written not with the use of IT. At this stage, you are still expected to be the scribe for the examination and present your hand-written work. Many of use find this increasingly difficult as we spend more and more time using our computers to present information. Spidery handwriting is often offputting to the examiner.

When you are ready to write your answer in full – ensure you do the following.

- **Identify and use the communication method** requested by the examiner

- **Always have three key parts to the paper** – an introduction, middle section where you will develop your answer in full, and finally a conclusion. Where appropriate ensure that you have an introduction, main section, summary/conclusion and if requested or helpful – recommendations.

- **Never forget to answer your question in the context or role set.** If you answer the question void of either of these, then you will fail to gain marks.

- **Always comply with the nature and terms of the question**

- **White Space** do not overcrowd your page – make sure there is white space. There is always plenty of paper available for you to use. Make sure you leave space between paragraphs, and that your sentences do not merge into one blur.

- **Count** how many actions the question is asking you to undertake and double-check at the end that you have met the full range of demands of the question.

- **Use Examples** – to demonstrate your knowledge and understanding of the particular syllabus area. These can be from journals, the Internet, the press, or your own experience – this really helps you add value to your answer.

- **The Senior Examiner is your customer** – or indeed future employer, as we have previously said. Consider carefully what is wanted to satisfy their needs and do your best to deliver. Impress them and show them how you are a 'cut above the rest'. Let them see your vigour and enthusiasm for marketing.

- **Use the specimen exam papers and specimen answers** to support your learning and see how you could actually improve upon them.

Practical actions

The critical path is becoming even more critical now as the exam looms. The following are vital points.

- Have you registered with CIM?

- Do you know where you are taking you examination – CIM should let you know approximately one month in advance.

- Do you know where your examination centre is? If not find out, take a drive, time it – whatever you do don't be late!
- Make sure you have all the tools of the examination with you. A dictionary, calculator, pens, pencils, ruler, etc. Try not to use multiple shades of pens, but at the same time make your work look professional. *Avoid using red and green as these are the colours that will be used for marking.*

Summary

Many of the hints and tips here are very generic and will work across most of the CIM. However we have tried to select those that are most helpful, in order that you take a sensible planned approach to your study and revision.

The key to your success is being prepared to give it the time and effort required, planning your revision, and equally important, planning and answering your questions in a way that will ensure that you pass your examination on the day.

The hints and tips presented are there to guide you from a practical perspective, the syllabus content guidance and developments associated to your learning will become clear to you while you work through this coursebook. Each of the authors have given subject specific guidance on the approach to the examination and how to ensure that you meet the content requirements of the question, in addition to the structuring issues we have been discussing throughout this unit.

Each of the authors and Senior Examiners will guide you on their preferred approach to questions and answers as they go. Therefore where you are presented with an opportunity to be involved in some activity or exam question either during or at the end of your study units, do take it, as it helps you learn in an applied way, but also prepares you for the examination.

Finally as a reminder

- Ensure you make the most of your learning process throughout
- Keep structured and orderly notes from which to revise
- Plan your revision – don't let it just happen
- Provide examples to enhance your answers
- Practise your writing skills in order that you present your work well and your writing is readable
- Take as many opportunities as possible to test your knowledge and measure your progress
- Plan and structure your answers
- Always take on the role and context of the question and answer in that context
- Adhere to the communication method selected by the examiner
- Always do as the question ask you
- **Do not leave it until the last minute!**

The writers and editorial team at Butterworth-Heinemann would like to take this opportunity to wish you every continuing success as you endeavour to study, revise and pass your examinations.

Introduction from the Senior Examiner

These Specimen Answers represent a combination of material prepared by the Senior Examiner and answers generated by candidates – answers which earned above-average marks and which therefore represent material of a benchmarking standard to which future students should aspire. There are a few considerations which should be strongly emphasized, however, before we go any further.

1. None of the Specimen Answers presented here are intended to be regarded as the definitive treatment for any given question. In a field that presents opportunities for qualitative judgements, there is no such thing as a truly definitive answer. On the other hand, there are answers that contain a positive blend of the five competencies which the examination seeks to assess, and which therefore qualify for creditable evaluations on the grounds that their authors clearly possess the attributes necessary for professional achievement in the marketing arena.

2. Similarly, because the field embraced by The Marketing Customer Interface is itself subject to change and progress, knowledge which was regarded as definitive at one period of time may be supplemented or even replaced altogether, as new thinking, experience and research refine what has gone before. At one time it was widely accepted that 'the customer is king', but organizations these days are more likely to accept the fact that some customers are more important than others, and some could profitably be discarded altogether; at one time Total Quality Management was seen as the principal route to competitive advantage, but few in the modern world subscribe unequivocally to that position.

3. Not all the Specimen Answers in this document are structured in conformity with the normal canons of business communication. Instead, the Answers contain key points indicating the issues which candidates should have raised, with elegance of style and presentation a secondary consideration. At the same time, it is important for future candidates to recognize that the appropriate 'packaging' of answers is a significant competency and can result in a sometimes crucial erosion of marks if ignored.

Previous reports by the Senior Examiner have highlighted and clarified the five competencies which the examination seeks to assess:

1. **Breadth of familiarity with the subject matter** – across the range of questions principally addressed in Part B. The Senior Examiner considers it entirely legitimate for part of the examination to focus on topics which have become important themes (such as electronic commerce), even though they may not be mentioned specifically in the Indicative Content.

2. **Depth of comprehension and understanding** – conventionally expressed by a willingness to challenge some of the conventional wisdom which surrounds the subject, to cite relevant examples of The Marketing Customer Interface in action, to draw upon personal experiences, and to reinforce empirical statements with evidential references to appropriate literature, textbooks, articles, Internet sources and other publications.

3. **Demonstration of a businesslike perspective** – through recognition of the fact that marketing initiatives have to be justified against resource/benefit criteria. Concern for customer satisfaction, therefore, derives from the belief that if customers are very satisfied they will re-purchase, and if they re-purchase then the organization becomes more profitable; accordingly, customer satisfaction is not an end in itself.

4. **Application capability** – reflected in treatments of the case study but also in responses to the more 'practical' or problem solving dimensions of many questions in Part B.

5. **Packaging skills** – represented by the readiness to adhere to the presentational obligations spelled out in many questions to produce answers in the form of a report, a memorandum, or a discussion document.

Ted Johns, Senior Examiner

Exam material

The Walters Chemical Company

Cleaning and rust preventative chemical compounds are the major products of the Walters Chemical Company, which has over 2,000 different formulations to meet all the expectations demanded by its customers (engineering companies and car manufacturers).

Frequently a Walters Sales Representative will be called in by a customer to resolve technical problems being experienced with the application of one of the Walters compounds. Although well trained, the Sales Representative commonly does not know the answer and telephones his Head Office for professional help. Calls of this nature are referred to the Technical Services Department.

Normally the trouble must be resolved within hours, if possible, in order to keep production moving in the customer's factory. Quick and responsive service is therefore important. Sometimes the Technical Services Department can give immediate help but more commonly it has to investigate further, thus necessitating a delay coupled with a promise to phone back once it is in a position to offer well-informed advice.

The Sales Representatives often complain that Technical Services do not fulfil their telephone promises. Follow-up calls from the Representatives lead to statements by Technical Services that there is no record of the previous request, or that additional information to be supplied by the customer has not yet been received, or that the problem is being worked on without the solution having yet been found.

The Technical Services Manager has devised a three-copy form which each Sales Representative is supposed to complete whenever they have a customer problem requiring specialized assistance. However, he claims that the Representatives do not use the form if they can avoid it: 'They would rather telephone, tell you about the problem and, if there is any trouble later, deny that they didn't supply you with all the facts. They then blame Technical Services for not doing its job. And every sales representative seems to think that his requests are the only ones that matter.'

The Sales Representatives, for their part, believe that they do give complete information to Technical Services, but that the department only hears what it wants to hear. The view of the Sales Representatives is that 'Filling out forms is fine for possible new customers, but for existing customers who run into trouble, we have to know the answer straight away. And Technical Services must have a poor filing system: they can never find any evidence of our previous calls. The only way to get them to do anything is to shout and make a nuisance of yourself.'

PART A

Question 1

Your answer should be written in the form of a report to the Chief Executive of the Walters Chemical Company. It is permissible to make assumptions by adding to the case details given above, provided that the essence of the case study is neither changed nor undermined in any way by what is added.

a) It appears that there is considerable hostility between the Sales function and the Technical Services Department. Suggest causes for the conflict and propose appropriate remedies.

(10 marks)

b) The interdepartmental conflict seems to be one factor which prevents the people in Technical Services from being sufficiently customer focused. What can be done to promote more customer-facing attitudes and behaviour amongst this group?

(10 marks)

c) The communication processes between the Walters Chemical Company and its customers are not efficient nor effective. How could they be improved?

(10 marks)

d) So far the Company has not created or applied any mechanisms for systematically soliciting customer feedback. Outline and justify the methods which you think they should use.

(10 marks)

(40 marks in total)

Marking scheme

It was stressed on the examination paper that answers had to be presented in the form of a report to the Chief Executive of the Walters Company. Candidates neglecting this instruction immediately deprived themselves of valuable marks.

The case study itself was deliberately built around a relatively old-fashioned enterprise, thus presenting able students with the opportunity to introduce new forms of electronic communication to facilitate interaction within the company and also between the company and its customers.

Within an overall framework of 40 marks for Part A as a whole, 10 marks were available for each of the four parts of the 'report'. Within those 10 marks, up to 2 marks were awarded for answers that complied in general with the normal rules of business report production.

Answer – Question 1a

Report

To: The Chief Executive, Walters Chemical Company

From: Marketing Director

Date: 12th June, 2000

Subject: Report on the Customer Interface

We spoke recently about the problem of hostility between the Sales Department and Technical Services. This report begins by looking at the causes of the apparent gulf between these two functions, and then suggests some remedies.

Internal conflict between highly motivated teams can and does happen in business, but it is costly and damaging, especially if it means that customers become the victims in a war which strictly speaking is nothing to do with them. The present difficulties seem to me to stem from a misunderstanding between Sales and Technical Services as to each other's role in servicing customers, and an overall lack of customer focus.

Specifically, the Sales Department alleges that Technical Services:

- Do not keep promises;
- Do not maintain full or easily accessible records;
- Are needlessly bureaucratic; and
- Do not listen to what is said to them.

Technical Services, for their part, counter that the Sales Department:

- Ignore agreed procedures;
- Do not consider the difficulties faced by staff in Technical Services.

There are various options open to us in resolving these problems, although some have budgetary (cost) implications.

First, we need to change our system for recording and handling customer problems. It is no longer reasonable to expect sales staff to complete a three-copy form and send it to Technical Services before a query can be dealt with. Frankly, this system does not benefit Sales or customers, but seems designed to narrow the channel through which queries flow, in the possible hope that this will lessen (or at least control) the workload of those in Technical Services. In other words, the three-copy form is a deterrent to effective problem solving rather than a contribution to it.

Sales staff should be encouraged to phone in directly with technical support questions. However, we must invest in providing Technical Services staff with the software to allow them:

- To log incoming calls systematically;
- To track the status of calls;
- To note when calls and queries have been resolved; and
- To remind technical staff when a query has been unresolved for too long.

Coupled with this, we must set defined targets for responding to technical complaints and queries. Saying that calls must be resolved 'within hours' is too vague. We need to specify how long a customer can expect to wait, and if we can't answer a question within the target time, then we must notify the customer of the delay and give them a firm promise concerning the next steps.

To speed up technical query resolution, we may need to look at expanding or developing databases of technical information, including perhaps a 'what has worked before' browser mechanism on our web site. I can let you have cost proposals for this if you accept the principle.

At a different level, we should instigate regular 'shadowing' of sales staff by technical staff and vice versa, in order to break down some of the hostile stereotypes that each has of the other. This will also allow each to gain a closer (plus, hopefully, a more sympathetic) perception of the other's difficulties, pressures and constraints.

Furthermore, we should consider allowing customers direct access to technical support staff by phone or email (once the latter have the improved IT support described above), so that salespeople can devote more of their time to what they should properly be doing.

Finally, we need to encourage a greater culture of customer awareness through a planned programme of internal marketing.

Senior Examiner's Comments

1a. Inter-departmental Hostility

The question invited clarification about the causes for conflict between Sales and Technical Services (5 marks), plus some appropriate remedies (5 marks). Factors to be mentioned should have included the incidence of stereotyping, the absence of any direct contact with the 'hated' entity, selective perception, and the negative impact of group cohesion. Possible remedies might have embraced the creation of joint problem solving teams, cross-fertilization and rotational assignments, deliberate exercises in perception sharing as part of a collaborative team-building exercise, and some training.

Answer – Question 1b

Promotion of Customer-facing Attitudes

Technical Services staff perform what is essentially a 'backroom' operation as presently constituted, and are insulated from customer contact in a way that sales staff are not. Shadowing salespeople on customer visits may help them to shed some of their insularity, but we can go further.

We can identify customers who have experienced regular problems requiring technical support and negotiate secondments from Technical Services to those customer organizations for a set period (generally 2-3 months). This will benefit our customers because they won't have to pay anything for the service, it will benefit our Technical Services function for obvious reasons, and most of all it will benefit our company because of the way in which it will tie our customers more closely to us.

Internal marketing efforts need to be given greater impetus and perhaps focused more on technical support staff and other non-customer facing people. We need to move to a very simple structure that allows no one at Walters Chemicals to forget that they exist either to serve customers or support those who do.

Using all the available media for internal communications – the Intranet, staff newsletter, briefing systems, the CEO's annual address to employees, the company's annual report, screensavers, noticeboards, mouse mats, telephone message pads and so forth – we must concentrate attention on the significance of the customer at all times. This will require positive role modelling from the top, and the enthusiastic endorsement of the senior executive(s) responsible for Technical Services.

It would help, too, if the HR infrastructure reinforced our customer service messages. For instance, the appraisal (performance review) system should specifically include customer-related competencies. As at SmithKline Beecham, individuals should be required to secure 'customer' feedback prior to appraisal from five individuals who qualify as their customers (whether internal or not). The performance management system should acknowledge customer service initiatives and achievements. We could create a non-pecuniary recognition and awards process targeted not only to Technical Services but also to other parts of the organization that do not deal directly with customers. Finally, our selection criteria should embrace the search for appropriate, customer-friendly attitudes.

General ideas for promoting customer-facing attitudes and behaviour could encompass 'adopt a customer' systems (in which teams visit customers in order to promote closer personal commitment), reward and celebrate initiatives, the explicit recruitment of customer-friendly people, an emphasis on the internal customer, incorporation of customer competencies into the performance review process, and so on.

Answer – Question 1c

Quality communication with our customers is essential to our business, as has already been suggested. We know that retaining our existing customers, encouraging their loyalty (through voluntary repurchasing and referral), and making them want to spend more with us in preference to other suppliers, are all key to our increased profitability and long term survival.

We are fortunate to operate in a business to business environment, in that we know exactly who our customers are. We know which companies we sell to and which individuals we normally deal with at those companies in the engineering and car manufacturing sectors.

We should capitalise on this knowledge. Our key contacts and key accounts (those 20 per cent of our customers who give us 80 per cent of our business) must be given privileged access to us. We can't expect them all to have to phone our switchboard and go through the same rigmarole as all our other customers (i.e., the 80 per cent of our customers who supply only 20 per cent of our business and profitability). If we have identified a customer as valuable to us, then we need to make them feel valued: we should offer direct line access to account handlers, and pager and mobile phone numbers to be used when account handlers are not immediately available.

More generally, we need to survey **all** our customers to see how they would most like to communicate with us and how they rate our existing communications, whether initiated by us or initiated by them. In the light of their replies, we should review:

- Telephone access – incoming calls to be answered within so many rings; staff who answer calls to be empowered to deal with the enquiry, up to an agreed cost level.
- Email access – with commitments to defined response times.
- The company web site – to ensure ease of navigation, downloading efficiency, 'stickiness' and adequate coverage for the frequently asked questions.
- Personal contacts – the ease with which personal appointments can be made, the extent to which they are kept, adherence to time promises, and out-of-hours access.
- Site visits.

We should be able to achieve far greater synergy in our communications with customers. For example, if we develop and expand our corporate database of technical knowledge, we will be able to offer access to it for our customers through a secure Extranet. Far from diminishing our value chain by allowing customers access to such information, we enhance it by offering them a valuable service which ties them more closely to our product range and our linked support activities.

Communication between the Company and its Customers

The Senior Examiner anticipated responses which suggested the creation of a problem solving 'hotline' direct to named client managers within Technical Services; the use of email and Internet communication processes (especially for the frequently asked questions); the production and wide dissemination of literature concerning typical customer problems and their resolution; or the re- alignment of Sales and Technical Services into a single entity. Other 'solutions' were welcomed, so long as it could be convincingly demonstrated that they would facilitate the ultimate objective.

Answer – Question 1d

Senior Examiner's Comments

Methods for Soliciting Customer Feedback

A brief overview of the qualitative and quantitative methodologies was appropriate, plus a reasoned case for the chosen approach or approaches.

The key to continued and enhanced profitability lies in getting even closer to our customers, understanding what they want from us, predicting what they are going to want next, learning what is becoming less significant for them, and then acting on the lessons before our competitors have a chance to do so.

We need customer feedback to allow us to achieve these goals. I have already described some methods for obtaining customer opinions and evaluations; some techniques we use already (salespeople feed back comments solicited from customers), and some we could easily develop.

Earlier in this report I have proposed a survey of customer attitudes to our communication and our responses to their queries/complaints. We could expand this survey into a more general investigation about customer perceptions, but we must be very careful to make it:

- Very specific and relevant;
- Easy and quick to complete; and
- Incentivised.

I suggest a telephone questionnaire, lasting no longer than 10 minutes, with the offer to call the customer back if the time is not appropriate, but with an appropriate, loyalty enhancing incentive or reward in order to boost response rates.

Furthermore, we need to make the systematic collection of customer feedback an integral part of our business processes.

With this in mind, we can issue customers with pre-paid comment cards and instigate a free telephone line for comments. In addition, our web site can be made more interactive and we can give much more publicity to our email address for customer evaluations. In all instances the requests for customer feedback should be personalised under the name of our Chief Executive, with responses addressed to him personally (rather than to the organization as a whole), because this will encourage individuals to co-operate.

We should record every customer comment received by whatever means, wherever possible, and analyze the information periodically in order to notice patterns. We cannot afford to be selective in this regard; in other words, we must record both positive and negative feedback. The information should be clearly identified internally as a valuable resource, not as a 'complaints file': in a sense, we should encourage more complaints, rather than set targets that imply the desire to keep the number of complaints to a minimum. If we do the latter, and our people think they might be 'punished' for producing complaints, we shall simply sweep the problem under the carpet.

We could consider holding an annual conference or convention for customers, at which feedback would again be sought both formally (through question and answer sessions, technical discussions, etc) and informally (through social networking). We could also arrange more regular and less formal events for key accounts – say, three or four times a year, hosted on our premises or at a local hotel.

We could also introduce a customer newsletter (whether in print or via our web site), featuring a 'We answer your questions' column. This publication would be free to all customers and we should outsource it to a contract publisher with the brief to make it as lively and readable as possible. Any letter or other comment to the customer newsletter would of course be fed into our Intranet database of customer reactions.

Finally, we must encourage proactive listening by our sales and other customer facing staff. It is a key sales skill, and one we evidently need to develop.

PART B

Answer THREE Questions Only

Question 2

It is predicted that in the future, for most societies there will be many more older people relative to other population categories. Assuming this prediction to be accurate, indicate what you would say if you were to speak at a Marketing Conference on the following issues:

What are the factors contributing to this trend?

In what ways can older people be usefully segmented?

What marketing opportunities are represented by the growing numbers of older people?

(20 marks)

Answer – Question 2

Older People – Marketing Implications; Speaker's Notes

1. Many commentators have noticed that we live in an ageing society. By the year 2025, around 30 per cent of people in the UK are expected to be over 60 years old; whereas at the moment there are approximately 3 people of working age to every 1 who is aged over 60. This proportion is expected to become 2:1 in the foreseeable future. So we not only have an ageing society; but this is also compounded by a declining number of younger people in absolute terms.

2. What are the reasons for the ageing society?
   - Better medical care, leading to increased longevity.
   - The availability of free medical care (in the UK and most European countries), via the National Health Service.
   - Greater self-consciousness about health and the physiological implications of lifestyle choices among people in general.
   - Improved facilities for public health: clean water, reduced air pollution (a decline in the heavy industries which would normally be responsible for much industrial pollution, plus more controls over pollution itself).
   - A long period of political stability (again in the UK, though not necessarily in some other parts of the world) without major wars to cause disruption and premature loss of life.
   - Continual and gradual improvements in overall prosperity.
   - Significant reductions in immediate post-natal death rates (once individuals have lived for their first year, their chances of dying in the subsequent 60 years are very remote indeed).

3. How might we segment older people for marketing purposes?
   - In segmenting older people, there are several variables we can consider. Some are derived from segmentation systems which can be applied to the population generally. For instance: gender, social class, income, educational attainment and, of course, demography itself.
   - Gender has relevance because although the gap is narrowing, women still (on average) outlive men. Older females in the population are therefore likely to remain customers for longer.
   - Social class can be used to segment older people too. It remains true that a large proportion of those in socio-economic groups D and E are retired people subsisting on the state retirement pension, possibly supplemented by a modest occupational pension. These individuals have little discretionary spending power and a disproportionate amount of their income is likely to be devoted to the purchase of food and fuel.
   - Other people in the 60+ age range constitute the so-called 'grey market' and have sometimes been described as 'silver surfers'. They are financially comfortable in retirement and may well remain in the same socio-economic group which they occupied prior to retirement. For this reason they constitute a potentially lucrative and attractive segment, which we may also describe, in family life cycle terms, as 'empty nesters' who have both money and leisure time, enabling them to indulge themselves in ways in which their state pension counterparts cannot.
   - A further consideration here is the fact that longevity is positively correlated with occupational status. In other words, those previously (or currently) in non-manual occupations are likely to live longer than those performing manual roles, whether skilled or otherwise.
   - Segmentation by educational attainment is allied to social class and income, although educational aspiration is perhaps a segment on its own. Some older people return to full-time or part-time education because they have the leisure time to do so and they wish to learn a new (possibly leisure-related) skill whilst keeping active mentally and physically.

o We can also segment older people geographically, to some extent. Unsurprisingly, older people are found in greater numbers in so-called 'retirement areas', such as the south coast of England, and are less populous in central London (those who do remain there are likely to be either very rich or very poor).

o However, it is perhaps most useful to segment older people psychographically, in terms of attitudes and aspirations. This will lead us to identify the potentially more profitable segment: the self-confident, the well-off and basically healthy over-60s, who still consider that they have many years of active life ahead and can now enjoy themselves because of the money and time they have.

4. The opportunities which older people present to the marketer.

o Many of you will have heard of some of the more successful ways in which products and services have been targeted towards older customers. Saga Holidays is one obvious example, although other specialist travel companies have followed in their footsteps. Thus Voyages Jules Verne sells to a predominantly older market, without ever making it explicit that they do so. The visual clues are present in their promotional material – watercolours instead of colour photographs – and in the kind of holidays they sell: luxury hotels, luxury cruises, long-haul destinations in which a sense of adventure is mitigated by low-risk cosseting, and locations which are well away from the 'youthful backpacker' area of the marketplace. Thus, indeed, the travel business has wisely focused increasingly on the grey consumer, taking its lead from North America where this has been standard practice for some time.

o There are other marketing opportunities, however. Financial services represents an obvious category for the older consumer. Financial considerations loom large even for the better-off older client (who is likely in any event to be more financially sophisticated), with the complexities governing state help for nursing home fees acting as a continuing worry for many. In this way financial services marketers have responded with a variety of tailored, mainly insurance-based products for older people, including:

  ▪ Policies to help pay towards the cost of nursing home fees;
  ▪ Equity release schemes;
  ▪ Pre-paid funeral plans;
  ▪ Life insurance; and
  ▪ Private medical treatment insurance.

o Some of the promotional activity for these products may still lack refinement or subtlety, but perhaps this is unavoidable. Sir Harry Secombe and Dame Thora Hird have been employed to promote insurance and pre-paid funeral plans respectively, and one television advertisement for a remortgaging (equity release) policy shows a 60+ man spending the money he has 'released' not on a new car but on a Harley-Davidson motorcycle: the 'silver surfer' connection is thereby made explicit.

o As mentioned earlier, educational courses can be targeted successfully at older consumers.

Some categories of educational programme do particularly well, such as:

  ▪ Art related tuition (painting, flower arranging, music, etc.);
  ▪ Genealogy ('discover your ancestors' – answering a need many older people have to feel 'part of a chain');
  ▪ Literature and foreign languages (perhaps as an adjunct to increasing opportunities for travel);
  ▪ IT; and
  ▪ Health and fitness.

o Magazines and to some extent newspapers can also be aimed specifically towards older readers. Both the Daily Telegraph and the Daily Mail have a relatively high proportion of readers aged over 60.

o Charities can certainly market themselves towards older people and anticipate a profitable response rate when they do. Statistics show that the over-60s are the biggest donors to UK charities when compared with other age segments; many are also prepared to give their time in the form of voluntary assistance to charities with which they personally identify.

o There are some other obvious categories, such as medicines and medical aids. There are some strange anomalies, too. For instance, no political party in the UK has deliberately tried to promote membership (as opposed to votes) from older people, perhaps reflecting society's widely remarked positive reaction to the concept of 'youth'. Some marketers, moreover, have been criticised for ignoring an obvious constituency for their products and services among older people: thus BUPA recently encountered adverse reactions within the marketing industry for its TV advertisements featuring a 20-something man when in fact it is the over-60s who are the heaviest consumers of medical insurance.

Senior Examiner's Comments

Increasing Numbers of Older People

Approximately one-third of the total marks was available for each of the three sections to Question 2.

Question 3

Your immediate Senior Marketing Manager, working for a large newspaper, has begun to express alarm about the effects of electronic commerce on the business. Write a report for her in which you examine the likely impact:

For the newspaper.

For the world of business as a whole.

(20 marks)

Answer – Question 3

Report

To Senior Marketing Manager

From: Marketing Manager

Date: 12th June, 2000

Subject: The Implications of E-commerce

E-commerce and Our Newspaper

As newspaper publishers, we have always been in the information business (though some would say that our primary purpose is entertainment). It would be tempting to conclude that we are better prepared for the implications of electronic commerce than most companies, because only the medium has changed.

That view would be too complacent, in my view. In common with almost all newspapers, we already have an Internet presence. However, we have not yet found a practicable way to make money from it – or, at least, no way of making money which is as straightforward as charging readers a price for each copy of the printed version.

Advertising is the obvious solution, but there is some danger that our web-based operation could be cannibalising existing sales of the paper version of our product. On the other hand, the web newspaper does have the advantage that it is instantly global in its reach, and this fact does represent some opportunities.

We can potentially position our web-based offering as a portal to other sources of information. We can raise revenue by this means and we can also offer to sell copies of reports and abstracts from previous issues.

We can equally develop the market for informational surveys on specific industries and geographical entities (like nation states, political regions or other groupings), making these available through our web site as we already do with our newspaper, and charging the relevant foreign ministry, industrial body or other corporate sponsor for our services.

Despite the fact that there are opportunities in E-commerce for this newspaper, behind all the Internet technology is the implied threat that making so much information available so easily to so many people will effectively shorten our value-chain, not only for information providers such as ourselves, but also for other publications and publishers. Even if this is so, there is nothing we can do on our own to stop the Internet momentum, because our competitors – the quality press within the UK, and major newspapers across the world – already have their publications online and already have affiliate programmes with, say, airlines, travel companies, book retailers, vintners, hotel operators and leisure businesses of all kinds.

As I began by implying, we might expect to be partially isolated from the threats, and although this is true it is of no great comfort. Our network of reporters, news gatherers, photographers, columnists and editors may be comparable with that of other newspapers, but no Internet business could easily replicate it or the infrastructure which enables it to function so smoothly every 24 hours.

Amazon.com had taken 7 per cent of the total US book market before 'bricks and mortar' rival, Barnes and Noble, realised what was happening and developed their own Internet bookstore. In the UK, W.H. Smith was even further behind, viewing Amazon as an 'American' phenomenon (and betraying a lack of comprehension about the precise nature of the World Wide Web). In the travel industry, e-bookers.com and lastminute.com have taken business away from traditional travel agents, and this process is bound to escalate as the airlines become fully Internet compatible in the near future (and this is despite the fact that the services of a travel agent have always been 'free' to the consumer).

Electronic commerce is making great inroads into the service sector and also within specific retailing arenas like books, CDs, videos, air travel and package holidays. Unless service providers or retailers can demonstrate that they are adding value to their product or service offering by existing in a physical (as opposed to a virtual) world, then they will continue to lose market share to the 'dot.com' newcomers.

One of our disadvantages which has to be faced is that because we are principally a 'bricks and mortar' operation we find ourselves moving more slowly in this Internet world than some of our newly emergent competitors. Recent research by the Bathwick Group has suggested that a 'dot.com' enterprise can move from the decision point about investment to the first transaction from its web site in as little as 14 weeks, whereas in a conventionally large organization it may take an average of 38 weeks even to make a strategic choice, let alone do anything about implementing it. So one of my principal caveats, therefore, is that we have to speed up our decision making processes if we are to keep pace with a rapidly evolving competitive scenario.

On the other hand, several things will work in favour of existing 'bricks and mortar' companies like ours.

Firstly, they (we) have woken up to the reality of E-commerce and are setting up their own web sites. Some are doing so reluctantly, some are uncertain about how far they want to go with it, some have tackled the task inefficiently, and some have done so with genuine creativity, enthusiasm and enterprise – but whatever the precise situation, they are all doing it. The new entrants may have already reached the end of their particular 'golden age' and will have to share the marketplace with the existing players.

Secondly, we know that most consumers are not Early Adopters or Innovators: they are resistant to new ideas that have not yet proved themselves. This is as true of companies as it is of products, and explains why 'dot.com' companies have to spend so much on marketing and promotion. So far as most consumers are concerned, they are unknown quantities and have no established credibility, whereas we have a powerful degree of brand value which we can exploit both as ourselves and as a portal into our affiliates.

This indeed is where 'bricks and mortar' companies will find that the value of their brands is ultimately reinforced by E-commerce rather than undermined by it. In cyberspace, nervous shoppers will look for the security of the familiar, and established brands are the badge of the tried and tested. This helps to explain the E-commerce success of companies like Tesco and Virgin, and makes it all the more remarkable that some newly developed electronic businesses have chosen to distance themselves from their reputable parents (e.g., 'IF' from Halifax plc, 'egg' from Prudential Assurance, and First Direct from HSBC).

Senior Examiner's Comments

E-commerce

Within the overall allocation of 20 marks, 10 could be awarded for an examination of the impact of e-commerce on the newspaper, plus 10 for a review of the implications for the world of business as a whole. A newspaper context was specifically chosen because of the direct connections between news-paper publishing and E-commerce: as it happens, virtually all major newspapers in the world have made their material available free of charge on the Internet, yet their circulation and sales figures appear not to have been seriously threatened. Moreover, these newspapers have added revenues through connections to affiliate web sites and through using their brand values as a basis for retailing in other sectors.

Question 4

How can customer service be used to create a genuinely sustainable competitive advantage? Illustrate your answer with relevant examples.

(20 marks)

Answer – Question 4

Using Customer Service for Competitive Advantage

In the current competitive climate, it is becoming increasingly difficult to keep customers loyal. This is because:

- Customers are themselves more willing to transfer their 'loyalty' from one product/service provider to another, whereas at one time their behaviour was characterised by inertia (an inertia which was mistakenly assumed to be a sign of genuine customer loyalty). In the financial services arena, for example, customers will more easily switch banks or building societies: it is physically possible to switch nowadays without excessive effort, and also the products of banks and building societies are much less similar, so the potential pay-off from a switching process can be worthwhile and significant.

- The arrival of new entrants into previously well-defined marketplaces has created a new degree of price competition which customers are prepared to exploit.

- Customers are more sensitive to poor, inept, misleading or incompetent customer service, and will more readily 'punish' their existing product/service supplier by taking their business elsewhere.

Customer Service as a Differentiator

All organizations are looking for ways to differentiate themselves. However, the introduction of quality standards in many sectors, and the legal requirements associated with compliance, often mean that product quality and functionality are much less likely to be meaningful differentiators so far as the customer is concerned. Some recent studies in the UK, for example, have demonstrated that people take an average of only 12 minutes to make decisions about the purchase of large consumer durables like refrigerators, washing machines and vacuum cleaners – largely because they believe that all of them will operate satisfactorily for an acceptable length of time. That being so, they will concentrate on design features, price and product availability.

The goal, therefore, is not customer 'satisfaction' – which is a kind of taken-for-granted acceptance that the product will work, and its appearance is acceptable – but customer 'delight', with expectations being exceeded to the point where the product or service is truly memorable. In some sectors, generating customer 'delight' presents a massive challenge because service levels are already very high; in others, customer 'delight' is easier to facilitate simply because the competition is slow, reactive, sluggish and unimaginative.

The situation is clearly illustrated within the field of E-commerce. Companies like Amazon.com (selling books, CDs, videos and other products) and Blackstar.co.uk (the Belfast-based purveyor of pre-recorded videos and DVDs) have established enviable reputations for the quality of their service precisely because many of their competitors are so indifferent. Amazon.com establishes a very personal relationship with its customers, notifying them of new publications similar to those which they have purchased before and keeping them up to date with the progress of their orders. Equally, Blackstar.co.uk produces automated responses to email enquiries, whereas many organizations, evidently inexperienced in an E-commerce environment, do not reply to emails at all, or take up to five days to do so.

There are three awkward but unavoidable complications about the creation of service ingredients which encourage customer 'delight'. First is the fact that if an organization raises its service offer – through the quality or speed of its response, through its pricing strategies, its customization, or anything else – then it will produce customer 'delight' initially, but after a while its customers will expect that standard of service all the time, and their reactions will accordingly slip back into mere 'satisfaction' once again. It then becomes necessary to create some new opportunity for 'delight', and so the competitive struggle continues. Unfortunately this is an unavoidable fact of life.

Secondly, once one competitor organization raises its service offer, others are virtually compelled to follow, whether they like it or not, because customer expectations will be raised right across the board. For some of these, therefore, service excellence is an exercise in defensive, reactive marketing, rather than something undertaken in search of performance superiority. Again, this is an unavoidable fact of life.

The third point is that new and innovative service benefits are rarely generated as a result of customer-focused research and feedback. Most of the great product/service ideas – the round Tetley tea bag, the Sony Walkman, 3M's Post-It Note – have been developed inside organizations by highly creative individuals. As Nishikawa pointed out in his seminal article for the Journal of Long-Range Planning in 1989, relying on customers as the principal source for service improvement or transformation will almost certainly mean that the organization concerned will never be higher than Number Two in the marketplace – precisely because most customers are relatively conservative in their thinking, and can only articulate preferences with which they are already familiar.

The Solution

The successful enterprises of today and tomorrow must recognise the truth of the comment made by Bill Gates in his 1999 book Business @ The Speed of Thought – namely that customer service will be the key competitive differentiator for the foreseeable future. This means that organizations must focus on the changing dynamics of customer attitudes and behaviour, must get very close indeed to their customers, and must learn to anticipate what customers might want next.

These successful enterprises, moreover, will embody the thinking behind Reichheld's Service-Profit Cycle, in order to integrate systems, people performance, and customers:

- Externally perceived excellent service quality leads to satisfied (and preferably delighted) customers.

- If customers are very satisfied or even delighted, they are more likely to repurchase, not only once but several times.

- Customer retention implies improved profitability, because it is always more cost-effective to retain existing customers than it is to find (and buy) new ones.

- Improved profitability means that more resources are available to enable internal service quality within the organization, to be both efficient and effective.

- If internal service quality is performed well, then employees will feel good about themselves, about the work they do, and about the organization which employs them.

- Employees who feel good are more likely to stay with the organization.

- Staff retention means that service quality is enhanced because of the effects of the learning curve.

Companies that ignore the Service-Profit Cycle do so at their peril, and are likely to become embroiled in a 'doom loop' in which service deteriorates, customers defect, money has to be diverted in an effort to replace them, internal service quality declines, staff morale plummets, labour turnover accelerates, and service deteriorates even more because it is delivered by new and inexperienced employees.

Senior Examiner's Comments

Customer Service as Competitive Advantage

Candidates are expected to discuss the argument that customer service excellence may be hard to copy. Some aspects can easily be emulated (e.g., software, systems, processes); others are much more idiosyncratic, 'soft' and culture-bound, e.g. the availability of direct access to the CEO (Kwik-Fit), the soliciting of complaints and feedback, the nature of the 'returned goods' offer (Lands End Clothing and the British Airports Authority Worldwide Guarantee); still others are crucially dependent on strong, consistent and visible leadership throughout the organization.

In the second part of the answer, candidates may explore ways in which organizations may turn their service offer into something that is sustainably unique, through very close customer relationship management, the creation of specific customer promises, and the implementation of a customer-centric structure.

Question 5

Answer only **one** of the following.

Outline and justify a marketing research plan for:

A fashion conscious clothing manufacturer that wants to find out which new designs will be most appealing to college students.

(20 marks)

A cigarette firm which wants to gain some insights into attitudes towards smoking among teenagers and young adults.

(20 marks)

Answer – Question 5

Marketing Research Plan: Attitudes Towards Smoking among Teenagers and Young Adults

Research Objectives

The broad aim of this exercise is to discover whether attitudes towards smoking are changing as a result of anti-smoking lobbyists and government campaigns; and to find out which situations induce smoking in young adults and teenagers.

More specifically, the objectives for the research are as follows.

- To establish which locations are most frequently associated with smoking or the desire to smoke.
- To determine the most common reasons why individuals take up smoking.
- To measure (and find ways of measuring) attitudes towards smoking. For example, how many smokers privately feel guilty about the practice and wish that they could give up?
- To identify the most popular smoking brands within the targeted age groups.
- To ascertain the extent to which smokers themselves are already familiar with the health risks involved.

Research Proposal

1. . Carry out secondary research in-house, using past research reports and company documents, e.g. current and recent sales figures, trends, geographical/demographic variations, seasonality, and so forth.

2. Commission a marketing research agency to carry out primary field studies into 'attitudes' about smoking. The agency will receive a detailed brief and will initially conduct pilot investigations.

Measurement Techniques

1. A combination of qualitative and quantitative techniques should be used, in order to ensure the objectivity of the process and the authenticity of the results.

2. One important method deployed will be **Focus Groups**, consisting of 6 to 10 people from the target age ranges, asked to attend group sessions where issues about smoking will be discussed. The Focus Group meetings will be held on premises provided by the research agency, with a two-way mirror and recording facilities. A moderator will prompt the group and take them through a series of issues surrounding smoking, according to the (yet to be prepared) brief.

3. The **advantages** of a Focus Group methodology are:

   o The dynamics of the group enable facilitators to discern subtle differences in culture, social class and other influences on behaviour, which would not normally be demonstrated through the medium of written questionnaires.

   o New insights and interpretations are more easily achievable.

   o Focus groups permit judgements to be made about the importance of different dimensions in the product/service offer; this is not so easy when more formalised techniques are used.

4. The **disadvantages** of Focus Groups are:
   - A possible 'follow my leader' climate in which more docile group members are content to follow the ideas put forward by dominant individuals within the group.
   - The group may take on a life of its own, totally unrepresentative of market segments at large.
   - The output of the group depends partly on the skills of the moderator.
   - Some contributions may be more welcome than others, and accordingly receive more emphasis in the subsequent interpretation about what has happened and the lessons to be learned.
   - The group may not incorporate some significant opinions.

5. I also recommend the use of Shopping Mall Intercept Surveys – i.e. a quantitative technique involving researchers positioned within a shopping centre and using quota-sampling approaches to obtain the correct numbers of respondents within each previously identified sector. Such surveys would be particularly relevant in this case, since teenagers and young adults are often seen in shopping centres.

6. A more detailed recital of the **advantage**s for Intercept Surveys should make the following points:
   - Respondents are screened before the questionnaire proper is initiated.
   - Because of the face to face structure, it is possible to use prompt material, such as information cards, packaging materials, pictures and so forth.
   - Generally speaking there is a high response rate.
   - The researcher can ensure that all questions are answered.

7. The disadvantages of Intercept Surveys are:
   - As with Focus Groups, there is possible researcher bias, because it is the researcher who records the responses, not the respondent himself/herself.
   - The structure of the questions can mislead some people.
   - The tone of voice and/or facial expression used by the researcher can consciously or unconsciously produce results which are not authentic.

Conclusion

I suggest that we combine in-house and research agency resources in order to gain a clear picture of attitudes towards smoking. I propose also that surveys are the best way to gain a meaningful and convincing insight into behaviour (as opposed to attitudes, bearing in mind that attitudes do not always coincide with actions).

Finally, it will be important to emphasise confidentiality when approaching all potential respondents, and also to investigate attitudes to smoking amongst non-smokers.

Senior Examiner's Comments

Marketing Research Plan

In the marking scheme, around 50 per cent of the total was allocated to the proposals for a marketing research plan, with the remaining 50 per cent available for an efficient, business-focused and cost-effective justification for the techniques to be employed. If candidates were to produce even a superficial project plan and timetable, so much the better.

Question 6

Sometimes companies move from healthy profitability to substantial profit erosion or even losses because, it is claimed, they have lost touch with their customers. Using recent examples in order to illustrate your argument, explain why organizations make mistakes of this kind, and show how they can be avoided.

(20 marks)

Answer – Question 6

Some of the monolithic business successes of the 1970s, 1980s and 1990s have come spectacularly unstuck in recent times, to the surprise of many, not least themselves. Yet the signs were there, and had they heeded them they might have been able to avoid the difficulties they now face. It may be over- simplistic to say that losing touch with their customers is the sole reason why companies like Marks & Spencer, Sainsbury's, British Airways and Rover are now in trouble; but it is certainly a significant factor, and probably the most significant.

Marks & Spencer, for example, has long been a very centralist organization, promoting from within and reluctant to learn from competitors in its own or in other sectors. It failed to listen to customers who said its clothes were becoming overpriced and dowdy, or that its premium-priced food was no better than that available from Tesco or Waitrose. For years Marks & Spencer refused to supply changing rooms in which its customers could try clothes before purchasing them, declined to provide customer toilets, and would not allow customers to pay for goods with their credit cards. Only when customers began to defect to retailers like Gap and Next, and to the supermarkets, did the Board of Marks & Spencer belatedly sit up and take notice.

So it appears that the Marks & Spencer management was guilty of taking its customers for granted and, as such, not listening to them. Yet other retailers – notably the John Lewis Partnership, which often gives the impression that it is run for the benefit of its staff (or 'partners') – has been guilty of the same fault without incurring the same degree of nemesis. What was different about Marks & Spencer and what could it have done differently?

The main problem was that it failed to hear customers telling it (or trying to) that there was a growing mismatch between what Marks & Spencer believed its brand stood for, and how customers perceived it. The mechanisms for gathering customer views were inadequate; customer-facing staff were ignored; recruitment and selection policies did not give high priority to customer-friendly attitudes and competencies; there were no reward or recognition systems built around customer service excellence; at the point of induction, new entrants were not told about the importance of customers, but were instructed about the company rules and procedures.

In the past couple of years, Marks & Spencer has fought back. Its previous Chairman and Chief Executive were forced into retirement; it now has an externally appointed Chairman but an internally promoted Chief Executive; several of the main Board directors have been ousted; several hundred administrative staff have been dragooned into front-line service roles; staff can now receive financial recognition for service achievements; and the company now has its first ever Marketing Director.

There are some delicious ironies here. Marks & Spencer has been a global operator for some years, using franchises in many markets, but throughout its activities insisting on the same degree of rigid, hierarchical, paternalistic, 'Baker Street knows best' control mechanisms over all its locations. When Marks & Spencer some years ago ran some poster advertisements in Israel featuring a young couple in M&S underwear caught *in flagrante delicto* in an elevator, management in London was horrified and ordered that the advertisements be withdrawn. Today, by contrast, it has commissioned designers deliberately to produce underwear which is sexy because they have at last heard what customers have been saying – namely that raunchy can be fun, but dull isn't.

Sainsbury's has been guilty of many of the same faults as Marks & Spencer, chiefly failing to realise that there has been increasing dissonance between its brand values and the aspirations or perceptions of its customers. The debate continues about the efficacy of so-called 'loyalty' cards, but the fact is that Tesco stole a march on Sainsbury's on this issue because Sainsbury's arrogantly assumed it knew more about its customers than it actually did. In a famous phrase, the Chief Executive of Sainsbury's described the Tesco Clubcard as 'electronic Green Shield Stamps' and then six months later was forced to approve the introduction of a virtually identical Sainsbury's card.

Rover, too, has decided to reposition itself as a mass market car maker following its sale by BMW to the Phoenix Group, because it now feels it has the ability to respond to what customers have been saying for several years – namely, that just because BMW owned Rover, Rover cars would not be viewed as BMW products. Image problems and brand misperception difficulties bedevilled Rover as they had Marks & Spencer, both companies suffering from a 'worthy but dull' view by customers but seemingly incapable of understanding genuine customer dynamics until almost the point of no return.

So: how can businesses avoid the pitfalls into which companies like Marks & Spencer have so spectacularly fallen?

Listening to what customers are saying is clearly a key requirement, but it takes more than traditional methods such as feedback forms (although they do have value) and the occasional survey. Businesses can use IT to record and track customer attitudes. They can deploy a range of qualitative and quantitative research techniques, from the incentivised customer questionnaire to the focus group or panel. All these approaches, of course, come with a price tag attached, but the price of not listening to the customer is potentially even greater – and much more damaging.

Clarity about brand values is important, but businesses need to apply a finely tuned ear to what customers feel and say about brands. Globally successful brands follow certain key rules, outlined for example by Damien Callaghan of Intel, makers of the hugely successful Pentium processor. He says the Intel brand must be:

- Clearly communicated
- Uniformly presented
- Protected legally in all jurisdictions and
- Standing for quality.

Above all, businesses must apply vigorous, consistent, thrusting and energetic leadership from the top, as does Tesco for example, which gives the impression of being endlessly turbulent and transformational. The importance of such leadership probably means that the CEO vacancy must be filled by new individuals every five years or so, and that potential CEOs should preferably come from outside so that they bring fresh thinking.

Finally, energetic businesses need energetic HR systems and a supportive people management infrastructure: individuals recruited against customer-related attitudes, regularly revitalised through induction, training and development, rewarded and recognised for customer service achievements, and so forth.

Senior Examiner's Comments

Organizations that Lose Touch with their Customers

In designing this question about organizations that have lost touch with their customers, the Senior Examiner was mindful of such recent high profile examples as Marks & Spencer, IBM, Storehouse (now renamed Mothercare), Laura Ashley, and Somerfield Supermarkets. Of course, this list is by no means comprehensive, and students may be able to contemplate similar instances within the business to business sector or within their own geographical environment.

Given 20 marks for the question as a whole, 10 were available for a discussion of the likely causes, plus 10 for an examination of the ways in which substantial profit erosion might be avoided. Points to be made might include: the complacent belief that the future will closely resemble the past; arrogance and perceived superiority which prevents the marketplace from being properly evaluated; a reward system which becomes increasingly anachronistic (e.g. IBM's continued incentivization emphasis on mainframe sales despite the overwhelming trend towards PCs); an inward-looking, bureaucratic culture; and pursuit of a sales-driven mentality rather than a truly marketing-focused orientation. In addressing the first half of the question, too, the more able students might list the seven 'learning disabilities of organizations' generated by Peter Senge in his book The Fifth Discipline; in the second half they could cite the advice offered by Andy Grove (formerly CEO and currently Chairman of Intel) in his 1996 book *Only the Paranoid Survive*.

Question 7

As the Marketing Manager for a soft drinks company, write a report for your Director in which you address the following issues:

The factors which your company should take into account when deciding which market segments to address and which ones to leave alone.

The processes which can lead to the discovery of new and potentially profitable segments.

The ways in which sales from existing segments may be developed incrementally.

(20 marks)

Answer – Question 7

Report on Segmentation Approaches for the Soft Drinks Market

Date: 12th June, 2000

Author: Marketing Manager

Introduction

Segmentation is an important factor in product development, marketing activities and the acquisition of competitive advantage. This report therefore examines segmentation in the soft drinks market and concentrates on the following issues:

- The factors to take into account when deciding which market segments to address – and, by implication, which segments to leave alone.
- The ways in which 'new' segments can be identified prior to exploitation.
- Methods for increasing our sales from existing segments.

Factors in the Selection of Target Segments

1. When segmenting markets in general, the criteria behind the identification of any given segment should be as follows:

   o **Measurable** – The segment should be capable of being quantified, and it should not be so large that in effect it appears excessively differentiated within itself.

   o **Accessible** – It should be possible for the company to gain access to the segment.

   o **Sustainable** – The segment should not be merely ephemeral or transient.

   o **Homogeneous** – The individuals comprising the segment should respond in broadly similar ways to the presence of marketing processes.

   o **Actionable** – The segment should be capable of being appropriately addressed and targeted; the segment may be 'perfect' in most respects but if we don't have the infrastructure to support it then we will have to leave the segment to one side.

2. Appropriate factors around which to segment the soft drinks market may include those identified below:

   o **Age** – The requirements of the youth market for soft drinks will have different characteristics from the expectations of those in more senior categories.

   o **Income/Occupation** – The availability of disposable income will affect product choice.

   o **Family Life Cycle** – The individual's position within the Family Life Cycle will influence the nature of the soft drinks purchased, and the reasons for purchase.

   o **Lifestyle** – Some people will buy soft drinks merely to quench their thirst, some as mixers, some as sources of nutrients and vitamins, and so on.

   o **Reference Groups** – The habits of role models will control the preferences of aspirational consumers.

3. Taking the above into account, moreover, it will be important to address those segments which are likely to be profitable. Although not a commodity market, there is little opportunity in the soft drinks field to build close and intimate relationships with individual customers, particularly as the products are often merchandised through a third party, such as retail outlets, supermarkets, off- licences, CTNs (confectionery, tobacco and newsagent shops) and leisure/entertainment venues.

4. The choice of a soft drink is likely to be a habitual purchase with little customer involvement, so brand equity is important.

5. The most desirable segments to address are those which have the following characteristics:

   o Above average levels of disposable income.

   o Above average levels of consumption for the product.

   o High levels of brand loyalty, once internalised.

   o Role modelling behaviour patterns.

The Discovery of New Segments

1. New segments may be discovered in a range of ways and can be a source of significant income and profitability, especially for the company which is first with the discovery.

2. The first necessity is for our company to keep reliable, detailed and accurate data about its customers and their profiles. We can secure such information through retail outlets and through sales records, and direct from our end-users through customer helplines, promotional competitions which encourage these customers to contact the company, Focus Groups, and links with the kinds of social environment within which our typical customers circulate.

3. Using the services of a data warehouse can deliver access to a wider range of consumer information; data mining techniques can be deployed in order to identify patterns, trends and potentially new segments.

4. Market research, both primary and secondary, may bring new information to light, especially if we examine in depth the reasons why people purchase our products, or why they purchase those of competitors, how their decision making processes operate, and the extent to which customers function as individuals or as members of groups.

5. We need to operate some brainstorming activities within the organization with the deliberate aim of creatively re-examining the established segmentation systems that we currently use. We may learn something useful by looking at the segmentation approaches adopted by companies in other similar fields (e.g. confectionery and fast food), and we should ask ourselves whether we can create entirely customised soft drinks designed around the tastebuds of each individual consumer.

6. Skilful environmental scanning will help us to keep up to date with demographic change, lifestyle modifications and all the significant dimensions of the PEST process.

Increasing Sales from Existing Customer Segments

1. It is well documented that it is cheaper, and often much more profitable, to convert light users of a product into medium users, rather than continually seek new customers who may in any event be purely transient.

2. If our attempts at such conversion are to succeed, we have to persuade existing customers to buy our current products more frequently and/or to try other related products within our range, in order to increase their overall consumption.

3. Ways in which this can be achieved might include:
   o Product development using information held about product preferences and the motivation to buy. In this way, for example, Kit-Kat has introduced adapted alternatives featuring plain chocolate, orange flavours and a 'chunky' option (which has been particularly successful, without significantly corrupting the market for the established four-bar version).
   o Given that product development is so costly (and involves high risk), it may be preferable to emphasise additional benefits from increased consumption of our existing products.
   o Brand promotions leading to enhanced brand awareness.
   o The use of 'limited edition', added value (through higher margin) products.
   o Sponsorship and endorsement from relevant individuals and organizations.
   o Advertising in appropriate publications, e.g. GQ magazine for drinks aimed at young, 'laddish' males.
   o 'Loyalty' schemes.

4. We need also to consider the opportunities created through the Internet. Forecasts of Internet usage in the UK indicate that some of its major clients are young people (especially young males); many of these are cash-rich and time-poor. We might easily establish a direct line soft drinks operation aimed at such individuals, perhaps in collaboration with an existing transactional web-based marketing company. For a price premium, moreover, we could offer our soft drinks with personalised labelling: this would never be a major source of revenue, but it would yield publicity and would certainly be something nobody else has ever done before.

5. Yet more opportunities can be created if we visualise our drinks brands as opportunities for brand extensions – into clothing, sports equipment, and so forth.

Introduction from the Senior Examiner

These Specimen Answers represent a combination of material prepared by the Senior Examiner and answers generated by the candidates themselves – answers which earned above-average marks and which therefore represent material of a benchmarking standard to which future students should aspire. There are a few considerations which should be strongly emphasised, however, before we go any further.

1. **None of the Specimen Answers presented here is intended to be regarded as the definitive treatment for any given question.** In a field that presents opportunities for qualitative judgements, there is no such thing as a truly definitive answer.

2. **On the other hand, these Specimen Answers do contain a positive blend of the five competencies which the examination seeks to evaluate.** These competencies are repeated below, with accompanying explanations: if they are a. acquired by students and then b. demonstrably displayed in their scripts, success is assured – not only in the examination, incidentally, but also within the marketing profession as a whole. This is because the same five competencies are equally applicable to the 'real' world as to the artificial world of the examination room.

3. **Because the Marketing Customer Interface is itself subject to change and progress, knowledge which was regarded as definitive at one period of time may be supplemented or even replaced altogether, as new thinking, experience and research refine what has gone before.** At one time, for example, it was widely accepted that 'the customer is always right' but organizations nowadays are more likely to argue that the customer can sometimes be wrong, or that even when the customer is right, restitution may not be appropriate. At one time too, Total Quality Management was seen as the principal route to competitive advantage, but few now believe this to be the case (and the few who do are misguided).

4. **Not all the Specimen Answers in this document are structured in conformity with the normal canons of business communication.** Instead, the Answers contain key points indicating the issues which candidates should have raised, with elegance of style and presentation a secondary consideration. At the same time, it is important for future candidates to recognise that the appropriate 'packaging' of answers is a significant competency and can result in a sometimes crucial erosion of marks if ignored.

5. **Where examination questions offer students a choice of thematic focus, these Specimen Answers do not always embrace all the alternatives.** Individuals may be asked to place their answer material into the context of either an airline or an international hotel group; the Specimen Answers will typically include only one of these choices.

6. **It is pointless and counter-productive for students to learn any of these Specimen Answers by heart.** Future examinations will not repeat any of the questions from the past (though question topics may appear very frequently). Reliance on memorising past answers actually means that candidates are disadvantaged, for three principal reasons. Firstly, an effective examination technique for this subject requires flexibility; secondly, the desire to reproduce ready made text will automatically mean that the specific requirements of any given question are being ignored; thirdly, as already made clear above, effective achievement at this level requires much more than straightforward descriptive knowledge.

The Five Competencies for Success

1. **Breadth of familiarity with the subject matter** – across the range of questions principally addressed in Part B. However, in addition to themes specifically listed in the syllabus, the Senior Examiner considers it legitimate also to pose questions on topics which have become significant since the syllabus was first written. It is for this reason that students must keep

up-to-date by reading relevant journals, periodicals and newspapers, or by systematically downloading relevant material from the Internet.

2. **Depth of comprehension and understanding** – usually expressed by a willingness to challenge some of the conventional wisdom which surrounds the subject, to cite relevant examples of the Marketing Customer Interface in action, to draw upon personal experiences, and to reinforce supposedly 'factual' statements with evidential references to appropriate literature, textbooks, articles and other sources.

3. **Demonstration of a businesslike perspective** – through recognition of the fact that marketing initiatives have to be justified against resource/benefit criteria. Customer satisfaction is therefore not an end in itself, but a possible route to increased profitability – and in some circumstances it may make better sense for customers to remain dissatisfied.

4. **Application capability** – reflected in treatments of the case study and in response to the more 'practical' and problem solving/opportunity seeking dimensions of many questions in Part B.

5. 'Packaging' skills – the readiness to adhere to the presentation obligations spelt out in many questions, and particularly as part of the brief for Part A. If asked to generate a report, candidates must comply. An 'essay' will not do.

Ted Johns, Senior Examiner

The copyright of all The Chartered Institute of Marketing examination material is held by the Institute. No Case Study or Questions may be reproduced without its prior permission which must be obtained in writing.

Exam material

The Davis Preston Group

The Davis Preston Group is a small group of 12 upmarket department stores, named after its market stall founder and located in prime city centre locations. It specialises in men's and women's clothing (including fashion wear, sports gear and shoes), furniture and furnishings and electrical goods; in addition, it sells male and female toiletries, garden equipment, toys and books.

Recently, the apparently unstoppable success of the company has faltered, for the following reasons:

1. About six months ago the Chief Executive issued a profits warning and indicated that worse was to come. He blamed the firm's poor performance on competition from cheap imports, high interest rates and general fears about the future of the economy.

2. Analysts and commentators have accused Davis Preston of being complacent, of ignoring changes in customer aspirations and of holding a lofty attitude towards competitors.

3. The previous Chief Executive, just retired, was an autocrat. He had been with Davis Preston all his life and had always been sceptical about innovation and change.

The company's people management policies reinforce the picture of an organization which is resolutely conformist:

1. Recruitment and selection systems are designed to seek out only those who will fit in with the Davis Preston culture and its current customer profile.

2. Each Davis Preston store is deliberately organized around the model of the nuclear family, with a father and a mother (i.e. a store manager and a staff manager if one is male the other is always female)), the inescapable inference being that the remainder of the staff are comparable with children. Certainly the atmosphere in the stores is paternalistic, with tight controls over appearance, behaviour and procedures.

3. All senior positions in the company are occupied by those who have spent their entire careers with Davis Preston. The previous Chief Executive had been with the firm for 40 years; the current one joined 34 years ago; the newly appointed Marketing Director (the first the company has ever had) has continuous service with Davis Preston for the past 29 years.

You are a Marketing Officer with the Davis Preston Group. Despite the company s stifling atmosphere, you have stayed because you hoped that the time would come when senior management might seriously contemplate the sorts of radical changes which in your view are needed. You now believe your time has come: there is a new Chief Executive, the outside world expects action and the profits warning has caused active concern among at least some of the company s executives.

PART A

Question 1

Write a report to the Marketing Director, which includes:

A SWOT analysis for the Davis Preston Group, with up to five Strengths, up to five Weaknesses, up to five Opportunities and up to five Threats.

(10 marks)

A commentary on the market segments which are currently the principal targets for the Davis Preston Group's operation and the feasibility of securing additional business through either market penetration or market development.

(10 marks)

Three initiatives which would enable the Davis Preston Group to establish much closer relationships with its customers.

(10 marks)

Suggestions for changes with regard to the internal management of the company in order to make its people significantly more customer focused.

(10 marks)

(40 marks in total)

Answer – Question 1

Report

Restoring Competitive Superiority for the Davis Preston Group

From: The Marketing Officer

To: The Marketing Director (and Board)

Date: 10th December, 2000

Introduction

This report has been written in the light of our company's recent profits warning. The areas to be covered will look at, firstly, the strengths, weaknesses, opportunities and threats facing the Davis Preston Group, then the market segments and feasibility of securing further business, initiatives for achieving closer relationships with customers, and finally suggestions regarding the improvement of the firm's internal management so that the Davis Preston group becomes more customer focused. A great deal needs to be covered, and therefore the report will deliberately be kept brief, with bullet points replacing what might otherwise be lengthy analysis.

Strengths, Weaknesses, Opportunities and Threats

The aim of this review is to ensure that the threats are anticipated and minimised (or, indeed, removed altogether), the weaknesses are undermined and the strengths are evaluated against the capabilities needed for the future in order to ensure that all potential opportunities are fully exploited.

Strengths

- Our quality market segments.
- Locations in prime, high traffic city centre settings.
- Wide range of merchandise, fashion wear, furniture, electrical goods, toiletries, garden equipment, toys, books, and so forth.
- A credible reputation for success, engendering impressive levels of customer loyalty and customer retention.
- A cultural 'style' which is immediately recognizable in the marketplace.

Weaknesses

- Our tendency to blame reduced profitability on the random impact of external influences, rather than a willingness to look at ourselves and our responsibility for the decline.
- A customer base which is only a small proportion of the population, and which itself may be ageing or diminishing for other reasons.
- Ignoring changes in customer aspirations and preferences, whilst subscribing to an arrogant belief that we do not need to learn from these customers and our competition.

348

- An autocratic (albeit paternalistic) style of management, causing problems for staff morale and motivation because of the tight controls over procedures, systems and personal appearance.
- Resistance to change at the top management level, amongst individuals characterised by complacency and belief in a series of 'best answers'.

Opportunities

- We have a wide range of products and therefore we could contemplate entry into additional segments of the marketplace as a route for profit enhancement.
- The Internet presents a magnificent opportunity for gaining access to new customers, not only throughout the UK but across the world; we could establish a web site to sell our goods online and thus build an e-commerce dimension for the Davis Preston business. Affiliations and links to other upmarket web sites could be established in order to stimulate our 'click' traffic, encourage cross-fertilization of customers, and transmit the asset of our reputation into new customer sectors.
- Closer customer liaison, especially through customer feedback processes, should enable us to find out more about changes in consumer fashion as well as developments in customer wants or needs.
- An integrated management information system should allow us to capture the data from questionnaires, focus groups and customer interviews, so that we can more easily discern trends and tailor our product/service offerings to credible portrayals of customer segment psychology.
- Hitherto we have concentrated on selling products, but many other organizations have acted on the argument that there is more added-value potential in the development of services for customers.

Threats

- Our competitors are beginning to notice that the Davis Preston Group has become detached from its customers; they are seizing the customer relationship initiative.
- Cheap imports – especially in competitive sectors which are largely price driven, such as consumer electronics and everyday clothing.
- Heightened price awareness amongst our existing customers, coupled with a willingness to go elsewhere if similar products are available at a discount.
- We have begun to move down the Reichheld 'circle of virtue' (or Service/Profitability Cycle); once this process is established, it is extraordinarily difficult to reverse.
- The prospects for a recession will always constitute a danger for our type of operation, causing some of our customers to stop purchasing altogether whilst others 'trade down'.

Market Segments

The Davis Preston Group continues to concentrate its efforts towards the 'upmarket' end of the population. This gives us a competitive advantage immediately but the possibility of problems in the immediate future, especially when one recalls that our existing segments comprise those in the A/B socio-economic categories; people with higher levels of disposable income (some of them male) and individuals who have time to shop during the day. We have to remember moreover that the existence of our store presupposes the existence of significant numbers in our target segments, who find shopping enjoyable and perhaps almost orgasmic; certainly there are not many males in this category, and there is also some evidence that more women are so 'cash rich, time poor' (as the phrase has it) that they prefer to do their shopping via the Internet, at times which our stores cannot match.

If we do wish to address ourselves to other segments, then our resources will only enable us to do so on a fairly selective basis. Indeed, if we were to seek to attract a comprehensive cross-section of the population, that would immediately alienate many of our existing clients; and I do not think we want that. Instead, I propose that we move forward through market development, by encouraging our customers to stay with us and to spend more of their resources with us than is currently the case.

One important point to note here is that although we have an ageing customer profile, the life expectancy of the UK population continues to rise and there are increasing numbers of those in the 50+ age range who are affluent with large amounts of disposable income, and also with impressive quantities of leisure time. By targeting these people – preferably with added value services as well as through our product ranges – we could easily restore our profitability.

I recognise that genuine marketing innovation frequently stems from intuitive thinking in the management team rather than through customer focused research. However, we should not ignore such research, and this obligation to get closer to our customers is part of my recommendations framework which follows:

- Focus groups will help us identify more rigorously what our existing (and potential) customers want and need, what they expect, and how we can exceed their expectations.

- Secondary research should concentrate on our competition and enable us to capitalise upon trends in demography and customer dynamics.

- Given that customers are enhancing their technological knowledge, then our Internet capability (especially transactional) needs to be stimulated.

- We may also derive opportunities through international expansion and the opening of representative stores or concessions at airports – again in view of the fact that our customers tend to be involved in holidays and so forth.

- Exploiting our database should permit us to formulate a loyalty scheme to help retain our customers. I acknowledge that most loyalty schemes are nothing to do with genuine 'loyalty' and are in reality disguised sales promotions, but that does not invalidate their value and their relevance; moreover, if our competitors run such schemes it is difficult for us to remain on the sidelines (remember that Sainsbury's felt compelled to introduce its own 'loyalty' card after initially dismissing Tesco's Clubcard with snorts of derision and contempt).

Closer Relationships with Customers

Investment in our staff would immediately give us an opening into competitive advantage. Encouraging excellent customer care is the fundamental ingredient for quality service, according to Clutterbuck. Training staff in customer relationships, how to deal positively with complaints, to be understanding, sort problems quickly and so forth, will enable the David Preston enterprise to shift from a product oriented culture to one which is primarily customer facing.

The business strategy needs to alter so that it concentrates unequivocally on the customer. Employees in the service 'front line' need to have roles which emphasise their service accountabilities; their performance and achievements need to be rewarded and recognised; their activities must be explicitly supported and endorsed by leadership from the top.

A commitment to customer based research will itself encourage customers to believe that their views matter. We should initiate face to face, one-to-one interviews with selected customers, plus focus groups and in-store 'events' like champagne breakfasts and special product/service promotions. Of course, we must simultaneously incentivise our customers to take part and supply us with relevant details of their purchasing habits and so forth – this means prizes of short holidays, flights, and products – but we can establish links with our suppliers in order to reduce the costs involved.

Once we have a convincing collection of customer information then we have to invest in a Management Information System which can manipulate the significant variables and permit a personalised approach to customer management. We may then approach individual customers proactively with details of products similar to those already purchased, or encourage them to put items into a 'wishlist' box on our web site so that we can then tempt them by tailor-made offers.

Internal Management Changes

To stimulate a more customer concentrated focus, the Davis Preston Group top management will need to 'walk the talk' and must show that closeness to the customer is vital for the future of the company.

In addition:

- They must explicitly encourage and motivate staff through team meetings which address current problems and involve staff in proposing new routes for competitive success.

- They must encourage feedback from staff, hold competitions for new ideas, and 'reward and celebrate' for innovation.

- The vision, values and mission of Davis Preston must be continually emphasised (and never mentioned cynically).

- Empowerment for 'front line' service staff must be facilitated so that they have more authority to offer immediate restitution in the case of customer complaints, or to take the initiative if any customer wants something a little different.

- Some of the very senior managers and executives will have to depart, either because they are incapable of assimilating the company's change of direction or because their behaviour (consciously or otherwise) is likely to undermine the probability of a successful outcome for the change. These departures must be handled humanely – after all, some of the resistance the company will encounter is not primarily the fault of the individuals concerned, since they have typically given loyal commitment to the firm for many years – but they must be implemented cleanly. In my view only a small number of high profile departures will be needed, because other 'doubters' will instantly realise that they must alter their attitudes and behaviour if they are to keep their jobs, and they will then do so.

- New role profiles should be constructed for all levels of staff, emphasising accountabilities rather than tasks and competencies rather than the more mundane requirements of a traditional person specification. These new role profiles should expect all employees to add value, and all employees to demonstrate a positive approach to their own individual 'customer' relationships.

- Recruitment and selection procedures should be adapted so that the organization deliberately seeks to identify applicants with the right attitudes: i.e. a positive 'can do' mentality coupled with high levels of Emotional Intelligence (empathy and interpersonal skills) which can be translated into customer facing performance.

Conclusion

The above report has covered all the aspects specified in the brief supplied. In essence, Davis Preston needs to look at each area carefully and decide which needs to be tackled first. My view is that the internal problems – of managerial behaviour, leadership and corporate 'culture' – need to be confronted very quickly, because our external, customer related difficulties require the introduction of some new approaches to management style and people performance. However, there is no reason why some of the customer focused investigations (focus groups and the like) should not be initiated soon, because the results of these studies may well supply additional ammunition to underpin the arguments for more strategic innovation.

Senior Examiner's Comments

This case study was loosely based on the recent experiences of Marks & Spencer which, like Davis Preston, has issued a series of profit warnings, has been accused of complacency, and has suffered under a succession of paternalistic and/or autocratic Chief Executives. Sir Richard Greenbury combined the roles of CEO and Chairman, against all the principles of corporate governance; though customer surveys were conducted in the company, results were concealed from him because of fears about his reactions. As a consequence, the company was unable to take pre-emptive action in order to stem the decline of customer perceptions about 'value for money', product ranges and product quality. Since the case was written, the performance of Marks & Spencer has deteriorated still further. Although the impact of organizational decline for Marks & Spencer has been more acutely felt in the UK than elsewhere, it is a global enterprise not only as a retailer but also as a purchaser of products (especially clothing) manufactured in various parts of the world.

There were four specific questions associated with the case study brief and each was marked out of 10, with assessments based on the coherence of any given response and the likelihood that genuine differentiation could be attained through pursuit of the advice proposed. Within each of the four questions, up to 20 per cent of the available marks were allocated for presentation.

PART B

Answer THREE Questions Only

Question 2

Many observers believe that commoditization is an inevitable consequence of the trends towards electronic commerce. Examine the arguments for this view and suggest ways in which the commoditization trap can be avoided by those entering an e-commerce environment.

(20 marks)

Answer – Question 2

To: Marketing Manager
From: E-commerce Specialist
Date: 10th December, 2000
Subject: The Commoditization of E-commerce

1. Introduction to the Commoditization Debate

It is currently being argued that the Internet is only useful for the purchase of low involvement goods, such as books and CDs. The world of e-commerce has been dominated by the success of companies like amazon.com which focus purely on 'commoditised' goods; recently the failure of more complex, high involvement goods and services to be successful when marketed online has fuelled the debate about whether e-commerce will reshape the economic landscape as much as anyone first expected.

2. Reasons Why Commoditization is so Significant in the E-commerce Sector

There are several key reasons why the Internet still succeeds mainly in commoditised areas:

2.1 There is a much higher level of customer 'comfort' associated with the purchase of standardised goods, and correspondingly a greater degree of uncertainty about goods which appear to be idiosyncratic.

2.2 Often up to 70 per cent of venture capital funding will be invested in the marketing, promotion and advertising of the transactional web site from which purchases can be made. This indirectly encourages the commercial start-up enterprise to focus on commoditised products and services, since these require minimal levels of individual attention prior to delivery.

2.3 The Internet itself involves transparent pricing, and it does appear that many online customers will shift suppliers as prices fall. If then, there is little else to differentiate any given Internet business, customers will gravitate to the lowest price option; and commoditization is by that time well established.

2.4 Many web sites and Internet enterprises underestimate the importance of connections but proceed, instead, as if the whole purchasing process can be anonymously automated. Their thinking may be technology dominated, in which case they unwittingly denigrate the significance of customer service; or their straitened resources may mean that they simply cannot major on service as a competitive differentiator.

3. Avoiding the Commoditization 'Trap'

Although currently 60 per cent of the e-commerce world is dominated by the pre-play start-ups, this looks set to change. As bricks and mortar enterprises transfer their activities online, they can use a 'follower' strategy and learn from the mistakes made by those who have gone before (and who have sometimes irretrievably damaged their credibility in the process). With 'brick' companies, their experience of building up a supply chain management system off-line can contribute strongly to success in the Internet arena.

4. Application of the Decision Making Model of Buyer Behaviour

Use of this framework shows how the commoditization 'trap' may be avoided.

4.1 Need recognition: the Internet is important here, because of its ability to target specific audiences and create hunger for a product or service.

4.2 Information search: the Internet is of particular value in this phase of the purchase process, and site navigability is a key determinant of a purchase outcome.

4.3 Evaluation of the alternatives: customers like to have control and need either a face to face email or telephone contact if they are to be persuaded to purchase high involvement goods and services over the Internet.

4.4 The purchase decision: many web sites which appear to be transactional do not in fact supply purchasing mechanisms, and this in itself is enough to encourage potential customers to go elsewhere.

4.5 The post-purchase decision period: the contact with the customer must be maintained, preferably proactively (as amazon.com does).

5. Examples of Online 'Winners'

Companies like amazon.com have enjoyed the benefits of 'first mover' advantage, but have also succeeded in creating very close relationships with their customers, with proactive emails, personalised communications and so forth. Other Internet businesses can achieve remarkably rapid response times for customer queries (e.g. blackstar.com, the Belfast based retailer of videos and DVDs) and have secured a reputation for being very customer focused, very trustworthy, and very accommodating when confronted with customers who want something a little different from the standard 'product'.

6. Conclusion

Entering the e-commerce environment should be carefully considered in terms of customer needs and probable trends in customer dynamics. The importance of integrating online and off-line customer service is crucial in the search for competitive advantage and avoidance of commoditization; it is equally vital to address the issue of channel choice and to enable customers to establish a two-way dialogue with the product/service supplier, particularly in respect of high involvement goods.

Senior Examiner's Comments

Within the 20 marks available for the answer as a whole, 10 could be awarded for a discussion of the claim that 'commoditization' might be an inevitable consequence of e-commerce, plus 10 for suggesting ways in which the 'commoditization' trap might be avoided.

Question 3

Assume that you are employed as a Marketing Officer within a not-for-profit organization. Write a report to your Chief Executive in which you:

    a.   Argue the case for creating a corporate culture which is much more customer focused.

    b.   Explore the special difficulties of creating a customer orientation in your type of business.

    c.   Suggest some practical routes through which customer focus might be achieved.

(20 marks)

First Answer – Question 3

From: Marketing Officer

To: Chief Executive, Donkey Sanctuary

Date: 10th December, 2000

Subject: Customer Orientation

1. Background

This report will highlight the need for customer focus in not-for-profit organizations generally, and at our donkey sanctuary in particular.

2. Why should our Culture be more Customer Focused?

Firstly, there is an increasing amount of competition in the not-for-profit marketplace, especially competition for limited funds, donations, gifts and legacies. Individuals who could be our customers are becoming increasingly aware of ethical and environmental issues. This trend has seen the numbers of not-for-profit organizations increase, in response to actual or predicted public concern.

In this context, it is crucial that we become more customer focused in our outlook, so as to sustain our position in the 'industry' and retain our 'share' of the market when confronted by new entrants.

3. Difficulties in Creating Customer Orientation in our Business and Type of Organization

As our enterprise does not aim to make a profit, it is difficult to secure a customer focus among our staff and among our senior management, for the following reasons:

3.1 Employees are not driven by the need to make (or contribute to) a profit, and may therefore lack direction.

3.2 They themselves may feel that phrases like 'customer focus' and indeed the word 'customer' are only appropriate to commercial companies.

3.3 Traditionally, our organization's 'customers' have come to us and so our culture has been responsive rather than proactive; it has not needed to engage in deliberate marketing.

3.4 Not-for-profit organizations are run principally by volunteers. We are therefore dependent on their goodwill. They are enormously valuable to us, but they are largely amateurs so far as marketing and customer focus are concerned, and are unlikely to submit themselves to the disciplines involved. For us to initiate a customer orientation campaign, therefore, could rapidly prove counter-productive if it were to drive some of our volunteers away.

3.5 Some people define the term 'customer' as one who pays. If asked to classify the 'customers' for a donkey sanctuary, many might think first of the donkeys; relatively few would mention our donors and sponsors.

4. Achieving Customer Focus

Some practical routes through which customer focus may be achieved can be suggested in the framework developed by Chris Daffy (*Once a Customer, Always a Customer*, Dublin: Oak Tree Press) as follows:

4.1 Vision and values. Our Chief Executive and senior management team should construct and then demonstrate commitment to a customer-centred vision and set of positive values related to customer orientation. This does not need to be done from scratch, since we could adapt similar vision/values systems already in existence for other not-for-profit entities.

4.2 Internal people issues. We should explicitly seek to recruit and select people with customer-facing attitudes, train and develop our existing staff in customer service and care, and stimulate employee contributions to continuous improvement and change in the arena of customer relationships.

4.3 External people issues. Customer feedback must be actively solicited, with the findings disseminated throughout the organization. Customers should be given the chance to become directly involved with the organization and not kept at a distance. We may build 'informational' customer databases, summarising customer opinions, feedback and donor behaviour preferences; we can (and should) appeal to linked potential customer categories, such as horse and pony lovers, encouraging them to pay visits to the sanctuary and play an active part in our affairs. Once we can build direct emotional relationships between customers and donkeys, then keeping the connection should be very straightforward!

5. Conclusion

Changing the donkey sanctuary's orientation to a customer focus must be done slowly in order to reduce resistance amongst our permanent employees and our volunteers. The change has to be led and directed by management however, seeping through to the staff and finally to the customers themselves.

Senior Examiner's Comments

There were three substantive sub-questions, each qualifying for 5 marks, plus a further 5 marks for the extent to which answers were presented as reports (to the imagined Chief Executive of a not-for-profit organization).

This answer is a typical approach to Question 3, written around the plausible scenario of a donkey sanctuary (in the UK). It is succeeded by another Specimen Answer which concerns itself with the Blood Transfusion Service, again in the UK.

Second answer – Question 3

To: Chief Executive

From: Marketing Officer

Date: 10th December, 2000

Subject: Creating a Customer Orientation within the Blood Transfusion Service

1. Introduction

This report is intended to explain the reasons behind the necessary move to a customer orientation. It will address the particular issues presented by the Blood Transfusion Service (BTS) and suggest some practical ways in which these might be overcome. Should my proposals be acceptable, I suggest a meeting to decide on timescales for the marketing plan.

2. The Change in Corporate Culture

In recent years, it has become increasingly obvious that another drift has occurred in market orientation. We have seen the focus move from product, to sales, and then to marketing; now the focus has shifted yet again, this time to the customer. Many businesses are beginning to reap the benefits of a 'customer orientation'. Increased choice within the market has coincided with limited consumer time and resources. In this case, they look for what Marshall has described as the greatest 'utility' from the range of options available. In today's terms, this could be rephrased as 'value for money'. In the case of the BTS of course, our customers do not spend money, because we are asking them to donate blood; however the same principle applies, because they must perceive the 'benefits' of blood donation as being sufficient to outweigh the 'price' involved.

3. Focusing on the Customer

If we focus on the customer, we can discover what his or her needs are. We can then work to fulfil these needs and satisfy our customers. It is widely acknowledged that it is five times more expensive to attract new customers than it is to retain current customers. It will therefore be of benefit to the BTS to adopt a customer focus, as this will help us to increase donation levels and also cut costs (because of the reduced need to find new volunteers).

4. The Difficulties of Creating a Customer Orientation within the BTS

4.1 Needles!

Many people are afraid of injections or surgical needles, which immediately put them off the idea of blood donation. We need to concentrate on the end benefits of donation for these customers and make them more valuable than the 'price' of enduring the needle.

4.2 Health issues.

There has recently been some bad press regarding infected blood transfusions. We must reassure our customers (the donors) and end-users (those receiving transfusions) that our methods are reliable. This may involve better training for our internal customers (in many cases volunteers) who run the donor sessions so that they have the relevant facts. At the same time we must make sure that anyone who is infected and therefore unable to donate is treated with respect and compassion, as a dissatisfied customer can tell twice as many people about their experiences as a satisfied one.

4.3 Capacity.

Although the ultimate aim is to increase donations, we must be aware of our current limitations and plan accordingly. It would be highly embarrassing were we to find ourselves in a situation where we had to turn away potential customers.

4.4 Effective targeting of customers.

We have a particular need for certain, rarer blood groups. It can sometimes be hard to locate members of these blood groups. It may be necessary to involve health authorities (as customers of ours) so that they can actively promote us to patients whom they know fit our requirements.

5. Practical Routes through which Customer Orientation might be Achieved

5.1 Research.

We could carry out research using secondary data at first, to establish past patterns in donation: e.g. how often people donate blood, the demographics of our donors, their lifestyles, and so forth. After establishing such information from our records, it may be necessary to conduct interviews with both donors and non-donors to assess their views, perceptions of the BTS, and their needs.

5.2 Training.

As I have mentioned earlier, better training may be required for our staff. This could cover issues such as privacy, how to deal with stressful situations, and how to explain the benefits of donation.

5.3 Location.

We already go to workplaces to obtain blood donations, but it may be desirable to review when we do this: would it be better, for example, to offer the service out of office hours, if some customers would prefer to complete a day's work and then go home immediately after the donation process is complete?

5.4 Promotion/feedback.

Increased promotion of the BTS may help us to improve relationships with customers, as they see greater importance being placed on their contribution. We already award badges for 25 years of donations, but a more short term method of customer recognition and feedback could be a newsletter explaining the benefits in each area of the country where the BTS operates.

6. Conclusion

Although it can be difficult to see immediate results, it is still important to remember that not-for-profit organizations such as ours can benefit from a customer focus. Closer contact with our customers and a two-way exchange can only help us, as we try to fulfil our end-users' needs.

This answer is an alternative Specimen Answer for Question 3, this time focusing on the UK Blood Transfusion Service.

Question 4

Identify an organization which in your view has world-class relationships with its customers and exceptional customer service performance and then answer the following questions:

a. What does your chosen organization do which makes it especially effective at managing and improving relationships with its customers?

b. How does your chosen organization maintain a strong customer orientation among its own people?

c. What lessons can be learned for other organizations seeking to achieve world-class excellence in customer relationships and customer service?

(20 marks)

First Answer – Question 4

Federal Express

The first indisputable factor that enables Federal Express to achieve a world-class relationship with its customers is that it instils and embraces a marketing orientation within its business. A marketing orientation is a fundamental business philosophy that places the customer unequivocally at the centre of the company's affairs and which, if properly applied, becomes an architectural process.

When that happens, the mission, vision, goals, objectives and plans all focus on what the customer needs and requires. The three key factors that an organization must have to enable it to be fully marketing oriented are:

-   A customer focus orientation.
-   Market-led activities.
-   A profit orientation.

Federal Express is a company which exemplifies all three of these elements in a combination which enables it to be truly world-class. Its characteristics are:

-   **Excellence of service provision:** Federal Express understands its customers. It has the correct systems, procedures and policies in place to ensure that all its customers are dealt with efficiently and effectively.

-   **Customer care as a business objective:** to ensure that customers feel important and valued. Training is given to staff to ensure they understand how to deal with customers; customer complaints and queries are dealt with quickly; customer facing employees are empowered to make decisions to help customers.

-   **Relationship marketing:** this is a key focus for Federal Express. Relationship marketing is the process which moves on from mass marketing; its aim is to have a one-to-one relationship with each of the company's customers. Understanding customer needs, listening to customers and then targeting customers more closely so that their exact needs are fulfilled: this is the route to customer satisfaction, customer delight and customer loyalty.

-   **Partnership processes with customers:** Federal Express wants to develop a partnership with its customers, and seeks to achieve this through the five stages of relationship marketing:

1. The basic transaction – a product or service is sold and there is no subsequent contact.

2. The reactive relationship – the customer is asked to call if he or she has a problem about parcel delivery.

3. The accountable contract – the company calls the customer to check that the parcel has arrived.

4. The proactive communication – the company regularly calls the customer and maintains periodic contact in order to build trust and mutual confidence.

5. The relationship – there is active dialogue between company and customer, with reciprocal feedback on improvement, restitution and transformational changes in service standards.

To summarise, the key elements that make Federal Express a world-class service provider are:

- A marketing oriented organization – that places customer satisfaction (and, better still, customer delight) as its main objective. As John Frazer-Robinson has argued in his book Customer-Driven Marketing, 'The object of a business is not to make money. The object of a business is to serve its customers. The result is to make money.'

- Excellent customer interaction – with general proficiency on the customer care front, rapid and positive handling of customer complaints, a company wide concern for service, a 'right first time' mentality, and the presence of an overarching strategic framework (mission, vision, goals, objectives and plans) which concentrate unequivocally upon the customer.

- Maintenance of customer focus among its own employees – through a Total Quality Management (TQM) culture with people knowing precisely what is expected from them whether they deal with external customers or not; and recognition of the fact that the only way to achieve competitive advantage is through the performance of people.

In essence, Federal Express believes that you should treat employees in the same way that you treat customers: i.e. you value them, you believe they can add value and you empower them. In this way Federal Express translates the Reichheld 'circle of virtue' into meaningful reality.

The lessons for other organizations which they can learn from Federal Express, are briefly as follows:

1. Customer satisfaction and customer delight are key determinants of competitive advantage.

2. Employee satisfaction is an essential prelude to customer satisfaction.

3. Customer orientation starts at the top, with the CEO and the corporate mission, and has to be communicated down the hierarchy both clearly and frequently.

4. Benchmarking is an excellent way to position yourself and work out what you need to do in order to get where you want to go.

5. World-class service does not stem from simply being reactive; instead, organizations must be proactive in order to devise better solutions and routes to innovative customer-focused transformation.

Senior Examiner's Comments

No specific form of answer construction was required; as a result, 6 or 7 marks were allocated to each of the three sub-questions, with up to 2 marks for an introductory paragraph identifying the organization which was to be the focus for the answer material.

Second Answer – Question 4

1. For the purposes of this question, I wish to use the supermarket retailer Tesco, to illustrate the main points of effective customer relationship management.

2. What makes Tesco effective at managing and improving customer relationships?

2.1 Keen customer focus – a dedicated customer service department.

2.2 Commitment to improving the shopping environment for customers: stores are well designed and well lit; there is a minimum of queueing; restaurants for refreshments are supplied; help at each checkout is typically available, with people to pack bags and carry purchases to the customer's car.

2.3 Store locations are convenient for population centres.

2.4 Tesco was the first supermarket to have dedicated child and parent parking spaces.

2.5 The majority of Tesco stores are open 24 hours, 6 nights a week.

2.6 Tesco offers a successful Internet shopping and home delivery service.

2.7 About three quarters of Tesco shoppers own a Tesco Clubcard. This has enabled Tesco to tailor its loyalty programme to individual shoppers, supplying them with money off vouchers relative to their normal purchasing patterns.

2.8 Regular customer feedback mechanisms are employed, with problems resolved very quickly before they have the opportunity to fester.

3. The principal ways in which Tesco promotes strong customer orientation.

3.1 Recruitment: Tesco has a thorough recruitment process which identifies suitable candidates for its customer focused environment.

3.2 Training: people are given the option to be trained in several different areas, and this helps the company when extra checkouts have to be opened.

3.3 Code of Conduct: Tesco has a set of customer focused values that employees are aware of and to which they are expected to adhere.

3.4 Standard of dress and appearance: as Tesco employees are instantly recognizable, they are made to feel part of a team, even though they are simultaneously allowed a measure of individuality because alternative uniforms are available.

3.5 Winning team: Tesco is a very successful company and its employees enjoy high morale because of their involvement.

3.6 Effective leadership: the company places great emphasis on interpersonal leadership from its managers and group leaders.

4. Lessons learned by other organizations.

4.1 Putting the customer first. Driving the business from the requests, aspirations and priorities of the customers, and adding value to these activities, provides differentiation and a high level of customer 'delight'.

4.2 Ensuring company cohesion and a unified customer facing culture. If all members of the organization are working towards the same goal – of customer service – then motivation is co-ordinated and leadership is single-minded, with no conflicting messages or ambiguities to get in the way.

4.3 Customer feedback. Allowing customers opportunities for feedback makes them feel appreciated and listened to; moreover, it enables the company to take corrective actions very quickly.

4.4 Problem solving. It is important to address all complaints quickly and efficiently. Wal-Mart has a similar 'sundown rule' which specifies that all complaints should be resolved by the end of the working day in which they occur.

4.5 Empowerment. Staff are encouraged to make decisions directly with the customers, so they can use their initiative, enjoy some degree of autonomy, and deliver positive results so far as customer perceptions are concerned.

Senior Examiner's Comments

This answer is an alternative Specimen Answer for Question 4, this time focusing on Tesco.

Question 5

A recent article in the Financial Times (20th January, 1999) claimed that Positioning is not a source of sustainable competitive advantage for any business, because it can easily be copied... Market positioning is a competitive advantage only when it is matched with competitive advantage based on brands and systems. Discuss and explain these statements, with specific reference to both an international airline and a fast food company.

(20 marks)

Answer – Question 5

There are a great many ideas concerning what creates competitive advantage and what makes a company successful. The Financial Times article claims that 'positioning is not a sustainable competitive advantage'. Positioning involves the company deciding where to pitch its products and to whom, based on its target market. Bill Gates (from Microsoft) has said, 'If the 1980s were about quality and the 1990s about re-engineering, the 2000s will be about velocity.' This highlights the speed at which companies need to change and adapt in a fast evolving marketplace. It is true to say indeed, that positioning can be easily copied; any company can produce a similar quality product at a similar price to the same target audience – and many do! It is therefore also true to say that other factors need to be present to ensure competitive advantage; brand value, for instance, can play an enormous part in securing profitability.

To illustrate the point that many factors can create competitive success, rather than just market positioning on its own, let us firstly look at an international airline.

The arena of air travel is historically a very competitive environment which has expanded over time, and continues to do so. There many key players in the UK, but they can all survive for differing reasons. Threshold competencies (basic service features) are similar across the industry. Core competencies (key differentiators) quickly become threshold competencies. For example, in order to differentiate itself, Virgin offered excellent in-flight entertainment and television screens in the rear of each seat; now, virtually all long-haul airlines have this feature. Virgin then introduced a limousine service for business customers, and again this has been quickly copied.

Overall, market positioning keeps the basic 'bread and butter' revenue coming in. British Airways focuses on the business traveller; Virgin on the 25-35 year old; and easyJet on low cost. However, longer term differentiation and competitive advantage are reinforced by carefully promoted brands and key specialisms. Promotions, service levels, loyalty programmes and efficient operating systems can also give companies the edge.

Fast food chains are very similar. They all offer similar products, at similar prices, and in largely similar locations. Perceived brand identity is an important feature for customers, and reinforces both values and benefits. Mintel reports have recently showed that different fast food products are targeted towards different customer segments: McDonalds concentrates on children, Burger King on teenagers and KFC towards young adults. In this industry, companies find success by targeting various people, although market position does not guarantee long term advantage. Thus a recent promotion and advertising campaign helped Burger King to steal a substantial amount of the market from McDonalds.

In conclusion, consumers are generally quite fickle. The fragmentation of previously large customer segments, and the availability of more suppliers, have led to increased price sensitivity and lower levels of customer loyalty. Market position has helped some companies by giving them significant advantages over the competition and enabling them to fend off price driven initiatives from elsewhere.

However, because of enhanced levels of customer mobility, companies must search for more than mere market position. Excellent service, strong brands, efficient company systems and processes, all provide excellent opportunities for long term success.

Relevant to this whole discussion are the arguments advanced in a new book Differentiate or Die by Trout and Rivkin (Wiley, 2000). As the authors point out, there are some supposed differentiators which in practice do not differentiate; among them are:

- Quality and customer orientation – which only work as sources of competitive advantage when the competition is sluggish. Once the competition catches up and quality becomes universal, then key players have to look for something else.

- Price – which only works when accompanied by structural advantages (e.g. SouthWest Airlines).

- Category-killing product breadth – which again only works when the competition is sluggish.

Instead, say Trout and Rivkin, there are some winning differentiators to which organizations like airlines and fast food enterprises should turn in their never ending search for supremacy:

- Market specialization – or 'positioning', in other words, enabling the organization to claim some special expertise.

- Customer preference – reflecting the fact that many customers will buy what they think they should be buying, in order to reassure themselves and possibly to impress others (e.g. Science Diet pet food).

- How a product is made – especially if the customers can be made to believe that the product incorporates some 'magic' ingredient, like Sony's Trinitron and McVities digestive biscuits.

- Newness – for the innovative customer, product innovation is itself a vital factor.

- Being first – the pioneer is able to enjoy the benefits from being the sole supplier, and imitators appear inadequate.

- Leadership – at least so far as customer perceptions are concerned.

- Attribute ownership – so, for example, Crest toothpaste 'owns' cavity prevention.

- Heritage – in other words, leadership through longevity, as in the case of Budweiser which dates from 1876.

At least in some circumstances, market positioning can count as a Critical Success Factor rather than a mere Critical Failure Factor – i.e. an aspect of organizational performance like quality, which the company has to perform well merely to remain in competitive contention.

Senior Examiner's Comments

Up to 10 marks could be secured through a general discussion of the sentiments expressed in the quotation from the Financial Times; the remaining 10 marks were earned through completion of the 'application scenarios' involving both an international airline and a fast food company.

Question 6

p>It is often argued nowadays that customers today don't want choice and don't want to be satisfied. Write a report for your Marketing Department of a car manufacturer in which you evaluate the relevance of these arguments for the car industry and explore the practical implications for the company s marketing strategy.

(20 marks)

Answer – Question 6

To: Marketing Department, Harrison Autos

From: Marketing Executive

Date: 10th December, 2000

Subject: Customer Choice and Customer Satisfaction

1. Introduction

There is a myth that customers don't want choice and don't want to be satisfied. This is misguided, and I seek to challenge the myth in the following report.

2. The Customers who Don't Want Choice

About a year ago, Smart (a division of Mercedes) introduced a new small car. There was only one model, but within months it was being seen in every main town across the UK. Whilst the car only came in one format, its target audience of young people had the option to choose various colour combinations and body panels, therefore personalising the model to their own individual preferences. By contrast, when the Ford Model T rolled off the assembly lines, Henry Ford was famed for saying that buyers could have it in any colour so long as it was black.

The simple fact is that cars today are used to express and articulate the personalities of the purchasers driving them. A businessman earning £200,000 a year will not want to be seen in a standard Ford Focus, for example. By contrast, a low income earner may love Jaguars but can only afford a mass production vehicle. In each case some level of personalization is achieved even in the purchasing process, but can then be accentuated through accessories, registration plates, and so forth.

Choice is imperative to most customers and without it their motivation to buy will be negligible or even non-existent. On the other hand, from a manufacturer's standpoint there are costs associated with customization, and most cannot afford to deploy more than around 5 model ranges at any one time. If you consider Ford and Renault, for example, they already use the same engines in different models, and use the same floor pan for different vehicles: they have sought deliberately to maximise the variety of their product offer whilst minimising the expenditure incurred.

Customization is important not only for the customer but also for the car dealer, since accessories represent a valuable source of high margin sales. Car owners will seek to acquire vehicles appropriate to (what they imagine to be) their lifestyles; some vehicles will reflect personal aspirations and even a degree of fantasy.

Choice is crucial, in short. Our customers demand it more and more; we must cater for their desires and ambitions, or we shall inevitably lose business. The only sense in which it might be accurately claimed that 'customers don't want choice' is that customers want precisely and exactly what they want – and so if they are offered a product choice which does not include precisely and exactly what they seek, then they are as dissatisfied as they would be if they had not been offered any choice at all. Telling a customer who wants a two door vehicle with automatic transmission that automatic transmission is only available on four door models is no way to attract clients.

3. The Customers who Don't Want to be Satisfied

People who are not interested in the product or service offered will be unconcerned about whether they are satisfied or not. You may wonder why such people would buy cars from us in the first place; however, there are some who simply want 'a car' and who do not regard it as a major part of their lives. A few too, need a car because their employer wants them to have one; again, they are purchasing under duress and not of their own volition.

Such instances are relatively exceptional and rare. For those who are potential customers, we should be concentrating our efforts towards generating customer delight.

A large proportion of customers who are merely satisfied will be susceptible to supplier change unless something else can be done to attract (and retain) them. In the UK, it is not uncommon to wait up to 10 weeks for a new vehicle, and this occurs because customers seek to specify a precise model rather than simply purchase whatever option is immediately available.

Dr. Naraki Kano, a marketing theorist, suggests three levels concerned with the concept of customer satisfaction: the 'Must Be' factors, the 'More is Better' factors, and the 'Delighters'.

The 'Must Be' factors are those items that must exist before a customer will be satisfied. Thus a new car must have an engine that works, wheels, and be ready to drive. The presence of the 'Must Be' factors does not produce customer enthusiasm, since they are expected; it is their absence which would become a cause for (adverse) comment.

The 'More is Better' ingredients are those elements which move a customer towards satisfaction and ultimately towards delight. Within a car such elements may include brand identity.

The 'Delighters' are factors that surprise and impress the customer more than he or she expected. Perhaps the car moves more smoothly than expected; perhaps it is equipped with satellite navigation, air conditioning or an exceptional music system.

Unfortunately for us, yet unavoidably, we have a constant struggle to find new sources of customer 'delight', because any given model innovation rapidly moves into the 'Must Be' quadrant and therefore ceases to be a source for customer amazement. I propose, in fact, that we concentrate our efforts on improvements to the service dimension; e.g. rapid response times, vehicle valeting as a regular part of the service package, and so forth.

Senior Examiner's Comments

Evaluating the relevance of the two statements (that customers don't want choice and don't want to be satisfied) was worth up to 10 marks; assessing the implications for a car company's marketing strategy could account for the remaining 10 marks. Within the general framework, however, answers had to be produced in the form of a report to the Marketing Department, and 4 marks could be awarded for answers which fulfilled this requirement.

Question 7

You have been recruited by a company in **EITHER** book/magazine publishing, **OR** over-the-counter medicines. The company, though international, is not yet active in your region but wishes to evaluate the market potential of the country where you reside. Write a report for your client in which you address the following:

a. The secondary information sources which should be consulted by the client.

b. The methods which your client could use in order to establish directly the extent to which its products or services would be successful.

(20 marks)

Answer – Question 7

Report on Assessing the Market Potential of the UK Magazine Market

To: Manager, Onion Publishing

From: Marketing Officer, Onion Publishing

Date: 10th December, 2000

Subject: Attractiveness of the Marketplace for Magazines in the UK

1. Introduction

As the UK is not yet one of the territories targeted by Onion Publishing, it is necessary to consider its market potential in advance of its potential entry. In this report I will outline some of the sources and methods by which this can be established. I will look firstly at secondary (or 'desk') sources which can indicate the potential size of the entire market, and then at some primary methods (or 'field' studies) which could be commissioned in order to determine more precisely the market demand for Onion publications.

2. Secondary Information Sources

2.1 ABC circulation statistics: These show how other companies' publications perform in the UK.

2.2 Government published demographic information: Including sources such as the UK Census (held every 10 years), Social Trends (annual publication) and all information held by the Office of National Statistics.

2.3 Geo-demographic information: Tools such as ACORN (A Classification Of Residential Neighbourhoods), Pinpoint and Experian contain large amounts of data which can be used to gain a picture of the UK population, its consumption preferences, lifestyle characteristics, and so forth.

2.4 Market reports: These are carried out by companies like Mintel and Datamonitor. It should be noted that, although generally reliable, as with all secondary sources the date of the investigation and also the rationale for its execution (i.e. if it were paid for by a specific enterprise) could have implications for the significance of the results.

2.5 Competitor information: Published accounts (from Companies House) could be useful in assessing performance; also the advertising rate cards issued by current publications can suggest comparative achievement and circulation/readership quality.

3. Problems with Secondary Data

Secondary data such as from the sources mentioned above should be sufficient to prove the potential market size for the Onion portfolio of publications. Caution should always be exercised, however, when dealing with secondary sources, to ensure that there is no biased information. As with primary research methods for example, the use of hypothetical questions is especially dangerous, since respondent replies may be equally hypothetical; in which case they cannot be used in order to predict customer behaviour in any specific scenario.

4. Primary Research Methods

Once the market potential is established, it will be necessary to undertake some primary marketing research to determine the precise demand for Onion publications. The main methods are questionnaires and interviews.

4.1 Questionnaires: These tend to constitute a quantitative method of research, providing data which can be directly measured. Questionnaires can be useful for understanding basic attitudes and opinions, and also for gathering some demographic information with a degree of local 'colour' not normally achievable from secondary material.

4.2 Interviews: These tend to be more qualitative and take two main forms – individual depth interviews/discussions, and focus groups. Either way, interviews are more suited to the exploration of motivation, needs and underlying attitude patterns, but the results (and the interpretation of the results) can be affected by interviewer bias or an interviewee's desire to please the interviewer. After all, as Nishikawa famously said (in his article for the Journal of Long Range Planning in 1989), 'the consumer is only sincere when spending'. By inference, therefore, statements about what a potential customer might do in the future, if a certain product became available and if his/her financial resources were adequate, are automatically misleading and possibly even completely false. They may reflect little more than wishful thinking, the public portrayal of politically correct opinions, or a genuine intention which ultimately becomes frustrated by the individual's readiness to succumb to the opinions of others.

4.3 Design of questions and interview samples: All questions have to be carefully developed so that they address every conceivable option and are not intentionally misleading or prejudicial; moreover, samples used for marketing research must be carefully selected so that they are representative of the ultimate customers for our products. This could be achieved by making use of demographic information.

4.4 Focus groups: This approach requires special mention and a paragraph to itself. They include up to about 10 people per group and you can ask questions about behaviour, opinions on products, service, price and the competition. You will require a trained facilitator and will need a good idea of who, what and where you want to benchmark against. Feedback is easily collated and analyzed; focus groups can also help to generate ideas for subsequent application. You have to beware of strong opinion leaders however, and individuals who talk too much.

5. Conclusion

Onion will be able to assess the UK market effectively by first using the available secondary information and then carrying out its own primary marketing research. It is important to refer to secondary data first as primary research can be expensive and certain aspects may be deemed unnecessary once secondary sources have been consulted.

Senior Examiner's Comments

Listing appropriate secondary sources could earn 10 marks; the remainder were allocated for an examination of the primary research techniques which could be used (in order to assess the market potential for book/magazine publishing or over the counter medicines).

Debriefing Activity 1.1

A more detailed approach to analyzing an organization will be found in the section on the customer care audit in the unit 'Strategy and methods to produce customer focused behaviour'

1. **Driving forces for change in the oil additives industry**

   Globalization

Car company	*Oil company*	*Additive company*
Consolidation of companies and technologies	Consolidation	Fewer more powerful customers
Some regional differences	Companies in transition	Centralized customer purchasing
		Customers want global pricing

   Legal, regulatory, environmental

Car company	*Oil company*	*Additive company*
Reduced exhaust emissions	Low emission fuels/lubes	Need for low emission systems
Drive to replace the car – low growth in traditional markets	Low market growth in traditional markets	Low growth in traditional markets

   Customer expectations

Car company	*Oil company*	*Additive company*
Lower cost cars	Lower-cost lubes/fuels	Lower-cost additives
	Less frequent oil change	Lower sales volumes
New models	Reduced product life cycle	Reduced product life cycle
No field failures	Fuels/lubes as commodity	Limited product differentiation
	More harms testing	Higher development costs
	Strong Competition	Customers want tailoring
		Higher service element required

   Economic

Car company	*Oil company*	*Additive company*
		High crude prices, weak euro
		Strong competitors and suppliers

2. **How is the organization responding**

   i. Globalization
      - Organization structured globally marketing, R&D, manufacturing, IT, etc., operations in 80 countries
      - Strategic Business Units established
      - Expansion in newer markets – focus on Asia Pacific, China, identification of opportunities in the Middle East, Russia etc.

   ii. Legal regulatory and environmental
      - Development of products which result in improved exhaust emissions
      - Annual environmental performance targets

   iii. Customer expectations
      - Dedicated customer support teams for key customers
      - Partnerships for product development
      - New regional customer service centres established
      - Strong cost focus within product development

   iv. Economic

- Partnerships established with suppliers
- Push for price increases

3. **How does this affect the way people are organized and managed**
    i. Organization
        - Global structure – matrix of business teams and functions
        - Implementation of cross-functional, cross-regional teams
        - Development of flexible systems and processes
        - Less hierarchy
    ii. Training/performance review systems
        - Goals-based review process
        - Improve interpersonal effectiveness – 360 feedback, etc.
        - Worldwide training on customer focus – educate all on their role in providing customer service
        - Promote the concept of a learning organization
        - Promote 'leadership' at all levels in the organization
    iii. Culture
        - Importance of core values – everyone understands what is important to the company
        - Openness about business results – everyone should be committed to how the company is doing
        - Encourage formation of external partnerships

4. **How does this affect managers**
    i. More global thinking and interregional travel
    ii. Less control – more empowerment
    iii. Responsibility for motivation and skill development rather than task and process
    iv. Complex matrix structure with many interfaces – line and technical responsibilities may involve different people
    v. Shift in emphasis – marketing led rather than manufacturing and product led – conflict

5. **How Does this affect employees**
    i. More change and uncertainty
    ii. Less 'paternalism' by company
    iii. More freedom and flexibility
    iv. More responsibility for own career and development
    v. Multiple managers – functional and project
    vi. More complex interfaces
    vii. More customer focus for product development functions

Debriefing Activity 2.9

People tend to expect the functional, social, experiential and emotional benefits from a service. They also take into account certain cost facts:

- Price
- Perceived risk
- Switching cost
- Fear of technological complexity
- Learning lot
- Future expectations.

The decision to buy the service is also affected by their AIO (attitude, interest and opinions) about the service and computers, the substitute available and complementary products they also consume, their engagement in relevant usage situations and their demographics.

Debriefing Question 2.5

MEMO

To: **Marketing Director**

From: **Lucinda and Rosie**

Date: **January 2000**

Re: **1 Market segmentation for the toy market – a fresh look**

       2 The customer/user distinction and its relevance for us

       3 Key roles in the DMU – how we can exploit them to our advantage

1 The market segmentation systems relevant for a toy manufacturer

A market segmentation exercise for your market would be an effective way of achieving a better understanding of your customers and how to position your marketing activities appropriately. It will also help to identify the prospects that are most likely to purchase your toy products and ensure your sales activities are also aligned to these customers.

By working through the following systems you will find the correct segment of potential customer which you can then plan your marketing mix around. From our point of view there are five ways of segmenting the market.

1. **Geographic**

   This is a very simple start to the process and is important if you market your products across a wide geographic area. It enables you to divide your market into nations, countries, regions and cities. Having analyzed this you can identify areas where you wish to concentrate your marketing and sales activities. Your decisions regarding marketing mix can then be adapted to suit each territory.

   For example, some regions may show greater interest in educational toys, whereas in other areas play value may be of greater interest. Some geographic variations will be linked to climate and the use of outdoor and indoor toys.

2. **Geodemographic**

   Alone this system will not give you a detailed enough profile of your customer. However, it will provide a useful platform for further research. This system is based on the belief that people in particular areas will have similar lifestyles, economic and social circumstances. Profiling this in connection to your particular products will give you direction on where future shops should be situated, sales structures and market campaign focus (e.g. where direct mail campaigns would be most useful). One of the most popular ways to produce a geodemographic profile is to use ACORN (A Classification of Residential Neighbourhoods) which uses financial, socio-economical and census data.

   If you have products already established in the market, this system can identify in what geodemographic area the brand is strongest and where other opportunities lie in similar market segments in which people with similar profiles are living.

3. **Socio-demographic**

   This method of segmentation has two sides to it, the socio-economic aspect which divides people according to social class, status and occupational classifications and the demographic (considered below). Generally speaking, it may appear that people with higher incomes have more disposable income, but this in itself does not imply that toy expenditure will have a high priority. It is the attitude of indulgence that needs to be looked for and that can be found in many working-class families through grandparents and other family members.

   Demographic segmentation is an easy and inexpensive way to identify:

   o   Trends in population (very relevant for targeting of child segments).

   o   Provides you with a better understanding of your market structure and potential customers.

   Demographics uses information on age, gender, education, family life cycle (i.e. measurable aspects of society). This may be particularly useful in making decisions about what age of child the toy(s) should be positioned to. This is particularly relevant to the toy market as there are a declining number of children in out society, and therefore we need to look at new product/market extensions such as toys aimed at adults.

4. **Behaviour in the product field**

   This is an important system that is based on a number of behavioural measures, e.g.:

   - Attitude to product
   - Loyalty to product
   - Purchasing frequency
   - Usage rate
   - Knowledge of product
   - Benefits sought from the product.

   Again this is fairly easy to achieve via customer questionnaires and inventories. The only challenge may be gaining questionnaire feedback from the users (i.e. children) depending on their age.

   Benefits segmentation is particularly useful as it addresses the expectations of either the purchaser or the user or both. Purchasers may be much more interested in the degree to which any toy has educational value, whether it is safe, its durability and its cost. Users (the children themselves) are much less activated by cost, but will be heavily influenced by peer pressure and the requirement of sustained interest through repeated playings without breaking.

   Purchasing patterns would also be of interest as visits to shops may occur at times that are relevant to the family, e.g. birthday, Christmas, or they may become something that is routinely done, toys can also be purchased via direct marketing and also across the web.

5. **Motivation, psychographics and social value groups**

   This is a very qualitative technique that explores the more 'emotional side' of purchasing decision making. Once completed you will have a more accurate picture of the 'personality' of your future and existing customers and what they really want from the toy. AIO analysis links motivation with other dimensions, as does social value analysis.

   In my view I think we should think about family life cycle and benefit segmentation. With this in mind we can develop an ongoing relationship with our customers, building a database so that we are able to create life-long customer relationships. The motivational aspects need to be researched along the lines of education, play and entertainment.

2 Relevance of the distinction between 'customer' and 'purchaser'

In marketing toys it is important to recognize that there is a difference in the person who uses the product (a child) and the person(s) who pays for the product (typically an adult) who is referred to as the 'customer'. This is typical of a market where the user (in this case because of age) lacks buying power, access and expertise to make the purchase.

Some purchases of toys may be a reflection of the donor's wish to get peace and love themselves, and to bring peace and love to the recipient – the gift of a teddy bear from a grandparent may want the child to fall in love with the bear and reflect love in return. This could be the motivation of many givers.

Alternatively you could get a child who pesters the parent for a skateboard – the payoff is peace for the parent from the relentless nagging!

A different example could be where a parent is satisfying their unfilled need for something – a father who was never given a train set, a mother who never had ballet lessons, very often the gift will provide a release for the parent being about to satisfy something within themselves.

Depending on the type of toy you are marketing the user and the purchaser may, in some circumstances, be the same (e.g. if the toy is aimed at teenagers), but more likely the purchaser will be an adult.

When thinking about the marketing mix for the product it will be essential to meet the needs of both roles. Failing to do this may result in a child who wishes to use the toy but has no 'buy-in' from the ultimate decision maker (the buyer). Alternatively you may have an adult who sees the benefits of the toy but the user (the child) who has no desire for the product.

There are many examples of toy manufacturers who address this decision-making unit by positioning promotion to both. For example, an advert for a toy will be appealing to the user (bright, visual, fun and noisy) but also present benefits appealing to the purchaser (value for money, safe, educational). The same principle should apply to all packaging, promotion, etc.

Both roles are equally important in making a purchase (and future purchases) and this dual positioning will be essential for sales success.

Until recently the toy market was an example of a market where an autonomous purchase used to be rare. Parents used to do the choosing and the paying – this is reflected in Early Learning Centres where parents chose what was good for their child, e.g. stimulated their development. But now much of the choosing is not done by parents, although many still pay. Children have more pocket money, permissive parenting, television advertising, skilful marketing, video, and the web have combined to take the decision out of parents' hands into their children's. Popularity of toys is very dependent on trends and fashions (i.e. 'toys of the moments' like Teletubbies). Children will be very influenced by the toys their peer group play with and talk about, especially since toys become a key part of children's interaction with them. Indeed, the future user (the child) can, in turn, become an influence to the final decision maker (the purchasing adult).

The distinction between user and customer (payer) makes good sense. We need to research what children want and what motivation and emotional values underpin the behaviour of our paying customers. This will give us a competitive edge over companies who only think in terms of one or the other role in the DMU.

3 The importance of other roles in the DMU

The DMU for a toy product purchase may be constructed as follows:

- User: Child
- Influencer: Peer group of child and other influencers/other adults/future users
- Decision maker: Child's parents/adult purchasing product
- Purchaser: Adult purchasing product.

This DMU would very much vary depending on the nature of the toy. For example, a toy designed for a teenager may see the actual child as the decision maker and purchaser and the child's peer group may still be an influencer.

Failure to recognize that in the toy market the DMU is more complex than with other products would lead to incorrect positioning of the marketing mix. It is essential to meet the needs of each role within the DMU, who will all have different motivations, interests, and behaviours.

For a product such as a toy the DMU is not as simple as just the user and the purchaser. You will also have to consider the following:

- Who influences the purchaser?
- Who initiates the process?
- Who influences future purchases?
- Who advises – the adviser who supplies technical assistance – within the toy shop itself?

There are a number of other roles within the decision-making unit which will contribute towards the decision to purchase a product. The following are consumer-referent groups which have significant impact on consumer behaviour:

- *Family* Different family members occupy different roles within the DMU. For example, a middle child may be bought a particular type of product, such as a bicycle, because their elder sibling received one at their age. They contribute to the DMU in this way. It is also interesting to note the general differences between male and female purchases. For example, the male of the household has greater influence on the purchase of items such as insurance and cars, whereas the female has greater influence over children's clothing and food. Items in the 'middle' are holidays and alcoholic beverages (Adcock, Bradfield, Halberg and Ross, 1994). Having this information on influences means that marketers can target certain products more towards the individual with greater influence on a particular purchase.

- *Peer groups* As mentioned previously in this report, peer groups are particularly important to the toy industry, as success in different product lines is often assured by their fitting the latest trend. People naturally want to belong to certain groups, and having the latest toy that their peers own may make them feel that they do conform. In conjunction with family, peer groups are of primary influence on consumer behaviour.

- *Consumer groups* The consumer has become more powerful as their awareness of what they want and expect to receive in terms of product and service has become increasingly prevalent.

This is exemplified by the burgeoning number of consumer watchdogs which have grown over recent years. It is imperative in the toy industry that products meet certain safety standards as defined by the government. Having a reputation of not meeting these standards will certainly affect the decision-making process.

- *Work groups* Work groups can be both formal and informal, defined by professional or departmental groups and the social groups formed with colleagues. If one is to assume that a high percentage of toys are bought by adults for children, then the adult's peers must also be considered as influencers within the DMU, as well as the child's peers. It may be that there is some competitiveness between adults as to their children's performance – artistically, educationally or socially. They may then want to buy them toys which help them to succeed or conform to certain social groups. Similarly, if one parent has a particularly good or bad experience when buying a toy, they are likely to tell their colleagues. In this respect, marketing to avoid post-purchase dissonance may be highly valuable.

Market activities may be influenced by these roles within the decision-making unit.

The individual players within the decision-making unit do vary, but they need to be considered in order to tailor marketing most effectively.

- *Aspirational appeal* This method uses a celebrity or well-known figure to endorse a product. It was documented recently that Stephen Hawking is an advertiser's 'dream figure' to endorse a product because he is so well known and is universally respected. In terms of the toy market, individuals who are known to have children and are viewed to be morally respected may hold aspirational appeal. Alternatively, the product can be placed in a particular context which appeals to the purchaser. For example, this may be a family sitting around a table playing with a particular game, or a product which encourages educational advancement through being fun.

- *Peer appeal* Having children who look popular and 'trendy' advertising a product may encourage children to aspire to owning the same product themselves. Peer appeal works on the basis that the consumer can relate to the context or individual who is advertising the product. For example, a mother of young children who is at home would probably relate to adverts depicting similar situations to her own. This particular demographic profile would also affect the scheduling of advertisements. A television commercial would probably suit the demographics of a morning programme such as GMTV or *Good Morning*, or a print advert would suit a predominantly female magazine such as *Chat* or even *Mother and Baby*, depending on the age of the child which the product was intended for.

- *Expert appeal* Again, this marketing strategy uses individuals to which the consumer can identify. It works on the basis that the consumer recognizes them as an expert in their field and they therefore believe them about the functions or pleasure of a particular product. A good example of this is Dorling Kindersley's use of Dr Miriam Stoppard on point-of-sale material. She is a highly branded author, and provides expert appeal to consumers because of her professional profile. If she advocates a particular range or type of toy for 1-3 year olds, parents are likely to follow her advice.

These three referent groups exemplify how different types of marketing appeal to different customers with varying needs and influences. It is essential to realize that these types of marketing do vary with the market segment. Whereas a parent of small children might follow the expert 'advice' of a doctor or child specialist, a teenager who is both the end user and purchaser is more likely to be influenced by peer appeal. Understanding the make-up of a decision-making unit and their process of actually making a purchase is essential in order to accurately target specific market segments. One could argue that it is especially important in an industry such as the toy market, where there is often such a clear distinction between the customer or purchaser and the end user.

When we sell into stores this concept needs to be extended to include:

- The decider – who takes the purchase decision
- The financer – who supplies the resources or who reports on their availability
- The gatekeeper – who allows information into the organization.

You also need to think about the type of decision:

- Straight rebuy
- Modified rebuy
- New purchase.

In deciding on the correct marketing mix for a toy product, all the above need to be researched. The result is an understanding of your full decision-marking unit (the group of people who decide whether to buy a product).

Debriefing Activity 3.10

When you approach an organization it is important to look at the whole system and not only at one aspect of it. You start with what has gone before, past history. You then go on to look at the organization from the outside – external factors affecting it within the macro- and micro-environment (see Unit 8, Additional techniques for mobilizing performance), then the inside of the organization – first as a whole, then the DMU groups within it and lastly the individuals. In any situation possible unforeseen circumstances should be taken into account.

Forces influencing organizational behaviour
1. The selling organization
    o Past history
2. The buying organization
    External factors
        o Macro-environmental factors (PEST)
        o Micro-environmental factors (competitors, suppliers, distributors, customers)
    Internal factors
        o The organization
        o The group
            i. What happens in the DMU group as a whole (intragroup)
            ii. What happens between groups (intergroup)
        o The individuals
            i. What happens between individuals in the group (interpersonal)
            ii. What happens in the individuals' minds (intrapersonal)
3. Unforeseen circumstances

Debriefing Activity 4.7

Answer

Attitude formation
- Classical conditioning (the association of the product with an event/feeling) – we would associate the new shaving product with luxury and pampering, for example, by placing the product in luxury hotel rooms.
- Operant conditioning:
    i. Positive reinforcement – we would emphasize that this method of shaving is quicker and leaves you feeling groomed.
    ii. Negative reinforcement – this could be that this method of shaving does not give you a rash.
    iii. Punishment – if you use this product you will not cut yourself shaving. Continuing using your existing product can lead to cuts and rashes.
- Modelling – a role model would be used in advertising, such as an actor or sports personality that our target audience admire.

Attitude change
- Theory of reasoned action:
    i. The formation of attitude is dealt with above
    ii. The subjective norm (the opinions of the customer's reference groups and how important these are to the customer) – we would target those reference groups important to the target segment we are trying to reach in order to increase motivation to purchase our new technology. We could do this by targeting opinion leaders such as journalists for men's magazines like *FHM* or consumer magazines like *Which*. This should also reinforce our message, as the customer's peer group should talk about/recommend the product.

369

- Theory of planned behaviour:

  We would have to ensure that nothing stops the customer from trying our product once they are motivated to do so. We have to ensure adequate distribution in stores and could back this up with a promotional mailing of a sample of the product to our target audience or through in-store demonstrations.

Debriefing Question 5.1

It is most likely that the:

- Independent variable is whether or not a customer has the 'cheap rate' service.
- Dependent variable is the measure of customer satisfaction. This could be obtained via questionnaire.
- Experimenter is most likely to be you.
- Control group is most likely to be those customers that have not had the cheap rate service installed. They are the best persons to act as a comparative group.

The study is a field study as the experiment is carried out in people's own homes.

Debriefing Question 5.2

There are a number of experimental designs that can be used to test the effectiveness of an advertising campaign. The exact choice would depend on financial limits, resource constraints and the broadcast pattern of the advertisement. It is most important to test before and after the advertisement is broadcast and, presuming times series data is not available, you are left to decide between pre-test/post-test, non-equivalent control group and the classical experimental designs. First choice would be the latter which provides more opportunity to eliminate the effect of intervening variables. However, if the advert was on trial in a particular region (as is usually the case) it will not be possible to randomly select people from this region (as some may have seen the advert some may not have). We would thus be forced to use one of the other two designs. Of these, the non-equivalent control group is preferred because of the presence of a control group to eliminate the effects of intervening variables.

Debriefing Question 5.3

It is certain that time series data will be available from past political opinion polls. In this case all that is required is a single test (case study or survey design) which can be compared with secondary data from previous polls. You could determine from this whether the trend in voting is up or down and thus make your prediction on the likely outcome of the next election (you might also wish to take other historical trends into account which could be picked up from the secondary data). Of course, if the resources were available, you might wish to commence your own time-series survey.

Debriefing Question 5.4

Your classmates may be a biased sample. Certainly, they are unlikely to be representative of the population in general, and would probably not match any quotas for this sort of survey (which would require a high number of parents as subjects).

Debriefing Question 5.5

To determine the extent of any cognitive dissonance induced changes in service quality evaluations you should use a control group.

For example, a courier company wants to know which aspects of their delivery service are important to their recently signed-up customers but are concerned that post-purchase dissonance might affect the results. To try and determine whether such dissonance significantly altered ratings they could use a matched control group of potential new customers and compare the rankings.

Debriefing Question 6.1

With limited time, a group discussion is likely to be the most productive technique. It would be possible to gather information from approximately 20 people per day (two groups of 10) so it would take approximately one week to survey 100 people. However, analysis time is likely to take at least another week (depending on the information you require).

Depth interviews will provide more information but take approximately twice as long. Projective techniques may be an option where only a limited amount of information is required allowing use of one of the techniques described.

Debriefing Question 6.2

Postal surveys are generally lower cost than telephone surveys and the respondee can be sent literature (such as photographs, fabric swatches, perfume samples) which could not be provided over the telephone. Postal surveys also have better coverage than telephone survey (not all people have a phone), interviewer bias is eliminated, and respondees can complete the survey form at their leisure.

CAI allows more personal questions to be asked than with a face-to-face interview. Responses are also quicker to analyze and interviewer bias is eliminated.

Debriefing Question 6.3

They broke Rule 14 – by failing to first introduce themselves and the purpose of the survey.

Debriefing Table

Sample answer

To: US Management Team

From: Client Manager (Europe)

Date: 20XX

Terms of reference: 1.   To make proposals to build the KAMs and NBDEs into an effective team 2. To outline recommended actions to improve customer care for clients.

Strategy

A series of meetings to discuss strategy will be held. This will take the form of workshops in which the macro- and micro-environment and the internal environment will be audited and a SWOT analysis carried out. Objectives will be agreed and strategies for growth considered alongside competitive strengths and core competences. A customer care programme will be introduced to cover issues such as customer acquisitions and retention. A business strategy for extranets, intranets and the internet will be discussed.

Shared values

A mission statement will be formulated that puts the customer at the centre of the business.

We also need to think about how we can go about creating an organizational culture that will override the sense of nationality and the identity people get from their different areas of work.

Structure

We should consider the appointment of a marketing director who will act as a unifying figure for both groups and be responsible for customer retention and new business.

We may also like to think about organizing around customers instead of geographical areas.

Style

The new marketing director will be a champion of customer care and ensure there is consistency and harmony between the two groups. Time will also be spent on customers.

Systems

A task force needs to be established to look at key issues on pay. Policies such as the linking of the bonus system to new business and customer retention will allow both KAMs and NBDEs to participate. Managers need to be given discretion in awarding pay increases.

Information about clients' needs to be communicated so that the same information is readily accessible. An extranet and internet strategy will be developed to aid in this process.

Staff Skills training

1. **Inter-group**

    Sessions will be run in which each group will be able to reverse roles. KAMs and NBDEs will be able to explore how each group perceives the other.

    Entertainment and a fun evening out will give people the chance to mix socially.

Key outcomes:

- o Help groups to reach a more realistic idea of what each group does
- o Provide an opportunity to reduce psychological and physical distance
- o Get some understanding of the dynamics of inter-group behaviour.

2. Group

A series of sessions will be held by a consultant to help the group to look at the processes taking place within the team in the normal flow of work, meetings, and informal and formal contacts. Of particular relevance here will be individuals' own actions and their impact on other people.

Key outcomes:

- o An opportunity to discuss cultural differences
- o An opportunity to talk problems out
- o An opportunity to discuss things that may be difficult to talk about under normal circumstances
- o Get some understanding of group behaviour.

Team building

A series of team building days will be held.

Key outcomes:

- o Bonding
- o An opportunity to create culture
- o An understanding of how our actions impact on other people
- o An understanding of some of the key skills needed in order to work effectively in a team.

Belbin role analysis

Key outcomes:

- o An understanding of team roles
- o An understanding of strengths and weaknesses (our own and the team)
- o An understanding of how people behave in different team roles
- o An opportunity to restructure the teams and balance out the team roles.

3. Individual Role analysis

Any failure to fulfil the individual's needs will lead to frustration and an unwillingness to consider change. We should therefore give each individual the opportunity to settle down with a consultant to talk about their role.

Key outcomes:

- o An understanding about the motivation of the individual.
- o An understanding of weakness where the job is not being done properly and for which training can be arranged.
- o The opportunity to talk through career plans.
- o The opportunity to ascertain whether the individual is constrained by anything else.

Appraisal scheme training

An appraisal scheme must be set up around the key result areas in the job description relating to sales, customer retention and customer satisfaction.

Leadership training

Group leaders should go on a series of team leader workshops.

Recommendations to improve customer care for clients

Month 1

1 Following on from the strategy day we will already have in place:

- A senior director on the group

- A task group to oversee the customer-care programme
- The outline of a tactical programme for customer care
- A task group to oversee the cyberstrategy – internet, intranet and extranet.

2 A focus group consisting of a mixture of clients, KAMs, NBDEs, and supporting staff should be set up. The subjects under discussion will be competitor service and customers' complaints. A video will be made of these sessions and circulated within the company.

Month 2

3 Following this a list of key areas of performance will be drawn up. Areas such as:

- Telephone answering
- Time from enquiry to quotation
- Frequency of client contact.

4 Measures will then be drawn up to enable us to evaluate our success in reaching our targets.

Months 3, 4 and 5

5 Training for staff on dealing with objections, negotiation, handling complaints and creating a good atmosphere will be organized.

Months 3 and 4

6 A promotional campaign will be organized to show our target market that we are happy, polite, efficient people to deal with. This will reinforce this new identity to our employees.

Month 6

7 Customers will be encouraged to visit out sites.

Budgets

Budgets need to be discussed and allocated. However, we first need to establish if these outline proposals are acceptable.

Conclusion

This report covers a wide range of activities the organization needs to consider. The final change that could be considered would be to make the same people responsible for new business and for customer retention. This would need to be done on a group basis so that the client's decision-making unit was approached with a relationship network in mind.

Debriefing Activity 9.6

1 The nature of innovation

Innovation as a term defines anything which is new, whether transformational or incremental, radically different or merely a development from what has gone before. The processes of innovation are applicable to the organization itself, its structure and 'modus operandi', but also, of course, to its products, services, marketing techniques and segmentation models. In short, innovation deals with the management of change.

Innovation is strategy based, it depends on good internal and external linkages, and it only happens when the organizational culture supports it and provides the enabling mechanisms for it to take place.

2 Analysis

By using the 7S McKinsey model, the analysis will seek to expose the links between the structures, processes and culture of an organization, the opportunities for innovation and the competitive and market environment in which the organization works.

2.1 External factors – macro and micro

A full analysis must be undertaken of the environmental factors impacting on your business.

   i. Macro factors

      Political, legal, economic, global, socio-cultural and technological factors must be examined. For example, what macro factors are preventing your organization from introducing new products speedily; has your organization embraced key technology developments relevant to their industry; is your organization aware of any advantages they could get by working in a specific local or international environment? (Some nationalities have particular skills.)

ii. Micro factors

The market, the competition, customers, suppliers, distributors and stakeholders must all be explored for their impact on your organization's performance. For example:

- o Do employees have a sufficient understanding of current market conditions and the needs of their customers?
- o What is happening in the market and what are your competitors doing?
- o Does your organization know how they compare to their competitors
- o Is your organization benchmarking – 7Ps, R & D, and other areas? And are they learning from their competitors?
- o Is your organization carrying out lengthy product research that enables the competition to steal their ideas?
- o Are you locked into a distribution relationship that prevents you from providing delivery promises such as 'same day service'?
- o Have you an established network of relationships that provide you with a constant supply of suggestions about new product developments and ways in which to improve their services? For example, has your organization developed any relationships with: universities, customers, distributors, suppliers, joint ventures, partnerships, etc.?
- o Has an analysis been done on the key opportunities and threats emerging from this?

3 Internal factors – based on the 7S McKinsey Framework

3.1 Strategy – Successful innovation is strategy based

- Is there a director in charge of innovation on the board?
- How does innovation strategy link to corporate strategy?
- Are there clear objectives on what your organization wishes to achieve?
- Is the search systematic?
- Are there formal or informal procedures? Do they work?
- How many man hours are given to innovation?
- How many products have been launched over the past one, two and three-year periods?
- What is their rate of success?
- How much revenue and profit has been generated by new products?
- Is your organization adopting a follower position (me too) or is it taking a truly innovative stance and establishing a market leader position?
- How much money is invested in innovation?
- How is your organization ensuring they keep their competitive advantage?
- What does the product portfolio look like? If you could draw a Boston Consulting Group matrix, would they be dogs, question marks, cash cows, stars?
- What do their product life cycles look like?
- If you mapped them on to the innovation and diffusion curve would their end users be innovators, adopters, early majority, late majority or laggards?
- Has the perception of their users been tested? And if so, have the products been repositioned?
- Are there customer satisfaction measures in place – was it what the customer wanted?

3.2 Shared values

Successful innovation involves a learning process which integrates key behaviour into effective routines.

- Is there top management commitment?
- Is there a clear sense of ownership and shared vision? Is innovation placed at the heart of the company culture?
- Are employees market-focused and encouraged to think of new ideas and how to approach their work in a more innovative way?

- Is the culture of innovation translated into job descriptions, targets and day-to-day activities?
- Is success rewarded? And are key people recognized and supported?
- Is there a willingness to celebrate failure by learning from what goes wrong rather than punishing those involved?
- Does the culture support a degree of freedom that allows staff to experiment?
- Is there a culture of can do, and decision making – or are things always waiting to be actioned?
- How quick is the decision making – do people do what they say – or do people have to leave in order to carry them forward?
- Time management is an aspect of culture – does your organization set realistic frameworks? And are people given time to think, reflect and be creative?

3.3 Structure

Successful innovation needs the appropriate structure.

- Does your organizational structure support innovation – is it flexible?
- Is it common practice to create 'project teams' when an idea for a new product or service is conceived?
- Is there a board appointment – an innovation director?
- Does your organization lend itself to secondments of key staff if the need arises?
- Is it possible for all employees to make decisions and/or request advice or authorization in 'real time'?

3.4 Style (of leadership and management)

- Is the leadership in your organization sending out the right messages about responding to market and customer needs through their communications and by setting examples?
- Does the leader model the right behaviour?
- Does the leader support innovative behaviour by ensuring there is an atmosphere of trust, honesty, reliability, stability – so that ideas can be developed, people have the freedom to speak up and be creative?
- Does the leader support the empowering of staff?
- Are managers committed to managing change or preserving the status quo?
- Are multi-skilling and training supported?
- Do the leaders know which values they support and which are mirrored in the organization:
    a. Innovation
    b. Cost reduction
    c. Market share
    d. Profit
    e. Sales turnover
    f. Training
    g. Creativity
    h. Customer satisfaction
    i. Customer loyalty
    j. Initiative
    k. Entrepreneurial spirit
    l. Team working?

3.5 Systems

Successful innovation depends on good external and internal linkages

Is communication effective – does it go vertically, horizontally and in a two-way mode?

Are there formal and informal procedures for collecting information internally and externally?

Are there formal and informal procedures for supporting relationships with the external environment?

How far are employees involved in continuous incremental innovation. For example are there formal mechanisms for finding and solving problems, are these methods linked to monitoring, measurements and appraisal? How successful is this? And are these linked also to customer satisfaction?

- Are systems compatible with innovation and speed? (This applies to recruitment, induction and reward policies as much as methods of disseminating information or making decisions.)
- Does the induction process introduce staff to the type of innovative behaviour the organization expects them to exhibit?
- Are new staff told the rewards this type of behaviour receives?

3.6 Skills

Some people may not be naturally innovative – they will need to be trained. Innovation involves change, change can be painful – are people introduced to the notion of dealing with a more ambiguous environment?

- Are people trained to be innovative and creative?
- The nature of the training needed might cover areas such as creativity, speaking in public, making presentations, technology, coaching, time management, handling difficult customers, negotiation and conflict and the ability to deal with differences of opinion.

3.7 Staff

Individual

- How well do individuals and groups within your organization function in their roles?
- Has any role analysis been carried out with staff to ascertain any of the following:
  - How they perceive their role and their responsibility to innovate? Are they self imposing barriers on their own creativity, making unwarranted assumptions, failing to challenge what is obviously wrong, being negative?
  - Whether they feel there are barriers in your organization preventing them from being more innovative? Are staff encouraged to think up new ideas? And when they get new ideas are the ideas acted upon? Are there pressures to conform that inhibit new ideas, does the group process make people feel foolish if they step out of line?
  - Whether they are resisting showing more innovative behaviour because they feel insecure? Frontline staff may feel motivated and have the competence to make speedy decisions to resolve customer queries – but without the willingness of line managers to empower them, staff will be frustrated in taking the initiative
  - Are people involved early enough?

Intra group and inter group

- Is there any intra or inter group conflict preventing innovation and processes from speeding up?
- If there are tensions within or between departments these need to be addressed. An unwillingness to consult, communicate and liaise will certainly result in misunderstandings and delays.
- Is enough time and other resources given to people to do this? In a marketplace where speed is all-important this will have a direct impact on business survival and success.
- Do you need a specially dedicated team that concentrates on innovation?
- Are there mixed role teams? (see Belbin)
- Do they use cross-functional teams?

How to create an organizational climate characterized by innovation and speed

- Execute research into the external factors affecting the organization as outlined in the analysis of the macro and micro environment. There may be opportunities to adapt competitors' products, exploit technological developments or research customer segments. Make sure you do some benchmarking.
- Execute research into the internal factors affecting the organization as outlined in the Innovation Audit above. There may be opportunities to develop dedicated innovation teams, reduce systems bureaucracy, decrease the research timescale, outsource tasks and build better relationships.

- Analyze gaps between customer-centric goals and reality – through individual interviews, group interviews – a service gap analysis.
- Managing change

Based on what is found, for example, the blockages are coming from outside the organization, then within the organization processes, group and inter group and individual behaviour . This will enable the organization to help define what the problems are and help them to buy into the process of change. Implement a training programme that focuses on innovation and introducing a creative climate along the following lines:

- Define core competences, shared values and strategic vision that will endorse an innovative culture in both product development and process innovation
- Identify how success will be measured
- Ensure structure and systems support this
- Develop the style of managerial behaviour needed to support core competences and values through skills training
- Implement standards and further skills training; motivate staff to participate through linking into job descriptions, appraisal and reward schemes
- Make sure that all new staff who are recruited have profiles conducive to the culture and are inducted into it
- Develop an internal marketing plan to ensure two-way communication so that the process of change is kept in mind and becomes part of the culture so that:
    a. The organization makes up new stories and myths about itself
    b. People say 'yes' instead of 'no' or 'yes but'
    c. People learn how to turn negative experiences into positive ones and make them something they can learn from
    d. People break through habitual ways of thinking and find new ways of looking at things
    e. They find ideas themselves and are encouraged to talk about and develop them
    f. Train people to learn ways of handling people who may disagree with them so that they learn how to manage conflict and get the resources they need to develop ideas
    g. Train people how to present and talk in public
    h. Teach them how to manage projects and make a plan
    i. Encourage people to improve themselves
    j. Help people to recognize the individuality of their customers so they can be truly innovative in meeting their needs – so we get Real Relationship Management
    k. Create a climate of trust where being different does not mean possible exclusion from the group.

Debriefing Case History

To: John Rush, Managing Director, Platinum Print

From: Maureen Davidson, Marketing Officer

Date: 6 December 1999

Re: Methods of investigating customer perceptions about our products and services

Introduction

Being able to capture, analyze and react to customer feedback is an essential element in the provision of a customer-focused business environment. At the moment, I imagine that you only gain customer feedback when something goes horribly wrong and the customer has complained – or the customer has simply gone elsewhere.

There are clear benefits to be gained from soliciting feedback from customers, whether they have complained or not. Some will be dissatisfied, and thinking of defecting to other suppliers, but they have not yet told you that: so, if you invite their comments, you will be given the opportunity indirectly to ensure that they are retained. Some customers will be satisfied, but only barely so: at the moment they see no particular reason why they should continue to place orders with Platinum Print when there are so many other printing companies available, all of them supplying products and services in more or less the same way as you. Talking to your customers – or, better still, listening to them – might generate some thoughts about mechanisms for producing genuine customer loyalty. Then again, there will be some customers who are very satisfied with Platinum Print but who feel mildly disgruntled because you don't nurture them enough: a questionnaire or membership of a focus group may be just what they're looking for.

On the other hand, you should be aware of the limitations associated with customer feedback. By and large, you should not expect to learn about new products and services not yet invented, because the vast majority of customers are not themselves innovative or creative thinkers. Also, customers sometimes don't know themselves and their own motivational patterns particularly well, so the answers they produce are not always authentic. As Nishikawa wrote in his seminal article for the *Journal of Long Range Planning* in 1989, 'Customers are only sincere when spending, not when talking' – in other words, if you ask them hypothetical questions ('Would you be prepared to pay for particularly rapid service?'), their answers may be equally hypothetical and would not reflect their actual behaviour. So surveys are best used in order to elicit customer feelings and perceptions, not as routes for market research.

Possible methodologies for investigating your customers

There are several options available for obtaining, analyzing and acting on customer feedback. The first is quantitative analysis, which can be performed with the use of questionnaires, telephone and/or face-to-face interviews, and surveys. The second option is qualitative analysis, which involves more in-depth interviews or focus groups. For Platinum Print, I recommend searching for some secondary (readily-available) information first, through sales figures and trends, printing costs, customer information, average spend per customer, and so forth.

In addition, the company may use one or more of the following:

1. *Satisfaction survey forms issued with each customer delivery* The forms do not need to be over-complicated (indeed, if they are it will simply mean that they won't be completed), but they can allow customers to rate your service in several key dimensions, such as the ordering process, staff helpfulness, staff efficiency, delivery times, product quality, and customer support. You should make sure, however, that although the forms require respondents simply to tick boxes, you always include an opportunity for them to offer comments about anything else which they consider important.

2. *Focus groups* Given the nature of your customer base, you could easily invite between six and ten of your major clients, selected randomly, to attend a session at which they can supply reactions to every aspect of your service and, moreover, can do so in depth. If the session is videotaped it will provide an excellent source of feedback and may identify common issues which are shared by groups of your key accounts. Customers who may not speak out individually may be more inclined to do so in a focus group setting, provided the group is properly managed so that it is not dominated by one or two particularly talkative contributors.

3. *Freephone customer support* In setting up this facility, which customers can call if they have a problem, you will be able to invite feedback whenever the opportunity arises. Periodically you must gather all the data from a sequence of separate phone calls and try to disentangle the principal lessons to be learned for the future.

Part b.

The outline of a generic rationale for relationship marketing could earn six marks, with the four remaining marks available for an assessment of the potential for relationship marketing within Platinum Print.

What is Relationship Marketing?

Many critics have pointed out that the traditional view about marketing – based on the marketing mix and the concept of exchange – was developed using assumptions derived from the huge American market for consumer goods. This short-term transactional focus is increasingly inappropriate for industrial and services marketing, where the establishment of longer-term relationships with customers is critical to organizational success. Gronroos, therefore, has formulated a relationship-based definition of marketing: 'The purpose of marketing is to establish, maintain, enhance and commercialize customer relationships (often, but not necessarily always, long term relationships) so that the objectives of the parties involved are met. This is done by the mutual exchange and fulfillment of promises.'

Payne and his colleagues (*Relationship Marketing for Competitive Advantage*, Butterworth-Heinemann, 1998) summarize the key elements of relationship marketing as follows:

1. The emphasis on the interaction between suppliers and customers is shifted from a transaction to a relationship orientation.

2. The relationship marketing approach concentrates on maximizing the lifetime value of desirable customers and customer segments.

3. Relationship marketing strategies are concerned with the development and enhancement of relationships with a number of key 'markets', both inside the organization and externally (involving customers, suppliers, referral sources, influence markets and recruitment markets).

4. Quality, customer service and marketing are closely related, but are frequently managed separately. A relationship marketing approach brings these elements into a much closer coherence.

How is a marketing relationship with customers achieved?

As we have seen above, Relationship Marketing is about building trust with customers and the generation of feelings of 'delight'. Customers have come to expect certain standards from companies, such as quality and product features. They will expect the same print quality from your company as from the print company down the road. It is therefore vital that the service you supply is impressive, memorable and spectacular, so that the customer will choose you and not somebody else.

The following elements are crucial in the development of a Relationship Marketing approach:

- The regular acquisition of customer feedback through questionnaires, surveys, interviews, focus groups, and so forth.

- Demonstrable commitment to customer service from the top of the company downwards, including frequent interactions between senior executives and customers in order to prevent that remoteness from customers which seems to characterize some large organizations. It may be helpful, too, if senior executives sometimes perform frontline service roles, so that they know what it is like to engage with customers in both reactive and proactive scenarios.

- Provision of customer-service training for everyone working in the company, even if they don't have direct contact with 'proper', paying customers themselves. Each employee has their own part to play in the delivery of superb service performance, and they need to internalize the concept of the internal customer in order to maximize their contribution.

- Recruitment and selection of people who have the right customer-facing attitudes (remember Professor Jim Heskett's injunction to 'Select for attitude, train for skill'), like empathy, emotional intelligence, social maturity, altruism and the willingness both to own and to solve customer problems.

- Reward, recognition and retention procedures which celebrate service delivery and restitution.

- 'disaster recovery' procedures to handle all customer difficulties before they get out of hand.

- Clear understanding about which customers generate higher levels of profitability, or have the potential for doing so: these are the customers who warrant optimum levels of service. Conversely, if you have some customers who don't generate profit for you, and show no likelihood of generating profit, then you may want to consider encouraging them to go elsewhere, though this can be dangerous if (a) they take others of your customers with them, and (b) the loss of their business means that your fixed costs are now distributed over a slightly smaller customer base.

Examples of relationship marketing in action include the use of so-called 'loyalty' cards by companies like Tesco and Sainsbury's. These schemes (now beginning to fall into some disrepute as they proliferate) are meant to encourage customers to be delighted and become loyal to the brand; the companies themselves benefit from the opportunity to construct a very detailed customer database, crucial for marketing, product research, and the development of personalized communications.

Part c.

Answers to Question 1.c may range over the creation of reward and recognition schemes based on customer-service performance levels (as measured by customer perceptions rather than through internally-generated indices), role-modelling of customer focus from the top of the company, the use of customer-centric teams, 'adopt-a-customer' projects plus visits to customers to get to know them firsthand, the deliberate recruitment of customer-friendly employees, and publicity about the benefits of a 'customer' mentality so far as internal customers are concerned. Professor Jim Heskett of Harvard points out that if organizations are serious about promoting a customer-facing culture, then they should 'select for attitude, train for skill' on the grounds that it is easier to equip new employees with technical proficiency than it is to change their underlying attitudes.

It is important to realize that internal customers are (nearly) as important as your external customers. True, the latter are the ones who generate income and profit for you, but on the other hand the willingness of these external customers to give you business will depend on their expectations and experiences with Platinum Print's people.

The Reichheld Service/Profit Cycle is relevant in making connections between customer perceptions, company performance, and employee achievement. If our external **customer service** is good, it leads to **customer satisfaction** and, better still, customer delight. Customers who are satisfied or very satisfied will come back for more: in other words, they exhibit **customer loyalty**. Organizations which retain the vast majority of their customers will have reduced costs, because it is always more expensive to find new customers than it is to keep your existing ones, so customer loyalty leads in turn to **increased profitability**, which means that the organization can allocate more resources to **internal service performance**. If your people feel good about working for your company, then they will experience high levels of **employee satisfaction** which spills over into **employee retention and commitment**. So the cycle starts again as **customer service** continues to improve.

Just as some companies enjoy the benefit of a rising curve of favourable results, others can reverse into a 'doom loop'. Customer service levels drop (as perceived by customers), or remain the same while service levels delivered by competitors are rising and eventually overtake yours; customers become dissatisfied or alienated; they defect; you have to work harder to acquire new customers as your existing customer base is eroded; your profitability declines; you allocate fewer resources to your internal service mechanisms; employees become demoralized; labour turnover accelerates, and you have to spend time inducting new people, who inevitably are less familiar with your customers, so your customer service performance falls further. As I write this report, organizations in a 'doom loop' scenario include Marks & Spencer, Sainsbury's, Laura Ashley, Storehouse and Somerfield: they may all recover eventually, but it will be a slow and painful process.

Thus it is important in Platinum Print to ensure that all employees are made aware of the importance of customer service. The message must be delivered from top management downwards, and must be reinforced by suitable role-modelling everywhere. It will be particularly helpful if a member of Platinum Print's top team (preferably the Managing Director) identifies himself as the 'champion' for customer focus.

Providing employees with customer feedback can itself be a motivating factor. As they see the results improving, they will make even more effort to secure better performance in the future, and this process can be enhanced if we introduce an 'Adopt-A-Customer' programme, enabling all the people working at Platinum Print to meet customers and develop the sort of personal networks which ultimately generate a customer-facing commitment to action.

Empowering employees so that they can resolve customer difficulties immediately should also improve the internal culture. Empowerment not only means that we have a better chance of retaining otherwise dissatisfied customers, but it also supplies higher levels of job satisfaction to people in frontline service positions.

Part d.

Little credit is available for ideas which simply replicate what other companies already do, or ideas which could be replicated more or less immediately. Instead, Platinum Print should seek to differentiate itself through the creation of distinctive (and not straightforwardly reproducible) competencies, such as superior customer service, the creation of new customer segments attacking different marketplaces, the development of total customer solutions involving, say, internet website design, mail-order processing support, and mailshot distribution. One entirely pragmatic proposal (generated by the Senior Examiner) is for Platinum Print to offer the "100/100 Guarantee": 100 per cent of any order to be delivered in 100 hours, with the offer of a 25 per cent price reduction on the next order if this guarantee is not fulfilled in any single instance. Given the cost of underpinning such a delivery promise, it may attract a price premium, but eventually this would be unnecessary as the company's employees become more accustomed to achieving such deadlines.

As you have already identified, Platinum Print currently has no identifiable competitive advantage over its direct competitors. Your product on its own is no longer sufficient to ensure that you will stay in business: all printing firms offer much the same quality, much the same service, much the same delivery promises, and much the same pricing. Indeed, you are in danger of operating purely as a commodity supplier and if that happens you can only compete on price – which means that you will go bankrupt because your customers are increasingly able to source their own printing requirements (through the internet) or even do it themselves.

There are some opportunities, however, which you should explore seriously in order to prepare effectively for the future.

1. Create a 'personal touch' through appropriate techniques of Relationship Marketing so that, for example, your important customers have a direct link to their own, named key account adviser or manager in Platinum Print.

2. Offer an apparently customized and special printing service to organizations within specific business sectors, e.g., private hospitals, so that these customers believe you to be equipped with a level of expertise which cannot easily be matched elsewhere.

3. Given that many of your customers now want very rapid response and delivery times above all else, offer a guaranteed service with discounts off subsequent orders should you fail to fulfil your promises.

4. Take advantage of the degree to which you can create a 'total customer solution', incorporating design, website development, mailshot distribution, or any other services which you could undertake on behalf of your commercial customers in particular. One possibility, for instance, is to offer facilities for the design and printing of menus for the restaurants which already purchase 'café pads'.

5. Locate some friendly, helpful and customer-facing employees in your front office so that casual, first-time customers are not intimidated. If you can find other ways of enticing potential customers into your front office in the first place, then so much the better, e.g., by racks of greeting cards and so forth.

6. Establish mutually-beneficial relationships with organizations which promote new business start-ups (so that you can acquire contracts concerned with letter-head printing or other forms of corporate literature), including banks.

7. Develop an internet website presence facilitated through an affiliate arrangement with a relevant portal. In time, too, the website may become transactional, so that customers can place orders direct with you via electronic communications.

8. Control and reduce your own costs through ensuring that 'distress' printing work is contracted out elsewhere, perhaps to other countries with significantly lower overheads. In this way you may achieve a powerful (but, it has to be said, temporary) pricing advantage.

Author – Ted Johns

Index

Product life cycle 24, 223
Product/service classification 19
Projective techniques 125
Promo*Focus 34
Proportions 120
Psychoanalytic theory 65
Psychographic segmentation 34
Psychographics 33
Psychological tests, recruitment 201
Public relations 261
Public sector
  customer 16
  performance management 163
  policy 17

Q

QS-9000 184
Qualitative research methods, comparison 129
Quality 109
Quality of life 288
Quantitative methodologies 129
Quantitative research methods 135
Question pairs 132
Question types 136
Questionnaire design 115, 135
Questionnaires 140
Quotas, setting 108

R

Radical resource productivity 294
Radio and television 142
Raw materials 22
Recruitment 198, 201
Recruitment and induction systems 158
Referent groups 69, 72
Reinforcement 91
Relationship marketing 237
  organizational markets 242
  risks 248
Relationship potential, influences 241
Relative advantage 224
Reliability of measurement 116
Reperatory grid (rep grid) 99, 128
Research
  casual 145
  internal versus external 123
  primary versus secondary 123
  qualitative versus quantitative 124
  quantitative methodologies 129
Research findings
  acceptability 116
Research report, structure 121
Residential neighbourhood classifications 26
Respect for diversity 298
Response scales 137
Responsibility, hierarchy 6
Rice's PV/PPS model 87
Risk 84
Rituals 52, 53
Role
  changes 249

  subjective psychological aspect 250
Role ambiguity 66, 252
Role analysis 210
Role behaviour 165
Role conflict 66, 252
Role defence 251
Role definition 252
Role interdependence 252
Role management 250
Role of women 284
Role relationships 14, 241, 251
  personal and professional dimensions of 248
Role signs 66
Role suction 252
Role theory 66
Role training 207
Role-playing 128

S

Sales promotion 260
Sample 107
Sample size 109
Search engines 147, 309
Secondary data, limitations 147
Secondary groups 69
Secondary information sources 141
Sectional interest group 294
Segmentation, value of 25
Self, concept of 64
Self assessment 160
Self-actualization 213
Self-directed teams 187
Semantic differential 137
Service and flow economy 295
Service level agreements 218
Service quality 110
  benchmarking 113
  measurement 112
Services 20
SERVQUAL 131
Shop surveys 132
Shopping goods 21
Simple random sampling 107
Social class, criticisms of 30
Social or ethical rating schemes 292
Social value groups 35
Socialization 55
Socio-cultural factors 282
Speciality goods 22
Sponsorships 309
Staff 159
Stanford Research Institute's life ways 36
Statistics
  use and abuse 149
  using 120
Status 28, 29
Stimulus-response (SR) model 82
Stratified random sampling 107
Stress and anxiety 249
Subjective norm 92